DIABOLIKA:
Supercriminals, Superheroes and the Comic Book Universe in Italian Cinema

DIABOLIKA:

Supercriminals, Superheroes and the Comic Book Universe in Italian Cinema

by Roberto Curti

Midnight Marquee Press, Inc.
Baltimore, Maryland, USA, London, UK

Copyright © 2016 Roberto Curti
Interior layout by Gary J. Svehla
Copy Editing by Janet Atkinson
Cover Design by Timothy Paxton, based on the Italian *locandina* for *Lo scoiattolo*, poster art by Volpi

Without limiting the rights under copyright reserved above, no part of this publication may be reproduced, stored in or introduced into a retrieval system, or transmitted, in any form, or by any means (electronic, mechanical, photocopying, recording or otherwise), without the prior written permission of the copyright owner or the publishers of the book.

ISBN 978-1-936168-60-6
Library of Congress Catalog Card Number 2015912388
Manufactured in the United States of America
First Printing June 2016

Dedication

**This book is dedicated to my wife Cristina
… my partner in crime, my Eva Kant.**

DIABOLIKA

TABLE OF CONTENTS

8 Acknowledgments

9 A Note on the Entries

Part One—An Overview of Italian Comics on Film

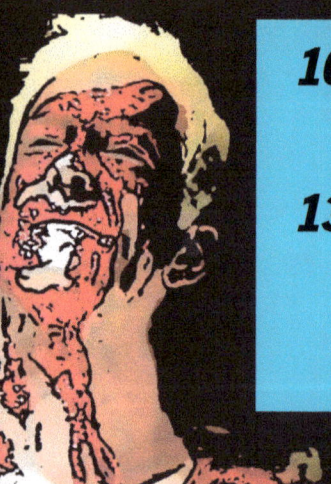

10 Chapter One—
   Comics: Italian Style!

13 Chapter Two—
   The "K" Factor: The "fumetti neri" Controversy

21 Chapter Three—The Myth of the Italian Superhero

26 Chapter Four—Forbidden to Minors ... The Adults-Only Comics

32 Chapter Five—Spoof, Satire and Social Criticism

36 Chapter Six— The Television Years

42 Part TWO— The Films

226 Appendix: The Turkish "Melting Pot": When an Italian Antihero Meets an American Superhero in Turkey by Kaya Özkaracalar

241 Essential Bibliography

243 Index

263 Author Biography

Acknowledgments

First and foremost, I would like to thank from the bottom of my heart the people who in one way or another helped make this book possible: Canadian film critic Steve Fenton, co-editor of the amazing magazines *Weng's Chop*, *Monster!* and *Monster! International*, who did a tremendous job in helping locate and/or improve upon the images for the book, and came up with many outstanding and rare ones. Without his help, this book wouldn't be half as good as (I hope) it is; my Maltese cinephile friends Mario and Roderick Gauci, who assisted me in the final editing and proofreading stage, and whose help has been invaluable as ever; fellow Midnight Marquee author and longtime pal Troy Howarth, who gave me friendly advice all the way through and proof-read the whole thing when it was still a rough-edged mess; Turkish film scholar Kaya Özkaracalar, who penned an incredibly engrossing and informative essay on the Italian *fumetti* influence in Turkish cinema, which I am honored to include in this volume and Gary J. and Susan Svehla, who believed in this project and enthusiastically supported it since the very beginning. *Mille grazie, Gary and Susan!*

I am also immensely grateful to the following: actor and film producer Roel Bos, aka Glenn Saxson, the man behind the Kriminal mask in the movies, who graciously provided interesting anecdotes and memories from his days in the Italian film business; novelist, scriptwriter and film director Ernesto Gastaldi, whose vivid recollections of the Golden Age of Italian genre cinema are a never-ending source of inspiration for movie fans; film scholar and head of the invaluable Mondo Macabro label, Pete Tombs, for kindly helping me with precious advice; actor Robert Woods, the star of many Euro cult films, who was kind enough to share his memories about the making of Paolo Bianchini's *Massacre Mania*.

My most sincere gratitude goes to those who in some way or other helped me throughout this book: Mark Thompson Ashworth, Lucas Balbo, Nicola Bassi, Stefano Isidoro Bianchi and *Blow Up* magazine; Francesco Cesari, Domiziano Cristopharo, Pierpaolo De Sanctis, Alessio Di Rocco, Antonio Marchesani, Domenico Monetti, Emiliano Morreale and Mort Todd. Last but not least, very special thanks to Tim Paxton who did a stunning cover design.

Photographs and illustrations are the copyright of their respective holders and are reproduced here in the spirit of publicity.

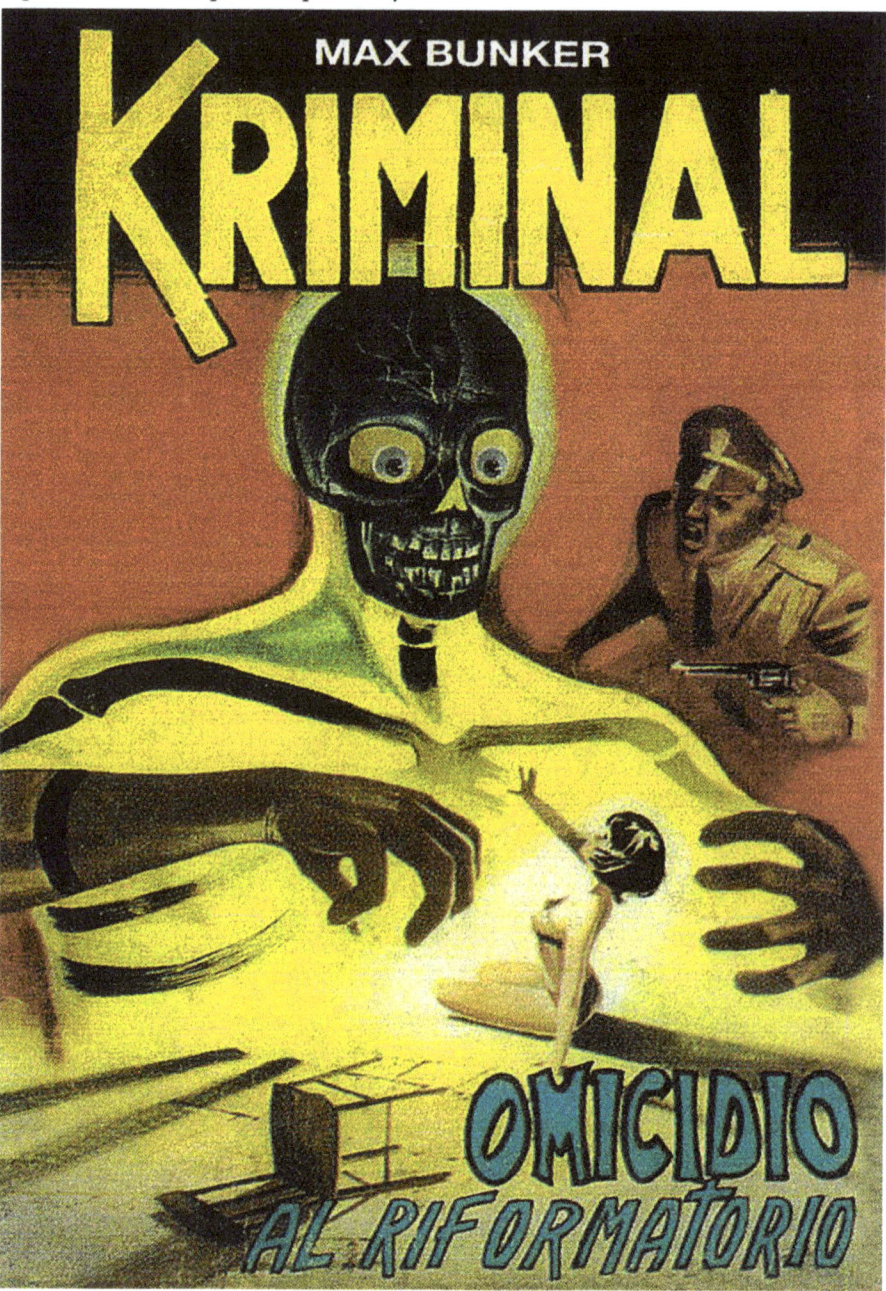

Cover art by Luigi Corteggi from *Kriminal* #5 (December 1964)

A Note on the Entries

This book lists the Italian films and TV series based on (or unofficially "inspired by") comic books, comic strips or photonovels, as well as those titles, which, even though they were not directly adapted from comics, sport a distinct comics feel in their style, characters and plot.

In a way, it can be said that during a certain point in Italian film history the whole genre industry was conceiving and churning out movies as if they were live-action comics of sorts. However, I decided to stick with the most blatant examples. That is the case with the Italian superhero movies included in the book, which had very strong roots in the comics universe, as well as the movies inspired by *fumetti neri* (even though not directly based on one). On top of that, I also chose to include several titles that dealt with the comics' social and cultural impact—such as the anthology comedy *Caprice Italian Style* (*Capriccio all'italiana*, 1968) or *Questo e quello* (1983, Sergio Corbucci)—and which I feel will help readers better understand the whole phenomenon.

Italian comics proved successful in other countries as well, and over the years there have been some foreign adaptations, such as a French production based on Hugo Pratt's graphic novel *Jesuit Joe* (*Jesuit Joe*, 1991, Olivier Austen) and a truly horrid and unfaithful film version of Italy's most popular comic strip, *Dylan Dog: Dead of Night* (2010, Kevin Munroe), of which the least said the better. Even though mentioned in passing in the text, they are not included as entries, as they are not Italian productions.

As for co-productions, I decided to include almost exclusively major Italian ones, directed by Italian filmmakers. That is why, for instance, Jesús Franco's *Lucky the Inscrutable* (*Lucky, el intrépido/Agente speciale L.K.: Operazione Re Mida*, 1967) is not listed, being a Spanish/West German/Italian co-production, helmed by a Spanish director and only partially filmed in Italy. Similarly, despite employing a number of Italian actors (including the female lead, Monica Vitti) and locations, Joseph Losey's *Modesty Blaise* (1966) was a completely British production and as such it is not included in the book. The sole exceptions are Turkish/Italian co-productions such as *Three Supermen at the Olympic Games* (1984) and *Lo scoiattolo* (1979). The former is fully part of the Italian *Three Supermen* series, and the latter pertains to the above-mentioned *fumetti neri*-inspired adaptations.

On the other hand, Roger Vadim's *Barbarella* (1968) is a special case. Despite being directed by a Frenchman, it was an Italian/French co-production whose importance is vital in many ways. It was produced by Dino De Laurentiis, shot at Rome's Dinocittà back-to-back with Mario Bava's *Danger: Diabolik* (with John Phillip Law playing a key role in one film and the lead in the other), and it was an example of De Laurentiis' attention to the phenomenon (in a period where he produced a number of films related to comics), as well as testimony to the vital influence that Jean-Claude Forest's creation had on the Italian comic book universe, a notion that will be discussed later on in the book.

A collateral yet very interesting topic is the impact of Italian *fumetti* on Turkish cinema—a whole universe which may well be something of an acquired taste to many, but which nonetheless sported a genre film production that had some very peculiar things in common with the Italian one, not least the presence of Italian filmmakers who moved to Istanbul during the 1970s. I am therefore deeply grateful to Turkish film scholar Kaya Özkaracalar, who has kindly agreed to write an exhaustive essay on the Turkish-made motion pictures based on Italian comics and photonovels, such as the *Zagor* films and the *Kilink* series, as well as other Turkish movies based on or inspired from Italian movie franchises which have a comics-feel. It is included as an appendix and I think it fits in rather well with the book's content and scope.

The entries are arranged in chronological order—based on the release dates in Italy—and under their English language title. Such English titles were intended for the original American theatrical run, the home video release or worldwide distribution. Those films that never made it to an English-language audience are listed under their original Italian title. For *Three Supermen at the Olympic Games*, a production so obscure that it remained unreleased in Italy *and* Turkey and only had a marginal home video release for the Turkish language community in Germany, I have made a further exception and listed it under the literal English title under which it is commonly known among film buffs, this being the more reader-friendly option.

Each entry features an essential crew and cast list (with each main player associated to the character's name). To conserve space I opted for abbreviations, which are as follows: *D*: Director; *S*: Story; *SC*: Screenplay; *DOP*: Director of photography; *M*: Music; *E*: Editor; *Prod*: Produced by.

The information bits provided throughout the text are the result of a thorough research from a variety of sources such as academic texts and essays and other assorted material—interviews with filmmakers and actors, newspaper reviews, etc.—which are listed in the bibliography.

Part One
An Overview of Italian Comics on Film

Chapter One
Comics: Italian Style

When he was still very young, Federico Fellini dabbled as a comic book writer for some time. Since Mussolini had banned American comics, Fellini penned the scripts for the Italian version of *Flash Gordon*, printed in Florence by a publisher named Nerbini. The Maestro told documentary filmmaker Damian Pettigrew during a lengthy 1994 interview (that became the film *Fellini: I'm a Born Liar,* 2002):

> Giove Toppi was the drawing artist, and I wrote the texts, introducing a certain Romagna flavor, which was not in Alex Raymond's original work. We were paid 10 *lire* a week, and when the series took off Nerbini doubled our salary to 10 *lire* … every two weeks![1]

Fellini was a great comics fan. He had his actors behave and talk like comic book characters (like Marcello Mastroianni in *8 ½*, who utters onomatopoeias such as "Swissshh" and "Gulp!"); he centered the first feature film he directed by himself—*The White Sheik* (*Lo sceicco bianco*, 1952)—on a fictitious photonovel character played by Alberto Sordi; he was a friend of Lee Falk's and at a certain point in the 1960s he even considered the idea of a "Mandrake" adaptation. Finally, his 1987 film *Intervista* features a sequence where Marcello Mastroianni is dressed as the popular comic book magician. On top of that, in the early 1990s, Fellini even resurrected his old unfinished project *Il viaggio di G. Mastorna, detto Fernet* (which he was initially set to direct in the mid-1960s, starring Mastroianni) as a graphic novel, illustrated by his friend Milo Manara. In the comic, Mastorna has the face of Paolo Villaggio, the popular comedian who starred in Fellini's final film *The Voice of the Moon* (*La voce della luna*, 1990).

The director talked at length about the comparison between the two forms of expression while discussing his collaboration with comic artist Milo Manara on the graphic novel *Viaggio a Tulum* (1989).

> Many years later, when I was working with Manara on *Viaggio a Tulum,* I found out that there really is no difference between making a movie and a comic strip. They both require the same logistic organization, the same tight deadlines, the same solutions to lab problems and, above all, the same means of expression. […] As we all know, a motion picture is essentially composed of a series of small panels in which one delineates a situation involving several characters organized

The first issue of *Corriere dei Piccoli* (December 27, 1908), Italy's first comic magazine

Photonovels ("Fotoromanzi") were all the rage in the Italian post-war years. Federico Fellini's *The White Sheik* (1952), starring Alberto Sordi (right), offered a fond yet biting view of the photonovel industry.

into space, where light and shadow, perspective and volume, are handled with attention. The story progresses when the panels are set into motion. In the case of a comic strip, one has to deal with the same panels, except that they are frozen on a page. [...] It is very suggestive since the reader must imagine the movement between a panel and the next. In a sense, the comic book's form of expression is artistically purer than cinema, since it is less definite, more allusive, less dependent on reality.[2]

The birth of comics in Italy dates back to December 27, 1908 with the publication of the first issue of *Il Corriere dei Piccoli* (Courier for the Little Ones), the children's weekly illustrated supplement of the daily newspaper *Il Corriere della Sera*. For many years, Italian comics were aimed exclusively at kids; they were simple one-page stories and did not even have balloons, which were replaced by captions in rhyme under each vignette. This detail may help us understand how they were primarily seen as an educational tool rather than a form of entertainment.

The Fascist regime actually turned comics into instruments of propaganda; such was the case with the notorious magazines *Il Balilla* (*Opera Nazionale Balilla* was the name of the Italian Fascist youth organization, which functioned as

A late 1960s portrait of the great Italian novelist and artist Dino Buzzati in his house; on the left is Buzzati's painting *La vampira*, obviously inspired by adult comics

an addition to school and education, named after an 18th-century young patriot) and *L'avventuroso*. However, the film industry did not really take any interest in them, and it was not until 1941 that the very first Italian comic adaptation was put into production. *Princess Cinderella* (*Cenerentola e il signor Bonaventura*, directed by Sergio Tofano) was an offbeat mixture of comic book, fairytale and musical. Something of an oddity, it was a rare bird within Italian cinema of the period, despite keeping up with the detachment from reality that was commonplace in the movies produced during the regime.

Post-WWII Italy saw the birth of another peculiar form of illustrated magazine akin to the *fumetti*, which soon enjoyed an enormous popularity: the *fotoromanzi* (*fotoromanzo* in the singular), that is, "photonovels." In *fotoromanzi* the stories were structured as comic books, with a succession of panels inclusive of speech balloons and captions. Yet they were composed of stills featuring real actors instead of illustrations.

The photonovel was an Italian invention. The first ones debuted in 1947, when the country was recovering from the destruction and the moral and economical desolation of the war years. Their creators were Cesare Zavattini and Luciano Pedrocchi, who had the idea of substituting drawings with pictures for the first magazine entirely dedicated to photonovels, *Bolero Film*. The first *fotoromanzi* editor, for the magazine *Il mio sogno*, published on May 8, 1947—the mag's subtitle was *Settimanale di romanzi d'amore a fotogrammi* ("The weekly mag of love stories in stills") as the term *fotoromanzo* had not yet been coined—would become a renowned film-maker: Damiano Damiani. Most *fotoromanzi* were simple love stories, usually variations on a basic plot and were aimed mainly at a female audience. However, by the early 1960s the photonovel had become a real industry, and several publishers were ready to jump on the bandwagon and explore uncharted territories, such as the horror and the Gothic genres, appearing parallel with the advent of the first adults-only comic books.

Chapter Two
The "K" Factor: The "fumetti neri" Controversy

In the mid-1960s it was not uncommon to read newspaper articles with such vehement titles as: "It is right and necessary that the *fumetti neri* end up before the criminal judge."[3] In this context, readers could find heartfelt tirades on the moral damage being perpetrated on the gullible minds of Italian youths by these sensationalized narratives; one could also be sure to read much pontification on the measures that needed to be adopted in order to put a halt to such moral decay … at any cost and by any means necessary.

But, what exactly were those *fumetti neri*? And what exactly were they doing to the defenseless readers?

First, an explanation on the name is necessary. *Fumetto*, in Italian, means "comic" (the term actually refers to the dialogue balloons: *Fumo*, in Italian, means smoke, hence the visual analogy between balloons and clouds of smoke) and *fumetti neri* literally means "black comics." The color-coding implied a moral judgment on their content. It was not only a nod to the *noir* genre (which they partly fit into) but it implied something sordid, vulgar and morally reprehensible. Something evil.

The idea of an amoral antihero was not new in Italian popular culture. Za-la-Mort, the French "Apache" (gangster) created and played by the slender, angular Emilio Ghione (who modeled the character on the French mystery crime serials by Victorin Jasset and Louis Feuillade), had appeared in many silent pictures starting in 1915, with phenomenal success. Described by Gino Moliterno as "a ruthless master criminal with a haggard face but a noble heart,"[4] Za-la-Mort underwent quite a singular trajectory. He started as a violent, cold-blooded murderer and ended up as an avenging figure, that protected the innocent and the helpless with the aid of his female sidekick, Za-la-Vie. It was a patent example of the need to temper down the character's excesses so as not to disturb the common moral. Therefore, exit Za-la-Mort the criminal and enter Za-la-Mort the investigator. However, when he made his last appearance, in Raffaello Matarazzo's *Fumeria d'oppio* (1947), Za-la-Mort was already old-hat, a relic from a past which the war had wiped out almost entirely.

After the difficult post-war years, Italy had finally recovered from a tremendous letdown and its economy looked healthier than ever—much more than anyone had expected. Those were the years of the so-called economical "Boom." Relieved as they were by the sudden burst of prosperity, Italians wanted to have fun. Along with fun came transgression. And with the loosening of censorship, they were beginning to savor it—and not only in the movies. After the end of the war, the ban of the Fascist party and the 1947 popular referendum that declared the fall of the monarchy, the Democrazia Cristiana, a center-right party with a strong Catholic backbone, governed the country, while Italy's Communist Party PCI (Partito Comunista Italiano) occupied the opposition. Democrazia Cristiana took control of film censorship, which operated under strict rules in order to grant the people a "morally responsible" cinema.

However, by the start of the 1960s, film censorship was gradually loosening its grip. It was not so much a matter of relaxation on the part of the commissions as a result of the changing mores and costumes. With the growth of the industrial economy and a wave of emigration toward the big cities, the less educated, mostly country-based

A lurid cover of the popular weekly magazine *Tribuna Illustrata* shows comic book personalities in jail awaiting trial.

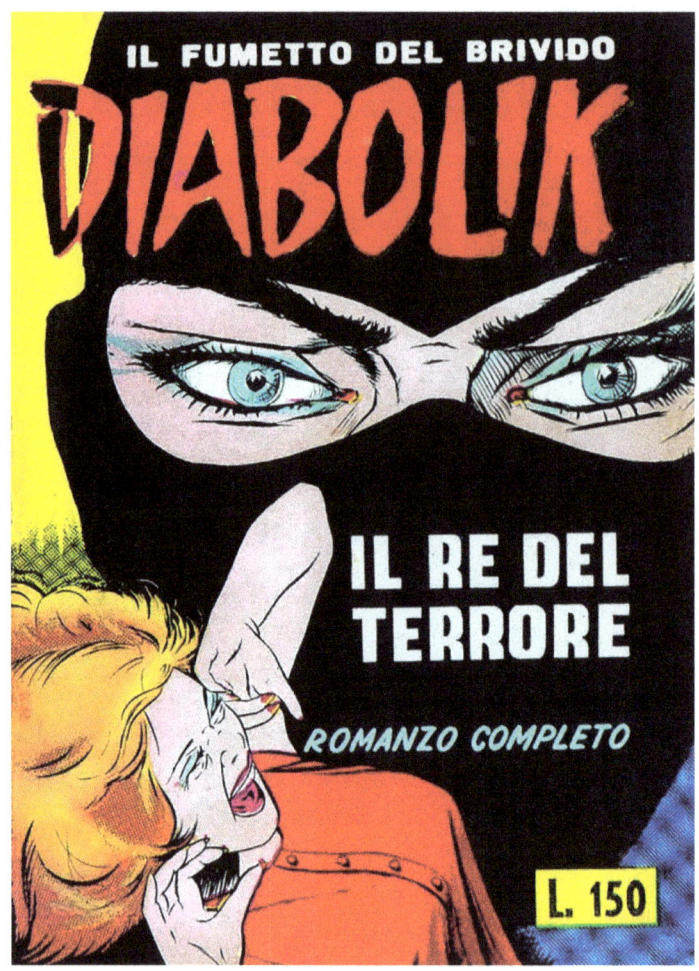

Cover art for the legendary *Diabolik* #1

The masterminds behind *Diabolik* were two sisters, Angela and Luciana Giussani.

Southerners moved to the North where they came across a more relaxed, family-free way of life. Huge patriarchal families suddenly dissolved, and their Catholic-based value systems became less stringent. Women grew more emancipated; men discovered that city life brought a variety of answers to their sexual urges (brothels had become illegal in 1958 with the Merlin Law, but prostitution was spreading throughout the cities, from nightclubs to the "street workers" that allured drivers in suburban streets). Marriage itself was no longer seen as an unbreakable bond as many voices started demanding a law on divorce, which was still not permitted by Italian law.

The movie industry somehow absorbed all this, and the results emerged on screen. Cinema can become a powerful instrument of self-reflection, even as presents itself in the form of popular entertainment. In *Big Deal on Madonna Street* (*I soliti ignoti*, 1958, Mario Monicelli), one of the pillars of the so-called *Commedia all'italiana*, one particular subplot follows the troubled love story between a would-be thief (Renato Salvatori) and one of his accomplices' sister, a beautiful Southern girl (Claudia Cardinale) who is kept locked inside her house by her morbidly protective brother (Tiberio Murgia). The situation is carried out on screen as a recurring gag, as the young man has to come up with all sorts of tricks to meet his beloved, but in the meantime it confronted the audience with a situation that—although it had been commonplace just several years earlier—was now seen as an abnormal and absurd legacy of the past.

Another similar example can be found in Pietro Germi's *Divorce—Italian Style* (*Divorzio all'italiana*, 1961). Marcello Mastroianni plays a Sicilian baron who, being unable to divorce his wife and marry a younger and more desirable woman (Stefania Sandrelli), resorts to killing his wife, counting on an article of the penal code which—incredible but true—considered "honor killing" (that is, committed by someone who discovered his or her spouse with a lover) to be punishable far less severely than murder.

Monicelli and Germi's depiction of the male propensity for objectifying women was basically humorous in tone, whereas Luchino Visconti explored similar terrain in a very different key in his masterpiece *Rocco and His Brothers* (*Rocco e i suoi fratelli*, 1960), which is set among Southern immigrants in Milan. Authorities seized the film because of its frank and realistic portrayal of sex, including a rape scene involving a prostitute (Annie Girardot), who is later murdered by her ex-lover.

Soon *Diabolik* and other *fumetti neri* raised a scandal for their approach to violence, as portrayed by the April 1965 issue of the weekly magazine *Domenica del Corriere*.

That same year, Federico Fellini's *La Dolce Vita* (1960) presented the audience with an openly sensual, sexually aggressive female character: Sylvia (Anita Ekberg), the Hollywood diva whom Marcello (Marcello Mastroianni) accompanies throughout Rome at night. Fellini's film caused a sensation, not only because of its portrayal of a city filled with prostitutes, extramarital sex, orgies and general amorality, but especially for the scene in which Sylvia bathes in the Trevi Fountain like a Pagan goddess. It was a frank image of remorseless, sin-free sexuality if ever there was one, as opposed to the way Italians looked at their own women—equally divided between saints and sinners, either virginal creatures submissive to the male or family-destroying, man-eating whores.

Times were changing, indeed. People were hungry for transgression. They demanded sex; they needed to feel the thrill of sin. Yet, at the same time, Catholic guilt could not help but resurface in terms of anger and violence toward the female body. A groundbreaking example would be Mario Bava's *Black Sunday* (*La maschera del demonio*, 1960) and its ferocious opening scene in which Barbara Steele is horribly tortured and punished in a graphically gory, over-the-top way that had not been seen in any Italian film be-

Luciano Secchi, aka Max Bunker (standing), and Roberto Raviola, aka Magnus (sitting), were the creators of *Kriminal* and *Satanik*, two of the best (and most controversial) *fumetti neri* of the decade.

fore—nor in a foreign one, for that matter. The subsequent Gothic horror thread would often focus on the duplicity of women as both alluring and damning angels, while at the same time offering excess and transgression … as far as censors would allow—that is, very little. But the audience's demand was on the increase. It was evident in films, where moderate nudity was starting to break in, as well as in other fields of popular entertainment.

Then, in November 1962, audiences were exposed to a new kind of "adults-only" pocket-sized comic books.

Since then, the world of Italian *fumetti* had known only positive heroes. The most popular comic strips were Western stories such as *Tex*, a series created in 1948 by Gian Luigi Bonelli and Aurelio Galeppini, which remains Italy's most durable comic book to date and is still published after almost 70 years. Tex Willer was a Texas ranger with the features of a young Gary Cooper and a staunchly moral code of honor, and the series was characterized by a revisionist approach toward native Americans, compared with the racial stereotypes in American films. Other comic books, such as *Asso di Picche* (Ace of Spades), featured masked heroes similar to those of the Golden Age of American comics. There were also rather shady characters, such as the protagonist of the grim Western series *Kinowa*, a man who has been scalped by Indians and becomes a masked avenger wearing a skin mask that represents a horned devil. But

Cover art for *Kriminal* #11, March 11 1965: An accomplished painter and designer, Corteggi created most of the covers for Magnus and Bunker's comics since 1965.

els). Most had a "K" in the name—menacing, mysterious, malicious, almost a code signal between the makers and the consumers that hinted at the dangerous, forbidden content.

The first and better of the lot were the skeleton-costumed, skull-masked *Kriminal* and the sexy dark lady *Satanik*. The latter was particularly significant, since the eponymous character was evil, unscrupulous and lethal, but beautiful, signaling that the tormented had become the tormentor. Furthermore, the world as portrayed in *Kriminal* and *Satanik* was dominated by corruption, murder, greed and sex, hidden under a hypocritical "respectable" façade, a world in which, paradoxically, the titular criminals would ultimately turn out as the less despicable characters.

Quality-wise, these were vastly superior to the many that followed, due to the skills of their creators, artist Roberto Raviola and scriptwriter Luciano Secchi, aka Magnus & Bunker—that is, Italian *fumetto*'s answer to Lennon & McCartney. What made them revolutionary was not simply the emphasis on sex and violence but the graphic way these were portrayed on paper, with a conception of the comic panels paralleling film editing. The story be-

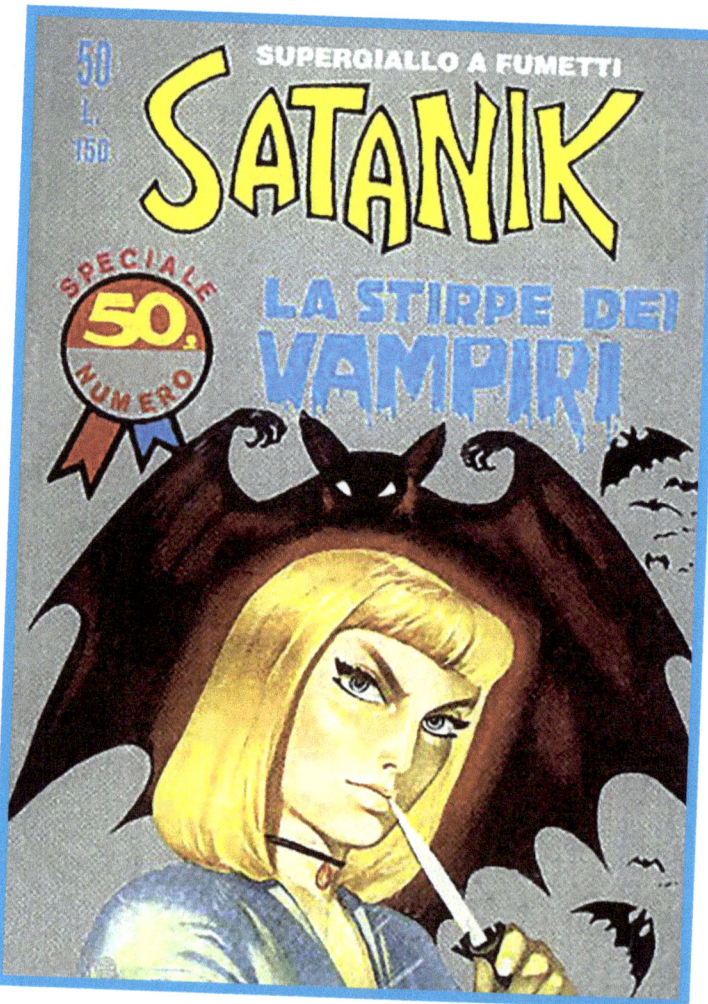

Cover art by Luigi Corteggi for *Satanik* #50, December 7 1965, featuring the character of Baron Wurdalak, the vampire

overall the main theme was that of the good guys against the bad guys, and it was out of discussion on whose side the reader was supposed to be.

Starting with *Diabolik*, things suddenly changed.

Diabolik was in many ways the opposite of an American superhero. He was a super*criminal* with a trendy costume, futuristic gadgets, a gorgeous female sidekick and an insatiable desire for money. And, most importantly, readers were invited to side with him.

Without the limitations given by flesh-and-blood actors and real-life situations, comics existed in a universe totally of their own, self-contained and fantastic, where anything could happen, and readers could project all kinds of fantasies, with even ampler freedom than films would allow.

Soon the market was flooded with cheap *fumetti* whose main characters practiced theft, robbery, rape and murder and had bizarre names such as Fantax, Demoniak, Sadik, Spettrus, Mister-X and Zakimort, often derived from pejorative adjectives and made to sound exotic by ending in consonants (whereas almost all Italian words end in vow-

Demoniak was one of many *fumetti neri* born in the wake of *Diabolik* and *Kriminal*.

world of 1960s Italy—a world of mass consumption and cheap dreams. There were even adults-only photonovels in the same vein, such as the notorious *Killing*, whose titular character also wore a skeleton costume and a skull mask.

In another rule-breaking move, these criminals had ravishing female sidekicks (who served as partners in bed as well as in crime), while their opponents where upright police officers who would inevitably be defeated by the antihero. Overall, the good guys were banal, insignificant characters without any distinctive or sympathetic trait. The bad ones proved to be much more interesting. And, above all, they were proof that crime *did* pay—in money and beautiful women ready to fall at their feet. "If you make love like you kill, you must be a superb lover!" a brunette lying naked on a bed whispers to Fantax in a typical *fumetto nero* scene, which pairs murder and sex.

However, at the core these comics were exacting a dual, ambiguous influence. As critics pointed out:

> On one hand they satisfied their inhibited readers' demand for transgression;

came secondary; the dialogue was often unnecessary. The style became just as important—actually, even more important—than the content itself.

The other *fumetti neri* were definitely not in the same league, starting with the simplistic drawings and the bottom-of-the-barrel stories and dialogue. Whereas mainstream comic books featured a high level of skills and efficiency, due to the key presence in the market of such huge publishers as Mondadori and Rizzoli, the smaller *fumetti neri* were born and operated in a less polished way. Sometimes these smaller "publishing houses" just consisted of improvised typographers-turned-publishers, who hired inexperienced artists, fresh from art school, to churn out comics in a hurry and jump on the bandwagon.

Ruthless criminals, rapists, torturers—these masked figures with unlikely (and usually highly significant) names—were a cheap updating of the myth of the decadent superhero, the very last and least in the vein of such controversial writers and intellectuals as Swinburne, Barbey D'Aurevilly and Barrès on one hand and Nietzsche and D'Annunzio on the other. They were remorseless beings who embodied an ideal of superiority transposed from a romantic and decadent setting to the chaotic, greedy

The controversial photonovel *Killing* featured a masked criminal whose costume was nearly identical to Kriminal's.

Satanik eventually became a film directed by Piero Vivarelli and starring Magda Konopka, released in 1968.

cesses, to avoid bloody scenes, overly strong images, horrific visions, torture scenes, sadism and to ban the use of knives (which, as a domestic utensil, were easily accessible to everyone and therefore might be used in a spirit of imitation on the part of the most gullible readers). Also, to have the protagonists act for the ultimate triumph of good over evil and employ cleverness rather than brute force.

Meanwhile, producers were starting to adapt the most popular *fumetti neri* for the screen, starting with *Kriminal* (1966, Umberto Lenzi) and its follow-up *Il marchio di Kriminal* (1967, Fernando Cerchio), *Avenger X* (*Mister-X*, 1967, Piero Vivarelli), *Satanik* (1968, Piero Vivarelli) and naturally *Danger: Diabolik*, which had a troubled production history and eventually became a film directed by Mario Bava for mogul producer Dino De Laurentiis, released in 1968.

If one considers that Italy's only other comic book adaptation had been 1941s *Princess Cinderella*, the transition from paper to the big screen of the most popular *fumetti neri* gives an idea of how things had changed in the film industry by that time. Producers, scriptwriters and filmmakers were absorbing and exploiting whatever impulse would seem profitable, in a frenzy of sorts that characterized the current and next decade.

Suddenly, *fumetti neri* were everywhere. Along with film adaptations—or even before them—came the parodies (such as the *Diabolik* spoof *How to Kill 400 Duponts*), the rip-offs (Ruggero Deodato's *Phenomenal and the Treasure of Tutankamen* and Guido Zurli's *Psychopath*), the tongue-in-cheek references, the knowing nods to the audience and the "K"s in the names. Consider, for instance, a TV commercial that featured an animated masked character dubbed Sorbolik, or the cheapo Western *The Bang-Bang Kid* (1967, Luciano Lelli and Giorgio Gentili), whose main villain (played by a black-dressed Riccardo Garrone) was called Killer Kissick. Even the spy film *FX 18, Secret Agent* (*Agent Secret FX 18*, 1964, Maurice Cloche), released in Italy as *Uccidete agente segreto 777—Stop*, was advertised with posters featuring characters taken from Magnus & Bunker's *Kriminal* and *Satanik*.

Coming three or four years after the birth of the *fumetti neri* craze, the first movie adaptations were not just a matter of censorship issues but also of an evolution in taste and aesthetics. Their explosion further underlined comics' centrality in everyday life and popular culture. It was in that period that the national film industry started looking at *fumetti* as a source of inspiration. Earlier on, elements drawn from comics had made occasional appearances in Italian films, often in comedies, where they would underline the protagonists' gags. For instance, *Totò, Peppino e le fanatiche* (1958) features a sequence where Totò and his family cannot communicate because of the overwhelm-

on the other hand, they exasperated it even further, by stressing the fact that pleasure equals evil, woman equals devil, body equals sin. Only a great criminal does have the strength to go beyond these boundaries. […] These heroes in black leotards are the heirs of a tradition and degeneration that goes from the Byronic hero through Rocambole to the Third Reich's SS.[5]

Fumetti neri caused a big fuss. The public opinion was outraged. Many accused them of corrupting the youth and blamed the supposedly negative morals they heralded, not to mention the daring erotic content. Soon, following a wave of seizures, trials and heated press campaigns, the publishers had to come up with a self-imposed "moral code" in order to put some limits to the most blatant ex-ing noise produced by the appliances in their new kitchen. Their inaudible dialogue appears on the screen in the form of comics-style balloons.

In the 1960s, *fumetti* became a recurrent presence in motion pictures—often carrying a symbolic meaning. For instance, the characters played by Vittorio Gassman in *Hard Time for Princes* (*La congiuntura*, 1964, Ettore Scola) and Rossano Brazzi in *Engagement Italiano* (*La ragazza in prestito*, 1964, Alfredo Giannetti) are revealed to be avid *Superman* readers—a habit which in Scola's film hints at the protagonist's Peter Pan complex, whereas in Giannetti's at his impotence, as Brazzi prefers reading his favorite comic rather than going to bed with a young girl. Massimo Franciosa's *Il morbidone* (1965) features a *Flash Gordon* fanatic, while Marcello Mastroianni's character in *The Tenth Victim* (*La decima vittima*, 1965, Elio Petri) has a whole bookshelf packed full with comics, which he considers classics. Vittorio Caprioli's *Scusi facciamo l'amore?* (1968) includes a scene in which Massimo Girotti dresses up as Batman, while Clint Eastwood, in Vittorio De Sica's episode *Una sera come le altre*—from the omnibus comedy *The Witches* (*Le streghe*, 1967)—is reproached by his embittered, unsatisfied wife (Silvana Mangano), who compares him unfavorably with the comic book antiheroes: "Those are real men! All you can do is bore me to death!"

Even more significantly, in Salvatore Samperi's vitriolic anti-bourgeois parable *Come Play with Me* (*Grazie, zia*, 1968), the neurotic and wheelchair-bound Alvise (Lou Castel) compulsively reads *Diabolik*, while Elio Petri's thought-provoking Gothic mystery *A Quiet Place in the Country* (*Un tranquillo posto di campagna*, 1968) is centered on an alienated, possibly schizophrenic Pop Art painter (Franco Nero), who is an avid consumer of risqué photonovels such as *Supersex* and *Sexybell*. While satirizing the way art has become a commodity in the modern-day world, Petri hints at the similar way the capitalistic system exploits sexuality and eroticism.

If comics were commonly used by filmmakers as a way of expressing their characters' lack of maturity—a common theme in Italian films of the period, best summed up by Dino Risi's unforgettable *The Easy Life* (*Il sorpasso*, 1962), the vast majority of popular cinema shared its escapist approach, with the rise of such genres as the Eurospy, the Western and the *giallo*—all of them more or less influenced by (as well as actively influencing, of course) Italian comics of the period.

Moreover, it was also a matter of style.

The 1960s was the decade of Pop Art all over the world. Pop Art was close to comics and vice versa. And intellectuals started looking at comic books in a different way, no longer considering them as a lower form of entertainment, but now as an art form. 1965 saw the birth of *Linus*, Italy's first "serious" monthly comic magazine. On its pages, one could find such diverse material as Charles Schultz's strips, Guido Crepax's *Valentina* and essays by Umberto Eco. In 1969 the renowned writer Dino Buzzati published *Poema a fumetti*, a work featuring Buzzati's favorite themes in the form of a graphic novel inspired by the myth of Orpheus, with homage to Dalí, Fellini, Warhol … and to popular *fumetti*. A famous photograph of the period shows Buzzati at work in his study. Behind him a poster featuring Diabolik can be glimpsed.

In those years, films often attempted to reproduce the comic book aesthetics—the colors, the use of camera angles and close-ups, the pacing and editing, the acting and so on. To some extent, comics were considered as an object of design, a matter of shiny surfaces and colors. Take Petri's sci-fi Pop Art confection *The Tenth Victim*, for instance, or Luciano Salce's *I Married You For Fun* (*Ti ho sposato per allegria*, 1967) and *Basta guardarla* (1970), where characters sometimes speak through balloons, in a reference to the soapy melodrama of the photonovels, which both films poke fun at.[6]

The *fumetti* influence was all over the place, sometimes in utterly surprising ways. Take Mino Guerrini's hard-boiled/whodunit hybrid *Date for a Murder* (*Omicidio per appuntamento*, 1967), a film characterized by an extremely refined visual style that is filled to the brim with Pop Art references that range from Tom Wesselmann to Domenico Gnoli (Guerrini was an accomplished painter before dabbling in filmmaking). The result shows how Guerrini was a much more promising filmmaker than his subsequent output would suggest. Alberto Cavallone (1930-1997), a former documentarian and advertiser, employed the language and style of *fumetti* in his 1971 low-budget spy spoof *Quickly, spari e baci a colazione*, which featured animated and comic book-like inserts, as well as a scene where the two protagonists, Sergio Leonardi and Jane Avril, start communicating through balloons in order not to be heard by the villain. Romano Scavolini's experimental short films often resorted to *fumetti* as a visual commentary. Take the hallucinated, self-explanatory *L.S.D.* (1970) and *Attacco! (Zen-Shin)* (1970), where the training of martial arts fighters is juxtaposed with panels by the comic artist Magnus to set against each other two different aspects of violence, the primary instinct and the language of the body, where the latter becomes a sort of grotesque *fumetti*-like synthesis.

Tinto Brass took inspiration from comics on several occasions. His Pop Art Western *Yankee* (1966) makes an almost abstract use of close-ups and camera angles, treating shots as if they were comic book panels; the *film noir Deadly Sweet* (*Col cuore in gola*, 1967) featured the collaboration of the renowned comic book artist Guido Crepax and *Attraction* (*Nerosubianco*, 1969) paid homage to Crepax as well as to Michael O'Donoghue and Frank Springer's *The Adventures of Phoebe Zeit-Geist*.[7]

Dino De Laurentiis' film version of *Diabolik*, directed by Mario Bava, was released in 1968.

Still, most of the films directly inspired by *fumetti neri* were disappointing when compared with their source. It was as if the moving image betrayed the one on paper. The stories were often variations on the typical heist film such as Jules Dassin's *Topkapi* (1964)—or, to name a successful Italian example, Marco Vicario's *Seven Golden Men* (*7 uomini d'oro*, 1965)—with a little bit of the James Bond-inspired gadgetry thrown in for good measure, and a man in a funny outfit to top it all.

To put it bluntly, these "geniuses of evil" did not look so menacing on screen. They were deprived of their most violent edges and were reduced to mere thieves or cat burglars, albeit with a weird taste for clothes. What is more, they were often more interesting as "Pop" exhibits than as significant attempts at capturing the language of comics. All in all, they looked like pale versions of Simon Templar—or, better still, the Fantômas character as revived (and reinvented in an openly parodist way) in the three French films directed by André Hunebelle and starring Jean Marais and Louis De Funès between 1964 and 1967. Ultimately, there was little or no difference between, say, *Diamonds Are a Man's Best Friend* (*Ray Master l'inafferrabile*, 1966, Vittorio Sala), a mediocre heist film about a womanizer international thief set in Bangkok, and the *fumetti neri*-based *Avenger X*—save for the protagonist's outfit. The few films that were not based on but simply inspired by the *fumetti neri*, such as *Phenomenal* and *Psychopath*, which further reduced the distinctive trait to just one thing, the costume, heightened such affinity.

By the end of the 1960s, though, the *fumetti neri* boom was over. Most disappeared as quickly as they had popped up (*Diabolik* is still being published to this day, though). They had exhausted their vital energy and function in a way. The mixture of thrills and violence would soon develop within a powerful movie genre, the Dario Argento-inspired *giallo*, whose black-gloved, masked assassins were faceless reincarnations of the "kings of crime" of the previous decade. Significantly, the thirst for material goods and wealth had been replaced by out-and-out sadism. The red thread between the two genres is dramatically shown in such films as the low-budget, bizarre early *giallo* *The Embalmer* (*Il mostro di Venezia*, 1966, Dino Tavella), which echoes the demented sadism and feverish dreamlike setting of the most lurid *fumetti neri*, with its cloaked villain wearing a skeleton mask, kidnapping young women and keeping their embalmed bodies in a subterranean Venetian crypt. Similarly, *The Girl in Room 2A* (*La casa della paura*, 1974, William A. Rose) features a hooded and cloaked executioner who kidnaps, tortures and kills "immoral" girls with the help of torture devices that look as if they were borrowed from a *Killing* photo shoot. Last but not least, Mario Moroni's trashy *giallo Ciak si muore* (1974) is focused on the shooting of a bizarre film-within-a-film whose climax features a plethora of Diabolik impersonators, each wearing an exact replica of the famous leotard and hood, among whom the murderer is hiding.

Meanwhile, audiences were looking for something more explicit; the call of the (naked) flesh was overwhelming. Soon a new trend began, that of erotic pocket comics. If the *fumetti neri* had been a key moment in the evolution of the sexual mores, they had soon become obsolete. Just as Italian erotic cinema was moving full sail toward the hardcore, the pocket comic strips would similarly evolve into pornography. By the end of the 1970s, the triple Xs had replaced the Ks.

Chapter Three
The Myth of the Italian Superhero

Besides the *fumetti neri*-inspired flicks, the mid-1960s also saw the emergence of another cinematic trend closely related to comic books: the superhero films.

The concept of the superhero in Italian cinema can be traced back to the early days of *Cabiria* (1914, Giovanni Pastrone) and the creation of Maciste, perhaps the country's first superman. As played by former dockhand Bartolomeo Pagano, the muscular Maciste was characterized primarily by the display of an exceptional, almost superhuman force that allowed him to perform extraordinary feats. Pagano/Maciste went on to become the star in a series of silent films that soon moved on from the Ancient Rome setting of Pastrone's film. A friendly giant who protected the weak and downtrodden, Maciste became the embodiment of patriotic values during Fascism, literally a "strong man" as the Duce loved to portray himself.

The late Fascist years, incidentally, saw the Italian debut of Superman … even though, due to the regime's habit of rejecting foreign names, the Man of Steel was rebaptized *Ciclone* (Cyclone) and his appearance was slightly redesigned. The Italian flag replaced the "S" on his chest and the costume sported different colors. The stories published in 1939 were taken from the daily strips destined to appear in U.S. newspapers, and the dialogue and drawings were drastically retouched so that the action appeared to take place in Italy. In the immediate post-war years, an Italian superhero also named Ciclone, created by Carlo Cossio, appeared. It was a rip-off of sorts of Siegel and Shuster's Superman character, but with an ironic, irreverent vein that made it closer to a parody than to a serious superhero. In subsequent years, Superman would again be published in Italy with a different name, *Nembo Kid*.

The resurfacing of muscle-bound heroes in the sword-and-sandal cycle of the late 1950s and early 1960s could also be seen as an Italian retelling of the typical superhero motifs. Hercules, Maciste, Ursus and their like not only performed incredible feats with superhuman strength, but they also faced arch-villains whose plans of deceit and

Asso di Picche, created in 1945 by Alberto Ongaro and Hugo Pratt, was one of Italy's first comic superheroes.

The Comic Book Universe in Italian Cinema

Gianfranco Parolini's *The Three Fantastic Supermen* (1967) was the first in Italy's longest-running superhero series. It starred Brad Harris (left), stuntman Nick Jordan (aka Aldo Canti, center) and Tony Kendall (aka Luciano Stella, right).

domination were ultimately overthrown by the hero at the very last minute. Italians did not know about Marvel comics yet, and their picture of the superhero was heavily influenced by an ideal of classical strength, not devoid of a homoerotic feel in the depiction of these demigods and their well-oiled bodies. Still, the sword-and-sandal genre (or *peplum*, as commonly defined in Italy) often contained fantasy, horror and even sci-fi elements—take Giacomo Gentilomo's *Hercules Against the Moon Men* (*Maciste e la regina di Samar*, 1964), for instance—that made these movies closer to their American counterparts, albeit within decidedly different environments. Stan Lee's *The Mighty Thor*, created in 1962, was in many ways an answer to Italian sword-and-sandal heroes, with Northern Europe mythology instead of the Greek and Roman ones.

Then came the spy films, which pushed the pedal of the fantastic much more often than their Anglo-Saxon models, incorporating sci-fi elements. The Eurospy genre proved influential on the Italian comic book universe. Examples were Magnus and Bunker's *Dennis Cobb—Agente SS 018* (41 issues, from May 1965 to February 1968) and the *Agenti segreti* series published by the Milan-based Sepim, namely the photonovel *Joe Crack* (7 issues, from April to October 1965) and *OS 117* [sic] inspired by Jean Bruce's character (15 issues, from July 1965 to September 1966).

It seemed just the right moment for a superhero *filone* (or stream) to blossom—and yet the advent of *fumetti neri* allowed a generation of fans to discover that siding with the bad guys could actually be more fun than cheering on the heroes. This perhaps explains why the superhero trend that eventually germinated in the mid-to-late '60s was not that successful in the first place. If the *fumetti neri* hinted at more adult entertainment, their masked counterparts were the remnants of a juvenile approach, which was gradually being put aside by genre cinema, more intent on discovering eroticism and violence.

There had indeed been Italian comic books featuring masked heroes, like *Asso di Picche*, created in 1945 by Alberto Ongaro and Hugo Pratt. A hooded avenger in the vein of *The Phantom*, who wears a yellow costume and fights organized crime, Asso di Picche has no superpowers but is an exceptional fighter and practices martial arts as well. The series lasted just 20 issues but proved to be successful abroad, especially in Argentina, where Pratt published new stories and the character was renamed As de Espadas. *Asso di Picche*—no relation to Nick Nostro's spy flick *Operation Counterspy* (*Asso di Picche operazione controspionaggio*, 1965) starring Giorgio Ardisson—was reprinted in 1967.

Ultimately, Italian superheroes on film—Superargo (*Superargo vs. Diabolicus*, 1966, Nick Nostro; *Superargo and the Faceless Giants*, 1968, Paolo Bianchini), Flashman (*Flashman*, 1967, Mino Loy), Argoman (*Argoman the Fantastic Superman*, 1967, Sergio Grieco), Goldface (*Goldface, the Fantastic Superman*, 1967, Bitto Albertini), The Three Supermen (*The Three Fantastic Supermen*, 1967, Gianfranco Parolini) and so forth—were a mixed bunch, benefitting from a number of diverse influences.

They were not directly based on *fumetti* but were often the patchwork result of a multiple cut-and-paste job, as scriptwriters and filmmakers put together characteristics of several different American superheroes, sometimes blatantly. The protagonist of *Flashman* ended up like a cross between Superman (finally published in Italy under its proper name from 1966) and Batman. Most borrowed from heroes of the Golden Age of American comics, yet with a distinctly Italian flavor. The over-reliance on such aged models as Lee Falk's *The Phantom* can be easily explained if one considers that Marvel Comics and its legion of masked heroes would reach our country only in 1970, thanks to Milan's Editoriale Corno (the same publisher as *Kriminal* and *Satanik*). By that time the idea of a subgenre dedicated to superheroes was out of the question within a movie industry that was committed to exploring eroticism.

Spanish poster for *Superargo vs. Diabolicus* (1966): Superargo was Italy's first masked superhero on film.

A major influence were the many films based on or inspired by the Zorro character, which were very popular at that time among the kids. Besides the many Italian/Spanish adaptations (brought about by the success of the 1957 TV series starring Guy Williams), there were also such rip-offs as Umberto Lenzi's *Terror of the Black Mask*, aka *The Invincible Masked Rider* (*L'invincibile cavaliere mascherato*, 1963) or Vertunnio De Angelis' *The Black Pirate* (*L'uomo mascherato contro i pirati*, 1964), starring Tony Kendall and George Hilton. Both films were about masked heroes with secret identities who fight against the baddies. Even though the *fumetti* references were superficial, these films signaled the concept of an incognito vigilante was taking place in popular culture.

Another strong source of inspiration came from the Mexican wrestling flicks. Even though Italians were rather unfamiliar with professional wrestling, several superhero films were Spanish co-productions aimed at South American markets. Superargo, the first true Italian superhero on film, was actually an Italian rendition of the typical South-of-the-border *luchadores enmascarados*, such as El Santo—ditto for the garishly costumed Goldface.

Cinematically speaking, the affinities between the superhero flicks and the *fumetti neri*-based ones were obvious. For one thing, both came close to the contemporaneous Eurospy thread of the mid-1960s. Sometimes the references would be only nominal. Giorgio Ferroni's *Super Agent Super Dragon* (*New York chiama Superdrago*, 1966) featured a spy with a name starting with "Super," played by Ray Danton, as well as a pair of starlets (Margaret Lee and Marisa Mell, who both appeared in other *fumetti*-related movies, respectively *How to Kill 400 Duponts* and *Danger: Diabolik*) wearing hot comic book-like outfits, replete with a mask on the eyes …

Other spy films contained more pointed nods to the *fumetti* imagery. Sergio Sollima's *Agent 3S3, Massacre in the Sun* (*Agente 3S3 massacro al sole*, 1966) featured a female secret agent (Evi Marandi) who at a certain point changes her looks with the help of a Diabolik-style latex mask. Similarly, the titular character of *The Spy with Ten Faces* (*Up-*

French poster for *Superargo and the Faceless Giants* (1968), the second Superargo film

U.S. poster for *Super Stooges vs. The Wonder Women* (1974), a spurious entry in the Three Supermen series

perseven, l'uomo da uccidere, 1967, Alberto De Martino) can change his looks at will—just like The Phantom, Fantômas and Diabolik. Mario Sequi's *The Cobra* (*Il cobra*, 1967) starred a down-on-his-luck Dana Andrews (looking lost in an alcoholic fog throughout the film) as a secret agent on the track of a mysterious masked villain named Cobra—the same name as the villain in Bitto Albertini's *Goldface*. Alberto Lattuada's spy spoof *Mission Top Secret* (*Matchless*, 1967)—concocted by producer Dino de Laurentiis as a vehicle for princess Ira von Fürstenberg—featured a magic Chinese ring that makes the protagonist (Patrick O'Neal) invisible. Lattuada's film employs the idea of invisibility for malicious gags, since the aforementioned ring is useful only when O'Neal's character is in the nude, but the script (by Lattuada, veteran genre screenwriter Piero Regnoli and the renowned novelist Luigi Malerba … an odd team indeed) throws in tongue-in-cheek gags, such as the scene where Henry Silva (in a surprisingly amusing performance as a bumbling spy) stops torturing O'Neal to watch cartoons on TV, laughing like a kid.[7]

However, the aforementioned titles ultimately featured more or less limited references to the comics universe; on the other hand, with their over-the-top masked villains concocting elaborate plans to rule the world and deliriously childish scenarios, Paolo Bianchini's sci-fi low-budget oddities *The Devil's Man* (*Devilman Story*, 1967) and *Massacre Mania* (*Hipnos follia di massacro*, 1967) shared a much deeper comic book feel which put them in the same category as the proper film adaptations, much more so than the spy films with which they were often paired.[8]

Then there was, of course, the influence of the *peplum*, which was evident in Gianfranco Parolini's *The Three Fantastic Supermen*. Parolini's film had the merit of launching Italy's longest superhero series, with no less than seven sequels. The Three Supermen's adventures around the world reflected the nomadic quality of Italian popular cinema and its capability of cashing in on whatever was "hot" from time to time, before jumping onto the next *filone*, from the exotic jungle adventure to the *gongfupian*, from the *Trinità*-style Spaghetti Western to the short-lived Amazons fever briefly sparked (at least in Italy) by Terence Young's film *War Goddess* (*Le guerriere dal seno nudo*, 1973).

German lobby card for *Argoman the Fantastic Superman* (1967, Sergio Grieco), one of the funniest Italian superhero films of that period

The results, understandably, were less cinematically successful than symptomatic of the decline of the Italian film industry. After a number of co-productions (including one with Hong Kong's Shaw Brothers) the series was taken over by producer-cum-director Italo Martinenghi and the *Three Supermen* series landed in Turkey, a market where the idea of adults acting silly in colorful costumes still made for profitable results at the box-office.

All in all, however, Italian superheroes were quite a different breed than their overseas counterparts. Most of them were actually amoral figures, such as Argoman or the Three Supermen (two of whom are in fact thieves temporarily recruited by the F.B.I.). It was as if Italian spectators could not take sides for out-and-out good guys—just like in Italian comedies, where the most recurring characters were morally questionable protagonists whose flaws became the films' strong points.

This also partly explains why such heroic figures never really took root. Their lack of popular success was due also to the scarce appeal of the juvenile-oriented science-fiction genre, so much so that Alberto Margheriti's *Mr. Superinvisible* (*L'inafferrabile invincibile Mr. Invisibile*, 1970) was, despite its suggestive title, just a kiddy comedy modeled upon Disney live-action flicks of the period, a blueprint blatantly acknowledged by the casting of Dean Jones in the lead as an absent-minded professor who perfects an invisibility serum. Meanwhile, moviegoers were leaning toward the more violent, unscrupulous Spaghetti Western gunslingers, with their almost supernatural skills with weapons and often-sinister sense of humor. On the other hand, a more realistic incarnation of the hero would emerge in the early 1970s, with the crime film and the fearless—though not quite invulnerable—cops that populated them.

A second wave of Italian superheroes briefly surfaced by the end of the 1970s, after the worldwide success of Richard Donner's *Superman* (1978). However, these efforts only showed the quick deterioration of Italian genre output. Having to compete with costly, special effects-ridden products further emphasized the economical crisis that the film industry was undergoing. Significantly, Martinenghi's last entries in the *Three Supermen* series in the 1980s were not even released to theaters; on the other hand, Italian cinema found a new unlikely superman of a different kind in the hardcore porn *Bath-man dal pianeta Eros* (1982, Antonio D'Agostino).

The time for heroes had long gone.

Chapter Four
Forbidden to Minors ... The Adults-Only Comics

Once again, it all started in 1962. This time in France, though—and it took three years before Jean-Claude Forest's scandalous *Barbarella* produced its effects in Italy. As film director Corrado Farina recalled:

> In the Summer of 1965, however, *Barbarella* was known only by those few who had the chance to buy Jean-Claude Forest's book in France, despite the censors' lightning that immediately struck it.[9]

Forest's uninhibited heroine was still an elitist phenomenon, totally unknown to the large majority of the public. Which meant it was a field day for Italian comics publishers, "because," as Farina put it:

> Here in Italy, with the ease of assimilation (but it would be better to say plagiarism) that has always distinguished us, many had the idea of making easy money by ripping off Forest's creation. It was simply a matter of finding her a new name, so as not to incur the wrath of the French publisher, and beat the others on time.[10]

The Summer of '65 saw the descent from space of many alluring astral bimbos. The first of the lot was *Selene*, written by "Victor Newman" (a collective pseudonym under which hid Corrado Farina as well as others) and drawn by "Paul Savant," alias Marco Rostagno[11], but the list comprises *Astrella*, Magnus & Bunker's *Gesebel* and then *Uranella*, *Cosmine*, *Venus*, *Alika*.

Of all these, the one that came closest to a film adaptation was *Alika*. A young French director, Jean Rollin, noticed it in a newsstand during a trip to Italy. Rollin immediately wrote to the Roman publisher to gather information about acquiring the film rights, stating that he was looking for "stories for science-fiction films that we hope to shoot as co-productions with a British company."[12] A contest to find a leading actress was advertised on the comic's pages, claiming that the film would be released in 1968, but the project was shelved. Rollin would soon try his hand at comics, writing the celebrated *Saga de Xam*, with illustrations by the elusive Nicholas Devil.

Curiously, *Alika*, subtitled *Il thrilling dello spazio* (The space thriller), originally mixed suspense, sci-fi and mild eroticism, whereas—starting with issue #8—it unexpectedly veered toward satire. The stories became littered with characters inspired by popular actors, singers, TV personalities and politicians. Issue #14 (*Aiuto! I Beatles*) even had the Fab Four posing as "interstellar musketeers" and battling against a popular Italian melodic singer, Claudio Villa. If this new course was a gimmick to avoid censorship, it proved unsuccessful. *Alika* met a similar fate as the *fumetti neri* of the period. In November 1966, issue #12 (*Il cavaliere mascherato*) was seized, together with a number of other comics, because of its content:

> Erotic scenes and even homosexual couplings; scenes of sadism and violence with horrific and gruesome details, such as to disturb public order, the order of the family and incite to criminality and crime.

Jean-Claude Forest's *Barbarella* (made into a film starring Jane Fonda) proved to be a huge influence on Italian comic books

Among Barbarella's offspring came Magnus and Bunker's saucy space opera, *Gesebel*.

A German poster for Bruno Corbucci's *Ms. Stiletto* (1969), based upon the very first Italian erotic *fumetto Isabella*, published in 1966

On the other hand, the Venetian Guido Crepax offered a different kind of erotic *frissons*, aimed at a more refined audience and far more significant artistically. Crepax's fascinating *Valentina*, about a fashion photographer resembling the silent diva Louise Brooks, who experiences all kinds of morbid daydreams and adventures, debuted in 1965 in the magazine *Linus*. It was adapted into a film by Corrado Farina with *Baba Yaga* in 1973.

Several years passed before Dino De Laurentiis produced a film adaptation of Forest's comic, which came out in 1968. When *Barbarella* went into production, the eponymous heroine had just landed on the pages of the thinking man's comic mag *Linus*, and by that time the imitations had long gone. Nevertheless, even though those sci-fi erotic paperbacks were short-lived, they paved the way for another revolution in the world of Italian comics—and, even though to a lesser extent, in genre cinema itself.

The basic idea was Columbus' egg. Science-fiction had never been a favorite genre among Italian readers, and the few onscreen examples had been either little-known B-flicks which failed to generate much interest—such as Paolo Heusch' *The Day the Sky Exploded* (*La morte viene dallo spazio*, 1958)—or *auteur* projects such as *The Tenth Victim*, which in turn bore a distinct comic book influence in the Pop Art set-pieces as well as in Ursula Andress' striking outfits. Anyway, if the future was not a good option, why not look back to the past? The spark came yet again from France, with yet another blonde heroine, Angelica, the female protagonist of *Angélique, Marquise des Anges* (1964, Bernard Borderie), based on the popular paperback novels by Anne and Serge Golon, starring Michèle Mercier. The imitation of 19th century serial novels, the so-called *feuilletons*, with their damsels-in-distress, sadistically cruel villains, adventures and passion—but with an emphasis on nudity and morbidity—would prove the starting point for the birth of Italy's very first out-and-out erotic comic, *Isabella*. It was 1966.

In some ways, it was the logical step forward after the *fumetti neri*. Audiences were hungry for nude flesh—either in film, pictures or comics. It took three years for *Isabella* to be adapted into film with Bruno Corbucci's *Ms. Stiletto* (*Isabella, duchessa dei diavoli*, 1969). Around the same time came Ruggero Deodato's *Zenabel* (1969), patently inspired by *Isabella* and more explicit both in its comic book refer-

The influence of adults-only comics can be found in films featuring scantily-dressed jungle heroines, such as *Luana, The Girl Tarzan* (1968, Roberto Infascelli).

ences, due to the use of balloons and the like, and eroticism. Meanwhile, the screens—and not just them—were flooded with female nudity. As satirized by Dino Risi's omnibus comedy *Vedo nudo* (I See Naked, 1969), sex was literally everywhere, and newsstands were overflowing with all kinds of erotic material. Even a publication like the photonovel, originally aimed at female audiences, had veered toward adults-only material by "allying with other male-oriented genres such as the Western, horror, the war film and then the sexy thread."[13] This favored the apparition of a new kind of *fotoromanzi*, such as the quarterly *Cinesex*, which offered photonovels based on films that heightened the latter's erotic content and actually reshaped their plots with an emphasis on the sex scenes.[14]

The adults-only *fumetti* were a wild and varied bunch. Most had period settings, like *Messalina* (launched in October 1966, it ran for 185 issues until August 1974), *Belfagor—L'arcidiavolo* (March 1967), the Arsène Lupin-type *Dominò il vendicatore* (May 1967), *Lucrezia* (1969, named after the notorious Lucrezia Borgia) and *Jolanda* (loosely based on the female pirate created in the early 1900s by novelist Emilio Salgari). Some, like *Goldrake Playboy* (March 1966) and *Cap* (November 1966) were set in the present. The former drew on Eurospy while the latter flirted with the phenomenon of the so-called "longhairs." Others, like *Al Capone* and *Bonnie*, sported a 1930s setting and hinted at *Bonnie & Clyde* (1967, Arthur Penn), which also spawned a short-lived period crime subgenre in the late 1960s. A number of adults-only comics, like *Jacula*, *Lucifera* and *Zora la vampira*, flirted with horror, whereas *Hessa* predated the Nazi-SS subgenre of the mid-1970s, with an uncomfortable over-reliance on the Nazi imagery (and with excerpts from Hitler's *Mein Kampf* as an appendix to the stories!) that eventually caused its premature end in 1972, after 42 issues, due to the insistence of the artists themselves. Then there was the Western, with *Vartan* (named after the French singer Sylvie Vartan) and *Walalla*; the spicy fairy tales (*Biancaneve*, created in 1972 by Rubino Ventura—real name Giorgio Pederiali—and Leone Frollo, based on Snow White, was one of the decade's very best) and so on …

The relationship between adult-oriented comics and cinema was, ultimately, a mutual influence. A number of comics had their roots in film. *Belfagor—L'arcidiavolo*, for instance, was loosely inspired by Ettore Scola's film *The Devil In Love* (*L'arcidiavolo*, 1966), starring Vittorio Gassman and Mickey Rooney. With *Lucrezia* Barbieri and Cavedon possibly drew from Osvaldo Civirani's film of the same name, starring Olinka Berova. Furthermore, the artists used to take inspiration from movie stars. *Goldrake* was about a secret agent whose features resembled those of French actor Jean-Paul Belmondo and whose partner looked just like Ursula Andress, and the bawdy *Lando* (a reference to comedian Lando Buzzanca, famous for his roles as a Southern, sex-obsessed Alpha male) had the face of singer-cum-actor Adriano Celentano. Ditto for the girls: *Zora la vampira*'s eponymous vampire bore a passing resemblance to Catherine Deneuve, the female devil *Lucifera* (published between 1971 and 1980, with 170 issues overall) was inspired by Marisa Mell and the super sexy bloodsucker *Sukia* (launched in 1977, 156 issues) was a dead ringer for the drop-dead gorgeous Ornella Muti.

Despite their popularity, most of these comics were not adapted into film, even though a number of projects seemed about to materialize over the years. A motion picture based on *Messalina* and starring the British pin-

Many adults-only comics flirted with the horror genre. One of the most popular was *Zora la Vampira*.

gin" raised in the wild jungle. The two *Gungala* films were emblematic in such respect. Ferrara and Deodato had their female lead, Dutch actress Kitty Swan, run through the African savanna in the nude in long shots, but whenever there was a medium shot or close-up of Swan's body, it was partially obscured with leaves or other props in order to cover the "offensive" parts—just like De Laurentiis had done with Jane Fonda's striptease at the beginning of *Barbarella*. Piero Regnoli's little-seen *La principessa sul pisello* (shot in 1973 but released only in 1976) was an anthology comedy that featured spicy versions of *Cinderella* and *Snow White*, inspired by adults-only comics of the period such as *Cappuccetto Rotto* and *Biancaneve*. Ventura and Frollo's comic was also the uncredited source for Mario Bianchi's 1982 sex comedy *Biancaneve & Co.*

To a lesser degree, the Gothic horror flicks made in the early 1970s were inspired by the sex-horror comics that represented a further step toward out-and-out hardcore. Take, for instance, *The Night of the Damned* (*La notte dei dannati*, 1971, Peter Rush [Filippo Ratti]), *The Devil's Wedding*

up Dolly Reed was announced in 1968, while *Walalla* #9 (April 1970) included a promotional pic of actress Katia Christine in the titular role during the making of a film that never saw the light of day. *Jacula* (one of the most durable of the lot; its publication ran from 1969 to 1982, with a total of 327 issues) was supposed to be adapted for the big screen in 1980 by director Vittorio De Sisti, with the participation of its creators.

Still, the influence of adults-only comics on the Italian movie industry went far beyond the explicit film adaptations. Take, for instance, the mini-thread about scantily-dressed jungle heroines: *Gungala la vergine della giungla* (1967, Romano Ferrara) and *Gungala, the Black Panther Girl* (*Gungala la pantera nuda*, 1968, Ruggero Deodato), *Luana, the Girl Tarzan* (*Luana la figlia della foresta vergine*, 1968, Roberto Infascelli), *Eva la venere selvaggia* (1968, Roberto Mauri), *Samoa, regina della giungla* (1968, Guido Malatesta) and *Tarzana the Wild Girl* (*Tarzana, sesso selvaggio*, 1969, Guido Malatesta). These "wild girls" openly recalled comic book heroines such as *Pantera Bionda*, Italy's first jungle girl created in 1948 by Enzo Magni (aka Ingam), as well as Renzo Barbieri's spicier *Jungla*, published between September 1968 and December 1971 and centered on a white "African vir-

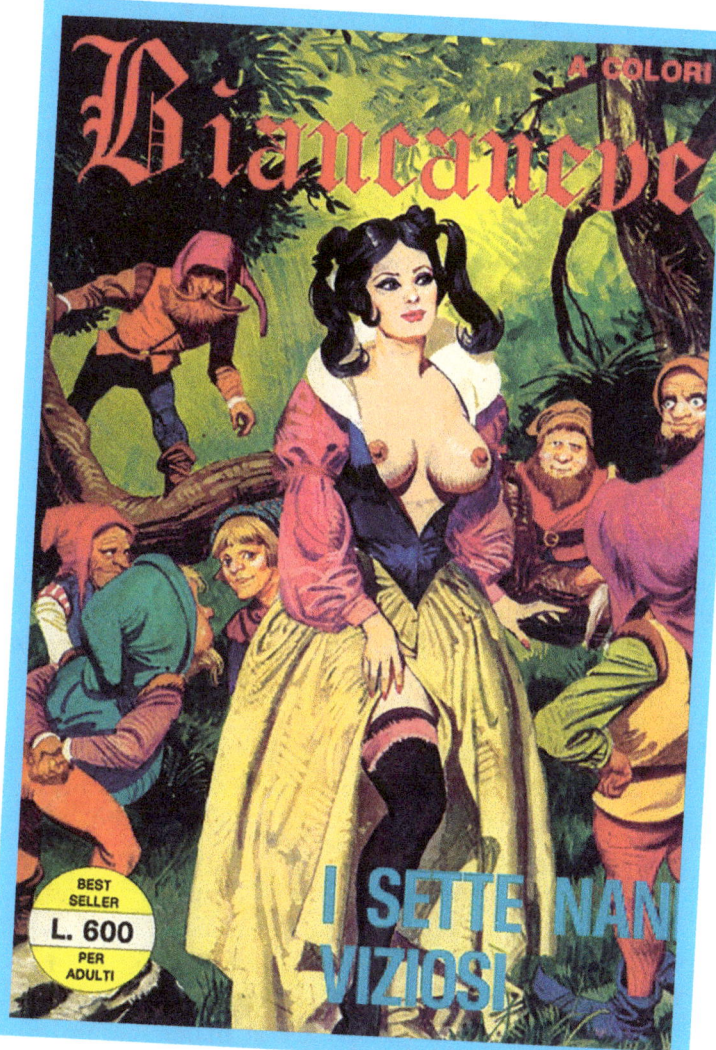

Biancaneve, by Rubino Ventura and Leone Frollo, was one of the best adults-only comics of the 1970s.

The Comic Book Universe in Italian Cinema

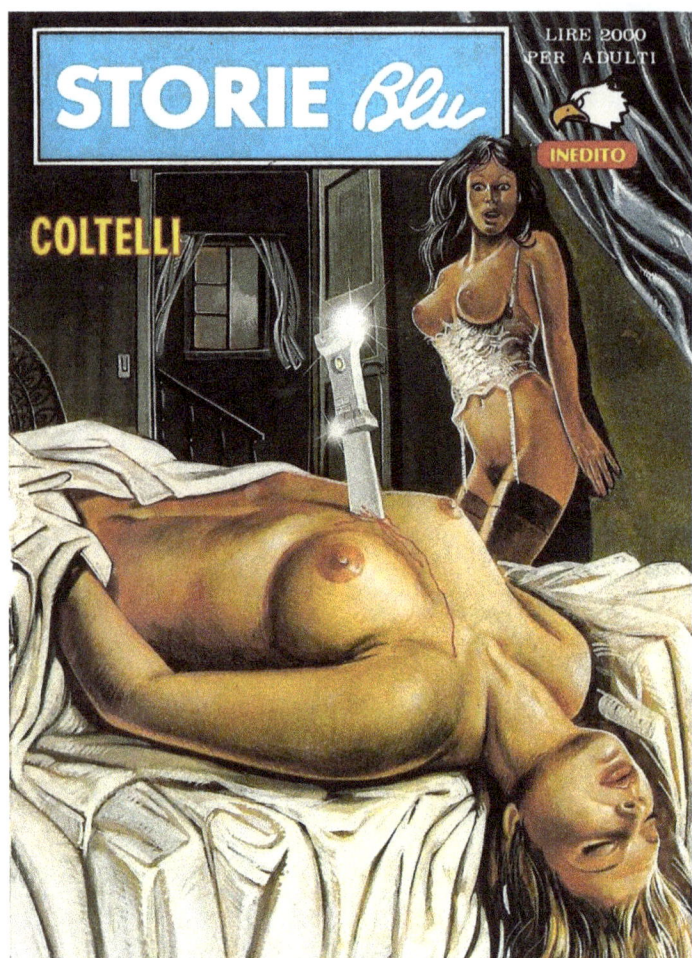

The sleazy *Storie Blu* series mixed hardcore sex, over-the-top gore and sci-fi elements into sordid bliss.

Night (*Il plenilunio delle vergini*, 1973, Paolo Solvay [Luigi Batzella]) and *Nude for Satan* (*Nuda per Satana*, 1974, Paolo Solvay [Luigi Batzella]), with their scantily-dressed *ingénues*, libidinous witches and female vampires who looked more like men-eaters and were less scary than they were exciting. In those films, the Gothic imagery became an accessory, similar to what happened in the comics of the period, which often used horror as a pretext to push the pedal of sadomasochism and assorted perversions, while hardcore porn films were still officially prohibited in the country (although filmmakers had started shooting explicit inserts for foreign markets).

Indie filmmakers have paid homage to *Oltretomba* with interesting results, namely *Bloody Sin* (2013, Domiziano Cristopharo) and the anthology *Catacomba* (2016, Lorenzo Lepori, Roberto Albanesi). On the other hand, its title notwithstanding, *Zora la vampira* (2000, Marco and Antonio Manetti) bears no relation whatsoever to the comic book by the same name. It is a horror comedy set in contemporary Rome that deals with topics such as clandestine immigration (Dracula arrives in Italy on an immigrants boat) and the local hip-hop scene (Zora is a graffiti writer, and hip-hop songs are amply featured in the soundtrack).

Overall, the weight that comics imagery had in Italian popular culture of the decade is best summarized in Pasquale Squitieri's *Viaggia, ragazza, viaggia: hai la musica nelle vene* (1973), one of the very first Italian films about drug addiction, where Squitieri interspersed or partially replaced the sex scenes with panels from adults-only comics. Anyway, as far as the direct relationship between comics and film scripts goes, there is still much to be unearthed, as the history of Italian *fumetti* is littered with little-known, surprising connections. Scriptwriter Fabio Piccioni recently revealed one. In an interview Piccioni recalled the vicissitudes of a scenario he wrote, *Il grido del capricorno* (The Cry of the Capricorn), which paved the basis for several adaptations, both as a comic and on film. First it was used for an eponymous special issue of *Oltretomba Gigante* (#9, February 1974, with drawings by José María Bellalta). Set in late 19th-century Germany, *Il grido del capricorno* is the story of a young orchestra director, Ludwig von Mayer, who lives in the shadow of his late father, a great composer, and is oppressed by a domineering mother who wants him to follow in his father's footsteps and become as famous as him. Meanwhile, a black-gloved killer begins to dispatch von Mayer's lovers and friends in suitably gruesome ways (and with ample display of nudity and sadism). The police and a criminologist start suspecting Ludwig, who is revealed to have killed his own father as a child, but bears no memory of the event. Then, after Ludwig's wife-to-be Helga is horribly murdered too, a shocking truth is revealed.

Being in severe shortage of cash, Piccioni approached Salvatore Argento, with whom he was on good terms and whose office was just in front of his house in Rome, and sold him *Il grido del capricorno* for 500,000 *lire*. The deal had an ironic side which perhaps came unnoticed to both parties, given that a couple of scenes in the comic were blatantly stolen from *The Bird with the Crystal Plumage*. Namely, the killer terrorizing a woman in bed and ripping off her panties, and the maniac attempting to break into Helga's house, by jimmying the door with a knife, as the woman watches in terror.

Very little of *Il grido del capricorno* ultimately appeared as the basic core that became *Deep Red* (*Profondo rosso*, 1975), but it was vital to the film's architecture. The relationship between Carlo (Gabriele Lavia) and his oppressive mother (Clara Calamai) comes from it, as does the brief opening flashback in which a child is seen picking up the knife that just killed his father, an image taken almost verbatim from Piccioni's story (and the *Oltretomba* comic). The rest, of course, was all Dario Argento's invention. And it is no surprise that Argento chose not to follow the outrageous final twist in which the murderer is not only revealed to be Ludwig's mother, but the elderly woman turns out to be a man in disguise, the late von Mayer's longtime lover—shades of Gunnar Hellström's *The Name of the Game Is Kill!*

(1968). Piccioni recycled the basic story once more a few years later in a contemporary setting. Again a young man becomes obsessed by the memory of his late father, an orchestra director; again a domineering, overly possessive mother becomes paramount and a flashback reveals the child's apparent role in his parent's murder. The result was Riccardo Freda's *Murder Obsession* (1981), which pushed the story toward even darker territories by accommodating black magic and incest.[15] The case of *Il grido del capricorno* is probably not a solitary occurrence; many screenwriters also dabbled with un-credited work in the fumetti industry (Piccioni himself wrote a number of stories for the *Terror* series) and turned their unproduced scripts into comic book scenarios.

Curiously, the taboo of hardcore pornography was officially broken in a *fumetto* before it was on screen. Magnus' *Lo Sconosciuto* was the first Italian comic book featuring the sight of an erect male sex organ and graphically depicted intercourse. It happened in issue #2, *Largo delle Tre Api*, published in August 1975, two years before the first "red light" theater—the Majestic Sexy Movie in Milan—opened.[16] In the following years, an impressive amount of hardcore comics were commercialized: Renzo Barbieri's company Edifumetto (and later Edizioni Lo Squalo/Squalo Comics, as well as a number of other brands, all traceable to Barbieri) cranked out adults-only pocket-sized strips with assembly line rhythms. The quality was often rushed and sloppy, and the contents were wildly outrageous, mixing horror, science fiction and pornography with an insistence on gory sexual-oriented torture scenes, such as in the infamous *Storie Blu* series. The results were akin to the Z-grade *gialli* and horror flicks produced near the end of the decade by Gabriele Crisanti, such as *Malabimba* (1979, Andrea Bianchi), *Giallo a Venezia* (1980, Mario Landi) and *Patrick Still Lives* (*Patrick vive ancora*, 1980, Mario Landi), with their over-the-top gruesome excesses.

With the gradual waning of the pocket hardcore craze, the 1980s and 1990s offered more examples of ambitious adults-only comics, such as Paolo Eleuteri Serpieri's *Morbus Gravis*, which featured the buxom Druuna, Franco Saudelli's *La Bionda* or Magnus' truly extraordinary *Le 110 pillole*, based on the 16th-century Chinese erotic novel *Jin Ping Mei*. This thread was strengthened by the appearance of glossy comic magazines such as *Blue* and *Selen*—named after Selen (Luce Caponegro), Italy's most sought-after porn star of the decade (after the death of Moana Pozzi). After years of undifferentiated mass consumption, eroticism in comics was becoming something close to elite.

The most popular Italian erotic comics artist today is probably Milo Manara, whose exquisite soft-core graphic novels, featuring his trademark pouty, slinky women, arrived on the screen in the 1980s with a French production. *Le Déclic* (1985, Jean-Louis Richard), based on *Il gioco*, allegedly featured scenes directed by Bob Rafelson after Richard was fired, was a critical disaster but launched the gorgeous French starlet Florence Guérin. Much more interesting, however, was Manara's collaboration with Federico Fellini. The artist illustrated Fellini's script *Viaggio a Tulum* (1989) and later the first part of *Il viaggio di G. Mastorna, detto Fernet* (1992), based on Fellini's legendary un-filmed project that dated back to the mid-1960s. Manara also collaborated with Alejandro Jodorowsky and Neil Gaiman, among others.

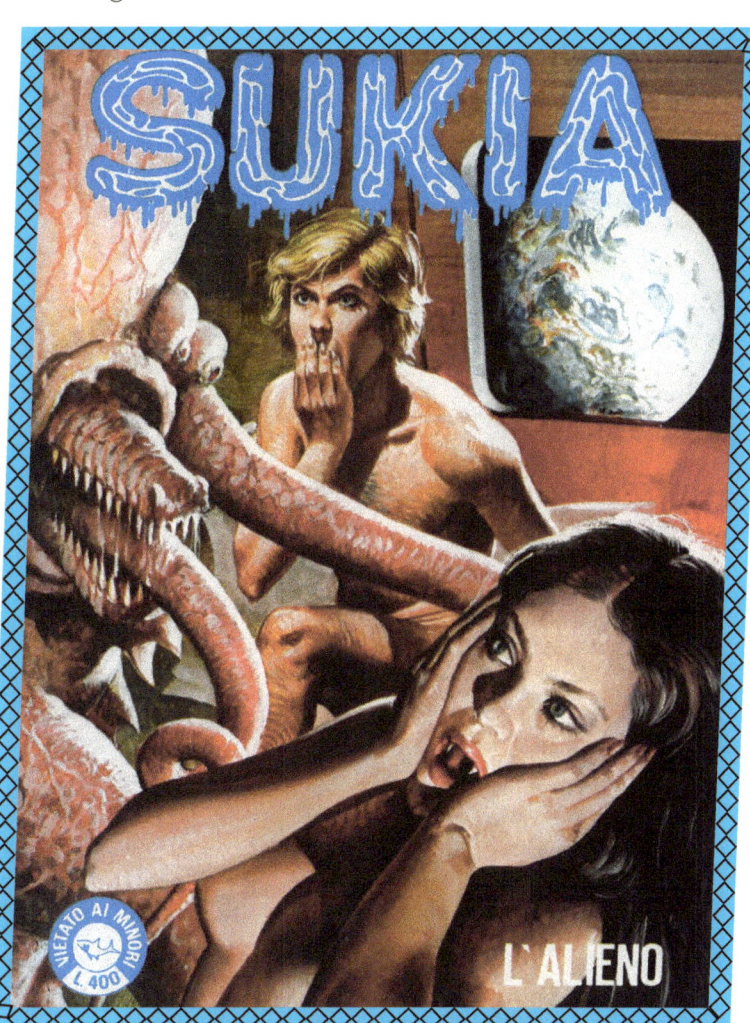

Sukia was another adults-only comic book. Here the heroine has the features of Italian movie star Ornella Muti.

Overall, though, the Italian porn industry did not dwell on comic books for inspiration. Partly, it can be blamed on the nature of Italian hardcore itself, and especially on the shoestring budgets, a fact that is evident when one considers the abysmal XXX Batman parody *Bath-man dal pianeta Eros* (1982). The only real attempt at blending explicit sex with *fumetti* was Max Bellocchio's ill-fated *DiaboliX (Colpo internazionale)* (1992), plagued by legal issues after *Diabolik*'s creator Luciana Giussani sued the makers.[17]

CHAPTER FIVE
SPOOF, SATIRE AND SOCIAL CRITICISM

The Italians have always been a deeply disenchanted people. How could it be otherwise, after thousands of years, which saw the country undergo countless dominations, wars and assorted political turmoils? As Harry Lime (Orson Welles) put it in *The Third Man* (1949, Carol Reed):

> In Italy for 30 years under the Borgias they had warfare, terror, murder and bloodshed, but they produced Michelangelo, Leonardo da Vinci and the Renaissance. In Switzerland they had brotherly love; they had 500 years of democracy and peace, and what did that produce? … the cuckoo clock.

The anthology comedy *Thrilling* (1965) poked fun at the *fumetti neri* phenomenon.

Along with violence and suffering came art, but with art came also its antidote—mockery, parody and laughter.

In Ancient Rome, there was the *satura* (later *satira*), a literary genre and a form of stage play. Partly inherited from the Greeks and perfected by such writers as Horatio, it was their favorite way to criticize society and politics in an often-edgy way. In the Middle Ages there were the heroic-comic poems. And so on, and on, from the pamphlets of the age of Enlightenment to the satirical magazines that flourished between the end of the 19th century and the early 20th century. With the discovery of the new medium—cinema—it was inevitable that filmmakers would try their hand at satire, parody and spoof as a means of reading and commenting on whatever might come handy, from politics to social trends.

Often such a humorous approach preceded the serious efforts. Take Steno's *Uncle Was a Vampire* (*Tempi duri per i vampiri*, 1959). Italy's first *real* vampire film—given that Riccardo Freda's *I vampiri* (1957) dealt with a different kind of bloodsucker than Dracula and the like—was a parody. That said it was understandable that such a phenomenon as the *fumetti neri* boom gave way to its share of spoofs, starting with the most popular of the lot—*Diabolik*.

First there was television. Singer-cum-TV show host Johnny Dorelli launched his own version of the character, Dorellik in the first installment of his television show *Johnny Sera*, on April 28, 1966. Even before Dino De Laurentiis could release the official film version of the comic book, Dorelli starred as Dorellik in *How to Kill 400 Duponts* (*Arrriva Dorellik*, 1967), directed once again by Steno.

Then there were the TV commercials. In the late 1950s, the brandy Vecchia Romagna had launched a successful advertising campaign based on the slogan "the brandy that creates an atmosphere" (a catchphrase in 1960s Italy, which made Vecchia Romagna a staple in every bourgeois home) and it benefitted from the presence of the famous veteran actor Gino Cervi[18]. In 1967 the Vecchia Romagna TV spots flanked Cervi by an animated character named Sorbolik, a funny looking, clumsily masked superhero which poked fun at *Diabolik* and all the *fumetti neri* characters with a "K" in their name.[19] Sorbolik was drawn directly on each frame, thus interacting with Cervi in a most primitive way—*Who Framed Roger Rabbit* (1988) it surely was not. However, the teaming up

Johnny Dorelli appears as Dorellik

Bonvi (real name Franco Bonvicini) was the creator of the extraordinary comic strip *Sturmtruppen*.

was a winning one, and soon Sorbolik became a children's favorite. The advertising continued up to 1972.

And then, of course, there were the comic book parodies from the short-lived Diabetik to the far more successful Paperinik (that is, Donald Duck moonlighting as a masked vigilante—closer to Batman than to Diabolik, actually) launched by the Disney Italia company in 1969 and introduced in the magazine *Topolino* (Mickey Mouse)—not to mention Bonvi's exhilarating *Cattivik*. The 1990s saw the debut of Parabolik, created in 1996 by Moreno Burattini, and we must not forget the recent, eccentric 44-page volume *Pasolik—Il fumettok del brividok* (2010), the result of a joint venture of several comic artists.

Fumetti neri, for all their sociological implications, were the target of the ever-biting *commedia all'italiana*—so much so that the first real apparition of a comic book-inspired character came not in one of the official adaptations, but in the comedy anthology *Thrilling* (1965), which dedicated one episode to *Sadik*, one of the most violent—yet artistically less remarkable—of the lot. Even more interesting was 1968's *Caprice Italian Style*, where the allusions to *fumetti neri* were employed as a way of reflecting on the ongoing generational conflict.

As for Italian superheroes, they included a quantum of mockery and humor in their DNA right from the start, as can be noticed in the straight examples of the sub-genre, such as *Flashman* or *Argoman the Fantastic Superman*—not to mention the amiable *Three Supermen* series. Yet those were simply genre flicks aimed at an unpretentious teen audience, whereas Sergio Spina's *Fantabulous Inc.* (*La donna, il sesso, il superuomo*, 1968) was a different matter altogether, and closer in tone to such thought-provoking oddities as William Klein's *Mr. Freedom* (1969). Beneath the surface of a spy/superhero yarn, Spina's film was a sociological and political satire that mixed such different topics as the Vietnam war and the influence of advertising on the silent majority. Similarly, Bruno Bozzetto's *The SuperVIPs* (*VIP, mio fratello superuomo*, 1968) spoofed the superhero craze in cartoon form, as a pretext to discuss the effects of the age of consumerism. Interestingly, several comics writers, such as Corrado Farina and Pier Carpi, also dabbled in advertising (as Ruggero Deodato would do in the early 1970s) before moving on to film directing. The insistence on such staples of popular culture as comics and advertising was a sign of the political awareness that marked the production of fantastic films in the late 1960s, such as Roberto Faenza's *H2S* (1969), Marcello Aliprandi's *La ragazza di latta* (1970), Farina's own *They Have Changed Faces* (*Hanno cambiato faccia*, 1971) and Silvano Agosti's *N.P. il segreto* (1971), to name a few.

On the other hand, Italy's most popular comic strip of the 1970s *was* a spoof. *Alan Ford*, created in 1969 by Magnus & Bunker, was born as a parody of the James Bond fever. It focused on an unlikely special counterspy squad (Gruppo TNT) composed of an exhilarating mixture of derelicts and lowlifes—an octagenarian hypocondriac, a cleptomaniac Count, an elderly ex-SS soldier —led by an irascible

It was one of the few Italian films of the decade that took direct inspiration from the world of comics after the flood of references that characterized the '60s. Curiously, the oddest examples of this scarce lot featured foreign comic characters, reprised and reworked in a jaw-dropping way. Bruno Corbucci's *The Three Musketeers of the West* (1973) was a potboiler filled with many ingredients—basically, Dumas' *The Three Musketeers* loosely adapted in a comedy western scenario *Trinity*-style, spiced with martial arts fight scenes—which even included elements possibly taken from Al Capp's comic strip *Li'l Abner*.[20] Much more explicit in its comic book references, Emimmo Salvi's jaw-droppingly bad *Pugni, dollari & spinaci* (1978) was focused on an entre-

The brilliant comic artist Andrea Pazienza was one of the leading figures in the New Wave of comics of the late 1970s.

and greedy old man in a wheelchair (the "Number One") and based in a down-at-the-heel flower shop that looked a lot like the one portrayed in Roger Corman's *The Little Shop of Horrors* (1960). The titular hero, Alan Ford, was a striking variation on Voltaire's Candide, an angelic blond young man (with the features of Peter O'Toole) whose naivety and kindness made him the most unlikely of spies. The group's adventures and recurrent characters allowed for a mordant social satire that often aimed at class struggle. Take the arch-villain Superciuk, an alcoholic street-sweeper who hates the lower classes (because they throw their dirt on the street …) and turns into an anti-Robin Hood who steals from the poor and gives to the rich, and whose trademark superpower is his fetid alcoholic breath. Despite many attempts, *Alan Ford* never made it to the big screen, and considering what happened to Magnus & Bunker's previous creations, it was better that way.

Traces of a similarly biting approach could be found in other comic strips of the period, such as Bonvi's *Sturmtruppen*, a darkly comic satire set in the trenches of World War II, which was adapted into film twice, in 1976 and in 1982 by Salvatore Samperi. It even paved the way for a spurious rip-off, Marino Girolami's awful *Kakkientruppen* (1977).

Tanino Liberatore and Stefano Tamburini's *Ranxerox*, published in the magazine *Frigidaire*, soon became a cult phenomenon, in Italy and abroad.

preneur (Maurizio Arena), who plans to launch a spinach brand featuring Popeye on the label and was filled with references to Elzie C. Segar's characters.

By the late 1970s, with the advent of U.S. blockbusters such as *Star Wars* (1977, George Lucas) and *Superman*, Italian genre cinema was mainly reduced to a mere assembly line-style affair, churning out low-budget rip-offs in an attempt at settling on a thread as successful as the

Western and the crime film had been during the decade. Within such a gasping film industry there was little room for parodies—even more since the straight attempts were so shaky. Take, for instance, *The Pumaman* (*L'uomo puma*, 1980, Alberto De Martino), which is just as (albeit unintentionally) hilarious as the proper spoof *SuperAndy, il fratello brutto di Superman* (1979, Paolo Bianchini). On the other hand, Sergio Corbucci's *Super Fuzz* (*Poliziotto superpiù*, 1980) was a Terence Hill vehicle in which the added elements of the superpowers acquired by the pale blue-eyed hero merely served to replace the usual slapstick brawls, within the same bland cop flick framing story as Corbucci's previous Bud Spencer/Terence Hill comedy, *Trinity: Gambling for High Stakes* (*Pari e dispari*, 1978), also shot in the United States.

The late 1970s marked a harsh political and generational clash in the country, and comics played a vital part in it. With the rise of a new guard of artists and writers, such as Tanino Liberatore and Andrea Pazienza, comics became a tool for protest, by means of an aggressive (and very politically incorrect) satire, which often took the form of metaphor, paired with a tendency at experimentation, both in plot structure and in visuals. The result was a magazine, *Cannibale*, which was unlike anything seen before in Italy.

In 1980 Stefano Tamburini, Vincenzo Sparagna and Filippo Scòzzari created another landmark magazine: *Frigidaire*, which gave ample room to experimentation and the counterculture by mixing comics and journalism. It was a new kind of *fumetto*, open to suggestions from other art forms, such as music. Liberatore and Pazienza drew many record sleeves, the most memorable being Liberatore's for Frank Zappa's 1983 album, *The Man From Utopia*, while Tamburini used to write music reviews under the aka Red Vinyle and even assembled a cut-and-paste experimental tape, *Thalidomusic for Young Babies*, influenced by industrial bands such as Throbbing Gristle and Cabaret Voltaire and by New York's No Wave scene. It also conveyed a bitter disillusion after the failure of the political far-left movements, which too often ended with drug-addicted artists, resulting in the untimely deaths of both Tamburini and Pazienza.

Frigidaire's stories presented outrageous, grotesque characters such as a green, muscle-bound masochistic and immortal superhero named Ramarro (Green Lizard) and the hyper-violent Ranxerox, a drug-addicted android, assembled with bits and pieces from a photocopying machine, no less! Such paradoxical adventures offered a harsh view of the period. Ranxerox was created by Tamburini, who initially also drew the stories, but soon he entrusted the drawings to Tanino Liberatore, the "hardcore Michelangelo of the *bande dessinée*,"[21] as one critic labeled him. Originally the character was called Rank Xerox, but Tamburini modified its name after the Italian subsidiary Rank Xerox asked that it be changed in order to avoid that the brand be associated with a character "whose exploits are a concentrate of violence, profanity and foul language," announcing that, otherwise, they would take legal action. Ranxerox became a cult favorite in Italy and abroad. In the United States the stories were published in the prestigious *Heavy Metal* magazine, until Tamburini's death from a drug overdose in 1986 caused them to brusquely halt.[22]

Incredibly, Ranxerox even turned up in Sergio Corbucci's 1983 comedy *Questo e quello*, where Renato Pozzetto plays a bizarre, nonconformist comics artist. The panels that can be glimpsed in Pozzetto's workshop and in the office of his boss, played by Gianni Agus, are unmistakable portraits of Liberatore's character. That an underground comic—or rather, the *milieu* surrounding it—would be the object of such a blatant appropriation is on one hand evidence of Ranxerox's popularity; on the other, it is a visual metaphor of the way the mainstream was consuming and swallowing the avant-garde—with its protest and rebellion—turning them into commercially viable commodities for the masses.

Sergio Corbucci's 1983 comedy *Questo e quello* featured Renato Pozzetto as an idiosyncratic comics artist, a character inspired by *Frigidaire*'s Stefano Tamburini. The drawings on the wall are by Tanino Liberatore.

Chapter Six
The Television Years

Tiziano Sclavi's *Dylan Dog*, Italy's most popular comic of the 1980s

A German poster for *Yor, The Hunter of the Future*

in line with foreign outings, such as the science-fiction saga *Nathan Never*. Yet, all this was lost on the Italian cinema of the period, which was gradually stagnating and falling victim to the growing moneymaking power of television. Their now-dominant economical position in the market allowed TV companies to take active part in production, and several *fumetti* were considered for adaptation. However, the results invariably suffered from either the small screen destination or the attempt at creating a commercially viable product, resulting in anemic copies of their paper models.

RAI television co-financed two ill-fated projects: Antonio Margheriti's *Yor, the Hunter*

Whereas *Questo e quello* took inspiration from the more rebellious and unconventional Italian comics, the previous year's *Sogni mostruosamente proibiti*, starring Paolo Villaggio, depicted the regimented side, an industry in full productive boom. Besides the steady sales overall, the 1980s was a period of great creativity and artistic freedom that led to some of the most significant efforts in the world of Italian comics. But there was more. Popular *fumetti*—represented mainly by the pocket series published by Sergio Bonelli, such as *Tex, Zagor, Mister No*—were also experiencing a renaissance of sorts among the younger generations, which culminated with the commercial exploit of Bonelli's horror-oriented *Dylan Dog* and the launch of many other series which were more from the Future (*Il mondo di Yor*, 1983), based on the Argentinian comic by Juan Zanotto and Ray Collins, and Duccio Tessari's *Tex and the Lord of the Deep* (*Tex e il signore degli abissi*, 1985). The latter was initially an attempt to launch a TV series of Italy's most popular comic book, a project swiftly abandoned in the wake of the film's disappointing box-office performance. On the other hand, Silvio Berlusconi's company Fininvest invested in the TV series *Valentina* (1989), based on Guido Crepax's character and aimed at an adult audience. *Valentina* was launched as a classy soft-core product, a sort of *Playboy Show* with plot and acting … well, sort of, since the gorgeous American model Demetra Hampton, who played Valentina, was no Katharine Hepburn in that respect. Berlusconi's company also co-financed Terence Hill's *Lucky Luke* (1991), the pilot for a TV series inspired by the Belgian comic book of the same name, an amiable and surreal Western comedy.

Despite a short-lived interest in the horror genre, which resulted in such directors as Lamberto Bava landing steadily on the small screen, the many issues regarding the protection of minors from violence in the media resulted in a taming of the more gruesome contents. Meanwhile, history was cyclically repeating itself, with a heated controversy regarding hyper-violent horror comics that exploded at the turn of the decade. Filmmakers did little to exploit it though. Traces can be found in Bruno Mattei's low-budget *giallo Madness*, aka *Eyes Without a Face* (1992).

Just a few years earlier, Dario Argento was playing the pied piper to crowds of teens with one of his biggest hits, *Phenomena* (1984), and so was Lamberto Bava with his two *Demons* films, which he produced, while *Dylan Dog* was selling like hotcakes. Half a decade later one could not even hurt a fly on film. It was not just a matter of the incapability on the part of Italian cinema to keep up with the demands of the younger generations, as the 1991 Mammì law *de facto* acted as an instrument of economic censorship, posing severe limits to the broadcasting of films rated V.M.14 and forbidding the V.M.18 ones to be shown altogether, thus forcing the producers to fall back on harmless entertainment, deprived of any edge (read: sex, violence and assorted controversial topics). The box-office disappointment of *Cemetery Man* (*Dellamorte Dellamore*, 1994), Michele Soavi's ambitious attempt at bringing the universe of *Dylan Dog* to the screen, albeit from a slightly different source, a metaphysical horror novel written by *Dylan Dog* mastermind Tiziano Sclavi, practically prevented any other live-action version of a comic book to be produced in the following years.

The box-office disappointment of *Dellamorte Dellamore* stalled production on future comic book movies.

Epilogue and Notes

Of the few Italian films made in the new millennium that bear a relation to comic books, most of them are either web series or zero-budget amateurish shorts which struggled to find an audience via alternative distribution channels. Examples were the fan-based films inspired by *Dylan Dog*, the regional diptych about an unlikely Ligurian superhero by the name of Capitan Basilico (*Capitan Basilico*, 2008, and *Capitan Basilico 2—I Fantastici 4+4*, 2011) concocted by a no-profit musical combo for benefit purposes and the crazy low-budget web series *Iros* (2011), which poked fun at the popular American series *Heroes*.[23] Since it was obviously an impossible task to compete with Hollywood's big-budget hits, the playground of these homemade and often fan-based projects was mostly television, home video and the web.[24]

Today, with the big-budget adaptations of Marvel and DC Comics concocted by the Hollywood studios, we are fully immersed in a comic book universe on film—not to mention the many independent and *auteur* pictures inspired by graphic novels and the like: Terry Zwigoff's *Ghost World* (2001) and *Art School Confidential* (2006), David Cronenberg's *A History of Violence* (2005), Edgar Wright's *Scott Pilgrim vs. the World* (2010) and Abdellatif Kechiche's *Blue Is the Warmest Color* (*La vie d'Adèle—Chapitres 1 et 2*, 2013), just to name a few. Cinema itself is being more and more influenced by the aesthetics and narrative modes of comics as a way to tell "adult" stories. Still, even though Italian comics are experiencing a renaissance of sorts due to a new generation of *fumetti* writers and artists, this tendency failed to take root in Italian cinema and was reduced to a few attempts—namely, Renato De Maria's offbeat *Paz!* (2002), inspired by the universe of Andrea Pazienza's counterculture underground comics, and Gian Alfonso Pacinotti's *The Last Man on Earth* (*L'ultimo terrestre*, 2011), based on a graphic novel and directed by a well-known cartoonist. Both films gained a marginal cult status but failed to attract much of an audience.

The future, however, looks rather promising. With *The Invisible Boy* (*Il ragazzo invisibile*, 2014), Gabriele Salvatores—who won an Academy Award for Best Foreign Film in 1992 with *Mediterraneo*—relies on a comic book-inspired theme and style in order to tell the story of a troubled boy and his relationship with the world, and does so in a recognizable, realistic Italian setting. Ditto for Gabriele Mainetti's impressive *Lo chiamavano Jeeg Robot* (2016), which breathes new life into the basic superhero with super problems plot. Still, television seems to be the favorite format for comic book adaptations. The much-awaited, big-budgeted *Diabolik*, produced by Sky Television, has not yet been given a broadcasting release date. The choice of Diabolik is a risky but inevitable bet. Over 50 years after his debut, the character created by Angela and Luciana Giussani is as popular as ever, and remains a marketable name abroad as well. Times have changed, though, and it would be useless to envision something in the vein of either Mario Bava's *Danger: Diabolik* or some other *fumetti* adaptation from the past. Expectations are high, as recent Italian TV series such as *Romanzo criminale* (2008-2010) and especially *Gomorra* (2014) have proven that a competition with foreign products is possible in terms of quality and spectacular value. Whether the forthcoming *Diabolik* series will represent a resurrection for comic book adaptations in Italy or a bitter disappointment, only time will tell.

Terence Hill's *Lucky Luke* (1991) brought to the screen the comic character by Morris and Goscinny.

Overall, the relationship between cinema and *fumetti* is a wild, fascinating and often unpredictable one and well worth investigating, not just because of the peculiar nature of many Italian *fumetti* and the motion pictures that were based upon them, but also because of the very tight interaction that existed between the evolution of comics and that of popular culture and mores in the country over the years. It can also be a frustrating one, as even the most accomplished adaptations can leave an odd taste in the mouth—a sense of incompleteness, perhaps, that can be summarized again in Fellini's words:

> Even though the comic book universe will generously lend its set-pieces, its characters, its stories to the movies, it won't be able to give away its most secret, ineffable suggestion—that of fixity, the same stillness as the butterflies pierced by a pin.[25]

An impressive close-up of the titular superhero in Gabriele Salvatores' *The Invisible Boy* (2014)

Notes:
1. Fellini, Federico and Pettigrew, Damien, *Federico Fellini: sono un gran bugiardo* (Rome: Elle U Multimedia, 2003), pp. 108-109.
2. Ibid.
3. Ghirotti, Gigi, "Giusto e necessario che i 'fumetti neri' finiscano davanti al magistrato penale," *La Stampa*, 9/21/1966.
4. Moliterno, Gino, *The A to Z of Italian Cinema* (London: Scarecrow Press, 2009), p. 341.
5. Mataloni, Federico, "Il fumetto nero nell'Italia del Boom," www.fuorileidee.com.
6. On the other hand, a number of comic book authors who started in that period would take the reverse path and tried their hand at scripting and directing over the years: Corrado Farina, Pier Carpi, Giorgio Cavedon and Max Bunker (with the little-seen *Delitti, amore e gelosia*, 1982) come to mind. Another top-notch author, Hugo Pratt, the creator of *Corto Maltese*, allowed himself several apparitions as an actor, in such idiosyncratic works as Luigi Scattini's film on the porn business *Blue Nude* (1977) and Leos Carax's *Bad Blood* (*Mauvais sang*, 1986).
7. Among the comics-inspired Eurospy films of the period, Jesús Franco's *Lucky the Inscrutable* stands out. Franco literally fills the film with references to the comic book universe. The opening sequence has Ray Danton, dressed in a costume that makes him look like a cross between The Spirit and Superman, standing still like in a freeze frame while a balloon proclaims: "Sono il re dei fumetti!" ("I am the king of comics!"), and a love scene between Danton and Rosalba Neri is an amusing spoof of the erotic photonovels of the period. The many nods to comics in Franco's career were a typical sign of the Spanish director's uniquely anarchic attitude toward filmmaking. Other Franco films openly flirted with the language of comics, most notably *The Erotic Rites of Frankenstein* (1972), *Los blues de la Calle Pop* (1983), *Bangkok cita con la muerte* (1985) and *El infierno virtual del Dr. Wong* (1998). What is more, his production company Manacoa took its name from a Spanish comic, *Anacleto, agente segreto*, which was also the main source of inspiration behind *Lucky the Inscrutable*.
8. Even though not directly based on a comic book, Primo Zeglio's *Mission Stardust (4 … 3 … 2 … 1… morte!*, 1967) was partially related to them. Zeglio's film was a loose adaptation of the German paperback series of novels starring Perry Rhodan, which in turn were made into comic books due to their immense popularity in their home country.
9. Farina, Corrado, "Selene bionda meteora," *Sgt. Kirk* #23, May 1969.
10. Ibid.
11. Rostagno (Turin, 1935—Juan Les Pins, 2004), a talented graphic artist and painter, later worked with Pier Carpi on the satirical erotic Middle-

Capitan Basilico (2008) was a low-budget superhero spoof concocted by the no-profit combo Buio Pesto.

Age strip *Beatrice*, published in the magazine *Horror*, about a (naked) witch tied to a stake who meets various Medieval characters, either real or fictitious. He became one of Italy's most sought-after illustrators.
12. See Piselli, Stefano, ed., *Cinefumetto—Bizarre Sinema Archives* (Florence: Glittering Images, 2008), p. 5.
13. D'Acquisto, Pina, "Ondata di calore. Gli ultimi fuochi del cineromanzo," in Morreale, Emiliano, ed., *Gianni Amelio presenta: lo schermo di carta. Storia e storie dei cineromanzi* (Turin—Milan: Museo Nazionale del Cinema-Il Castoro, 2007), p. 221.
14. Such an approach marked the rest of the issues as well. Besides the photonovel there were "topical articles and 'hot' news from the world, with a particular fondness for the reports from Europe's most famous nudist camps and small-town scandals; short stories with a high rate of sensuality (which in later years would become out-and-out pornography); the inevitable readers' corner, filled with (morbid) questions on sex and bouts of verbal exhibitionism on the part of the authors of the (true or false) letters […]." Maina, Giovanna, "Cine & Sex. Sessualizzazione dei media e cineromanzo tra gli anni Sessanta e Settanta," *Bianco & Nero* #573, May-August 2012.
15. "It is a basic scheme, in which, from time to time, you can put everything," Piccioni commented. See Pulici, Davide, "Il grido del capricorno," *Nocturno Cinema* #147, January 2015, p. 95.
16. It must be added, though, that filmmakers had started shooting explicit scenes for the foreign markets since the early 1970s.
17. On the other hand, one of the most celebrated U.S. porn filmmakers, who specialized in hardcore spoofs focused on American superheroes, is the very Italian Axel Braun (aka Alessandro Ferro)—the son of the legendary porn pioneer Lasse Braun (Alberto Ferro)—who helmed such epics as *Batman XXX: A Porn Parody* (2010), *Superman vs. Spider-Man XXX: An Axel Braun Parody* (2012) and *Man of Steel XXX: An Axel Braun Parody* (2013).
18. Cervi (1901—1974) had starred in a range of great films such as *La corona di ferro* (1941, Alessandro Blasetti) as well as the 1950s/1960s series *Don Camillo*, alongside the French comedian Fernandel, based on Giovannino Guareschi's satirical novels. In the mid-1960s he played Commissioner Maigret in a very successful string of TV films based on Georges Simenon's character.
19. The name Sorbolik hinted at a popular dialectal

expression ("Sorbole" used to indicate amazement and surprise) typical of the Bolognese dialect, thus poking fun at Cervi's own Bolognese accent.

20. The opening scenes of *The Three Musketeers of the West* are set in the peacefully (and stinky) Cheese Valley, and contain several elements that are most likely borrowed from Capp's strips. The protagonist, Dart Jr. (Giancarlo Prete), is introduced as a Li'l Abner lookalike, while his diminutive yet dominating mother recalls Mammy Yokum. What is more, Cheese Valley's inhabitants talk in a mock dialect that is inspired by Capp's use of dialogue. Another nod to comics in Corbucci's film is the representation of twin Black Barts, a pair of black-dressed comic thugs modeled upon *Lucky Luke*'s Daltons (or, more likely, the twin killers Frit and Frut as seen in *Alan Ford* #20, *Frit, Frut*, January 1971).

21. Mattioli, Valerio, "Ranxerox. Quando l'Italia guidò l'avanguardia del fumetto mondiale," *XL* #80, October 2012.

22. Ranxerox was resumed in 1996. French writer Alain Chabat completed Tamburini's last unfinished story, and he would later direct a comic book adaptation, *Asterix & Obelix: Mission Cleopatra* (*Astérix & Obélix: Mission Cléopâtre*, 2002), on which Liberatore (now residing in Paris) designed the costumes.

23. The weirdest of the lot is perhaps 2009's *Capitan Novara—Un giorno da supereroe* (Captain Novara—A Day as a Superhero). Capitan Novara (Novara being a town in Piedmont, Northern Italy) was created in 2004 by Fabrizio De Fabritiis and billed as "Italy's first superhero," about an insurance agent who has grown extraordinary powers after being exposed as a child to a cosmic source of energy, the "Nova Rays," and who secretly leads a double life as a superhero. The most interesting thing about the comic was De Fabritiis totally embracing a provincial Italian environment for his stories, which blends with the author's drawing style (openly influenced by such American comic artists as Jim Lee) in an imaginative (and obviously tongue-in-cheek) way. For instance, the hero gains his superpowers after falling into a paddy field (rice cultivation is Novara's main agricultural resource). As De Fabritiis commented, "Unfortunately, here in Italy, it was always thought that there can be no "Made In Italy" superheroes, but I actually think the opposite is true. We Italians love superheroes, as proven by the success of so many superhero movies in theaters—still, being mostly xenophiles, we have always been fascinated by the heroes that were imported from abroad. I once read a comment from a guy on a blog who said that the character was cute, but in a comic book you cannot do stories set in Novara. Others commented that a character so deeply tied to a region was itself an absurd idea. If you think about it, though, many superheroes have a precise place of action, for example if you take away Spiderman from New York and put him in the Nevada desert you may lose about 90 percent of its appeal. So why can't an Italian boy grow superpowers, and since his life takes place in a small Italian town, decide to help others by wearing a costume and defending his own city?" The self-produced comic found a marginal audience in a radically unusual form. Capitan Novara's one-page stories were published on advertising placemats distributed in bars, restaurants etc. before Fabritiis came up with *Capitan Novara Magazine*. The hero eventually changed name into a more audience-friendly Capitan Nova (perhaps in a nod to Marvel's cult superhero created by Marv Wolfman, Len Wein and John Buscema). In 2009 De Fabritiis teamed up with Luca Baggio and concocted a 20-minute short based on his own character in order to take part in a national short film competition. Besides co-directing, De Fabritiis also drew the storyboards. A zero-budget independent effort by a small video editing company named MadMirror, *Capitan Novara—Un giorno da supereroe* won the prize as best short film at said competition. Shot on video, with non-professional actors, it is an unpretentious, enthusiastic effort by a team of very young cinephiles, and it shows. Despite its blatant shortcomings, it is a reminder of the passion it takes to make films, at all levels.

24. On the other hand, the Australian miniseries *Italian Spiderman* (2007) directed by "Alrugo Entertainment" (a collective comprising Dario Russo, Tait Wilson, David Ashby, Will Spartalis and Boris Repasky) must not be confused with the Italian superhero films it spoofs—although it is actually closer in spirit to the awkward, mean-spirited Turkish rip-offs which misappropriate popular American superheroes, with its paunchy mustached hero (Ashby, hiding under the alias "Franco Franchetti") wearing a cheap mask and unlikely T-shirt with a spider drawn on it.

25. Festi, Roberto and Scudiero, Maurizio, eds., *Cinema & Fumetto. I personaggi dei comics sul grande schermo* (Trento: esaExpomostre, 2006), p. 29.

Part Two
The Films

1941

Princess Cinderella
(*Cenerentola e il signor Bonaventura*)
Italy, b/w, 72 minutes
D: Sergio Tofano. *S:* Sergio Tofano; *SC:* Edoardo Anton [Edoardo Antonelli], Vittorio Metz, Sergio Tofano; *DOP:* Manfredo Bertini; *M:* Renzo Rossellini; *E:* Italo Cremona.
Cast: Paolo Stoppa (Il signor Bonaventura/Mr. Goodluck), Silvana Jachino (Cinderella), Roberto Villa (Prince Charming), Guglielmo Barnabò (The King), Mercedes Brignone (The Queen), Sergio Tofano (The Doctor), Rosetta Tofano (Pasqualina), Mario Pisu (Il bellissimo Cecè), Camillo Pilotto (The Ogre), Piero Carnabuci (Barbariccia).
Prod: Arno Film (Rome).

After her marriage to Prince Charming, Cinderella spends her days in the luxurious royal palace, being affable with all the people around her. However, her two envious sisters manage to get her away from the palace. The Prince falls into a state of despair. Mr. Goodluck and his friend, "the beautiful" Cecè, promise to go in search of the girl and bring her back to her husband. After fighting such archenemies as Barbariccia and the Ogre, Bonaventura and Cecè succeed in the attempt, with the help of a good Fairy.

Il Signor Bonaventura (Mr. Goodluck) was one of Italy's most popular comics characters in the first half of the 20th century. Sergio Tofano (signing as "Sto") created the character in 1917 for the children's magazine *Il Corriere dei Piccoli*. Drawn in a patently child-like style, the naive and honest Bonaventura almost looked like a clown, with his red frock coat and bowler hat, large white trousers and a dachshund by his side. His adventures—usually consisting of just eight vignettes, accompanied by rhyming captions—followed a simple, recurring pattern: Bonaventura found himself with no money and in an unfortunate situation, but thanks to his good-natured attitude and honesty, he managed to overcome calamities, and in the end received the princely sum of one million *lire* (in a period when 1,000 *lire* a month was considered a big salary) in the form of a huge, sheet-like banknote.

The immediate success turned Bonaventura into a mass phenomenon. The opening phrase of all his stories, "Qui comincia l'avventura del signor Bonaventura" (Here begins the adventure of Mr. Goodluck), became of common use in everyday life. Bonaventura's strips appeared every week for 26 consecutive years. Publications were interrupted after the armistice of 1943, which left Italy in chaos, occupied by the Nazis, and with the Allies slowly fighting their way from Sicily to the North, with the support of Italian partisans.

Tofano also brought his character to the stage, in six musical comedies that he wrote and directed between 1927 and 1953. He also concocted a film adaptation, *Princess Cinderella*, in which he paired Bonaventura with the eponymous fairytale heroine, taking inspiration from his second *Bonaventura* musical stage play, *La regina in berlina* (1929), songs included. The great stage actor Paolo Stoppa (seen in Sergio Leone's *Once Upon a Time in the West*, 1968) played Bonaventura, and he wore a curious and decidedly weird-looking make-up in order to look exactly like the character.

An eight vignette Bonaventura story in the magazine *Il Corriere dei Piccoli*

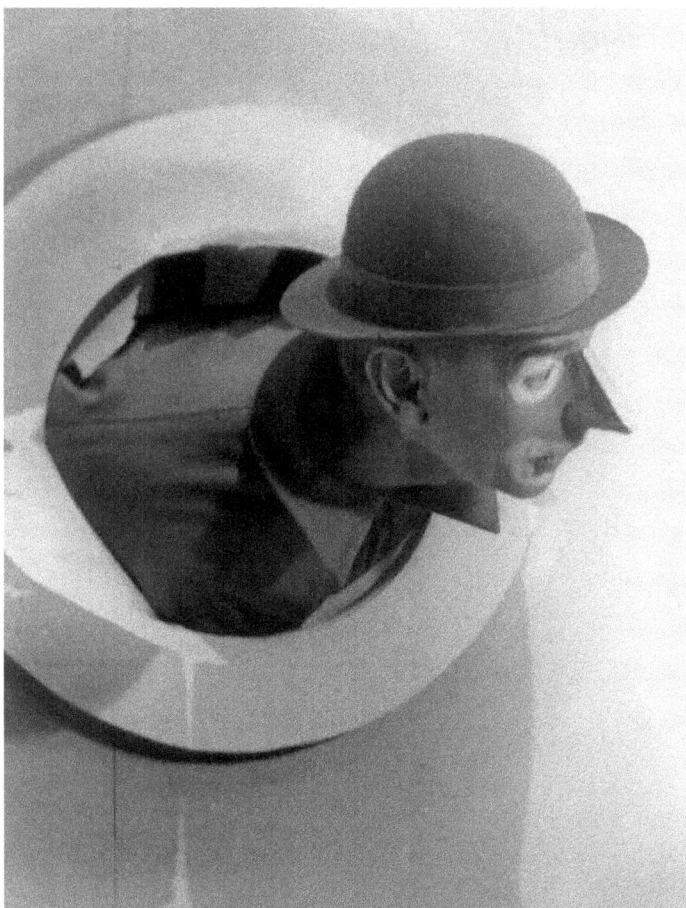

Paolo Stoppa in Bonaventura make-up in Sergio Tofano's film version of his most popular character, *Princess Cinderella*, directed by Tofano himself

Tofano surrounded him with many characters taken from the scripts. Mario Pisu was cast as one of Bonaventura's recurring sidekicks, a vain damp young man named "Il bellissimo Cecè" (The Beautiful Cecè), and Piero Carnabuci played the recurrent villain Barbariccia. Besides writing and directing, Tofano also played a secondary role as a doctor; he also drew the opening titles, which portrayed the characters beside the actors' names, further underlining the film's comic book source.

With its stylized fairytale-like studio sets (it was entirely shot at Pisorno Studios in Tirrenia, Tuscany, Italy's oldest film studios), gaudy costumes and over-the-top make-up, *Princess Cinderella* has evident debts to the Laurel & Hardy classic *Babes in Toyland*, aka *March of the Wooden Soldiers* (1934, Gus Meins, Charles Rogers) and fascinating nods to German Expressionism. Even though the picture was aimed at children, there are some notably bizarre inventions throughout, such as a witch with a sidecar on her broom and an ogre who has to undergo a dental session to replace his fallen teeth. Tofano's film also displays ingenious special effects, with an intelligent use of stop-motion (such as a bed remaking itself) and double-exposure.

Princess Cinderella surfaced in the U.S. only in 1955. It was virtually invisible in Italy for decades, until it was restored and screened at the 2009 Venice Film Festival, in the retrospective dedicated to "lost" Italian films.

1965

Okay sceriffo
Italy, b/w, 37 minutes
D: Angio Zane. *S and SC:* Arnaldo Bonfadini, Ignazio Colnaghi and Angio Zane; *DOP:* Diego River [Diego Fiume]; *M:* Juan Falenito; *E:* Angio Zane.
Cast: Frank Senis (Sheriff Preston), Bruno Salvatori (Jo Bapee), Ignazio Colnaghi (Uncle Gary), Dario Cipani (Dick), Osiride Pevarello.
Prod: Ona Film.

Kock City is a small mining town in Nebraska, near the border of Kansas. The mines and their product support a great number of shady and scheming characters, so that Sheriff Preston must always stay on his guard. Preston does not like to use a gun in his mission of justice and usually reverts to shrewd methods to keep the town peaceful. Optimist Jo Bapee, a former stable boy, a good and likeable old man named Gary and his grandson Dick help him.

Of all the films included in this volume, *Okay sceriffo* is probably the weirdest, if only for its origins. The main character, the "Sheriff of the Silver Valley,"—a mixture between the Lone Ranger and Tex, with references to another Italian comic, *Il Piccolo Ranger*—appeared in a series of comic strips conceived as part of the advertising campaign for a brand of cold cuts, Negroni. They were published in the weekly magazine *Topolino* since 1963 and consisted of one-page adventures, with just a handful of vignettes. The stories inevitably ended with a cliffhanger, and a line that read: "To know the end of this exciting adventure, follow on TV the *Carosello* offered by Negroni."

Carosello was one of the most popular TV programs: a 10-minute series of commercials—conceived as short films—broadcast on prime time, right after the eight o'clock news. For children, it was an appointment not to be missed, before going to bed, as the commercials were often aimed at the younger audiences, with plenty of comic characters and amiable gags. Negroni's "Sheriff of the Silver Valley" soon became one of the most popular of the lot. Film historian Marco Giusti described them as a "great, funny series of TV commercials, famous for their (more or less …) intentional sloppiness. Small, easy and funny Western stories, featuring a sheriff and his deputy, who seem to come straight out of the set of an Italian film of the 1940s. Over many years of broadcasting, the stories did not change much. With B-grade sets and bad actors they always ended up with the sheriff uttering the same lines over and over again: "Once again we have to thank our lucky star," while his deputy, holding a gun in both hands, sends kisses to the sky and replies: "Thank you, lucky star!" [Author's note: Negroni's brand logo was a star, here conveniently shaped as a sheriff's star.] Then comes Negroni's famous jingle that advertises the product [...]"[1]

If the mixture between *fumetti* and advertising was not enough, the "Sheriff of the Silver Valley" knew a further incarnation, and a most surprising one indeed. Angio Zane, the filmmaker responsible for all the commercials, assembled several adventures of the Sheriff for a short film titled *Okay sceriffo*, in an attempt at cashing in on the success of the rising Spaghetti Western genre. Of course, the result had little to do with Sergio Leone's films and their over-reliance on violence. It was an unpretentious movie for the whole family, destined to play the parish theater circuit. It was even screened at a collateral section at the 1965 Venice Festival.

Unlike the TV spots, which went on for years, actually into to the mid-'70s, *Okay sceriffo* soon disappeared from sight and resurfaced in Italy in the early 1980s on a much-sought after videocassette which became a collectors' item. The same happened with the only DVD release, distributed in newsstands by the label Hobby & Work.

Zane (1925-2010) was a former documentary filmmaker who made his feature film debut in 1957 with *La capinera del mulino*; he specialized in children's films before directing TV commercials. His last feature film was a documentary on the partisan war, *Ribelli, Brigata Perlasca* (1986).

Another *fumetti*-style series of commercials worth mentioning is *Gringo* (1966-1976), which was patently inspired by the Spaghetti Western and featured a bunch of comic book-like characters, starting with the eponymous hero. The advertised product was a brand of canned meat with a definitely Western name, Montana.

Note:
1. Marco Giusti, *Il grande libro di Carosello. E adesso tutti a nanna ...* (Milan: Sperling & Kupfer, 1995), p. 388.

Thrilling
Italy, b/w, 117 minutes
"Il vittimista." *D:* Ettore Scola; *SC:* Ruggero Maccari, Ettore Scola; *DOP:* Alessandro D'Eva; *M:* Ennio Morricone; *E:* Marcello Malvestito.
Cast: Nino Manfredi (Nanni Galassi), Magda Konopka (Luciana), Luigi Battaglia (Franco), Luciano Bonanni, Tino Buazzelli (The Shrink), Carlo Cerioni.
"Sadik." *D:* Gian Luigi Polidoro; *SC:* Ruggero Maccari; *DOP:* Pier Ludovico Pavoni; *M:* Ennio Morricone; *E:* Nino Baragli.
Cast: Walter Chiari (Renato Bertazzi), Dorian Gray [Maria Luisa Mangini] (Veronique).
"L'autostrada del sole." *D:* Carlo Lizzani; *SC:* Rodolfo Sonego; *DOP:* Roberto Gerardi, Pier Ludovico Pavoni; *M:* Ennio Morricone; *E:* Franco Fraticelli.

Cover art for a 1970s reissue of *Sakik*

Cast: Alberto Sordi (Fernando Boccetta), Sylva Koscina (Paola), Giampiero Albertini, Federico Boido.
Prod: Dino De Laurentiis Cinematografica (Rome).

"*Il vittimista.*" Nanni Galassi is convinced that his wife is planning to murder him. He goes to a shrink who explains to him that his fantasies are generated by a sense of guilt due to his extramarital affair. Galassi then breaks up with his lover, who takes her revenge by killing him. "*Sadik.*" Stressed businessman Renato Bertazzi not only has to settle a difficult deal which might be vital for his career, but he must also cope with his sex-obsessed, comics-addicted wife Valeria and her bizarre erotic fantasies. Valeria asks Renato to dress up as Sadik and pretend to rape her, just like in an adults-only comic book. The consequences will be disastrous for both ... "*L'autostrada del sole.*" Fernando Boccetta ends up spending the night in an ominous looking inn after his car breaks down. There, he finds out that a family of homicidal maniacs occupies the place.

From the time of its inception in March 1965, *Sadik* was one of the most controversial *fumetti neri* of its time. Publisher Ugo Del Buono asked his collaborators Sergio Garassini and Francesco Paolo Conte to find a good writer who would create a character in the vein of Diabolik, but with a more explicit emphasis on sex and violence. Enter Nino Cannata, a writer well versed in humorous comics

Walter Chiari and Dorian Gray in a publicity still from *Thrilling*

who had never tried his hand at the *giallo* genre. Cannata, who in that period was working for a well respected publisher (Universo) whose products were very far from the much-discussed *fumetti neri*, accepted the task but asked not to sign *Sadik* under his real name. The same occurred with the artist who drew the comic, also requesting to stay anonymous, signing the comic only as "Gian." Even Cannata did not know who was hiding behind that pseudonym. It later turned out that the mysterious artist was Giancarlo Agnello, who specialized in children-oriented comics.

Cannata and Agnello had a field day with *Sadik*. The titular character was a masked villain whose costume was nearly identical to Diabolik's. The main difference was Sadik's almost caricatured features, with a square jaw that would have made Chester Gould proud (and even recalled a bit the notorious profile of Benito Mussolini, Il Duce). Yet, compared with Sadik's criminal behavior, Diabolik was as quiet as a lamb. Sadik is a genius of evil, a criminal mastermind who does not hesitate in getting rid of whoever stands in his way. His identity is unknown and his powers—which make him virtually invincible—are mysterious. His love interest is the equally ferocious Loona, while his archenemy, secret agent 003 Eddy Castle, is graphically modeled upon Eddie Constantine's Lemmy Caution.

Sadik was an immediate hit. The first issue, *Il castello del terrore* (The Castle of Terror), sold over 100,000 copies. Equally resounding was the reaction on the part of the authorities. Issue #2, *Il mistero del bonzo* (The Mystery of the Bonze) was seized because of its allegedly "morally harmful" content. Del Buono, whose publications had already been the target of denunciations and seizures, decided to yield *Sadik* to Garassini, who, together with Fulvio Scocchera, founded another publishing house named Antares.

However, the ongoing trouble with the authorities, in the form of further seizures, eventually led to a third takeover. In March 1966 *Sadik* changed hands again, ending up at Alhambra Edizioni. There, the character was drastically redesigned in order to soften its violent content. Two new artists, Victor Hugo Arias and Emilio Uberti, replaced Agnello and the hero's features were made less aggressive. Last but not least, Cannata was explicitly asked to write stories that were less outrageous and turn the character into some sort of masked avenger. This brought *Sadik* to an early death, as audiences no longer felt attracted to a comic book that had completely lost its edge. Meanwhile, Scocchera and Del Buono were found guilty (punished with fines and suspended jail time) in the notorious Milan trial against the *fumetti neri*, which ended in early 1967. However, this was the last straw. *Sadik* was later reprinted by Alhambra in 1968 with its name changed into *Cobra*. More reruns followed, this time with the original name, dating from 1971 to 1989.

Its *success de scandàle* made it inevitable that *Sadik* ended up on the big screen. Yet its journey was quite peculiar. As often happened in Italian cinema, parody predated the real thing.

A seven-inch record of the film's theme song, with cover art featuring the stars of the three episodes: Walter Chiari, Nino Manfredi (left) and Alberto Sordi

Anthology comedies became the huge commercial trend in Italian cinema of the early 1960s. Thanks to the works of such filmmakers as Dino Risi, Mario Monicelli and Luigi Comencini, the so-called *commedia all'italiana* (Comedy Italian-style) had become the convenient way to analyze post-war Italy, its lifestyle, its larger-than-life characters and its newfound hedonism. Films like *The Easy Life* (*Il sorpasso*, 1962) and *Opiate '67* (*I mostri*, 1963) used laughter as a sharp weapon to cut like a knife into the country's economical boom and the monsters it generated. The latter movie, in particular, hit upon a winning formula. Short skits, each of them just a few minutes long, were characterized by a vitriolic black humor, in which two famous stars such as Vittorio Gassman and Ugo Tognazzi played a number of picturesque and over-the-top characters. The episode formula became a staple in *auteur* cinema as well. *Boccaccio '70* (1962) saw the teaming up of Vittorio De Sica, Federico Fellini, Mario Monicelli and Luchino Visconti for a modern-day conceptual take on Boccaccio's short stories, centered around sex as seen in 1960s Italy.

Soon other film anthologies flourished, often putting together acclaimed directors and stars. They centered on a common theme (usually sex) and turned into commercially profitable items at the box-office. One such case was *Thrilling*, where—as the title suggested—the recipe was spiced up with hints of the thriller genre. Ettore Scola's episode *Il vittimista* dealt with a Latin teacher, played by Nino Manfredi, who is convinced that his wife is planning to murder him, while Carlo Lizzani's segment *L'autostrada del sole* focused on the misadventures of a man (Alberto Sordi) whose car breaks down during a trip on Italy's A1 motorway[1]. The film flirted with black humor, with amusing touches such as the use of the Italian version of Petula Clark's *Downtown* (re-titled *Ciao ciao*) as the mocking commentary to the murderous punch line in *Il vittimista*.

The central episode, *Sadik*, was directed by Gian Luigi Polidoro and starred Walter Chiari, one of Italy's most underrated comedians. It was not only the best of the trio but the closest to *fumetti neri*. The story focused on a petty businessman who has to deal with his wife's bizarre erotic fetishes. Here the *fumetti neri* are a pretext to ridicule the immature and hypocritical mentality of the emerging middle class, whose long-repressed sexual appetites are finally unleashed in a child-like manner—the solace of a generation that still sees sex as something "dirty" and can cope with it only by overemphasizing its most ludicrous and over-the-top aspects.

The funniest aspect in all this is that it's the protagonist's unsatisfied wife who turns out to be the sexually dominating half in the story, similarly to what happens in Marco Ferreri's pungent satire on Catholic marriage mores *The Conjugal Bed* (*Una storia moderna—L'ape regina*, 1963). To quench the woman's fantasies (and, she implies, save their prematurely sex-less marriage) poor Renato Bertazzi has to wear Sadik's costume—albeit the one as portrayed in the film is notably different from the comic book, starting with the "S" on the chest—and perform a series of grotesque feats, in a badly-assembled sex pantomime conceived by the terminally comics-obsessed woman (who has filled their apartment with *fumetti neri*, which pop up even in the fridge).[2]

As often with Italian comedies, the plot takes a decidedly grim turn, blending tragedy and farce. After a number of hilarious incidents (he is forced to burst into the apartment through a window in order to spice up the masquerade, and so on) Bertazzi finally succumbs to the fictional character he is playing and strangles his wife … after he finds out that she has just rejected an important phone call because she did not want to be disturbed during their foreplay.

Screenwriter Ruggero Maccari satirizes the controversies that accompanied the *fumetti neri* phenomenon, by aping their supposedly negative effects on gullible minds due to their mixture of sex and violence. Maccari's script also emphasizes the inner mediocrity of the Italian male, by juxtaposing the sexually unimaginative Bertazzi and his masked alter ego, with whom he eventually identifies in the final scene. Bertazzi's incapability of facing his economical issues, as he lives above his possibilities and continually escapes his creditors' solicitations like William H. Macy in *Fargo* (1996), is a grim footnote after the illusory years of the Boom.

Although working on what is ultimately little more than an extended sketch (the episode runs less than 20 minutes), Polidoro makes the best use of stylized black-and-white lighting and weird camera angles to suggest the visuals of a comic strip, even employing balloons instead of dialogue at times. The result is an underrated gem of 1960s Italian comedy, and a worthy addition to the whole *fumetti neri* phenomenon as well.

Interestingly, Vittorio De Sica's episode *Una sera come le altre*—from the De Laurentiis-produced omnibus comedy *The Witches* (*Le streghe*, 1967)—sort of reprised the same theme, with an embittered wife (played by Silvana Mangano) who fantasizes about comic book heroes seducing her in front of her boring and decidedly not very passionate husband (played with self-ironic wit by Clint Eastwood). However, Sadik was the only *fumetti neri* antihero briefly glimpsed in the scene, alongside iconic comic book characters such as Mandrake and The Phantom.

Note:
1. The title *L'autostrada del sole* refers to Italy's longest motorway, the A1, inaugurated in October 1964, which ran from Milan to Naples, thus virtually unifying the North and the South of the country. The A1 quickly became one of the symbols of Italy's Boom.

1966

Kriminal, aka *La máscara de Kriminal*
Italy/Spain, color, 98 minutes
D: Umberto Lenzi. *S and SC:* Umberto Lenzi; *DOP:* Angelo Lotti; *M:* Raymond Full [Romano Mussolini]; *E:* Jolanda Benvenuti, Antonio Gimeno.
Cast: Glenn Saxson [Roel Bos] (Kriminal), Helga Liné (Inge/Trude), Andrea Bosic (Inspector Milton), Ivano Staccioli (Alex Lafont), Esmeralda Ruspoli (Lady Gold), Dante Posani (Frank), Franco Fantasia (Commissioner Murad), Susan Baker [Maria Luisa Rispoli] (Margie Swan), Armando Calvo (Kandur), Mary Arden (Gloria Farr).
Prod: Filmes Cinematografica (Rome), Estela Films (Madrid), Copercines (Madrid).

The ruthless thief and cold-blooded murderer known as Kriminal escapes from a London prison just a few moments before he is to be hanged. Hounded by Scotland Yard's Inspector Milton, Kriminal is sheltered by his ex-wife Margie, who is currently the secretary of Lady Gold, the owner of an import/export jewelry firm. Kriminal learns that a large amount of diamonds will be shipped to Turkey the next day, and he sets up a plan to steal them at the airport. There, however, he is dismayed to discover that Lady Gold has hired a pair of twins, Inge and Trude, to carry the diamonds. Kriminal is able to snatch one of the two sisters' purse, which is empty, while the other girl leaves undisturbed headed toward Istanbul. When he learns from the newspapers that the insurance company paid Lady Gold one million pounds for the theft, Kriminal realizes that the woman exploited him in order to get the insurance money. He approaches Lady Gold and finds out that the diamonds are in Inge's possession. Kriminal traces her and manages to get hold of the jewelry, getting rid of the woman's accomplices in the process. Pursued by the police, he covers his tracks, but in the end it is Milton who will have the upper hand …

A key date in the history of Italian comic books was August 1964. That month saw the release of another *fumetto nero*, inspired by *Diabolik*'s phenomenal success and published by Milan's Editoriale Corno. Originality was not its strong point, but the story *Il re del delitto* introduced the most astonishingly spectacular—not to mention controversial—comic antihero of the decade: Kriminal.

The new pocket-sized comic book marked the first teaming of the 25-year-old writer Max Bunker (real name Luciano Secchi, born August 24, 1939) and his regular illustrator Magnus (real name Roberto Raviola, 1939–

Writer Max Bunker (left) and comic artist Magnus, the men who brought *Kriminal* to life

The impressive opening panel for *Kriminal* #58 (April 8, 1966)

1996). Bunker's debut as a comic book writer had been a Western, *Maschera Nera*, a rather humorous and slightly violent variation on the theme of the masked avenger *à la* Zorro and The Lone Ranger. An eclectic and incredibly prolific writer, Secchi also tried his hand at science-fiction with *Atomik*, whose adventures were included as an appendix in *Maschera Nera*; then he concentrated on the growing thread of the so-called *fumetti neri*. Magnus (who took his pseudonym from the Latin motto *magnus pictor fecit* of Bologna's Academy of Fine Arts where he graduated) was a former graphic designer who was making his first steps in the world of *fumetto*, and had arrived in Milan in the Spring of 1964, looking for a job as a comic artist. He knocked at the door of a small publisher named Editoriale Corno and, as they say, the rest is history …

The name Kriminal was possibly inspired by the successful pop song *Kriminal tango*, released in 1959 by Piero Trombetta, which had been one of singer Fred Buscaglione's most popular numbers, and even inspired Géza von Cziffra's 1960 film *Kriminaltango*. What is more, it had the essential "K" factor, since it immediately brought *Diabolik* to mind. Secchi and Raviola realized the potential of the concept behind *Diabolik* and the improvements they could add to it. These improvements could be summed up in two words: sex and violence.

On a creative basis, *Kriminal* was ultimately more successful than *Diabolik*. Its makers understood that they had to wipe away all the protagonist's positive aspects and push the controversial negative elements as far as possible, so as to create the immoral antihero par excellence. If Diabolik is ultimately a Fantômas clone, albeit an exceptional one, then Anthony Logan (aka Kriminal) is so much more than that, starting with his grinning skull mask and skeleton costume that make him a living icon of death, like some sort of a *Dia de los muertos* fetish puppet that has come to life. A former circus acrobat abandoned by his father, growing up first in an orphanage and then in reform school, Logan was marked by a life of hardship and became a ruthless, cold-blooded murderer who kills people copiously, as if it is the most natural thing in the world, and who brutally takes from others what life had always denied him. He did not even become an embodiment of evil, but rather a symbol of the dissolution of any moral tenant in a society where violence, murder and assorted cruelty had become an end game.

But there was more than that: sex. Diabolik was rigidly monogamist, whereas Kriminal was promiscuous to the extreme. He seduced scantily dressed, provocative women and then callously strangled or stabbed them so as to conceal his identity. No remorse; no regrets. In one of the comic's most daring plot twists, Kriminal even rapes his arch-enemy Inspector Milton's fiancée Gloria Farr (herself a cop). Farr in turn is irresistibly driven to Logan despite what he has done to her … so much for romanticism.

Secchi came up with grand pulp ideas for *Kriminal* which Raviola—an original, innovative artist with a peculiar, almost self-parodist style—managed to expand and visualize. Kriminal's skull mask and trademark black and yellow skeleton costume—a result of Logan's circus days as an acrobat—were a stunning, unforgettable Pop Art creation, an icon worthy of the most celebrated examples of Italy's "Bel Design" and "Linea Italiana," and one that would soon be copied by other comics … even though Magnus & Bunker were not the first to come up with such a concept. *Fantax*, published just a couple of months earlier (June 1964), also featured a character wearing a very similar (albeit far more crudely executed) white skeleton costume and skull mask.[1]

Whereas *Diabolik* was ultimately based on the same Manichean worldview of the old serial novels, *Kriminal* was totally extraneous to such a moral dichotomy. Ultimately, Anthony Logan becomes a hero of sorts for the reader not because he is any good—he is cruel to the bone—but sim-

A panel for *Omicidio al riformatorio*, where Magnus went as far as censorship would allow … and even further

picaresque, satirical, dramatic and grotesque, Secchi and Raviola revealed a discursive depth quite unusual in Italian comics.[2]

Traditional values were joyously destroyed by the duo's iconoclast approach, which was characterized by a taste for the grotesque and the mocking black humor. They explored the boundaries between horror and satire—and at the same time displayed a cynical attitude that concealed a social commentary on an increasingly hollow and empty society founded on greed and moneymaking—where there were no moral values to be found.

Moreover, Secchi's stories were very much reminiscent of contemporaneous B-movies, so much so that issue #5, *Omicidio al riformatorio* ("Murder at the Reform School," December 1964) almost looked like a novelization of Mario Bava's *Blood and Black Lace* (*Sei donne per l'assassino*, released in Italy nine months earlier) set in a reform school. The story was Magnus & Bunker's first minor masterpiece ply because the world he moves in is even crueler. And unlike Diabolik, he is not a winner; he is fallible and often fails because of miscalculation, bad luck, sheer chance … or human stupidity. And when he goes back to his lair, there is no Eva Kant waiting for him. He is, and will always be, a reject, born with the Mark of Cain on his forehead, forever barred from the rest of humanity.

However, despite *Kriminal*'s ultra-violent, erotic and politically incorrect content, Secchi and Raviola always kept their tongues firmly in cheek. As Italian comics historian Simone Castaldi put it:

> The narrative ability of Secchi, a mediocre novelist but brilliant scriptwriter for comics […], and the graphic strength of Raviola (who, a few years later, became one of the greatest signatures of European comics) united in a constant exchange of narrative intuitions. Moving with ease between

Spanish poster for Umberto Lenzi's film version of *Kriminal* (1966)

Dutch actor Glenn Saxson was cast in the leading role as *Kriminal*. Director Umberto Lenzi preferred a younger Kriminal to the older version in the comic.

Inevitably, *Kriminal* soon became one of the main targets of the press campaign against the *fumetti neri* that caused a number of their issues to be seized. This forced Secchi and Raviola to mitigate its violent and erotic content (ditto for their twin creation, *Satanik*) and give more room to standard whodunit and mystery elements. Starting with issue #55 (*Dramma in collegio*, July 1966) the character of Lola Hudson was introduced. She would become Kriminal's lover and then his wife—a unique fate for a *fumetti neri* hero. However, Secchi and Raviola had not lost their knack for biting punch lines and pointed satire. Issue #90 (*Quello che non ti aspetti*, March 1967) features several self-referential in-jokes inspired by the *fumetti neri* trials. A panel shows a bad guy yelling, "Kriminal and Satanik together! That's too much! It's an obscene situation like in one of those *fumetti neri*!" Kriminal stabs him in return, replying, "The obscene thing is that someone really believes we are obscene!" and later on, while punching a thug: "If I'm not killing you now that is because it's the editor-in-chief who's going to jail instead of me!"

It took a couple of years before *Kriminal* got to the big screen. The blond-haired, handsome Anthony Logan was played by the Dutch actor Glenn Saxson (real name Roel Bos), one of the many good looking foreign actors who were finding their way in Italian cinema of the period. As Saxson recalls today:

> I arrived in Italy in the spring of 1964 and started pretty soon doing photo-novels and TV commercials (*Caroselli*). Coming from the Academy of Dramatic Arts, my hope was a film career.[3]

His first film appearance was an uncredited bit role in Luchino Visconti's *Sandra of a Thousand Delights* (*Vaghe stelle dell'orsa ...* , 1965).

> It was only one day's work but interesting because it was with Claudia Cardinale and I was being directed by the great Visconti.

Bos' exceptionally good looks—blond hair, blue eyes, square jaw, athletic presence—soon gained him his first starring roles in a couple of Westerns. He recalls the origin of his pseudonym:

> My first movie as a leading man was *Go with God, Gringo* (*Vaya con dios gringo*, 1966, Edoardo Mulargia), shot in Cinecittà ... As you know, those days all Western actors were obliged to

and introduced a shockingly daring novelty. "*Diabolik* was still stuck to portraying female dancers in order to show their legs. I couldn't stand it!" as Raviola explained:

> So, the first time a girl's skirt was raised, I showed her embroidered panties, which no one had ever dared to show. They were so accurately drawn that they impressed even Bunker.

A colorful Italian lobby card for *Kriminal*

have American names. I liked Roel Bos but my producer wanted a more American-sounding name, so finally we agreed on Glenn Saxson. Ironically, later on the name was sometimes misspelled as Saxon, especially in foreign editions of my films.

Saxson went on to play one of the many Djangos in Italian cinema in Alberto De Martino's *Django Shoots First* (*Django spara per primo*, 1966) before donning the skeleton outfit.

> For *Kriminal*, which was my third movie after the two Westerns, I made a screen test that Umberto Lenzi liked, as he preferred a younger Kriminal to the older Kriminal in the comic strip.

The then 35-year-old Lenzi was by that time an established director in the realm of Italian popular cinema. Born in Tuscany in 1931, he started out as a journalist for various local newspapers and magazines, such as the prestigious *Bianco e Nero*, and eventually put off his law studies to pursue the art of filmmaking. Lenzi enrolled at Rome's Centro Sperimentale di Cinematografia in 1956, and debuted in 1958 with a picture shot entirely in Greece (*Mia Italida stin Ellada*, "An Italian Woman in Greece," 1958). With his following output he proved to be an affordable, efficient director who got to display his eclecticism by jumping from one genre to the next, according to what the market required: grim melodramas (*Duel of Fire/Duello nella Sila*, 1962), adventure stories (*The Triumph of Robin Hood/Il trionfo di Robin Hood*, 1962), historical dramas (*Catherine of Russia/Caterina di Russia*, 1963), pirate films (*Sandokan the Great/Sandokan la tigre di Mompracem*, 1963), sword-and-sandal flicks (*Messalina vs. the Son of Hercules/L'ultimo gladiatore*, 1964) and even weird crossovers such as *Samson and the Slave Queen* (*Zorro contro Maciste*, 1963), which featured the titular muscleman (actually Maciste in the Italian version) opposed to swashbuckler legend Zorro.

Lenzi's technical prowess made him the ideal director for action and spy movies, with such titles as *008: Operation Exterminate* (*A 008, operazione sterminio*, 1965), although his notorious bad temper made him a somehow difficult type with which to deal. Saxson recalls:

> Working with Lenzi was easy although I was warned in advance that he could be a bit hysterical.

Shooting went on for about two months and, as was customary with that type of co-production, a number of exotic locations were worked into the film. Interiors were shot in Rome, while exteriors were filmed in Madrid, Istanbul, the Black Sea and London. Despite having his own double (the great Attilio Severini) for the scenes in which he wears the skull mask, Saxson had to perform his own stunts in the film's most spectacular scene, where Kriminal runs atop a speeding train, because Severini had just injured his ankle and there was no time to find a replacement.

Lenzi explained:

> I wanted to make my debut into this type of genre with *Diabolik*, but we couldn't get the rights, since De Laurentiis had already bought them. Thus I made *Kriminal* […]. [The Tuscan director had originally set his eyes on another Magnus & Bunker comic: *Satanik*, which was eventually adapted for the screen by Piero Vivarelli in 1968.] As a comic book, *Satanik* is better than *Kriminal*. It was more morbid, more erotic, but since I could not make that into a film, I fell back on the other one.[4]

Still, for *Kriminal* Lenzi opted for a lighter tone in jarring contrast with the comic book's explosive mixture of sex and violence:

> I saw it recently on TV and it seemed even better than when I shot it in 1966. Then I was a bit perplexed; now I appreciate the aspect of irony in it, something which comic strips didn't have, because they were vulgar, horrible."[5]

Lenzi went further, explaining that he argued with Bunker about some major changes he made to the eponymous character, "because it was a bit Nazi-skin fascist [sic!]. We made a fun film."[6]

Lenzi's claims about *Kriminal*'s fascist ideology are debatable to say the least, and it is unlikely that the Tuscan filmmaker ever took more than one or two distracted glances at the comic book, otherwise he would have noticed its undeniable tongue-in-cheek attitude. Anyway, if the movie is none too convincing, that is precisely because of this overly light approach.

The comic-strip style opening titles are very promising, anyway, as they epitomize the plot through a series of panels depicting Kriminal at work, while a driving, easy-listening score provides us with an instantly recognized guitar riff, courtesy of composer Raymond Full … aka Romano Mussolini.

However, from then on things start to get worse. Kriminal's costume has been redesigned due to practical (and budgetary?) reasons, though and looks rather impoverished, while the trademark skull mask has been replaced by a cheap-looking hood and a yellow-and-black suit which is closer to the comic book's covers (by Luigi Corteggi) than to Magnus' panels. However, Saxson acts most of the film without the skeleton costume on, and perhaps it is better that way.

The storyline chronicles Kriminal's last-minute escape from execution and his tribulations on the track of a bunch of stolen diamonds, which lead him face-to-face with such lovely ladies as Helga Liné and Mary Arden, as well as genre stalwarts like Ivano Staccioli, in one of his usual scumbag roles, and Andrea Bosic as Inspector Milton (looking rather different than his comics counterpart).

Lenzi claimed:

> It was an interesting experiment, as I tried to toy with the technical aspects of the language of comics, trying to apply them on a silver screen, as in the final sequence, featuring the typical balloons.[7]

However, there is actually little of all this in the film, and the aforementioned ending—where live-action is abruptly replaced by comics-type panels, which do not recall Magnus' style at all—looks more like the producers having run out of money than a way to emphasize the umbilical cord between *Kriminal* and its comic book source.

Kriminal, for most of its running time, is actually closer to one of those travelogue James Bond rip-offs that were flooding the screens during that period. Saxson moves from London to Spain and then to Istanbul like a '60s version of Arsène Lupin, seemingly more concerned with his peculiar disguises than anything else. What is more, despite a profusion of fashionable female *decollétees* and hairdos, Kriminal's sex adventures are very mild and chaste; the same can be said about violence, with the exception of a suitably nasty moment when Kriminal takes his revenge on Staccioli by secretly replacing his shaving foam with acid.

Although *Kriminal* benefits from tight pacing and judicious direction, its indifferent, undistinguished script ultimately bogs the film down. Saxson could well have been anybody else instead of Kriminal and that would not have changed matters one bit. All things considered, *Kriminal* is fast, fun and entertaining overall, but it is also disappointingly tame.

The film was moderately successful, leading to a follow-up, *Il marchio di Kriminal*, directed by Fernando Cerchio. Sadly, though, as of today there is no official English language DVD release of the movie.

Lenzi moved on to a decidedly more adult genre, which proved to be one of the most influential of the following years—the *gialli*. He directed a triptych of erotic thrillers starring Carroll Baker that were heavily influenced by French *film noir* of the period and took advantage of Italy's relaxing censorship: *Orgasmo* (1969, released in the U.S. as *Paranoia*, which led to a somewhat confusing situation in years to come), *So Sweet … So Perverse* (*Così dolce… così perversa*, 1969) and *Paranoia* (aka *A Quiet Place to Kill*, 1970).

In the 1970s Lenzi became one of the leading directors in the crime genre, with such titles as *Gang War in Milan* (*Milano rovente*, 1973), the extraordinarily grim *Almost Human* (*Milano odia: la polizia non può sparare*, 1974), *Assault with a Deadly Weapon* (*Roma a mano armata*, 1975), *Violent Naples* (*Napoli violenta*, 1976), *Free Hand For a Tough Cop* (*Il trucido e lo sbirro*, 1976) and the crepuscular *From Corleone to Brooklyn* (*Da Corleone a Brooklyn*, 1979).

The Tuscan director also paved the way for one of Italian cinema's most controversial sub-genres, the cannibal film, with *The Man from Deep River* (*Il paese del sesso selvaggio*, 1972), starring Ivan Rassimov. He would continue with a pair of films that are perhaps among his best-known among horror fans, although far from his best work: *Eaten Alive* (*Mangiati vivi!*, 1980) and the infamous *Cannibal Ferox* aka *Make Them Die Slowly* (1981). The early 1980s saw the release of some of his most notorious pictures, such as the trashy gory horror *Nightmare City* (*Incubo sulla città contaminata*, 1981) and the aforementioned *Cannibal Ferox*. Lenzi dabbled again with horror and thriller during the decade, albeit with disappointing results, before ending his career in the early 1990s with a couple of passable yet nondescript cop flicks in the vein of American movies of the period.

Kriminal was one of the most memorable *fumetti neri*. Its sales peaked to over 300,000 copies in its heyday, and it survived the new tide of blatantly erotic comics of the late 1960s and early 1970s. However, its overall quality had long since declined, given that other and less gifted artists replaced Magnus. He and Secchi mostly dedicated themselves to *Alan Ford*, the spy spoof they had launched in 1969 and which proved to be one of the milestones of Italian *fumetto*. *Kriminal* ceased publication with issue #419, *La fine?* (November 1974). However, Secchi would episodically reprise the character again in the following years, even with a tone of parody, in *Alan Ford* (issue #150, *Kriminalissimo*, December 1981).[8]

Magnus moved on to an eclectic and often iconoclastic career. After parting ways with Secchi, he moved to Edifumetto (the then-leading publisher of adults-only comic books in Italy) where he worked on a number of blatantly erotic comics before creating his masterpiece, *Lo Sconosciuto* (1975), an incredibly nihilistic *noir*

The Belgian poster for *Kriminal* actually censored the skull mask and minimized the costume's skeleton appearance.

about a mercenary named Unknow (sic) which lasted just six issues, from July 1975 to January '76 (Magnus later reprised the character in the following decades with new stories). *La Compagnia della Forca*, released in 1977, was a Medieval picaresque adventure that somehow recalled *Alan Ford* with its array of bizarre characters. Both, however, were commercial flops.

In a bold move, Magnus then tried his hand at out-and-out hardcore porn with the grotesque, no-holds barred *Necron*, centered on a necrophile female scientist who creates a hugely endowed monster out of body parts in order to satisfy her sexual needs. Due to its excessively gory and graphic content, *Necron* caused a sensation at the time of its release in 1981, but comics scholars praised Magnus' stylistic evolution, with a more experimental and stark trait which recalled the French *ligne claire* and proved highly influential on the new generation of European comic book artists. Other creations of the period were the elaborate, astonishingly exquisite erotic graphic novel *Le 110 pillole* (The 110 Pills) and the equally remarkable science-fiction epic *I Briganti*.

Magnus' final masterpiece was a special, huge format issue of *Tex*, a colossal, painstakingly detailed work that was seven years in the making and which he completed just days before passing away of liver cancer in February 1996.

On a final note, there is no connection at all between *Kriminal* and later films released in Italy with the word *Kriminal* in the title. Hubert Frank's *Das Teufelscamp der verlorenen Frauen* (1978) came out in 1980 as *Kriminal Love—Amore carnale*, and the Turkish film *İnsanları Seveceksin* (1979, Melih Gulgen) was submitted to the board of censors in February 1981 with the alluring title *Kriminal Porno*. The former was an erotic thriller set on a remote island, about a girl who is taken prisoner by a gang of thugs. Whereas Gulgen's was a Turkish/Italian production, a violent crime drama starring local star Cüneyt Arkın as well as TV starlet Gloria Piedimonte, who enjoyed a short-lived popularity after her

***Kriminal* is perhaps the very best of all *fumetti neri* (art by Magnus).**

appearance as the dancing girl in the opening credits of the TV show *Discoring*. Following a film totally dedicated to her (1979's *Baila Guapa*, the name of the song Piedimonte was dancing to) she soon fell into soft-core limbo. For the home market version of the film, the Italian co-producers added several erotic scenes shot by Sergio Bergonzelli. *Kriminal Porno* received a V.M.18 rating.

Notes:
1. Published by Edizioni Cofedit, *Fantax* featured a private detective who moonlights as the titular assassin. Unlike Kriminal, however, Fantax only persecuted other criminals. The comic strip lasted 17 issues (June 1964/October 1965) before changing its name into *Fantasm* because of legal troubles (a character with the same name was being published in France since 1946). *Fantasm* ran 23 issues and ceased publication in August 1967.
2. Castaldi, Simone, *Drawn and Dangerous: Italian comics of the 1970s and 1980s* (Jackson MS: University Press of Mississippi, 2010), p. 14.
3. Glenn Saxson, email interview with the author, February 2014.
4. Gomarasca, Manlio, *Umberto Lenzi* (Milan: Nocturno Libri, 2001), p. 222.
5. Giorgi, Andrea, "Eating Lenzi. Umberto Lenzi interviewed," *Necronomicon* #5, 1994, p. 21.
6. Ibid.
7. Ibid.
8. In September 2015, Mondadori—which bought the rights from Secchi—launched another incarnation of the character in a weekly magazine. In addition to the different format (the old pocket size has been abandoned) and the use of color, the "new" Kriminal looks quite different from the original one, and contemporary American comics patently influence the stories. Fans of the "old" Kriminal have been warned.

Superargo vs. Diabolicus

(*Superargo contro Diabolikus*, aka *Superargo, el hombre enmascarado*)

Italy/Spain, color, 88 minutes

D: Nick [Nicola] Nostro. S: Mino Giarda; SC: Jaime Jesús Balcázar; DOP: Francisco Marín; M: Franco Pisano; E: Teresa Alcocer.

Cast: Ken Wood [Giovanni Cianfriglia] (Superargo), Gérard Tichy (Diabolikus), Loredana Nusciak [Loredana Cappelletti] (Diabolikus' mistress), Mónica Randall (Lidia), Francisco Castillo Escalona (Col. Alex Kinski).

Prod: Liber Film, S.E.C. Film (Rome), Producciones Cinematográficas Balcázar (Barcelona).

After accidentally killing an opponent in the ring, the masked wrestler Superargo falls into a deep personal crisis. He is given a chance to redeem himself when Colonel Kinski of the OSS recruits him on an important mission. Someone is stealing large quantities

The Spanish poster for *Superargo vs. Diabolicus*

Stuntman Giovanni Cianfriglia (billed as Ken Wood) played the masked hero, wrestler-cum-special agent Superargo.

of uranium and mercury from merchant ships, killing the crews in the process. Superargo is assigned to find out who is responsible. He sneaks into the gang's hideout and finds out that the mastermind is a mad scientist named Diabolikus, who has found a way to turn those elements into a gold isotope …

By the mid-'60s, Italy was ready for its first homemade masked superhero on film. It is not surprising, however, that Superargo was a wrestler. Besides the recurring element of brute force that somehow had marked the concept of the hero in Italian films since the silent era, the fact that *Superargo contro Diabolikus* was an Italian-Spanish co-production revealed the producers' intent to focus on the Spanish and South-American markets, given that wrestling has never been one of Italy's favorite sports. Spanish-speaking audiences, on the contrary, were familiar with another wrestler hero: El Santo, whose real identity was a mystery, and who fought against evil masterminds in order to save the world.

Whereas the paunchy Mexican hero went on to star in a plethora of films, his Italian counterpart appeared in just a couple of flicks before falling into oblivion after the superhero fever vanished. El Santo was not so popular in Italy anyway; only a few outings starring the Mexican *luchador* arrived in the country, and El Santo had his name changed into Argos, so that moviegoers would not confuse him with Simon Templar "The Saint" ("Il Santo" in Italian).[1] Proving the producers' intentions, Superargo was originally to be called Super-Argos.

However, for the character of Superargo, scriptwriters Mino Giarda and Jaime Jesús Balcázar drew on other sources. Superargo's back-story (he has killed a fellow wrestler in the ring and is tormented by guilt) looks like it was lifted from John Ford's *The Quiet Man* (1952), while the additional fact that he is also a concentration camp survivor is quite an unexpected touch and hints at a realistic background that the film never fully exploits. The main inspiration was comics, namely Lee Falk's *The Phantom*, which provided the blueprint for the red costume with black belt, gloves and boots worn by the leading man Ken Wood (real name Giovanni Cianfriglia).

Born in Anzio in 1935, Cianfriglia is one of the unknown soldiers of Italian cinema. He debuted as Steve Reeves' double in *Hercules* (*Le fatiche di Ercole*, 1958) and became a reliable stuntman and character actor who appeared in dozens of genre movies, from Westerns to crime flicks. Cianfriglia's casting as Superargo was most likely a budget-saving choice. Since he was an unknown performer (not necessarily an accomplished or even a hand-

Superargo and Lidia (Spanish actress Mónica Randall) in Diabolikus' secret lair.

some actor) who would not demand too high a salary and could perform his own stunts,[2] the fact that Superargo never takes off his mask during the film helped overcome Cianfriglia's shortcomings. Add an English pseudonym, as it was customary in Italian popular cinema in those days (the surname "Wood" possibly recalled Giuliano Gemma's early alias Montgomery Wood), and there you have it—Superargo!

As the director himself recalled about Cianfriglia:

> I had him act like a Zorro. By showing only his eyes you could not see his acting, nor his face, what he was saying or the expressions on his face. Then, when we dubbed the film, I gave him the best voice actor I could find, and despite his shortcomings, he made a good impression on screen."[3]

Unlike El Santo and the Phantom, though, the Italian superhero has superpowers, as his friend Kinski demonstrates to the government authorities in the film's most amusing scenes. Superargo can stand extreme heat and cold, is able to hold his breath for over seven minutes and is virtually invulnerable due to the quick coagulation of his blood. His Achilles' heel is electricity, which causes him extreme pain even though he cannot be electrocuted to death. Too bad he lacks Rodolfo Guzmán Huerta's opulent belly.

The *fumetti neri* was obviously drawn upon, as proven by the name of Superargo's opponent Diabolikus (with the "K" spelled in capital on the posters), a detail that is lost in the English language prints. The reference did not pass unnoticed. In the spring of 1966 producer Ottavio Poggi received a formal notice from Dino De Laurentiis, who was preparing *Danger: Diabolik*, which warned him not to use the original title *Super-Argos contro Diabolicus*. However, it is debatable whether the title change satisfied De Laurentiis' demands ...

The name, together with the bizarre costume (with an octopus logo on the chest), is the only thing that distinguishes such an uninteresting villain as Diabolikus, a sort of modern-day alchemist who has found the method of turning other metals into gold and plans to overthrow the world economy by flooding the market with gold, using the plethora of bad guys who populated Italian spy films of the period. The Bond connection, on the other hand, is emphasized by the scene where Superargo visits the government's secret research lab and collects the usual array of bizarre gadgets, including a bulletproof costume, a TV/radio transmitter disguised as a pin and uranium detectors in the guise of cocktail olives (!).

Overall, *Superargo vs. Diabolicus* is a straight, simple-minded adventure yarn that brings to mind 1930s and 1940s serials, as the hero has to face deadly perils about every 10 minutes or so. Unlike most of his contemporaries, though, Superargo does not shy away when it comes to handling a machine gun. Such skill pushes him closer to Bond than Batman.

Director Nicola "Nick" Nostro (Gioia Tauro, 1931-2014) was a former assistant director who debuted in 1962 with the drama *Blood and Defiance* (*Il sangue e la sfida*) and directed 10 films in a decade—all within the realm of genre cinema—before retiring for good. His direction is competent and he almost conceals the low budget through a clever use of atmospheric lighting, such as in the scenes set in Diabolikus' underground lair, a labyrinth of caves and cool labs. The film also features a suitably pleasant animated opening sequence à la Roger Corman and an underwater battle that looks like a poor man's answer to the celebrated scene in *Thunderball* (1965). Nostro recalled in an interview:

> We chose the locations carefully. We shot the exteriors in Barcelona, Spain. The interiors were shot in Rome, at the De Paolis studios. The caves were about 20 miles from Rome. However, Poggi was one of those stingy producers who tried to save as much money as he could, on everything. He would not even rent a studio, if he could come up

with something else. He used to shoot the indoor scenes in his villa in Frascati![4]

If Cianfriglia is at least physically adequate in the leading role, the rest of the cast is nondescript, with the exception of the German actor Gérard Tichy, a recurrent face in Spanish cinema, as Diabolikus. Many familiar Italian stuntmen (including Pietro Torrisi, Gilberto Galimberti, Bruno and Franco Ukmar) pop up in uncredited bits, while the Spanish Mónica Randall and the red-headed Italian Loredana Nusciak fill in the main female roles, respectively as Superargo's fiancée and Diabolikus' mistress.

Cianfriglia would reprise his role in the sequel *Superargo and the Faceless Giants* (*L'invincibile Superman*, 1968).[5]

Notes:
1. Both *Santo contra las mujeres vampiro* (1962) and *Santo en el museo de cera* (1964) were released in Italy in 1965, respectively as *Argos alla riscossa* and *Argos contro le 7 maschere di cera*. Then it was the release of *Santo en el tesoro de Drácula* (1969)—which came out in both a straight and a more erotic version as *Il tesoro di Dracula* (in 1977) and *Vita sessuale di un vampiro*. While 1975's *Santo contra los asesinos de la Mafia* was released (in 1977 as well) as *Argos il fantastico Superman*.
2. However, it must be noted that Cianfriglia was replaced by a double in the wrestling scenes. The two fighters in the opening match are the stuntmen Roberto and Emilio Messina.
3. Albiero, Paolo, "Un ragazzo di Calabria a Cinecittà," *Cine 70 e dintorni* #9, 2005, p. 55.
4. *Ibid*.
5. Besides the name Superargo, there is more than a passing connection between Nick Nostro's film and the Brazilian comic book, created by Italian-Brazilian artist Eugenio Colonnese in 1967 and published by Miguel Penteado's GEP. Superargo, replete with a red and yellow costume, is a secret agent and *capoeira* fighter, *capoeira* being a form of dance developed by African slaves in Brazil, with the agility they thereby gained being used as part of their resistance to their Portuguese owners; today, *capoeira* is taught in schools as a form of martial arts.

1967

Argoman the Fantastic Superman, aka *The Fantastic Argoman*, aka *The Incredible Paris Incident*
(*Come rubare la corona d'Inghilterra*, aka *Argoman superdiabolico*)

The Italian poster for *Argoman the Fantastic Superman*

Italy, color, 93 minutes
D: Terence Hathaway [Sergio Grieco]. S and SC: Dino Verde, Vincenzo Flamini; DOP: Tino Santoni; M: Piero Umiliani; E: Renato Cinquini.
Cast: Roger Browne (Sir Reginald Hoover/Argoman), Dominique Boschero (Regina Sullivan/Jenabell), Eduardo Fajardo (Shandra, the butler), Nadia Marlowa (Samantha), Dick Palmer [Mimmo Palmara] (Kurt), Richard Peters [Nino Dal Fabbro] (Inspector Lawrence), Edward Douglas [Edoardo Toniolo] (Inspector Martinet), Andrea Bosic (Admiral Durand), Tom Felleghy (General Headwood).
Prod: Fida Cinematografica (Rome).

In London St. Edward's crown has been stolen. Inspector Lawrence of Scotland Yard, who is in charge of the investigation, is convinced that the elusive Argoman performed the hit; Lawrence asks the noted criminologist Sir Reginald Hoover—who, unknown to him, is actually Argoman—to assist him in the case. Sir Reginald meets a mysterious woman Regina Sullivan who was sailing in front of his luxurious villa on her hovercraft and seduces her—thus temporarily losing his superpowers. In the meantime, the crown is delivered back with a note signed by Jenabell, "Queen of the World," who demands

Sir Reginald (Roger Browne) and Regina (Dominique Boschero) enjoy each other's company

in exchange a gigantic diamond that is capable of refracting the sun's rays with incalculable effects. Even though he discovers that Jenabell and Regina Sullivan are the same person, Sir Reginald cannot prevent the woman and her gang from getting hold of the jewel. What is more, Jenabell has created humanoids that are dead ringers for the world's leading politicians and which she maneuvers at her own will. Argoman penetrates Jenabell's lair just in time to thwart her devilish plan …

If there is a film that perfectly captures the spirit of 1960s Italian superheroes, *Argoman the Fantastic Superman* is the one. Sergio Grieco's movie retains the *fumetti neri*'s delightful amorality while squeezing the best from the many Italian James Bond rip-offs in terms of tongue-in-cheek, fast-paced action.

For one thing, whether Argoman is a good or bad guy is highly debatable. Sure, he helps the police capture the ravishing but dangerous Jenabell, who has stolen St. Edward's crown from the Tower of London and plans to conquer the world, but in the opening scene he is about to be executed by a Chinese army,[1] and his personal art collection includes such items as Leonardo Da Vinci's painting "La Gioconda" …

A multimillionaire, criminologist and art collector, Argoman's *alter ego* Sir Reginald Hoover is a playboy whose only interest seems to be his own pleasure. The hero's amorality and ribald sexism make him an irresistible cross between a sexually voracious Batman—replete with an imperturbable butler (Eduardo Fajardo) wearing a leopard cape à la Lothar—and a super-powered James Bond. In his sumptuous villa by the sea, Sir Reginald has a personal harem of bikini-clad beauties constantly waiting for him to summon them whenever he feels like it.

Argoman the Fantastic Superman is full of gleeful plot twists, tongue-in-cheek humor (Argoman temporarily loses his powers after having sex) and Pop Art *décors*. Argoman's superpowers are an odd bunch to say the least and include the ability to hold his breath underwater for over half an hour ("Not bad, but I get bored down there") and telekinesis. Yet his lemon yellow costume (replete with a visor that curiously resembles X-Men's Cyclops) verges on self-parody while Dominique Boschero, as Jenabell, the self-proclaimed "Queen of the World," sports a different outfit—and invariably a sexy one—in each scene she appears.

Much of the credit for the film's amusement must be given to co-scripter Edoardo "Dino" Verde, a former satirical writer who was a contributor to the renowned magazine *Marc'Aurelio*, together with such personalities as Cesare Zavattini, Marcello Marchesi, Vittorio Metz,

Stefano "Steno" Vanzina and Federico Fellini. Besides writing a huge number of theater shows (the so-called "Varietà," which mixed comedy and musical numbers), in the 1950s Verde became a prolific screenwriter. Among his works are such gems as Dino Risi's *The Widower* (*Il vedovo*, 1959) and Steno's Gothic parody *Uncle Was a Vampire*, plus a number of Franco & Ciccio vehicles.

Given Verde's input, the film's campy content is hardly surprising. Humorous dialogue and visual jokes abound: "Poor Sir Reginald ... who knows which torture he is being submitted to just now," the Chief of Police sighs after learning that Hoover has been taken prisoner by Jenabell. Cut to Browne and Boschero languidly kissing in bed. The sci-fi angle of the plot is also tongue-in-cheek, as Verde and co-scriptwriter Vincenzo Flamini throw in a device capable of duplicating human beings (as in *The Three Fantastic Supermen*), a giant diamond with outstanding powers and an unlikely tin robot which looks like it came straight out of a cut-rate 1950s space opera.

Executive producer Edmondo Amati was not too keen on the result, though:

> The idea was to make an Italian Superman of sorts, but we did not have the means or the technique.[2]

However, other parties involved were not as dismissive about the film. Dominique Boschero claimed it was the funniest of all the spy flicks in which she appeared.

> I had to play the Queen of the World. But when they tell you, "You will be the Queen of the World," you ask yourself how are you gonna play that role! However, it was something new, a film ahead of its time. Sergio Grieco was a rather good director and we had a higher budget than usual, and more locations as well—including London.

Boschero was right about Grieco, one of the more solid and accomplished genre filmmakers to emerge from Italy's Bond fever. A veteran director who had debuted behind the camera in 1950, Grieco (1917-1982) had dabbled in many genres—from melodrama to comedy, from swashbuckling adventures to sword-and-sandal efforts. His spy movies of the decade, such as the two *Agent 077* films starring Ken Clark, were technically well made and reasonably entertaining. In the following decade Grieco would also try his hand at crime pictures, with the hyper-violent *Terror in Rome* (*I violenti di Roma bene*, 1976) and the cult favorite *Beast with a Gun* (*La belva col mitra*, 1977) starring Helmut Berger and spy veteran Richard Harrison, the very same movie Robert De Niro and Bridget Fonda are watching on TV in Quentin Tarantino's *Jackie Brown* (1997). In *Argoman* Grieco makes good use of the Techniscope format with the help of cinematographer Tino Santoni, while Piero Umiliani's score is as catchy and frivolous as ever, thus perfectly capturing the film's spirit.

With his square jaw and arrogant macho smile, Roger Browne is quite effective as Argoman. One of the many American actors who crossed the ocean and settled in Italy during the Golden Age of Cinecittà, Browne specialized in sword-and-sandal epics (*Vulcan Son of Jupiter*, *The Ten Gladiators* and *The Revenge of Spartacus*) due to his impressive physique before moving on to Eurospy fare (*Super Seven Calling Cairo*, *Operation Poker* and *Rififi in Amsterdam*). His output thinned out in the '70s, where he had to cope with the outgrowing amount of erotic films being produced in Italy. Among others, he appeared in Rino Di Silvestro's *Women in Cell Block 7* (*Diario segreto da un carcere femminile*, 1973) and Aristide Massaccesi's notorious *Emanuelle in America* (1977).

Argoman the Fantastic Superman is available on DVD in the United States on the Dorado Films label.

Notes:
1. Curiously, the Italian version is missing said prologue, which introduces Argoman in an amusing manner. He is just about to be executed by a Chinese firing squad but saves himself by way of his psychic powers. He keeps muttering: "Kill each other ... kill each other ... kill each other ..." until the soldiers just turn around and shoot one another dead.
2. Giusti, Marco, *007 all'italiana* (Milan: Isbn Edizioni, Milan 2010), p. 106.

Avenger X

(*Mister-X*, aka *Mister X*)

Italy/Spain, color, 90 minutes

D: Donald Murray [Piero Vivarelli]; S: Adriano Bolzoni, Augusto Caminito; SC: Eduardo M. Brochero; DOP: Emanuele Di Cola; E: Gian Maria Messeri; M: Manuel Parada.

Cast: Norman Clark [Pier Paolo Capponi] (Mister X), Gaia Germani [Giovanna Giardina] (Timmy), Armando Calvo (George Lamar), Anna Zinnemann (Dolly), Umi [Umberto] Raho (MacDoug), Renato Baldini (Jack Caruso), Franco Fantasia (Inspector Roux), Dante Posani (Jim), Helga Liné (Gloria).

Prod: Terra Film (Rome), Copercine (Madrid).

The powerful Lamar, President of Trad Chemical Industries, is actually the head of a huge opium ring. When his lover Veronica demands a piece of the cake, Lamar has her killed by his men and pins the murder on Mister-X, a thief and master of disguise who is sought by the police all over the world. Understandably angry for being accused of a crime he did not commit, Mister-X—who is actually the wealthy American multi-millionaire Bob Rockson—moves to the isle of Capri with his beautiful fiancée Timmy. There, Lamar is meeting two gangsters, MacDoug and Caruso, who will join him for a huge opium deal. After Caruso is mysteriously killed, Lamar grows increasingly suspicious. Mister-X gets vital evidence of Lamar's traffic, but his adversary abducts Timmy. After MacDoug is murdered as well, it turns out that Lamar's right-hand man Jim is trying to take his boss' place, in cahoots with Lamar's new lover Gloria. In the end, however, Mister-X saves Timmy and defeats the drug lord.

Created by Cesare Melloncelli (writer) and Giancarlo Tenenti (drawing artist), *Mister-X* was published by Milan's Edizioni Cervinia, headed by Gino Balzarini. Publication started in October 1964—a mere two months after the debut of Editoriale Corno's *Kriminal*. However, Melloncelli soon left because of creative differences with the publisher and was replaced by the husband-and-wife team of Alfredo Saio and Andreina Repetto.

Mister-X—labeled with the catchphrase "È un giallo a fumetti" (It's a comic book *giallo*)—was quite different from the other *fumetti neri* of the era, mainly for one reason: the almost total absence of violence. The titular character, based in Paris, is actually a gentleman thief once again in the vein of Arsène Lupin (to the point that he leaves a card with his name at the site of his spectacular thefts). What is more, his victims are usually members of the élite, but Mister-X is also capable of good deeds, bringing gangsters and other assorted criminals to justice, much to the dismay of his archenemy Inspector Roux (the umpteenth variation on *Diabolik*'s Inspector Ginko).

It was possibly the lack of explicit violence that allowed the character to end up on television in 1967, in a series of TV spots for a renowned brand of detergent, Dixan. That very same year *Mister-X* became a film, directed by

A Spanish poster for *Avenger X*, Piero Vivarelli's adaptation of the comic book *Mister-X*

Piero Vivarelli (1927-2010), a peculiar filmmaker/songwriter who, after enrolling with the Fascists during World War II, had become a militant Communist after the conflict. Vivarelli wrote the lyrics for several of singer Adriano Celentano's most famous songs (such as *24.000 baci* and *Il tuo bacio è come un rock*) and co-directed Celentano's film debut, the ambitious caper film, *Robbery Roman Style* (*Super rapina a Milano*, 1964).

Much like its source, *Avenger X* (the English title abandoned the character's original name) is a hopelessly tame affair. Although the opening credits display a titillating series of suitably lurid panels, the film turned out a lackluster, half-baked potboiler with almost no references to the comic book world it came from.

For a start, Mister-X is an uninvolving, unsympathetic hero, who is completely lacking the edgy working-class appeal of his contemporaries. His jet-set attitude ("I won the last eight editions of the World Golf Championship," he boasts to his girlfriend), good table manners and general stiff upper-lipped demeanor are a far cry from the genuine sadism of Kriminal, so much so that he looks visibly less uncomfortable wearing a tuxedo and sipping a glass of champagne than donning his costume. Speaking of which,

Mister-X was played by Pier Paolo Capponi, billed as Norman Clark, perhaps to cash in on the popularity of Ken Clark, the star of many Italian spy movies.

the cinematic Mister-X wears quite a different outfit than his comic book counterpart. Instead of the red adhesive costume, complete with a hood that fully hides his face, red cape, white boots and gloves, Vivarelli has his titular character don an anonymous black-hood-and-leotard which makes him look like a third-rate Diabolik, plus he sports a belt with an "X" on it that recalls The Phantom. The result is so awkward and disappointing that said costume makes its appearance only 40 minutes into the film and is featured in merely a couple of scenes.

Even if Interpol is hot on his heels, Mister-X is ultimately one of the good guys, and this makes him a thoroughgoing bore. And the fact that the script carefully excuses him from indulging in controversial activities does not help. Sex is merely hinted at in a few lines of dialogue ("Our days will be very busy," Timmy observes, to which Mister-X replies, "And our nights, too ...") that would have been old-fashioned in 1930s Hollywood screwball comedies, and Gaia Germani gets to barely show her legs and shoulders while in a bathrobe.

Violence is also kept to a minimum, since it is not Mister-X's habit to kill people. The nastiest bit, so to speak, has Mister-X being tortured with a blowtorch that barely blackens his shirt. However, Vivarelli claimed that the most violent scenes were excised from the Italian version to avoid a V.M.14 rating and were maintained in the copies aimed at the foreign markets. The director was highly exaggerating, as according to the Board of Censors' verbals, the cuts amounted to a total of 47 seconds and involved two scenes: the blowtorch approaching Mister-X's naked chest and a subjective shot of a man on a boat driving at full speed toward the reef.

The allegedly low budget does not allow for many distractions. After an opening bit in Rome, with a murder filmed at the Stadio dei Marmi at the Foro Italico (the same location depicted in a celebrated scene of Mario Bava's *The Girl Who Knew Too Much*, 1963), much of the film takes place in Capri. Yet the indoor sets will look familiar to fans of Italian genre cinema, as they belong to the same villa in Rome where Bava shot *Blood and Black Lace*. Vivarelli stages a few tepid fistfights and even tries to show off his technical prowess in a lengthy fight scene shot in one long take, but the result only highlights how haphazardly put together the rest of the film is.

The cast is a mixed bag. As the titular hero, the slightly balding Pier Paolo Capponi (billed as Norman Clark) looks definitely out of place, as he has neither the looks nor the *physique du rôle* for the character. Capponi—a fine actor nonetheless, but more at ease in drama than in adventure—would soon become one of crime films' recurring presences, often as the hard-boiled police inspector, after playing the role of Duca Lamberti in Fernando di Leo's first adaptation of a Giorgio Scerbanenco novel, *Naked Violence* (*I ragazzi del massacro*, 1969). Capponi also showed up in *gialli* (Luciano Ercoli's *The Forbidden Photos of a Lady Above Suspicion*, 1970; Dario Argento's *The Cat O' Nine Tails*, 1971; Umberto Lenzi's *Seven Bloodstained Orchids*, 1972—in

Gaia Germani and Pier Paolo Capponi in a rare publicity still for *Avenger X*. Unfortunately Capponi only wears the costume in a couple of scenes.

The Comic Book Universe in Italian Cinema

the latter two titles he reprised his typical commissioner role), but his best performance was as Tony, Martin Balsam's ignorant, sadistically violent right-hand man in Di Leo's powerful gangster drama, *Blood and Diamonds* (*Diamanti sporchi di sangue*, 1978).

The ravishing Gaia Germani, already seen in Bava's *Hercules in the Haunted World* (*Ercole al centro della Terra*, 1961), Bernard Borderie's Lemmy Caution flick *Your Turn, Darling* (*À toi de faire ... mignonne*, 1963) and Warren Kiefer's *Castle of the Living Dead* (*Il castello dei morti vivi*, 1964) among others, was a rather popular starlet in the 1960s. Other familiar faces of Italian genre cinema turn up in minor roles: master of arms and character actor Franco Fantasia as Inspector Roux, the ubiquitous and suavely menacing Umberto Raho and Renato Baldini (who was also featured in the *Killing* photonovels). Since *Avenger X* was an Italian-Spanish co-production, Iberian bombshell Helga Liné is a welcome presence in one of her tailor-made nasty bitch roles. Liné also has the film's best line, as she hisses to the captive Timmy: "Nothing kills more than sex, you gotta be updated!"

Avenger X was tepidly received at the Italian box-office, with a scant 112 million *lire*. The following year Cervinia closed down and *Mister-X* ceased publication in February 1968. The last issue, #53, saw the return of Melloncelli as the writer. However, Tenenti (who had been the titular artist for almost all of the issues) offered the character to another publishing house, Renato Bianconi's Alhambra, which was publishing similar *fumetti neri* such as *Cobra* (a rerun of *Sadik* under a different name). The new series, this time subtitled "Brivido—avventura—mistero" (Thrill—adventure—mystery), resurfaced just a few months later, in September 1968, with monthly publication, and offered a revised version of the hero's costume. This time a small Lone Ranger-style, old-fashioned mask that only covered the character's eyes replaced the full-head hood. Another debatable alteration regarded the covers, which were all rather similar and boring portraits of Mister-X brandishing a gun, with no mention of the stories' titles on the front.

This rather *retro* restyling did not help, though. The new series was not anywhere near as successful as the first one, and Alhambra's *Mister-X* closed down for good in May 1969, after just nine issues.

Deadly Sweet, aka *I Am What I Am*
(*Col cuore in gola*, aka *Dead stop—Le coeur aux lèvres*)
Italy/France, color, 107 minutes
D: Tinto Brass. *S:* loosely based on the novel *Il sepolcro di carta* by Sergio Donati; *SC:* Tinto Brass, Francesca Longo, Pierre Lévy, with the participation of Guido Crepax; *DOP:* Silvano Ippoliti; *M:* Armando Trovajoli; *E:* Tinto Brass.

Cast: Jean-Louis Trintignant (Bernard), Ewa Aulin (Jane Burroughs), Roberto Bisacco (David), Charles

A Spanish poster for *Deadly Sweet*

Kohler (Jerome Burroughs), Luigi Bellini (Jelly-Roll), Vira Silenti (Martha Burroughs), Skip Martin, David Prowse.
Prod: Panda (Rome), Les Films Corona (France).

Bernard, a French actor who is in London for work, one night finds a girl, Jane, standing horrified by a dead man named Prescott, the owner of a night club. Bernard immediately decides to help her. First, though, he needs to find a compromising photograph that he believes Jane's brother has taken. While looking for the photo, Bernard kills a hitman whom he caught at Prescott's home, thus putting himself in danger too—however, he is willing to do anything for Jane. After a mysterious gang kidnaps the girl, Bernard locates Jerome and the two men team up to find Jane. Eventually, Bernard finds out that it was she who murdered Prescott. Jane confesses that she did it because he was blackmailing her. Then she pulls out a gun and shoots Bernard, as he is the only one who knows the truth ... and also because she realizes that she is falling for him.

In 1945, when he was just 12, Guido Crepax drew his first comic based on a film, a juvenile rendition of James Whale's *The Invisible Man* (1933).

I saw it in Milan. When I got back to Venezia I drew it. I had an extraordinary visual memory then, in fact I immediately drew the story after watching the film just once![1]

Twenty years later Crepax invented *Valentina*, once again drawing inspiration from cinema—this time, the titular heroine was modeled upon silent film star Louise Brooks. Crepax loved movies ("I was a movie maniac. I used to be there all the time. My two passions were music and films"), and it was natural for him to finally become part of one, even though in a quite peculiar way.

In 1966 fellow Venetian filmmaker Tinto Brass called Crepax to draw the storyboards for his new project, *Deadly Sweet*. Brass had already flirted with the medium in his previous effort, *Yankee* (1966), an idiosyncratic Western starring Philippe Leroy. Brass stated:

> I wanted to make a film in ideograms—like in Chinese writing, where a symbol indicates a whole concept. So I did not film a horse but an eye, or a spur. […] The characters seem two-dimensional, as in a comic.[2]

However, Brass experienced lots of trouble with the producers in the editing process, where the director's vision was not respected. He sued the production company and eventually took his name off the film.

For *Deadly Sweet*, Brass adapted a paperback novel by Sergio Donati, *Il sepolcro di carta*, published in 1955. Brass explained:

> It is funny to think how the film was born. I was offered to make a movie out of the novel, which I did not like very much. The producers wanted [Jean-Louis] Trintignant in the lead. I went to meet him, but I didn't feel like telling him a story that did not convince me. So I invented another one. And he accepted. Then I sent him over the real script, telling him I had changed my mind.[3]

Yet the director radically changed the plot, most importantly by moving the story from Rome to London—a city whose spirit and style were saturating Italian culture, after the success of Michelangelo Antonioni's *Blow-up* (1966) as well as Alberto Sordi's *Smoke Over London* (*Fumo di Londra*, 1966). Brass continued:

> At that time London represented what Paris had represented before it: the place of transgression and freedom. Lots of things were happening. The Beatles were only one of them. It was Europe's liveliest urban center.[4]

Besides the patent nods to the *Nouvelle Vague*, the smell of Swingin' London is all over the film, best exemplified by the cover of The Beatles' album *Revolver* on display in one scene. However, Brass also repeatedly pays homage to Antonioni, by showing the poster for *Blow-up* as well setting a scene in a photographer's study. One character even refers with admiration to "Michelangelo … Antonioni, of course."

The nephew of a famous Venetian painter, Brass had the intuition of reinventing the *film noir* as a comic strip. And that is where Crepax came in handy, and he stated:

> I drew a storyboard of one scene and gave it to Tinto Brass. I went to Rome, met Tinto and brought these drawings. It was a drawn screenplay, so to speak.[5]

Even though he was used to working with black-and-white, Crepax concocted color storyboards (or "graphic suggestions," as they are termed in the end credits) for the film, which Brass faithfully reproduced. Crepax used warm colors, with lots of reds, which were unusual in his work. Even though the storyboards (50 panels, about 16 by 20 inches each) retained his peculiar style, they are structured like movie shots, with no words except for the typical *fumetti* onomatopoeia.

Almost every image in *Deadly Sweet* is conceived as a comic book panel, from the many extreme close-ups to

Jean-Louis Trintignant and Ewa Aulin, the would-be hero and the damsel-in-distress of *Deadly Sweet*

the wide-angle shots, to the way Brass reframes the shot in order to accommodate, for instance, Trintignant's eyes in a small rectangular portion of the screen, totally surrounded by black. And then there are the forced perspectives, the colored filters, the sequences shot in primary colors or black-and-white and the onomatopoeia—"Ough!" "Slam!" "Thud!"—that Brass retains from Crepax' storyboards and which fill the screen whenever there is a fight scene, or somebody is shooting someone else, and so on, as if they belonged in a Roy Lichtenstein panel. "The script was written while keeping in mind the patterns of *fumetti*," as Brass pointed out. "The onomatopoeic sounds were already in the script. The producer used to ask me, "But how do you write?" "Oh well, I write this way!"[6]

If the use of fetish objects (such as a Nazi hat and uniform) are nods to Crepax's *oeuvre*, Brass packs the film to the brim with references to the comic book universe, from *Tarzan* (when Ewa Aulin tells him her name is Jane, the hero replies, "Me, Tarzan") to *Batman* (a panel from Bob Kane's comic pops up while Bernard is walking around London) and even stuff aimed at more acquired tastes. In an amusing bit, Trintignant even points to a poster of Alfred E. Neuman, *Mad Magazine*'s fictitious mascot-cum-cover boy, uttering the famous line—"What? Me worry?"—just as he is about to be punched by a couple of thugs.

The protagonist becomes a comic book character of sorts—an empty, walking stereotype who moves as if he was being drawn by a comic artist, making poses, changing his voice, acting like the hard-boiled type he desperately fails to be.

Even though he deludes himself that he is the hero, Bernard is doomed from the start. He is punched, tricked, beaten, cheated, ridiculed (even by Brass himself. One scene juxtaposes Trintignant being chased by hoods with a dog race), betrayed, tortured and ultimately murdered, in one of the director's most darkly ironic endings. The other characters are just as one-dimensional, including a malevolent, sex-crazed dwarf (played by Anthony "Skip" Martin) and assorted hit men.

And then, of course, there is the leading lady, Brass' reimagining of the *femme fatale* archetype. Even though she shows very little by today's standards, the then 17-year-old Ewa Aulin is absolutely gorgeous as the "deadly sweet" *ingénue* Jane, who—just like *Blow-up*'s Vanessa Redgrave—is after a compromising picture and will stop at nothing to get it. Brass stages an amazing striptease scene in which Aulin undresses behind a white panel, so that we only get to see her silhouette (Trintignant becomes so excited that he takes off his clothes too, and then jumps on a vine and then onto her, just like Tarzan would …). Another scene has a thug lasciviously caressing Aulin's body with a gun as she is bound and gagged—enough to earn the film a V.M.18 rating (forbidden for those under 18 years old) in Italy.

A lot of *Deadly Sweet*'s charm is the result of Silvano Ippoliti's outstanding cinematography. As Brass recalled:

> Barcarol[7] had died and I needed to find another director of photography. That's how I worked; I had already

written the script. There was a scene where somebody threw a cigarette and I wanted the embers to be seen in the half-light. I submitted this dilemma to various directors of photography. Somebody said, "Well, we'll put an electrical resistance inside the cigarette … " and so on. Silvano Ippoliti just said, "We'll film it." He was a bit like Barcarol.[8]

Even though it exists in a universe of its own, it would be unfair to say that *Deadly Sweet* is oblivious to the outside. When Trintignant and Aulin meet in a theater, they watch a newsreel about the Six-Day War fought by Israel, Egypt, Jordan and Syria in June 1967. Brass had not lost his knack for incorporating vitriolic political commentary into his work, which caused his 1963 film *Chi lavora è perduto* to be banned by the Italian Board of Censors.

Despite the presence of Trintignant (then at the apex of his popularity after Lelouch's *A Man and a Woman*, 1966), *Deadly Sweet* was not a hit in Italy. Trintignant and Aulin, on the other hand, met again on the set of Giulio Questi's weird *giallo Death Laid an Egg* (*La morte ha fatto l'uovo*, 1968). Brass' next film, *Attraction*, was also shot in London, with the same crew as *Deadly Sweet*, and also featured references to comic books and Pop Art … that is, of course, besides Tinto's ever-growing obsession: sex.

Deadly Sweet is available on DVD in the United States on the Cult Epics label.

Notes:

1. Caneppele, Paolo and Krenn, Günter, "Guido Crepax, cinefilo artista del fumetto," in Festi and Scudiero, *Cinema & Fumetto*, p. 61.
2. Codelli, Lorenzo, ed., *Nerosubrass* (Udine: Dino Audino Editore/Centro Espressioni Cinematografiche, 1996), p. 47.
3. *Ibid.*, p. 52.
4. *Ibid.*, p. 50.
5. Caneppele and Krenn, "Guido Crepax, cinefilo artista del fumetto," p. 63.
6. Codelli, *Nerosubrass*, p. 52.
7. Bruno Barcarol had been Brass' director of photography on the director's early films.
8. Codelli, *Nerosubrass*, p. 56.

The Devil's Man
(*Devilman Story*)
Italy, color, 87 minutes
D: Paul Maxwell [Paolo Bianchini]. *S and SC:* Paul Maxwell, Max Caret; *DOP:* Alan Jones [Aldo Greci]; *M:* Patrick Leguy; *E:* Constance Elliot.

Cast: Guy Madison (Mike Harway), Liz Barrett [Luisa Baratto] (Christine Becker), Diana Lorys (Yasmin), Alan Collins [Luciano Pigozzi] (Kew), Bill Vanders (Prof. Becker), Lawrence Marchal [Valentino Macchi], Ken Wood [Giovanni Cianfriglia] (Devilman).

Prod: Lion International (Rome).

Reporter Mike Harway decides to help the young Christine Becker in the search of her father, Professor Becker, who has mysteriously disappeared in Rome. The investigation leads them both to Africa where, when traveling through a deserted area, they are captured and taken to the abandoned fort of El Faium. There, they find a subterranean scientific laboratory where the crazy Devilman is conducting horrible experiments on people. Devilman's dream is to replace his own brain with an artificial one that will make him able to rule the world. The villain keeps Professor Becker under his mind control, and is planning to have the professor complete the transplant on Christine first. Devilman's right-hand, Kew, allows Mike to flee and look for reinforcements. The reporter joins forces with a Tuareg tribe, but in the final battle, the Tuareg warriors clash in a furious struggle with Devilman's soldiers …

The first of three films Paolo Bianchini shot for producer Gabriele Crisanti, *The Devil's Man* is something of an oddity within Italian cinema of the period. It is often labeled as a spy film, and misleadingly so. With its mixture of exotic adventure, mystery and science fiction, it is actually closer to 1930s and 1940s U.S. serials—yet with a nod to the *fumetti neri* as well as to the superhero thread. This time, though, it is not the hero who wears a mask, but a weird-looking supercriminal, Devilman, in the Italian version—no relation to Go Nagai's *manga* of the same name.

According to Crisanti, *The Devil's Man* was designed as means of recovering costs and recycling scenes from another film he produced, *I predoni del Sahara* (1965, Guido Malatesta). Bianchini was practically given *carte blanche* and said:

> Crisanti showed me the footage he filmed in Morocco, with riders galloping, and he told me, "I sold the title already, and I have this usable footage; you shoot whatever you want. You can also add up to 6,500 feet of blank footage—as long as you keep the scene of the riders, it will do."[1]

This may partly explain the plot's tortuous and often decidedly illogical pattern. The opening scenes in Rome seem to belong to a low-par Hitchcockian thriller, as a young woman finds out that her father—a renowned brain surgeon—has mysteriously disappeared and she discovers a dead man who might have been killed by the missing scientist. Bianchini throws in every trick in the book (a stairwell shot from below, an eerie looking Santa Claus, a men-

Guy Madison and the mysterious masked villain in an Italian *fotobusta* for Paolo Bianchini's *The Devil's Man* (1967).

acing chestnut vendor, etc.) to build tension. The results are naive and yet strangely entertaining, as they heighten the film's strictly one-dimensional approach, which becomes evident with the abrupt introduction of Guy Madison's character—claiming to be a reporter but behaving more like a spy. Hence, the many plot synopses labeling him a secret agent.

Then the story moves on to Morocco in order to stitch together those scenes Crisanti cared so much about, and eventually we move to the core of the film, with the appearance of the titular super-villain. As played by *Superargo*'s Ken Wood, hiding his scarred features behind a silver mask (which makes him look a bit like Fantômas as portrayed by Jean Marais in André Hunebelle's films) and wearing lethal gloves with blades over the dorsum which come handy when it is time to cut someone's throat, Devilman is an impressive villain, even though his experiments and purpose are rather shady (to put it mildly) and the character's background is never explained.

All in all, Devilman looks like a cross between the *fumetti neri* antiheroes and early serial villains seen in the likes of *The Fighting Devil Dogs* (1938) or *Mysterious Doctor Satan* (1940), with a little bit of Dr. Mabuse thrown in for good measure. His zombie-like thugs have distinctively blank pupils, while director of photography Aldo Greci lights the underground lab beneath the Sahara desert, with a reliance on primary colors and shade/light effects. A case in point are the shots in which Mike or other characters walk though an intermittently lit corridor, or the sarcophagus-like cells which contain the victims of Devilman's experiments, flooded in a bright red light.

The cast is merely adequate. Guy Madison, well into his forties, is a mildly convincing, if not a particularly fascinating lead. Whereas Luisa Baratto—seen in Massimo Pupillo's *Bloody Pit of Horror*—fails to make much of an impression as the requisite damsel-in-distress. The gorgeous Diana Lorys is a bit underused, while the ubiquitous Luciano Pigozzi does his usual "slimy villain" routine. However, Bianchini's direction is svelte, with lots of hand-held shots, extreme close-ups and weird camera angles that are obviously patterned after comic book panels. Despite the low budget (which makes for a rather poor looking lab, full of sporadic red lights that ought to suggest state-of-the-art technology), the director makes good use of miniatures that are enthusiastically blown up, Antonio Margheriti-style, at the end.

The Devil's Man garnered a minor cult following in later years, together with the third film Bianchini directed for

Crisanti, the offbeat sci-fi thriller *Massacre Mania* (*Hipnos follia di massacro*, 1967), which also has definite comic book undertones. However, the self-deprecating Bianchini was not too fond of the results:

> Guy Madison was the only one who took the whole thing seriously. It was such crap![2]

Notes:
1. Giusti, *007 all'italiana*, p. 117.
2. Ibid.

Flashman
(*Flashman*)
Italy, color, 96 minutes
D: J. Lee Donan [Mino Loy]. *S and SC:* Ernesto Gastaldi; *DOP:* Floriano Trenker; *M:* Franco Tamponi; *E:* Eugenio Alabiso.
Cast: Paul Stevens [Paolo Gozlino] (Lord Alex Burman/John Smith/Flashman), Claudie Lange (Alika), John Heston [Ivano Staccioli] (Kid), Jacques Ary (Inspector Baxter), Micaela Cendali [Micaela Pignatelli] (Nevenka), Anne Marie Williams (Sheila), Seyna Seyn (Flower).
Prod: Zenith Cinematografica (Rome).

In London Professor Philips has discovered a serum that turns people invisible. However, a gangster named Kid murders Philips and steals the invention and tests it on himself. This way, he robs the Bank of Ireland. At the same time, a criminal competitor Alika and her female gang of forgers defraud the same bank and take advantage of their friendship with the bank officials, replacing the money with counterfeit banknotes. Chief Inspector Baxter of Scotland Yard is fumbling in the dark, but a mysterious masked vigilante who calls himself Flashman intervenes and sides with the law. Flashman is actually a rich nobleman, Lord Alex Burman, who fights crime in his spare time. Passing off as the bank's cashier, Alex is able to find the gangsters' next target. Meanwhile, Kid and Alika have joined forces in order to get hold of a Maharajah's fortune. After the latter's unexpected death, they set their eyes on his beautiful daughter (and heiress) Nevenka. It is up to Flashman to thwart their plan …

Despite bearing a similar *nom de plume* as D.C. Comics' The Flash, *Flashman*'s titular hero has a very different costume and superpowers. With his threadbare yet shiny red-and-silver attire, replete with cape and a bulletproof vest, he is a nice pop creation, the evidence of how Italian B-cinema could do wonders out of virtually nothing.

Flashman looks more like a cross between Superman—we first see him disguised as a bespectacled, clumsy bank clerk—and Batman; he is actually a millionaire of Russian origins, has a butler named Jeeves—who welcomes him back after missions and asks which salon he would like his tea to be served—and retainers dressed in 18th-century liveries. What is more, he has a sassy "yé-yé"

The German poster for *Flashman* (1967)

sister who paints eyes on her cheeks, wears bright yellow miniskirts and calls her brother a Tory. Another nod to Bob Kane's character, who was enjoying vast popularity due to the contemporaneous American TV series starring Adam West and Burt Ward, is the theme song by Franco Tamponi, graced by a groovy Farfisa organ, a killer bass line and a descending surf guitar riff.

The funniest touch about *Flashman* is that the eponymous superhero does not have any particular agenda. He has become a masked vigilante simply out of sheer boredom. "You see, my dear, when one has so much money as I do, he must come up with something to make life interesting," he explains to his sister. "Some collect Chinese prints, others collect butterflies … me, I collect criminals!"

This way Burman's relationship with his opponent, Kid (Ivano Staccioli), takes on interesting class notations. "I always dreamed of becoming a Maharajah," the proletarian bandit daydreams. "A hundred wives, splendid palaces, tons of gems …" Unlike the many evil geniuses of comic fiction, Kid has no plans to rule the world whatsoever. He is just another son of the Boom who dreams of making a quick and easy buck. On the other hand, Claudie Lange's gang of female crooks is a nice spicy touch, which

Paolo Gozlino (aka Paul Stevens) demonstrates how his dance skills contribute to his action hero ones.

is sadly left undeveloped, whereas the foolish Inspector on the case, played with farcical frenzy by the French-born Jacques Ary, is run-of-the-mill comic relief.

For the plot, scriptwriter Ernesto Gastaldi took inspiration from H.G. Wells' novella *The Invisible Man*, revisiting it in a humorous way, with such dialogue as, "An invisible man! How do you do that?"

"I undress!" [In a nice spicy touch, Lange as well has to take off her clothes near the end to become invisible when Flashman pursues her.]

Curiously, invisibility was also featured in Alberto Lattuada's pop-tinged spy extravaganza *Mission Top Secret*, released just a few months later. As with so many spy films of the period, a detour in the Middle East was inevitable, and for the third act Gastaldi and Loy let their hero loose amid the ruins of Baalbeck in Lebanon.

Gastaldi recalled about the film's genesis:

> The starting point was the comics, but the impetus was Mino Loy's desire to grapple with the technology of partially reflecting mirrors. Mino is a skilled technician, and at that time the special effects were not easy to do on camera. Mario Bava was a monster, and Antonio Margheriti was a close second. *Flashman* relied more on the cameraman's skills than on the story.[1]

However, the special effects vary wildly in quality. The transitions-to-invisibility bits are nicely made, whereas the animated objects (i.e. a gun) dancing in the air often sport visible fishing wires attached to them. On the downside, an explosion within a palace's façade is clumsily portrayed through a cardboard picture of the building, behind which a small fire can be seen, and the climactic boat chase-cum-explosion is rendered through patently fake miniature boats (and a flying Flashman puppet). The poor set-pieces also hint at the picture's low budget.

As the lead, blue-eyed Paolo Gozlino (1929-1992), hiding under the alias of Paul Stevens and bearing a passing resemblance to Guy Madison, sports the requisite straight face and charming macho looks, but he cannot overcome his wooden acting. An accomplished dancer and choreographer, Gozlino became popular in Italy due to his appearances in many TV shows. He worked in the movies as choreographer as well, on such titles as Riccardo Freda's *Caltiki, the Immortal Monster* (*Caltiki il mostro immortale*, 1959), and as a supporting actor. The same year as *Flashman* he popped up as Mandrake in *Una sera come le altre*, an episode from the anthology comedy *The Witches*, directed by Vittorio De Sica and starring Silvana Mangano and Clint Eastwood. Gozlino would maintain his anglicized pseudonym on a number of Westerns made during the early 1970s before gradually giving up on acting.

Born in Sardinia in 1933, Loy (real name Guglielmo Loy Donà) was a producer-director who dabbled in popular cinema. He helmed a number of erotic documentaries in the early 1960s, plus the spy story *Fury in Marrakech* (*Furia a Marrakech*, 1966), also written by Gastaldi. As usual with Loy's films, Sergio Martino's older brother Luciano (1933-2013) produced *Flashman*. It was Loy's third-from-last film, followed by the Gastaldi-penned war yarn *Desert Assault* (*La battaglia del deserto*, 1969) and the mondo flick *Questo sporco mondo meraviglioso* (1971).

Note:
1. Ernesto Gastaldi, email interview with the author, March 2014.

Goldface, the Fantastic Superman

(*Goldface, il fantastico superman*, aka *Cara de oro*)
Italy/Spain/Venezuela, color, 100 minutes
D: Stanley Mitchell [Adalberto "Bitto" Albertini]. S and SC: Ambrogio Molteni, Bitto Albertini, Italo Fasan; DOP: Carlo Fiore; M: Franco Pisano; E: Jordan B. Matthews [Bruno Mattei].
Cast: Robert Anthony [Espartaco Santoni] (Dr. Vilar/Goldface), Evi Marandi (Olga), Big Matthews [Attilio Severini] (Pamela's assassin/Goldface), Micaela Pignatelli (Pamela), Jan Foster Lothar (Kotar, Goldface's assistant), Manuel Monroy, Hugo Pimentel (Matthews).

Prod: Cineproduzioni Associate (Rome), Balcázar Producciones Cinematográficas (Barcelona).

In Venezuela Matthews, a wealthy industrialist, moonlights as a lucrative gangster under the name of Cobra, extorting large sums of money from his colleagues, threatening to blow up their factories. To convince the most reluctant victim, Matthews pretends to be blackmailed by the Cobra too. However, a masked wrestler superhero named Goldface steps in and spoils his plans. Thereafter, the Cobra tries by every means possible to retaliate by attempting to kill Pamela, the daughter of the industrialist he was blackmailing. He does not succeed, though, as Goldface—who hides under the identity of a scientist, Dr. Vilar—repeatedly saves the girl. Matthews then tries to get rid of Goldface, but to no avail. The masked wrestler—assisted by Kotar, his faithful servant, and by a comely counterintelligence agent—eventually defeats the dangerous criminal.

As director Adalberto Albertini recalled, *Goldface* was offered to him by Giuseppe Maggi, the head of distribution company Filmar, who was very much impressed by his debut film *Supercolpo da 7 miliardi* (1966). Albertini wrote in his autobiography, *Tra un ciak e l'altro*:

> He invited all his employees, drivers, porters and friends to the screening. At the end of the film he asked their opinion. Everyone in the audience loved it. So he immediately had me sign a contract with a conspicuous advance to shoot a film in Venezuela. I had to agree to have Ambrogio Molteni as co-scripter. I jumped for joy: Ambrogio was a dear friend ... And I left for Venezuela.[1]

Even more than the two *Superargo* movies, *Goldface, the Fantastic Superman* was conceived as an answer to the Mexican *El Santo* series. Shot in and around Caracas and featuring a group of professional wrestlers, Albertini's film closely follows the typical outline of the wrestling superhero pictures, replete with a couple of lengthy fight sequences in the ring.

"The plot was some sort of Zorro or Scarlet Pimpernel rehash," Albertini admitted, giving away a couple of the most obvious influences in Italian adventure films of the decade.[2] The basic storyline is nothing more than a bare-bones good vs. evil routine, about an evil industrialist/supercriminal posing as a blackmail victim (and blowing up his own industries) in order to collect money from another industrialist he is blackmailing. On top of that, the script is injected with a juvenile humor that is quite silly at times. Goldface has a peanut-munching black sidekick named Kotar (!) who speaks exactly like the "poor negroes" in 1930s films, while the wrestling scenes have commentary by an off-screen sportscaster (who in the Italian version has

The spectacular Italian *locandina* for Bitto Albertini's *Goldface, the Fantastic Superman* (1967)

the voice of Oreste Lionello, Woody Allen's Italian voice dubber) who creates all sorts of grating howlers. However, several scenes definitely work, such as when Goldface and Kotar (who is dressed up in the Goldface costume for the occasion) blow up inflatable Goldface-shaped balloons to confuse the gun-toting villains. Another amusing moment has Goldface defeat some baddies on a motorboat by using a remote controlled toy plane, which he borrowed from a kid and loaded with dynamite.

If the film's pompously named antagonist The Cobra (replete with a cape with a snake silhouette designed on the back) has been best described as "a bargain basement

The Italian newspaper ad for Albertini's film stressed "live footage of wrestling matches for the first time on screen."

tion scenes are *Goldface*'s shining light, including a lengthy motocross race, a motorboat chase and a car-versus-plane scene à la *North by Northwest* (1959).

The climax, in which Goldface is suspended from a helicopter while the baddies kick his hands and face until he falls into the sea from no less than 100 feet, is another outstanding example of Severini's recklessness. Albertini recalled an amusing anecdote on the set:

> The Venezuelan producers chose the best location, a beautiful gulf surrounded by tropical vegetation. They summoned the press and television to film the shooting of that important scene. I had placed two cameras at ground level, one of them filming in slow motion. As soon as we were ready, I yelled "Action!" on my walkie-talkie. The helicopter took off, with Severini hanging from it, and we reached the established spot. Severini dropped down into the sea.
>
> My goodness—what a fall! It seems like he would never touch the water! Then, with a huge squirt, he disappeared into the sea. The crowd cheered loudly. The cameras were still rolling as we waited for that formidable athlete to reemerge, but I was terrified when I saw several motorboats rapidly converge upon that spot.
>
> "Damn!" I yelled. If they entered the shot my scene would be ruined. We zoomed in so as to make the shot narrower. Then eventually Severini appeared on the surface. The scene was safe. I got angry at the Venezuelan producers. "Who's that imbecile who sent the motorboats over?"
>
> "I did," the production manager replied candidly.
>
> "But why?" I yelled. "Severini is a great swimmer!"
>
> "I know," he replied, "but this spot at sea is full of barracudas!"
>
> "So, did you choose this very spot to feed my stuntman to your damned barracudas?"[4]

Bondian super-villain" (despite his claims that "one Cobra is born every 1,000 years!"), Goldface is nothing special himself. He has no superpowers and his outfit (pale blue leotard, red cape and golden mask) is rather ugly. Unlike Superargo, his true identity is soon revealed in the shape of the apparently meek scientist played by the co-producer, the Venezuelan Espartaco Santoni (1937-1998), who openly plays with his Don Juan off-screen persona.[3] Most of the time, however, Santoni is replaced by his stunt double, the outstanding Attilio Severini, who also directed the many stunts and plays a small role in the film.

Despite the low budget—a number of sequences were shot at the local Sheraton hotel, which most likely provided for the cast and crew accommodations as well—the result is impressive. Severini performs all sorts of spectacular stunts, especially on a motorbike, which at times make Goldface resemble a cut-rate Captain America. The ac-

Severini was one of Cinecittà's unsung heroes, a stuntman who would perform every trick in the book, yet he rarely got noticed, let alone had his name in the credits. Here he is third-billed as "Big Matthews," but he is actually the star, whether he is donning the Goldface costume or not. A funny story occurs about him when he got the news that *The Fall of the Roman Empire* (1964, Anthony Mann) was about to be shot in Cinecittà. Severini ran to the production office in a hurry. "I'm doing that one; I'm doing *The Fall of the Roman Empire!*" he claimed. "By the way, how *high* is that *fall* going to be?"[5]

A former cinematographer, Adalberto "Bitto" Albertini (1923-1999) directed a number of unpretentious adventure yarns and Westerns, before going over to erotic flicks, first with a couple of period farces and then with 1975's *Black Emanuelle*, the first in a successful series starring Laura Gemser as an uninhibited photographer, which he signed with the pseudonym Albert Thomas. Albertini directed a sequel in name only (*Black Emanuelle 2*, 1976, not even starring Gemser) before passing the buck to Aristide Massaccesi. In the mid-'80s he helmed several trashy late *Mondo* films, *Naked and Cruel* (1984), *Naked and Cruel 2* (1985) and *Mondo senza veli* (1986), which remained his last directorial effort.

Interestingly, there are Italian *fotobuste* for *Goldface, il fantastico superman* that actually feature stills from *3 Dev Adam* (1973, T. Fikret Uçak), providing evidence that the Turkish film, which was never released in Italy, was actually picked up by a distributor called Mercator at some point. Since *3 Dev Adam* was made in the early 1970s, it is likely that these lobby cards were prepared for a *Goldface* theatrical re-release in the late 1970s, during the *Superman* fever.

Notes:
1. Albertini, Bitto, *Tra un ciak e l'altro. Storielle di Bitto Albertini* (Catania: Edizioni Boemi, 1998), p. 83.
2. Ibid., p. 71.
3. One allusive line of dialogue between Goldface and the girl (Micaela Pignatelli) whose life he has just saved goes as follows: "I'd have a nice idea on how to repay you," she says. "I'm sorry but I'm training," he replies. "I'm going to wait!" "Good, I'll put you on my waiting list."
4. Albertini, *Tra un ciak e l'altro*, p. 72.
5. Giusti, Marco, *Vado l'ammazzo e torno: Diario critico semiserio del cinema e dell'italia di oggi* (Milan: Edizioni ISBN, 2013), p. 65.

Johnny Dorelli (as Dorellik) and the gorgeous Margaret Lee (as Baby Eva) in *How to Kill 400 Duponts* **(1967)**

How to Kill 400 Duponts
(*Arrriva Dorellik*)
Italy, color, 96 minutes

D: Steno [Stefano Vanzina]. *S:* Castellano & Pipolo [Franco Castellano, Giuseppe Moccia]; *DOP:* Mario Capriotti; *M:* Franco Pisano; *E:* Ornella Micheli.

Cast: Johnny Dorelli [Giorgio Guidi] (Dorellik), Margaret Lee (Baby Eva), Alfred Adam (Inspector Saval), Jean-Pierre Zola (Antoine Le Duc), Rossella Como (Barbara Le Duc), Riccardo Garrone (Vladimir Dupont), Piero Gerlini (Raphael Dupont), Agata Fiori (Charlotte), Didi Perego (Gisèle Dupont), Terry-Thomas [Thomas Terry Hoar Stevens] (Inspector Green of Scotland Yard).

Prod: Inter Jet Film (Rome), Mega Film (Rome).

Master criminal Dorellik's diabolical laughter echoes during his most audacious crimes and his criminal rampage plagues the French Riviera. The French police call in Scotland Yard's aid in the person of Commissioner Green. Dorellik, however, is actually in dire straits financially, so much so that he is even abandoned by his secretary (and lover) Baby Eva and has to place a job ad in a newspaper. This leads Dorellik to be entrusted by a man named Raphael Dupont with a hard task. He must kill all the other Duponts of France in order for Raphael to become the sole heir of a Brazilian multimillionaire. Dorellik begins his work, and in the meantime he tries to win Baby Eva back. However, things will not go exactly as planned …

Inevitably, the success of *Diabolik* spawned a spoof of the titular character—a practice which was very much alive in the '60s, as shown by the flood of Franco & Ciccio movies churned out assembly line-style to capitalize on the latest box-office hit, from Westerns to war films. Shot

The film included Dorelli's hit song *Arriva la bomba*.

between April 10 and mid-June 1967 and directed by the experienced Steno, *Arrriva Dorellik* was, however, mainly a vehicle for the popular singer and TV host-turned-actor Johnny Dorelli, who had been one of Italy's most successful crooners for over a decade. The title and script made reference to Dorelli's TV character of Dorellik, which had debuted in his TV show *Johnny Sera*, a caricature of and idiotic Diabolik lookalike with an asinine laugh and a selection of gadgetry borrowed directly from *Batman—The Movie* (1966).

The result was an amiable, amusing farce that unpretentiously tied a number of Dorelli's diverse sketches together. The plot, a sort of extension and expansion of Robert Hamer's classic black comedy *Kind Hearts and Coronets* (1949), has Dorellik offing one-by-one all the Duponts (one of France's most common surnames) so that the only heir left will receive an enormous inheritance—a feat that gained the film its U.S. title, *How to Kill 400 Duponts*. As Dorellik's adversary, the equally idiotic Inspector Green, the gap-toothed Terry-Thomas, turned up in one of his usual pompous Englishman characterizations, while the lovely Margaret Lee plays Dorellik's lover.

Many gags are actually better than expected. The ending, in which the two antagonists are deliriously switching their identities while unmasking one another, is an imaginative piece of nonsense. It was reprised verbatim more than 20 years later in Ezio Greggio's awful *The Silence of the Hams* (*Il silenzio dei prosciutti*, 1991). Dorelli—who gets to sing the catchy title song *Arriva la bomba*, one of the hits he had launched on the TV show *Se te lo raccontassi*—is surprisingly effective himself. He would go on to star in more than 40 films in the following decades, proving to be an accomplished actor, and not just in comedy, as shown by his intense performance as the ruthless petty reporter in Luigi Zampa's outstanding stab at the *giallo*, *Il mostro* (1977).

The reference to *Diabolik* did not pass unnoticed to Dino De Laurentiis, who owned the rights to the comic book and was producing the official film version, directed by Mario Bava (for which Terry-Thomas would also be recruited!). The mogul producer sued the filmmakers, which resulted in the Italian title changed from *Dorellik* to *Arrriva Dorellik* (Here Comes Dorellik) just before release.

Il marchio di Kriminal, aka *Los cuatros Budas de Kriminal*

Italy/Spain, color, 92 minutes

D: Fernando Cerchio. *SC:* Eduardo Manzanos Brochero; *DOP* Emilio Foriscot, Angelo Lotti; *M:* Manuel Parada [actually Piero Umiliani]; *E:* Gianmaria Messeri.

Cast: Glenn Saxson [Roel Bos] (Kriminal), Helga Liné (Mara Gitan), Andrea Bosic (Inspector Patrick Milton), Frank Olivier [Armando Francioli] (Robson), Tomás Picó

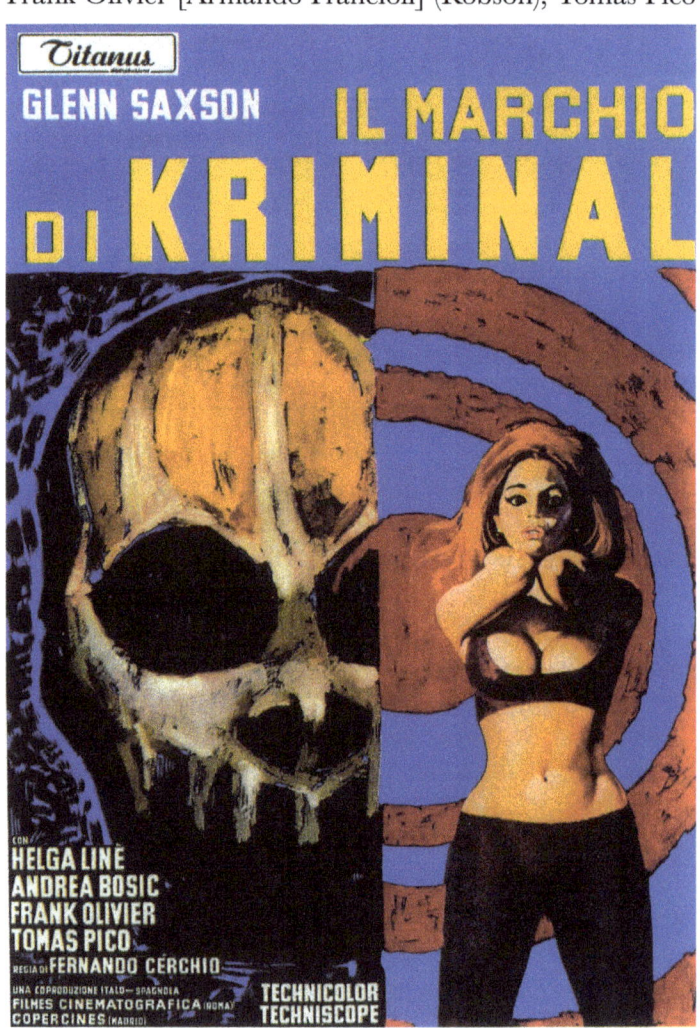

The Italian poster for Fernando Cerchio's *Il marchio di Kriminal* (1967), the sequel to Umberto Lenzi's *Kriminal*

Glenn Saxson (as Kriminal) and Helga Liné returned from the first film

(Thomas Patterson), Evi Rigano (Janet), Anna Zinnemann (Gloria), Franco Fantasia.

Prod: Filmes Cinematografica (Rome), Copercines (Madrid)

After discovering a fragment of a map inside an old porcelain statue, which is also the hiding place of two precious paintings, Kriminal immediately sets out to retrieve three other statuettes, similar to the one in his possession, which contain the other fragments. His search is successful, and soon Kriminal is only missing a part of the map to locate the hidden paintings' whereabouts. The fourth statue, however, is in the hands of two adventurers, Mara and Robson, who, in turn, try to steal Kriminal's parts of the map. The three eventually join forces and agree to share the proceeds equally. Kriminal, Mara and Robson locate the treasure in an archaeological area outside of Beirut. Kriminal then dispatches his two accomplices, who selfishly had tried to keep the entire booty, and prepares to return to his hideout. However, the unexpected arrival of Inspector Milton, who has been on his trail for some time, messes up his plans. In an attempt to escape capture, Kriminal falls to his death, his car falling into a ravine.

Despite a disappointing second half, which again transforms the movie into a banal travelogue adventure, *Il marchio di Kriminal* (The Mark of Kriminal), again starring Glenn Saxson, is ultimately more successful than its predecessor in conveying the feeling of Magnus & Bunker's grimly ironic comic book.

The story picks up with an appropriately tongue-in-cheek gag, as Kriminal's familiar silhouette appears behind a window while an elderly lady is sleeping in her bed. The king of crime crawls inside. When she notices him, the poor woman has a fatal heart attack. It turns out that Kriminal is now heading a home for the aged, and together with his mistress (who lovingly calls him "My little skeleton"), he takes advantage of his costume and mask to provoke heart attacks among the guests and collect the insurance money.

The genius of evil has been reduced to a third-rate boogeyman who only scares defenseless old ladies, a biting, positively irreverent touch that is definitely in the same spirit as Secchi and Raviola's subsequent works, namely *Alan Ford*, and sets the tone for a more humorous yet nastier plot.

All in all, the Dutch actor makes for a suitably cool villain/hero, extremely dangerous yet gifted with a charming ironic vein. Andrea Bosic and Helga Liné pop up again, the former as Inspector Milton and the latter in a role totally unrelated to the first film. The black humor

A colorful Italian *fotobusta*

in Eduardo Brochero's script is also more in keeping with the comic book. In one scene, Kriminal's lover attempts to dispatch him by poisoning his tea; meanwhile he is setting up a deadly ambush for her, by turning her bathtub into an electric booby trap. Saxson's smile as he hears the woman's off-screen demise, accompanied by a sudden flash of light from behind a door, is a perfect comic book moment, as is the scene in which Kriminal sneaks into Milton's house, where the pre-nuptial party is taking place, to steal one of the Buddhas that has just been bought at an auction by Milton's bride-to-be. Posing as one of the Inspector's colleagues, he brings a present that turns out to be a deadly trap—a box concealing a gun that fires as soon as the container is opened. This cruel gesture (could not Kriminal simply steal the Buddha and leave?) sums up perfectly the character's indifference to violence and his playfully sadistic attitude.

The strip's flair for offbeat, grotesque secondary characters is also rendered rather successfully, while Kriminal's trademark costume shows up a bit more often than in Lenzi's film. As with the previous chapter, the shooting was the pretext for a travelogue parade of exotic exteriors. Saxson recalls:

> We shot the film in Rome, on a cruise from Genoa to Beirut, Baalbeck, Byblos and Madrid ....[1]

But it is the style that displays *Il marchio di Kriminal*'s degree of success. Cerchio makes pointed use of its comic book source, by frequently ending scenes with transitions from live-action to drawn panels. The mocking ending looks like a poster for *Hellzapoppin'* (1941), as devils armed with forks are ready to greet Kriminal in hell. Rather than closing the film on a moralistic note, it comes off as a juicy punch line. Another asset is the musical score, credited to the Spanish composer Manuel Parada but actually the work of Piero Umiliani.

Cerchio (1914-1974) was a veteran of many sword-and-sandal epics and several tongue-in-cheek parodies (as well as the excellent *film noir Il bivio*, 1951). *Il marchio di Kriminal* was his penultimate work, the last being the Western *Death on High Mountain* (*Morte sull'alta collina*, 1969, signed as Fred Ringold), starring Peter Lee Lawrence. Some sources claim that on *Il marchio di Kriminal* the young Nando Cicero, the director of several interesting Spaghetti Westerns who later specialized in lewd comedies, aided Cerchio ... but Saxson is adamant:

According to my knowledge Cicero had nothing to do with the movie.[2]

After the two *Kriminal* films, Saxson's career somehow stagnated. He starred in the sub-par jungle adventure flick *Luana, the Girl Tarzan* (1968, Roberto Infascelli) and in three more Westerns—*Il magnifico texano* (1967, Luigi Capuano), *Il lungo giorno del massacro* (1968, Antonio Cardone) and *Carogne si nasce* (1968, Alfonso Brescia)—none of which left much of an impression. By the end of the decade he starred in a couple of erotic German comedies directed by Franz Antel and in Sergio Bergonzelli's *School of Erotic Enjoyment* (*Io Cristiana, studentessa degli scandali*, 1971) before virtually disappearing from the big screen for over a decade.

The actor explains:

> Since I had more artistic ideas in mind, I started producing and that was the reason I didn't do much acting during those years, although I did [appear] in commercials. *Sogno*, a popular photo-novel publisher, paid me well to do a *fotoromanzo* once in a while … At the same time I got involved with a TV company which produced some programs for RAI and the TV film *Donnarumma all'assalto* (1972), directed by Marco Leto.[3]

As a producer, Saxson financed a couple of very interesting and original works:

> My second film as a producer was *Il Saprofita* (1974), directed by Sergio Nasca. It was entered in many festivals—Cannes, Taormina, San Francisco, Chicago, Brussels among others. It got great reviews all over the world and, being a low-budget movie, it was a big commercial success. After that I produced *Vergine, e di nome Maria* (Virgin, and by the name of Mary, 1975), again directed by Nasca. It was another festival film and it had great international reviews … but it also had trouble with the censors for no reason at all because the film was not at all blasphemous as they claimed.[4]

Nasca's film, the thought-provoking story set in a Northern town slum of an underage proletarian girl who becomes pregnant, even though she is apparently a virgin, was seized by the authorities and had to be re-titled *Malia*—*Vergine e di nome Maria* before finally being distributed again.

Notes:
1. Glenn Saxson, email interview with the author, February 2014.
2. *Ibid*.
3. *Ibid*.
4. *Ibid*.

Massacre Mania
(*Hipnos follia di massacro*)
Italy, color, 90 minutes

D: Paul Maxwell [Paolo Bianchini]. *S and SC:* Paolo Bianchini, Max Caret; *DOP:* Henry Marchall [Erico Menczer]; *M:* Carlo Savina; *E:* Angel Coly [Otello Colangeli].

Cast: Robert Woods (Henry Spengler), Rada Rassimov (Nicole Bouvier), Fernando Sancho (Professor Kenitz), Ken Wood [Giovanni Cianfriglia] (Inspector Griffi), Lino Coletta (Maurice), Piero Gerlini, Nino Vingelli, Maurizio Merli (First suspect).

Prod: Cinecris (Rome).

Rome is plagued with a series of inexplicable, apparently unrelated murders that always take place on Thursdays. After surviving a

The Spanish poster for a Spanish co-production

The French VHS cover art for Paolo Bianchini's *Massacre Mania*

murderous attempt on his life by his fiancée Nicole, psychiatrist Henry Spengler realizes that all the victims were hypnotized while watching a TV series that is broadcast every Thursday. He investigates on his own and finds out that the film contains subliminal frames in which a mysterious masked man appears. Meanwhile Nicole is investigating as well and she locates a scientist, Professor Kenitz, who has now retired and poses as a sculptor. It turns out Kenitz had perfected a device which could hypnotize people at a distance via television. A mysterious masked villain who heads a secret organization and is planning to conquer the world murders Kenitz …

Paolo Bianchini's third and last film for producer Gabriele Crisanti following *The Devil's Man* and *Superargo and the Faceless Giants*,[1] was shot in eight weeks in and around Rome, between February and March 1967. *Massacre Mania* is one of the weirdest Italian films of the decade, and once again it's an odd mixture of science-fiction, thriller and comic book-style adventure.

For the first half, *Massacre Mania* works like an offbeat, engrossing thriller. The opening scene, with a murder shown through the killer's POV shot (a man shoots a woman in front of a TV set, without any apparent reason), predates the sense of uneasiness to be found in several *gialli*, namely the unexplained opening suicides in Armando Crispino's *Autopsy* (*Macchie solari*, 1975) and the seemingly unrelated murders at the start of Paolo Cavara's excellent *Plot of Fear* (*E tanta paura*, 1976). It does not take long before the hero (Robert Woods, misspelled in the credits as Robert "Wood") realizes that there is something wrong with the murders, which take place during the broadcasting of a seemingly very bad adventure TV series called *La donna dei sogni* (Dream Woman).

The dialogue serves as mere throwaway: "What if they kill you?" Rassimov asks Woods, after he tells her he is going to investigate on his own. "Next year I won't pay taxes," is the answer. Bianchini seems interested only in the visuals, in such a way that at times his film seems almost improvised. As Woods himself recalls:

> These were nearly always collaborative efforts (where almost everyone involved had input) and improvisation was the *status quo* for most as well … There were, as I recall, no trial and error scenes removed, because once we agreed on a plan of attack, we executed … and except for the editing, our intentions became reality and remained in the film … not much waste …[2]

As the French critic Jean-Marie Sabatier pointed out[3], the result recalls early Dario Argento in the way the script eschews coherence in favor of a nightmarish atmosphere that builds upon logic of its own. Take the sequence where Woods follows a lab technician who appears to have some vital information about an abandoned, dilapidated and decidedly menacing factory, which is completely deserted … save for a small lab with a moviola which the technician claims to be his own. If this was not unlikely enough, the man leaves Woods alone to study a vital piece of film evidence … only to return minutes later with a pair of thugs and beat the hell out of him in order to find out what he has discovered.

This is all strangely compelling somehow. Perhaps it is because of the lackadaisical pacing, or Bianchini's frenetic style, all hand-held camera shots to make up for the lack of budget. Another factor is the casting. Woods, then quite popular after his role in the successful Spaghetti Western *Seven Guns For The MacGregors* (*7 pistole per i MacGregor*, 1966, Franco Giraldi), is quite convincing in an unusual casting choice. Yet even more off-putting is Fernando Sancho turning up as a sexually ambiguous professor who is the film's main red herring. As Woods recalls:

> Sancho was always the macho, comic relief/antagonist in the Westerns we did together … I was surprised he ac-

cepted this role. It was a departure from his usual self, but I, for one, thoroughly enjoyed his performance in the film, as a gay man ... what an amusing departure![4]

Then there is the setting. Even though the main characters are foreigners—an American shrink, a French psychoanalyst and a German professor—*Massacre Mania* takes place unequivocally in Rome. And what a Rome this is! The way Bianchini depicts the Eternal City is as surprising as it is eerie. The dilapidated factory (later also to be seen in Luigi Bazzoni's top-notch *giallo The Fifth Cord*, 1971) is a striking location, and even though it is patently absurd, the idea of concealing a sci-fi like underground lab amid ancient Roman ruins is undoubtedly a treat for the eyes and provides a nice setting for the silly scenes in which Woods and the police are searching the lab's whereabouts.

It is only halfway into the movie that *Massacre Mania* turns into the same kind of science-fiction extravaganza as *The Devil's Man*, with the appearance of a nameless masked villain, a Dr. Mabuse type who wears a disturbing golden mask and controls people's minds through hypnotic subliminal messages. Several writers have pointed out a connection with David Cronenberg's *Scanners* (1981) and *Videodrome* (1982)[5] ... that is definitely too much weight for *Massacre Mania*'s weak shoulders to bear. A closer reference might be Emilio Vieyra's *Stay Tuned for Terror* (*Extraña invasión*, 1965), which features a similar idea, but this might well be yet another coincidence, especially since Vieyra's film never made it to Italy. However, the whole thing has a definite comic book feel, as Woods himself acknowledged:

> I actually loved doing that film, because it was a departure from Westerns. And I loved the comic book implications![6]

There is a chance Bianchini might have concocted the script as a follow-up to *The Devil's Man*, as the two supercriminals look very similar to each other. Devilman's wrestler-like silver mask has been replaced with a golden, expressionless one which resembles a sculpture Nicole notices in Kenitz' workshop. Information about the film is scarce, and it is unclear who is the actor behind the mask. There has been speculation that it was Giovanni Cianfriglia (or Ken Wood, if you prefer), who also plays the Inspector aiding Woods in rescuing his fiancée (and who, in a bit of unintentional hilarity, offers him a machine gun to help himself against the bad guys ... just as if 1967 Italy

The ravishing Rada Rassimov, the female lead in *Massacre Mania*

was the Wild West). However, according to Woods it is more likely that the man behind the golden mask (who was not named in the script either) was actually stunt coordinator Nando Poggi.

Crime film *aficionados* will jump at the appearance of a very young, mustache-less Maurizio Merli, who plays the first suspect questioned by the police in one of the early scenes. In the mid-1970s Merli would briefly become one of Italy's most popular film stars after his roles in a number of violent, grim crime movies (the so-called *poliziotteschi*).

As a thriller, *Massacre Mania* is admittedly filled with plot holes. As with his earlier *The Devil's Man*, Bianchini piles up scene-after-scene with little care for logic, yet, when closely scrutinized, the whole story does not really make much sense. Who the hell is the masked man? What exactly is he planning to do by hypnotizing people and turning them into assassins? What part did *La donna dei sogni* have in all this? What exactly was Professor Kenitz's (Fernando Sancho) involvement with the conspirators—if there was any? Unfortunately many questions are left unanswered,

The Comic Book Universe in Italian Cinema

or the answers that come up tend to be put under the old "mad villain planning to rule the world" umbrella.

Overall, even though it is often labeled as a spy flick, *Massacre Mania* is actually a lot closer to the superhero films of the era, of which it represents a darker version, and very Italian too, due to its recognizable setting and details. Even though the result is just plain silly, it is one of the very few science-fiction films ever made to feature a battle between the ultra-technological baddies and *Carabinieri*.

Today, *Massacre Mania* has gained a small yet growing cult status in Italy. Upon its release, though, it was virtually ignored. As Crisanti admitted:

> It was a flop … I made the mistake of giving it to a distributor—Vecchioni, the owner of United International Films—who went bankrupt before the film was released. Without a normal distribution, it came out in just a few theaters. This way, we couldn't even recover the costs.[7]

As with his other efforts of the period, Bianchini did not have a high opinion of *Massacre Mania*, though:

> I have been invited to conventions and film schools concerning this film. But every time I watch it again, it's such a terrible thing. Perhaps people notice that there's a certain high craft about these pics, as they were literally made out of nothing.[8]

Woods, on the other hand, was extremely impressed by the director's working method.

> Paolo Bianchini was an exemplary filmmaker with great energy [and was] fun to work with. It took no time at all on the set with him to be convinced that I wanted to be his friend and work for him again … Paolo and I became good friends during the shoot, so when Dr. Amati of Fida Films asked me to do another Western and gave me *carte blanche* to find a script, hire a director and cast the major roles in another project, I immediately called Paolo. In a very short time, he came up with the script for *Gatling Gun* (*Quel Caldo Maledetto Giorno Di Fuoco*, 1968). We hired George Rigaud, who had played my father in *Seven Guns For The MacGregors*, as a principal heavy in it and John Ireland as the character Tarpas, and we were off and running again … To this day, I am convinced that Paolo is one of the most talented directors I had the opportunity to work and become friends with. Except for the "science-fiction" aspect of *Hipnos*, the film occupies a very special place in my memory. I believe that without that element, it was a fantastic film …[9]

Notes:
1. *Massacre Mania* was submitted to the Italian board of censors in October 1967, one month after *Superargo and the Faceless Giants*, but was eventually released earlier. The Italian title is actually *Hipnos follia di massacro*—not *Hypnos*, as it is often misspelled in reference books.
2. Robert Woods, email interview with the author, June 2014.
3. Sabatier, Jean-Marie, "Hypnose ou la folie du massacre," *La Saison 74—Revue du Cinéma/Image et son* #288/289, October 1974.
4. Woods, email interview, June 2014.
5. Incidentally, Bianchini's film was released to home video in France as *Teledrome*.
6. Giusti, *007 all'italiana*, p. 139.
7. Woods, email interview, June 2014.
8. Giusti, *007 all'italiana*, p. 138.
9. Woods, email interview, June 2014.

The Three Fantastic Supermen
(*I fantastici 3 Supermen*)
Italy/Yugoslavia/France/West Germany, color, 94 minutes

D: Frank Kramer [Gianfranco Parolini]. *S:* Frank Kramer; *SC:* Marcello Coscia, Frank Kramer; *DOP:* Francesco Izzarelli; *M:* Ruggero Cini, Jimmy Fontana; *E:* Edmondo Lozzi.

Cast: Tony Kendall [Luciano Stella] (Tony), Brad Harris (Brad McCallum), Nick Jordan [Aldo Canti] (Nick), Charles Tamblyn [Carlo Tamberlani] (Professor Schwarz), Jochen Brockmann (Golem), Patricia Carr [Rossella Bergamonti] (Diana), Bettina Busch (Zizi), Gloria Paul (Havana Scott), Salvatore Borgese.

Prod: Cinesecolo (Rome), Parnass Film (Munich), CFFP (Paris), Avala Film (Belgrad).

F.B.I. agent Brad McCallum recruits two masked thieves, Tony and the mute Nick, to steal an amount of money that will allow him to expose a gang whose leader, Golem, plans to rule the world. Due to their physical strength and exceptional acrobatic qualities, Brad, Tony and Nick succeed in the heist, thanks also to their bulletproof costumes

The Marvel comics-style bombastic U.S. poster for Gianfranco Parolini's *The Three Fantastic Supermen* (1967)

created by Professor Schwarz. However, Golem has his henchmen take Schwarz prisoner, in order to get hold of his most recent discovery: a device that duplicates everything—including human beings. Schwarz, however, does not want to use his invention, but the criminals force him by kidnapping his daughter as well. The three supermen come to their rescue. They discover that the gang hides behind an apparently harmless institution for children, and they sneak into the lair and destroy the deadly machinery.

Conceived in the midst of the superhero craze that briefly caught Italy during the mid-'60s, Gianfranco Parolini's *The Three Fantastic Supermen* marked the beginning of a long running if far from world-shattering series.

Parolini's concept was as simple as it was shrewd. Born in 1925 (and not 1930 as many reference books state), the director had already set the trend for a different approach to the sword-and-sandal genre. In *The Ten Gladiators* (*I 10 gladiatori*, 1963), Parolini emphasized the *peplum*'s tendency at multiplying the hero—see the many films that featured not just one but two or more musclemen facing and eventually helping each other—by churning out a sort of answer to Hollywood's *The Magnificent Seven* (1960). With *The Ten Gladiators* he introduced the audience to no less than 10 different heroes, each with a well-characterized personality, presented as an army of superheroes *ante litteram*. The idea also allowed the director to display his sense of humor and playful attitude—a constant presence in his work.

Parolini perfected the formula with *3 Avengers* (*Gli invincibili tre*, 1964), which went even further in its genre contamination, by injecting ample doses of comedy into a usually more serious framing narrative. *3 Avengers* would be Parolini's last sword-and-sandal opus, as the genre was fading by then, choked to death by the new-born Spaghetti Western as well as (to a lesser extent) the technological James Bond rip-offs which the director embraced with his German co-produced spy saga of *Agent Jo Walker/Kommissar X*, starring Tony Kendall and Brad Harris.

For *The Three Fantastic Supermen*, Parolini simply took *3 Avengers*' basic concept and turned the previous film's three muscle-bound protagonists into superheroes of sorts, thus detaching from the declining sword-and-sandal genre with its period settings and clichés, and embracing a quite different aesthetic model, borrowed from spy and sci-fi films of the period—not to mention the frothy, pop-oriented TV shows centered on superheroes such as *Batman* and *The Green Hornet*. All this, while retaining the amiable mixture of light-hearted adventure and humor which somehow set *The Three Fantastic Supermen* aside from its peers.

Parolini's film was explicitly aimed at younger audiences, with lots of childish action scenes and the obligatory comic relief provided by the mute of the trio, played by Nick Jordan (real name Aldo Canti). The amusing musical score enhanced the cheerful and at times openly parodic tone. One almost forgets that two of the three supermen are actually thieves who are recruited by the F.B.I. but never become out-and-out "good guys" as their ultimate aim is to keep the money for themselves. It is a bit of amorality that makes them quite different from the ordinary superheroes and becomes a recurring element in the series' subsequent entries.

Like its contemporaries, *The Three Fantastic Supermen* was a mixed bag, which cannibalized and recycled many different inspirational sources. For instance, the heroes' outfits owe a lot to Lee Falk's *The Phantom*, with the addition of Zorro-style black capes; the supermen handle Mexican *bolas* and climb up walls like Spiderman (and like Diabolik will do in Bava's film the following year) thanks to suction cups in their shoes. On the other hand, Jochen Brockmann's Golem is the umpteenth variation on the Goldfinger mold; the naive technological gadgetry on display also pays homage to Ian Fleming's hero. But there is more, as fans will recognize homages (or rip-offs, depending on one's point of view) to *Batman*, *The Green Hornet*, spy

The three supermen in action: Brad Harris (left), Tony Kendall (center) and Nick Jordan (right)

capers and much, much more, including the human cloning device—one of sci-fi's most recurrent topics, both in literature, comics and films.

The humor is often puerile, with many slapstick gags that were already old-hat in the silent era, and special effects are cheesy. An experiment gone wrong with the human duplicator device is visualized through crude animation. However, Parolini's dynamic direction turns the movie into a sort of live-action cartoon, full of chases, fistfights and spirited stunts, with a conspicuous use of trampolines to amplify the actors' acrobatics (choreographed by Parolini's trusted master of arms Giuseppe Mattei, featuring a number of Italy's very best stuntmen) just like in Hong Kong action movies. *The Three Fantastic Supermen* climaxes with a big fight that features the heroes facing their own replicas. It is all rather silly (*very* silly at times), nonetheless entertaining—and never boring.

Tony Kendall and Brad Harris had both starred in Parolini's *Kommissar X* films. The Rome-based Kendall (real name Luciano Stella, 1936-2009) was a good-looking baker who had found his way to showbiz almost by accident due to his handsome features. Kendall started doing photonovels and got his first important role in Mario Bava's *The Whip and the Body* (*La frusta e il corpo*, 1963), alongside Christopher Lee and Daliah Lavi. Kendall would later star in several Spanish horror cult classics, such as Amando de Ossorio's *Return of the Evil Dead* and *The Loreley's Grasp* (both 1973). The American-born Harris (born in 1933) was a former bodybuilder who tried his luck in Italy at the peak of the sword-and-sandal fever. While his fellow musclemen suffered the decline of the *peplum* genre, Harris managed to find a niche of his own in spy and adventure flicks, thanks to a much welcome self-ironic approach.

Of the three protagonists, Canti is by far the most athletically gifted ... as well as the most annoying acting-wise, constantly grimacing, giggling and cackling in every shot he is in. A former circus acrobat with his brothers and a top-notch stuntman who debuted in Parolini's *The Ten Gladiators*, Canti (nicknamed "Robustino" in the biz for his outstanding physical qualities) enjoyed a short-lived popularity after the *Three Supermen* series.

Canti performs a number of show-stopping stunts in the film. Parolini commented:

> Today these effects are done digitally, whereas back then they were performed on the set, and stuntmen were personally taking the risk. Aldo would jump out of a window, 20 feet high, do a somersault, bounce on the floor, land on a wooden trampoline and jump into a Ford which started at full speed ..."[1]

One realizes that Parolini was not over-exaggerating.

In the subsequent entries, however, Canti was usually replaced by fellow stuntman Sal Borgese—who briefly appears *twice* here, first near the beginning as a bazooka-toting F.B.I. agent and later on as one of Golem's shade-wearing thugs, this time shooting a machine-gun—and he popped up again only in the Turkish co-production *3 Supermen Against the Godfather* (1980), which was one of his last screen roles. Canti disappeared from sight in the late 1970s. One of his last memorable appearances was as the spirited villain "Totonno 'o pazzo" in Alfonso Brescia's Neapolitan-based crime story *Napoli … serenata calibro 9* (1979) starring Mario Merola. Canti was reportedly linked to the Italian underworld. In 1966 he was arrested in Rome when police agents found him driving a car with no license and a bag full of lock picks. Later on, he served some time in prison and was found murdered with a bullet to the head at Rome's Villa Borghese Park, on January 22, 1990.

Due to financial reasons, *The Three Fantastic Supermen* was shot entirely in Yugoslavia, which resulted in decidedly different visuals from the usual Italian and Spanish landscapes. Singer and dancer Gloria Paul (the then-wife of Italian film composer Piero Piccioni) provides the necessary dose of womanly charm. She would return in the series' second installment, *3 Supermen a Tokyo* (1968).

The Three Fantastic Supermen was a reasonable box-office success in Italy and was sold worldwide, spawning a number of sequels that had the trio moving all around the world in a "Road To …" spirit: Japan (*3 Supermen a Tokyo*, 1968), Africa (*Three Supermen in the Jungle*, 1970), Hong Kong (*Supermen Against the Orient*, 1973), the Wild West (*The 3 Supermen in the West*, also 1973) and even an undefined Prehistoric Age in Alfonso Brescia's spurious *Super Stooges vs. the Wonder Women*, aka *Amazons Against Supermen* (1974). By the end of the 1970s, producer/director Italo Martinenghi tried to keep the series alive by moving to Turkey where he made *3 Supermen Against the Godfather*, followed by the awful *Three Supermen at the Olympic Games* (1984) and, finally and mercifully, *Three Supermen in S. Domingo* (1986).

None of these were directed by Parolini, who moved on to other genres, while retaining his favorite mixture of action and irony. The World War II film *5 for Hell* (*5 per l'inferno*, 1969) basically reprised the same formula as his earlier films, spiced with a little bit of *The Dirty Dozen* (1967), as the commando led by Gianni Garko displays impressive acrobatic qualities during their search for the secret plan held by a cruel Nazi general (played by the usually reliable Klaus Kinski).

Parolini then settled on Spaghetti Westerns—with such amusing results as the two Sabata movies (*Sabata* and

An Italian *photobusta* shows the three supermen in action.

Return of Sabata) starring Lee Van Cleef, *Adios Sabata* (*Indio Black, sai che ti dico: Sei un gran figlio di ...*, 1970) starring Yul Brynner and 1976's *Diamante Lobo* with Van Cleef and Jack Palance—and later on to comedies in the vein of Bud Spencer and Terence Hill films. His last effort in the 1970s was the ill-fated *Yeti* (*Yeti-Il gigante del 20° secolo*, 1977), a juvenile *King Kong* rip-off destroyed by inept, laughable special effects that marked the director's commercial swan song. Parolini would direct one more film in the late eighties, the little-seen *Secret of the Incas' Empire* (*Alla ricerca dell'impero sepolto*, 1987).

Note:
1. Norcini, Matteo and Ippoliti, Stefano; "Piacere, Kramer... Frank Kramer," *Cine 70 e dintorni* #6, 2004, p. 9.

Tom Dollar
(*Tom Dollar*)
Italy/France, color, 90 minutes

D: Frank Red [Marcello Ciorciolini]. *S*: John Connery and Pierre DeVries, based on the photonovel "Tom Dollar" by Al Petre; *SC:* John Connery and Pierre DeVries; *DOP:* Rino Filippini; *M:* Giosy Capuano, Mario Capuano; *E:* Mario Anconetani.

Cast: Maurice Poli (Tom Dollar), Giorgia Moll (Samia/Louise), Erika Blanc [Enrica Bianchi Colombatto] (Lady Barbara Crane), Franco Ressel (Mr. Gaber), Jacques Herlin (Jerome Osborne), Jean Rougeul (Crisantemo), Calisto Calisti.

Prod: Tigielle 33 (Rome), Les Films Jacques Leitienne (Paris).

The Iranian prince Barancan is killed just as he is about to sign an agreement for the sale of a uranium deposit to the United States. The C.I.A. is convinced that Barancan's heiress, Princess Sania, is also in peril. Special agent Tom Dollar is sent on a mission to dispatch the conspirators. Lady Barbara Crane follows Tom, she is a Brit agent as well as one of Tom's lovers. To make the investigation easier, and with the help of plastic surgery wizard Jerome Osborne, Sania is replaced with a lookalike named Louise, a shop assistant who agreed to act as a stand-in for the princess. Nevertheless Sania, reluctant to put an innocent in deadly peril, takes Louise's place. A first attack by unknown assassins ends with the murder of Yasmin, the princess' maid. Tom Dollar chases one of the killers and discovers the existence of a secret sect composed of masked fanatics, the Singh. Tom ventures into their hideout, but he is captured and tortured. Eventually he discovers that the head of the sect is Gaber, Sania's cousin ...

At first glance, there is nothing that sets apart *Tom Dollar* from the many Italian spy flicks of the period: a leading man modeled upon James Bond (that is, as skillful in action as he is with the opposite sex), an exotic setting, a pair of beautiful actresses, a half-baked action plot and a good dose of nice lounge music on top. Yet Marcello Ciorcio-

The French poster for Marcello Ciorciolini's *Tom Dollar*

lini's film is something unique, as it was actually based on the photonovel of the same name, published in the magazine *Bolero Film* in 1965.

Tom Dollar was one of the first photonovels centered on a secret agent, and reportedly, "The scenes were shot with plenty of money, in scientific labs (perhaps recycling movie sets), on steep rocks or underwater; but the success was scarce or however not enough to justify the huge costs."[1] Other similar photonovels were launched in that period. *Le avventure di Jacques Douglas* (1965) and *Le avventure di Lucky Martin* (1970) were both produced by *Bolero*'s main competitor, *Lancio*. However, due to their higher costs, these types of *fotoromanzi* were soon dropped in favor of the standard sentimental stuff.

Tom Dollar is sort of a jigsaw character, as is often the case with Italian rip-offs. Besides the Bond influence, Dollar has a Japanese butler who recalls Inspector Clouseau's Kato, to the degree that he keeps his master in shape by attacking him by surprise, so that Tom can practice his Kendo moves. The script—co-written by a ... John Connery—is basically routine, a mildly interesting spy who-

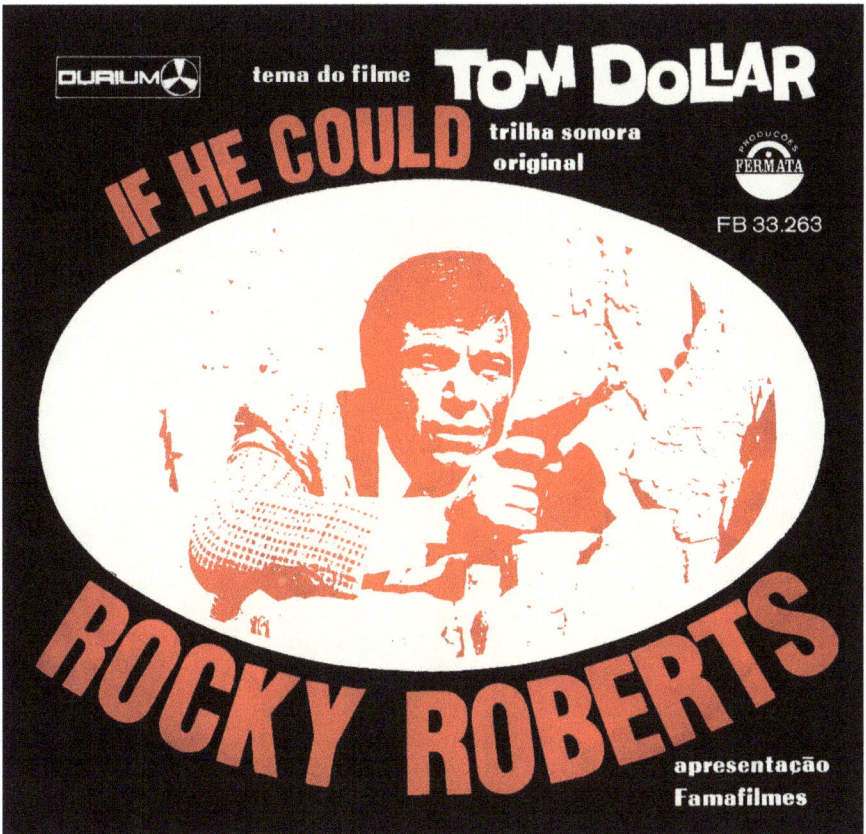

Rocky Roberts' title song for *Tom Dollar* also had a Portuguese release.

dunit (with a villain whom the attentive viewer will recognize as soon as he pops up, not least because he is played by a supporting actor specializing in portraying villains …) with a bit of exotic feel. For example, the secret sect's members have an "S"-shaped serpent branded on their chest, an idea which seems to come straight out of some old serial or paperback adventure novel.

The direction is obviously rushed. Scenes in the streets with passers-by looking directly at the camera are the norm. Yet, Ciorciolini—who had just directed another spy film, *Black Box Affair* (1966, credited as James Harris)—conjures up a number of good moments. The opening sequence echoes the killing of John Fitzgerald Kennedy, as the Iranian prince is shot by a sniper while passing through the city in his open white limo (Ciorciolini even has his bodyguard jump to the back seat to protect him), while another suggestive scene has Tom chasing a baddie into a waxworks museum whose exhibits suddenly turn out to be the white-masked sect members, a moment that would not have been out of place in a Georges Franju film. The best bit, however, is a chase scene between Tom and an assassin that climaxes with a shootout on a hill covered with Persian rugs baking in the sun.

As the titular hero, French actor Maurice Poli is quite effective. Born in Zarzis, Tunisia, in 1933, Poli was a recurring face in Italian films of the period. Due to his hard-boiled, sun-tanned face and magnetic eyes, he would usually play hard-edged types, and gained a certain fame after his role as Alfred the French in the amusing heist film *Seven Golden Men* and its sequel *Seven Golden Men Strike Again* (*Il grande colpo dei 7 uomini d'oro*, 1966), both directed by Marco Vicario. Poli had been Tom Dollar in *Bolero*'s photonovels, which allowed him to make the transition from supporting to lead actor—something that would not often happen to him again in his career. Poli kept working in Italy, sometimes billed as "Monty Greenwood" and mostly in Westerns, war and crime films. He was one of the unscrupulous characters in Mario Bava's *5 Dolls for an August Moon* (*5 bambole per la luna d'agosto*, 1970), and worked again for Bava as the "Doctor," the head of the robbers in the director's ill-fated grim action thriller, *Wild Dogs* (*Cani arrabbiati*, 1974).

As for the rest of the cast, actress-cum-singer Giorgia Moll plays yet another exotic type (she had been Audie Murphy's Vietnamese love interest in Joseph L. Mankiewicz's *The Quiet American*, 1958), while Erika Blanc is given almost nothing to do except looking ravishing as Tom's vapid love interest ("Did you recognize me from far away?" she coos when they meet at the airport; "I recognized your luggage," is Dollar's curt reply). The best of the lot is French character actor Jacques Herlin, in an amusing over-the-top turn as a manic plastic surgeon whose dream is "to turn Fanfani [one of Italy's most famous politicians, a former Prime Minister and well-known because of his short stature] into De Gaulle."

Despite the exotic setting, most of *Tom Dollar* was shot in Rome, namely in the luxurious Villa Miani, a location that often popped up in movies of the period (it is the French museum in Deodato's *Phenomenal*, for instance). The upbeat jazzy, vibrophone-based score, by Giosy and Mario Capuano, is instantly catchy, and R&B singer Rocky Roberts, who provides the requisite title song, was immensely popular in Italy at that time. His version of *T-Bird* had been chosen as the signature tune for a famous radio program, *Bandiera gialla*, and he won the singing contest *Festivalbar* with the hit *Stasera mi butto*. He even starred in a few *musicarelli*, Italian musical comedies built around popular singers and/or hit songs of the period.

Marcello Ciorciolini was a prolific screenwriter who specialized in comedies, mostly Franco and Ciccio films, and directed a few of them. Of the 10 features he helmed between 1965 and 1982 (the last, *Settefolli*, was a made-for-TV work), five starred the two Sicilian comedians.

Note:

1. Anelli, Maria Teresa, Gabbrielli, Paola, Morgavi, Marta and Piperno, Roberto, *Fotoromanzo: fascino e pregiudizio* (Milan: Savelli Editori, 1979), p. 215.

1968

Barbarella, aka *Barbarella—Queen of the Galaxy* (*Barbarella*)
Italy/France, color, 98 minutes
D: Roger Vadim. *S:* based on Jean-Claude Forest's comic *Barbarella*; *SC:* Terry Southern and Roger Vadim, in collaboration with Claude Brule, Vittorio Bonicelli, Clement Biddle Wood, Brian Degas, Tudor Gates, Jean-Claude Forest; *DOP:* Claude Renoir; *M:* Bob Crew Generation, Charles Fox; *E:* Victoria Mercanton.

Cast: Jane Fonda (Barbarella), John Phillip Law (Pygar), Anita Pallenberg (The Great Tyrant), Milo O' Shea (Concierge/Durand-Durand), Marcel Marceau (Professor Ping), Claude Dauphin (President of Earth), David Hemmings (Dildano), Ugo Tognazzi (Mark Hand), Serge Marquand (Captain Sun).

Prod: Dino De Laurentiis Cinematografica (Rome), Marianne Productions (France).

In the 41st century, space traveler Barbarella is sent on a secret mission by the president of Earth. She must locate a scientist named Durand-Durand, who has disappeared in the Tau Ceti galaxy. Durand invented the lethal Positronic Ray, which transports its victims to the Fourth dimension. After her spaceship crashes on the planet Lythion, Barbarella is saved from certain death by the hairy Mark Hand and then meets a blind angel named Pygar. Barbarella discovers that Durand is located in the city of Sogo, ruled by a female "Great Tyrant," which Durand is planning to overthrow in order to become Master of the Universe. The people of Sogo revolt, but Durand uses the deadly ray to quell the insurrection. Barbarella and the former Queen escape with Pygar's help.

For one of those unfathomable coincidences written in the stars, the world's first sexually liberated heroine saw light on the very same year as *Diabolik*. She was blonde, curvaceous and erotic to the bone—starting with a name that sounded like someone tickling you under your armpit. Barbarella came with the spring, like a breeze. She was the creation of the Parisian comic book artist and writer Jean-Claude Forest (1930-1998)

The founder (together with film director Alain Resnais) of the French Comic-Strip Club, Forest devised for *Barbarella* a science-fiction setting, inspired by his work as a cover artist for the paperback imprint *Le Rayon Fantastique*, published by the prestigious Gallimard. The titular heroine is a young woman who travels in space and has all kinds of erotic adventures. She is seduced by aliens, sleeps with robots and is even submitted to an experiment involving an "orgasmotron," a machine that provokes excessive plea-

Roger Vadim's film was scripted by the great satiric novelist Terry Southern, shown here.

sure. Forest surrounded Barbarella with all kinds of weird and funny characters, such as a one-eyed man named Duran, a blind ornithanthrope (bird-man) named Pygar, the acquatic man Narval, a villainess named La Reine Noire (The Black Queen), a female prostitute robot called Mado, etc. Forest himself turned up in a tongue-in-cheek self-portrait as the "Artist" who has a child with Barbarella.

It was 1962 when Forest's creation ("The first comic strip for grown-ups") appeared in the quarterly *V—Magazine*, but *Barbarella* really came to prominence after the Belgian-French publisher Éric Losfeld (1922-1979) reunited the strips in a 70-page folio book, published in December 1964 by his own Éditions Le Terrain Vague.

The publication provoked a scandal. Unlike the previous adults-only comics (such as the notorious "Tijuana Bibles" that poked obscene fun at newspapers' most popular strips), *Barbarella* was an official release by an important publisher. However, Losfeld was used to stirring controversies by adding provocative titles to his catalogue. Besides publishing such well-known magazines as *Positif* and *Midi-Minuit Fantastique*, he released—often anonymously and clandestinely—"obscene" works by the likes of the Marquis De Sade, Leopold von Sacher Masoch, Guillaume Apollinaire, Boris Vian, Mario Mercier, Ado Kyrou, as well as essays like Georges de Coulteray's *Le Sadisme au cinéma* (interdicted by the Ministry of the Interior in July 1964) and avant-garde, daring strips such as *Epoxy* (by Paul Cuvelier and Jean Van Hamme) and *Saga de Xam* (by Jean Rollin and Nicholas Devil).[1]

The popularity of Forest's character paved the way for such female-based comics as *Jodelle* (1966), *Pravda* (1967), the aforementioned *Saga de Xam* (1967), *Vampirella* (1969) and *Paulette* (1971), as well as all sorts of variants and imitations—including the Italian *Selene* and *Gesebel*. Understandably, it also raised film producers' interest. With the relaxation of censorship, it was inevitable that sooner or later *Barbarella* would land on the big screen. After all, Forest had taken inspiration for his character from a real movie star, Brigitte Bardot, then the world's sex symbol par excellence.

Eventually it was Dino De Laurentiis who bought the rights. Italy's most ambitious movie mogul joined forces with France's Marianne Productions and secured a deal with Paramount for U.S. distribution, planning to shoot *Barbarella* and a less expensive feature (Mario Bava's *Danger: Diabolik*) to cover the costs. Even though it was basically an Italian production with the participation of French investments, *Barbarella* became an international bandwagon, accommodating people of different countries in what was one of the first erotic big-budget efforts in cinema history.

There were less than six degrees of separation between Barbarella and the actress who would eventually portray her on screen. Forest had given his heroine the features of Brigitte Bardot; BB was married to Roger Vadim; Vadim's third wife was … Jane Fonda. The American actress granted an earthier, perhaps more playful approach to the role; what is more, she displayed an unpredictable ease at exhibiting her body before the camera, which definitely surprised audiences and contributed to the film's success.

Fonda was the fourth actress contacted for the role. De Laurentiis' first choice had been Virna Lisi, then came Bardot, who was tired of playing "sexy" roles; the third was Sophia Loren, who refused because she was pregnant and felt she was not fit for the part. Fonda herself was not too sure about the film, but Vadim convinced her by explaining that science fiction was a rapidly evolving genre. He was quite right. At that time Stanley Kubrick was working on *2001: A Space Odyssey* (1968) …

For the script, Vadim brought on board Terry Southern, the celebrated satirical writer who had worked with Kubrick on *Dr. Strangelove or: How I Learned to Stop Worrying and Love the Bomb* (1964). Southern's wife Gail Gerber explained:

> After Terry finished writing Peter Sellers' lines for *Casino Royale*, we flew to Paris to meet with Roger Vadim and

Jane Fonda's star-making turn as Barbarella made her into an international celebrity.

his wife Jane Fonda. Terry had known Vadim from the time he spent in Paris during the early fifties. [...] Tackling a science fiction comedy based on a comic book would be a new challenge for Terry, and he was interested in doing it.[2]

Southern was not new to eroticism. He co-authored (with Mason Hoffenberg) the notorious novel *Candy* (1958), whose heroine shared several points with Barbarella ... starting with her willingness to sleep with whoever crossed her path. Due to the lessening of censorship that characterized the period, Vadim's compatriot Christian Marquand made *Candy* into a film as well. Gerber continued:

> Overall, Terry loved writing *Barbarella* because he felt it was his *Candy*—a brave girl trying to do the right thing but in outer space. She was liberated and was her own woman just trying to get along.[3]

Later on Southern would openly flirt with pornography with the novel *Blue Movie* (1971), about the misadventures of a big shot director named Boris Adrian (patterned on none other than Stanley Kubrick), who shoots an ambitious, big-budget artistic pornographic film.

Like *Candy*, *Barbarella* was essentially built around a series of sexual encounters, whose pretext is a fragile story about the search for a vanished astronaut named Durand-Durand. Southern threw in several funny bits, especially at the film's beginning. Gerber recalled:

> He enjoyed writing for Jane Fonda. Terry was particularly pleased with the opening scene that he created where she enters the spaceship and floats

weightless while removing her spacesuit, which facilitated a kind of striptease as the theme song played over the credits. Jane had studied ballet and to me it was one of the most elegant and sensual stripteases ever seen on the silver screen. Furthermore, it was a valid moment. Terry would never write something frivolous or capricious. Jane disagreed and I think has regretted doing the scene to this day in spite of how beautiful she looked.[4]

Southern had a field day playing with references to sexual liberation and ironic bits of pseudo-science. Early on, in a scene that recalls *Dr. Strangelove's* awkward phone calls between the U.S. and Russian Presidents, Barbarella and the President of Earth (Claude Dauphin) salute with the word "love"; later on Barbarella explains to Mark Hand (Ugo Tognazzi)—who imposed his desire for sexual favors in retribution for him having saved her from a bunch of evil kids and their deadly dolls—that no one has been making love for centuries except the poor, as sex "was proven to be distracting and a danger to maximum efficiency." Of course, Mark manages to persuade Barbarella, and afterwards she comments: "It was rather … interesting. Still I see what they mean by saying it's distracting."

The cast was a mixed bunch. There was the young American star, or soon-to-be one, John Phillip Law, who had made an impression as the Russian sailor in the satirical comedy *The Russians Are Coming, the Russians Are Coming* (1966, Norman Jewison) and had played alongside Fonda in Otto Preminger's *Hurry Sundown* (he would work again with Preminger in the ill-fated *Skidoo*, 1968). Law had started his career in Italy, with an episode of the film *High Infidelity* (*Alta infedeltà*, 1964) directed by Franco Rossi. Among his Italian films of the 1960s, Giulio Petroni's cult Western *Death Rides a Horse* (*Da uomo a uomo*, 1967), co-starring Lee Van Cleef, stood out. De Laurentiis had signed Law for two pictures, the other being Mario Bava's *Danger: Diabolik*. Then there was the British David Hemmings, fresh from Antonioni's *Blow-up* (1966)—a great choice to please the art-house crowd. And, of course, a home-made star for the Italian audiences was needed:

moreover, Ugo Tognazzi was used to playing offbeat roles, such as in Marco Ferreri's *The Ape Woman* (*La donna scimmia*, 1964). Incidentally, here he sports a decidedly ape-like costume. And let us not forget a renowned French mime (Marcel Marceau) in his first on-screen speaking part, and a Swingin' London supermodel (Anita Pallenberg). Everything smelled fresh and young as the audiences the film was aimed at.

Pallenberg was the most impressive presence of the lot as the Black Queen and a perfect erotic counterpart to Fonda's Barbarella, even though, due to her strong Cockney accent, Marpessa Dawn (*Black Orpheus*, 1959) dubbed her voice. Pallenberg was not the first choice for the role,

"It was rather … interesting. Still I see what they mean by saying it's distracting." Jane Fonda's pillow-talk in *Barbarella*

actually, but came on board after a curious episode at Paris' hot spot disco Régine's. Gail Gerber added:

> Terry and Vadim were talking about casting for Barbarella when a beautiful young black woman passed by our table on her way to the ladies room … Vadim got excited and shouted, "There is my Black Queen!" In the comic book *Barbarella*, the Black Queen is evil, not African, but Vadim insisted that Jane and I follow her to the restroom and ask her if she would like a role in the movie. We did, and in French she said that her father was a king and that she would never be allowed to work in the

Durand-Durand (Milo O'Shea) submits Barbarella to the Excessive Machine.

cinema. We returned to the table with the bad news and Vadim was crestfallen. He was not used to being turned down, and in his own city! I immediately thought of my friend Anita, who resembled me somewhat but had more sparkle and a more adventurous persona, so I suggested her. A beaming Vadim replied, "What a good idea! I'm so glad I thought of it!"[5]

At that time Pallenberg was engaged to Keith Richards. According to Law, Dino De Laurentiis even tried to get The Rolling Stones on board to write the score. The outlandish idea never took off, however, as the Italian producer would not pay the conspicuous sum the English band asked for the job. De Laurentiis had to fall back on Charles Fox and the band The Bob Crewe Generation. The notoriously stingy producer even managed to persuade Law to work one extra week for free to cut costs.

Shooting took place at De Laurentiis' own studio, Dinocittà, immediately after *Danger: Diabolik* had wrapped. As Law recalled:

> The shooting of *Diabolik* finished on a Friday, and *Barbarella* started on a Monday. They even used some of the same sets [referencing the scene in Valmont's nightclub in Bava's film], as well as the same special effects man, the great Carlo Rambaldi [...].[6]

Rambaldi created many props and effects in the film, including the eerie cannibal dolls with sharp teeth that menacingly surround Barbarella in one of the early scenes. One of *Barbarella*'s most striking inventions was Pygar, the blind angel, a mixture of innocence and sexual innuendo, enhanced by Law's angelic features. The actor was not blindfolded as in the comic, and had his hair dyed blond for the role.

> I wanted my wings to match my hair so I would look like a comic book character and not someone in an opera.[7]

Working with De Laurentiis was not easy for many involved in the film—Southern included. As Gerber pointed out:

> Dino De Laurentiis (whom Terry nicknamed "Dino D") caused some minor problems. Terry felt that De Laurentiis was only interested in making a profit and producing movies on the cheap. He had no interest in creating good cinema.[8]

Even though several sources state that Southern was the only writer around, the film's opening credits show a list of no less than eight scriptwriters, with the author of *The Magic Christian* and Vadim alongside six other names. Gerber explained:

> It was a surprise to us when *Barbarella* was released that the screenplay credit included not only Vadim but also a number of Italian names unknown to Terry. [...] Though I can't verify because I never set foot on the soundstage during filming, I know that Terry wrote such tight scripts that there was no room for change. To the day he died, Terry never mentioned collaborating with anyone regarding *Barbarella*. When he did work with another writer, he always gave them their due.[9]

Despite the American writer's friendship with Vadim and Gerber reporting how pleased he was by his own contribution, one wonders whether this can be said about the finished film. In a 1973 interview, when asked about his experience in the movies, Southern claimed:

Suffice it to say that, with the exception of *Dr. Strangelove*, of the films I've worked on there isn't one which would not have been infinitely improved by the absence of the director.[10]

That could as well be the case with *Barbarella*. Today, Roger Vadim's big-budget erotic extravaganza looks like a hollow, self-indulgent minor work, and one that has aged badly. One of the most obvious problems is Vadim's awkward approach to Southern's humor. Take the would-be comic scenes, such as Mark Hand's wind-propelled ship going round and round on the icy lake as he and Barbarella are having sex inside. This becomes a heavy-handed gag worthy of Benny Hill, which just looks clumsy and unfunny.

However, for all its spicy bits the result failed to achieve Forest's vision. Whether Southern and Vadim did not want to push the pedal of eroticism to the limit or De Laurentiis was content with just a mildly titillating film, *Barbarella* is quite tame by today's standards. Besides Fonda's opening strip (carefully camouflaged with the opening credits in order to cover the actress' private parts), there is surprising little nudity in it, and despite the many sexual innuendos (such as the Sogo nightclub—an acronym for Sodom and Gomorrah—and the S/M-style outfits worn by the characters), most of the saucy parts are either relegated offscreen or played for laughs—or both. Such as when Dildano the lead rebel (David Hemmings, whose character allows Southern yet another mordant satirical bit) insists on making love to Barbarella in the way that people used to in the future, using the "exaltation transference pellet." The two lovers sit opposite one other and place the palms of their hands together. Then, according to the instructions, they wait "for one minute or until full rapport is achieved." Later on, Durand-Durand captures Barbarella and forces her into a giant musical organ, then proceeds to play his *Sonata for Executioner and Various Young Women …* which results in the girl being stripped nude and sexually fondled by the musical device (incidentally, the British pop-music band Duran Duran reportedly got their name from O'Shea's character here …). Durand's aim is to kill Barbarella by way of ever-increasing sexual pleasure, but the Excessive Machine eventually breaks down, defeated by the heroine's sexual resistance …

However, Vadim does not go nearly as far as Forest did. He keeps the Excessive Machine from the comic but drops one of its more memorable moments, the scene in which the uninhibited heroine sleeps with … a robot, Diktor. An oft-quoted panel has them engaging in post-coitus talk, with a visibly satisfied Barbarella commenting, "Diktor, you have real style!" and the robot replying modestly,

"Oh! Madame is too kind … I know my shortcomings … There's something a bit mechanical about my movements!"

Despite its timidness, *Barbarella* was rated R at the time of its U.S. release (the 1977 re-release got a PG rating, though). And yet, there is no doubt that everything in the film leads to one thing: sex. That Vadim had little else in mind is something that even his actors recall. Speaking about the director's obsession with eroticism, John Phillip Law observed:

> There was one problem, and that was Vadim was crazy about sex, on and off screen. The fantasies, the perversions and he was crazy about women … he only cared about the actresses on the set; he doted on them, fussed over them and he didn't pay any attention to the [male] actors.[11]

Dildano (David Hemmings) and Barbarella make love the futuristic way.

Law was adamant in stating that Vadim was not quite up to Bava's standards as a filmmaker.

> Bava was like a European cross between Alfred Hitchcock and Roger Corman. And he was extremely modest. He didn't even consider himself a real film director. He would say things like, "I don't know anything about directing; I just know a few tricks with the camera." But he was very talented and in the end he knew what he wanted. He was a genius. [He was] … one of the last great artisans. Vadim, on the other hand, considered himself a conceptual artist, refined, special; he thought he was very vanguard: an *auteur*. But he was obsessed with eroticism. Once he told me, "I'm not gay, but I'm very feminine. That's why I can get women to do anything I want, both in film and in real life."[12]

Even though it is quite enjoyable at times, the problem with *Barbarella* is that it is less a film than a series of (admittedly striking) set-pieces. It looks stunning, thanks to Claude Renoir's cinematography, and the nine million dollar budget De Laurentiis put at Vadim's disposition make for a colorful yet hollow universe, all glaring colors and glamorous costumes (by Paco Rabanne, no less). The result is as fascinating as it is hopelessly superficial, like its would-be refined cultural references that range from Impressionism (Georges Seurat's 1884 painting *A Sunday Afternoon on the Island of La Grande Jatte* can be spotted in Barbarella's spaceship) to Pop Art: the bubbling liquid magma lake that threatens the planet is called Mathmos, after the British company that manufactured one of the most instantly recognizable fetishes of the 1960s, the lava lamp.

Furthermore, for all its apparent breeziness, *Barbarella* is very badly paced. Vadim is so enamored of Fonda that he practically has the film stop dead in its tracks whenever she is onscreen—that is, in almost every scene. Overall, *Barbarella* looks more like a fashion catalogue of the era, a reminder of how our fathers' (erotic) imagery looked like. And this, for a science fiction film, is not a good thing.

The story goes that Charles Bludhorn of Paramount Pictures did not like the finished product and was skeptical about its release. He was wrong; released in October 1968 (with the tag "Suggested For Mature Audiences," as the MPAA motion picture rating had yet to be introduced), *Barbarella* grossed 5.5 million in North American theater rentals and became the year's second most popular film in Britain. It was a huge hit worldwide, and gained a growing cult status, especially after a 1977 re-release as *Barbarella: Queen of the Galaxy*. This PG-rated version was toned down and had nudity removed.[13]

According to Gail Gerber, Dino De Laurentiis tried to involve her husband in a follow-up, which never got made.

> Decades later, De Laurentiis called Terry about writing a low-budget sequel to *Barbarella* and mentioned casting Jane Fonda's niece in the lead since he felt that Jane was now "over the hill." Terry, who was ill at this time, was not thrilled with this offer and it never came to fruition.[14]

Eventually, in early 2013, scriptwriters Neal Purvis and Robert Wade (who co-wrote five James Bond films, including 2012's *Skyfall*) were announced to be working on an adaptation for a *Barbarella* TV series produced by Gaumont International Television, to be directed by Nicolas Winding Refn, who called Barbarella "one of the ultimate counter-culture characters." The Danish director would also be the executive producer, alongside Dino De

A pair of bizarre looking guards captures Barbarbella.

Laurentiis' widow Martha. However, at the time of this writing the project seems stalled.

Barbarella is available on DVD in the United States on the Paramount label; despite the subtitle *Queen of the Galaxy*, it is the original uncut version.

Notes:
1. Due to a 1949 law that sought to protect minors from "sensational" literature, *Barbarella* was later subject to restrictions. In November 1969 it was banned by the Ministry and declared "interdit aux mineurs, d'exposition et affichage et de publicité" (forbidden to minors, also in exhibition, display and advertising). A similar fate struck Losfeld's publication of Guido Crepax's *Valentina*.
2. Gerber, Gail and Lisanti, Tom, *Trippin' with Terry Southern: What I Think I Remember* (Jefferson NC: McFarland, 2009), p. 53.
3. *Ibid.*, p. 70.
4. *Ibid.*
5. *Ibid.*
6. Aguilar, Carlos and Haas, Anita, *John Phillip Law. Diabolik Angel* (Pontevedra/Vizcaya: Scifiworld/Quatermass, 2008), p. 82.
7. *Ibid.*
8. Gerber and Lisanti, *Trippin' with Terry Southern*, p. 70.
9. *Ibid.*
10. Southern, Nile and Friedman, Josh Alan, *Now Dig This. The Unspeakable Writings of Terry Southern* (London: Methuen, 2002), p. 68.
11. Aguilar and Haas, *John Phillip Law*, p. 82.
12. *Ibid.*
13. Hughes, Howard, Outer Limits: Thev Filmgoers' Guide to the Great Science-fiction Films (London: I.B. Tauris, 2014), p. 103.
14. Gerber and Lisanti, *Trippin' with Terry Southern*, p. 70. After relocating to the U.S., De Laurentiis produced a big-budget adaptation of Alex Raymond's *Flash Gordon*. The film, directed by Mike Hodges and released in 1980, was not well received but eventually became a cult favorite due to its campy approach (including a rock score by the British band Queen).

Caprice Italian Style
(*Capriccio all'italiana*)
Italy, color, 95 minutes
"La bambinaia." *D:* Mario Monicelli; *SC:* Age [Agenore Incrocci], Scarpelli [Furio Scarpelli], Bernardino

The Italian DVD sleeve for the omnibus comedy, *Caprice Italian Style* (1968)

Zapponi; *DOP:* Giuseppe Rotunno; *M:* Marcello Giombini; *E:* Adriana Novelli.

Cast: Silvana Mangano (The Nanny).

"Il mostro della domenica." *D:* Steno [Stefano Vanzina]; *SC:* Steno, Roberto Gianviti; *DOP:* Silvano Ippoliti; *M:* Gianni Sanjust, Ricky Gianco; *E:* Adriana Novelli.

Cast: Totò [Antonio De Curtis] (Elderly gentleman), Ugo D'Alessio (police commissioner), Regina Seiffert (Girl).

"Perché?". *D:* Mauro Bolognini; *SC:* Age, Scarpelli, Bernardino Zapponi; *DOP:* Giuseppe Rotunno; *M:* Piero Piccioni; *E:* Nino Baragli.

Cast: Silvana Mangano (Wife), Renzo Marignano (Husband).

"Che cosa sono le nuvole?" *D:* Pier Paolo Pasolini; *SC:* Pier Paolo Pasolini; *DOP:* Tonino Delli Colli; *M:* Domenico Modugno; *E:* Nino Baragli.

Cast: Totò (Iago), Ninetto Davoli (Othello), Laura Betti (Desdemona), Franco Franchi (Cassio), Ciccio Ingrassia (Roderigo), Adriana Asti (Bianca), Domenico Modugno (Street-sweeper).

"Viaggio di lavoro." *D:* Pino Zac [and Franco Rossi, uncredited]; *SC:* Age, Scarpelli, Bernardino Zapponi; *DOP:* Giuseppe Rotunno; *M:* Sergio Battistelli; *E:* Giorgio Serralonga.

Cast: Silvana Mangano (The Queen).

"La gelosia." *D:* Mauro Bolognini; *SC:* Cesare Zavattini; *DOP:* Giuseppe Rotunno; *M:* Carlo Savina; *E:* Nino Baragli.

Cast: Ira Fürstenberg (Silvana), Walter Chiari (Paolo).

Prod: Dino De Laurentiis Cinematografica.

"La bambinaia:" A nanny discovers that her group of children are reading *fumetti neri*, so she throws them away and tells the children classic fairy tales … with unexpected results. "Il mostro della domenica:" An elderly gentlemen is so obsessed with hippies that he becomes a maniac who kidnaps young men with long hair and gives them drastic haircuts. "Perché?:" A woman incites her boyfriend to drive faster and not pay attention to road signals as well as other cars … with tragic consequences. "Che cosa sono le nuvole?:" A puppet master is staging a version of *Othello* for an audience of kids, but the puppets start asking the reasons behind their acts. "Viaggio di lavoro:" A queen arrives in an African country, but she makes a speech designed for another country, causing the people's outrage. "La gelosia:" Silvana believes her husband is cheating on her, and she keeps following the man with the intention of killing him.

Produced by Dino De Laurentiis and conceived mainly as a vehicle for the producer's then-wife Silvana Mangano, who stars in three of the six episodes, *Caprice Italian Style* did not feature a strong central theme as De Laurentiis' earlier anthology comedy *The Witches*, but it was perhaps more experimental, both in the tone and in the choice of stories. As the title indicated, the film was meant to be a "Caprice," an almost abstract diversion of sorts, with the scriptwriters and directors focusing on whatever issue they liked. De Laurentiis even allowed the introduction of a mixture of cartoon and live-action in the episode *Viaggio di lavoro* (Work Trip), directed by Franco Rossi and discarded from *The Witches*, which was completed with animation by Pino Zac (who already provided *The Witches*' outstanding animated opening credits).

The result was terribly uneven, even for such a slippery terrain as omnibus comedies usually were—even downright bad at times (namely, Mauro Bolognini's two segments), yet with several sparks of genius throughout, and at least one minor masterpiece: Pasolini's *Che cosa sono le nuvole?* (What Are Clouds?). The episode also marked the last screen appearance of the brilliant Totò, Italy's greatest film comedian, who died in April 1967 just after finishing his scenes with Pasolini (the film was released in 1968, one year after his death). Co-starring Franco & Ciccio, Pasolini's favorite Ninetto Davoli and singer Domenico Modugno, *Che cosa sono le nuvole?* was a poetic fantasy centered on a group of string puppets playing Shakespeare's *Othello* (Davoli, in blackface, plays the Moor while Totò, with green make-up, is Iago) who start asking themselves about the meaning of Truth. Eventually, after the angry audi-

Totò conceives his diabolical plan against longhairs in the episode *Il mostro della domenica*.

ence assaults the stage and the puppeteer has thrown the puppets into the garbage, the puppets look up at the clouds and discover the "heartbreaking wonder of Creation."

Interestingly, one of the film's most interesting aspects is its take on the *fumetti neri*, even though the days when these were the target of judges and newspapers for their excessive violence were basically over by the time *Caprice Italian Style* was released. Whether this was the result of an in-joke aimed at De Laurentiis (who produced *Danger: Diabolik* and *Barbarella* around the same period) or a serious commentary on the passing times is debatable. The fact is that two episodes focus expressly on the *fumetti neri*'s alleged transgressive power as perceived by the common man, and these are about the most interesting reflections on the whole phenomenon.

La bambinaia (The Nanny), directed by Mario Monicelli, is centered on a haughty nanny (Mangano) who is understandably horrified when she discovers that the little children she is taking care of are reading *Kriminal*, *Diabolik* and *Satanik*—and are enjoying them greatly, too. She throws away their comics and reads them Charles Perrault's fairy tales instead. As a result, the children start crying, being scared and shocked by the horrific excesses of *Little Red Riding Hood*. It is just a quick joke, but a sharp one indeed, and with a delicious punch-line.

Steno's *Il mostro della domenica* (The Sunday Monster) is much more articulated and also subtler as a social satire. The term "capelloni" (longhairs) was used in a pejorative sense in Italy to indicate all those young males who were letting their hair grow long as a means of marking protest against fathers and families. As Pier Paolo Pasolini wrote:

> Longhairs became a rather large number—like the first Christians—yet they kept being mysteriously silent; their long hair was their one and only language, and to add anything else mattered little to them.[1]

Totò plays an elderly bourgeois who just cannot stand their sight—the epitome of the fathers' attitude against their sons. He is introduced while coming out of a barbershop, looking in disapproval at the hippies in the street; then we see him at a public phone, disgusted by a nearby young male who presumably smells quite bad. His social hypocrisy is soon unmasked, as we see him with his young lover (posing as his "niece") driving on the way to his country house, refusing to help a couple of longhairs whose car has stopped and commenting that "one cannot tell whether you are men, women or something in between!" Unfortunately for him, his car breaks down as well, and it will be the two hippies who will help him out ... in exchange for a lunch at his villa.

Soon, though, the place is invaded by a multitude of longhaired youth who prepare a gigantic bowl of spaghetti (which they eat with their hands, echoing a famous scene in Totò's earlier classic *Miseria e nobiltà*, 1955) before dancing to some music that the man considers mere noise. Earlier on, the young hippie had dismissed Totò's records of Verdi, Bach and Beethoven as "stuff that's got no use with women."

Such a violation of private property—not to mention the spoiling of his much-anticipated sexual encounter—has unpredictable effects on the man's psyche. But guess what sparks Totò's reaction ... an issue of *Diabolik* peeping from the back pocket of a longhair's jeans. In a brilliant moment, Steno has the frame suddenly freeze and turn into a comic strip of sorts, with Totò dressed (more or less) as Diabolik, while a balloon on his right shows his thoughts, informing us that he is conceiving a plan against the "damned longhairs." It is a striking sight gag, which turns a symbol of transgression into a symbol of repression, and sneers at the narrow-minded moralists in so doing, by turning them into their own worst enemy.

Such deeds, however, are definitely more amusing than those of the *fumetti neri*'s antiheroes. Dressed up in a variety of disguises as a priest, a flamboyant queer type, a (female) prostitute, a bagpiper, Totò lures and then kidnaps young hippies, whose hair he trims as if he was plucking chickens. The vignette with Totò posing as a blond homosexual is rather explicit for the time, as he openly picks up a pair of male hustlers. Homosexuality was still a taboo subject matter in Italian cinema, and acceptable only when approached in a farcical manner. The bagpiper bit is also memorable, and a nice comic reference to The Pied Piper—only this time the longhairs run away from Totò and up to Rome's famous Trinità dei Monti stairs …

Even though it does so in a humorous way, *Il mostro della domenica* is significant both in the way it hints at the generational conflict that was putting the country into turmoil (a commonplace in many Italian films of the period) and for Steno's satirical allusion to the police's reactionary behavior toward the younger generations in the episode's biting punch-line. The commissioner who arrests Totò eventually lets him go when he finds out that his own son has become a longhair, and even allows the maniac to prowl on the teenager and cut his hair as well—just like the commissioner played by Farley Granger will let the sex maniac (Chris Avram) kill the former's unfaithful wife in Roberto Bianchi Montero's sleazy *giallo So Sweet, So Dead* (1972). What is more, the maniac is recruited in the armed forces as an *agent provocateur*, namely "Agent K07" (note the "K" …), with "licenza di rapare" (license to crop). Considering that Steno helmed (signing it with his real name) the committed political crime film *Execution Squad* (*La polizia ringrazia*, 1972), about a subversive Neo-Fascist conspiracy that employs a self-dubbed "Anonymous Anti-Crime" in order to pave the way for a Fascist dictatorship, the final joke obviously has a vitriolic political commentary.

If one considers that *Caprice Italian Style* came out in theaters just one month after a furious clash between left-wing militant students and the police in Rome (the so-called "Battle of Valle Giulia," March 1, 1968), one of the key moments in Italy's 1968 revolts, Steno's episode is all the more remarkable and thought-provoking.

The Italian poster for *Totò Diabolicus*

Note:
1. Pasolini, Pier Paolo, "Il "discorso" dei capelli," in *Scritti Corsari* (Milan: Garzanti, 1975).

Danger: Diabolik
(*Diabolik*)

Italy/France, color, 101 minutes

D: Mario Bava; *S:* Dino Maiuri, Adriano Baracco; *SC:* Dino Maiuri, Brian Degas, Tudor Gates and Mario Bava; *DOP:* Antonio Rinaldi; *M:* Ennio Morricone; *E:* Romana Fortini.

Cast: John Phillip Law (Diabolik), Marisa Mell (Eva Kant), Michel Piccoli (Inspector Ginko), Adolfo Celi (Ralph Valmont), Claudio Gora (Chief of Police), Mario Donen (Sgt. Danek), Terry-Thomas (Minister of Finance), Renzo Palmer (Minister's assistant), Andrea Bosic (Bank manager), Carlo Croccolo (Lorry driver)

Prod: Dino De Laurentiis for Dino De Laurentiis Cinematografica (Italy), Marianne Productions (Paris).

Despite the precautions taken by Inspector Ginko, Diabolik steals 10 million dollars and returns to his secret lair, a cave furnished with all sorts of technological gadgets, where he lives with his partner Eva Kant. Ginko forces a supercriminal, Valmont, to help him catch Diabolik. Meanwhile, for his lover's birthday, Diabolik plans to steal a valuable emerald necklace that belongs to Lady Clark, and once again ridicules the police in the process. However, Valmont kidnaps

Eva and demands a 10 million dollar ransom plus the emeralds. Diabolik manages to release Eva and kill Valmont. To escape capture he swallows a pill that induces apparent death; he wakes up just in time before the autopsy. After the umpteenth hit (he robs a 10-ton gold ingot) the police discover Diabolik while he is melting the ingots and is submerged by a wave of molten gold. However, his asbestos suit protects him from certain death …

Our story begins in 1957. Roman novelist Italo Fasan published the novel *Diabolic—Uccidevano di notte* (Diabolic—They Killed By Night), written under the pseudonym Bill Skyline. It was a mystery novel, a *giallo* (the term, literally "yellow," identified the narrative genre, named after the color of the popular paperbacks that had been published since the late 1920s), the story of an actor who, after discovering he is terminally ill, decides to commit a series of perfect murders, challenging the police to stop him. The murderer signs himself as "Diabolic."

One year later, in Turin, a young man—Mario Giliberti, a worker at a Fiat car factory—was found murdered. The local newspaper *La Stampa* received an anonymous letter from someone who claimed to be the murderer, and signed himself as "Diabolich." The enigmatic figure would send eight more letters to the newspaper, à la Zodiac, before vanishing. Giliberti's murderer was never caught.

Fasan's novel was immediately reprinted with a tagline that referenced the Turin killing, and a few years later Italy's most renowned comedian, Totò, starred in a film called *Totò Diabolicus*, released in April 1962. The plot—basically a rip-off of Robert Hamer's *Kind Hearts and Coronets*—centered on a mysterious assassin named Diabolicus, who kills all the members of a noble family (in order to get hold of the inheritance) and sends threatening letters to the police. *Totò Diabolicus* allowed Totò to play no less than six different roles, including that of an elderly baroness, with exhilarating results. Diabolicus, the mysterious serial murderer, wore a hood and a black leotard with his name written on the chest, and dispatched his victims while laughing hysterically. A remarkable anticipation of the *fumetti neri* antiheroes if there was one, albeit with decidedly grotesque undertones. The film grossed almost 500 million *lire*, with over 2,200,000 tickets sold.

Seven months later, on November 1, 1962 the first issue of *Diabolik* (*Il re del terrore*, "The King of Terror") came out. The cover for *Il re del terrore* was striking. It featured an extreme close up of a man's face, his features completely hidden by a black mask that left only the eyes uncovered—pale blue, icy and cruel— towering over a screaming young woman in the foreground. By just a quick glance, it was obvious that *Diabolik* was not an ordinary comic strip for children. And to remove all doubts, the subtitle read "Il fumetto del brivido" (The Comic book of Thrill).

It is not unlikely to guess that this new comics character was partly inspired by the "Diabolic(h)" Turin kill-

The Parisian arch-criminal Fantômas, created by Marcel Allain and Pierre Souvestre, was one of the main inspirations for *Diabolik*.

ing as well as Totò's grotesque murderer, even though the creators claimed they took the name from "Diabolo" (medieval for "Diavolo," Devil). However, it was the final "K" that made all the difference.

No one would suspect that two members of the weaker sex committed the perfect crime. The writers' names were initially kept secret to the public, as the stories were simply signed by "A. and L. Giussani." The initials stood respectively for Angela and Luciana. Angela Giussani (Milan, 1922-1987) was quite a peculiar figure in the history of Italian *fumetti*. Born from a middle-class family in 1947, Angela married the renowned publisher Gino Sansoni and started working as a fashion model at her husband's advertising agency. She appeared in adverts for Ducati radios and Bemberg fabrics. Then Sansoni founded a publishing house, Astoria, and Angela followed him in this new adventure, working as a secretary, editor and, once again, as a model for kitchen manuals aimed at housewives. In 1961 Angela founded a new publishing company, Astorina,

Angela and Luciana Giussani created the concept of the *fumetti neri* and *Diabolik*.

aimed at a younger audience, and launched an American comic book centered on a prizefighter, *Big Ben Bolt*, created by Elliot Caplin and John Cullen Murphy. This attempt turned out a flop, as the Italian version of *Big Ben Bolt* lasted a scant two years, but Giussani did not give up and perfected the formula by turning the hero into an antihero.

Besides the aforementioned reference to the real-life Turin murder, an indisputable influence on *Diabolik* were such fictional characters as Rocambole, the gentleman thief created in 1857 by Pierre Alexis Ponson du Terrail, and especially Fantômas, the Parisian arch-criminal introduced in 1911 by French novelists Marcel Allain and Pierre Souvestre. Fantômas starred in a series of 32 novels (followed by 11 more by Allain writing solo) and soon debuted on the big screen in a quintet of serials directed by Louis Feuillade and produced by Gaumont in 1913-1914, followed by more adaptations, both French and American.

Legend has it that the spark of creation caught Angela Giussani while reading a Fantômas novel she had found abandoned in the next seat during a train trip, and the similarities between the French model—ruthless, megalomaniac, diabolically smart and a true master of disguise, who is pursued by his sworn enemy, Inspector Juve—and its Italian descendant are readily apparent. Like his predecessor, Diabolik can change his features at will through special skin-like masks which he perfected, and he has his own nemesis in the person of Inspector Ginko, the smart, stubborn policeman who is continually baffled and outwitted by his opponent. The first *Diabolik* stories even took place in France, in Marseille, before the Giussani sisters created the fictional city of Greville as the theater for their antihero's deeds.

With Fantômas, Allain and Souvestre took the tradition of the *feuilleton*—a Manicheist world view for the masses, with the characters rigidly divided into good and bad, heroes and villains, redeemed and damned—and spiced it with a generous dose of unadulterated crime fiction, similarly in turn (but with a decidedly stronger tone) to what Maurice Leblanc had done with Arsène Lupin. What is more, they abolished the happy ending and described the world as a demented place where anarchy rules—a trait which made Fantômas beloved by the Surrealists (so much so that René Magritte repeatedly used the famous Fantômas iconography in his paintings), precisely because of the way he broke the rules, thus allowing the readers to finally (and gleefully) take sides with a character that represented out-and-out evil.

Giussani took a similar path with her own creation, but had the brilliant intuition of changing the basic format by applying the repetitive pattern of the *feuilleton* formula to the comic strip, and, most of all, making the result a pocket-size item. Giussani noticed that many commuters traveling through the Milan train station had the habit of carrying with them cheap novels which they bought at the station newsstands, and reading them while waiting for their train or during the trip, before putting them back in their pockets. Size mattered, indeed. The smaller the better, the 6.7 by 4.7 inch format proved to be just perfect and would become the standard format for the *fumetti neri*.

However, the reference to Fantômas was not simply a lucky accident. Giussani actually had marketing research done in order to better understand the public's tastes, and she found out that *gialli* were the most popular literature genre (hardly surprising, given the enormous popularity of the "Gialli Mondadori" paperback novels and their many imitations). Yet a *giallo* novel was too long for a short train trip. Readers needed something they could read and finish quickly before stepping off their car—something that would not keep their mind and attention too busy. "I wanted to make *gialli* for people who could barely read," Giussani later claimed.

The character's development was also evidence of a well thought out commercial step. For once, graphically, Hollywood movie star Robert Taylor inspired Diabolik's features, yet they soon started bearing a strong resemblance to a more contemporary model as well as one of the period's most striking sex symbols, Sean Connery's Agent 007 … square jaw, hard and cruel blue eyes, ample forehead, not to mention an array of futuristic and often unlikely gadgets, including Diabolik's luxurious car, a Jaguar E-Type (which actually predated Bond's Aston Martin, first seen in 1964's *Goldfinger*).

Souvestre and Allain's novels heavily inspired *Diabolik*'s first issues, the ones drawn by artist Gino Marchesi. *Il re del terrore*, *L'inafferrabile criminale* and *L'arresto di Diabolik* liberally borrowed plot elements and characters from the novel *Fantômas*, whereas *L'atroce vendetta* (#4) portrayed a fake decapitation taken from *Les amours d'un prince* (1912). In *Il genio del delitto* (#5) Diabolik killed a painter named Radié and used the skin from his hands to commit killings and leave the dead man's fingerprints on the bodies, just like Fantômas had done with the painter Jacques Dollon in *Le mort qui tue* (1912, later made into a film as well). Issue #8 (*Sepolto vivo!*) featured a serum that allows Diabolik to reach a state of apparent death for 36 hours, similarly to what Fantômas had done in *Le pendu de Londres* (1911). And so on …

However, Diabolik was more in tune with the present. For once, he was younger (in the novels, Fantômas has a daughter, Hélène, who is the love interest of his other opponent, the journalist Fandor) and less formal in his trademark attire. Whereas Fantômas was presented in illustrations wearing a tuxedo and top hat (not to mention a monocle), Diabolik sported an outfit more in tone with the comic book tradition: an adherent black leotard, vaguely reminiscent of the one worn by The Phantom. Some scholars point out a few decidedly humorous references: Floyd Gottfredson's Phantom Blot and especially Zagar, the "genius of evil," created by the Italian comic book artist Jacovitti for the strip *Cip l'arcipoliziotto* in 1945. In a brilliant graphic inversion of the typical "eight-shaped" mask, Diabolik wore an adhesive hood that completely covered his face except for the icy blue eyes. Nevertheless—thanks to the unfathomable inner logic of comic book fiction—his features were still fully recognizable to the reader. A reference to Lee Falk's hero can be found in Diabolik's origins—revealed in #107, *Diabolik, chi sei?* (Diabolik, Who

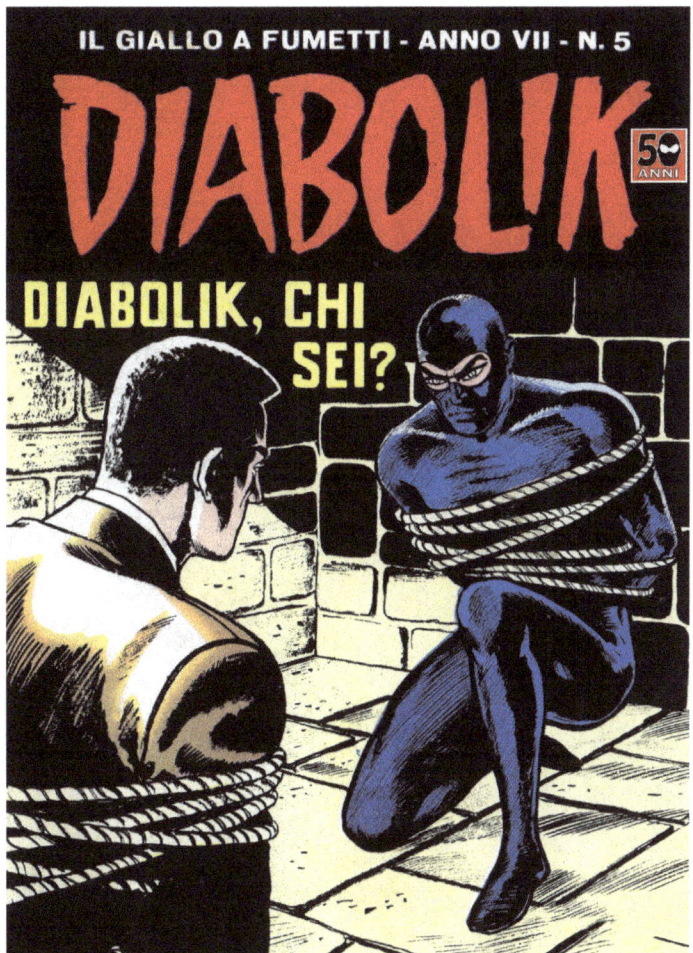

Diabolik **#107 explained Diabolik's almost mythical origins.**

Are You?), published in early 1968— which also have a mythical and almost biblical halo to them. The nameless infant was abandoned on a boat adrift at sea after a shipwreck, and a crime kingpin named King raised the child on a desert island. Diabolik took his *nom-de-plume* after a ferocious panther.

Another less noticeable reference was *Fantax*, a French comic book created in 1946 by writer "J. K. Melwyn Walsh" (aka Marcel Navarro) and artist "Chott" (Pierre Mouchot). Besides the similar half-hood worn by Fantax (who sported a red-and-black costume with an "F" on the chest), the French superhero's stories had a violent content which led to Mouchot being prosecuted by the French censors.

Last but not least, *Diabolik* offered—although in a mild, mild way—another key ingredient: sex … mainly focused on the person of Eva Kant, who makes her first apparition in issue #3 *L'arresto di Diabolik* (Diabolik's Arrest), where she is named "Lady Kant." The ravishing blonde, an ambassador's widow, soon becomes Diabolik's partner in one of the comic's most enduring *ménages*.

However, although he was born according to the stereotype of the lone wolf, and made very brief appearances

For the film version Dino De Laurentiis cast John Phillip Law as Diabolik and Marisa Mell as Eva Kant.

commercial boom. *Diabolik* earned cover stories on the most prestigious tabloids, and newspapers started a heated campaign against that new form of entertainment, labeled as anti-educational and dangerous for the gullible minds of the (supposedly underage, despite said warning …) readers and, in general, portrayed as an example of the decadence of Italian society caused by the decline of traditional values. "It seems that heists and robberies take place only because of *Diabolik*," the Giussani sisters stated after an issue (*Il tesoro sommerso*, #82, 03/20/1967) was seized primarily because of a woman in a bikini on the cover:

> It's easy to fault society's issues on a comic book. Now it's getting absurd. We are being attacked politically—right-wing newspapers accuse us of fomenting revolutions, whereas for the left-wing ones we are fascists![1]

On the other hand *Diabolik* even inspired a song, released in 1966 as a 7" single and sung by Betty Curtis (real name Roberta Corti). By 1966, each issue saw a print run of no less than 300,000 copies, and its readers were not just the train commuters at which Giussani was aiming. Readership also included middle and high-class professionals, representing an easy way to escape from the tedious daily routine and give free rein to the imagination.

At first, Diabolik actually was a ruthless, immoral hero, who left behind him a series of dead bodies—never using a fire weapon but instead an array of knives, poisons, strangling laces … and did not hesitate when it came to dispatching a potential eyewitness. However, the newspapers' moral crusade soon had its effects on the comic book's content: Diabolik was no longer the cold-hearted murder machine as seen in the first episodes, and he became a more conventional criminal with a proper "ethical" code. He no longer killed indiscriminately but targeted his victims in the criminal underworld; even then, he replaced his lethal weapons with a hypodermic needle with soporific effects. Moreover, he concentrated on stealing goods that belonged to other criminals, becoming some sort of a deviant, hyper-technological and far more egotistical Robin Hood. A free spirit, who "openly defies law, rules and the established order, and not to undermine it, but simply for the pleasure of making fun of it."[2]

Overall, however, *Diabolik* had its share of issues and challenges. Despite its continuous and ever-growing success, it was a case of the concept overwhelming the stories—not to mention that the artwork was far from striking. A quick comparison between *Diabolik*'s first issue (drawn by an elusive artist named Zarcone, who then disappeared) and Magnus & Bunker's extraordinary *Kriminal* is simply shattering in this sense, although the Giussani sisters soon

in the stories, just as if he was a phantom of sorts, Diabolik drastically evolved after the appearance of Eva. Initially submitted to the criminal, soon—see issue #15, *Lotta disperata* (Desperate Struggle)—she became his partner in crime … as well as in bed. It was a slight move on the part of the Giussani sisters, and one that won the comic strip even more fans in its smart reworking of the typical criminal couple clichés which somehow predated women's claims of equality. By that time, starting from issue #14, Angela's younger sibling Luciana (1928-2001) joined her, leaving her job at a dustbin factory to become the second half of the dynamic scriptwriting duo behind *Diabolik*. Eva Kant (to be pronounced "Kant"—a homage to the great 18th century German philosopher, no less!) was soon to become an icon of female beauty. Her facial features were patently inspired in turn by Grace Kelly, whereas the hairstyle came from Marchesi's own wife.

Sales were disastrous at first. It took over a year (after a pre-cautioning "adults only" warning appeared on the cover starting with issue #2) before *Diabolik* became an unexpected *success de scandale*. Starting with July 1963's *Terrore sul mare*, sales started growing and 1964 saw the character's found in Enzo Facciolo an efficient and reliable drawing artist.[3]

What is more, *Diabolik* has not aged gracefully. Despite the participation of such important scriptwriters as Alfredo Castelli, Pier Carpi and Giancarlo Berardi[4], the stories were often repetitive in their stretched-out "police and thieves" theme, and the sex-and-violence content was ultimately tamer when compared with the many imitations that followed. In many cases these overwhelmed *Diabolik* in sheer inventiveness (such as *Kriminal* and *Satanik*) and luridness, no doubt due to that old Italian over-the-top fast approach: rip them off, do it quickly and do it 10 times the amount as the original.

in the person of the renowned comedian Louis De Funès, who played opposite Jean Marais as a decidedly cartoonish Juve. Hunebelle followed *Fantomas* with two sequels, *Fantômas se déchaîne* (1965) and *Fantômas contre Scotland Yard* (1967).

Cervi—a rather accomplished director on his own, with such films as *Today We Kill ... Tomorrow We Die!* (*Oggi a me ... domani a te!*, 1968), *Queens of Evil* (*Il delitto del diavolo*, 1970) and *Nest of Vipers* (*Ritratto di borghesia in nero*, 1978)—was rather ambiguous when referring to *Diabolik*.

> I definitely like the comic book hero created by the Giussani sisters, and I think that with a few retouches he

Marisa Mell replaced Catherine Deneuve after just a week of shooting. According to John Phillip Law, Bava and De Laurentiis decided that Deneuve was too bland and that Mell was hot.

With sales growing steadily despite (or maybe because of) seizures and assorted controversies, it was just a matter of time before *Diabolik* would make it to the big screen. The first film producer who became interested was Tonino Cervi, the son of Gino Cervi and the head of the company Italy Film. In the meantime, the Fantômas character was experiencing a second rebirth of sorts, due to the success of André Hunebelle's *Fantomas* (*Fantômas*, 1964), starring Jean Marais in a dual role as the titular character and his adversary Fandor. The Italian title for Hunebelle's film was, significantly, *Fantomas 70*, hinting at the way the titular character was being reshaped to please the younger generations, with more than a nod to the current spy and sci-fi trends, but also not forgetting an emphasis on humor

> could turn into an extraordinary character for the silver screen. He is neither a cop, nor a spy, nor an executioner or a gentleman-thief. He is a superman, beyond every law and every rule.[5]

In other interviews of the period, Cervi sounded less than enthusiastic about the project:

> I'd been thinking of a film based on a comic book for a while. Something like *Flash Gordon* or *The Phantom*. However, these characters work on the screen only if they are represented in a cer-

Mell and Law have an obvious screen chemistry, which allows for a palpable erotic mood throughout.

tain manner, with big budgets. I think that nowadays a good film based on *Flash Gordon* would be a sensational success [...] but it would cost as much as *Cleopatra*. I have to settle for something more modest, so I'm doing *Diabolik*.⁶

Cervi was actually hoping that *Diabolik* would help him put together an anthology film directed by three of cinema's greatest filmmakers: Fellini, Bergman and Kurosawa. Italy Film acquired the rights from Astorina for 20 million *lire* and proposed a distribution deal to Dino De Laurentiis: a hundred million *lire* advance in exchange for the exploitation rights for the film in perpetuity. De Laurentiis granted only 70 million, but in a short time he managed to put together a co-production between Italy, France (Les Films Marceau-Cocinor) and Spain (A.S. Film Producción and Impala).

The first draft of the story was concocted by two young comic book writers, Pier Carpi and Corrado Farina, who were both also working in the TV advertising field, on the so-called "Caroselli." Then the project passed on to other hands. Since the controversies about violence in comic books were reaching a peak, the scriptwriters entrusted with the adaptation (Giampiero Bona and Fabrizio Onofri) were specifically instructed to tone down the violence, whereas a non-essential emphasis on comedy was added, just like in the French *Fantomas* adaptations. News articles about the oncoming project looked far from auspicious.

> On film, Diabolik will be a little less cruel than the original, to avoid trouble with the censorship commission, and he will fight criminals of his own class, leaving in peace honest people as well as the hapless Inspector Ginko, the head of the homicide squad who has been chasing the phantom criminal for years to no avail. Instead of Ginko, who will play a secondary role in the film, we'll have a super antagonist in the vein of 007's Goldfinger.⁷

Another article noted:

> When Tonino Cervi announced that he would bring *Diabolik* to the screen, he pointed out that he would completely rework it [...]. Diabolik will not perform any criminal deed, and he will move in a world without police. In a certain way, he will become a literary character, a romantic superhero that will use the prestigious weapons of talent, intuition, inspiration and divination. Not coincidentally, he reads Nietzsche and Freud. He will display no sign of the sadomasochism that characterizes certain contemporary heroes, not only in comic books but in literature, theatre and cinema as well.⁸

Predictably, the Ministerial Commission, devoted to preliminary analysis of scripts, passed the script without any objections. Brit director Seth Holt was attached to the project, while—despite early claims at casting an unknown actor as the protagonist⁹—the French Jean Sorel was ultimately chosen to play the leading role, after Cervi unsuccessfully attempted to cast Alain Delon, whose demands were too high for the 500 million *lire* budget. Elsa Martinelli would play Eva Kant because, once again, Cervi's first choice, namely Virna Lisi, turned out to be unreachable. The then 64-year-old George Raft would co-star as Diabolik's antagonist, "Richness," while other prominent parts would be played by Marilù Tolo, Venantino Venantini and the midget Jimmy Karoubi.

Principal shooting began in Malaga, Spain on September 20, 1965 … and soon came to a halt on October 18. Raft got ill and was forced to leave the set. Gilbert Roland replaced him, and Holt had to abandon all the footage that featured Raft and reshoot the scenes with the substitute.

The scenes set in Spain were ultimately wrapped up, but on November 13 shooting was once again interrupted, and this time for good, due to "technical and script-related reasons." The real reasons for such an abrupt halt were never officially cleared up, and many rumors circulated at the time. "The fate of *Diabolik* [...] is still shrouded in mystery," noted the weekly magazine *A.B.C.* in a piece dated January 9, 1966:

What's certain is that shooting was suspended indefinitely. As for the reason, there are quite different versions. According to the one peddled by the entourage of director Seth Holt, what has happened must be charged upon producer Tonino Cervi, who ended up penniless after a few days of shooting. To make up for the inconvenience, Cervi devised a curious trick: let's have the director quit and get the insurance money, then finish the film. Quite a simple plan, as one can see, except for one detail: why would the director have to leave? Throwing somebody out of a film is easy, but having him go away of his own accord is rather complicated. For this purpose, the producer ordered that the crew be party to a kind of "conspiracy of silence": nobody would talk to the director or answer when he would ask something. However,

The movie script drew from several stories, and this was one of the main inspirations.

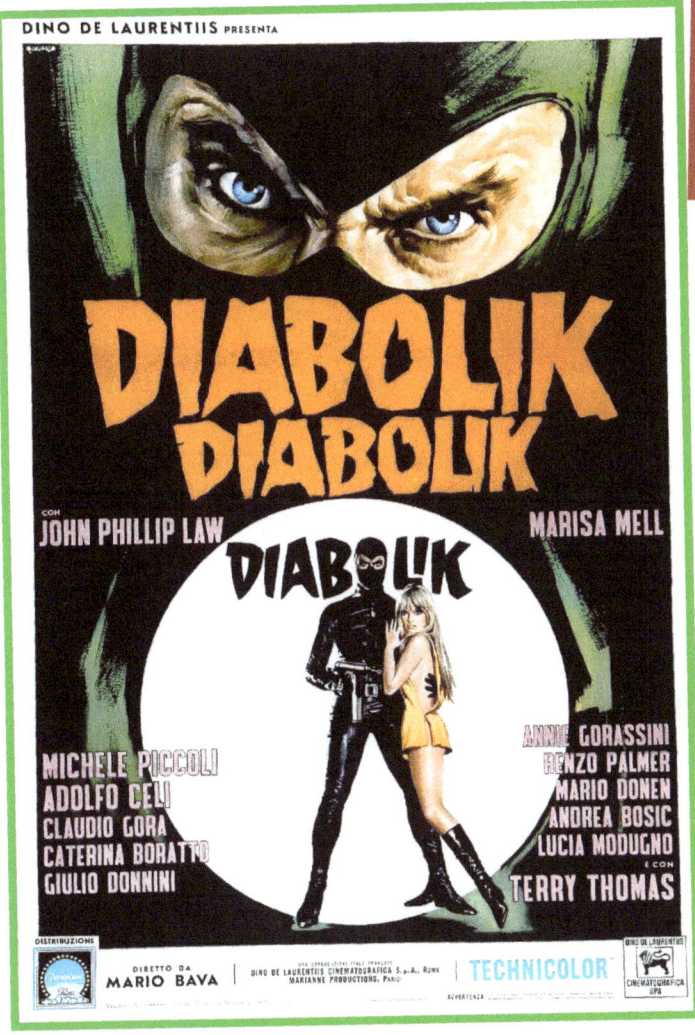

An Italian poster for *Danger: Diabolik*

Cervi had not considered the proverbial British phlegm: Seth Holt smelled a rat, and therefore he quit only after his adversary surrendered and gave up on the film, leaving it in the hands of distributor Dino De Laurentiis. According to Tonino Cervi's friends, on the contrary, it was not the crew who did not address the director, but the latter who talked to nobody, for the simple fact that he had nothing to say. The crisis broke out on the day that the film's star, Jean Sorel, stated loud and clear that he would not stand any longer a director who was much more concerned in downing bottles of whiskey than directing actors.[10]

As it eventually turned out, the final decision came on the part of Dino De Laurentiis, after he watched Holt's footage. As De Laurentiis explained to his financers in a letter kept at Rome's State Archive:

A tower-climbing sequence from *L'ombra nella notte*, the original comic story

weapons), thus provoking a financial loss that brought the company to the brink of bankruptcy. Once again it was up to De Laurentiis to act as a *deus ex machina*, by taking care of all Italy Film's contractual expenses and liquidating the various parties.

However, Cervi's company was ousted from the project. Furthermore, it was also prohibited to reuse—even partially—the filmed footage.

In retrospect, such a clumsy series of missteps on the part of the producer is almost unbelievable. Holt, a competent director himself, was definitely not the right man to bring to the screen such a dynamic character. Sorel was a rather wooden actor, and Martinelli was yet another wrong choice as Eva. What is more, if Holt's footage was reportedly below par, a large part of the fault had to be laid on the script. The story, which is completely different from the one later brought to the screen by Mario Bava, centers on a couple of heists involving famous paintings and artificial diamonds and sounds like a bad rip-off of a *Batman* TV episode, complete with a jaw-dropping scene in which Jimmy Karoubi dresses up as Diabolik. Furthermore, Diabolik's opponent is characterized as an almost comical character, Ginko is absent and sex and violence are kept to a minimum as expected. The scene where Diabolik helps a poor boy to recover his senses before he flees—the same boy he previously knocked unconscious—speaks volumes about the producers' cowardly attitude.[11]

Determined not to give up on the project, De Laurentiis started from scratch. He managed to find a strong financial backing with Paramount as a distributor, and opted on Mario Bava as a director, partly because of the latter's solid reputation in the fantastic film genre, but most likely in order to save money as well, due to Bava's ability of doing wonders with virtually nothing, as amply demonstrated by his earlier works, particularly *Planet of the Vampires* (*Terrore nello spazio*, 1965). Consequently, the budget was far from huge (about 200 million *lire*, less than a half that afforded Holt) while "name" actors like Adolfo Celi (*Thunderball*, 1965) and Michel Piccoli were cast in supporting roles—the former as the jinxed villain Valmont, the latter as Ginko. The masked antihero had the Adonis-like features of John Phillip Law, whom the producer wanted to reward after *Barbarella* (where Law would play Pygar) was postponed due to technical difficulties. Law explained:

> Shooting was interrupted to save everyone's money ... This is because the footage that had been shot so far was of a level so low, both from an artistic and commercial point of view, as to make us clearly understand that to continue on that path meant heading toward disaster ... that would surely have led to the completion of a product doomed to failure ... it has been decided to repair the error by interrupting the shooting in order to look for a new director and correct the script.

De Laurentiis' good intentions were not enough to quell the spirits of the other parties involved, who resorted to strong-arm tactics. The French companies denounced Italy Film and demanded the immediate termination of the contract, while the Spanish A.S. Film Producción confiscated the footage and seized the technical equipment rented by the Italian company (cameras, costumes,

> Dino De Laurentiis offered to extend my contract, so I could do another comic book film that needed to be made quickly in those weeks that were left before starting *Barbarella*.[12]

However, the actor was adamant in admitting he did not know either *Barbarella* or *Diabolik*.

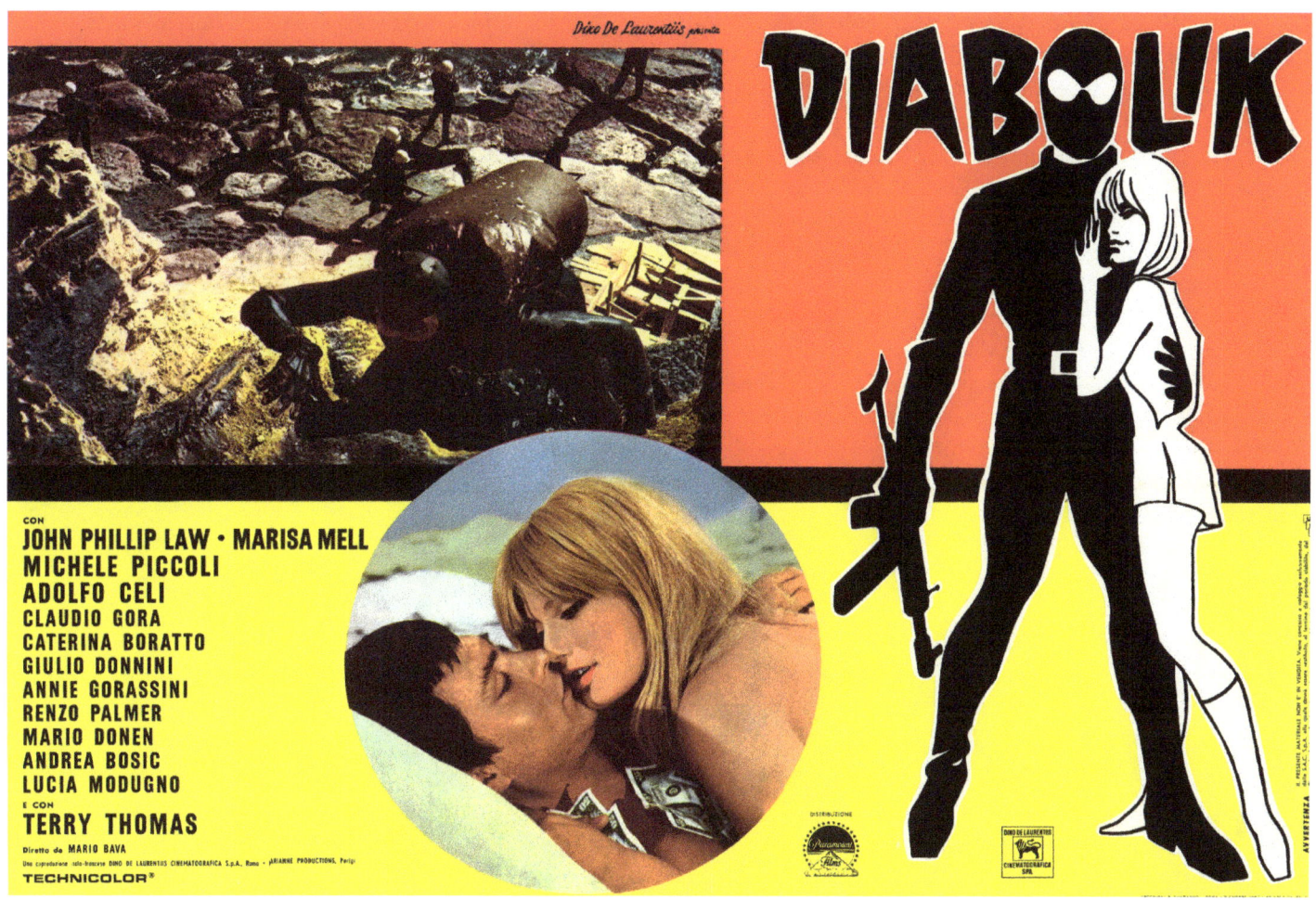

A lobby card for *Danger: Diabolik*

I always loved comics, I grew up with them, but the American ones. Then when I agreed to do the movies, I picked up loads of copies of both *Diabolik* and *Barbarella* to become familiar with the characters. They were very, very different. *Barbarella* was all about kinky eroticism, while *Diabolik* was all about being bad. […] He is the perfect antihero. A supercriminal, who in some ways is like what we consider today a terrorist, like when he blows up government buildings and so on. […] Anyway, only in Italy, in the sixties, could they make a superhero out of a character like that. The opposite of the American superheroes.[13]

To find the perfect Eva Kant was a tougher nut to crack. Initially, Eva was to be played by a still unidentified American model, the "friend" of Charles Bludhorn, one of the heads of production at Paramount. The girl was fired before shooting started because, as one newspaper maliciously suggested, "the 'qualities' magnified by her pictures did not correspond to her 'real' appearance." Then it was Roger Vadim's turn to push De Laurentiis to cast Vadim's ex-*fiancée* Catherine Deneuve. As Law recalled:

> Bava didn't like the idea, but he gave in, so we started shooting … It wasn't long before it became obvious that Catherine wasn't Eva Kant, and that there was no chemistry between us. She was very sweet, and a very good actress, but she was simply not right for the part. So, after just a week of shooting, Bava and De Laurentiis watched the rushes and they decided that Catherine seemed bland, she wasn't "hot," and didn't fit in this kind of a film. So they decided to replace her and start again.[14]

The producer then allowed Bava to choose whichever actress he thought he would work well with, and the director pointed at two names: Marilù Tolo and Marisa Mell. It was the Austrian actress (real name Marlies Moitzi, 1939-1992) who finally got the role … whereas Deneuve went on to shoot Buñuel's *Belle de jour* (1967), where she played alongside Sorel *and* Piccoli. Small world …

The script for *Danger: Diabolik*—by Dino Maiuri, Tudor Gates, Brian Degas and Bava, from a treatment by Adriano Baracco—adapted and stitched together three different episodes, *Sepolto vivo!* (#8, August 1963) *Lotta disperata* (#15, March 1964) and *L'ombra nella notte* (#35, May 1965). Filming started on April 11, 1967 and went on for nine weeks, until June 18, 1967. Bava—who was used to much tighter shooting schedules—later described the experience as a nightmare. He would even go so far as to tell Luigi Cozzi in a 1970 interview that when De Laurentiis called him with an offer to direct a sequel, he answered: "I am sick, disabled in bed, permanently."[15] He complained that De Laurentiis had him tone down the violence, and it is widely reported that the producer and the director had opposite ideas on how to bring the comic to the screen. As John Phillip Law put it:

Diabolik and Eva make love in their money-covered bed …

They each had a different movie in their heads. De Laurentiis wanted to make a cosmopolitan super-production for family viewing, with an elegant, worldly thief, something like Raffles. But he was wrong then, because *Diabolik* was a specifically Italian creation, and Bava wanted to stay true to the comic book, so that the comic book fans, and there were millions of them, wouldn't be disappointed. I agreed with Bava, with his idea to make a dark, violent, very Italian film. In the end, after loads of controversy, they made a hybrid version […].[16]

This is undoubtedly true, yet Bava's reaction to De Laurentiis' demands was astute. In his film, suspense becomes over-the-top showiness, whereas violence becomes mockery. *Danger: Diabolik* was submitted to the Italian Board of Censors in December 1967. The film was given a "Per Tutti" (All audiences allowed) rating, after the producer agreed to five brief cuts; it saw release in Italy on January 24, 1968.

Reportedly, the Giussani sisters did not like Bava's film one bit. Nevertheless, and despite the budgetary limits and an episodic screenplay, *Danger: Diabolik* remains an impressive, remarkable work that seems to get better with time, like a prestigious vintage wine. Bava did not demystify the main character by pressing the pedal of irony, nor did he try for a "knowing" approach. Everything in *Danger: Diabolik* is strictly one-dimensional: a series of colored, shiny surfaces and moving objects filling the screen with no inner logic except being there for the viewer's pleasure. A case in point is the scene at Valmont's nightclub (a set-piece recycled in *Barbarella*), with a parade of hippie extras dancing at Ennio Morricone's score amidst Bava's trademark color schemes and gels. Part of the credit must be given to the outstanding set-pieces designed by Flavio Mogherini, as well as the costumes designed by Luciana Marinucci and Giulio Coltellacci, but there is more. According to Bava scholar Alberto Pezzotta:

> Bava does an even more subtle and sound operation, by making a truly Warholian film … not only because he reproduces the iconography of consumerism's stereotypes, but because he does so in a non critical way, accepting the void and the bad taste, and giving up not only irony and parody, but every sociological criticism or rebellious façade.[17]

What many reviewers did not get at the film's release is that *Danger: Diabolik* is not simply a reinvention of the comic book character, but a re-imagination of it as seen by the common man. Gone are the thief's cold, methodical, scientific prep work, his isolation and seclusion, his relationship with Ginko, an obstinate, obsessed man with no other goal in life than to catch his arch-enemy (and *doppelgänger*). Despite killing people by the dozen, in Bava's version Di-

... a far less daring version of the same scene was later featured on the cover of *Colpo alla zecca*, published four months after the release of the film.

abolik becomes an exuberant, colorful adventurer full of joy of living and gifted with a much-welcomed irony, plus a childish attachment to all things technological. Diabolik's main aim is to make his lover happy (so that she returns the favor in bed …), and his biggest act of rebellion is blowing up the income tax building—an ordinary man's notion of protest against the government. Thus, Diabolik becomes the perfect hero for mediocre times.

Despite Law's claim that when he showed up on the set made up as Diabolik, with combed hair and retouched eyebrows, Bava greeted him with the words: "Ma questo è Diabolik!" ("But this is Diabolik!"), the director was reportedly not satisfied with his lead. Several critics also objected that the actor was too young for the role. Yet Law proved to be an almost pitch-perfect Diabolik. With his permanent cynical grin, feline movements and limited facial expressions, he becomes a perfect counterpart to Bava's style, an object among other objects in a world apparently devoid of "normal" people and literally painted on the screen in gorgeous primary colors. Ennio Morricone's extraordinary score, a composite of very different influences and suggestions, perfectly fits this concept.

Diabolik and Eva, so physically similar that they almost look like siblings, exude an overt sensuality that bursts out of almost every sequence. Bava is more interested in filming his protagonists while they are showering, making love or caressing each other, with the accompaniment of a sensual female voice (Edda Dell'Orso) in Morricone's score rather than in their criminal exploits. The two criminals are linked by a relationship that is exclusive, passionate and totally devoted. They live for each other, and behave as if the rest of the world is merely an instrument for their own happiness. Law and Mell had an obvious screen chemistry, which their real-life love affair during the shooting no doubt helped strengthen. Their perfect bodies are continually explored by the camera yet left untouched, as in the chilling autopsy scene, when Diabolik is in a state of apparent death and about to be sliced open by the coroner, where the director shows his skill as a master of suspense with Diabolik's "resurrection" at the very last moment. This sequence openly recalls several of Bava's most celebrated ones, such as Asa waking from the dead in *Black Sunday* or the dead astronauts coming back to life in *Planet of the Vampires*.

Danger: Diabolik is definitely much more erotic than its comic book source, and joyfully so, as exemplified by the scene in which Eva, lying naked on the bed, has her body covered with money by Diabolik—perhaps a nod to Alberto Moravia's scandalous novel *La noia* (1960), which featured a similar scene[18]—before they make love, and the one where he places the stolen emeralds over her naked flesh. The hero's carnality is sublimated yet again in the

Danger: Diabolik featured outstanding costumes designed by Luciana Marinucci and Giulio Coltellacci.

ending, where he is covered from head to toe with molten gold, thus becoming a living statue, a monument to himself. Bava would have probably laughed when asked about this, but the image of Eva Kant kneeling before Diabolik, silently crying and caressing his new shining skin, seems like a tribute to a famous Surreal sequence in Luis Buñuel's *L'Âge d'or* (1930).

If Diabolik is a master of disguise, Bava proved once again that he was the Grand Master of Illusion, by creating the hero's hidden cave with the help of a handful of props, some paper-cut models and a few mirrors. The supremacy of appearance over reality is continually underlined in the film through the use of cartoonish images and gags. To steal the emeralds, Diabolik takes a picture of a room and puts it in front of a closed-circuit camera, thus replacing the real view with a phony one. Then, to escape the police, he uses a mirror-like reflective sheet that looks like one of Wile E. Coyote's "Acme" devices. Bava even pokes fun at the audience and himself in a priceless sight gag that has a fake model train suddenly enter the frame. Just as the viewer is thinking how shoddy a special effect this is, the train is revealed to be … a model that the archcriminal is playing with.

Law later declared that working with Bava had been nothing short of "fantastic":

A lot of people didn't take him seriously, but he was a genius. I did anything he wanted; I was so impressed by his ability. One time he said to us, "You and Marisa concentrate on your characters, and I'll look after the camera." He had these great tricks; he'd create sets where there weren't any. One day he said, "Take a few days off while I make your cave-home." When I entered the cave with my car and didn't see anything, I thought, "What's going on here?" Bava said, "Come upstairs," and he showed me that with paper cutouts on glass panels, he had designed exactly what he had in mind for Diabolik's "bat cave." He would pan the scene from behind the glass panels, and you would swear you were inside a cave. Of course, then he would have to explain in great detail where I had to step. "Walk along that catwalk, then go slowly up those stairs as you were going up in an elevator." Later, when we saw the rushes, De Laurentiis shouted, "I'm going to tell Paramount that this set cost 100,000 dollars!"[19]

Bava conceived another similar trick for the scene in which Diabolik rescues Eva in a cabin. The director was dissatisfied with the set he had been provided with, so he told his actors to take a break and then proceeded to cut a picture out of a magazine, which he then placed on a glass in front of the camera. As Law recalled:

Then he said to me, "John, when you go up the hill, turn your hand as if you are opening a door." And when you see it on film, you'd swear I was going into a house. What Bava did is a lost art. Today they do everything with computers. Cut here, add there … [20]

Danger: Diabolik is a popular film in the purest sense of the term, because not only does it come from popular culture, but is also made with a popular attitude employing cheap, popular material. By resorting to painted glass panels and paper-cut silhouettes, Bava's work bore curious similarities with the contemporaneous "Arte Povera" (Impoverished Art) movement, although his was not a philosophical quest but merely a money-saving necessity. Still, the director's nods to the art world were apparent. As Corrado Farina pointed out in an essay:

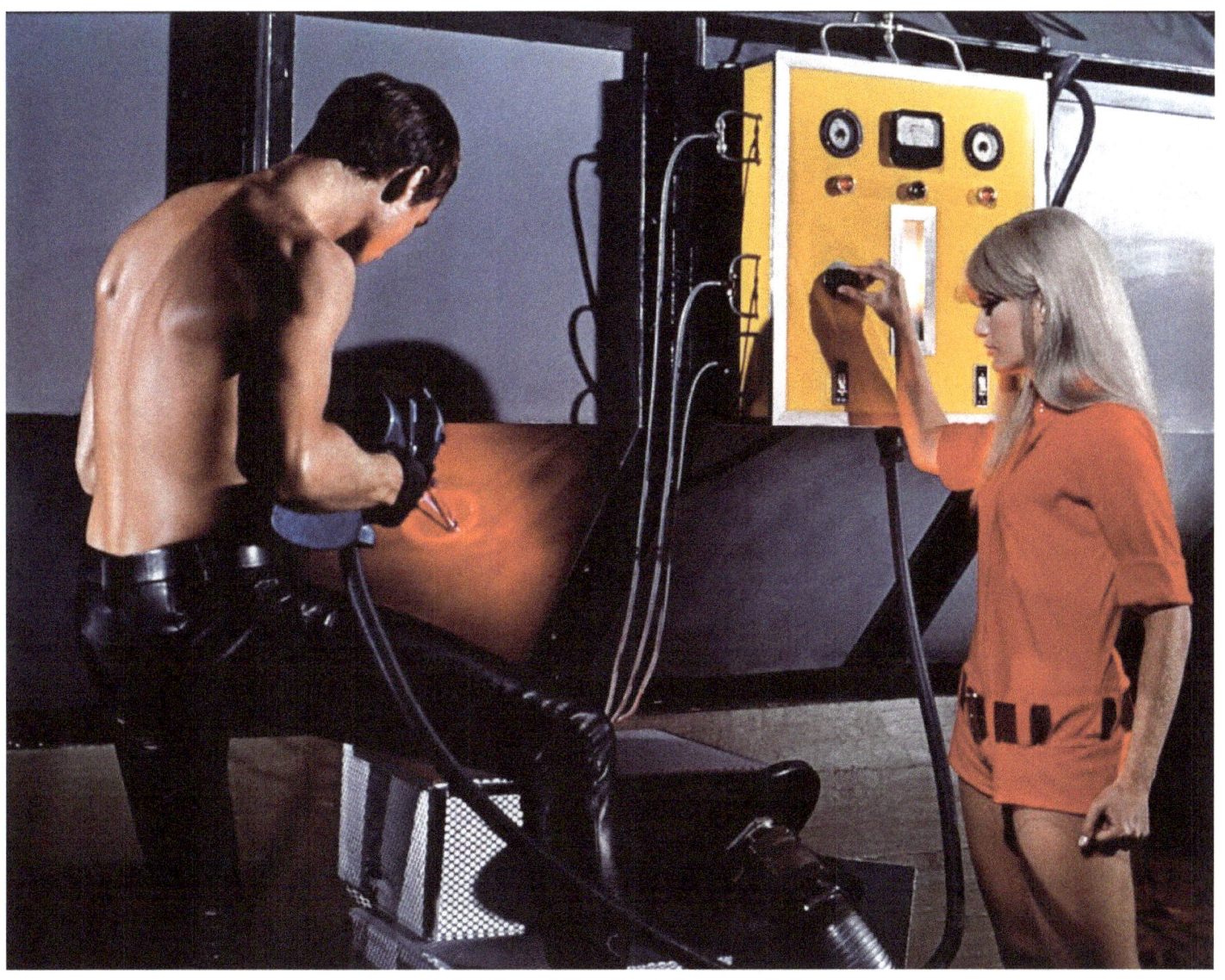

Diabolik and Eva in their secret lair

This film cheerfully betrays its source […], but luckily there is a director (and director of photography) of proven skills who has the gift of irony and makes the story enjoyable by winking not only at the *007* series but also at Pop Art, as well as all the cultural fashions of the period. The scene where Eva's face is sketched in an identical drawing in a funny animated sequence is nothing short of an homage to such artists as Roy Lichtenstein (as well as a nod to De Laurentiis' soon-to-be-filmed *Barbarella*, whose appearance Eva resembles in the artist's sketch). Seen at its release, *Danger: Diabolik* could seem an attempt (rather uncertain between copy and parody) at cloning the James Bond films. Today, it gains a very enjoyable *retro* taste.[21]

Law rightly pointed out:

> Part of the success of the film had to do with the sexy clothes, black leather and rubber masks or in how girls like bad boys.[22]

On the other hand, Diabolik's adversaries (including the "good guys") are nondescript, anonymous, caricatures or just plain ugly. No doubt who to take sides with … As the Italian novelist and film scholar Giuseppe Lippi stressed, Bava's film even influenced Diabolik's graphic portrayal in the comic book series. Labeling Diabolik "a fetishistically interesting thief," Lippi noted:

> Being made of latex, the black mask (white in the memorable tower climbing scene) penetrated between the lips, allowing viewers to see Diabolik's

The Comic Book Universe in Italian Cinema   107

Mario Bava told John Phillip Law: "You and Marisa concentrate on your characters, and I'll look after the camera."

mouth. The leading artists in the series, Enzo Facciolo and Sergio Zaniboni, would remember such a detail. They never tried to copy the "latex effect" but since then they gave up shading the mouth and neatly outlined it in perfect evidence under a transparent veil.[23]

Danger: Diabolik was highly anticipated in Italy, so much so that De Laurentiis threatened to sue a couple of production companies which were producing a superhero film (*Superargo vs. Diabolicus*) and a spoof (*How to Kill 400 Duponts*) to prevent the use of names or titles too similar to *Diabolik*. Yet the Italian distributors did not give up. In late 1968, the 1966 Japanese film *Ogon batto* by Hajime Sato, starring Sonny Chiba, was released in Italy as *Il ritorno di Diavolik*, only one consonant away from the Giussani sisters' character. However, *Danger: Diabolik* was a financial disappointment for De Laurentiis. Its box-office gross was below expectations in Italy as well, with slightly more than 265 million *lire* taken in. The film barely broke even in Europe and was a flop in the United States, but it garnered a considerable cult status over the years. Today it is available on DVD on the Paramount label.

Diabolik's popularity was such that the character lived a parallel life on the radio. In 1972, Radio Monte Carlo broadcast a series of 30-second sketches every 15 days that accompanied the release of a new Diabolik issue. Ettore Andenna (Diabolik), Liliana Dell'Acqua (Eva) and Antonio Devia (Ginko and occasionally Diabolik) provided the voices. From April 7 to July 2, 1981, Radio 1 RAI broadcast 26 episodes, running between 20 and 25 minutes each, written by Lamberto Lambertini and Sergio Scapagnini and directed by Lambertini. The voice actors were Daniele Formica (Diabolik), Bianca Maria Voglio (Eva) and Paolo Falace (Ginko). The episodes, broadcast twice a week were a "free adaptation"—and very likely demystifying—of the comic book; the voices were deformed and distorted, sometimes in falsetto, the stories accompanied by weird noises and the characters spoke various Italian dialects. The series ended with Diabolik and Eva on their way to the guillotine, without mentioning whether they would be executed or if they would manage to escape. Several episodes were replicated over the following years in the radio show *Audiobox* (November 24 to December 29, 1982) and *Doppiogioco* (July 21 to August 25, 1984). Radio 2 ran another series of 20 radio dramas from November 13 to December 8, 2000, starring the renowned voice actor Luca Ward (Diabolik), Roberta Greganti (Eva) and Francesco Prando (Ginko). A second series, featuring the same actors and consisting of 10 episodes, was broadcast daily from June 7 to June 18, 2004.

More recently, The Beastie Boys' video clip for the song *Body Movin'* (1998) directly referenced Bava's film, by mixing footage from the movie—the celebrated sequence in which John Phillip Law climbs a tower to steal Lady Clark's emeralds—and scenes featuring the three New York rappers. In 2004, the Italian pop band Tiromancino (headed by film director Federico Zampaglione) also paid homage to *Danger: Diabolik* with the video for their song *Amore impossibile*, directed by Lamberto Bava and featuring *The Bold and the Beautiful*'s Daniel McVicar as Diabolik and Claudia Gerini as Eva Kant, plus a cameo by Law himself as a museum guard. Further references to Bava's film can be seen in Roman Coppola's film *CQ* (2001), in which a young film editor (Jeremy Davies) is working on a science-fiction film called *Codename: Dragonfly*, produced by a mogul (played by Giancarlo Giannini) who is a photocopy of Dino de Laurentiis. The style and sets in Coppola's film also openly pay homage to *Danger: Diabolik*. The moment in which Angela Lindvall is rolling around on her bed covered with banknotes is a replica of the aforementioned scene in Bava's film, and even John Phillip Law pops up in a supporting role.

An animated series based on the Giussani sisters' character was produced in the late 1990s by Saban En-

The image of Eva Kant kneeling before Diabolik, silently crying and caressing his new shining skin, seems like a tribute to the famous Surreal sequence in Luis Buñuel's *L'Âge d'or*.

terprises International, and premiered in Europe on Fox Kids. It was directed by Jean-Luc Ayach, with Paul Diamond and Larry Brody as head writers, and was inspired by the *Batman* animated series on Fox. Composed of 40 episodes lasting 20 minutes each, the series referenced only vaguely themes and characters of the comic book, adapting them to a much younger audience than usual. Most notably, the main differences are as follows: the rejuvenation of Diabolik and Eva Kant, who become much younger than they are in the comics; the replacement of Diabolik's trademark E-type Jaguar with a more modern and fanciful car; the victims of Diabolik's thefts are only criminals; Inspector Ginko belongs to Interpol and not to the local police; the adventures take place in the real world instead of imaginary places such as Clerville and Ghenf and the creation of the Brotherhood, a criminal organization headed by Dane, Diabolik's half-brother, a character who does not even exist in the original comic book. The series was aired on the French TV network M6 but never made it to the U.S.

In the early 2000s it seemed that a feature film was in the planning stages, to be directed by Cristophe Gans and starring Mark Dacascos and Monica Bellucci, plus Billy Crudup (as Ginko) and Deborah Kara Unger. Gans, whose idea was to hire Donald Westlake for the script, wanted:

> To take this character and place him in an erotic, very adult caper movie, as far away from any Austin Powers' feel as possible ... [...] The Bava film is unique and I'd never, ever want to copy it. But let's see where we can take Diabolik today for a totally new and different Pop Art experience.[24]

It eventually came to nothing.

Along the years there were recurrent rumors of a *Diabolik* TV series. First announced in 1991, based on scripts by Mario Gomboli and Alfredo Castelli and featuring a financial joint venture between RAI and Silvio Berlusconi's TV company Fininvest, it was quickly shelved. The following year news came of a script being commissioned to Rospo Pallenberg, but it took five years before the announcement, at Cannes' MipCom, of a TV pilot. However, the news was soon belied by *Diabolik*'s publishing house Astorina. In 2002 *Diabolik* became a hot topic again, as the series' main scripter Mario Gomboli announced a big-budget picture to be produced with French money, faithful to the comic but set in the present day. The script was commissioned to the renowned mystery novelist Carlo Lucarelli and Giampiero Rigosi. According to Lucarelli, the story focused on Diabolik's first encounter with Eva. The script was completed in April 2007, and principal shooting was scheduled to start in January 2008, but then the project stalled.

More rumors ensued, first of a six-part TV series produced by RAI Due (RAI's second TV channel), then of a two-part miniseries starring Raoul Bova, one of Italy's

Covered from head to toe with molten gold, Diabolik becomes a living statue, a monument to himself.

most popular actors. Eventually, in November 2012, *Diabolik*'s 50th anniversary was celebrated on the Italian Sky Cinema channel with the screening of a two-minute trailer starring Italy's swimming champion Lorenzo Benatti as Diabolik. A 50-minute, 10-episode series—produced by Sky Italia with the British BSkyB and Sky Deutschland—has been announced for late 2016/early 2017.

Notes:
1. Scaringi, Carlo; *Il mito Diabolik* (Rome: Gremese, 2003), p. 49.
2. Ibidem, p. 14.
3. Among the other artists that took turns drawing *Diabolik*, we must not forget Sergio Zaniboni, Franco Paludetti, Flavio Bozzoli, Lino Jeva, Giorgio Montorio and Leone Cimpellin.
4. Castelli (born in 1947) and Pier Carpi (real name Arnaldo Piero Carpi, 1940-2000) would later create the groundbreaking magazine *Horror*, published by Sansoni. Castelli would also create *Martin Mystère*, one of Italy's most popular and enduring comic series. Carpi dabbled with movies as well, directing a couple of weird films, the Gospel allegory *Povero Cristo* (1975) and the controversial occult horror flick *Ring of Darkness* (*Un'ombra nell'ombra*, 1979). Berardi would also become an important name in the world of Italian comics, thanks to the impressive *Ken Parker*.
5. Quaranta, Antonio, "Produrrò il film "Diabolic" [*sic!*] per fare il ragazzo cattivo," *La Gazzetta di Latina*, 05/16/1965.
6. Minuzio, Nero, "Mandrake Ciak," *L'Europeo*, 05/09/1965.
7. Martini, Giorgio, "Gli occhi di Diabolik," *Bella*, 08/26/1965.
8. C. M., "Il fumettistico Diabolik legge Nietzsche e Freud," *Telestar*, 08/13/1965.
9. *L'artiglio del demonio* (issue #9, second series, 03/05/1965) featured an ad by Italy Film: "Looking for a new actor." The ad invited anyone who would meet the characteristics required ("Masculine and handsome features—bright eyes—height 5'10" (minimum)—athletic physique") to get in touch with the production. However, this was most likely a publicity stunt on the part of Cervi in order to steam things up a bit about the upcoming film.
10. Anonymous, "L'inglese flemmatico e l'italiano nei guai," *A.B.C.*, 1/9/1966.
11. For a thorough history of the "lost" *Diabolik* film, see Curti, Roberto and Di Rocco, Alessio, "'Maledizione!' The True Story Behind Seth Holt's Accursed Version of Diabolik," *Video Watchdog* #176, p. 22.
12. Aguilar and Haas, *John Phillip Law. Diabolik Angel*, p. 71.
13. Ibid.
14. Ibid.
15. Cozzi, Luigi, "Intervista a Mario Bava," *Horror* #13, December 1970/January 1971, p. 101.
16. Aguilar and Haas, *John Phillip Law. Diabolik Angel*, p. 72.
17. Pezzotta, Alberto, *Mario Bava* (Milan: Il Castoro, (1995) 2013), p. 91.
18. A less daring version of the same scene is featured on the cover of issue #113 *Colpo alla zecca*, which—contrary to what several Bava biographers write—was *not* an inspiration for the script, for the simple reason that it was published on May 27, 1968, four months after the release of *Danger: Diabolik*.
19. Aguilar and Haas, *John Phillip Law. Diabolik Angel*, pp. 74-75.
20. Ibid.
21. Farina, Corrado, "Cinema italiano e fumetto: piccola cavalcata al confine tra gli anni 60 e 70," *FilmCronache* #2, 2006, pp. 19-22.
22. Aguilar and Haas, *John Phillip Law. Diabolik Angel*, p. 72.

23. Lippi, Giuseppe, "Maschere e pugnali. Recital in tre parti," *Nocturno* #133, October 2013, p. 55.
24. Jones, Alan, "Danger: The Adventurer," www.fangoria.com, July 2002.

Fantabulous Inc.

(*La donna, il sesso e il superuomo*, aka *Fantabulous*)

Italy/France, color, 95 minutes

D: Sergio Spina; *SC:* Furio Colombo, Ottavio Jemma, Sergio Spina; *DOP:* Claudio Ragona; *M:* Sandro Brugnolini; *E:* Giancarlo Cappelli.

Cast: Richard Harrison (Richard Werner), Judi West (Deborah Sands), Adolfo Celi (Dr. Karl Maria Van Beethoven), Gustavo D'Arpe (Prof. Krohne), Fabienne Fabre (Alice, the nurse), Nino Fuscagni (Leonard MacFitzroy), Enzo Fiermonte (General Van Pelt), Gislaine Barbot (Young nurse), Silvio Bagolini (French General), Arturo Dominici (Captain Fenninger).

Prod: Summa Cinematografica (Rome), Procinex (Paris).

After spending the evening with his fiancée Deborah, a model and an actress in advertising spots, Richard Werner is kidnapped and taken to a mysterious Swiss firm, Fantabulous Inc., headed by Dr. Karl Maria Van Beethoven. Werner undergoes a painful surgery that turns him into some kind of obedient automaton with a superhuman strength and intelligence. With the help of a huge calculator (named "SS"—that is, Servus Servorum) created by professor Krohne, Van Beethoven plans to manipulate the human brain in order to create the perfect individual. Werner—officially dead and renamed "F-17"—is now a tool in the hands of Van Beethoven, who orders him to steal the "atomic plasma," a revolutionary new form of energy discovered at the Atomic Center in Geneva, and show the powers of his "superman"—whom Van Beethoven plans to turn into a military weapon and sell to foreign governments. Beethoven's idea is simple. Common citizens, worried by the ever-growing criminality and frustrated by the frequent protest marches, strikes and demonstrations, need new heroic figures to protect the status quo. Fantabulous Inc. has thus created the perfect product and is already conditioning the public opinion through TV spots that feature the heroic superman. However, when he recognizes Deborah as the protagonist of one of these spots, F-17 goes berserk. Richard eventually recovers his memory and personality and turns against Van Beethoven, Krohne and the electronic brain ...

One of the crucial moments in Italian post-war history was January 3, 1954. On that day, at 11 o'clock in the morning, RAI—Italy's national public television—started broadcasting all over the country. A pretty female announcer presented that day's schedule and, from then on, the life of millions of Italians would never be the same again. Even though the country's economy was so poor that not many families could afford a TV set, television became immensely popular all the same. Audiences gathered in bars or other public places and soon became addicted to the small screen, changing their lifestyle accordingly, electing new idols and becoming themselves new targets for mass advertising. Sergio Spina was one of the key figures in the blooming Italian television industry; he was the director behind one of the most popular early TV programs, *Strapaese*. The Milan-born writer and filmmaker had the chance to observe the phenomenon from behind the scenes and take note.

Spina started working in the movie business in the late 1950s, in parallel with his television assignments, first as artistic supervisor on an exotic documentary (*Moana l'isola del sogno*, 1959), then as scriptwriter. He penned a couple of sword-and-sandal pictures, *War Gods of Babylon* (*Le sette folgori di Assur*, 1962, Silvio Amadio) and *Slave Queen of Babylon* (*Io Semiramide*, 1963, Primo Zeglio). A mass-media expert and a university teacher, Spina developed a view of the new media that eventually crystallized in the script for his feature film-directing debut, *Fantabulous Inc.*

Even though it has many elements in common with contemporary genre flicks—as announced by the presence of familiar faces from Italian spy and adventure films such as Richard Harrison (not the greatest actor but suitably effective) and Adolfo Celi (*Thunderball*; *Danger: Diabolik*) as the suave villain—*Fantabulous Inc.* is quite different from the typical commercial stuff the audience would expect and is closer to the overtly political films made by the new generation of young cineastes.

Spina and his co-scriptwriters Furio Colombo (who later became the editor-in-chief of the Italian Communist party's official newspaper *L'Unità*, and an MP for the Left, which he remains to this day) and Ottavio Jemma use the comic book storyline as a pretext for a grotesque discourse that touches a number of themes which would become crucial in 1968, from consumerism and advertising to the social clashes that were starting to happen following the impact of such events as the Vietnam War.

Spina's depiction of consumerism and the modern "society of spectacle" feel at least partly indebted to the ideas of the French philosopher Guy Debord. But there is definitely more than that, as cinematic, literary and artistic references abound, including Jean-Luc Godard's *Alphaville* (1965), Stanley Kubrick's *Dr. Strangelove* (as evident from the grotesque mad scientist Krohne, whose hands have been replaced with mechanical claws), Wilhelm Reich's theories, Roy Lichtenstein's paintings … and, of course, comics: Lee Falk's *The Phantom* and *Mandrake*, Marvel and DC's superheroes, Pierre Bartier and Guy Peellaert's Pop Art erotic comic *Jodelle* and so forth.[1]

The film's look and style exude a Pop Art era feel, with garish colors, disjointed and syncopated narration and quirky editing, and Spina has a knack for impressive comic book-like imagery, with bits of animation, weird camera angles and visual tricks, resulting in a number of effective scenes. Werner's kidnapping, which comes at the end of

The Italian publicity material for *Fantabulous, Inc.* tried to pass the film off as an erotic drama of sorts.

Krohne underlines), Werner is something more than the typical comic book hero. He wears a mask, a golden costume and a silver cape, and his superpowers are an odd mixture cobbled together from many different sources—he is invulnerable to bullets and flame-throwers as well as extreme cold, he can fly, is able to perform elaborate mathematical calculations ... Yet, his "creators" have brainwashed him so as to become a super-soldier, *Robocop*-style, remorseless at killing innocent women and children. The references to Vietnam are all too obvious.

On the other hand, even though he quotes Goethe's *Faust*, Celi's Van Beethoven is not the typical madman with delusions of grandeur, but rather a devilish entrepreneur, a hi-tech arms merchant who funnels his Nietzschean babblings into a decidedly capitalistic enterprise—to exploit the ongoing wars throughout the planet and sell his "super-soldier" to the best bidder. Rather than ruling the world, he merely aims at profit. He knows that free will has already been eliminated by consumerism. He rants:

> You are all attached to such a useless tiring freedom ... to think, to choose, to doubt, to decide ... all the time, every minute ... what a grueling burden ... do let others, more expert and illuminated than you, think in your place, Mr. Werner!"

Fantabulous Inc. is surprisingly unpleasant at times—witness the cringe-inducing scene in which a man has his fingers crushed under machinery by Van Beethoven's men in order to destroy his fingerprints, or the brain-surgery sequence which features stock footage of an authentic skull-drilling. Most upsetting, too, is the inclusion of graphic real-life executions, war killings and street revolts, accompanied by Van Beethoven's monologue about the uncertainty and disorder of present times, which gives away the movie's anti-war message and puts it closer to the political films of that era than to mere genre entertainment.

The erotic elements—including mild female nudity—are also present in pure 1968 spirit. For a villain who proclaims: "Make war, not love!" we have a hero who recovers his personality after having sex with his girlfriend (played by Judi West, seen in Billy Wilder's *The Fortune Cookie*, 1966): love—*physical* love, as emphasized in the opening sequence—wins over everything. Another scene, in which Werner is subjected to the sight of naked women in order to test his reactions, even predates a celebrated sequence in John Boorman's *Zardoz* (1974).[2]

Fantabulous Inc.'s most dated aspect is the dialogue. The script is chockfull of quips, witticisms, wordplay and slangy bits which are very much the product of their time, like a second-rate take on Anthony Burgess' reshaping of

a rather elaborate sequence, is a crescendo of paranoia as the unsuspecting hero is repeatedly approached by Van Beethoven's men, all wearing dark shades and taking the place of gas station attendants, cops and so on. Another high point is the lively lounge score by saxophonist Sandro Brugnolini, the leader of Rome's prestigious Modern Jazz Gang.

As the titular everyday man-turned-superman ("Only a mediocrity can be turned into an übermensch," as the English vocabulary in *A Clockwork Orange* and the Kubrick/Terry Southern verbal inventions of *Dr. Strangelove*—characters often talk in rhyme, while Krohne speaks in a bizarre mixture of neologisms and mispronunciations—which eventually becomes rather annoying. The film is also somewhat let down by its meager budget, which is especially evident in the ample use of stock footage; what is more, the most spectacular scene—F-17's stealing of the atomic plasma—is solved through crude optical prints.

In order to make Spina's film more commercially palatable, the distributors resorted to one of the oldest tricks in the book … they dropped the puzzling original Italian title *Fantabulous* and replaced it with the allusive *La donna, il sesso e il superuomo* (Woman, Sex and the Superman), with an emphasis on the double-entendre of the term "superman"… not that this helped, since the film performed poorly at the box-office.

Spina's second and last film was *L'asino d'oro* (The Golden Ass, 1970), an adaptation of Apuleius' ancient Latin novel *Metamorphoses* made in the wake of *Fellini—Satyricon* (1969), set in Ancient Rome and starring Barbara Bouchet and John Steiner. Despite the director's ambitions, it was an unremarkable effort, wavering between lewd and picaresque comedy, drama, fantasy and grotesque, with a handful of weird ideas and twice as many indigestible moments. It had problems with the censors and did just as badly at the box-office. Spina then returned to what he knew best—the small screen. The director did not think much of it. To an interviewer who confessed that he had actually liked *L'asino d'oro*, he curtly responded: "That's because you don't know anything about movies!"

Notes:
1. Spina includes quick shots of Jack Kirby's unmistakable panels for *Captain America*, *X-Men* and *The Fantastic Four*, even though Marvel comics would be introduced to the Italian audience only in 1970, by the Milan-based Editoriale Corno, starting with Spiderman and Daredevil.
2. The Board of Censors demanded that the violent and erotic elements be drastically toned down, resulting in cuts of one minute and 51 seconds, and gave the film a V.M.14 rating.

Phenomenal and the Treasure of Tutankamen
(*Fenomenal e il tesoro di Tutankamen*)
Italy, color, 95 minutes

D: Roger Rockfeller [Ruggero Deodato]. *S:* Aldo Iginio Capone; *SC:* Ruggero Deodato, Aldo Iginio Capone; *DOP:* Roberto Reale; *M:* Bruno Nicolai; *E:* Luciano Cavalieri.

Cast: Nicola Mauro Parenti (Count Guy Norton/"Fenomenal"), Lucretia Love (Lucretia Perkins), Gordon Mitchell (Gregory Falkov), John Karlsen (Prof. Mickewitz), Carla Romanelli (Anna Guillaume), Cyrus Elias (Julien), Agostino De Simone (Lord Baxter), Maurizio Merli (Pino).

Prod: Italiana Cinematografica Artisti Riuniti (I.C.A.R.) (Rome).

Despite the sophisticated alarm system that should protect it, the valuable mask of the Pharaoh Tutankamen is stolen from a museum in Paris. The sensational hit was performed by Gregory Falkov, the head of a criminal gang specializing in spectacular thefts that have been hired by an expert Egyptologist, Lord Baxter. However, just as Falkov is handing Baxter the mask, a mysterious man named Phenomenal intervenes, retrieving the treasure and mailing it back to the museum's director, Count Norton. However, the mask turns out to be a copy. When Falkov is murdered, the plot thickens. Phenomenal discovers the real culprit, and the mask finally returns to its original location …

"Do not ask me the story because I don't remember it!"[1] Ruggero Deodato told an interviewer when asked

The international poster for Ruggero Deodato's *Phenomenal and the Treasure of Tutankamen* (1968) emphasized similarities with *Diabolik*.

about *Phenomenal and the Treasure of Tutankamen*, which says a lot about the opinion he has about his first "official" film, signed under the pseudonym Roger Rockfeller[2]. One of the lamest, less remarkable entries in the supercriminal/superhero trend of the late 1960s, *Phenomenal* was actually Deodato's second directorial outing. *Gungala la pantera nuda* (1968), an exotic jungle film which was part of another small trend loosely inspired by the world of Italian comics, had marked Deodato's *de facto* debut, as he was called on mid-shooting to replace the director, Romano Ferrara.

Although openly reminiscent of the *fumetti neri* antiheroes of the period, Phenomenal is actually a vigilante who hides behind an above-suspicion identity. The story unfolds almost as a whodunit, as the real mastermind villain is disclosed only near the end. Similarly, Deodato's game is to keep the audience guessing who Phenomenal might really be … even though, needless to say, the masked hero's secret identity is pretty clear from the start.

All in all *Phenomenal* (spelled Fenomenal in the Italian prints) is a lame, forgettable creation. His costume is boilerplate to say the least: black trousers, adhesive black sweater and a black sock on his face—with no eye sockets. One wonders how this guy is able to walk his way without stumbling every two steps, let alone fight criminals.

Phenomenal's most distinctive trait turns out to be his manic laughter (another mannerism borrowed from *Diabolik*), which definitely does not add much. What is more, the story is completely devoid of violence and lacks the campy factor that made similar entries (such as Mino Loy's *Flashman*) at least mildly enjoyable. The only spicy bits are the Turkish bath scenes, in which Deodato makes good use of the handheld camera … and has the opportunity to show a number of scantily clad ladies.

As expected, the plot draws from various sources: the caper film in the vein of *Topkapi*, the James Bond series (note the technological gadgetry on hand) and the exotic Italian spy rip-offs, with the inevitable trip to Tunisia. Yet the storyline is so confused it is difficult to tell what is going on at times. The opening heist, for instance, turns out to be an elaborate set-up on the part of the museum's security service in order to test the alarm system.

In the early 1960s Deodato had worked as an assistant director to such filmmakers as Antonio Margheriti and Sergio Corbucci, and he had learned how to do his homework. He directs *Phenomenal* with some verve, and often tries to recapture the feel of comic book panels through close-ups and unusual camera angles. He even has a cameo as the bespectacled guy who falls off a bycicle in one of the early scenes, but not due to Hitchcockian ambitions: "We were penniless and we needed an extra," he explained[3]. However, the svelte direction cannot overcome the many shortcomings in the plot, acting and budget.

As Phenomenal, Nicola Mauro Parenti is one of the cinema's worst superheroes. Blame it on the producer—Parenti himself, who had delusions of becoming an actor. As Deodato recalled:

The Turkish bath scene provided for one of the film's few *frissons*.

He used to put on airs. He was a nice guy, but took himself too seriously. He was too stiff, a dog of an actor; I treated him like shit on the set, but then he called me again for *Zenabel*. He had this fixation about action films [...]. He was specialized in finding private investors for his pictures, and they almost always turned out to be sleazy types [...]. He used to have them put money in [the production in] exchange for small roles in the films.[4]

Parenti also cast his gorgeous wife Lucretia Love as his co-star. Carla Romanelli, on the other hand, was Deodato's fling at that time. Gordon Mitchell, with platinum blond hair, steals every scene he is in with his manic laughter and evil grimace, while a very young Maurizio Merli, who would become Italy's most popular crime film star due to vehicles such as *Violent Rome* (*Roma violenta*, 1975) and *Violent Naples* (*Napoli violenta*, 1976), has a small role as one of Mitchell's henchmen.

Despite the Parisian setting, *Phenomenal* sports such typical Roman locations as Villa Miani (the museum where the treasure of Tutankamen is exposed), a recurrent sight in many films of the period, seen, for instance, in *Argoman the Fantastic Superman* as well as in Camillo Mastrocinque's Gothic horror film *An Angel for Satan* (*Un angelo per Satana*, 1966). As for the usual amount of travelogue footage, Deodato had an amusing anecdote to tell:

I was shooting a scene in Paris, on the Champs Elysées, with my handheld camera, while President De Gaulle was passing by in his car during the July 14 parade, the celebration for the taking of the Bastille. I was panning on the crowd and the passers-by, when I framed a guy ... and I stopped. I put the camera down and asked that man, "Can I use you in my film?" And he said, "Yes ... yes of course." Do you know who he was? Rex Harrison. Can you believe that? I got Rex Harrison as an extra in my film! He was there by chance, watching the parade, and ended up in my film (laughter).[5]

And, indeed, Harrison can be spotted for about a couple of seconds, wearing shades and understandably disinterested in Deodato's camera.

Overall, the best thing about the film—which even surfaced on home video in the States on the VCI and Wizard labels—happens to be Bruno Nicolai's score, replete with an infectious title song that repeats the protagonist's name *ad libitum*.

Notes:
1. Fenton, Harvey, Grainger, Julian and Castoldi, Gian Luca, *Cannibal Holocaust and the Savage Cinema of Ruggero Deodato* (Surrey: FAB Press, 1999), pp. 11-12.
2. As for the pseudonym, Deodato later said: "I didn't give a shit about the film ... I was asked, "What name do you want to put on the credits?" and I thought, "A rich man's name ... so who is a rich guy? Rockfeller!" See, I was as dumb as a rock." Gomarasca, Manlio, "Fenomenal e il tesoro di Tutankamen," in Gomarasca, Manlio and Pulici, Davide, eds., "Monsieur Cannibal. Il cinema di Ruggero Deodato," *Nocturno Dossier* #73, August 2008, p. 15.
3. Gomarasca, "Fenomenal e il tesoro di Tutankamen," p. 14.
4. Ibid.
5. Aramu, Daniele, "Il ragazzo dei Parioli. Intervista a Ruggero Deodato," *Nocturno* #1, Summer 1996, p. 19.

Psychopath

(*Sigpress contro Scotland Yard*, aka *Mister Zehn Prozent—Miezen und Moneten*)

Italy/West Germany, color, 96 minutes

D: Guido Zurli. SC: Arpad De Riso, Enzo Gicca Palli; DOP: Franco Villa; M: Gino Peguri; E: Romeo Ciatti.

Cast: George Martin [Francisco Martínez Celeiro] (Alan/Harry Caldwell/Sigpress), Ingrid Schoeller (Muriel), Karin Field (Priscilla), Paolo Carlini (Inspector Harold Bennett), Orchidea De Santis (Manuela), Andrew Ray [Andrea Aureli] (Themistocles Niorkos), Nick Jordan [Aldo Canti] (Pedro), Dick Palmer [Mimmo Palmara] (Maurice), Klaus Kinski (Pierluigi/Periwinkle), Gloria Paul (Joselita Del Filar, nightclub singer), Tony Candela [Donato Canti] (Maurice's henchman).

Prod: Rekord Films (Rome), Cinesecolo (Milan), Parnass Film (Munich).

Sigpress, a mysterious international thief, is a specialist in stealing valuable jewels, which he then returns to the owners as a means of collecting the reward money. Scotland Yard is after him, in the person of Inspector Bennett, but to no avail. Sigpress learns that a Greek ship owner, Themistocles Niorkos, will travel from London to Paris carrying a fabulous gem, "The Eye of Allah." Bennett is escorting the jewel incognito, but during the trip the "Eye of Allah" disappears. However, the stolen jewel is only an imitation as the real "Eye of Allah" is still in the hands of its owner. The Inspector suspects some-

The U.S. Force Video box art tried to pass off the film as a straight thriller, emphasizing Klaus Kinski's presence.

thing is fishy and investigates on his own. In the meantime Niorkos is ambushed and shot by mysterious individuals. Sigpress, disguised as a journalist, anticipates Bennett's moves and uncovers the truth. Niorkos' private secretary Muriel and her lover/accomplice Maurice murdered Niorkos and intend to take possession of the jewel. Sigpress intervenes and manages to eliminate the two murderers when they are about to dispatch Niorkos' daughter Manuela.

Together with Ruggero Deodato's *Phenomenal and the Treasure of Tutankamen*, Guido Zurli's *Sigpress contro Scotland Yard* is one of the few examples of Italian genre cinema transposing the feel of the period's *fumetti neri* without actually resorting to one of them. The script (by Arpad De Riso and Enzo Gicca Palli, the latter uncredited)[1] introduces a character who is patently modeled after Diabolik in his appearance (the Spanish George Martin looks very much like the Giussani sisters' character, and Zurli has him dressed in tight black clothes when he is at "work") and in the use of outlandish gadgets, such as the latex masks or a bulletproof turtleneck sweater.

However, the way Zurli's film deals with its antihero once again shows just how much Italian cinema of the period ultimately tamed the comics' edgy contents. For one thing, Sigpress (not the most striking of names, admittedly) is some sort of a gentleman thief à la Arsène Lupin who steals the haul from actual thieves and returns it back to its owners, charging a 10% fee for his services. In the German prints he was renamed "Mister Zehn Prozent," Mister Ten-Per-Cent. His relationship with his archenemy Inspector Bennett (this time a bit more intelligent than usual) is portrayed as an amiable cat-and-mouse game, with Sigpress poking fun at his unfortunate rival by appearing like a bespectacled journalist (shades of Clark Kent) who keeps following Bennett everywhere. What is more, the plot is yet another variation on the worn out storyline as seen in many heist and spy films of the period—not to mention the actual *fumetti neri* adaptations—with a little bit of *The Pink Panther* (1963) thrown in for good measure.

However, unlike Deodato's mediocre *Phenomenal*, Zurli's film is ultimately quite enjoyable. It has an ironic punch which most of its contemporaries lacked, and it is too bad Zurli leaves some ideas underdeveloped, such as Sigpress addressing the camera in the opening scene, telling the audience: "I can't say this is a hard job, but someone has to make a living, huh?" A couple of visual gags center on Zurli paying homage to Agent 007, as Sigpress defeats a gang of thugs while wearing a Sean Connery/James Bond mask, while another funny touch has Sigpress making mocking phone calls to poor Inspector Bennett in which he introduces himself with the sound of Wagner's *Ride of the Valkyries*.

Another rather amusing thing about *Sigpress contro Scotland Yard* is the way Zurli hints at the hero's allegedly closet homosexual tendencies. In the credits sequence Zurli has Martin perform somersaults and gym exercises on the beach, by way of a hidden trampoline, wearing only a pair of leopard shorts. This is more than campy—it's best classified under "beefcake." Even though adoring girls surround him, Sigpress looks rather indifferently at their charms, and throughout the film he is usually dismissive toward the weaker sex. He even abandons the gorgeous Ingrid Schoeller (wearing just a bathrobe) after she proposed a deal regarding a precious jewel and implying her willingness to have sex with him as part of her reward for giving him precious information. In an early scene, we find Sigpress being massaged by his butler/factotum Pierluigi (Periwinkle in the English prints), played by Klaus Kinski, and warning him not to "annoy" the gardener's niece, daughter … and wife. A revealing dialogue goes like this:

"How long have you been divorced, Pierluigi?"

"Two years, sir"

"And it's two years since you have been exaggerating with girls … don't you think it's time to calm down a bit?"

As the imperturbable butler, Kinski—who appears for no more than five minutes overall, despite being marketed as the lead in the version released on VHS in the States on the Force Video label, misleadingly titled *Psychopath*— makes no mystery that he was in it just for the money, and he looks out-and-out bored. In the final scene we see him lying on a couch, sipping a glass of whisky (J&B, perhaps?) while lazily activating a tape recorder that serves as his master's alibi, and it perfectly sums up Kinski's attitude throughout the film.

Zurli had some amusing anecdotes about working with the notoriously mercurial thespian.

> He showed up on the set driving a Rolls Royce (laughs) and, while he was being made-up, I went and asked him, "Can I borrow your car keys?" He gave me the keys, I took the car and drove away, and he almost had a stroke (laughs). I stopped just behind the corner, 50 yards away, but he thought I had left for who knows where …[2]

Having been warned about Kinski's bad behavior on set, Zurli devised a funny trick in order to keep the actor quiet and follow his acting directions.

> The first day Kinski came on the set— we were shooting at a villa in Frascati—I asked my assistant director Carlo Potenza, "When Klaus shows up, let me know!" After a while Carlo came over and said, "He's coming!" "Really? Okay then, let me know when he's about to enter the room!" "He's climbing the stairs just now!" Then I started acting mad (laughs). Everyone on the set was looking at me, "What happened to this guy?" (laughs) I threw away the script, yelled, kicked the floodlights … (laughs) When Kinski came into the room and saw me like this, he probably thought, "This guy is even more nuts than me, better keep quiet … "[3]

Besides the athletic and likeable Martin and the excellent Paolo Carlini (usually a dramatic actor, here showing first-rate comic skills) in a show-stealing turn as the obtuse Inspector Bennett, the cast features Aldo Canti, aka Nick Jordan of the *Three Supermen* series, in a small comical role as a petty, garishly-dressed South-American criminal named Pedro, who is overly jealous of his hat. Zurli also cast Canti's brother Rosato, here hiding under the alias Tony Candela. The female cast is no less than spectacular. Besides Schoeller, Karin Field (seen also in Radley Metzger's *The Alley Cats*, Antonio Margheriti's *Web of the Spider* and Jess Franco's *The Demons*, among others) and Gloria Paul (in a small role, doing her usual nightclub singer routine), there is a very young and ravishing Orchidea De Santis, who went on to become one of Italy's most fascinating sexy starlets of the 1970s.

The tight budget has Zurli intersperse the few London and Paris exteriors (one such has Martin coming across the "Cameo Moulin" London grind house, playing Kaneto Shindo's *Onibaba*) with such unmistakably Roman locations as the oft-seen Villa Miani (the Greek ship owner's villa) and the Testaccio slaughterhouse used in several mid-1970s Italian Nazi movies, as well as Fernando di Leo's *Mr. Scarface* (1976), and here it serves as a London alley where Sigpress kidnaps Pedro and takes his place. The result is strangely endearing, as when Martin moves from the aforementioned Testaccio location to the outside of a seedy Soho bar and then inside a mind-blowing Cinecittà interior, which looks like a Surrealist rendition of a Middle-East tavern—all this within a handful of shots.

Born in Foiano della Chiana, Tuscany, in 1929, Zurli was a much more capable filmmaker than most of his *oeuvre* might lead one to suspect. He started his directing career in the early 1960s, with *Slave Girls of Sheba* (*Le verdi bandiere di Allah*, 1963), which initially had been offered to Sergio Leone. His following output included the 1966 black com-

Spanish actor George Martin plays the film's hero, Sigpress, usually surrounded by adoring ladies.

The Comic Book Universe in Italian Cinema

Sigpress, seemingly a ladies' man, prefers to relax at home, sipping a cup of tea served by his butler Periwinkle (Klaus Kinski).

edy *È mezzanotte, butta giù il cadavere* (It's Midnight, Throw the Corpse—a wordplay on the Italian phrase "It's noon, throw the pasta"), the Western adventure *Zorro the Fox* (*El Zorro—La volpe*, 1968) and the Dick Randall-produced grotesque horror comedy *The Mad Butcher* (*Lo strangolatore di Vienna*, 1971), starring Victor Buono.

In the early 1970s Zurli moved to Turkey to shoot a thriller for producer Türker Inanoglu (*The Little Eye-Witness*, 1972) and stayed in the country several years to direct more films. He returned to Turkey by the end of the decade, tired of being offered only erotic or porn flicks[4] and helmed a few crime pics such as *Polizia selvaggia* (1977), *Target* (*Bersaglio altezza uomo*, 1979) and *Lo scoiattolo* (1979). In the 1980s he worked as a TV director for RAI, and in the 1990s the directed a few TV movies and a couple of violent adventure films, *Born to be a Warrior* (1995) and *Welcome America* (1997), made in Serbia, starring and produced by a prizefighter named Gidra Stone. Zurli died in 2009.

Notes:
1. Werner Hauff and Zurli are actually credited as co-writers, but according to Zurli their presence was only nominal, due to co-production needs.
2. Grattarola, Franco, "Il dissacratore dei generi. Intervista con Guido Zurli," *Cine 70 e dintorni* #10, 2008, p. 30.
3. *Ibid*, p. 31.
4. Contrary to what most reference books state, Zurli did not actually direct *Black Deep Throat* (*Gola profonda nera*, 1977, signed by "Albert Moore"), which was filmed by his assistant Vito Bruschini and completed by Mario Bianchi. Throughout the shooting Zurli (who had written the script and was slated to direct it) was hospitalized, recovering post-surgery.

Satanik
(*Satanik*)
Italy/Spain, color, 86 minutes
D: Piero Vivarelli. *S:* Eduardo Manzanos Brochero; *DOP:* Silvano Ippoliti; *M:* Manuel Parada [actually Romano Mussolini and Roberto Pregadio]; *E:* Gianmaria Messeri.
Cast: Magda Konopka (Marny Bannister/Satanik), Julio Peña (Inspector Trent), Humi [Umberto] Raho (George Van Donen), Luigi Montini (Dodo La Roche), Armando Calvo (Commissioner Gonzalez), Mimma Ippoliti (Stella Dexter), Isarco Ravaioli (Max Bermuda), Piero Vivarelli (Commissioner Le Duc).
Prod: Rodiacines (Rome), Copercines (Madrid).
The middle-aged, ugly and disfigured Marny Bannister works as an assistant to professor Greeves, a well-known biologist who has

perfected a serum that restores beauty and youth. To get hold of the portentous drug, Marny does not hesitate to kill the professor. After drinking the potion, she turns into a beautiful young woman. The police immediately focus their suspicion on Marny, who seems to have disappeared without a trace. Marny makes the acquaintance of a wealthy jeweler, Van Donen, and the two become lovers. One evening, during a sexual encounter with him, Marny suddenly resumes her previous appearance, since the drug has a limited effect in time. After killing Van Donen, Marny once again regains her beauty, thanks to a new dose of the serum. She then takes on a new identity, that of stripper Stella Dexter, whom she murdered, and hooks up with gangster Dodo La Roche at a strip club in Geneva. However, the police are on her trail, and Dodo finds out about her true identity. Marny escapes both the police and the gangsters, but runs out of the precious drug, thus returning to her ugly old self. Desperately trying to evade capture, she steals a car, but falls to her death in a ravine.

Debuting in December 1964, *Satanik* was the second *fumetto nero* created in a row by Magnus & Bunker. In a way, *Satanik* was even more important than *Kriminal* in the history of Italian comics. By making their evil antihero a woman, Secchi and Raviola broke the ultimate boundary—gender.

As one scholar put it:

> Satanik is alone in a violent and corrupt society, having been rejected by her father and scorned by her sisters because of her deformed face. Unlike the beautiful, good, passive and conformist popular heroines of the *fotoromanzo*, the prey of heroes and villains, Satanik nevertheless transforms herself into a beautiful and sensual woman with a magic potion. She becomes a criminal with neither morals nor sexual inhibitions, and she turns her repressed anger into open revenge.[1]

Furthermore, as it has been noted:

> Despite Satanik's cruelty and the often paradoxical stories […], she is a believable character, frustrated by the unhappiness caused by her loneliness and need for approval: one must not forget, after all, that Marny tries to win the respect and consideration of those who surround her by working hard (she is introduced as a talented university researcher), but she realizes how much her ugly looks prevent her not only from finding a male partner, but also from establishing and being successful

Cover art for the first issue of *Satanik* (December 1964), art by Luigi Corteggi

> at work. Satanik, besides conveying a will for total freedom […], finds herself living a life that pushes the reader to sympathize with her rather than condemn her. In ugliness and in beauty, she is alone […].[2]

Like they did with *Kriminal*, Secchi and Raviola often took inspiration from films and novels. The first issue *La legge del male* (The Law of Evil) perversely drew on a fairytale-like concept. The red-headed Marny, humiliated by her mother and her gorgeous sisters, is very much a revised version of Cinderella, while the serum of beauty she perfects (according to the theories of an alchemist named Masopust) is an update of the Fairy Godmother's magic spell—and similarly loses its effects at the most inopportune moments.

Furthermore, there are references to classic novels such as *The Picture of Dorian Gray* as well as *The Strange Case of Dr. Jekyll and Mr. Hyde*, but the subterranean umbilical cord between *fumetti neri* and genre cinema is also evident throughout. The horrific angle is the perfect counterpart to erotic *frissons* in the adventures of Marny Bannister,

Satanik (aka Marny Bannister) in a panel from *Satanik* #51 (December 1966)

Two panels from *Satanik* #47 (October 1966) demonstrate Magnus' skilled blend of eroticism and the grotesque. Such imagery caused *fumetti neri* a lot of trouble at the time.

who becomes an even more unscrupulous incarnation of duchess Du Grand, the evil man-eater of Riccardo Freda's *I vampiri* (1957), continuously mutating from old hag to ravishing red-haired vixen.

The beautiful Satanik embodies all the qualities of the *belle dame sans merci*. Just like the ravishing but deadly Asa played by Barbara Steele in Mario Bava's *Black Sunday*, Marny embodies the duplicitous nature of seduction. On the surface, she is alluring, irresistible and sports an aggressive sensuality—high cheekbones, upturned nose, a curvaceous body heightened by adhesive outfits—but her beautiful features conceal an ugly truth. It is a clever move on the part of the creators to play on the concept of Catholic guilt, by making their antiheroine such a desirable witch. Readers know well about Satanik's real nature, yet they cannot help but fall victim to her deadly charm, just like the male characters in the stories.

Even more than in *Kriminal*, horror blooms within the family, and outside respectability hides corruption and perversion. *La legge del male* culminates in a family massacre (Marny humiliates one sister, disfigures the other, kills her mother and pushes her father to suicide) that sounded like a loud sneer to the moral majority and the preserved Catholic and family values. No wonder *Satanik* caused a fuss when it first came out.

Similarly to Anthony Logan, Marny's deeds are dictated by a deep feeling of hatred and vengeance against the whole world, and since the story is narrated through her point of view, the male characters inevitably end up looking unsympathetic or just plain despicable, with their hypocrisy openly displayed through their disgusted looks toward the poor ugly woman which become lustful once she has turned into a beautiful lady. It is a striking jibe at a male-dominated society which judges the weaker sex based on appearance alone and one that shows how *Kriminal*'s apparent misogyny was actually part of a much subtler and problematic worldview.

On top of that, this time Secchi's stories ventured into the realm of supernatural horror. Gradually Marny turns into an out-and-out witch with supernatural powers, and faces monsters and vampires. One of her adversaries is a bloodsucker named Wurdalak, very likely a reference to the episode of Mario Bava's *Black Sabbath* (*I tre volti della paura*, 1963). Interestingly, Secchi and Raviola would reprise Wurdalak in a comic way, possibly under the influence of Roman Polanski's *The Fearless Vampire Killers* (1967), in *Alan Ford*.

Magnus' panels for *Satanik* were a highlight, as his Expressionist and almost parodist style allowed him to maintain a moral distance from the lurid, over-the-top stories. The artist would further develop his tendency to the grotesque in his most popular and successful collaboration with Secchi, the spy spoof *Alan Ford*. However, *Satanik*, even more than *Kriminal*, proved a key influence for the next generation of comic artists.³

Although relatively tame by today's standards (there was scarcely a bare breast, but the eroticism that came from Magnus' deliciously long-legged women in suspenders and bra is still irresistible), *Satanik* was yet another punch in the stomach of respectability, as well as a loud, lewd jeer to the superficial times to which it belonged. However, just as had occurred with *Kriminal*, Secchi had to tone down the most anarchic elements of his own comic book. Legend has it that the writer received anonymous phone calls, warning him that he had to stop showing a woman who took such "liberties" with the opposite sex as Marny did.

The difference between *Satanik* and its (scarce) imitators is obvious, as the latter either lacked the over-the-top amorality of the model or its stylistic accomplishment. The first, *Zakimort*, was a pale female version of *Diabolik*—whose sleeve design the comic patently resembled—created by future film director Pier Carpi for the publisher Sansoni. It was about a rich heiress, Fedra, the daughter of a notorious gangster, who moonlighted as a masked vigilante named Zakimort to avenge her father, and cultivated an impossible love for her adversary, police lieutenant Norton. Unlike Satanik, Fedra/Zakimort is a much more conformist antiheroine, starting with the fact that she willingly conducts a dual life, keeping her good and evil side drastically separated. It was miles removed from Satanik's tormented existence based on appearance and temporary yet always changing characters.

Zakimort lasted until 1974, almost as long as its model. Other far less successful female-based *fumetti neri* were *Samantha* (seven issues, from January to July 1966), *Kristine la Superdonna* (seven issues, April to October 1966) and *Masokis* (five issues, March to September 1966). The latter, with its jaw-dropping emphasis on sadomasochism—the eponymous character is a beautiful woman who has a dual sex life and enjoys being tortured by her partners—predated the second wave of adults-only comics, which would focus primarily on sex.⁴

However, after the inevitable seizures (issue #45, *L'isola dei mostri*, published in September 1966, was one of the victims) Bunker too had to stoop to compromises:

> As the author of the scripts, I lived through all those moments when orders and counter-orders overlapped with such speed that it became impossible to remember which was the right one to follow. No revealing négligés, no naked backs, the "No's" were followed by a long list which became thicker and thicker—it took two hours to wade through it!⁵

After the wave of seizures and trials, in 1966 Secchi moved the stories toward traditional crime and mystery, the way he also did with *Kriminal*. Satanik's appearance gradually changed from buxom and provocative to a slim and somehow less enticing teenager. Number 100 (*Il regno del silenzio*, November 1968) even went as far as showing Marny sign a deal with the chief of police and become a peculiar kind of secret agent, a female James Bond of sorts. It was the beginning of the end. *Satanik* closed down in November 1974, with issue #231. Despite Secchi returning to write the stories since issue #149, the series' quality had dropped, especially after Magnus gave up illustrating it in 1970 to focus solely on *Alan Ford*.

Little of the above, however, was to be found in the film adaptation (yet another Italian-Spanish co-production) shot in 1967 by Piero Vivarelli, soon after *Avenger X*, and released in early 1968. Officially scripted by the Spanish co-producer Eduardo Manzanos Brochero, also responsible for *Il marchio di Kriminal*, almost everything is

The Polish-born Magda Konopka was chosen to play the role of Marny Bannister for Piero Vivarelli's film.

The Italian *locandina* for *Satanik*

wrong with *Satanik*—starting with the fact that the character's nickname is not even mentioned once throughout the film.

The opening titles try to convey a comic book feel through the (admittedly crude) use of colored frames arranged as panels, but the effect is soon dissipated once the story sets into motion. Completely eschewing the fascinating fantastic overtones of Bunker's stories, Brochero only keeps Marny Bannister's transformation from old hag (in the comic book, however, she is actually 25) to gorgeous man-eater and drops all the rest. Despite Konopka's greenish-looking, awfully bogus make-up (so carelessly conceived one wonders whether anybody was taking the whole thing seriously), there is still enough material for the viewer to hope for a more promising development. However, things get just worse and worse, as Vivarelli abandons fantastic territory for a depressingly banal story involving a diamond necklace (again!), the heroine's murder of a horny jeweler (Umberto Raho, billed as Humi Raho) and her teaming up with a gang of crooks in Geneva.

Critics lashed out at Vivarelli's inadequate casting of Polish actress Magda Konopka in the lead. Despite her long legs and passing resemblance to Marisa Mell, the ravishing Konopka was not the most gifted actress, and her wooden screen persona fails to convey the explosive, morbid eroticism of the comic book character. What is more, Vivarelli (who pops up as the French Commissioner Le Duc) leaves her with nothing to do except bitch around in sexy outfits—yet the outstanding costume Satanik wore in the comic book is sadly lost—and perform a strip-tease and an enticing nightclub act (shot in slow-motion and easily the film's best bit) while donning a Diabolik-style black hood and costume.

Despite some mild nudity (Konopka's breasts are briefly exposed at the end of said strip act), *Satanik* is ultimately tame and mild to the point of self-sabotage. Not only is it badly scripted and paced (witness the flamenco dancers scene, a totally useless diversion if there was one) but it is so scared of its potentially anarchic content that it proceeds to deny it meticulously as it goes along, nullifying every spark, every idea, every single interesting moment with an indifferent routine approach that is jarringly inept and worthless. Last but not least, the ending is easily one of the most anti-climactic (not to mention stupidly moralistic) ever committed to celluloid.

Despite being moderately successful at the Italian box-office, the result was perhaps the most disappointing of all the flicks based on the *fumetti neri* phenomenon. One wonders what a filmmaker like Umberto Lenzi (who was originally interested in developing it into a movie) would have done with the material, given the fact that during the same period Lenzi was starting a new trend with his erotic, morbid thrillers such as *Paranoia* (*Orgasmo*, 1969).

Despite being credited to Manuel Parada, the music score was actually written by Roberto Pregadio and Romano Mussolini (the Duce's fourth son). The latter also produced (incognito) the picture, a fact that helped shooting in Francisco Franco's Spain. Pupi Avati, who was the assistant director (only for the scenes shot in Italy) and went on to make his film debut that same year with the grotesque *Balsamus l'uomo di Satana* (released in 1970), was so disappointed with his experience on the set that he later claimed that watching Vivarelli direct had taught him how *not* to make a movie.[6]

Vivarelli's film was not the only stab at *Satanik*. Luciano Secchi later revealed in an interview about a projected

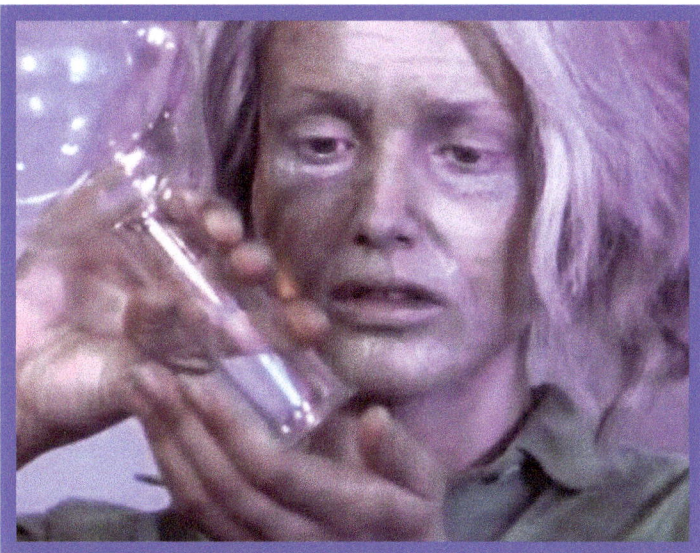

Konopka's awkward make-up as the unattractive Marny Bannister before her transformation

TV series that never took off, even though the unreleased pilot was not bad. Almost 40 years later, the character of Satanik was featured in the amateur short film, *Satanik, il volto del male* (2003, Giacomo Dimarno).

Vivarelli went on to make *The Snake God* (*Il dio serpente*, 1970), an exotic drama with voodoo overtones produced by Alfredo Bini, which was a smash hit at the box-office; its female lead Nadia Cassini became a star in Italy, and Augusto Martelli's musical theme *Djamballà* became immensely popular. Vivarelli's subsequent career as a director was erratic at best; he directed a couple of so-called "Decamerotics" inspired by Pasolini's "Trilogy of Life" (*Il Decamerone nero*, 1972; *Codice d'amore orientale*, 1974), but his most ambitious effort, *Nella misura in cui …* (1979), an ironically autobiographical reflection on sex, politics and filmmaking set in the Caribbean, turned out a commercial flop. In the late '80s Vivarelli also directed porn star Moana Pozzi in *Provocazione* (1988), an erotic (but not hardcore) flick very loosely based on Arthur Machen's *The Novel of the White Powder*. His last film was *La Rumbera* (1998), yet another exotic comedy/drama set in Cuba. He died in 2010.

Satanik is available on DVD in the U.S. on the Retro Media label and also is part of Image Entertainment's "Euro Fiends from Beyond the Grave" triple feature disc (with *The Faceless Monster* and *The Red Headed Corpse*).

Notes:
1. Manai, Franco, "Satanik," in Moliterno, Gino, ed., *Encyclopedia of Contemporary Italian Culture*, 2003 (London: Routledge, 2003), p. 528.
2. Zanatta, Sara, Zaghini, Samanta and Guzzetta, Eleonora, *Le donne nel fumetto: l'altra metà dei comics italiani. Temi, autrici, personaggi al femminile* (Latina: Tunué, 2009), p. 99.
3. As Filippo Scòzzari, the co-founder of the cult magazine *Frigidaire*, recalled: "I cannot help but consider Magnus [Raviola] a luminous figure. […] The early *Kriminal* and *Satanik* stories were absolutely fantastic because, from an artistic point of view, they represented an innovative and rebellious slant in the context of the worn-out Italian comics scene. They were ribald and belligerent, both in their characters and in the way they proposed themselves to the market. There's no doubt they were satisfying a demand that had grown very strong. […] Magnus was our forefather, a progenitor in front of which I humbly bow down in reverence." Castaldi, *Drawn and Dangerous*, p. 18.
4. Meanwhile, the omnivorous (and decidedly prolific) Secchi and Raviola even approached the spy genre (*Dennis Cobb—Agente SS018*) and space operas (*Gesebel*). Even if these met a decidedly less exciting commercial response, they are noteworthy as they play with genres the way the juiciest B-movies did. *Dennis Cobb* recalls the sauciest spaghetti James Bond imitations, whereas *Gesebel* features Margheriti's Gamma One spaceships as well as interstellar busty Amazons inspired by Forest's *Barbarella*.
5. Federico Mataloni, "Il fumetto nero nell'Italia del Boom (1962-1970)," www.fuorileidee.com.
6. *Balsamus l'uomo di Satana*—a grotesque tale about a dwarf (played by Avati regular Bob Tonelli) who is believed to be a modern-day reincarnation of Cagliostro—featured the uncredited collaboration of Avati's fellow Bolognese citizen Magnus, who drew sketches for the film, depicting *Balsamus'* bizarre characters.

Superargo and the Faceless Giants, aka *Superargo* (*L'invincibile Superman*, aka *Il re dei criminali*, aka *Superargo, el gigante*, aka *Superman el invencible*)

Italy/Spain, color, 102 minutes

D: Paul Maxwell [Paolo Bianchini]. *S and SC:* Julio Buchs; *DOP* Alan Jones [Aldo Greci], Godofredo Pacheco; *M:* Berto Pisano; *E:* Juan Pisón.

Cast: Ken Wood [Giovanni Cianfriglia] (Superargo), Guy Madison (Prof. Wendland Wond), Liz Barrett [Luisa Baratto] (Claire Brand), Diana Lorys (Gloria Devon), Harold Sambrell [Aldo Sambrell] (Kamir/Pao-Ki), Thomas Blank [Tomás Blanco] (J. G. Stafford), Aldo Bufi Landi (Dewey).

Prod: G. V. Cinematografica, Società Europea Cinematografica (Rome), Ízaro Films (Madrid).

Superargo, a masked wrestler-cum-secret service agent gifted with incredible strength, is inquiring about the strange disappearance of several strong athletes. It turns out an army of invincible zombie-like creatures have kidnapped them. Superargo returns to the ring in order to pose as bait and eventually finds out who is the mastermind behind the kidnappings: Professor Wendland Wond, a mad scientist who performs terrible experiments on the victims, turning them into indestructible cyborgs …

Paolo Bianchini's keen eye for the strange and the bizarre makes this, the second in a diptych dedicated to the eponymous wrestler/superhero, less a comic book style diversion than a one-of-a-kind science-fiction/adventure hybrid. Superargo (again played by stuntman Giovanni Cianfriglia, aka Ken Wood) is an Italian version of El Santo who divides his time between the ring and the struggle against crime; his costume definitely brings to mind The Phantom, and so does the introduction of a sidekick (played by the renowned Spanish character actor Aldo Sambrell). His car, on the other hand, is a Jaguar E-Type, the same model owned by Diabolik.

Superargo (Giovanni Cianfriglia) and his sidekick (Aldo Sambrell) examine one of the faceless giants.

Like the first installment *Superargo vs. Diabolicus*, Bianchini's film was an Italian-Spanish co-production, presumably aimed at those markets where Santo films were more popular. Therefore, it is no surprise that *Superargo and the Faceless Giants* opens during a wrestling match, as its predecessor had done. What seems like a useless digression in homage to the audience's tastes quickly sets the plot in motion. A small army of weird zombie soldiers kidnaps the winning athlete. Bianchini later inserts another lengthy wrestling scene, again justified by a vital plot point—something that did not happen often in El Santo films.

Compared with the first chapter, Julio Buchs' script has a decidedly more comic book quality. Invulnerable and mysterious, his face always covered by a black mask—slightly different (and better-looking) than the one in Nick Nostro's *Superargo vs. Diabolicus*—Superargo investigates the disappearance of many athletes. The victims are kidnapped by villainous scientist Wendland Wond (Guy Madison) and turned into cyborgs, devoid of blood, organs and will.[1] They are electrically rechargeable and commanded by a sort of ultrasonic device—the kind of naive prop that would not have been out of place in a 1950s sci-fi flick. It is a rather common theme in science fiction and spy films of the period. See for instance Jess Franco's delightful spy spoof extravaganza *Attack of the Robots* (*Cartes sur table*, 1966), starring Eddie Constantine.

The "faceless giants," as the U.S. title would have it, are indeed impressive. They wear weird helmets with tubes protruding from them and their expressionless features are deformed by the simple trick of having the extras wear a nylon stocking on their faces; the cinematographer films them using extreme low-angle close-ups. The sequence where they attack Superargo within the woods that surround Wond's villa, with dozens of hidden cameras on top of trees filming the struggle, is suitably eerie, ditto for the sight of the cyborgs standing behind a plate of glass in Wond's lab, immersed in a gas that makes them insensitive to pain. A few colored lights can do wonders, sometimes.

Superargo and the Faceless Giants features more weird elements. Superargo's sidekick Kamir is a cross between a butler and a Mystic, who has enhanced his master's psychic qualities by teaching him levitation, transcendental meditation, ESP and telekinesis (which allows for such throwaway dialogue exchanges as "That's a good idea!" "Did you guess it?" "No, I just read inside your mind!"). The mad doctor's underground lab even has a medieval torture chamber inside it, just in case it's needed. Even though the violence quota is light, it is surprising how the hero does not hesitate when it comes to dispatching his opponent in cold blood, by throwing Wond into conveniently nearby quicksand (rendered through a laughably cheap visual trick).

The low-budget is evident throughout, and Bianchini does not spare the zooms, yet the film moves at a brisk pace. Action scenes make ample use of trampolines—a staple in Hong Kong martial arts films and a recurring trick in the *Three Supermen* series. The overall pop quality is underlined by Berto Pisano's score, which bears a passing resemblance to Nelson Riddle's theme for the *Batman* TV series.

As Wond, the film's villain, Guy Madison is a rather offbeat mad doctor, wearing a suit and tie and thick black glasses that make him look more like a university professor.

The impressive Spanish poster for *Superargo and the Faceless Giants*

A former TV Western star in the series *Wild Bill Hickok*, Madison (real name Robert Ozell Moseley, 1922-1996) left Hollywood for Europe where he played the lead in a number of Spaghetti Westerns and adventure films. The ravishing Diana Lorys (a regular presence in such Jess Franco cult epics as *The Awful Dr. Orlof*, *Residencia para espías* and *Nightmares Come At Night*) plays Madison's assistant, while the undistinguished Luisa Baratto is Superargo's love interest. The fact that Madison, Lorys and Baratto all co-starred in Bianchini's previous film, the spy story *The Devil's Man*, suggests that the two movies might have been shot back-to-back.

The end titles announced a third chapter, *Superargo e i giganti senza volto* (thus necessitating a new title for its potential U.S. release!), which was never made, no doubt due to the film's disappointing box-office takings. *Superargo and the Faceless Giants* was submitted to the Italian film censorship in September 1967, nine months after *Superargo vs. Diabolicus*, but was released not until January 1968, when the masked superhero trend was already waning. Bianchini would move on to direct several moderately interesting Spaghetti Westerns, and returned to superhero territory, albeit in a parodic way, with 1979's *SuperAndy, il fratello brutto di Superman*.

Unlike its predecessor, *Superargo and the Faceless Giants* is currently available on home video in the United States in several different editions. Besides Code Red's double feature with *Wacky Taxi*, Apprehensive Films released it on DVD as part of the "Cinema Insomnia" collection—that is, with excerpts from the film interspersed with an annoying comic commentary by a "Mr. Lobo," in the vein of *Mystery Science Theatre 3000*.

Note:
1. Curiously, the basic plot about the disappearance of athletes would be reprised in issue #3 of *Alan Ford*, *Operazione Frankenstein* (Operation Frankenstein), published in July 1969—a mere coincidence?

On the other hand the U.S. one-sheet poster made Superargo look like an action figure toy.

SuperVIP, the fearless hero in Bruno Bozzetto's *The SuperVIPs*

The SuperVIPs, aka *VIP, My Brother Superman* (*VIP, mio fratello superuomo*)
Italy, color, 79 minutes
D: Bruno Bozzetto. *S:* Bruno Bozzetto; *SC:* Bruno Bozzetto, Attilio Giovannini, Guido Manuli; *DOP:* Luciano Marzetti; *M:* Franco Godi (songs by Johnny Gregory); *E:* Luciano Marzetti, Giancarlo Rossi.
Prod: Bruno Bozzetto Film.

Since the dawn of mankind a family of superheroes, the VIPs, have protected the weak and the oppressed. However, due to a genetic defect, the last descendants of the species are two very different brothers. The handsome SuperVIP is a prime specimen—he is invulnerable, incredibly strong and can even fly. On the other hand, the small, myopic and complex-ridden MiniVIP has extremely limited powers—including a pair of underdeveloped and rather ridiculous-looking wings. However, the VIPs team up when MiniVIP ends up on a deserted island where the warped lady tycoon Happy Betty is experimenting on lethal "brain-missiles" which will turn the world population into robot-like consumers. After SuperVIP is taken prisoner, it is up to MiniVIP to save his big brother and foil Happy Betty's plans …

Bruno Bozzetto's second feature cartoon, following the success of his Western spoof *West and Soda* (1965), was an outstanding satire on the age of consumerism, in the form of a humorous take-off on the superhero film. Born in 1938, the Milanese cartoonist soon proved to be a rare bird in Italy's none-too-sparkling world of animation films. Norman McLaren was reportedly very impressed with his first short film, *Tapum! La storia delle armi* (1958), and a couple of years later Bozzetto created one of his most popular characters, Signor Rossi, a middle-aged rather ordinary citizen who became the protagonist of many short films.

If *West and Soda* was quite a feat, being Italy's first animated feature film in 16 years, it was a lucky bet for Bozzetto. Due to technical difficulties, the project took two years to materialize, and when the film came out in theaters, Italy was experiencing the Spaghetti Western fever. *The Super VIPs* was a more ambitious effort, though. As Bozzetto explained its genesis:

> It all started like this … I had completed *West and Soda* and we sold it in the United States—I only found out afterwards they picked the film up for tax reasons, not because they cared about it. […] Probably for the same reason, when shortly after I started *The SuperVIPs*, the Americans, and in particular this Lady Robinson, who was the wife of a Nobel prize winner, got interested in the project. She was the one who followed everything, and she was a real pain in the ass! Every now and then she came over to Milan, and since she had to justify her presence, she felt entitled to talk about the film, and came up with mind-blowing bullshit! Anyway, she made one good observation, related to the fact that initially the picture was centered entirely on MiniVIP, which was a parody of Lee Falk's *The Phantom*. She rightfully pointed out that it was too little for a feature film … and so SuperVIP was born.[1]

Bozzetto's winning idea was to turn the superhero into an ordinary figure. If Peter Parker's motto was: "With great power comes great responsibility," MiniVIP—the weakest superhero in the universe, in the director's own words—has even greater problems. Looking like a masked early incarnation of Woody Allen's unlikely bespectacled antiheroes[2], MiniVIP is overwhelmed by his responsibilities even though his powers are laughable. He is incapable of coming up to others' expectations; he epitomizes the modern ordinary man, stressed and strained and unable to find his way in a society where beauty and appearance are vital, and where the weaker and most vulnerable are marginalized.

For a cartoon, *The SuperVIPs* is extremely sharp and thought provoking in its political commentary. The sequence in which a scientist explains the characters of today's "automated life" is a meditation of sorts on the ideas divulged by philosopher Herbert Marcuse in his 1964 book *One-Dimensional Man*, expressed in a grimly funny way. Modern men are seen as automatons, whose only connection with residual functions are the right hand (to eat and use remote-controls), right foot (to push the accelerator), the eyes (to watch TV, even though "Intellectuals also use them to read book *covers*") and the mouth, "mainly for smiling and smoking," as Bozzetto has his character say, adding:

> Those who use it for speaking become politicians. Those who don't use it at all become subtle humorists.

The SuperVIPs may not be subtle, but it is nevertheless incredibly entertaining, and definitely not intended solely for children.

Bozzetto's main targets are consumerism and the manipulation of consensus on the part of capitalism. The villain is a supermarket tycoon named Happy Betty (predating *Futurama*'s Mom), whose aim is not to conquer the world but to create the perfect customers through "brain-missiles" that penetrate into people's heads, affecting and conditioning their will—a paradoxical representation of the psychological mechanics in advertising. As the consumer/slaves proclaim in a funny yet chilling musical number, "We are those who represent progress/we don't mind being fools nonetheless."

Another outstanding invention are Happy Betty's slave employees, modeled after Willy Wonka's Oompa-Loompas and portrayed as Asian types who are exploited in a way that makes Charlie Chaplin's factory worker in *Modern Times* (1936) look relaxed. They are given limited time for eating, going to the bathroom (if they stay too long they will most likely be reduced to ashes by a ray-gun), resting (they are put to sleep by a bang on the head and awakened 15 minutes later) and are provided with hilarious surrogates for holidays and sex—all this, as Happy Betty underlines, at the expense of a reasonable quota of their salary.

Bozzetto's not quite politically correct portrayal of said slaves had his U.S. financers make objections.

> Since the Japanese slaves were all yellow, Lady Robinson was not happy with that because she said the film couldn't be sold in Japan—so she wanted us to make them green. There were two tanned characters sunbathing on the boat in the cruise scenes and she said, "No, no, they look like colored people and that's no good!"[3]

Besides its political, satirical and sociological undertones, *The SuperVIPs* is a joy to watch. Despite the apparent simple animation style, the attention to detail is painstaking, and Bozzetto's inventions are often extraordinary examples of creativity on a tight budget. An undisputed influence on Brad Bird's much-acclaimed *The Incredibles* (2004), *The SuperVIPs* was one of Italy's best-known and most successful cartoons. It also appeared in comic book form in the magazine *Il Giorno dei Ragazzi*.

However, it took eight years for Bozzetto to helm his third cartoon feature film, the extraordinary *Allegro non troppo* (1976), inspired by Disney's classic *Fantasia*, which mixed animation and live-action. Over the years Bozzetto has been awarded many prizes, among which the Golden Bear for the short *Mister Tao* at the Berlin Film Festival in 1990, while in 1991 his animated short *Grasshoppers* received an Academy Award nomination. In 1987 he directed his only live-action feature film, *Sotto il ristorante cinese*.

In 2007 Bruno Bozzetto released the 3D short *PsicoVIP* which reprised the characters of his 1968 film and became a TV series.

The Comic Book Universe in Italian Cinema

In 2007 Bozzetto created *PsicoVIP*, a short 3-D film (only four minutes long) which reprises the characters of MiniVIP and SuperVIP. The former has ended up with an inferiority complex toward his brother and is now undergoing analysis from an incompetent, dishonest shrink named Doc who does not help him in any way (but in the end demands an 80-euro fee for his services). *PsicoVIP* gave way to a TV series (26 episodes, four minutes each) released to DVD in Italy.

The SuperVIPs is available on DVD in the United States on the DigiView Entertainment label, under the title *VIP, My Brother Superman*.

Notes:
1. Azzano, Enrico and Meale, Raffaele, "Intervista a Bruno Bozzetto," www.quinlan.it, April 2014.
2. Oreste Lionello, who later became Woody Allen's Italian dubber, provided the voice for MiniVIP.
3. Azzano and Meale, "Intervista a Bruno Bozzetto."

3 Supermen a Tokyo, aka *Drei tolle Kerle*
Italy/West Germany, color, 100 minutes
D: Bitto [Adalberto] Albertini. *S:* Mario Amendola; *SC:* Mario Amendola, Bitto Albertini, Evroni Ebert; *DOP:* Umberto Grassia; *M:* Ruggero Cini; *E:* Vincenzo Vanni.

Cast: George Martin [Francisco Martínez Celeiro] (Lieutenant Martin), Dick Gordon [Salvatore Borgese] (Dick), Willy Newcomb [Willy Colombini] (Willy), Gloria Paul (Gloria), Lisabeth Wu (Yamita), Mino Doro (Jacob Ferré), Attilio Severini (Henchmen Chief).

Prod: Cinesecolo-I.N.D.I.E.F. (Rome), Terra-Filmkunst (Munich).

Trusted with the task of locating a compromising film about a British authority that may cause a scandal, agent Martin of the F.B.I. teams up with Dick and Willy, two skilled acrobat thieves who perform their routine in a costume. The three move from Hong Kong to Tokyo, where they overcome great difficulties and dangers, and they avoid death thanks to their bulletproof vests. With the help of a Japanese scientist who has built a machine capable of miniaturizing things, Dick is subjected to the test, and, in his miniaturized state, is able to locate the film's whereabouts. However, it all turns out to be a stratagem on the part of their opponents, who are in London and ready to expose the film to the press. The three supermen then use again the miniaturizing machine to avert the scandal …

The first in a long series of follow-ups to *The Three Fantastic Supermen*, Bitto Albertini's *3 Supermen a Tokyo*[1] punctuates the action with comic interludes more so than before, including huge, spectacularly choreographed fistfights—a formula that would be perfected in the Western comedies starring Bud Spencer and Terence Hill, such as the *Trinità* films—and classic slapstick gags like the mandatory Keystone Kops-style car chases.

The exotic locations are little more than an excuse to pad out the running-time with the expected travelogue footage, while the simple, basic humor sometimes recalls Franco & Ciccio comedies. Such as a scene has the superheroes treated to dinner in a Japanese restaurant, whose menu lists such dishes as "dog stew," and they have predictable difficulties in using the chopsticks. Silly as it may have been, though, the sight of three grown men in red costumes running around and behaving like three-year-old kids on the streets of Tokyo was met with utter indifference by the Japanese passers-by during the shooting of the aforementioned car chase sequence, much to the director's surprise, even though the scene was filmed using hidden cameras in order to capture the crowd's reaction[2].

The fantastic angle is still present in *3 Supermen a Tokyo*, in the form of a miniaturizing device that takes the place of the earlier film's duplicating machine. The three buffoons are reduced to Lilliputian dimensions so that they can steal a compromising film, which provides the McGuffin around which the plot revolves. There is also a charming Asian villainess who kills people with her kisses, by way of a lethal lipstick—a trick that looks like it could have come straight out of any number of stereotypical Fu Manchu films.

Although Albertini was a less accomplished filmmaker than Parolini, he does a competent job on the whole, even though the budget was allegedly too scant to allow for elaborate set-pieces. Overall, the film's best scene may be the one in which the Lilliputian Sal Borgese sneaks into a room and climbs a table. Albertini makes good use of his floor-level camera with a POV scene of the miniaturized hero, and he shows Borgese amid oversized props such as books, matches, ashtrays and table clocks (echoes of *The Devil-Doll*, *Dr. Cyclops* and *The Incredible Shrinking Man* here). Another effective moment is the funhouse sequence, which has Albertini employ all the tricks in the book, including an array of colored lights as our heroes confront a bunch of gangsters among skeletons, grim reapers and assorted horrific apparitions.

3 Supermen a Tokyo did not feature any of the original cast members, save for the beautiful singer/showgirl Gloria Paul. Spanish actor George Martin, who took over Brad Harris' role in the first film, was a regular presence in Euro Westerns. He would return in several subsequent installments. Stuntman Sal Borgese steals the film as the idiot of the trio, even popping up in drag as a Geisha in one scene—an occurrence that would become a staple in the following *Three Supermen* films. Borgese would become the series' longest-lasting member, co-starring in five more entries (including the final episode, 1986's *Three Supermen in S. Domingo*). On the other hand, *3 Supermen a Tokyo* marked Willy Colombini's only appearance in the series. The following year Colombini (who had debuted in Pietro Fran-

The three supermen in action ... We can almost hear the mad cackling as their bulletproof vests defy bullets.

cisci's *Hercules*, 1958) played his most popular role among film buffs, the beatnik-hippy painter Arcibaldo Spadafora in the bawdy comedy, *Let It All Hang Out*, aka *The Man with the Golden Brush* (*Der Mann mit dem goldenen Pinsel*, 1969, Franz Marischka), alongside Edwige Fenech.

Notes:
1. The title is often misspelled as *3 supermen in Tokio*, even on the Italian DVD sleeve.
2. Albertini, *Tra un ciak e l'altro*, p. 136.

1969

Ms. Stiletto

(*Isabella, duchessa dei diavoli*, aka *Isabella - Mit blanker Brust und spitzem Degen*)
Italy/West Germany, color, 93 minutes
D: Bruno Corbucci. *S and SC:* Giorgio Cavedon, Mario Amendola, Elisabeth Forster; *DOP:* Fausto Zuccoli; *M:* Sante Romitelli; *E:* Luciano Anconetani.
Cast: Brigitte Skay [Brigitte Johanna Riedle] (Isabella De Frissac), Mimmo Palmara (Baron Eric Von Nutter), Fred Williams (Gilbert De Villancourt), Elina De Witt (Marguerite Fontaine), Mario Novelli (Mayer), Tino Scotti (Malicour), Sal Borgese (Diego), Lucia Modugno (Fabienne).

Prod: Cinesecolo/I.N.D.I.E.F. (Rome), Hape-Film (Munich).

Isabella is the only survivor of the noble De Frissac family, whose members were all slaughtered by an Alsatian adventurer, Baron Von Nutter, who has taken over all their properties. Raised by a tribe of Gypsies, Isabella eventually becomes aware of her origins. Von Nutter repeatedly has his men try to dispatch her, but to no avail. Determined to take revenge and regain possession of her wealth, Isabella penetrates Von Nutter's castle where she attacks the usurper and disfigures him, cutting off his nose and one ear. Forced to hide his scarred face behind a leather mask, Von Nutter manages to take Isabella prisoner. Just before he can exact his revenge, he is captured and sentenced to death. However, Von Nutter eventually escapes ...

Four year after the *fumetti neri* revolution, the masked villains were already losing their impact on the audience, mainly due to the wave of magazine seizures and controversy, which caused their authors to tone down the sexual and violent content. It was time for a turn of the screw.

The apt move came from a small Milanese publisher, Edizioni Sessantasei. The founder Renzo Barbieri and his co-manager Giorgio Cavedon decided to get rid of the mystery and *giallo* elements and push further the erotic content. Nudity was quickly catching on, despite the censors, and there was a feeling that times were definitely changing. The younger generations were becoming wilder and wilder to the eyes of their parents, their hair was get-

The French pressbook for Bruno Corbucci's *Ms. Stiletto* (1969), based on the adult comic book *Isabella*

ting longer and the skirts were getting shorter. Barbieri—a former reporter for the newspaper "La Notte"— and Cavedon were the right men at the right place and time.

In April 1966 Edizioni Sessantasei published two new comics, *Goldrake* (also known as *Goldrake Playboy*) and *Isabella*. *Goldrake* was a Venetian C.I.A. agent modeled after James Bond. He had the features of the French actor Jean-Paul Belmondo and a name that recalled both gold and Sir Francis Drake, the pirate—not forgetting Goldfinger, of course. His sidekick was a ravishing spy who looked just like Ursula Andress.

The prime inspiration for *Isabella* was once again the *feuilletons*, the popular serial novels of the 18th century. Another obvious inspiration was the saucy swashbuckling melodrama scenarios of Bernard Borderie's *Angelica* series … with the addition of a conspicuous amount of sex and sadism, according to the lesson of the Marquis de Sade. Barbieri created the character, Cavedon wrote the stories, and artist Sandro Angiolini brought them to life with his pencil and ink. Although pretty tame in its erotic content by today's standards, barely showing a nipple now and then, in 1966 *Isabella* (nicknamed "The Duchess of Devils") became a phenomenon of sorts. As Italy's first openly erotic comic strip, it paved the way for a number of similar magazines starring virginal and desirable *ingénues* who were ready to drop their clothes whenever possible.

A film adaptation was in the air, and as soon as the barriers of censorship collapsed, it finally materialized in 1969. "Soixanteneuf année érotique," as sung by Serge Gainsbourg and Jane Birkin on the 7" single of the same name (which was seized because of obscenity laws in Italy), was the year that marked a leap in the representation of sexuality on the screen and in the media. 1969 saw the release of many genre films that were blatantly oriented toward eroticism, while *auteurs* such as Fellini and Visconti displayed a more problematic approach toward the subject matter within the historical frescos of *Fellini—Satyricon* and *The Damned*. As film critic Callisto Cosulich noted:

> The sexualization of film is nothing but an aspect of the sexualization of mores, which in turn is strictly connected with the gradual emergence of the society of well being.[1]

This was evident when looking at other media. The first issue of the photonovel *Cinesex* came out, which displayed complete films in photonovel form (the first being Fernando di Leo's *A Woman on Fire/Brucia ragazzo, brucia*, 1969)

The French book tie-in ad for *Ms. Stiletto*

and—as the title suggested—gave ample room to the erotic interludes.

It was up to Bruno Corbucci, Sergio's younger (and less gifted) brother, to bring *Isabella* to the big screen. Despite being a rather nondescript filmmaker, with *Isabella, duchessa dei diavoli* (titled *Ms. Stiletto* on its home video release in the U.S. in the mid-1980s) Corbucci helmed one of his better pictures. In the movie, he makes clever use of comic book wide-angle shots and forced perspectives (such as in the prologue, where Isabella watches as her parents are brutally killed), and the script offers plenty of humorous dialogue. Whether they have the characters deliver such over-the-top lines as, "Your eyes are like two pools of pure limpid water, sometimes I wish I could jump in," or "You are a creature born to be loved and make men happy"—the scriptwriters (Cavedon plus Corbucci's regular writing partner Mario Amendola) never take their tongues out of their cheek.

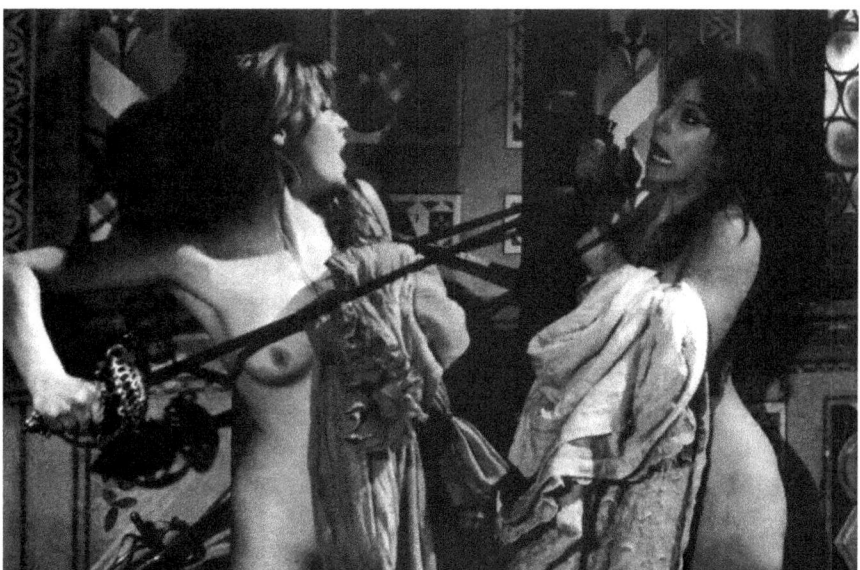

Fabienne's (Lucia Modugno) attempted seduction turns into a deadly peril for Isabella (Brigitte Skay) in *Ms. Stiletto*.

Even though Brigitte Skay makes for a pleasing but not particularly charismatic presence as Isabella, her interplay with the other cast members allows for at least one memorably erotic sequence in which the heroine barely escapes the attentions of a woman (Lucia Modugno) whose attempts at a lesbian seduction conceal a homicidal purpose. Corbucci perfectly captured the spirit of Cavedon's comic book in the scene where Von Nutter has one of his female lovers try and arouse a muscle-bound black servant in front of all his guests, causing bets on whether she will succeed or not. The woman caresses and teases the imperturbable naked man while the diners are ogling the scene, voraciously feeding on chicken legs.

As Von Nutter, Mimmo Palmara is a suitably evil villain, sadistic and ruthless: "I'd gladly keep you as a plaything, but I fear you must join your husband," he sneers before murdering Isabella's mother in cold blood. After being horribly disfigured by the heroine, Von Nutter wears a leather mask that makes him look like some sort of *fumetti neri* villain—another hint at how the erotic comics of the mid-to-late sixties were following a similar path as their predecessors. On the other hand, Salvatore Borgese, in a supporting role as a knife-throwing Gypsy, recklessly performs somersaults and stunts in almost every scene he is in, as if he just stepped out of one of the *Three Supermen* films. The parade of female beauties is impressive, but the cast also includes Jess Franco regular Fred Williams (as Isabella's beau) and veteran character actor Tino Scotti, who would work with Federico Fellini on *The Clowns* (1970). Too bad that at the time of this writing the film is available in the United States only in the form of an old and badly cropped VHS, on the Force Video label, sold at a very high price among collectors.

Skay (born in 1940 in Mannheim, West Germany) enjoyed short-lived popularity as a sexy starlet by the decades' end. She had a brief but memorable role in Mario Bava's *A Bay of Blood* (*Ecologia del delitto/Reazione a catena*, 1971) and was in another Bava film, the less successful *Four Times That Night* (shot in 1969 but released in Italy in 1972 after being initially banned by the Board of Censors), but within five years she would appear in such dreck as Luigi Batzella's *Blackmail* (*Lo strano ricatto di una ragazza perbene*, 1974) and *The Beast in Heat* (*La bestia in calore*, 1977) before retiring.

Born in 1930, Cavedon, who would later create other popular erotic comics such as *Lucifera* and *Zordon*, before parting ways with Barbieri in 1972, also wrote six novels inspired by *Isabella*, which came out in the series *Isabella—Le memorie* (Isabella—The Memoirs) and emphasized the comic's erotic content. An eclectic personality as well as an accomplished jazz musician, Cavedon also tried his hand at filmmaking, with the little-seen ghost story *Ombre* (1980), which he scripted and co-directed with Mario Caiano, starring Lou Castel. Cavedon died in 2001.

Note:
1. Cosulich, Callisto, *La scalata al sesso* (Milan: Immordino, 1969), p. 187.

Zenabel

Italy/France, color, 90 minutes

D: Ruggero Deodato. *S:* Antonio Racioppi, Gino Capone; *SC:* Antonio Racioppi, Gino Capone, Ruggero Deodato; *DOP:* Roberto Reale; *M:* Bruno Nicolai; *E:* Antonietta Zita.

Cast: Lucretia Love (Zenabel), Lionel Stander (Pancrazio), Mauro Parenti (Gennaro), John Ireland (Don Alonso Imolne), Fiorenzo Fiorentini (Cecco), Nassir Cortbawi, Cristine Davray.

Prod: I.C.A.R. (Rome), Gemini Pictures International (Rome), Pierson Production (Paris).

In 1627 the young Zenabel learns that she is the daughter of a Duke who was ousted and killed by the Spanish Baron Imolne. A defiant fighter, always ready to challenge the alleged superiority of men, Zenabel gathers a small army of women and leads them against Imolne, determined to exact revenge. During the annual "Festival of the Virgins," Zenabel sneaks among the girls that the Baron offers as solace to his guests, releases them and takes the fugitives to the mountains. There she meets a bandit called Gennaro, who joins her in the fight against Imolne. However, when she recklessly sneaks all alone again into the Baron's castle, Zenabel is taken prisoner and sentenced to death. On the same day of the execution, however, Gennaro rescues her. Zenabel unleashes her women against Imolne's Spanish guards and, with the help of a whimsical inventor, manages to defeat them. The Baron is reduced to powerlessness, and Zenabel regains the rulership of the duchy. Eventually, though, she renounces it to marry Gennaro.

The German DVD cover art for Ruggero Deodato's *Zenabel* (1969)

After the Western comedy spoof *I quattro del pater noster* (1969), Ruggero Deodato teamed up again with producer-cum-actor (well, sort of) Mauro Parenti for yet another stab at the world of Italian comic books. As with *Phenomenal and the Treasure of Tutankamen*, however, the resulting film was not directly based on a comic book. Still, the inspiration was blatant. Whereas the previous effort flirted with the *fumetti neri* phenomenon, by providing audiences with a black-dressed thief who openly recalled *Diabolik*, *Zenabel*—presented with the subtitle *Davanti a lei tremavano tutti gli uomini* (All men trembled before her)—was a shameless rip-off of Giorgio Cavedon's saucy adults-only period adventure *Isabella*, which was being adapted to the screen that same year by Bruno Corbucci, as *Ms. Stiletto*. The plot was basically the same: a beautiful young girl discovers that she is actually a Duchess, deprived of her title and wealth by an evil opponent, and fights to regain her status.

Compared with Corbucci's film, *Zenabel* is definitely more of a comedy, filled to the brim with humorous episodes and caricatures, and plays its revenge story in an amiably picaresque manner. Deodato's 17th century (benefitting from stunning locations such as Bracciano's castle and the village of Tuscania) is colorful and picturesque, populated by dwarves, flamboyant gay types, sex-hungry dirty old men (an amusing performance by Lionel Stander) … and stunning young ladies who seem just too anxious to take their clothes off.

The opening sequence sets the tone, as several girls are taking a bath in an idyllic country setting, near a waterfall (the Monte Gelato fall, a recurrent sight in so many Italian movies of the period). Deodato films the scene in slow motion, with plenty of wide-angle shots, accompanied by Bruno Nicolai's alluring score (this time the roles reversed, as Ennio Morricone merely conducted it). Not only does the scene convey a sense of beauty, it also predates the joyously erotic atmosphere of so many "Decamerotics."

What is more, *Zenabel* is even closer to the atmosphere and feel of a *fumetto* than Corbucci's film had been. Deodato came up with every trick in the book to convey a sense of comic panels coming to life. This is particularly evident in the flashback that shows the slaying of Zenabel's family, perpetrated by the evil Baron Imolne (John Ireland), which Deodato filmed as if it was a silent one-reel comedy, red-tinted, with comically speeded-up shots and actors "talking" through balloons, while Nicolai's score plays like a Benny Hill-style march.

Another interesting element is the political content of the film. Zenabel is one step ahead of Isabella, as she is openly portrayed like a proto-feminist leader, who is well aware of the injustice and the abuse her gender is suffering and is thoroughly convinced of women's superiority above men. She wants to affirm "Women's freedom and independence," and claims that, "Women won't have to obey men and submit to their whims." Her motto is, "The way we want or without us!"

As Deodato recalled:

> The script was by Gino Capone, perhaps it was his very first one, and it was delightful. I really put my heart and soul into *Zenabel*, but the film was affected by the lack of a popular lead actress.[1]

Watching the film, it is hard to believe that the Texas-born Lucretia Love (Parenti's wife at that time) never did rise to stardom in Italy. A stunning-looking blonde with magnetic eyes and a breathtaking figure who had made her debut in the mid-'60s in the spy flick *Da Istanbul ordine di uccidere* (1965, Carlo Ferrero), Love was also a better actress than many of the sexy starlets that populated Italian cinema of the period—a quality she did not have many chances to prove, one exception being Luigi Vanzi's grim period crime film *1931: Once Upon a Time in New York* (*Piazza pulita*, 1973) where she played alongside Tony Anthony and Adolfo Celi.

Love's career was erratic; she appeared among others in the undistinguished *giallo The Devil Has 7 Faces* (*Il diavolo a sette facce*, 1971, Osvaldo Civirani), the trashy women-as-gladiators flick *The Arena* (1973, Steve Carver), the atmospheric Gothic *giallo The Killer Reserved Nine Seats* (*L'assassino ha riservato nove poltrone*, 1974, Giuseppe Bennati), the *Exorcist* rip-off *The Eerie Midnight Horror Show* (*L'ossessa*, 1976, Mario Gariazzo) and the ghost story *A Whisper in the Dark* (*Un sussurro nel buio*, 1976, Marcello Aliprandi), usually in supporting roles. Her last film appearance was in Charles B. Griffith's dreadful horror comedy *Dr. Heckyl and Mr. Hype* (1980).

As for the rest of the cast, Parenti once again demanded a role for himself, that of the Neapolitan bandit Gennaro—this time, luckily, not assuming center-stage, given the abundance of lovely ladies surrounding him. As the evil Baron Alfonso Imolde, John Ireland provided the requisite villain. Deodato recalled:

Lucretia Love, producer Mauro Parenti's wife, as the heroine in *Zenabel*

> There was a very funny episode concerning Ireland … We had prepared a stake in Tuscania's main square, for the scene in which Lucretia Love is about to be burnt alive. Everything was ready: the extras, the horses, and Lucretia already tied at the stake. Only John Ireland was missing. Why was John Ireland missing? Because he was still at the Hilton Hotel in Rome, waiting for his check. Since the producer had not paid him yet, he decided he would not show up on the set until he got the check. I had to shoot in a hurry; I was running out of time and I had about 400 people on the set. Meanwhile, Lucretia—tied to the stake, ready to shoot—was yelling at me: "Ruggeroooo! What is happening, Ruggero? Why aren't we shooting?" "We're waiting for John Ireland!" "And what am I doing here, all tied up?" and she yelled, and yelled … Eventually, it was 12 o'clock, John Ireland showed

up. I placed the camera at a distance for a long shot, and all Ireland had to do was to give the signal for the stake to be set on fire. Everything was ready, but he did not give the signal.

Since I was standing quite far from him, I couldn't understand what was going on, so I sent the two dialogue coaches to check out what the problem was. Ten … minutes passed, and they were still talking without anything happening … meanwhile, Lucretia had started yelling again. So I came over and asked what was it all about. Mickey Knox, one of the dialogue coaches, told me that John belonged to the American school of acting, and in order to play a scene, he needed to know what his character was thinking. Keep in mind that he only had to make a gesture with his hand! Then I really got pissed off—and Lucretia was still yelling. So I turned back, noticed a dwarf among the extras, grabbed him and put him in Ireland's hands, telling him: "Well, now you are going to give the signal while holding this dwarf in your arms like a baby!" He stood there, open-mouthed, and told me, "Wow, Ruggero … Great idea!" … and from then on he played all his scenes in the film holding that dwarf![2]

According to Deodato, Stander too always wanted to be holding someone … mainly young girls.

> As soon as Lionel finished a scene he sat down claiming he was feeling hot and didn't want to go on shooting. But since he was crazy about girls and there were so many and often scantily dressed, as soon as I finished a take I sent one to him, to flirt with Lionel a bit. He was so happy that he calmed down, and I placed the camera for the next scene and we moved on …[3]

Zenabel was a commercial disaster in Italy. It was released in the same week as the notorious bombing at Piazza Fontana in Milan, in December 1969. People were scared to go out and theaters were empty. However, the film provided Deodato with a working opportunity for the next few years. An advertising production company in Milan, Gamma Film, noticed the scene of the "Festival of Virgins," in which naked girls are running through the woods, backlit and in slow motion and soon Deodato started making "Caroselli," short Italian advertising films which were immensely popular in the country. The 10-minute "Carosello" broadcast in the evening slot at about nine o'clock gathered an audience of adults and children alike.

Deodato kept working in advertising for the next few years. His next film was *Wave of Lust* (*Ondata di piacere*, 1975), starring his then-wife Silvia Dionisio and John Steiner. Then came the violent crime flick *Live Like a Cop, Die Like a Man* (*Uomini si nasce poliziotti si muore*, 1976) and the grim adventure film *Last Cannibal World* (*Ultimo mondo cannibale*, 1977). It was time for Deodato to sow the seeds that in a few years would earn him the nickname "Monsieur Cannibal," after the release of the shocking jungle epic *Cannibal Holocaust* (1980).

Poor Lucretia was filming on set while star John Ireland was back at the Hilton Hotel awaiting his check.

Notes:
1. Gomarasca, Manlio, "Zenabel," in Gomarasca, "Monsieur Cannibal," p. 21.
2. *Ibid.*, p. 20.
3. *Ibid.*, p. 21.

1970

Three Supermen in the Jungle
(*Che fanno i nostri supermen tra le vergini della jungla?*, aka *Los 3 supermen en la selva*)

Italy/Spain, color, 95 minutes

D: Bitto Albertini. S: Mario Amendola; S: Mario Amendola, Santiago Moncada; DOP: Santiago Crespo; M: Sante Maria Romitelli; E: Luciano Anconetani.

Cast: George Martin [Francisco Martínez Celeiro] (Martin), Sal Borges [Salvatore Borgese] (Dick), Brad Harris (Captain Scott McCall), Femi Benussi (Jungla), Alan Parker [Pasquale Simeoni] (Klaus Krunsky), Francisco Braña (Zumakov).

Prod: Cinesecolo (Rome), Pan Latina Films (Madrid).

On the day of his marriage, Captain Scott McCall of the F.B.I. is sent on a mission to a Uranium mine in central Africa. He must arrive there before a Russian expedition that is already on the way. Scott releases his two friends, thieves Dick and Martin, who had been imprisoned by an Indian sheik, and together they reach Africa. After a victorious battle with the Russians, the three supermen encounter an all-female tribe of wild white women who offer their help. Scott and his friends refuse but then are taken prisoner by the tribeswomen as their queen intends to marry Scott, with whom she is in love. The heroes manage to escape, and after further adventures they get to the mine just in time to beat the Russians. But it is not over yet, as Dick and Martin try to sell the property to the Chinese ...

The third entry in the *Three Supermen* series marked the return of Brad Harris, costar of the first episode, alongside George Martin (who here turns from F.B.I. agent to thief, in a role switch from *3 Supermen a Tokyo*) and Sal Borgese. The plot, about a valuable Uranium deposit which the Supermen must get hold of before the Russians (who wear fur hats, eat caviar and are always ready to burst into a Kozachok dance) do, almost turns Albertini's film into a predecessor of John Landis' *Spies Like Us* (1986).

The sci-fi angle is pretty lame, being confined to a scene in which Harris drives a powerful drilling vehicle and digs an underground tunnel in order to release his friends, and the humor is as puerile as ever, relying heavily on the expected acrobatic fistfights. As in the previous episode, Albertini does not spare us the sight of the three supermen laughing and making faces in their bulletproof costumes as their adversaries vainly attempt to dispatch them via machine-guns.

The Italian DVD cover art for *Three Supermen in the Jungle* (1970)

However, the most noteworthy thing about *Three Supermen in the Jungle* is the way the script blends the superhero theme with the contemporaneous exotic jungle subgenre. Despite the show-stealing presence of Femi Benussi, who just stepped out of *Tarzana the Wild Girl* (*Tarzana sesso selvaggio*, 1970) and here wanders about in a breathtaking leopard bikini as the "Queen of the jungle," the erotic factor is really mild and does not go beyond the sight of several scantily-clad girls and a tepid catfight. The suggestive Italian title, which translates as, "What are our supermen doing among the virgins of the jungle?" makes the film sound like a sex romp, which it definitely is not. Funnily enough, the Italian tagline hailed it as, "Worthy of Walt Disney," replete with the Disney logo ... a bitter irony, considering that in his late years Martinenghi would be held in judgment in a case involving video piracy of Disney films (see the entry for *Three Supermen in S. Domingo*).

Racial stereotypes revisited in a farcical key abound, such as the cannibal tribe which the trio stumbles upon, whose chief speaks a mixture of Southern Italian dialects. As for the African setting, it is represented by stock footage of assorted wildlife, interspersed with counter-shots of the actors filmed at the Rio Alberche in Aldea del Fresno, near Madrid, due to the film being an Italian-Spanish co-production.

Sal Borgese (billed as "Sal Borges" in the U.S. prints), as the mute of the trio, even gets to utter real words instead of mumblings, courtesy of a local wizard, and acts over-the-top from beginning to end, in a non-stop collection of cartoonish grimaces.

The series was revived in 1973 with two titles, *The 3 Supermen in the West* and *Supermen Against the Orient*.

1973

Baba Yaga, aka *Baba Yaga, Devil Witch*, aka *Kiss Me, Kill Me*

(*Baba Yaga*)

Italy/France 1973, color, 90 minutes

D: Corrado Farina. *S*: based on the comic *Valentina* by Guido Crepax; *SC*: Corrado Farina; *DOP*: Aiace Parolin; *M*: Piero Umiliani; *E*: Giulio Berruti.

Cast: Carroll Baker (Baba Yaga), Isabelle De Funès (Valentina Rosselli), George Eastman [Luigi Montefiori] (Arno Treves), Ely Galleani (Annette), Daniela Balzaretti (Romina), Angela Covello (Toni), Corrado Farina (Carabiniere/Nazi General/Prussian General), Franco Battiato (Man in white in the cemetery), Michele Mirabella (Man in white in commercial), Guido Crepax (White car driver).

Prod: 14 Luglio Cinematografica (Italy), Productions Simone Allouche (Paris)

In Milan fashion photographer Valentina Rosselli is almost run over by a car driven by a quirky middle-aged lady, Baba Yaga, who invites the young woman to her place to photograph a collection of jewelry and antiques. When Valentina shows up, Baba Yaga gives her a strange doll in a S/M outfit. Soon weird erotic nightmares plague Valentina where she is subjected to punishments and tortures. Baba Yaga, who turns out to be a witch, puts her under a spell. The doll, on the other hand, has weird supernatural powers. It kills several of Valentina's friends and then metamorphoses into a young woman, Annette. More mysterious events follow, as Baba Yaga seems to weave a dense network of seduction and death around the photographer, with whom she is morbidly attracted. Just as she is about to fall victim to the sadistic lesbian duo of Baba Yaga and Annette, boyfriend Arno rescues her. Annette goes back to being a doll and Arno shatters it into pieces, while Baba Yaga falls to her death through a hole in the floor. However, it turns out that the house has been uninhabited for years, and no one has ever heard of Baba Yaga ...

If 1962 marked the beginning of the renaissance for Italian popular *fumetti*, the year zero for adult-oriented comics in Italy was 1965, the year magazine *Linus* started its publications. Comics had began to be taken seriously as an art form by Umberto Eco, who—in his seminal essay *Apocalittici e integrati* (Apocalyptic and Integrated, 1964)—began to investigate this type of popular entertainment with tools that were formerly dedicated to "serious" literature, thus taking the stale intellectual Italian world by surprise. But it was *Linus* that made the difference.

By presenting the works of Al Capp (*Li'l Abner*), George Harriman (*Krazy Kat*), Charles Schultz (*Peanuts*) and other renowned comic book authors and artists, together with monographic essays on the history of comics and their most important exponents, *Linus* (the name came from one of Schultz's most memorable characters) was aimed at an audience of literate, intellectual readers. Its formula mixed entertainment, quality and experimentation in its gallery of "graphic literature," as editor-in-chief Giovanni Gandini put it. He was proven right. *Linus* is still being published today—a testament to the quality of the concept behind it.

It was in *Linus* that Guido Crepax's *Valentina* took her first steps. A former graphic designer who had created successful advertising campaigns, Crepax (1933-2003) entered the world of comics in 1963. Valentina appeared for the first time in *Linus* as a secondary character in a science-fiction story about

The Italian poster for Corrado Farina's *Baba Yaga* (1973)

Isabelle de Funès played Valentina. Director Farina had her dress, move and act just like in Crepax's panels.

an art critic, Philip Rembrandt, who moonlighted as a superhero by the name of Neutron.

With her androgynous figure, slightly anorexic body and trademark short bobbed hair inspired by Louise Brooks in G.W. Pabst' 1929 film *Pandora's Box*, Valentina was a striking creation. An independent woman, a fashion photographer who moved in the chaotic, superficial world of contemporary Milan, Valentina had a darker side which emerged more and more among the years. Soon Valentina rose to prominence at the expense of Neutron, becoming the protagonist of Crepax's stories—which, on the other hand, abandoned the early crime content, turning more and more complex, ambiguous and surreal. And erotic.

Crepax had Valentina waver between everyday reality and dream, her daily job and the unbridled fantasy of her nightmares filled with fetishism and sadomasochism, which in turn reflected the idea of woman as a sex object that Valentina exploited in her photo shoots. In her dreams she became the victim of Nazi officers, sadistic torturers, soldiers and witches.

If *Valentina* belonged to the same period as the *fumetti neri*, and also retained the emphasis on eroticism, it was worlds removed from them, both in conception, context and execution. Crepax's style was as complex as it was refined, influenced by the works of Ben Shahn and David Stone Martin, with hints of Liberty, Expressionism, Surrealism, homages to movies and plenty of literary references, from De Sade to Verne, from Melville to Collodi's *Pinocchio*.

What is more, Crepax destroyed the comics' traditional syntax by amplifying the depth-of-field, emphasizing weird angles and forced perspectives, and above all splitting up the linearity of action into a myriad of fragments, while at the same time dividing the human body into multiple portions, in a sort of parallel to cinema's experimental use of the split-screen format. Each vignette had a size and composition that resorted to cinematic editing. In one of his stories, he even replicated the famous battle scene in Eisenstein's *Alexander Nevsky* (1938) almost shot-by-shot, with astonishing results. His qualities did not go unnoticed. Tinto Brass commissioned Crepax to do the storyboards for his experimental Pop Art thriller *Deadly Sweet*, and for some time considered the idea of adapting one of *Valentina*'s stories for the screen—namely *La forza di gravità*, one of Crepax's first efforts, with a sci-fi angle to it—but eventually abandoned the project, as he thought it would be impossible to portray the artist's visual universe on the big screen. However, it was Corrado Farina who eventually gave it a try it a few years later, with *Baba Yaga*.

A former film critic, copywriter and advertising director, who was well aware of the world of publicity and its aesthetics, Farina had always loved Crepax's work, which he had examined at length in essays published on various magazines as well as in a short documentary film, *Freud a fumetti* (1970). The idea of adapting *Valentina* into a motion picture was a somehow logical progression of Farina's discourse on the connections between cinema, advertising

De Funès (comedian Louis' niece and a rather popular singer in her native France) was cast as Valentina because of co-production reasons and eventually prevailed over Stefania Casini.

and comics, which he had first explored in his film debut, *They Have Changed Faces*, an inventive rendition of Bram Stoker's *Dracula* set in contemporary Italy and filled with references to Herbert Marcuse's book *One-Dimensional Man*.

They Have Changed Faces starred a modern replication of Jonathan Harker, who is summoned to the villa of Engineer Nosferatu (Adolfo Celi), the president of FIAT, Italy's greatest car manufacturing industry. Nosferatu then proceeds to drain the hero of his freedom and free will, by turning him into a part of the capitalistic system he represents. The metaphor of the capitalist as a vampire may be worn out nowadays, but Farina peppered his low-budget film with neat visual ideas, such as a couple of Fiat 500 posing as watchdogs in the park of Nosferatu's mansion. *They Have Changed Faces* did not perform well at the box-office, but the most attentive critics noticed that a peculiar *auteur* was born. Farina's second film would be his baptism of fire.

Farina's aim was to capture and heighten the cinematic quality of Crepax's style, while in the meantime experimenting on the relationship between *fumetti* and film syntax. The director recalled:

> So far, I was disappointed by the works based on comic books. None of the filmmakers who embarked on that task had been able to deepen the relationship between the language of comics and that of films.[1]

The choice of *Baba Yaga* was dictated by its self-contained storyline as well as the presence of fantastic elements—which Farina wanted to explore and expand, as he had done in his debut—as opposed to Crepax's later, more erotic-oriented stories. The emphasis on the Fantastic is evident in the theme of the "living doll," which harks back to E.T.A. Hoffmann's short story *The Sandman*, also the inspiration for Freud's celebrated 1919 essay *The Uncanny*.

Farina made several changes in the script; he eliminated the character of Philip Rembrandt and turned a marginal character in the comic, film director Arno Treves, into the male co-protagonist. Pre-production seemed to go smoothly at first, as Farina signed a deal with producer Turi Vasile, and through him got in touch with Franco Committeri, who then took Vasile's place as the film's main backer. Then, just as Farina finished writing the script, disaster happened—the first of many. Committeri backed away after the fiasco of Marco Bellocchio's *Sbatti il mostro in prima pagina* (1972), which he had produced, and Farina had to start anew in search of a producer. He eventually sealed a deal with a company named "14 luglio Cinematografica": a French co-investor was also credited, but mainly for tax reasons. However, the French presence on the film eventually led to the casting of Isabelle de Funès (comedian Louis' niece and a rather popular singer in her native France) as Valentina—a choice Farina was never very happy with. His first choice was Elsa Martinelli, and until the very end he was torn between De Funès and Stefania Casini (*Blood for Dracula*; *Suspiria*).

For the role of Baba Yaga, the lesbian witch from hell who goes after Valentina, the director originally wanted Ornella Vanoni, a popular Italian singer who had been only in a handful of films until then—a daring move which was doomed to be just wishful thinking. Farina eventually cast Anne Heywood, who then backed away when shooting had begun, leaving him to find another lead actress in a hurry. Farina eventually settled on Carroll Baker, mostly out of necessity. Even though Baker had little of the comic's Baba Yaga in her, shooting went on smoothly. Arno was played by George Eastman aka Luigi Montefiori, who did not impress the producers. Farina recalls ironically:

> When they told me I would have George Eastman in my film I said, "Who?" He had only done Spaghetti Westerns, and I had never heard of him. However, he proved to be fit for the role. He had the right looks.

The U.K. Shameless DVD cover for *Baba Yaga*.

Having completed principal shooting and post-production, Farina allowed himself a brief vacation. When he came back, he was in for a big—and decidedly unpleasant—surprise.

> My cut of *Baba Yaga* was one hour and 40 minutes. I wrapped the film up, edited it and gave it to the producer, who approved it: "How beautiful!" he said. Then I went on holiday for one week. When I came back I got a call from the producer, who said: "Well, you know, we cut out half an hour from the film." I beg your pardon? I'm not sure I understand … "We showed the film around and they told us it was too slow …"[2]

Adding insult to injury, the cuts had been made on the negative, thus compromising the director's original cut for good. Farina, furious, denounced the producers' behavior to the media and threatened to take his name off the film. He achieved at least the opportunity of re-editing *Baba Yaga*, with his assistant director Giulio Berruti. However, since the original version was lost, he could only come up with a compromise of sorts.

A couple of scenes left off the final cut were particularly interesting. Farina opted to omit the prologue, which catches the viewer off-guard, as at first it looks like some sort of soft-porn Western: a half-naked Indian girl, her breasts exposed, is pursued by a pair of Yankee soldiers in an abandoned cemetery at night. Just as they are about to rape her, the scene is revealed to be a clandestine counterculture happening, as a man with a white caftan and long white wig (singer-songwriter Franco Battiato) steps in and recites verses from John G. Neihardt's *Black Elk Speaks*, surrounded by people on motorbikes. Meanwhile, the girl takes her own revenge—and symbolically avenges her own people—by castrating (off-screen) the soldier that had attempted to violate her. The happening abruptly ends when a Carabinieri squad shows up. One of the officers is Farina himself, in one of the three small roles that he played in the film—all of them authoritarian incarnations, appearing in Valentina's sadomasochistic nightmares, the others being a Nazi general and a Prussian high officer.

It was an off-putting, thought-provoking introduction, which portrayed Valentina's spoiled world of bourgeois protesters … who all end up later at Valentina's place, discussing cinema, philosophy and revolution with a glass of wine in hand, perfectly integrated into the hollow society they were condemning earlier on. At the same time the prologue revealed Farina's intention to play with the audience by mixing reality and appearance. Another scene that ended up on the cutting-room floor was one of Valentina's erotic nightmares, a boxing match between her and a hippie, in which Baba Yaga (as her coach) performs some definitely ambiguous "massages" on her.[3]

It was not over, though, as the Italian Board of Censors demanded two cuts: a brief long shot of De Funès' full frontal nudity and the moment where Baker undresses in front of Valentina. As for the latter scene, Farina recalled bemusedly:

> It was a nice experience, since I didn't actually ask Carroll to do a full frontal nude scene (laughs). At some point, we were about to shoot and Carroll came over and asked: "Corrado, do you think it's okay if I play the scene like this?" … and she opened her nightgown. "Well, that's absolutely fine with me! No problem, no problem at all …"[4]

Despite its troubled genesis and poor critical and commercial results—most critics panned the film and the

Valentina and Arno face the unexplicable death of a model (Angela Covello)·

box-office results were disappointing, due also to bad distribution—Farina gave up filmmaking.[5] *Baba Yaga* is an impressive little film which captures the spirit of its time in a peculiar way. If *Valentina* was a product of the 1960s, *Baba Yaga* has a very 1970s look and feel, with plenty of late Pop Art oddities and hints at the cultural climate of the era, as in the aforementioned prologue. Even though Farina chose not to push the sexual element too far, some of the film's most memorable images do indeed have an erotic quality. Ely Galleani's appearance as the "living doll," wearing a S/M outfit that leaves little of her stunning body to the viewer's imagination, is worthy of Alain Robbe-Grillet.

Farina kept Crepax's habit of scattering references throughout his vignettes: books and posters pop up everywhere, and one key scene has Valentina realize the true nature of the doll while watching a screening of Paul Wegener and Carl Boese's Expressionist masterpiece *Der Golem* (1920) in a *cinema d'essai*. The director even adds some of his personal favorites, such as the early 20th century writer Emilio Salgari, whose novels can be glimpsed in a shot and whose character "Il corsaro nero" (The Black Corsair) inspired the sexy outfit donned by the model played by Angela Covello in the enticing photo shoot scene. Two decades later Farina would write a mystery novel about Salgari's alleged suicide.

What is more, several panels of Crepax's stories are recreated to the minutest detail—including the Surrealistic clock without hands in Baba Yaga's house; other sequences recall the artist's stylistic experiments, namely the ones where the action is replaced by black-and-white stills—a case in point is Valentina and Arno's lovemaking scene. Several moments have a distinct *fantastique* flavor which positively juxtaposes with the rational world of early 1970s Milan. Take Baker's memorable screen entry as she steps out of her luxurious Bentley, which materialized like a modern version of Dracula's carriage in a deserted street at night. Farina explained:

> I tried to do something similar to what Brass did with *Deadly Sweet*. Not so much by respecting, betraying or reinventing the *fumetti*'s code, but on the other hand by trying to reproduce their language and graphics to the letter. However, I did not try hard enough, mainly for production reasons. I didn't have the time, the technology and perhaps the courage either. The parts that still convince me the most are the sequences where I juxtaposed a series of burnt stills, thus obtaining an effect that is close to *Valentina*'s spirit. Even more than the stills placed next to each other as in one of Crepax's panels, I think the ones that work best are the parts where I had an image fade into another, creating a movement effect which, even though it comes from still-frames,

is akin to Crepax's panels, which are very similar to each other, where we see an eye closing, a mouth opening or a hand moving over a woman's body.[6]

Crepax (who had a cameo as a cab driver) was moderately happy with the results, but Farina was not particularly satisfied with *Baba Yaga*. He later judged his attempts at blending cinema and comics as only partially successful. Aiace Parolin's atmospheric cinematography, with its bright colors, was fascinating yet quite different from Crepax' monochromatic worldview. Had he the opportunity to electronically correct the color palette, Farina would have aimed for a starker, more stylized approach overall, in the vein of Fellini's *Juliet of the Spirits* (1965).

That said, however, *Baba Yaga*—available on blu-ray and DVD in the United States on the Blue Underground label—is a one-of-a-kind experience, and a reminder of how it was possible to experiment with film language within the boundaries of commercial cinema. It also proved Farina as an interesting filmmaker who had his own original vision and style. Unfortunately it has remained his last feature to date: Farina returned to television and advertising before embarking on a career as a novelist in the 1990s.

Notes:
1. Corrado Farina interviewed in *Valentina e la strega*, a featurette available as an extra on the Italian DVD of *Baba Yaga*.
2. Curti, Roberto and Pulici, Davide, *Corrado Farina* (Milan: Nocturno Libri, 2000), p. 132.
3. Both scenes were restored on the Italian DVD release of the film.
4. Curti and Pulici, *Corrado Farina*, p. 135.
5. Years later Farina tried to put together his third film with producer Franco Cristaldi, but the project was aborted at a late stage. Farina turned the script into his first novel, *Un posto al buio* (A Place in the Dark).
6. De Sanctis, Pierpaolo, "Valentina on screen. Conversazione con Corrado Farina," in Della Casa, Stefano and Viganò, Dario E., eds., *Pop Film Art* (Rome: Mibac/Centro Sperimentale di Cinematografia/Cinecittà Luce/Edizioni Sabinae, 2012), p. 204.

Supermen Against the Orient, aka *The Three Fantastic Supermen in the Orient*
(*Crash! Che botte strippo strappo stroppio*)
Italy/Hong Kong, color, 102 minutes
D: Bitto Albertini [and Kuei Chi-hung, uncredited]. S: Bitto Albertini; SC: Gino Capone, Bitto Albertini; DOP: Pier Luigi Santi; M: Nico Fidenco; E: Fausto Ulisse.

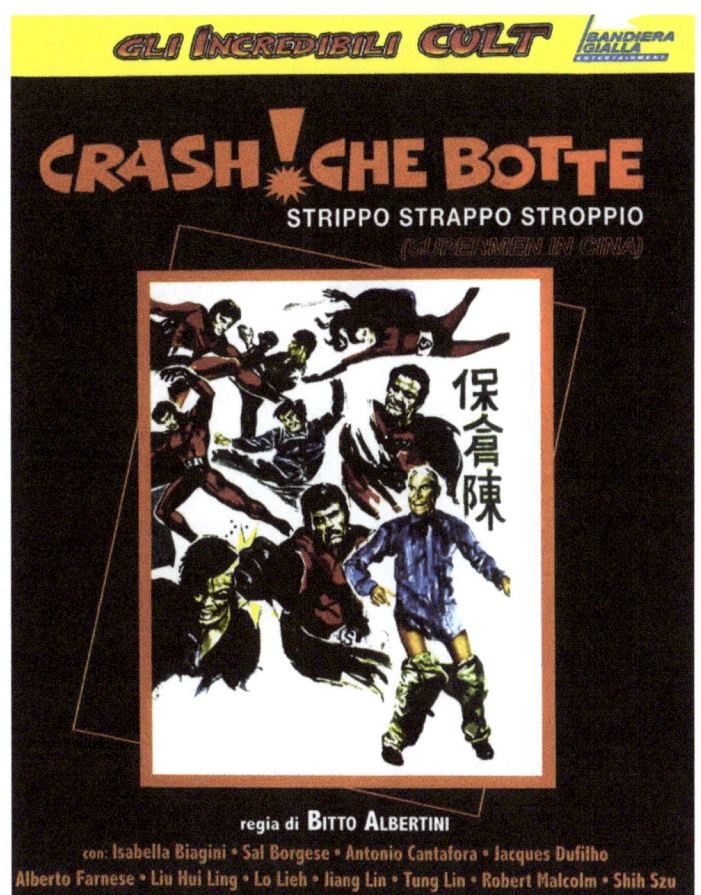

The Italian DVD cover for Bitto Albertini's *Supermen Against the Orient* (1973)

Cast: Robert Malcolm (Captain Robert Wallace), Antonio Cantafora (Max), Sal Borgese (Jerry), Lo Lieh (Master Tang), Shih Szu (Suzy), Alberto Farnese (Colonel Roger), Jacques Dufilho (U.S. Ambassador), Isabella Biagini (Ambassador's wife), Tung Lin (Chen-loh), Jackie Chan.
Prod: I.N.D.I.E.F. (Rome), Shaw Brothers (Hong Kong).

F.B.I. agent Robert Wallace is sent to Hong Kong to put an end to a cocaine smuggling ring led by Chen Loh's gang, which operates between Hong Kong and Bangkok. He must also rescue six secret agents who were captured by Chen Loh. Wallace finds unexpected help from a martial arts expert, Tang, a charming Chinese spy named Suzy and two of his old friends, the masked thieves Max and Jerry. However, in exchange for their support, the latter ask Wallace to help them loot the safes of the United States ambassador, Mr. Archibald. Bob and his acolytes then move to Bangkok where they overcome Chen's gang and release the prisoners (among whom there is also Suzy's brother). In the end Bob seizes Max and Jerry's loot, but the two thieves are given generous checks for their services on the part of the U.S. government.

The umpteenth entry in the *Three Supermen* series marked a weird team-up if ever there was one. As Pete Tombs explained in his essential book *Mondo Macabro*:

[after Bruce Lee's death] … the traditional markets for Hong Kong product

A publicity still from *Supermen Against the Orient*. From left to right: Sal Borgese, Antonio Cantafora, Shih Szu, Lo Lieh and Robert Malcolm

were becoming restricted. Censorship in Singapore and a quota system for local films in Thailand meant that there was less demand for product from the big Shaw Brothers and Golden Harvest operations. Both companies sought some respite in overseas co-productions.[1]

This led Shaw Brothers to form unlikely financial partnerships with Hammer Films (*The Legend of the 7 Golden Vampires*, 1974) and with the German-based Rapid Film for the erotic *Enter the Seven Virgins* (1974) and, last but not least, with the Italian I.N.D.I.E.F for *Supermen Against the Orient*.

The partnership led to an assorted cast that is notable for the presence of Lo Lieh, Hong Kong's first international superstar after *Five Fingers of Death* (1969),[2] as well as the lovely Shih Szu, also seen in *The Legend of the 7 Golden Vampires*. Sal Borgese was the only cast member returning from the preceding *Three Supermen in the Jungle*. Robert Malcolm starred in the Brad Harris role as the F.B.I. agent who recruits the other two amiable crooks, while Antonio Cantafora replaced George Martin—Cantafora had recently starred as the young Peter Von Kleist in Mario Bava's *Baron Blood* (*Gli orrori del castello di Norimberga*, 1972).

Cantafora would soon return to obscurity after co-starring (billed as Michael Coby) alongside Israeli actor Paul Smith (*Midnight Express*; *Popeye*) in a number of films featuring a pair of Terence Hill and Bud Spencer lookalikes, such as *The Diamond Peddlers* (*Il vangelo secondo Simone e Matteo*, 1976). He would also play a real superman in Juan Piquer Simón's campy gay superhero fantasy *Supersonic Man* (1978), and one of his latest screen roles was in Dario Argento's *The Card Player* (*Il cartaio*, 2004). Another notable addition to the cast was that of the French actor Jacques Dufilho (later seen in Herzog's *Nosferatu the*

Sal Borgese in action

Vampyre, 1979), who was quite popular in Italy at that time due to his role as the idiotic Colonel Buttiglione in a series of comedies. Dufilho provided further (and rather annoying) comic relief as the Richard Nixon-obsessed Ambassador.

Production-wise, *Supermen Against the Orient* did not resemble the previous *Three Supermen* entries—Italo Martinenghi's company Cinesecolo had nothing to do with it. This entry broke the series' narrative continuity, and it was up to Albertini and co-screenwriter Gino Capone to concoct a totally new storyline, by starting the Three Supermen's mythology from scratch (for instance, the supermen here try on their bulletproof costumes for the first time). Meanwhile, Martinenghi produced his own *Three Supermen* film, *The 3 Supermen in the West*, which also marked his directorial debut and came out in Italy a few months before Albertini's film.

So as to further detach itself from the original series, and in the meantime aiming for the kung-fu parodies that were then in vogue, *Supermen Against the Orient* was released under the mind-blowing onomatopoeic Italian title *Crash! Che botte strippo strappo stroppio* (which can be loosely translated as "Crash! What blows! Bim Bam Boom!" or something like that) that bore no reference at all to the three masked superheroes—who play a secondary role in the plot anyway, as their invulnerable costumes appear only one hour into the film.

However, the tongue-in-cheek approach was firmly in place, as proven by the demented title song courtesy of composer Nico Fidenco and singer Ernesto Brancucci, an astonishing trashy gem whose lyrics go as follows: "Smash 'em, punch 'em, bash 'em, grind 'em under!" The humor is as silly as ever, allowing the masculine Borgese the opportunity to dress up in drag—a recurrent gag in the series—as a particularly ugly stewardess, and we are not spared the supermen's customary mocking routine, leaping and laughing while being shot at by the bad guys. If the worn-out gags were not enough, there is also more than a little bit of racism involved in the depiction of the Asians—but political correctness was never a strong point in Italian genre cinema anyway.

On the other hand, the action bits are handled to better effect than in the other episodes, due to the presence (uncredited in Italian prints) of Kuei Chi-hung as co-director, who most likely took care of the martial arts stunts—which may explain why the style is so similar to Shaw Brothers films of the period, replete with crash-zooms and slow-motion bits. Kuei would go on to direct such sleazy horror films as *Killer Snakes* (1974) and *The Boxer's Omen* (1983). According to some sources, the film marked an early cameo appearance by a very young Jackie Chan, who worked as one of the choreographers as well, although his presence is impossible to detect amid the extras.

Shaw Brothers would team up with Italian producers again for Alfonso Brescia's downright bizarre *Super Stooges vs. the Wonder Women*/*Amazons Against Supermen* (*Superuomini, superdonne, superbotte*, 1974), which retained a number of elements from the *Three Supermen* series. The Hong Kong-based company churned out another totally unrelated *Supermen* film, the Taiwan/Hong Kong-produced *Superdragon vs. Superman*, aka *Bruce Lee Against Supermen* (*Meng long zheng dong*, 1975, Chia Chun Wu), released in Italy as *Bruce Lee contro i Supermen*. Despite the presence of the red-dressed, caped and masked superheroes, Wu's film also paid reference to *The Green Hornet*, the 1966-1967 TV series which had launched Bruce Lee as Kato.

Notes:
1. Tombs, Pete, *Mondo Macabro. Weird & Wonderful Cinema Around the World* (New York: St. Martin's Griffin, 1998), p. 17.
2. Lo would also co-star in another interesting Italian/HK co-production (with Spanish and U.S. participation as well), Antonio Margheriti's Western *The Stranger and the Gunfighter* (*Là dove non batte il sole*, 1974), alongside Lee Van Cleef.

The 3 Supermen in the West
(*…e così divennero i 3 Supermen del West*, aka *…y así la armaron los 3 superhombres en el Oeste*)
Italy/Spain, color, 95 minutes
D: Italo Martinenghi [Spanish version: George Martin]. *S and SC:* Italo Martinenghi, Anthony Blond [Antonio Cesare Corti], George Martin; *DOP:* Jaime Deu Casa; *M:* Bob Deramont [Roberto Pregadio]; *E:* Manlio Camastro.
Cast: George Martin [Francisco Martínez Celeiro] (George), Sal Borgese (Sal), Frank Braña (Brad), Ágata Lys (Yolanda/Agata), Gigi Bonos (Prof. Aristide Panzarotti), Cris Huerta (Jake Patch), Fred Harrison [Fernando Bilbao, aka Fernando Arrien Elgezabal] (Sheriff Canticchia), José Canalejas (Buffalo Bill), Pedro Sanchez [Ignazio Spalla] (Navajo Joe), Fernando Sancho (FBI director), Luis Barboo, Víctor Israel.
Prod: Cinesecolo (Rome), Transcontinental (Madrid).

In Rome the eminent scientist Aristide Panzarotti has perfected a time machine that allows him to travel back in time and witness the destruction of Pompeii. F.B.I. agent Brad and his friends Sal and George are sent on a mission to get hold of the device. The three sneak into Panzarotti's villa, activate the time machine and travel back in time to see the attack on Pearl Harbor and the Normandy landings. Then they end up in Kansas in 1867, where the bandit Navajo Joe steals their vehicle. To get the time machine back and return to the present, Brad and friends must face a series of farcical adventures in the Old West, helped by an undertaker named Oliver and Yolanda, the daughter of a Protestant priest. Back in Rome, before separating again, the three supermen witness the accidental destruction of the time machine.

The 3 Supermen in the West[1] was in some ways a key title in the context of the *Three Supermen* franchise, though not for its cinematic merits.

Apparently, there was not much to differentiate it from previous chapters, except for the noticeably lower budget. Sal Borgese and co-star George Martin reprised their roles from *Three Supermen in the Jungle*, but this time they teamed up with Spanish character actor Frank (Francisco) Braña in the role of the F.B.I. agent played by Brad Harris in *The Three Fantastic Supermen* and *Three Supermen in the Jungle* and by the same Martin in *3 Supermen a Tokyo*. It was an unwise bit of casting, indeed, as in the previous film Braña was one of the bad guys, and he was usually cast in villain roles throughout his career. Coherency was never the series' forte, anyway, but Braña looks uncomfortable in the role.

The rest of the cast, this being an Italian-Spanish co-production, is replete with familiar Spanish actors such as Fernando Sancho (as the director of the F.B.I.), Víctor Israel (as a banker) and the gorgeous Ágata Lys. Italian character actor Ignazio Spalla is graced—perhaps for the only time in his career—with a "special participation" credit under his customary aka Pedro Sanchez.

What really makes *The 3 Supermen in the West* a turning point in the series is the fact that it marked the debut of Cinesecolo's general manager Italo Martinenghi behind the camera, in what was probably an attempt to beat the concurrent Italian/Hong Kong co-production *Supermen Against the Orient*, which was released a few months later.

Unlike so many genre filmmakers in Italian cinema, who had undergone a long apprenticeship as assistant directors before debuting behind the camera, Martinenghi (1930-2008) was a former lawyer who got bitten by the bug and found the sacred fire of passion within. Yet he simply could not direct a film to save his life. What he lacked, he

The Spanish poster for *The 3 Supermen in the West*

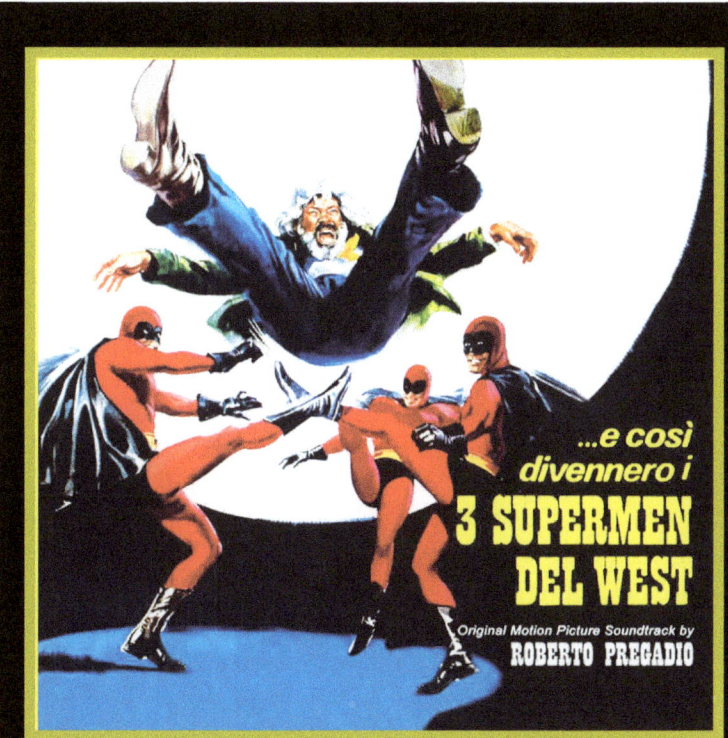

The Italian soundtrack album cover for Italo Martinenghi's feature debut as director with *The 3 Supermen in the West* **(1973)**

tried to remedy naively, and his efforts seem more like the work of a bizarrely imaginative kid than that of a grown-up professional. As a result, *The 3 Supermen in the West* rivals Ed Wood, Jr. schlockers in sheer ineptitude.

In order to add some spark to a by-then gasping formula, the script had the three heroes end up in Spaghetti Western territory courtesy of a time machine, thus basically predating the same concept as Robert Zemeckis' *Back to the Future Part III* (1990). However, the budget was so threadbare that the time travel sequences as seen in the first part of the production are represented via stock footage from other movies—from sword-and-sandal epics to black-and-white war documentary footage, and even, believe it or not, an excerpt from a *Gamera* flick, with the protagonists' off-screen voices commenting on what is going on. On the other hand, the "Western" elements are blatantly unconvincing. Spalla's character is named Navajo Joe, but bears no relation with the protagonist of Sergio Corbucci's 1966 Western of the same name. José Canalejas plays an idiotic Buffalo Bill.

Overall, the formula was basically the same as with previous chapters, including a suitably catchy title song (sung by Ernesto Brancucci, in English)—only done less effectively. Most scenes look as if they were shot in one take (with an over-reliance on zooms) in leftover sets, and the expected acrobatics and fistfights soon become tiresome. What is more, the Western parody is a third-hand reworking of everything from Franco & Ciccio films to Bud Spencer and Terence Hill's *Trinità* series, complete with saloon brawls, pie fights and even a Bud Spencer lookalike played by Fernando Bilbao.

The humor is as childish as ever. The scientist has a pair of mechanical gorillas (that is, extras in threadbare monkey suits) guarding his abode; some scenes are incongruously speeded up in an attempt to solicit laughter; the supermen dress up in various get-ups during the film (and Borgese even dresses in drag as some point—an inevitable occurrence in each and every entry in the series) and do their jumping and cackling routine as the baddies unload their guns on their bulletproof costumes.

The gags are invariably second-rate. In an early scene Borgese and Martin are trying to sell a tourist the Colosseum, in an ill-fated attempt at ripping off a gag in *Tototruffa '62* (1961, Camillo Mastrocinque) where a scam artist (played by Totò) sells the Fountain of Trevi to an unsuspecting buyer. Later on Borgese makes a passable impression of Totò's own puppet mime routine, and in another scene he also imitates Charlie Chaplin. Another gag repeats a moment from *Trinity Is STILL My Name!* (*Continuavano a chiamarlo Trinità*, 1971) when Martin demonstrates his prowess in grabbing the gun while slapping his adversary in the face.

Martinenghi even sets up a football match between the good and the bad guys—a scene that brings to mind what Sal Borgese had to say about the weight of the producer's directorial input into the series during an interview on the Italian TV show *Stracult*:

> As soon as Martinenghi showed up on the set, when we were shooting exteriors, we gave him a football and sent him playing elsewhere [...] The film's direction was a team effort, most notably by George Martin.

The co-protagonist is actually credited as the sole director on the Spanish version.

Martinenghi would helm all the series' subsequent entries: the threadbare Turkish co-productions *3 Supermen Against the Godfather* (1980) and *Three Supermen at the Olympic Games* (1984), as well as the series' swan song, *Three Supermen in S. Domingo* (1986).[2]

Notes:
1. Although the IMDb lists the film under the title *Three Supermen of the West*, the onscreen title on the foreign language prints is actually *The 3 Supermen in the West*.
2. On the other hand, there is no connection between the *Three Supermen* series and the German/Turkish *Three Superguys* films, a quintet

of comedy/action films starring "Robert Widmark," real name Alberto Dell'Acqua. The Italian actor was actually the only element that connected the first two entries—both West German co-productions directed by Ernst Hofbauer—to the other three, which were either Turkish or Turkish/Italian co-productions. Hofbauer's films were *Two Sane Nuts* (*Dschungelmädchen für zwei Halunken/Che matti … ragazzi!*, 1974), which was later marketed in West Germany as part of the series with the title *Zwei Teufelskerle auf dem Weg zur grünen Hölle*, and *The Three Superguys* (*Zwei Teufelskerle auf dem Weg ins Kloster/Che stangata … ragazzi!*, 1975). Then came *The Flying Superboy* (*Bas belasi/Bob il baro*, 1976, Atıf Yılmaz), *The Three Superboys Strike Again* (*Üç kagitcilar/Che carambole … ragazzi*, 1976, Natuk Baytan) and *Three Superguys in the Snow* (*Babanim evlatlari/Mettetemi in galera… ma subito*, 1977, Natuk Baytan, Ernst Hofbauer, co-starring Cüneyt Arkın).

1974

Super Stooges vs. the Wonder Women
(*Superuomini, superdonne, superbotte*)
Italy/Hong Kong, color, 94 minutes
D: Al Bradley [Alfonso Brescia]. *S and SC:* Aldo Crudo, Alfonso Brescia; *DOP:* Fausto Rossi; *M:* Franco Micalizzi; *E:* Liliana Serra.

Cast: Nick Jordan [Aldo Canti] (Aru/Dharma II), Marc Hannibal (Moog), Hua Yueh (Chung), Malisa Longo (Mila), Aldo Bufi Landi (Dharma I), Genie Woods (Beghira, Queen of the Amazons), Karen Yeh (May May Wong), Lynne Moody (Myra), Riccardo Pizzuti (Philonus), Giacomo Rizzo (Canicula), Magda Konopka (Waitress at the tavern).

Prod: A Erre Cinematografica (Rome), Shaw Brothers (Hong Kong).

In ancient times a tribe of Amazon women set out to meet a village god named Dharma and learn the secret of immortality from him. However, the masked Dharma is a fraud, and different men over the centuries have enacted his role in order to keep the peace. When

An Italian *fotobusta* for *The 3 Supermen in the West*

Dharma is mortally wounded by the Amazons, his place is taken by his young disciple Aru, who teams up with a couple of friends—the black, Herculean Moog and the martial arts expert Chang—to avenge his dead mentor …

The second strange fruit of the Shaw Brothers' venture in a co-production with Italy, namely with Ovidio Assonitis and Giorgio Carlo Rossi's company A Erre Cinematografica, *Super Stooges vs. the Wonder Women*, was yet another outlandish affair. The plot patently cashed in on Terence Young's *The Amazons*, aka *War Goddess*, a costly enterprise that producer Ovidio Assonitis had cleverly exploited by churning out a quick rip-off, *Battle of the Amazons* (*Le Amazzoni—donne d'amore e di guerra*, 1973), directed by Brescia. One of the original three supermen, Aldo Canti, returned in one of his rare starring roles, alongside former Harlem Globetrotters/Harlem Magicians star Marc Hannibal, who by then had built himself a solid acting career through many TV appearances as well as a role in *Airport* (1970), while the Shaw Brothers provided their own home-made star, Hua Yueh.

The rest of the cast is a delight for connoisseurs: Brescia's regular Malisa Longo is Canti's love interest, *Scream Blacula Scream*'s Lynne Moody is Moog's girlfriend, while Giovanni Cianfriglia, the unforgotten Superargo, has a small role as a bandit and Magda Konopka (*Satanik*) pops up in a blink-and-you'll-miss-it cameo as a tavern waitress. Aldo Valletti, a weird-looking extra who would soon be chosen by Pier Paolo Pasolini to play the President in *Salò, or the 120 Days of Sodom* (*Salò o le 120 giornate di Sodoma*, 1975), can be spotted during a fight scene in the village.

A Hong Kong poster for Alfonso Brescia's *Super Stooges vs. the Wonder Women* (1974)

Overall, it is hard to describe *Super Stooges vs. the Wonder Women* with any adjective other than "demented." The script—by director Alfonso Brescia and Aldo Crudo, according to the credits, although Assonitis claims the film was actually written by Brescia and Bruno Corbucci[1]—throws in a mind-boggling mixture of wildly diverse references, which turn the whole thing into a big ugly mess. Yet it is sort of endearing at times, at least for those viewers who belong to the so-bad-it's-good school of thought.

The opening features the warrior women engaging in violent and deadly sports which will lead to the election of the sole survivor as their queen. Said scenes—such as the Amazons throwing arrows at one another and wrestling to the death over a bed of spiky knives—are definitely not in the same humorous league as the rest of the film.[2] Then the tone changes abruptly, with the apparition of a cartoonish evil gang, "Le Tigri dei Boschi" (The Tigers of the Woods), who play a very similar role as Erich von Zipper and his biker acolytes in AIP's *Beach Party* series. Riccardo Pizzuti plays the leader Philonus. The bearded stuntman was also at the receiving end of Bud Spencer's punches and slaps in the *Trinità* films, and he played a similar role (albeit serious) in *Battle of the Amazons*.[3]

The Spencer and Hill films are paid an obvious reference when we are introduced to Moog (Marc Hannibal), a gigantic black muscleman intent on devouring a huge plate of bean stew in a tavern. The resulting fistfight sports the same slapstick stunts and Wile E. Coyote-style violence that could be found in the contemporary comic EuroWesterns, and which Gianfranco Parolini had first started developing in his sword-and-sandal movies and then in *The Three Fantastic Supermen*. However, the humor is definitely more on the demented side. In the aforementioned tavern scene Moog blows away the entire Tigers gang by way of an incredibly powerful belch. As with his previous period farce *Helen, Yes … Helen of Troy* (*Elena sì, ma … di Troia*, 1973), comedy was not Brescia's *piece de resistance*. He would fare much better with his Neapolitan-based crime melodramas of the late '70s, starring Mario Merola.

A U.S. lobby card for *Super Stooges vs. the Wonder Women*

With the introduction of Dharma (Aldo Bufi Landi), the god-like guardian of the eternal fire (which is actually oil), the script harks back yet again to Lee Falk's *The Phantom*, whose myth is basically recycled in a vague, non-historical primitive setting. Dharma is perceived by the natives as being immortal, as he has been present for centuries, while his role is handed down from generation to generation. Yet this would not be an Italian film if the scriptwriters did not throw even more ingredients into the cauldron. Dharma's hideout is some sort of prehistoric bat-cave (replete with a butler named Jeeves), and Dharma has a few tricks up his sleeve when it comes to illustrating his supernatural powers recalling Batman's gadgetry.

After Dharma is killed and young hero Aru (Nick Jordan, alias Aldo Canti) takes his place, the reference to the *Three Supermen* series kicks in as Aru teams up with Hannibal and Hua to fight the Amazons. Canti has plenty of chances to show his skills as an acrobat, with the help of some strategically hidden trampolines, reverse speed and slow-motion bits, while Franco Micalizzi's score nicely underlines the proceedings, with its overtly farcical tone. The third act, however, is yet another variation on the typical *Seven Samurai/The Magnificent Seven* mold, this time in a humorous vein, as the three heroes prepare to defend a village from the Amazons' attack by instructing the villagers and concocting a series of booby traps and amusing devices for protection (including primitive fire-throwing tanks).

Unlike in Bitto Albertini's *Supermen Against the Orient*, there is not much room for elaborate martial arts choreographies here. Hua, one of the titular "Super Stooges," (as the trio was re-baptized in the U.S. version to emphasize the comedy aspect), often plays like a placid sidekick to Canti and Hannibal. As for the fight scenes, it must be noted that the curvaceous Amazons are blatantly replaced with hairy, decidedly masculine body doubles. However, the action hardly ever lets up, and Fausto Rossi's widescreen cinematography is fairly competent.

The sets and costumes are an example of the film's totally anachronistic "period" setting, which borrows elements from different time frames. Despite the Amazons being a creation of Greek mythology, Dharma's attire consists of a Medieval-style metal vest, an incongruous-looking cape, shorts and a mask, while the locations are taken from Spaghetti Westerns—such as the countryside homestead where the initial fight between Moog and the Tigers takes place, which can be spotted in such films as Giorgio Ferroni's *Blood for a Silver Dollar* (*Un dollaro bucato*, 1965) and Mario Bava's *Roy Colt and Winchester Jack* (1970)—and *pepla* (the village where Aru meets his two companions).

Brescia's film performed modestly at the Italian box-office, but American-International picked it up for distribution in the U.S. It often played on a double-bill with Jim Clark's horror flick *Madhouse* starring Vincent Price, Peter Cushing and Robert Quarry. It is known under a variety of titles: *Barbarian Revenge*, *Return of the Barbarian Women*, *Amazons and Supermen*, *Amazons Against Superman* [sic!] and is available on DVD in the U.S. on the Rarescope label as *Amazons vs. Supermen*.

Aldo Canti (as Nick Jordan) plays the masked hero.

Notes:
1. Gomarasca, Manlio, "Beyond the Screen. Il cinema di Ovidio G. Assonitis," in Gomarasca, Manlio and Pulici, Davide, eds., "Controcorrente 4," *Nocturno Dossier* #82, May 2009, p. 20.
2. Curiously, this footage is not included in the German print, *Supermänner genen Amazonen*, which opens with the tavern scene.
3. Giacomo Rizzo, a Neapolitan comedian who would feature prominently in Brescia's so-called *sceneggiate*, plays Pizzuti's sidekick. Incidentally, Rizzo resurfaced from obscurity when he starred as a repellent loan shark in Paolo Sorrentino's *The Family Friend* (*L'amico di famiglia*, 2006).

1976

La principessa sul pisello
(The Princess on the Pea)
Italy, color, 95 minutes

D: Piero Regnoli. S and SC: Piero Regnoli; Dial: Vittoriano Vighi; DOP: Fausto Zuccoli; M: Nico Fidenco, arranged by Giacomo Dell'Orso; E: Adriano Tagliavia; AD: Gianni Siragusa.

Cast: Susanna Martinková (Cenerentola/Cinderella), Christa Linder (Biancaneve/Snow White), Gino Milli (Prince), Gianfranco De Angelis (Maurice Rampaldier), Amparo Pilar (Jeanne), Franca Maresca (Fairy Godmother), Liliana Chiari (Brothel's Madam), Gino Pagnani (Maurice's brother), Fausto Tommei (Monsieur Rampaldier, Maurice's father), Marisa Bertoni (The Queen), Luigi D'Ecclesia (Sozzolo), Adriano Cornelli (Ciucciolo), Franco Doria (Caccolo), Alessandro Perrella (Chamberlain), Bruna Celati (Old Woman), Salvatore Furnari (Mosciolo), Gaetano Guacci (Fregnolo), Jocelyne Chaquat (Jeanne), Tiziana Casoli (Prostitute), Anna Montanari (Prostitute), Antonio De Martino (Petolo), Domenico Imperato (Minchiolo), Luciano Pusineri (The Huntsman), Mar-

New Zealand video cover art features an unlikely Spiderman figure.

cello Bonini Olas (The King), Rossana Canghiari (Prostitute).

Prod: Enzo Boetani and Giuseppe Collura for Samy Cinematografica (Rome)

A group of prostitutes gather around a fire and listen to the fairytales told by an old woman, killing time waiting for customers. "Cinderella:" In 19th-century France, a libertine nobleman stages an orgy to "cure" his son Maurice, who seems disinterested in women. However, Maurice falls for Cinderella, a naive maid who works at a brothel and has joined the orgy, disguised as a high society whore, with the help of the Fairy Godmother. At midnight the spell ends and Cinderella flees from the palace, leaving her panties behind her. Maurice sets out to find her, no matter what … "Snow White:" The Evil Queen, jealous of her beautiful stepdaughter Snow White, entrusts a huntsman to kill her. However, Snow White escapes her fate and takes refuge in a shack in the woods, inhabited by the Seven Dwarfs. When she learns that Snow White is still alive, the Queen attempts to kill her with a poisoned apple, but the girl is smarter than she thought …

Looking at his incredibly prolific body of work—over 110 credits as a screenwriter, plus 11 as a director, in a career spanning over 40 years—one would find it hard to believe that Piero Regnoli (1921-2001) had once been the titular film critic for the Vatican newspaper *L'Osservatore Romano*. Eroticism was the driving force in many of his scripts, such as Brunello Rondi's *Tecnica di un amore* (1973), Roberto Bianchi Montero's *Caligula's Hot Nights* (*Le calde notti di Caligola*, 1977) and Mario Bianchi's *Satan's Baby Doll* (*La bimba di Satana*, 1982), and even though his directorial output was somewhat tamer in comparison, sex was often a primary element, resulting in such works as *The Playgirls and the Vampire* (*L'ultima preda del vampiro*, 1960). However, even when he churned out reviews for the austere Vatican newspaper, at a time where Italian movies were subjected to an oppressive, narrow-minded censorship, Regnoli showed an independent attitude and a vivacious intelligence. The same qualities characterized his film career as well, despite its ups and downs in quality, and led him to work and become friends with such peculiar, idiosyncratic filmmakers as Riccardo Freda and Lucio Fulci. Regnoli had known Freda since the late 1940s when he worked as vice artistic manager at the production company Universalia (also close to the Vatican), which produced Freda's period melodrama *Guarany* (1948). He co-wrote *I vampiri* (1957) and worked with Freda on some unreleased scripts in the 1970s. For Fulci, Regnoli penned *White Fang* (*Zanna bianca*, 1973) and some of the director's later horror pictures, namely *Demonia* (1990), *Voices from Beyond* (*Voci dal profondo*, 1991) and *Door to Silence* (*Le porte del silenzio*, 1991).

According to Regnoli's wife and collaborator Silvia Innocenzi, the idea for *La principessa sul pisello* came from Regnoli's friend, actor-director-producer Alfredo Rizzo (who played the sex-obsessed ballet manager Lucas in *The Playgirls and the Vampire*, and directed a number of erotic flicks in the mid-1970s), who, "following the success of the adults-only fairytale comics […] attempted to launch a new thread inspired by the re-imagining of fairytales in a comical-sexy way,"[1] similarly to such U.S. exploitation films as *The Erotic Adventures of Pinocchio* (1971, Corey Allen).

The customary words "Once upon a time …" introduce the viewer to a modern-day setting, at a park (the "Città della Domenica" in Perugia) whose attractions refer to such popular fairytales as Pinocchio, and which happens to be populated by prostitutes—the perfect audience for the twisted erotic tales told by an old lady, who maintains that "fairytales do exist. Fact is, you have to be able to understand them," hinting at the socio-cultural symbols and nuances that are littered all over them.

The starting point is, of course, the overturning of fairytales' characteristic elements in a malicious way. Instead of a slipper, Cinderella loses her panties while running away after the spell has ended, and her beloved "prince" goes around asking women to try and wear them in order to identify her. Similarly, the gentle and naive Snow White becomes a clever young woman, who fools her wicked stepmother into tasting a bite of the poison apple (imbibed with LSD) and seduces the Seven Dwarfs in order to steal their diamonds. The horny dwarfs themselves are replete with such names as Sozzolo, Mosciolo, Fregnolo, Caccolo, Petolo, Minchiolo, Ciucciolo, all of them leading to predictable sex jokes, while the talking mirror is recreated as a TV set of sorts (an idea reprised in 1982's *Biancaneve & Co…*).

The adults-only comics' influence is undeniable, but Regnoli throws in some unexpectedly cultured references as well. In "Cinderella," the prince's father and brother are depicted as two Sadean libertines who shoot arrows at half-naked maids, whereas a sequence openly quotes *Last Year at Marienbad* (*L'année dernière à Marienbad*, 1961, Alain Resnais) as Cinderella (Czech actress Susanna Martinková, then Gianni Garko's wife) walks across a villa's garden amid statue-like guests.

The premise is quite good, but Regnoli does little to develop it, and the shoestring budget does not help. The direction is flat, the sight gags range from silly to awful, including a cringe-inducing pie battle between the dwarfs and the verbal jokes often fall flat, although the title's admittedly bawdy double-entendre (the title means literally "The Princess on the Pea"—*pisello*, in Italian, is also slang for the male sexual organ) is played upon with deranged humor. The elderly lady never actually manages to tell the titular fairytale *The Princess and the Pea*, since her audience is formed of prostitutes who keep telling her they know all there is to know about it. On top of that, Regnoli fails to give his film a comic book-like quality. The affinities between the second episode and Rubino Ventura and Leone Frollo's *Biancaneve* are merely superficial. Snow White (played by the stunning-looking blonde Christa Linder) does not resemble Frollo's raven-haired creation, and the director fails to explore the subtle indictment of the country's retrograde mentality that was at the heart of Ventura and Frollo's comic.

Overall, the anthology format (although underplayed, the overlong second episode runs one hour alone) makes *La principessa sul pisello* closer in tone to the saucy "Decamerotics" produced around the same time in Italy—a thread to which Regnoli had contributed with his previous movie, *I giochi proibiti de l'Aretino Pietro* (1973), albeit with a tamer approach to eroticism. Despite the often-bawdy dialogue, there is actually little sex, with few bare breasts in sight, and no full frontal nudity at all.

This, perhaps, condemned the film to oblivion. Shot in 1973 and submitted to the Board of Censors in April 1974, *La principessa sul pisello* was given a bland V.M. 14 rating, and was eventually released in August 1976 to minimal distribution.[2] It was born old, at a time when hardcore pornography was about to burst out on Italian screens. *La principessa sul pisello* was Regnoli's last official feature film as a director; over a decade later, he helmed, uncredited, the 1986 melodrama *Giuro che ti amo*, starring the Neapolitan singer Nino D'Angelo.

Notes:
1. Grattarola, Franco, Norcini, Ippoliti, Stefano and Norcini, Matteo, "L'uomo delle stelle. Ricordo di Piero Regnoli," *Cine70 e dintorni* #2, Spring 2002, p. 38.
2. Regnoli's film was beaten in time by Oscar Brazzi's *Giro girotondo... con il sesso è bello il mondo* (1975), made later but released earlier. Written by Roberto Leoni and Franco Bucceri, and starring Rossano Brazzi and the buxom Patrizia De Rossi (aka Patrizia Webley), it was a more interesting variation on the theme of adult fairytales, which revisited *Little Red Riding Hood* as a malicious sci-fi comedy. However, like Regnoli's film, it failed at the box-office.

Sturmtruppen

Italy/France, color, 100 minutes
D: Salvatore Samperi. S: based on the comic strip *Sturmtruppen* by Bonvi [Franco Bonvicini]; SC: Renato Pozzetto, Cochi Ponzoni, Maria Pia Fusco, Vittorio Vighi; DOP: Giuseppe Rounno; M: Enzo Jannacci; E: Sergio Montanari.
Cast: Renato Pozzetto (Rookie), Cochi [Aurelio] Ponzoni (General), Lino Toffolo (Rookie), Teo Teocoli (Captain), Felice

The Italian DVD cover art for Salvatore Samperi's *Sturmtruppen* (1976)

Andreasi (Sergeant/The Pope), Massimo Boldi (Rookie), Jean-Pierre Marielle (The Unknown Soldier), Umberto Smaila (The Cook), Corinne Cléry (The Actress/The Wife/The Woman at the Villa), Bonvi (The Prisoner).
Prod: Irrigazione Cinematografica (Milan); Les Films Jacques Leitienne (Paris).

During World War II, a bizarre German battalion prepares to fight an unnecessary war under the command of a cocaine-riddled General, who stays in a luxurious palace disguised as a cabin, in the company of a Karl Marx puppet, a homosexual Captain who is always looking for recruits with blue eyes and a violent, stupid Sergeant. The soldiers are unruly, drug-addicted and sexually frustrated, and when finally reaching the front, their incredible behavior does not change. They even mistakenly kill their chaplain, who on Christmas Eve will be replaced by the General in person. In the midst of the war a messenger of God shows up with a message of peace. The Pope, with a poisoned host, kills the messenger. The General and the Captain rejoice: the war continues …

A brilliant cartoonist who had specialized in advertising on "Carosello," Franco Bonvicini, nicknamed Bonvi (1941-1995), had sporadically dabbled in the movie business as a make-up artist and costume designer, and even played a small role in the Franco and Ciccio film *Come rubammo la bomba atomica* (1967). His big opportunity came in 1968 when he participated in a contest held by the Communist newspaper *Paese Sera* for a new satirical comic strip to be published within. Bonvi contributed with *Stur-*

mtruppen, a comic strip set in the trenches of World War II, recounting the conflict from the point of view of the German army. He won the contest, leading to *Sturmtruppen* debuting in October 1968, with a steady and ever-growing success, which led to the strip becoming a regular presence in the comics magazine *Eureka*, created by Luciano Secchi and appearing from 1972 to 1975.

The format, which reprised that of the typical U.S. daily strips, was vital in the comic's success, but *Sturmtruppen's* main asset was Bonvi's use of language, employing a bastardization in which Italian terms were given pseudo-German suffixes so as to ape the German language—a linguistic experiment which recalled both the Medieval jargon employed in Mario Monicelli's *Brancaleone's Army*, aka *For Love and Gold* (*L'Armata Brancaleone*, 1966) and Dario Fo's stage plays based on the gibberish language style of Grammelot. However, Bonvi's was not simply a satire against war, but the expression of the artist's anarchic view of life and his negativity toward all ruling systems, thus emphasizing the madness and nonsense of the human condition, a point which the artist's caricatures and taste for detailed panel compositions made even more mordant. The characters were army recruits with identical features that are differentiated only by way of their first name, and their superiors—inevitably cruel, violent, stupid, sadistic or downright crazy. And the humor was grotesque and surreal, with the occasional bouts of poetry included as well as chilling reflections on the "banality of evil," to quote Hannah Arendt. It was as chilling as it was exhilarating, and vice versa.

The original idea to put Bonvi's strips on film came from Ermanno Donati and Luigi Carpentieri, the producers behind the very first Italian horror film, Riccardo Freda's *I Vampiri* (1957), as well as many other genre efforts. Donati had recently produced another movie set during WWII, Tinto Brass' scandalous *Salon Kitty* (1975). The two producers were amazed to discover that Bonvi was Italian and not French as they had thought, and got in touch with him through the scriptwriter Vittorio Vighi, who was a good friend of his. Ennio De Concini was involved in the project as the director, and Vighi and Maria Pia Fusco started working on the script. In spring 1976 the newspapers reported the news that Renato Pozzetto and Paolo Villaggio would be starring in the film: shooting was scheduled for June. Pozzetto specialized in an absurdist kind of humor, replete with nonsense monologues and a strong unrealistic feel. His staring, dazed looks and naive characterizations had turned him into one of the most popular Italian comedians of the decade, following his surreal TV appearances. What is more, the actor was looking for more unconventional roles as well as a more oblique kind of humor than most of his peers. On the other hand, Villaggio was enjoying a great success on TV with the character of German Professor Kranz, similar in spirit to Bonvi's moronic Nazis.

However, the project passed through several different hands during the prep stage. Donati and Carpentieri were not convinced about De Concini's vision, and for a short while, it seemed that Franco Cristaldi would be involved in the film as producer. *Sturmtruppen* eventually ended up on Achille Manzotti's desk. The script was rewritten, the sections authored by Vighi and Fusco were dropped and De Concini backed off and was replaced by Salvatore Samperi. Villaggio as well walked off to star in Sergio Corbucci's *Il signor Robinson, mostruosa storia d'amore e d'avventure* (1976).

In later interviews, De Concini sounded very embittered when talking about his involvement in *Sturmtruppen*:

> All of a sudden I felt that my relationship with cinema was running out. […] The strangest thing is that I made the decision when I was about to start the film. […] At first I had written the treatment for Donati and Sbariglia, the producers of *Salon Kitty*, then the whole thing ended up in the hands of Cristaldi, and I was supposed to shoot the film with unknown actors. Finally, everything ended up with Renato, Cochi … but I did not feel like doing it. I would have made a bad job and a bad movie.

It was all too natural that the project of a film adaptation of Bonvi's strips involved the new wave of young comedians who gravitated around the Milanese "Derby Club," on whose stage a whole generation of comedians took their first steps. Pozzetto co-wrote the script with his friend Cochi Ponzoni (the other half of the comic duo Cochi & Renato, which exposed Pozzetto to TV audiences) and surrounded himself with a cast featuring other fellow "Derby" regulars such as Ponzoni, Teo Teocoli, Massimo Boldi, Felice Andreasi and others, who are given almost equal screen-time as the undisputed star. Bonvi himself even showed up in a bit role as the prisoner sentenced for execution that acts before the firing squad as though he were a goalkeeper. The only female presence in the film is Corinne Cléry, who replaced Edwige Fenech due to co-production reasons, and whose role allowed Pozzetto to broaden his satirical darts toward marriage and the battle of the sexes. Another of Pozzetto's pack, musician-cum-actor Enzo Jannacci, wrote the title song.

The talented Samperi (1944-2009) made quite a sensation with his film debut *Come Play with Me*, ideally in the same vein of Marco Bellocchio's masterpiece *Fists in the*

Pocket (*I pugni in tasca*, 1965), albeit with a more evident erotic vein—a trait that characterized most of Samperi's work. An active participant of the student protests in 1968, he retained his anti-*bourgeois* vein in his following works, despite the many commercial compromises and a certain discontinuity in inspiration. His greatest commercial success was *Malicious* (*Malizia*, 1973), an erotic comedy that made Laura Antonelli *the* Italian sex symbol *par excellence* of the decade. Samperi's approach to the material is at once respectful and creative. For instance, he constantly resorts to sequence shots and long takes, so as to maintain the spirit of the strips. There is hardly any close-ups in the film, and the elaborate dolly shots are paradoxically closer to Jancsó than to the Italian comedies of the period. What is more, Samperi and his collaborators made a drastic choice, by shooting almost all the film in exteriors, in a large muddy quarry which, with the help of scarce yet intelligent set decoration, became a quite suggestive metaphorical *non-lieu* where to stage the script's surreal antics.

Samperi claimed that his main inspiration was Robert Altman's *M*A*S*H* (1970), and at times it shows, especially in the character played by Pozzetto, a rebellious type who's always intent on rolling himself a reefer and who at one point shows up nude at a gathering in protest and is eventually imitated by the whole platoon. The gags are as offbeat as they are outrageous. The General keeps in his luxurious, vast headquarters (which on the outside look like any other barracks) a Karl Marx puppet, which he tortures in all sorts of ways; a giant bottle of Coca Cola is placed right in the middle of a battle field; the trenches are reinvented as a Grand Hotel of sorts where each soldier is given the key to his "room" ... What is more, there are recurrent jokes on drug use, self-mutilation, homosexuality (the Captain dresses like Valentino in *The Sheik*, lusts over blue-eyed soldiers and always has some phallic-related object in his hand[1]) and cannibalism.

The result, albeit disjointed, lives up to Bonvi's anarchic fury and is perhaps—together with Pozzetto's directorial debut *Saxophone* (1978)—the closest thing to the spirit of the "Derby Club." Samperi's anti-militarist vein is apparent throughout and culminates in the mordant ending, in which the Unknown Soldier comes down to Earth with a message from God (who, the messenger says, is a woman) that would put an end to this and all conflicts. The Pope meets him and kills him with a poisoned wafer before he can deliver his peace message, so that war can continue forever, much to the General's (and the Church's) satisfaction. It is a thought provoking, daring ending which caused the film some trouble, culminating in a seizure from a magistrate with the accusation of being "insulting to religion"—which did not stop *Sturmtruppen* being one of the season's biggest hits, with over one billion *lire* grossed at the box-office.

The popular comic duo Renato Pozzetto (left) and Cochi Ponzoni pose on the cover of a 7-inch of the title song for the movie.

The film's success led to a dreary rip-off (*Kakkientruppen*, 1977, directed by Marino Girolami)[2] and to a sequel, *Sturmtruppen 2—Tutti al fronte*, written by Bonvi and again directed by Samperi, but minus Pozzetto, who by then had converted heart and soul to an easier, less experimental but very successful series of mainstream comedies.

Notes:

1. According to Teocoli, a number of scenes featuring his character were cut for fear of the board of censors. Teocoli, Teo, *Io ballo da solo: autobiografia comica* (Milan: Mondadori, 2010), p. 174.
2. On the other hand, Mino Guerrini's *Von Buttiglione Sturmtruppenführer* (1977) pays only nominal reference to Bonvi's strips, being the fourth entry in the series dedicated to the idiotic Colonel Buttiglione, a character created in the radio show *Alto gradimento*, played by the French comedian Jacques Dufilho.

1977

Kakkientruppen

Italy, color, 90 minutes

D: Franco Martinelli [Marino Girolami]. S and SC: Marino Girolami, Carlo Veo; DOP: Fausto Zuccoli; M: Renato Serio.

Cast: Gianfranco D'Angelo (Fitz), Lino Banfi (Otto), Oreste Lionello (Inspector General), Mario Carotenuto (Lieutenant), Donald O'Brien (Camp Commandant), Ric [Riccardo Miniggio] (Surgeon), Gian [Gian Fabio Bosco] (Surgeon), Francesco Mulé (Cook), Enzo Andronico (Sergeant), Dante Cleri (Adolf Hitler).

Prod: Kristal Film (Rome).

At the headquarters of a Wermacht battalion, lots of crazy types can be found, resulting in a variety of unlikely events. Soldiers Otto and Fitz continually end up in the punishment cell due to their impertinence; a pair of inept surgeons operate on the wounded soldiers with grotesque results; the Camp commandant seems preoccupied mostly by having the best toilet paper at hand and a cook serves meals prepared with human flesh …

Hastily put together to exploit the success of Samperi's *Sturmtruppen*, Girolami's film reflects in its concept and essence the worst habits of the Italian film industry of the period. Instead of attempting to recreate the style and substance of Bonvi's strips, it merely hints at its source through the title and the mocking use of ungrammatical German-sounding gibberish in the dialogue, whereas the script is actually an assembly of painfully unfunny (not to mention old) vaudeville sketches and jokes with an anything-goes attitude that now and then attempts the odd surreal effect. On top of that, whereas Bonvi's stories were a mordant and ultimately grim reflection on human nature, *Kakkientruppen* exhibits a worrying indifference toward its source material, which makes the attempts at satire leave a dreary taste in the mouth.

Girolami and co-scriptwriter Carlo Veo even come up with a number of awkward cinematic homages. A recurring gag, with a *bersagliere* on bike (presumably en route since World War I …) showing up now and then to ask directions, is a variation on a famous one in *Hellzapoppin'* (1941); a couple of Laurel and Hardy impersonators turn up in a scene, while later on a Sandokan lookalike (the character was extremely popular in Italy after Sergio Sollima's 1976 TV movie starring Kabir Bedi) asks to be enrolled in the battalion and fight against the British. In the ending, Adolf Hitler (character actor Dante Cleri) dresses up as Charlie Chaplin to escape capture from the Allies, but is immediately recognized by his troops. None of the above moments elicits a smile, let alone laughter.

The blatant sloppiness is all over the place: the sets are slapdash (the entire film takes place in several badly assembled locations and in the surroundings of Villa Mussolini near Rome, made up to resemble a concentration camp of sorts), the direction is constantly at a "one-take-will-do" level and the actors involved do their routine (Lino Banfi speaks in his usual Pugliese accent, for instance) without any enthusiasm. In a later interview, comedian Mario Carotenuto even admitted that he was ashamed of having taken part in such dreck.

The most remarkable thing about *Kakkientruppen* is its reliance on graphic and over-the-top gore—an occurrence to be found in other comedies of the period, such as Bruno Corbucci's *Messalina, Messalina!* (1977). In the opening sequence, a military orchestra director kills the soldiers who play the wrong note; he shoots one in the chest with a shotgun, resulting in the still-pounding heart splattering out of the wound and bouncing around. Recurring gags feature a cook who serves the soldiers meals prepared with human limbs and assorted body parts and organs. The commander is served "ham" sliced directly from a severed leg, for instance. Seemingly similar to Stanley Ellin's short story *The Specialty of the House*, this is actually closer to *The Undertaker and His Pals* (1966) … Another macabre comic riff features a pair of incompetent

The Italian DVD cover art for Marino Girolami's *Kakkientruppen* (1977)

surgeons who gleefully amputate limbs or randomly pull out inner organs from their unfortunate patients ("You know how to pull out the best in people," one victim who has just had his liver extracted says).[1]

The insistence on such material makes the result uneasily close to the contemporaneous Nazi-erotic sub-genre—especially a borderline title such as the grotesque *Liebes Lager* (1976, Lorenzo Gicca Palli) with which Girolami's film shares the same lack of taste, further emphasized by the title itself (a bad pun on the word "cacchio," a slightly less vulgar euphemism for "dick," which is given the Teutonic treatment, resulting in something roughly translatable to "crappy troops"). Incidentally, Girolami does not lose the chance to pay reference to the Nazi cycle. One line of dialogue goes like this: "No, this is not *Salon Kitty*! Even though it is a mess[2] all the same!" Indeed.

Notes:
1. Ric and Gian, a rather popular comic duo active in showbiz since the 1960s and who already appeared in several movies including the Western spoof *Ric e Gian alla conquista del West* (1967, Osvaldo Civirani), play the inept surgeons. *Kakkientruppen* was their last film appearance, and later on they mostly appeared on TV.
2. The gag plays on the double meaning of the word "casino," which means "brothel" as well as "mess."

1978

Pugni, dollari & spinaci
Italy, color, 101 minutes
D: Emimmo Salvi. *S and SC:* Maria Carla Bufalino, Emimmo Salvi, Aureliano Lippi; *DOP:* Oberdan Troiani; *M:* Ignazio Polizzi and Claudio Natili.
Cast: Maurizio Arena (Sammy Mannia), Charles Pendleton [Gordon Mitchell] (Frank Stilo), Sonia Viviani (Stilo's daughter), Ugo Bologna (The Count), Giacomo Furia (Stilo's lawyer), Richard Lloyd [Iloosh Khoshabe] (Leo Coppola), Pietro Torrisi (Jo Monumento).
Prod: Soilsub Cine TV (Rome).

Sammy Mannia, the owner of a spinach farm and a vegetarian restaurant, is planning to launch a new line of canned spinach by using Popeye's image as a brand. However, Sammy is deep in debt with the shady Frank Stilo, a ruthless industrialist who wants to take hold of Sammy's properties in order to build a skyscraper …

Emimmo Salvi was a former production manager who debuted behind the camera in the early 1960s with the sword-and-sandal *Vulcan Son of Jupiter* (*Vulcano, figlio di Giove*, 1962), starring the Libanese muscleman Iloosh Khoshabe. Of the nine films Salvi directed between 1962 and 1978, none are good, most are quite bad—albeit sporadically interesting: see the eerie Western *3 colpi di Winchester per Ringo* (1966)—but none reaches the appalling trashiness of his last effort, *Pugni, dollari & spinaci* (Fists, Dollars & Spinach).

Italian *locandina* for Emimmo Salvi's *Pugni dollari & spinaci*, featuring Popeye and other E.C. Segar characters

The story is basically a remake of Salvi's earlier musical comedy *Un gangster venuto da Brooklyn* ("A Gangster From Brooklyn," 1966) without the musical numbers—save for a couple of songs by the band Milk & Coffee, which were featured prominently on the credits and throughout the film[1]—but with the addition of another element. As suggested by the title's reference to spinach, Salvi and company drew on one of the world's most recognizable comic icons: Popeye (created in 1929 by Elzie Crisler Segar) the sailor who gains superhuman strength by eating cans of spinach.

Not only does the plot deal with a spinach farmer, Sammy Mannia (Maurizio Arena), who uses the Popeye character on his product's labels, and whose farm is filled with posters (painted by a crazy artist living in his home) portraying Popeye, Olive Oyl and other Segar characters. What's more, Salvi even has his protagonist speak to said posters just like Woody Allen did with the Bogart character in Herbert Ross' *Play It Again, Sam* (1972), as the comics character acts as a mentor and inspiration. On top of that, in the film's climactic boxing/wrestling match, Sammy's pal Jo (Pietro Torrisi) gains his strength back and wins over his adversary (Iloosh Khoshabe) after watching posters of Popeye eating spinach.

The advertising material for the film also has Popeye, Bluto and Olive Oyl in evidence, while several scenes feature a still-frame of a vignette with Popeye and Olive, and the comics characters' off-screen voices commenting on the narrative with a phony American accent. Luckily, Salvi does not go so far as to actually have lookalikes of Segar's characters—except for actor Ugo Bologna, who portrays a Wimpy clone, bowler hat and mustache included.

Pugni, dollari & spinaci was at least partially sponsored by a renowned Italian brand of canned and frozen vegetables, Surgela, which is also featured in several dialogue passages as a plug—keeping in line with the blatant "occult" advertising that plagued Italian cinema of the decade. Therefore, the idea of pairing the world's most famous cartoon sailor and spinach on film might have sounded winning to some. An advert for *Pugni, dollari & spinaci* featured Popeye, surrounded by a crown of spinach and with the Surgela brand well in evidence beneath him, while a line proudly announced that the film was "shot in Surgela's harvest fields." It is the kind of naive publicity stunt that was commonplace at that time.

Believe it or not, the filmmakers actually acquired the rights from Segar's estate. One wonders why they bothered, given the movie's palpable shoestring budget. The film's almost non-existent circulation did not have anything to do with legal troubles, since a copyright reference is featured in the end credits, and *Pugni, dollari & spinaci* was even advertized in the magazine *Braccio di Ferro* (Popeye's Italian name) in March 1977, with a three-page article. Furthermore, the drawings seen in the film appear to be the work of Italian artist Pierluigi Sangalli, who drew Popeye's Italian stories in the magazine. However, Salvi's picture met a sad fate nonetheless. The producer, Giuseppe Castagnini, went bankrupt and *Pugni, dollari & spinaci* disappeared into limbo. It resurfaced years later on home video, for the happy few who savored such an outlandish film experience.

This is not to say that the script lacks interesting elements. Sammy—who usually wears a white T-shirt with the line "Sammy Mannia for president" *handwritten* on the back—is the kind of dreamer that would not have been out of place in a Frank Capra film. He is a vegetarian and an ecologist who plans to build an ark and save all animals, and who dreams of a Utopian society that will no longer be dominated by banks and capitalism. What is more, his restaurant/farmhouse is actually some sort of commune that serves free meals to all the derelicts and homeless people around. On the other hand, his adversary Frank Stilo (Gordon Mitchell) is depicted as the quintessential capitalist-cum-gangster, always wearing striped suits and handling money as if the bills were napkins. There is obviously some sort of post-1968, anti-capitalist grudge at work here, which makes for pretty odd results, considering that *Pugni, dollari & spinaci* was basically aimed at children. The concluding song even features lines such as: "With money you won't buy our freedom … "

Too bad the film's jaw-dropping amateurishness is all over the place. *Pugni, dollari & spinaci* was mostly shot at Gordon Mitchell's Western village, providing squalid sets such as Sammy's "restaurant," while the skyscraper where Stilo has his headquarters is represented via a freeze-frame of some stock footage building, repeated over and over. The dialogue makes one's teeth grind, and the many fight scenes à la Bud Spencer & Terence Hill are so badly choreographed and shot that even experienced stuntmen such as Pietro Torrisi look lost. On the other hand, Mitchell (credited under his real name, Charles Pendleton) hams it up gleefully as the villainous Frank Stilo, while Salvi even retained Khoshabe in a supporting role.

A former teenage idol in the 1950s due to such films as Dino Risi's *Poor But Beautiful* (*Poveri ma belli*, 1957), Maurizio Arena (real name, Maurizio Di Lorenzo) saw his popularity brusquely diminish in the 1960s, in parallel to his gain in weight. In the last years of his life he claimed he had psychic powers and posed as a healer. He died in 1979, at just 45 years of age. *Pugni, dollari & spinaci* was his last film—a sad footnote to his career, indeed.

Note:
1. Milk & Coffee also published a 7" 45 rpm featuring the two songs, *Goodbye S. Francisco/Pugni, dollari & spinaci*. The item can be easily found at reasonable prices on eBay.

1979

Lo scoiattolo, aka *Mücevher Hırsızları*
Italy/Turkey, color, 83 minutes
D: Guido Zurli. SC: Fuat Özlüer, Erdogan Tünaş; DOP: Çetin Gürtop; M: Walter Rizzati; E: not credited.
Cast: Gülsen Bubikoglu (Jasmine), Bulut Aras (Murat), Alan Moore [Attilio Severini] (The Squirrel), Paolo Carlini, Karin Schubert, Edmund Purdom, Tanju Gürsu.
Prod: Erler Film (Istanbul), Mafi Cinematografica (Rome)

Several jewel thieves, including Jasmine and her father, a masked acrobat known as "The Squirrel," have their eyes on a collection of valuable jewelry. They follow the precious cargo from London to Istanbul, but the Squirrel's attempt at stealing the jewels is foiled by a rival thief, Murat. However, yet another gang intervenes, kidnapping both Jasmine and Murat. It is up to the Squirrel to release his daughter before the villains kill her …

By the late 1970s, the Tuscan-born director Guido Zurli had established himself in Turkey, a country where he could keep working without having to surrender to the overflowing trend in then current Italian cinema—the sex film. Backed as usual by producer Türker Inanoglu, with *Lo scoiattolo* Zurli put together a picture in the vein of the 1960s heist flicks à la *Seven Golden Men*, but which also featured a masked acrobat thief that recalled the antiheroes of the *fumetti neri* season.

Turkish audiences loved masked vigilantes and criminals, as shown by the amount of films that featured blatant rip-offs of the most popular comic books, from *Superman* to *Killing*, from *Batman* to *Spiderman*—needless to say, without the producers ever paying a dime to the rights' owners. Turkish cinema was a jungle, but it was also a safe environment for that kind of popular and unpretentious genre productions that were rapidly declining in Italy, partly because of the advent of private television broadcasting and partly for the ever harder competition with the big-budgeted, special effects-ridden blockbusters coming from the United States.

That is exactly what *Lo scoiattolo* is: a naive little crime film where villains all have ominous mustaches and the good guys always win in the end. Violence is bloodless, women are all gorgeous and love prevails even among thieves. The Turkish title *Mücevher Hırsızları* (Jewelry Thieves) was ultimately more pertinent than the Italian one *Lo scoiattolo*, which hinted at the titular masked cat burglar's rather awkward nickname (hence the squirrel's tail that he leaves as a signature in the place of the jewels he steals).

Even though he looks far from irresistible in his adhesive outfit and mask—which makes him look like Robin's uncle—the middle-aged Attilio Severini (here billed as Alan Moore) shows he has not lost his agility after almost two decades as one of Italy's top stuntmen. In one scene, the Squirrel climbs the side of a building, jumping from one balcony floor to the next with the help of a ladder stick, and it is quite obvious that there are no nets underneath, as Zurli is filming the scene with a hand-held camera from the ground floor, in the street below. Severini claimed he was also responsible for the film's scenario—speaking of which, even though some sources ascribe the script to Zurli, Turkish databases credit the screenplay to the expert duo formed by Fuat Özlüer and Erdogan Tünaş (the latter was also responsible for *Target*).

The stunning Italian poster for Guido Zurli's *Lo Scoiattolo* (1979)

Unlike Italo Martinenghi's *3 Supermen Against the Godfather*, made around the same time in Istanbul, Zurli's film looks at least more polished, no doubt due to the director's skills—if Zurli was no *auteur*, at least he knew how to set-up the camera for a shot, something that could not always be said about Martinenghi. Nevertheless, one cannot expect the action scenes being on a par with Hollywood standards. One laughable sequence has the Squirrel sneak into a safe chamber protected with infrared rays—that is, red threads that the thief must avoid touching, while crawling on his back on the floor, in a bargain-basement rendition of the typical heist film suspense routine. Too bad Severini very visibly touches one of the threads as he prepares to do his limbo routine: Zurli obviously did not bother doing a second take …

The cast features a mixture of local stars and familiar faces of Italian cinema. The still gorgeous Karin Schubert had seen her career go downhill because of her drug habits, and within a few years she would fall headfirst into the cauldron of Italian hardcore porn. Here she has a secondary role as a model that is also the lover of a sleek gangster played by Edmund Purdom (a part initially to have been played by Adolfo Celi), here looking as disinterested as ever in the proceedings. Paolo Carlini—who had been in several of Zurli's films, including *Psychopath*—steals the show as an insurance agent who must protect the jewels and fails miserably. Sadly, it was Carlini's last role, as he died of a brain aneurysm in 1979, soon after shooting had been completed. *Lo scoiattolo* was submitted to the Italian Board of Censors in December 1980, and it briefly surfaced in theaters in March 1981, almost two years after being made. As of today, it is available only in copies culled from Turkish TV broadcasts.

SuperAndy, il fratello brutto di Superman

Italy, color, 95 minutes

D: Paolo Bianchini. *SC:* Leone Colonna; *DOP:* Sergio Salvati; *M:* Paolo Casa; *E:* Paolo Boccio.

Cast: Andy Luotto [André Paul Luotto] (SuperAndy), Gino Santercole (SuperKid), Eurilla del Bono (Marthy), Christian Esposito (Tommy), Silvia Annichiarico (Andy's mother in Trypton), Michele Mirabella (Michael, Superkid's agent).

Prod: Filmedia Coop. (Rome).

Just as the planet Trypton is about to explode, the infant SuperAndy is launched in a rocket to planet Earth, as his parents have already done for his brother SuperKid. The alien boy lands in Italy, where Antonio and Maria and their 12-year-old son Tommy take him in. Even though he is psychically still a newborn, Andy looks like an adult—and a rather ugly one at that. However, aided by his adopted parents and stepbrother, Andy learns and acquires human habits without losing the extraordinary superpowers of his own race. After reaching maturity, Andy's purpose is to reunite with SuperKid, who has been hired by a Hollywood production company and earns a living by working in TV advertising. SuperAndy saves a girl named Marthy, who falls in love with him when she sees him dressed up as a superhero, yet she rejects him when Andy appears in the guise of an ordinary man. Aided by Marthy and Tommy, SuperAndy neutralizes all the efforts made by the Americans who fear him as a rival of their own superhero. He also manages to win Marthy's heart and marries her. He will earn his living as a human pony express, by transporting heavy packages all over the world.

Spoof has always been a favorite practice in Italian cinema. An industry focused on jumping on the bandwagon of almost every potential hit—be it Italian or otherwise—

Italian *locandina* for *SuperAndy, il fratello brutto di Superman* (1979)

would often churn out not just rip-offs of the most successful films, but also their parodist deconstruction. For instance, *SuperAndy, il fratello brutto di Superman* (SuperAndy, Superman's Ugly Brother) was submitted to the Italian Board of Censors in May 1979, that is, a mere three months after the Italian release of Richard Donner's *Superman* (1978). It was perhaps one of the last examples in the noble art of parody within a rapidly deteriorating movie industry.

The concept for the film came from scriptwriter Leone Colonna, whose father had been Folco Quilici's collaborator on a number of important Italian documentaries. Colonna had worked with Rodolfo Sonego, Alberto Sordi's favorite screenwriter, and took part—although uncredited—in devising such scripts as the wonderful *The Scopone Game* (*Lo scopone scientifico*, 1972, Luigi Comencini) and *The Cat* (*Il gatto*, 1977, also by Comencini). For *SuperAndy*, his first credited script, Colonna chose to focus the parody not on the Superman character, but on the actor who would play him—just as had been the case with, say, Johnny Dorelli in *How to Kill 400 Duponts*.

The choice of Andy Luotto was emblematic. Born André Paul Luotto, the bearded, hook-nosed American actor (born in New York in 1950, he would later assume Italian citizenship) had become a minor TV personality after the success of Renzo Arbore's non-conformist TV show *L'altra domenica* (The Other Sunday, 1976) which featured among others a very young Roberto Benigni (as an idiotic film critic who had not even seen the movies he was reviewing) and Isabella Rossellini.

Arbore had discovered Luotto in a local TV station and immediately cast him because of the young man's peculiar, angular face and weird ways. Luotto's previous experiences in the movie biz were as a voice actor in the English versions of such films as Enzo Castellari's *The Big Racket* (*Il grande racket*, 1976) and Fernando di Leo's *Mr. Scarface* (*I padroni della città*, 1976). Luotto reflected:

> I entered the cast with Benigni, in the show's third year. Renzo told me that the audience did not like him very much, so he needed someone as his comic relief. I played Renzo's Italian-American cousin, who couldn't understand a word of Italian. So I just remained silent the whole time ...[1]

Luotto's lunar look and idiosyncratic behavior immediately became hugely popular, as it was something audiences would not expect. He almost looked like a misfit—or an alien, for that matter.

> An old woman I met in the street told me "It's good that now deaf-and-dumb people can work on television!" Many actually thought I was some kind of freak, not an actor!

Eventually Luotto would sometimes utter just two words, "Buono" (Good) and "No buono" (No good), using them as a comment on whatever issue was raised during a conversation. It became a catchphrase.

Although the plot for *SuperAndy* partially recalls Bruno Bozzetto's extraordinary cartoon *The SuperVIPs*, Colonna built the film around Luotto's maladjusted persona. The opening scene blatantly remakes the prologue of Donner's film, as SuperAndy's parents send him away from planet Trypton to Earth (in a giant cradle, no less!) and the newborn Andy—who looks already adult, beard and everything—ends up in a *petit bourgeois* Italian family. The film then concentrates on Andy as the unlikely superhero, by juxtaposing his superpowers with his clumsy persona and following his love story with a girl who does not recognize him when he is not wearing his costume (as people normally do with Clark Kent ...).

Despite the film being aimed at an audience of all ages, there is something vaguely disquieting about Luotto—his demented looks, the way he feeds on his stepmother's breast, the surreal encounter with a psychoanalyst named Dr. Spock (sic!)—which suggests that the film might have benefitted from a looser, thought-provoking Monty Python-like approach. At one point, Colonna's script even throws in some sort of half-baked satire against America and capitalism. SuperAndy's handsome brother, SuperKid (played by singer Gino Santercole, replete with Superman's characteristic curl) has become a TV personality and an advertising model in Hollywood, and is exploited like a slave by an evil agent (played by none other than Michele Mirabella, the unfortunate librarian in Lucio Fulci's *The Beyond*).

The fact that neither Luotto nor the rest of the crew ever got close to Hollywood is hardly surprising, as *SuperAndy, il fratello brutto di Superman* looks like it was shot in the outskirts of Rome and never on a real film set for that matter. The overall drab look and slovenliness makes it hard to believe it was directed by such an expert filmmaker as Paolo Bianchini. The director had stayed away from sets since 1972's "Decamerotic" farce *Decameron n°4—Le belle novelle del Boccaccio*, and later turned to TV commercials.

Given that he had directed several competent sci-fi flicks in the previous decade, one assumes that Bianchini had the technical prowess to face a film featuring special effects involving flying people and the like. However, not even Fellini could have done anything with the shoestring budget, and the special effects are definitely forgettable. Yet the result has that same naive, endearing quality as Ciccio Ingrassia's amiable *Exorcist* parody *The Exorciccio* (*L'esorciccio*, 1975). Product placement is ribald (besides the inevitable J&B plug, there is room for other liquors that were everywhere in 1970s Italy such as Fernet Branca and Batida) and so are the attempts at meta-cinema humor. Luotto and his co-stars often comment on the film's score ("Good music! Who's that playing?"), and he and Santercole have an amusing song-and-dance routine to the sound of Paolo Casa's funky theme.

Ten years earlier, the transition from the small to the big screen would have been something rather common for an actor. However, by the end of the decade it was a risky move. True, TV's most popular shows drew in audiences of millions, but cinema was rapidly falling into a comatose state. What is more, filmgoers had become much more demanding in their tastes. No wonder such a rushed, cheap-looking production as *SuperAndy* turned out to be a flop, despite Luotto's popularity.

Bianchini would abandon cinema for almost two decades[2], before returning to the big screen with *La grande quercia* (The Wide Oak, 1997), a movie aimed at children. In interviews, he claimed that he was ashamed of his previous works and considered *La grande quercia* as his real feature film debut. Luotto, on the other hand, would continue his acting career in comedies. He wrote, directed and starred in *Grunt!* (1983), a parody of Jean-Jacques Annaud's *Quest for Fire*, which turned out to be another flop. Later on he took part in many TV shows (including Renzo Arbore's 1985 cult talk-show *Quelli della notte*), TV movies and films, somehow making the transition from comedian to "serious" actor due to his roles in Francesco Rosi's *The Truce* (*La tregua*, 1997) and Ricky Tognazzi's *The Inverse Canon* (*Canone inverso*, 2000). Luotto is also an accomplished chef and has published several books of recipes and personal memories.

Notes:
1. Cappelli, Valerio, "La seconda vita di Andy Luotto," *Il Corriere della Sera* 01/04/1998.
2. Bianchini's only film project in the 1980s was his participation to the collective documentary *L'addio a Enrico Berlinguer*, on the funeral of the leader of the Italian Communist Party who died in 1984.

1980

The Pumaman
(*L'uomo puma*)
Italy, color, 90 minutes
D: Martin Herbert [Alberto De Martino]. *S:* Alberto De Martino; *SC:* Massimo De Rita, Luigi Angelo; *DOP:* Mario Vulpiani; *M:* Renato Serio; *E:* Vincenzo Tomassi.
Cast: Walter George Alton (Professor Tony Farms/Puma Man), Donald Pleasence (Kobras), Miguel Ángel Fuentes (Vadinho), Sydne Rome (Jane Dobson), Silvano Tranquilli (Ambassador Dobson), Benito Stefanelli (Rankin).
Prod: ADM Films Department – DEANTIR (Rome).

The evil Dr. Kobras has found an ancient golden mask, the product of an alien civilization on Earth, which he uses to control people's minds, starting with the Dutch ambassador's daughter Jane Dobson. However, Kobras fears the interference of the Pumaman, a legendary "man-god" who is also the protector of the mask and who might be

The British video ad for *The Pumaman* (1980)

living in London. Kobras' henchmen start murdering all those whom they suspect may be the Pumaman—but who turns out to be the mild-mannered American paleontologist Tony Farms. Mysterious Vadinho, who reveals himself as an Aztec priest, gives Tony a magical belt that grants him amazing super powers. With the help of Vadinho, Pumaman releases Jane from Kobras' influence and ultimately defeats the latter by crashing the helicopter in which he is attempting to flee. Vadinho returns with the mask to his hidden temple in the Andes, aboard an alien spacecraft.

"You are the worst I've ever seen, but you are the Pumaman," his sidekick Vadinho tells the amazed—and definitely not amazing—titular character in one scene, and that pretty much sums up all about Alberto De Martino's *The Pumaman*. If his right-hand man diminishes the hero, that says a lot.

In the late 1970s, after such big hits as *Close Encounters of the Third Kind*, *Star Wars* (both 1977) and *Superman*, science-fiction was becoming "in" again in Italy, or so it seemed. Old classics were being re-released, while filmmakers injected sci-fi elements into their work. What is more, the superhero figure briefly returned to fashion, albeit in a bastardized way, after the wake of the sword-and-sorcery thread, with such titles as Antonio Margheriti's *Yor, the Hunter from the Future*, based on Juan Zanotto and Ray Collins' comic book. Luigi Cozzi's *Hercules* (1983) would also reprise the old *peplum* genre in an openly superheroic fashion, by enhancing the sword-and-sorcery elements.

De Martino's film, on the other hand, most likely germinated after the success of *Superman*, yet the script also paid reference to Erich von Däniken's books about an alien race having landed on Earth before civilization began, thus imposing its influence on early human culture (and, in the case of the Pumaman, injecting selected individuals with superpowers). After the obligatory post-*Star Wars* onscreen text informs us that "an ancient Aztec legend tells of a God who descended to Earth from the stars at the dawn of time and became father to the first Pumaman … ," the opening scene shows an alien spaceship descending over Stonehenge. The fact that the globe-shaped vessel looks like a giant disco mirror ball—not to mention that the megalithic landscape (why not an *Aztec* one, given said prophecy, one wonders?) seems like the set for Spinal Tap's song *Stonehenge*—gives an idea of the film's shortcomings right from the start.

As the director explained:

> *The Pumaman* was a production based on the trend of the moment. I had always done it that way and always done well. But regarding this genre of film, there was the audience's diffidence toward Italian movies featuring special effects. They knew we were not up to the task, and didn't take us seriously.[1]

The (too) many scenes involving the titular hero "flying" are a case in point. De Martino recalled that the special effects caused lots of problems on the set.

> We had to do them with a camera that Italo Zingarelli had purchased in Germany, but the technicians were not able to use it. On the last days of shooting, so as not to go beyond schedule, I hired a blue-screen crew and shot all the scenes that were required in just two days.[2]

The special effects' overall clumsiness gives away the low-budget and puts egg on the faces of the filmmakers further demonstrating that, with the growing budgets and technical proficiency of the major Hollywood blockbusters, for Italian genre cinema it was quickly becoming impossible to fight Goliath with a mere sling. In this case, the sling and bullets are cheap transparent backgrounds and rear projections, plus a pair of green contact lenses for the scene in which the Pumaman sees in the dark, which allows for an infrared-like POV shot of the hero defeating his enemies.

Not that Massimo De Rita and Luigi Angelo's script was riveting with original ideas. Once again the scriptwriters drew heavily on *The Phantom* (hinting at a generational issue that Italian superhero films—and their makers—never really left behind), imagining that the Pumaman role, as well as his power-inducing belt, have been passed on from generation to generation. The plot outline is yet again a bare-bones "learning to cope with powers" routine, as the unaware, meek paleontology professor Tony Farms learns that he is, indeed, The Pumaman.

Besides his ability to fly and see in the dark, the Pumaman can pass through solid matter like walls (which means more awkward special effects on display) and has ESP powers that allow De Martino to throw in a camera negative trip—à la the poor man's *2001: A Space Odyssey*. Tony can even stop his own heartbeat and fall into a cataleptic state

The U.S. video sleeve for *The Pumaman*

of apparent death for 10 minutes, which inspires a would-be suspenseful scene where Pleasence's sidekick (stuntman Benito Stefanelli) double-checks if Tony is actually dead as he seems to be. However, the hero's outfit is really a sight to behold. Once he has worn a prizefighter-like magical belt, Tony sports a brown sweater with a puma's muzzle on it, a pair of buckskin trousers and shoes. It is less a superhero costume than a casual outfit for a stroll in the park.

Meanwhile, as the required evil villain (graced with the ominous name Kobras), Donald Pleasence spouts his share of idiotic lines of dialogue while maneuvering a "golden" mask (a prop wrapped up in golden aluminum foil, that is) which allows him to control the minds of whoever comes close, thus enabling him to (yawn) rule the world. Perhaps the film's single weirdest idea is having Kobras keep in his lair wax replicas of the heads of the people whom he controls. As Kobras' mind grip weakens, the heads start cracking. The rest is so old-hat it almost looks like recycled footage from De Martino's earlier spy flicks of the 1960s: the same banal good vs. evil dichotomy, the same predictable adventures and cliff-hangers and the same stuntmen (now in their middle ages) doing their routine (Nello Pazzafini, Stefanelli, Giovanni "Superargo" Cianfriglia).

Alberto De Martino's memories about the motion picture that inaugurated his third decade as a filmmaker were not very fond. Putting it bluntly:

It was the only pic I did wrong in my whole career.[3] No one went to see it. Private TV stations were taking over. Beforehand, there was RAI, which used to broadcast one film with a commercial break in the middle. When *The Pumaman* came out the invasion had started. When I saw it was a flop, I started asking myself questions. I had made a film I shouldn't have. However, it did well abroad and managed to get the guaranteed minimum back, otherwise I'd have had to sell my house. It did not even gross half a billion *lire* in Italy. However, they still talk about *The Pumaman*, and no one understands why. It became a cult film.[4]

"Cult" is perhaps an exaggeration. *The Pumaman* is the type of flick that bad movie fans laugh at. The kind soon to appear on *Mystery Science Theater 3000*. De Martino claimed he had to inject humor into the film as that was the only way to save it[5], but attempts at irony do not help much, apart from a few humorous dialogue exchanges:

> Who's The Pumaman? A comic book hero? Never heard of him!
> Actually, he did not exist until yesterday!
> Does this at least provide you with something?
> Only trouble for now!

It is never clear whether something is conceived with laughter in mind or is accidentally ridiculous. Take the would-be mystical lines spouted by Vadinho, the Pumaman's sidekick (played by Miguel Ángel Fuentes, seen also in Herzog's *Fitzcarraldo*, 1982), such as: "Every man is a god, every man is free," which becomes a sort of mantra throughout the film. Furthermore, Renato Serio's cheesy keyboard score sounds like a theme for a kiddy TV show, and a bad one at that.

However, the film's casting is the final nail in the coffin. As the love interest, Sydne Rome (wearing black leather bodysuits with pointy shoulders that make her look like a dominatrix from the future) is indifferent at best, and the fact that she dubs her own voice in the Italian version does not help. As the Pumaman, Walter George Alton is, quite simply, a walking embarrassment. Alton was an aspiring actor when he had played a small role in Blake Edwards' *10* (1979), but he was blessed by this, his only leading role. Then, after another little-seen film (Lawrence Dane's *Street Dance*), he disappeared once and for all.

As Vadinho, the mystic/priest/mentor/sidekick, the Mexican Fuentes is perhaps the least banal character, if only because of his dime-store philosophical one-liners and his vocation to martyrdom, that in the pre-finale has him sneaking into Kobras' lair wearing a dynamite belt, ready to blow himself up in order to destroy the villain—an idea which would never pass the green light in today's age of political correctness.

As De Martino recalled:

> In the U.S. they searched for the leading actor everywhere, but he wasn't a real actor. I don't think he has done anything else in his career.

De Martino was right. After giving up on acting, Alton became a medical malpractice attorney in New York City. His "comeback" took place on the small screen, when he was interviewed in a satirical fake news piece aired on *The Daily Show with Jon Stewart* in November 2007.

Although there is no official DVD release of the film, *The Pumaman* is available to home video as part of the *Mystery Science Theater 3000* series. Joel Hodgson and company obviously had a field day with this one—and who could blame them?

Notes:
1. Gomarasca, Manlio, "Il cinema è quello che ci fa," in Gomarasca, Manlio and Pulici, Davide, eds., "Fatti di cinema. Controcorrente 3," *Nocturno Dossier* #51, October 2006, p. 9.
2. Ibid.
3. Ibid.
4. Ercolani, Eugenio, "Semplicemente cineasta! Intervista a Alberto De Martino," www.fascination-cinema.it.
5. Gomarasca, "Il cinema è quello che ci fa," p. 9.

Super Fuzz
(*Poliziotto superpiù*, aka *Supersnooper*)
Italy/U.S.A./Spain, color, 97 minutes

D: Sergio Corbucci. *S and SC:* Sergio Corbucci, Sabatino Ciuffini; *DOP:* Silvano Ippoliti; *M:* Michelangelo La Bionda; *E:* Eugene Ballaby [Eugenio Alabiso].
Cast: Terence Hill [Mario Girotti] (Dave Speed), Ernest Borgnine (Sgt. Willy Dunlop), Joanne Dru (Rosy Labouche), Marc Lawrence (Torpedo), Julie Gordon (Evelyn), Sal Borgese (Paradise Alley)
Prod: El Pico S.A. (Rome), Trans Cinema Tv (Madrid).
Rookie police officer Dave Speed falls into a top-secret nuclear experiment conducted by NASA in an Indian reservation in the Everglade. As a red plutonium rocket detonates, Dave is caught in the explosion, and as a result he acquires superpowers. Dave begins to use his powers—which he temporarily loses when exposed to the color red—in the line of duty, and together with his partner, Sergeant Willie Dunlop (whose daughter Evelyn he is in love with), he tracks down a master counterfeiter, Torpedo. Speed is framed for his best friend's murder and sentenced to the electric chair after Torpedo's goons imprison Dunlop in a freezer on a fishing trawler that is then sunk. He manages to escape, and discovers that Willie, still locked inside the underwater freezer, is not dead. The two cops set out to give Torpedo his just desserts ...

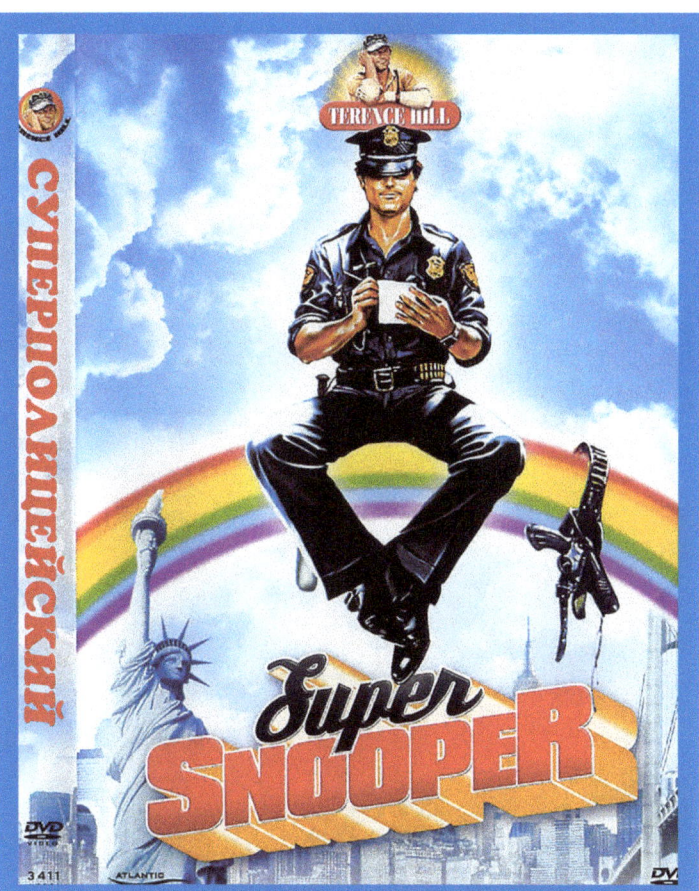

The Russian DVD cover art for *Super Fuzz*

In the early '80s, the days of the Spaghetti Western were just a vague memory for Sergio Corbucci. After helping define the genre in the mid-1960s and directing a handful of its most memorable (and darkly violent) examples, Corbucci quickly smelled its decline, and after the box-office failure of *Bandera Bandits* (aka *Sonny and Jed*, 1972), co-starring Tomas Milian and Susan George, he abandoned the Western genre, only marginally returning to it with the mildly amusing spoof *Shoot First ... Ask Questions Later* (*Il bianco, il giallo, il nero*, 1975), which teamed up Milian (in caricatured Japanese samurai make-up, spoofing Toshiro Mifune's character in *Red Sun*, 1971), Giuliano Gemma and Eli Wallach. Perhaps this was not Corbucci's best effort, but it was one that hinted at the direction his career would take.

Since the mid-1970s, Corbucci became one of Italy's most successful filmmakers within the comedy genre—

Terence Hill as superhero cop Dave Speed in an Italian lobby card for Sergio Corbucci's *Super Fuzz*

even though, quality-wise, his output was not comparable to his earlier works such as *Django* (1966) or *The Great Silence* (*Il grande silenzio*, 1968). Similarly, Bud Spencer and Terence Hill—aka Carlo Pedersoli and Mario Girotti, Italy's most profitable comedy duo since the release of 1970's *My Name Is Trinity*—had moved away from the Western and flirted with other genres, such as the modern-day "buddy cop" movie *Crime Busters* (*I due superpiedi quasi piatti*, 1977, Enzo Barboni), which nevertheless retained the recurring elements of their work: paper-thin plots, amiable family-friendly humor, lots of slapstick brawls and fistfights.

Corbucci first directed the couple in the 1978 action comedy *Trinity: Gambling for High Stakes*, his first film shot in the United States[1]. Even though it was a box-office hit in Italy, the typical Spencer/Hill formula was not exactly Corbucci's taste, as he himself recalled:

> I found myself working with two actors I was not familiar with, on a type of film which I actually did not like that much.

Corbucci correctly pointed out the comic book-like, cartoonish essence of Spencer and Hill's films:

> Take Mickey Mouse and Donald Duck—they can't be anything else, no matter what. The big guy is always the big guy, good-natured, who slaps the baddies and pretends to be angry, while the other guy is the smart one, who always gets into trouble. The problem is having them act in a context that is different from the previous one, because eventually the ultimate goal is having them slap the bad guys and win, whatever the situation.[2]

Corbucci teamed up again with the sole Hill for *Super Fuzz* (aka *Supersnooper*, the title that appears over the opening credits): Perhaps exaggerating things a little bit, the director recalled:

It was a success in the United States … [*Super Fuzz* became a staple on early '80s HBO rotation and today is available on DVD on the Somerville House label] Usually Spencer and Hill pics were not distributed in the States, since they were made for other markets. The Americans don't like Bud Spencer; they don't know who he is. Terence—blond, pale blue eyes, of German origins—is more akin to the Anglo-Saxon standard, so he could make his way into the U.S. market. He actually starred in a couple of American films as he speaks English without any accent, and so he can be accepted as the protagonist, whereas the other one wouldn't.[3]

This might explain why this time Corbucci put aside the seemingly endless brawls in favor of fantasy and cartoon-like elements which hinted at the then-current *Superman* craze, while keeping up with Hill's onscreen persona. The script, by the director and Sabatino Ciuffini, is a simple-minded affair, replete with stereotyped characters (including the expectedly idiotic baddies, with the usual array of familiar stuntmen popping up as the goons) and a half-baked crime/action plot about a counterfeit ring which in the writers' intention was supposed to be made marginally more interesting by the flashback structure. The film opens with Hill (as rookie cop-cum-superhero Dave Speed) about to be executed for the umpteenth time—he keeps surviving electrocutions—for a murder he did not commit.

Even though Hill is not the typical masked superhero, he does wear a police uniform, an element not to be underestimated, especially at a time when being a cop was a tough and ungrateful job in Italy, as shown by the so-called *poliziotteschi*. In many ways, *Super Fuzz* is a comic-like fantasy which plays in a humorous way several themes that were typical of the Italian crime genre, and which perhaps unconsciously—despite or possibly because of its American setting—emphasized a need for justice that was being frustrated by everyday news. In some ways, the blond "super fuzz" played by Terence Hill was the children-friendly, less problematic version of the martyr-like cops played by Maurizio Merli. He would come close to death and martyrdom, but he defeated the bad guys in the end. In *Super Fuzz*, Hill reprises his usual good guy character: simpleton at times and yet smarter than most other people in sight; he relies heavily on his angelic looks, disarming smile and magnetic blue eyes, which more than make up for his indifferent acting. He even keeps his eating habits in the Trinity series, devouring a bowl of beans with a heavy appetite as his last prison meal.

Corbucci did not spare the comic book elements. The superhero's genesis is in the vein of so many U.S. post-war comics, being the result of the exposure to nuclear radiation (coming from a supposedly secret NASA experiment … which nonetheless turns up in the local news!), whereas Dave's attitude is more akin to the good-humored Popeye. His "superpowers," invariably conceived to comic effect, are a weird bunch: super-speed, telekinesis, super-human strength, foresight, invulnerability, the capacity to breathe underwater and catch a bullet between his bare teeth or to inflate a bubblegum and create a floating balloon. Although the most amusing of all is Dave being able to walk on the water and speak the language of fish, which gives him a Messiah-like halo while in keeping with the movie's bland ecological message (a recurring theme in Hill's filmography). Similarly to Kryptonite having the effect of neutralizing Superman, Dave's powers temporarily disappear in the presence of the color red, which provides a few amusing or tepidly suspenseful moments. Predictably, the special effects are definitely less than special, and they

Ernest Borgnine (left) and Terence Hill in a German lobby card for *Super Fuzz*

often rely on awkward blue screen techniques; the climax features Dave and his partner inside the aforementioned floating bubblegum balloon and looks not much better than the dreadful blue backdrops seen in Gianfranco Parolini's inept *Yeti*.

Since the film was designed for U.S. consumption and shot on location in Miami, Corbucci managed to include a few familiar Hollywood faces in the cast. As Hill's sidekick, the late, great Ernest Borgnine provides the expected dose of hammy acting, while Marc Lawrence turns up in his requisite bad guy role. As the faded actress whom Borgnine has a crush on, and who is then revealed to be in cahoots with the main villain, the 58-year-old Joanne Dru makes an ill-fated comeback that has one yearn for the days of *Red River* (1948, Howard Hawks) and *She Wore A Yellow Ribbon* (1949, John Ford). Sadly, *Super Fuzz* was to be her last film.

Corbucci teamed up again with Spencer and Hill for 1981's *A Friend Is a Treasure* (*Chi trova un amico trova un tesoro*).

Notes:
1. "I found myself in this boundless and funny America, which I had so often created in my Westerns. I had invented an America that did not exist anymore, and perhaps never really existed. It was our own imaginary America, the one portrayed by the great American directors whom we all loved." Caldiron, Orio and Corbucci, Nori, *Sergio Corbucci* (Rimini: Ramberti, 1993), p. 92.
2. Ibid.
3. Ibid., p. 95. Corbucci is referring to Dick Richards' *March Or Die* (an English production, actually) and Jonathan Kaplan's *Mr. Billion*, both 1977.

3 Supermen Against the Godfather

(*3 supermen contro il padrino*, aka *Los tres supermen contra el padrino*, aka *Süpermenler*)

Italy/Spain/Turkey, color, 87 minutes

D: Italo Martinenghi. *S:* Italo Martinenghi; *SC:* Italo Martinenghi, Tony Blond [Antonio Cesare Corti]; *DOP:* Aldo Ricci, Çetin Gürtop; *M:* Nico Fidenco; *E:* Italo Martinenghi.

Cast: Nick Jordan [Aldo Canti] (Atak), Sal Borgese (Matrak), George Arkın [Cüneyt Arkın] (Detective Murat/Agent Brad), Aldo Sambrell (Baba Jackson), Güngör Bayrak (Agata), Übsak Emre (Agata's lover), Andrea Guzon (Miss Braun, the nurse), Tony Blond (Yavsak).

Prod: Barbatoja Film (Elba), Cinesecolo (Rome), Asbrell Productions (Madrid), Erler Film (Istanbul).

The time machine invented by Professor Panzarotti, which is now located in Istanbul, is at the center of many people's attention.

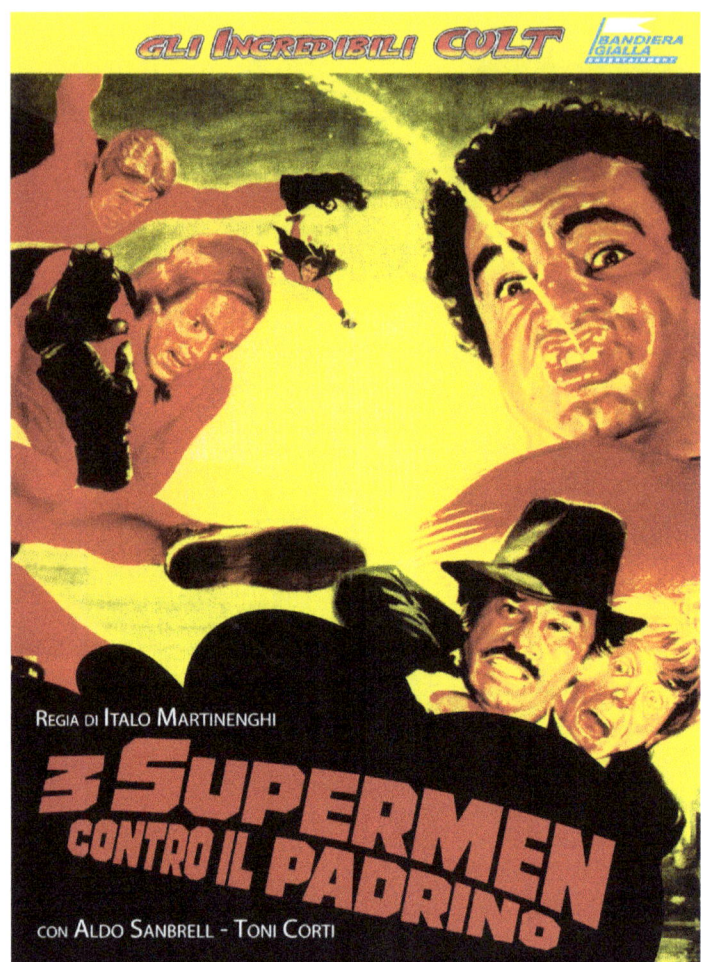

The Italian DVD cover art for Italo Martinenghi's *3 Supermen Against the Godfather* (1980)

A Mafia godfather wants to get hold of it so he can travel back in time and find out who has betrayed him by stealing a shipment of heroin. What he does not suspect, though, is that the traitor is his own daughter, Agata. F.B.I. agent Brad also needs the device in order to travel back into the past and dig out a treasure. Brad teams up with his old friends, Nick and Sal, but the godfather steals the time machine and kidnaps Panzarotti. However, the inept gangster inadvertently sabotages the invention, while the professor loses his memory. Brad and his acolytes disguise themselves as a doctor and paramedics in order to retrieve Panzarotti from the clinic where he is being taken prisoner, with the help of a sensuous nurse, who is actually an F.B.I. agent incognito …

The time lapse between Italo Martinenghi's feature debut *The 3 Supermen in the West* and *3 Supermen Against the Godfather* coincided with a severe backlash that struck the Italian film industry. By the mid-'70s, the Spaghetti Western was waning, while the crime film that had been the country's other major genre would last only a few years more. The birth of local TV stations marked the beginning of the end, as they attracted a larger number of moviegoers by offering a wide array of films throughout the day, plus stripteases and assorted erotic shows.

The three supermen (from left to right): Sal Borgese, Cüneyt Arkın and Aldo Canti

The number of spectators was steadily decreasing, with a figure of about a hundred million per year from 1975 onwards. Meanwhile, since February 1977 Italian television finally started broadcasting in color, an event that further alienated moviegoers. A comparison between box-office gross in 1976 and 1977 is self-evident, with a decrease from 455 to 374 million tickets sold. In 1979 said quota further diminished to 276 million—about half as much as four years earlier. Movie theaters raised the ticket price but did not improve their service. Many cinema houses were old if not decrepit, with uncomfortable seats and obsolete projectors.

The economical hemorrhage saw a dramatic turn of the screw within the movie industry. A small number of filmmakers even moved to Turkey to shoot their B-films, availing themselves of productive benefits and minimal costs. The results were often below average, yet they allowed small-time producers, former stars and directors to keep breathing, by aiming their output at a less demanding and decidedly more enthusiastic audience.

Through his friend Guido Zurli, who had been making films in Turkey since 1971, Martinenghi teamed up with Turkish mogul producer Türker Inanoglu to shoot his second *Three Supermen* flick. Turkey loved superheroes, as shown by the home-made renditions of popular masked characters such as The Phantom (who starred in three films starting with *Kızıl Maske*, 1968), Zorro, The Lone Ranger, Superman (see *Süpermen Fantoma'ya Karsı*, 1969, where he meets Fantômas), not to mention the outlandish trio of T. Fikret Uçak's *3 Dev Adam*, in which El Santo and Captain America team up to fight an evil Spiderman. Hence, Martinenghi's attempt at making his characters known to the local audience was, at least on paper, a wise one. On the other hand, the Italian market was by now practically unattainable for such productions as *3 Supermen Against the Godfather*. The film received a regular visa in Italy but was practically never distributed and surfaced to home video only a quarter of a century later.

The intervention of Turkish financers allowed for the presence in the cast of local movie star Cüneyt Arkın as the F.B.I. agent who enlists the two amiable acrobatic thieves on a dangerous mission, while Aldo Canti returned to his old bright red outfit (after the weird spin-off *Super Stooges vs. Wonder Women*) alongside the monolithic Sal Borgese as the mute of the trio. *3 Supermen Against the Godfather* was co-produced by Spanish actor Aldo Sambrell (who also played the unlikely godfather) with his company Asbrell, while Martinenghi took advantage of the presence of Italians residing in Turkey, such as production secretary Giovanni Scognamillo (who plays a doctor) and his daughter Sandra.

Production values were quite poor—a fact underlined by the title sequence, in which hand-written titles appear in balloons over crudely animated silhouettes of the three characters "flying"—while the story was a thin, barely fleshed out outline replete with the usual acrobatics and fistfights. Martinenghi recycled Professor Panzarotti and

3 Supermen Against the Godfather featured mild erotic elements. Spanish bombshell Andrea Guzon finds herself fought over by Aldo Sambrell (left) and Cüneyt Arkın.

his time machine from the previous episode (and he would use the gimmick again in the subsequent *Three Supermen at the Olympic Games*), but this time there is not even room for time travel, save for one sequence near the beginning. However, the action scenes—including a long chase and fight at the Istanbul dock—are at least passable, something that cannot be said about the following entries in the series. Arkın makes for a surprisingly apt lead, due to his martial arts skills (which he proudly displays in his introductory scene) and appealing screen presence, while Jordan and Borgese (who has his required scene in drag, this time as an ugly nurse) are at their athletic best.

What sets the film apart from its predecessors is the mild eroticism on display that makes it closer in style to 1970s Italian sexy comedies, which were very popular in Turkey by then. However, the local audience had already savored the mixture between superheroes and eroticism. A recent addition to the thread was Yılmaz Atadeniz' *Süper Selami* (1979), a Superman parody about a loser who acquires superpowers which nevertheless work only if he does not have sex (hints of *Argoman the Fantastic Superman* here). The film is stuffed with nudity and spiced together with stolen movie themes.

3 Supermen Against the Godfather is a decidedly tamer affair in comparison. No female nudity is included, but Martinenghi has the indigenous starlet Güngör Bayrak spend several sequences wearing only a breath-taking bikini, while the Spanish bombshell Andrea Guzon (seen in Jess Franco's *Sadomania* and in Joe d'Amato's *The Pleasure*, among others) plays a sexy agent/nurse who has to cope with Panzarotti's attentions, after the scientist's libido has been awakened via an electroshock designed to have him regain his memory. In one sequence Guzon ends up in her lingerie as well, while Arkın and Sambrell fondle her libidinously. Nico Fidenco's score adds the expected silly title song (co-written by Martinenghi and his co-scriptwriter Antonio Cesare Corti), this time with vague dance ambitions; it pops up again and again throughout the film.

The previous year Martinenghi had helmed the awful comedy *Lady Football* (1979), shot in Switzerland and starring singer-turned-actor Mino Reitano, Francesca Romana Coluzzi and the director's own son Stefano, where he had plenty of room to display his love for soccer. According to Turkish film scholar Kaya Özkaracalar, in 1981 Martinenghi was apparently again in Istanbul for location scouting for a sequel called *Lady Football Players*, which was never made. The producer-director would also cast his offspring in his subsequent films, *Three Supermen at the Olympic Games* (1984) and *Three Supermen in S. Domingo* (1986), which brought the series to a sad end.

1982

Bath-man dal pianeta Eros, aka *Klito-Bell*
Italy, color, 85 minutes
D: Richard Bennett [Antonio D'Agostino]; *S and SC:* Richard Bennett; *DOP:* Sam Martinez [Sergio Martinelli]; *M:* Ubaldo Continiello; *E:* Michèle Bourdon.
Cast: Mark Shanon [Manlio Cersosimo] (Bath-man/Erotikon), Nadine Roussial (Bath Baby/Klito-Bell), Riccardo Zamagni (Helios), Guia Lauri Filzi [Barbara De Massi] (The Commissioner's wife), Sabrina Mastrolorenzi (Rape victim), Giuseppe Alotta (Poker), Sandy Samuel [Ornella Picozzi] (Girl at the party), Pauline Teutscher (Poker's Pussy-girl #1), Cathy Ménard (Poker's Pussy-girl #2), Luigi Tripodi (Commissioner).
Prod: Cinematografica Roma Rama (Rome).
In New York a Commissioner fights organized crime, helped by a clumsy masked superhero named Bath-man. However, Bath-man

is actually an over-sexed alien from the remote planet Eros, where he was known as Erotikon, and who put his sexual proclivities aside after landing on Earth in order to struggle against evil. The same happened to his partner Klito-Bell, otherwise known as Bath Baby. The lord of planet Eros sends an idiotic robot agent named Helios to Earth in order to redeem the two superheroes. Meanwhile New York is experiencing a crime wave. Criminals hired by the evil Poker are raping young women. Catwoman turns the Commissioner into a homosexual with her raygun, while the Commissioner's wife is raped. Bath-man and Bath Baby intervene each time, but eventually it is Helios who restores order. He summons the main characters into a room and starts a huge orgy, after which they will no longer be enemies.

A man dressed in a Batman costume, his cape fluttering in the wind, is riding his bicycle down a hill in a muddy country road, amid placidly ruminant cows. The camera accompanies his descent from the distance, in a lingering excruciating shot, until the man almost gets stuck in a puddle of mud, then jumps down from the bike and proceeds on foot, pushing his bike beside him. The opening scene for *Bath-man dal pianeta Eros* deserves a place in the annals of bad cinema, no doubt about it. One wonders what reaction there might have been on the part of the raincoat crowd that populated "red-light" theaters, eagerly awaiting for sexually explicit material. Not that Antonio D'Agostino's film does not deliver the goods, thanks to such Italian porn regulars as Mark Shanon [sic!], aka Manlio Cersosimo—Italy's answer to Harry Reems, a stalwart presence of many Aristide Massaccesi porn epics and here donning Batman's cape and costume—as well as a bunch of other hardcore regulars. Yet, the effect is still today astonishing to the viewer.

Bath-man dal pianeta Eros was the third in a quartet of hardcore porn quickies shot and produced consecutively by Antonio D'Agostino between late 1981 and early 1982. Besides Batman, D'Agostino's inspiration might well have been the photonovel *Supersex*, originally published in 1967 (from an idea by Alan G. Ferguson, with the subtitle "Il fotofilm fantaerotico") and later re-launched in the 1970s in a hardcore version starring the French porn actor Gabriel Pontello as the eponymous character, a sexually insatiable alien who moonlights as a secret agent and whose sexual escapades are invariable accompanied with the immortal battle cry, "Ifix Tcen Tcen!" It is worth noting that in their earlier incarnation the *Supersex* photonovels also included the erotic adventures of a female alien named Sexybell.

Overall, *Bath-man dal pianeta Eros* is not so far from a live-action version of the legendary "Tijuana Bibles" that featured popular comic characters indulging in sexual activities. As Italian film critic Manlio Gomarasca noted:

> *Bath-man* curiously predates by at least a dozen years hardcore cinema's tendency to parody, and remains an isolated case in this period.[1]

Such a parody, it must be added, is decidedly not subtle in any way. Cersosimo's mustached Bath-man is shown in undershirt and underpants, complaining of back pain and jolting in fear when his female assistant pops up unexpectedly in his room. What is more, the fearless superhero speaks with a strong Roman accent and Ubaldo Continiello's overly jokey score underlines his athletic (and sexual) shortcomings. To add insult to injury for Batman fans, his opponents are a supercriminal named *Poker* (Giuseppe Alotta)—who wears a jester's costume and hat and has two Cat-Woman types nicknamed "Pussy-girls" (Pauline Teutscher and Cathy Ménard) as sidekicks—and a flamboyantly gay Penguin lookalike. (Incidentally, the idea of a ray that turns people into homosexuals clearly gives an idea of how little political correctness was taken into account).

Bath-man, the over-sexed alien from the remote planet Eros, now fights evil on Earth.

The filmmakers' disdain for copyright does not stop here. In a scene Bath Baby masturbates to the sound of a music theme that liberally "borrows" from Serge Gainsbourg's *Je t'aime, moi non plus*.

The elusive Rocco D'Amato, author of the picturesque dictionary on Italian hardcore porn *DizionHard*, commented:

> Even though we won't go so far as saying we are enthusiastic about the film, we acknowledge Bennett the courage (or straight face?) of repeatedly challenging the rules of good taste, which even in porn, does not happen frequently.[2]

That said, it would take guts (and quite debatable tastes) to call the effort noteworthy, let alone praise the film's technical qualities. Examples? Although the story takes place in New York City, the sets are obviously very much Italian. A police station is sparsely recreated in a room of the villa where most of the film is shot[3], whose walls are furnished with stars-and-stripes flags. But there is more than that.

Some of the hardcore scenes are set in somehow futuristic surroundings—which, given the shoestring budget, allows for laughable results. The first one features the performers in ancient Greece-like costumes and psychedelic lights. Another scene has a trio of thugs in *A Clockwork Orange*-like droogs outfits—that is, bowler hats and leopard singlets—raping a woman (Sabrina Mastrolorenzi) … in someone's kitchen. The skeleton-like plot eventually climaxes in the predictable orgy, after the robotic agent from planet Eros (Riccardo Zamagni, with his face painted silver) magically reunites all the main characters in a room and undresses them with his mind powers. For Italian hardcore completists, the film would produce Italian porn cinema's first DP, courtesy of Guia Lauri Filzi, alias Barbara De Massi. The not-so ravishing actress, one of Italy's earlier porn stars, would retire from the business in 1985.

D'Agostino (born in Catanzaro in 1938) had debuted in 1979 with the pretentious sex flick *La cerimonia dei sensi*, and soon became one of Italy's leading porn filmmakers of the decade. Amidst a plethora of hardcore flicks, he also directed two erotic pseudo-documentaries which were rather successful at the box-office, *Impariamo ad amarci: guida all'educazione sessuale* (Let's Learn to Love One Another: A Guide to Sexual Education," 1985) and *Mutant Sexual Behaviour* (*Noi e l'amore – Comportamento sessuale variante*, 1986). He gave up filmmaking in the late nineties.

The film was also distributed in Spain in 1986, as *Vicio en el planeta Eros*. It was released to home video in Italy under the title *Klito-Bell*.

Notes:

1. Gomarasca, Manlio, *Culthard*, Nocturno Book #1, 1997, p. 110.
2. D'Amato, Rocco, *DizionHard. Il porno italiano in pellicola e videocassetta dalle origini al 1990* (Rome: RD'A Editions, 2003), p. 36.
3. The villa, located in Rignano Flaminio near Rome, was the set of many other Italian hardcore flicks of the period, including D'Agostino's *Triangolo erotico* (1982).

Snow White and the 7 Wise Men
(*Biancaneve & Co...*)
Italy, color, 95 minutes
D: Mario Bianchi. *S:* Marino Girolami and Marino Onorati; *SC:* Luigi Petrini and Nino Marino; *DOP:* Umberto Galeassi; *M:* Ubaldo Continiello; *E:* Adriano Tagliavia.

Cast: Michela Miti (Biancaneve), Franco Bracardi (Innkeeper), Aldo Sambrell (King Agesilao), Damianne Saint-Clair (Queen Crimilde), Gianfranco D'Angelo (The Talking Mirror), Oreste Lionello (Magone the Magician), Gianni Magni (Jack the Silencer), Enzo Garinei (Stronzolo), Aldo Ralli (Dammelo), Tiberio Murgia (Godolo), Mireno Scali (Prince Charming).

Prod: Valiant (Rome).

After Biancaneve's mother the Queen dies giving birth to her, the sex-addicted King Agesilao is tricked into remarrying by the wicked Crimilde, who unknown to everyone—is actually a transsexual. The years pass and Biancaneve becomes a beautiful young woman. Resenting the threat she perceives her stepdaughter represents, Crimilde hires a killer named Jack to dispatch her. Jack, however, becomes smitten with Biancaneve and cannot bring himself to kill the girl. Instead he takes Biancaneve's virginity and presents a lock of her pubic hair to the queen as proof that Biancaneve is dead. Unable to return home, Biancaneve wanders the kingdom and meets the seven saviors, who accommodate her in their abode. Crimilde, who was turned into a man by the magician Magone, poisons Biancaneve, causing her to fall into a state of apparent death.

The Italian DVD cover art for Mario Bianchi's *Biancaneve & Co* (1982)

The saviors learn that Biancaneve will revive only by having intercourse with Prince Charming. However, the spell will be broken only if she is a virgin …

Clearly inspired by Rubino Ventura and Leone Frollo's adults-only comic *Biancaneve* (although the source is not indicated in the credits), *Biancaneve & Co…* is a cheap erotic farce whose main point of interest is the presence of the milk-skinned Michela Miti, in various states of undress, as the titular *ingénue*. The gorgeous Miti definitely looks like Frollo's creation, including the ribbons in the hair that make her look like the quintessential innocent little girl … at least while she has her clothes on. The rest of the cast comprises a number of comedians that were often seen in low-budget comedies of the period, such as Gianfranco D'Angelo and Oreste Lionello, and the Seven Dwarfs are replaced (possibly because of practical reasons) by seven "wise men" with such salacious names as Stronzolo (Assholey), another reference to Barbieri and Frollo's comic.[1]

Shot in and around the Lazio village of Manziana and at castle Arsoli (seen in Margheriti's *The Long Hair of Death*, 1964, and *Mrs. Stiletto*, among others), *Biancaneve & Co…* features anachronisms galore. Some are part of the filmmakers' attempt at soliciting laughter. The "talking mirror" is a TV set in which a newscaster appears to answer Crimilde's questions, the king views 8mm pornographic films which he seized from his subjects, the characters communicate by telephone and sometimes wear modern clothes. Others, such as cars passing in the background in the scene where Godolo (veteran supporting actor Tiberio Murgia, best-remembered for *Big Deal on Madonna Street*) is arrested in the village square, are just part of the film's overall sloppiness[2]. The camera filming the actors with the setting sun behind their backs ruins several scenes, such as the one where the saviors discuss how to save the cataleptic Biancaneve. This effect is downright amateurish.

The attempts at comedy include references to the early Italian private broadcasters, notably in the character of the "talking mirror" (D'Angelo) who apes some of the more awkward aspects of the period's naive local television. The film employs a voice-over impersonator of Diego Abatantuono (then at the peak of his fame), and features lookalikes of other popular comedians such as Carlo Verdone and Roberto Benigni. The latter, played by Mireno Scali as the ugly-looking Prince Charming, was a recurring presence in low-budget comedies of the early 1980s, once again underlining the frantic urge at imitation that was common to many films of the period. Despite the occasional offbeat or demented idea (such as Crimilde turning into a male and poisoning Biancaneve by having her perform fellatio on his poisonous member), the film is a dire, unfunny mess and further proof of Mario Bianchi's ineptitude as a filmmaker. Around the same time Roberto Montero's son would dive headfirst into hardcore porn.

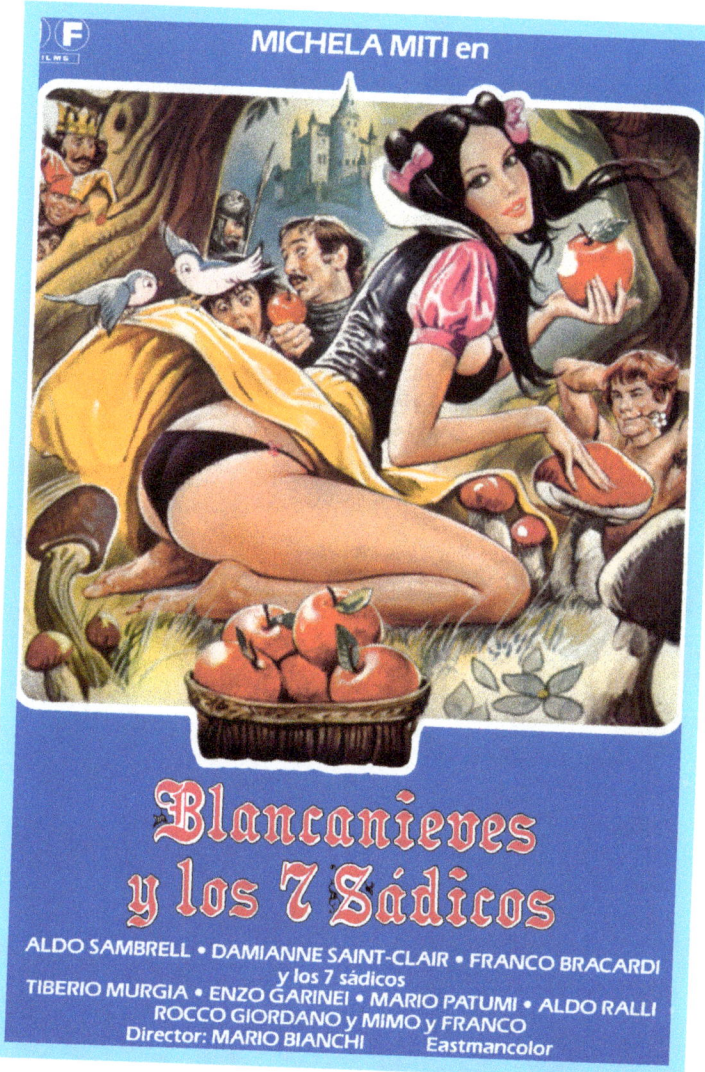

This Spanish poster emphasizes the comic book influences.

Rather incredibly, *Biancaneve & Co…* was even picked up for distribution abroad. It was released theatrically in Spain as *Blancanieves y los 7 sádicos*, and popped up in video in Germany (as *Schneefickchen und die Sex-Zipfelzwerge* and *Schneefittchen und die 7 glücklichen Zwerge*) and France (as *Blanche-Neige et les 7 sadiques*). It even surfaced in an English version titled *Snow White and the 7 Wise Men*.[3]

Notes:
1. The idea of the Seven Dwarfs having parodist names was also in Piero Regnoli's *La principessa sul pisello* and constituted, perhaps, the most explicit reference to the comic. Incidentally, Regnoli had the parts played by real dwarves. See the entry for *La principessa sul pisello* for further details on the similarities with the comic.
2. Even Ubaldo Continiello's music was recycled from Bruno Corbucci's *Il trafficone* (1974). It includes a theme that is a blatant rip off of the Swiss song *Der Ententanz*, which in 1981 became a hit

single in Italy as *Il ballo del qua qua*, sung by Al Bano and Romina Power.

3. Just for the record, it must be noted that the trashy porn flicks inspired by classical fairytales helmed in the 1990s by Franco Lo Cascio (under the alias Luca Damiano), such as *Alice nel paese delle pornomeraviglie* (1993), *Le avventure erotiX di Cappuccetto Rosso* (1993) and *Biancaneve e i sette nani* (1995), had nothing to do with 1970s adults-only comics.

Sogni mostruosamente proibiti
Italy, color, 89 minutes

D: Neri Parenti. *S:* Giovanni Manganelli; *SC:* Laura Toscano, Franco Marotta and Neri Parenti; *DOP:* Alberto Spagnoli; *M:* Bruno Zambrini; *E:* Sergio Montanari.

Cast: Paolo Villaggio (Paolo Coniglio), Janet Agren (Dalia), Chris Avram (Fonseca), Camillo Milli (Publisher), Paul Muller (Concierge), Alessandro Haber (Commissioner Rovere), Alida Valli (Marina's mother), Sofia Lombardo (Marina), Renzo Rinaldi (Killer), Mike Bongiorno (Himself).

The Italian DVD art for *Sogni mostruosamente proibiti*, Italy's answer to *The Private Life of Walter Mitty*, featuring references to the comic book universe.

Prod: Intercapital/Maura International Films.

Paolo Coniglio is a naive and clumsy comic book writer who works in a huge publishing house and is bullied by his boss and his soon-to-be mother-in-law. To escape the dreary daily routine, Paolo imagines himself as the protagonist of very vivid daydreams in the company of Dalia, the beautiful comics' heroine whose stories he is in charge of translating. In his visions Paolo plays (albeit with tragicomic effects) heroes of popular literature and comics, such as Superman, Percival and Tarzan. Each time his return to harsh everyday reality is abrupt and delusional. However, one day, while shopping at the supermarket, Coniglio meets a charming blonde girl who is a dead ringer for Dalia. The woman involves him, against his will, in shady spy intrigue. Paolo finds himself in possession of a box of chocolates in which Dalia has hidden a microfilm with evidence that the wealthy Fonseca is actually a powerful crime boss. Coniglio becomes the target of Fonseca's hired assassins, who also abduct Dalia. Will the meek Paolo be able to release his beloved one?

By the early 1980s Paolo Villaggio was Italy's most popular comedian. The phenomenal success of Luciano Salce's *White Collar Blues* (*Fantozzi*, 1975) and its follow-up *Il secondo tragico Fantozzi* (1976)—based on Villaggio's books about a sad, awkward and unfortunate accountant who is bullied by his bosses, colleagues and practically everyone he meets—provided Italian audiences with a working-class antihero whose non-stop humiliations and sufferings hinted at the dark side of the economical boom. Villaggio followed the *Fantozzi* films with more of the same, by churning out variations on the same basic scheme and revisiting *White Collar Blues*' most exhilarating gags over and over in a series of follow-ups and similar projects (which even included an un-filmed sci-fi comedy, *Il vagabondo dello spazio*, to be directed by Mario Bava and based on Philip José Farmer's novel *Venus on the Half-Shell*)[1].

The scheme soon grew tired, mainly because the other directors were not up to Salce's skills when it came to portraying Fantozzi as an ultimately tragic character, a sad clown whose faults and defeats are our very own. By laughing at him we are laughing at our own misery. This was soon lost in favor of unpretentious yet repetitive sight gags, mediocre filmmaking and lazy scripts. For *Sogni mostruosamente proibiti* (Monstruously Forbidden Dreams) Giovanni Manganelli's story simply borrowed the basic idea from *The Secret Life of Walter Mitty* (1947, Norman Z. McLeod), the Danny Kaye vehicle based in turn on James Thurber's short story. However, no one bothered to acknowledge the source of inspiration in the credits, even though it was obvious from the title, as McLeod's film had been released in Italy as *Sogni proibiti* (Forbidden Dreams).

Villaggio's appearance—paunchy, timid, deferential toward everyone to the point of self-loathing—makes him closer to Fantozzi than Mitty, a fact underlined by the character's name Paolo Coniglio[2], but the filmic and literary source eventually make *Sogni mostruosamente proibiti* a bit stronger than other Villaggio pics of the period. The idea of the main character daydreaming his impossible adventures perfectly interacts with the actor's typically clownish, comic book-like approach to sight gags, which usually end up with him badly injured, crippled or humiliated—yet ready for the next gag.

Another interesting thing about *Sogni mostruosamente proibiti* is the setting, which transposes the pulp magazine publishing house of the 1947 film into an Italian publishing company specializing in comic books of all sorts—from Superman (whose silhouette is on display in a couple of scenes) to horror stories about werewolves, not to mention romantic/erotic stuff. The comics industry was in full operating mode by the early 1980s, churning out all kinds of products, from experimental, underground projects (such as the monthly magazine *Frigidaire*) to no-holds-barred hardcore paperbacks. In *Sogni mostruosamente proibiti* the story revolves around a soft-core comic that recalls the ones drawn by Milo Manara, starring a beautiful (and often half-naked) heroine by the name of Dalia.

The daydream sequences have Villaggio play Superman, a medieval knight (replete with a heavy armor) and a clumsy Tarzan—even though the funniest bit is perhaps a surreal tennis match that pits him against a Björn Borg lookalike. In the Superman segment, Paolo flies from his office to save Dalia as she has been taken hostage by thugs; it is the pretext for a brief parody of Richard Donner's 1978 film about the popular D.C. Comics hero. However, the "flying man" effects are as crude as those seen in Alberto De Martino's *The Pumaman*, which says a lot about the movie's slapdash quality. No wonder, since Neri Parenti—Villaggio's usual collaborator as well as the director of many more comedies over the years—is a rough, ham-fisted taskmaster whose philosophy toward filmmaking can be condensed in the good old "one take will do" motto. Curiously, in the poster for the film Villaggio is wearing Superman's outfit—which underlines his not-so-athletic physical shape—but a "C" (standing for Coniglio) replaces the customary "S" on the chest, whereas in the film the "S" is on display.[3]

Horror film fans will be amused at the references to the old dark house sub-genre, as Coniglio lives in an eerie hotel appropriately named "Nosferatu." Alida Valli as Coniglio's insufferable mother-in-law is as stern here as she was in Dario Argento's *Suspiria* (1977) and *Inferno* (1980)[4], and she keeps recalling her long series of late husbands who all died in horrible ways. Paul Muller plays a ghost-like, silent and ubiquitous concierge who always seems to appear out of nowhere, and Chris Avram basically reprises his white-gloved crime boss character as seen in Mario Caiano's *La malavita attacca ... la polizia risponde* (1977). Another familiar name pops up in the credits: Paolo Gozlino (the titular hero in Mino Loy's *Flashman*) acts as choreographer for one

Paolo Villaggio and Janet Agren in a tender moment

of the best gags, a scene in which Coniglio (dressed in an ugly-looking adhesive tutu to escape a pair of thugs) finds himself on a stage, in the middle of a classical ballet set to the strains of a Strauss waltz.

Despite Villaggio's antics, however, it is the stunningly beautiful Janet Agren who steals the show. Even though she is often seen wearing horrid-looking and very 1980s costumes, the then 34-year-old blonde Swedish actress is ravishing as Coniglio's impossible love object, and she even has a couple of see-through nude scenes. Agren was one of the most popular erotic film stars during the early 1970s. She appeared in three films by Brunello Rondi (*Master of Love*, 1972; *Tecnica di un amore* and *Ingrid sulla strada*, both 1973), as well as in Mike Hodges' black comedy *Pulp* (1972) and Billy Wilder's *Avanti!* (1972). She was also a recurring presence in Decamerotics, *gialli* (*The Killer Reserved Nine Seats*, 1974; *The Perfect Crime*, 1978), crime films (*The Left Hand of the Law*, 1975; *Deadly Chase*, 1978; *Il commissario di ferro*, 1978), gory horror (Lucio Fulci's *City of the Living Dead*, 1980; *Panic*, 1982; *Rat Man*, 1987) and cannibal flicks (Lenzi's *Eaten Alive*, 1980). In the '80s, however, Agren mostly appeared in comedies, before her career eventually waned in the 1990s.

Notes:
1. See Curti, Roberto and Di Rocco, Alessio, "Mario the Wanderer" in Howarth, Troy, *The Haunted*

World of Mario Bava (Baltimore MD: Midnight Marquee Press, 2014), p. 158.

2. Literally "Paul Rabbit" in Italian; the term "rabbit" has the same meaning as "chicken" in English, that is, a cowardly faint-hearted individual.
3. Villaggio played a superman of a different kind in the episode *Italian Superman* in the anthology *Quelle strane occasioni* (1976). He is an Italian immigrant in the Netherlands who, thanks to his prodigious sexual endowment, becomes the star in a live sex show … much to his wife's chagrin, as due to his overworked appendage, he can no longer satisfy the woman. Nanni Loy directed the episode, but he refused to sign it, and "Anonymous" appeared on the credits.
4. Speaking of which, a small bit (Villaggio waking up in a dream to find his bathroom completely flooded with water) plays like a variation on Irene Miracle's exploration of the underwater apartment in Argento's film.

Sturmtruppen 2—Tutti al fronte
Italy, color, 95 minutes

D: Salvatore Samperi. *S:* based on the comic strip *Sturmtruppen* by Bonvi [Franco Bonvicini]; *SC:* Bonvi, Giancarlo Governi; *DOP:* Romano Albani; *M:* Umberto Smaila; *E:* Sergio Montanari.

Cast: Massimo Boldi (Rookie: Cicciobello Pannolino), Teo Teocoli (Rookie: Thief), Felice Andreasi (Sergeant), Franco Oppini (Rookie), Giorgio Ariani (Rookie), Francesco Salvi (Rookie), Bonvi (Captain), Giancarlo Magalli (Rookie: Otto von Nibelunghen), Enzo Cannavale (Galeazzo Musolesi), Bombolo [Franco Lechner] (Rookie: Poet), Giorgio Porcaro (Rookie: Austrian), Serena Grandi, Ramona Dell'Abate.

Prod: Clemi Cinematografica.

A bunch of crazy characters (a petty thief, a pathetic mama's boy and two idiot brothers who do a Laurel and Hardy impersonation) enroll in a ramshackle German battalion, headed by a homosexual general, a sadistic captain and a stupid sergeant. The rookies will perform all sorts of idiotic and demented acts …

Coming six years after the box-office success of the first film, Salvatore Samperi's sequel to his own *Sturmtruppen* proved an utter disaster on all fronts, despite the presence of the strip's creator Bonvi as both scriptwriter (teaming up with TV author Giancarlo Governi, with whom Bonvi had written the cartoon adaptation of *Sturmtruppen* for the TV show *SuperGulp!*) and actor, as the Aryan captain. Even though the cast featured a number of actors from the original film (but with the sole Andreasi reprising his role as the discipline-obsessed, idiotic sergeant), this time Samperi could not count on Renato Pozzetto and Cochi Ponzoni, whose presence had contributed to its biting tone. Instead, a number of young comics of various origins were amassed in the cast. Besides the stage comedians from Milan's "Derby Club" (such as Giorgio Porcaro, whose character inspired the antics of the much more popular Diego Abatantuono), there were such extraneous presences as Bombolo and Enzo Cannavale, Tomas Milian's comic sidekicks in the Nico Giraldi series, with Cannavale embodying one of Bonvi's recurring characters in the script, the Fascist-allied Galeazzo Musolesi.

Gone also was the sharp anti-militarist satire, replaced by indifferent, repetitive jokes which border on the stupid rather than the surreal. Oppini and Ariani's routine as painfully unfunny Laurel & Hardy impersonators is a low point, while Boldi (who would become one of Italy's most popular comedians in the 1990s with his appearances in the so-called *cinepanettoni*) is, quite simply, unbearable. On top of that, Samperi's direction is embarrassingly listless, obviously in tone with the film's shoestring production values. As a result, the tone was definitely close to the hit-and-miss, dreadful sketch anthology films of the period, such as *I carabbinieri* (1981, Francesco Massaro) and *I carabbimatti* (1981, Giuliano Carnimeo).

Sturmtruppen 2—Tutti al fronte was a deserved box-office flop. One review of the period even reported audiences demanding their money back and causing huge walk-

The Italian DVD cover art for Salvatore Samperi's *Sturmtruppen 2: Tutti al fronte* (1982)

outs from theaters. By then Samperi's career had gone downhill. No longer one of Italy's most idiosyncratic and genuinely provocative filmmakers, in the 1980s he settled into unpretentious comedies (*Un amore in prima classe*, 1980; *Vai alla grande*, 1983) and glossy erotic dreck with very little redeeming qualities, such as *The Dark Side of Love* (*Fotografando Patrizia*, 1984) and the Jean Genet-inspired *The Corruption* (*La Bonne*, 1986). His last work for the big screen was the disastrous *Malizia 2000* (1991), again starring Laura Antonelli in her last screen role. He resumed work behind the camera 15 years later for a number of successful but impersonal TV movies. Samperi died in 2009.

1983

Questo e quello
Italy, color, 102 minutes

D: Sergio Corbucci. *S and SC:* Bernardino Zapponi, Nino Manfredi, Renato Pozzetto; *DOP:* Sandro D'Eva; *M:* Gaio Chiocchio, Luciano Rossi; *E:* Amedeo Salfa.

"Questo … amore impossibile." *Cast:* Renato Pozzetto (Giulio Scacchi), Janet Agren (Lucy), Nino Manfredi (Doctor), Gianni Agus (Publisher), Michela Miti (Giulio's girlfriend).

"Quello … col basco rosso." Nino Manfredi (Sandro), Renato Pozzetto (Gregory), Desirée Becker (Daniela), Sylva Koscina (Daniela's mother).

Prod: Achille Manzotti/Faso Film (Rome).

"*Questo … amore impossibile*": *Giulio Scacchi, a punk comic book artist who lives with a community of drop-outs and specialized in violent, grotesque horror stories, is experiencing a creative crisis. Then, one day, he meets an angelic woman named Lucy, who forces him to abandon his scruffy lifestyle and focus on a romantic love story. However, the woman turns out to be paid by his own publisher in order to give Giulio a renewed inspiration … "Quello… col basco rosso": A 60-year-old writer, Sandro, is looking for inspiration to finish his latest novel. At a health resort, he meets a very young girl with whom he falls in love …*

> It went like that. In 1982 Frank Zappa was on tour in Italy, and after a show he met a would-be-groupie who managed to sneak into the dressing room. To justify her presence in the backstage, the girl pretended that she was a reporter for a magazine named *Frigidaire*. She gave Zappa a copy, he opened it and saw a *Ranxerox* story. He kicked the girl out and kept the mag.[1]

When Zappa set his eyes on *Frigidaire*, the magazine was already a (counter) cultural phenomenon in Italy.

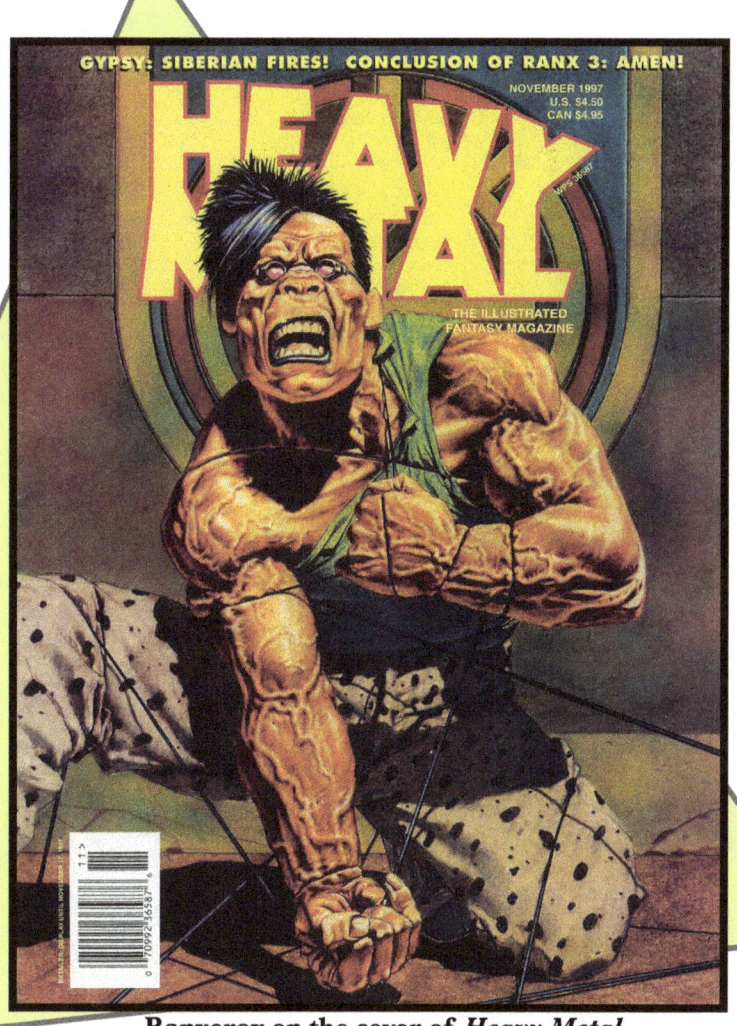
Ranxerox on the cover of *Heavy Metal*

Founded in 1980 by a small group of writers and artists (Stefano Tamburini, Vincenzo Sparagna, Filippo Scòzzari, Tanino Liberatore, Andrea Pazienza) after the experience of the underground comic magazine *Cannibale* and the satirical weekly *Il Male*, *Frigidaire* was nothing short of an atomic bomb that branded the decade with its mixture of grotesque comics, gonzo journalism, satire, music … As Liberatore recalled:

> Stefano had this simple yet brilliant idea, of a mag which would not be just about comics, but would also feature reports, stories, weird articles—in short, a container that left us free rein to our world view even beyond the comic panels. He wanted to call it *Frigidaire* and we were all excited about that.

Frigidaire's most emblematic comic was *Ranxerox*, about a synthetic android who lives in a postmodern Rome that looks like the rusty half of the cyberpunk Los Angeles as seen in *Blade Runner* (1982)—yet the character was actually created in 1978, four years earlier … with nods to J.G.

A panel from Tanino Liberatore's *Ranxerox*

Ballard's works such as *Crash*. The stories were written by Tamburini (who had created the character for *Cannibale* and initially drew it himself) and illustrated by the extraordinarily gifted Tanino Liberatore, whose detailed panel compositions and refined human anatomy were nothing short of outstanding. Liberatore went on to draw the cover sleeve for Zappa's 1983 album *The Man From Utopia*, portraying the guitarist like a variation of his trademark character. Ranxerox had become an icon, and one that survived his creator. Tamburini died of a heroin overdose in April 1986, and his body was found two weeks after his death. Two years later it was Pazienza's turn to succumb to a fatal overdose.

In a sense, it was a sign of the passing of time. The rebellious thrust that guided those counterculture artists had soon dissipated, in a decade marked by the sad end of all the revolutionary dreams and the emergence of a clean-cut, greedy generation of bourgeois sharks, attracted by the mirage of money, luxury and the easy life. It was the decade of the so-called "Milano da bere" (Drinking Milan), of the rampaging advertising, of Silvio Berlusconi's television empire and its anesthetic, disengaged TV shows.

As for movies, the 1980s in Italy were the decade of comedy. The market was dominated by the most popular comedians—Paolo Villaggio, Renato Pozzetto, Enrico Montesano, Adriano Celentano—who often co-starred in anthology films conceived like Italian versions of the "movie-movie" format reintroduced in Stanley Donen's 1978 film of the same name, the first example in the country being Pasquale Festa Campanile's *Qua la mano* (1980). For *Questo e quello* (This and That), Sergio Corbucci—who had directed many of said actors' box-office hits—teamed up with Bernardino Zapponi, the talented writer who had been Fellini's collaborator since *Toby Dammit*, in the Edgar Allan Poe-inspired anthology *Spirits of the Dead* (1968) and who co-scripted, among others, Dario Argento's *Deep Red*. The film's two episodes are basically excuses for the film's stars, Renato Pozzetto and Nino Manfredi, to do their comedy routine, and Corbucci's direction is sloppy and careless, not that it mattered to moviegoers, given that the film was a box-office hit nonetheless.

The first episode, starring Pozzetto, is in some way similar to the Villaggio vehicle *Sogni mostruosamente proibiti*, released the previous year, which gives an idea of how the comic book world was popular at that time (a popularity that in this very case allows for more than a little fantasizing over the artists' real life and working conditions…), as well as the overall laziness that had scriptwriters cannibalize the same ideas over and over. Pozzetto here plays a quite peculiar, almost clownish figure. Sporting a long, curly wig, a samurai-like band with the Japanese flag on the forehead, walking around with a goat (!) on the leash and looking visibly scruffy and unkempt, Giulio Scacchi is a successful yet highly idiosyncratic comics writer and artist who specializes in excessively gory and outrageous *fumetti* that refer directly to the kind of stuff one could find in *Frigidaire* … especially since the panels in Pozzetto's workshop are unmistakably drawn by Tanino Liberatore and portray none other than Ranxerox (the artist is thanked in the end credits).

As in *Sogni mostruosamente proibiti*, the story has the protagonist meet the girl of his dreams (once again played by the ravishing Janet Agren) who looks as if she just stepped out of a vintage comic book. The mystery woman makes the foul-mouthed, anarchic Giulio radically change his hygiene habits (starting with the use of soap and water) and appearance, turning him into an impeccably dressed, educated bourgeois. She also persuades him to write and draw a comic book version of their encounter, an old-fashioned love story that is in stark contrast with the artist's previous output. All this is interspersed with Pozzetto's surreal antics and one-liners ("What kind of car is this, a Maserati?" he asks while mounting … a horse-drawn carriage).

All this has an element of social satire, which does not pass unnoticed.

Even though Giulio is seen as a sincere artist, Corbucci and Zapponi have a field day satirizing the kind of comics

Comic artist Tanino Liberatore

he creates and the generation they are aimed at. A miracle court of freaks (punks, transvestites, slackers) surround Giulio and they camp at his place, a beautiful beacon on the sea, and spend their time doing drugs, eating spaghetti and having promiscuous sex. It is a very similar vision as that of the "longhairs" invading Totò's home in *Caprice Italian Style*. Only this time the filmmakers seem to be taking the side of the middle-class bourgeois, with a very obvious disdain toward the dropouts. It is quite a significant reversal that is as cynical as it is paternalistic. What is more, Giulio regularly takes inspiration from the punks (with more than a little help from hashish, amphetamine and whisky) but complains that, "These are hard times … I find it hard to work, the inspiration has gone …" Wealth makes inspiration falter, as Corbucci and Zapponi seem to be implying.

Yet the film's morale is somewhat ambiguous. Giulio is after all being exploited by his own publisher (Gianni Agus), who even resorts to an elaborate (and unbelievable) trick in order to make him go back to safer, more reassuring kinds of stories—an element which recalls what was happening in the movies after television's rise to glory, with producers demanding tame product that would be eligible for TV broadcasting.

However, in the end, Giulio gladly accepts a huge check from his publisher and he even returns to his ex-girlfriend, once a promiscuous, drug-consuming punkette, but now she shows up in a clean, "good girl" dress, meaning that she has cleaned herself up … a reactionary ending if ever there was one, or the bitter admission on the part of the filmmakers (especially Zapponi, who went on writing nondescript comedies that had little of the spark of his earlier material) that, to paraphrase Zappa, they were only in it for the money.

Anyway, neither Tamburini nor Pazienza would end up as Giulio Scacchi. Either you walk the line or you die—there is no other choice for rebels, and both conclusions translate to a defeat.

Note:
1. Mattioli, "Ranxerox."

Yor, the Hunter from the Future

(*Il mondo di Yor*, aka *Yor, le chasseur du futur*, aka *Yor*)
Italy/France/Turkey, color, 206 minutes (TV version), 98 minutes (theatrical version), 88 minutes (U.S. version)

D: Anthony M. Dawson [Antonio Margheriti]. *S:* from the graphic novel *Henga, el cazador* by Ray Collins [Eugenio Zappietro] and Juan Zanotto; *SC:* Anthony M. Dawson and Robert Bailey; *DOP:* Marcello Masciocchi; *M:* John Scott, Guido and Maurizio De Angelis; *E:* Alberto Moriani and Giorgio Serralonga.

Cast: Reb Brown (Yor), Corinne Cléry (Ka-Laa), Alan Collins [Luciano Pigozzi] (Pag), Carole André (Ena), John Steiner (Overlord), Ayshe Gul (Rea).

Prod: Diamant Film, RAI-Radio Televisione Italiana.

In a seemingly prehistoric age, a lone hunter named Yor rescues two cavemen, Ka-Laa and Pag, from a dinosaur attack. While the tribesmen are feasting over the beast's remains, a rival tribe attacks the village. Only Yor and Pag escape, while Ka-Laa is abducted. Yor and Pag track down the blue-skinned prowlers in a cave, where Yor releases Ka-Laa and destroys their captors. Ka-Laa and Pag join Yor in his quest to find his origins, which has them face many perils. First they meet a mysterious society of sand mummies led by a woman who wears an amulet similar to Yor's. Then they make friends with a peaceful tribe whose children they saved from dinosaurs, and they survive an attack perpetrated by flying saucers. Eventually Yor and his pals reach an island, where it turns out that their world is actually future Earth, which has turned back to a prehistoric age after a nuclear holocaust. The evil Overlord and his android army control all technology. Yor, Pag and Ka-Laa defeat the Overlord and his forces and fly off in one of the Overlord's spacecrafts, returning to the mainland where they will use their superior knowledge to help civilization begin again …

Coming after the war film *Tiger Joe* (*Fuga dall'arcipelago maledetto*, 1982) and the amiable *Raiders of the Lost Ark*-like adventure yarn *Hunters of the Golden Cobra* (*I cacciatori del co-*

Astonishing French movie poster for Antonio Margheriti's *Yor, The Hunter from the Future* (1983), art by Philippe Druillet

bra d'oro, 1982), Antonio Margheriti's *Yor, the Hunter from the Future* was the adaptation of the cult Argentinian comic book *Yor*, created in 1974 by writer Ray Collins (aka Eugenio Zappietro) and drawing artist Juan Zanotto. Originally titled *Henga, el cazador*, the saga (overall 48 episodes) appeared in Italy in the magazine *Lanciostory* in 1975. Margheriti told an interviewer:

> Zanotto's comic fascinated me. Productively speaking, it was a rather ambitious project, I must say. Unfortunately halfway through we experienced the usual problems, but there was an attempt at inventing a prehistoric setting, dinosaurs included ...[1]

With its (apparently) prehistoric age setting and a muscle-bound hero on a quest, *Yor, the Hunter from the Future* also fit in the sword-and-sorcery thread that had been started by the success of John Milius' *Conan the Barbarian* (1982), and which comprised such titles as Lucio Fulci's *Conquest* and Franco Prosperi's *The Throne of Fire* (both 1983). Yet, the plot evolved in a radically different way, as anticipated by the title song's cryptic lyrics: "There is a man from future ... ," as the attentive listener can discern buried beneath a flood of bad 1980s synthesizers.

Therefore, after a first half that more or less recalls Hammer's stone-age epics (dinosaurs included), the second part switches to full *Star Wars* mode, with the apparition of John Steiner as a Darth Vader clone, flanked by an army of black androids ... looking every bit like the soldiers in Lucas' film and even carrying laser guns (shooting red rays, in order to differentiate them from the green rays shot by the good guys). Nothing of this was to be found in Collins and Zanotto's stories. In the comic book, Yor discovers he is a member of the Atlantis race, a humanoid civilization who once inhabited the planet Mars. It is also revealed that his spaceship crashed before landing on Earth, and that he was adopted at an early age by a tribe of cavemen. The final battle between Yor and the Overlord is also absent in the comic book, as the "Supreme" briefly appears in just two vignettes. Obviously, the changes on the part of the scriptwriters were designed to cash in on the current post-atomic thread, in one of those typical blends that were commonplace in Italian genre cinema.

Interestingly, *Yor, the Hunter from the Future* was in Margheriti's own words:

> One of those attempts to combine the Italian and Turkish film industries, and the results are always something very special.²

Turkey provided the setting becoming the beautiful and savage-looking region of Cappadocia, with its rocky highlands and unmistakable natural stone towers. Originally, *Yor, the Hunter from the Future* was planned as a four-part miniseries, each installment being 50 minutes long, and the full version was broadcast in Italy on RAI television. However, the version that was distributed worldwide for theatrical release was a butchered 98-minute mess (reduced still further to 88 for the copy released in the United States), which cuts so much out of the original story that the result often looks pretty rushed.

Yor, the Hunter from the Future was widely distributed by Columbia in the United States, where it was a financial success, grossing almost three million dollars … despite soliciting hilarious response among viewers. It ended up in John Wilson's *The Official Razzie Movie Guide* in the "100 Most Enjoyably Bad Movies Ever Made" list, and was also nominated for three Golden Raspberry Awards in 1983: Worst New Star (Reb Brown), Worst Musical Score and Worst Original Song (the grating *Yor's World*). As often happens, such fury was excessive. True, the film has its shares of absurdities, from the low-budget special effects to some laughable plot holes. For instance, after Yor releases Ka-Laa in the cave where she was imprisoned, he starts flooding sections of it as a diversion that allows him to escape. The flood kills everyone else in the cave, not only the enemy tribe but also the other poor villagers who were kept in cages and could not run away. And yet, no one seems to give a damn about it.

Margheriti himself did not think much of the film. When asked by Peter Blumenstock about *Yor, the Hunter from the Future*, he just burst out laughing:

> Can you believe that Columbia distributed 1400 prints of that film in the United States? It was one of the most successful pictures of my life! And I mean, look at it; it's so *bad*! And they only saw bits of it in America; there exists a version made for TV which runs over three hours and is even more hilarious. […] Every once in a while,

Reb Brown as the titular hero Yor

> I enjoy looking for *Yor* in those movie guides and I always discover a "bomb" or a "turkey" rating. It was a fun project made with almost zero budget. It was a party film and I sometimes enjoy looking at it again.³

However, for all its shortcomings, *Yor, the Hunter from the Future* is at least better than most of the early 1980s Italian post-atomic war flicks. Margheriti took care of the special effects with his son Edoardo, with nice results. The creatures were in the spirit of Hammer's 1960s fantasy films set in the Stone Age, like *One Million Years B.C.* (1966, Don Chaffey), as the weird dinosaur with sharp teeth that Yor defeats near the beginning becomes a mixture of a Triceratops and a Stegosaurus. Margheriti also took care of the gigantic black crocodiles, made with rubber foam and animated on carts.

> It was very difficult. […] They were huge puppets, over 52-feet long.⁴

Margheriti resorted to his beloved miniatures for many scenes, including the aforementioned cave flood, which looks like the umpteenth version of the river of blood as seen in the sci-fi epic *Wild, Wild Planet* (*I criminali della galassia*, 1965) and the punishing flood in the outstanding ghost story *The Unnaturals—Contronatura* (1969).

The direction is svelte, with lots of hand-held camerawork and wide-angle shots in the interior scenes. Margheriti even comes up with several interesting showpieces like the scene in the mirror labyrinth, a nod to Orson Welles' *The Lady from Shanghai* (1947). However, the budget's shortcomings are pretty evident throughout, and the final part of the film, which takes place in what looks like a huge

Corinne Cléry as a ravishing cave-girl from the future

underground complex amid tubes and stairs, would not be out of place in a Bruno Mattei film. Another downside is the score (by John Scott and the brothers Guido and Maurizio De Angelis)—which was partly recycled from *Adam and Eve vs. Cannibals* (*Adamo ed Eva, la prima storia d'amore*, 1983, Enzo Doria and Luigi Russo) and was in turn re-used in other Italian post-atomic flicks of the period. The aforementioned opening song cannot be believed unless actually heard.

As Yor, wearing a terrible blond wig with little more than one single facial expression, Reb Brown makes for a pretty awful hero. The American actor had debuted in Bernard Kowalski's *Ssssss* (1973) and enjoyed a career on the small screen in the 1970s (including the two abysmal 1979 *Captain America* TV movies) before landing the lead role in Margheriti's film. That same year he was in Ted Kotcheff's *Uncommon Valor* (1983) and later on in Philippe Mora's *Death of a Soldier* (1986), but his career résumé comprised such titles as Bruno Mattei's war flicks *Strike Commando* (1987) and *Robowar* (1988)—not to mention the South African sci-fi would-be-epic *Space Mutiny* (1988) and Mora's appalling *Howling II: Stirba—Werewolf Bitch* (1985).

The rest of the cast is B-movie paradise: the lethargic-looking Carole André is some sort of blonde answer to *Star Wars*' Carrie Fisher, replete with a white outfit, while Corinne Cléry provides the love interest (and not much else) and John Steiner hams it up as required as the evil Overlord. The best of the lot features Alan Collins, aka Luciano Pigozzi, Margheriti's longtime friend and a constant presence in so many of his films, as Pag the caveman. Here, Pigozzi (with a little help from his stunt double) has a show-stealing scene where he rescues Yor by dangling from a rope over an abyss like a consummate trapeze artist. It is one of those over-the-top moments that made even the truly bad Italian genre films worth watching.

Once labeled "the Italian Peter Lorre," Pigozzi (born in 1927) was one of the most recognizable supporting actors in genre cinema. Besides working with Margheriti (who gave him one of his best roles as the ghastly Uriah in *The Unnaturals*), Pigozzi appeared in several Mario Bava classics, such as *The Whip and the Body*, *Blood and Black Lace* and *Baron Blood*. In the latter he had an amusingly horrific scene in which he was trapped inside a deadly "Virgin of Nuremberg" and suffered a similar fate as Barbara Steele in *Black Sunday*. His last movie roles were in Bruno Mattei's *Born to Fight* and Margheriti's *Alien from the Deep* (both 1989).

Yor is available on DVD in the U.S. as part of Sony's on-demand manufacturing service.

Notes:
1. Garofalo, Marcello, "Le interviste celibi: Antonio Margheriti. La tecnica e gli effetti," *Segnocinema* #85, May/June 1997, p. 11.
2. Blumenstock, Peter, "Margheriti—The Wild, Wild Interview," *Video Watchdog* #28, May/June 1995, p. 59.
3. *Ibid*.
4. Garofalo, "Le interviste celibi: Antonio Margheriti," p. 11.

1984

Three Supermen at the Olympic Games

(*Üç Süpermen Olimpiyatlarda*, aka *3 supermen alle Olimpiadi*) Turkey/Italy, color, 65 minutes
D: Yavuz Yalınkılıç [and Italo Martinenghi, Cavit Yürüklü, uncredited]. *SC:* Yavuz Yalınkılıç; *DOP:* Salih Dikisçi.
Cast: Yılmaz Köksal (Salih), Levent Çakır (Murat), Stefano Martinenghi (Cengiz), Filiz Özten (Artemis), Emel Özden (Crazy Girl), Daniel Darnault, Jocelin Davan, Georges Guéret, Alain Flick.

The supermen in the footage are borrowed from *Çılgın Kız ve 3 Süper Adam* (1973). Note the different costumes and the amazing papier-mâché robot.

Prod: Objektif Film (Istanbul).

Transported back in time yet again by an evil Chinese professor, the three supermen find themselves in the middle of the Olympic games in the ancient days of humanity, at the mercy of the goddess Artemis. More adventures follow, as the three get to fight the evil Great Satan and his accomplice Aphrodite and release a young girl who has been captured by them. Eventually, the supermen get back to the present, when one of them single-handedly defeats a gang of thugs …

The second-to-last entry in the *Three Supermen* series, *Three Supermen at the Olympic Games* is a Frankenstein-like mixture of scenes shot in Ephesus, Turkey by Italo Martinenghi, who gathered Turkish backing with the help of Guido Zurli, plus recycled and redubbed footage from the Turkish *Çılgın Kız ve 3 Süper Adam* (The Crazy Girl and 3 Super Men, 1973, also known as *3 Supermen and Mad Girl*) by Cavit Yürüklü, a carbon copy rip-off of the original Italian films[1].

For the occasion, Martinenghi teamed up with producer Kunt Tulgar and cast his own son Stefano, whom he was unsuccessfully trying to launch into the movie biz (see also *Three Supermen in S. Domingo*) as one of the three titular heroes, sided by the blond Levent Çakır (who, unlike other films, can even fly and brings to mind a Z-version of William Katt as *The Greatest American Hero*) and the mustached Yılmaz Köksal. A number of French actors, including Daniel Darnault and Georges Guéret, are also part of the game.

The result? As film historian Pete Tombs put it, "This was a film that even Ed Wood might have disowned."[2] Despite the brief running-time the plot is an incoherent, almost indecipherable mess—at least judging from the Turkish-language copy, which is the only print in circulation and looks in very bad shape (for one thing, the dialogue is constantly out-of-synch). Once again the three superheroes travel back in time as they did in *The 3 Supermen in the West*. However, due to budget restrictions, the time machine is a 12-channel mixer that a cast member (badly made-up as a Fu-Manchu type) is switching. Things become a bit difficult to follow when the superheroes end up in ancient times together with Professor Panzarotti, who invented the time machine in the 1973 film, and are endorsed by the goddess Artemis (Filiz Özten) to take part in the games. All this is supposed to be a comedy, mind you, and there is plenty of supposedly humorous footage featuring Turkish comedians interspersed.

Then the footage from *Çılgın Kız ve 3 Süper Adam* kicks in. The Turkish superheroes are masked, their costumes sport an additional "S" on the chest—and it is indeed Superman's "S" in a display of blatant indifference to copyright that was typical of Turkish cinema. Besides such discrepancies, the story takes a U-turn toward out-and-out sci-fi, with the appearance of a villain with a devil mask (named as The Great Satan) leading a sect of green-hooded men into some catacombs, an army of scantily-dressed girls and a princess (Emel Özden, the "Crazy Girl" of the title) being tortured with some sort of bizarre machinery … and an astonishingly bad *papier-mâché* robot. All in all, the inserted part is the most appetizing thing about the movie, at least for its trashy entertainment value, due to garish colors and outlandish costumes.

From time to time, however, it is back to the newly-shot scenes, with the supermen practicing the high jump, javelin and so on—all the while the score blatantly rips off John Williams' main theme from Richard Donner's *Superman* … redone on the cheap on a single keyboard.

The third part has the other supermen disappear and focuses on Levent Çakır, who defeats a gang of robbers that perform their hits at the racetrack. The footage includes some of the worst "flying man" sequences in cinema history, and the fights are terrible. Besides the alarmingly poor stunt choreography, Çakır has his cape continually covering his face because of the strong wind—something that apparently did not bother the filmmakers, who probably followed the golden "one take" rule throughout.

The Turkish version of the movie is credited to Yavuz Yalınkılıç, while other sources state differently. Pete Tombs' excellent book *Mondo Macabro* suggests that the film was co-directed by Martinenghi and Kunt Tulgar, while in their volume *Fantastik Türk Sinemasi* Giovanni Scognamillo and Metin Demirhan credit Martinenghi and Yalınkılıç as directors. Early posters, though—possibly pre-production publicity material—list the sole Martinenghi as director. Overall, *Three Supermen at the Olympic Games* looks like an unfinished effort on the part of Martinenghi that Yalınkılıç pulled together with the help of the *3 Supermen and Mad Girl* bits to make up for narrative holes and lack of footage.

The film was not even released in Turkey but came out directly to home video in West Germany, for the Turkish community. It was shown for the first time on Turkish television in 1994.

Notes:
1. In turn, *3 Supermen and Mad Girl* was also partly connected with *The Deathless Devil* (*Yilmayan seytan*, 1973), a Turkish remake of the U.S. serial *Mysterious Doctor Satan* (1940, John English, William Witney).
2. Tombs, *Mondo Macabro*, p. 107.

1985

Tex and the Lord of the Deep
(*Tex e il signore degli abissi*)
Italy, color, 104 minutes
D: Duccio Tessari. *S:* Gian Luigi Bonelli; *SC:* Duccio Tessari, Marcello Coscia, Gianfranco Clerici and Sergio Bonelli; *DOP:* Pietro Morbidelli; *M:* Gianni Ferrio; *E:* Lidia Bordi and Mirella Mencio.
Cast: Giuliano Gemma (Tex Willer), William Berger (Kit Carson), Carlo Mucari (Tiger Jack), Peter Berling (El Morisco), Aldo Sambrell (El Dorado), Isabel Russinova (Tulac), Charly Bravo (Pablito), Flavio Bucci (Kanas), Riccardo Petrazzi (The Lord of the Deep), Hugo Blanco (Magua), Frank Braña (Jim Bedford), José Luis de Villalonga (Dr. Warton), Gian Luigi Bonelli (Narrator).
Prod: RAI-Radio Televisione Italiana.

Aided by two friends—elderly ranger Kit Carson and Navajo warrior Tiger Jack—Texas ranger Tex Willer defeats a gang of outlaws who assault army convoys and sell the arms to the Indian tribes. Later on, however, Tex is forced to seek help from El Morisco, an extravagant Mexican scientist and half-sorcerer who reveals the true nature of a terrible weapon which is causing horrible deaths in the area. The victims are shot with little greenish stones with a blowgun and end up looking like dried-up mummies. The culprits are the Yaquis, a savage tribe that lives in the mountains. After the Indians take Carson and Tiger prisoners, Tex leaves for the Yaqui region in order to save his friends. The Yaqui leaders are Kanas and the beautiful princess Tulac, the daughter of the mysterious "Lord of the Deep," a scarred high priest who lives inside a huge subterranean cave from where the lethal green stones are extracted. Tex releases Kit and Tiger Jack and has the cave exploded with dynamite. Kanas and Tulac die in the explosion, while Tex leaves toward new adventures...

On September 30, 1948 Italians made the acquaintance of a new comic book hero: Tex Willer, an outlaw who is enlisted in the Texas Rangers, in a story titled *Il totem misterioso* (The Mysterious Totem). The comic book was called *Collana del Tex*. It was 36 pages long and cost 15 *lire*.

Writer Gian Luigi Bonelli (1908-2001) and comic artist Aurelio Galeppini (or "Galep" as he used to sign the stories; 1917-1994) had previously created another Western hero: *Il Giustiziere del West* (Avenger of the West) that had come out in newsstands just one year previously. Due to the flood of American movies that reached Italian cinemas in the years just after the war, the Westerns—many of which, like *Stagecoach* (1939) had been unseen due to the Fascist regime's embargo on American films since the late 1930s—became one of moviegoers' favorite genres, especially among the kids. What is more, *Tex* had yet another important predecessor. In 1937 Rino Albertarelli had created *Kit Carson*, which appeared in the weekly magazine *Topolino* and was characterized by a rather naive vision of the Wild West.

However, at first Bonelli and Galeppini considered *Tex* an experiment, as the character had been conceived basically as a support act to another comics hero, *Occhio Cupo* (Gloomy Eye), the protagonist in a classic swashbuckling story. At the beginning, Tex even reprised several of Occhio Cupo's traits: the close-fitting black jeans that looked like tights, the floppy boots and the shirt with fringes. Nevertheless, *Occhio Cupo* was soon forgotten, whereas *Tex* became Italy's comic book hero *par excellence*.

The name Tex was inspired, of all things, by a clothing store in Milan by the name "Tex Moda" (Tex Fashion). Originally, it had to be Tex *Killer*, but Bonelli and Galeppini chose to change the initial "K" at the very last minute so as not to have problems with the censors—a lucky move if ever there was one.

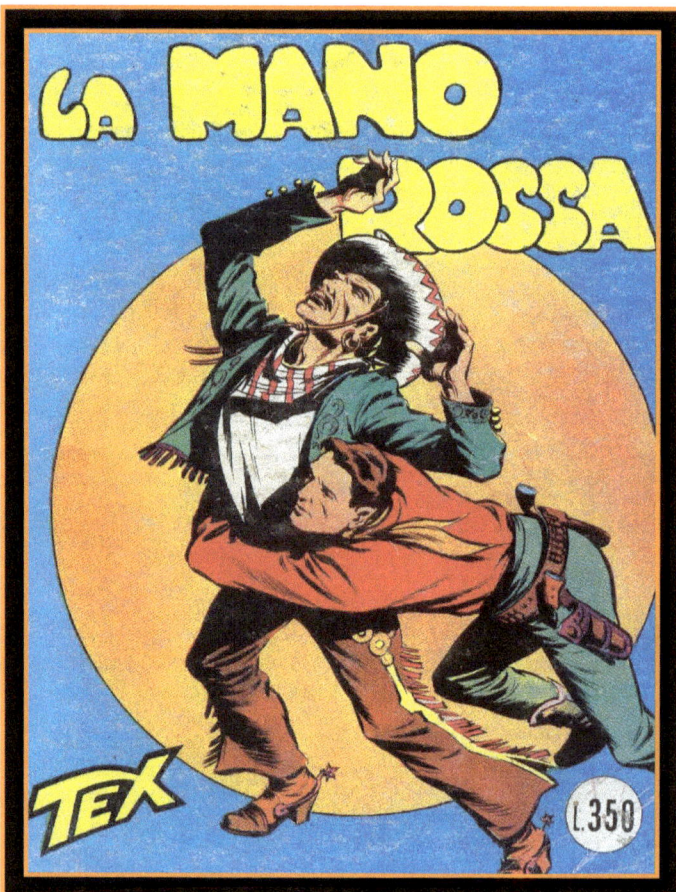

Tex Willer, Italy's most popular and long-lived comic hero, debuted September 30, 1948 in a 36-page comic.

Despite the setting and a lead character whose features were patently inspired by Gary Cooper, *Tex* showed many differences compared with its sources of inspiration. Bonelli had devised a peculiar Wild West, inspired by American films yet devoid of the racist overtones of so many horse operas. On the contrary, *Tex* offered a revisionist view of the Native Americans, often seen as more sympathetic and wiser than the cynical and violent "white people." Tex himself was depicted as the supreme chief of all Navajo tribes, and the tribes knew him by the name "Aquila della notte" (Night Eagle); he acted as an intermediary between the Navajo and the Federal government. He had married a Navajo woman named Lilyth (sic) and had had a son by her.

Another influence was Alexandre Dumas' *The Three Musketeers*, as the stories were usually centered on a quartet of friends—or "pards" as they were referred to in the comics: Tex, his elderly friend Kit Carson, Tex's son Kit and the Indian Tiger Jack, who is Tex's blood brother.

The style was also an important factor in Tex's success. Galeppini's trait was unmistakable: precise and fluid, a bit in the vein of Harold Foster's comics, enriched by thick shadows and sparse yet attentively sketched backdrops.

Collana del Tex was originally published in the "strip" format: the comic (soon renamed *Tex*) then adopted another format, which had a vital part in its popularity beginning in the late 1950s and continuing to this day. Its success was so wide that many other Western series followed, such as *Kinowa* (1950), *Capitan Miki* (1954), *Il Grande Blek* (1954), as well as Luciano Secchi's *Maschera nera* (1962) and *El Gringo* (1965), the latter possibly being the first Italian comic inspired by Sergio Leone's Westerns. In the 1960s, however, following a drafted law on the part of two MPs from the right-wing party Democrazia Cristiana regarding preventive control over comic book publications, most publishers adopted a self-censorship code, which resulted in the mark "MG" ("Garanzia Morale," Moral Warranty) on the covers. *Tex* was one of the comics that submitted to such a code, the repercussions from which affected the reprints. For instance, in the very first edition of *Il totem misterioso* Tex was initially described as a "fuorilegge" (outlaw), whereas in the subsequent reprints he became a "giustiziere" (avenger). Bonelli often recalled how censors were not happy with several of the hero's most characteristic catchphrases such as "Fiamme d'inferno!" (Flames of hell!) and "Al diavolo!" (To hell with it!), which sounded too much like … Satanic invocations.

Tex soon experienced an incredible success, and it was translated and published in many other European countries, such as France (as *Texas Boy*), Spain (as *Texas Bill*), Finland, Norway, Sweden, Yugoslavia and Greece. It became immensely popular in Turkey (as *Teks*) and landed in such exotic markets as India, Indonesia, South America (especially Brazil) and Israel. Its only apparition in the United States, on the other hand, was in a special issue drawn by the great Joe Kubert and published stateside by Dark Horse Comics in the early 2000s.

The idea of bringing *Tex* to the screen had been floating around for years. Sergio Bonelli started working on a film adaptation in the late '60s. He founded a production company named "Condor Cinematografica," based in Milan and concocted a script based on the 1969 story *Fort Defiance*. Among the actors considered for the main roles were Charlton Heston (as Tex) and Jack Palance (as Kit

Young Giuliano Gemma, one of the stars of the Euro Western and, at least on paper, the ideal choice to play Tex on screen.

Carson). Bonelli got in touch with directors such as Tonino Valerii and Enzo G. Castellari, two of Italy's main specialists in the Western genre. Valerii recalled having been summoned in the early 1970s by Gian Luigi Bonelli. As the director explained:

> I had never read *Tex* in my whole life. I bought a few issues to see what it was all about, and I liked *Sangue Navajo* very much. I told Bonelli that we could make a good film out of it, and he was glad to hear that—it was one of the stories he loved the most. […] Then it emerged that Bonelli wanted to take care personally of all the costumes and sets; what is more, he put aside the idea of *Sangue Navajo* and chose another story instead, about a stampeding herd of cattle that destroys a whole Western village, with all the stories of the main characters intertwined. That meant we would have to shoot scenes featuring 400 cattle … Besides, the costume thing was impractical. On paper, it is perfectly fine to have a character wear a yellow scarf, red shirt and black trousers, but on a screen it looks ridiculous. Eventually the project fell apart.[1]

Then came the 1980s, and *Tex* finally became a movie directed by another prominent Italian filmmaker who had helmed a number of Westerns in his career: Duccio Tessari. The project was originally conceived as the pilot of a TV series produced by RAI, Italy's national public broadcasting company, in partnership with Cinecittà Studios. Fans of the comic book debated the choice of Giuliano Gemma as the hero—after Tessari had discarded other options, including Patrick Wayne—but the then 45-year-old actor seemed born to play the role. Unlike other Italian Western stars, such as Franco Nero, Gemma had mainly played uptight fearless heroes with a stern moral code, such as Ringo in Duccio Tessari's *A Pistol for Ringo*, aka *Ballad of Death Valley* (*Una pistola per Ringo*, 1965) and *The Return of Ringo*, aka *Blood at Sundown* (*Il ritorno di Ringo*, 1965). It was Tessari who had turned Gemma into one of Italian cinema's most beloved stars. After launching him as a leading man in the amusing sword-and-sandal *My Son, the Hero* (*Arrivano i titani*, 1962), he directed the handsome actor in the aforementioned *Ringo* diptych, the ironic spy flick *Kiss Kiss, Bang Bang* (1966), the grim crime yarn *The Bastard*, aka *The Cats* (*I bastardi*, 1968), the Western *Alive or Preferably Dead* (*Vivi o, preferibilmente, morti*, 1969) and the exotic comedy *Safari Express* (1976). Being their eighth film together, *Tex and the Lord of the Deep* seemed to guarantee an exciting result.

The rest of the cast was a journeyman bunch, ranging from good to terrible. Austrian William Berger, a staple of European genre films during the 1970s, was an ideal casting choice as Kit Carson, Tex's right hand man (while the character of Tex's son Kit was put aside), whom he resembled in an amazing way. The little-known Carlo Mucari turned out a convincing Tiger Jack, replete with typical "wise-silent-Indian" clichés. Familiar Spaghetti Western faces such as Aldo Sambrell and Frank Braña provided solid supporting roles, whereas Flavio Bucci—an excellent actor who had worked with Elio Petri, Dario Argento, Aldo Lado and Mario Monicelli among others—was wasted in a thankless role (and with a ridiculous wig) as one of the main villains, Kanas. On the other hand, the casting of the ravishing but inept Isabel Russinova (a popular TV personality at that time, due to the TV music show *Discoring*) was a debatable choice on the part of the producers.

It must be added, though, that *Tex* was a tough nut to crack. Over the years, the comic book had perfected its own universe, which was difficult to faithfully bring to the screen, especially in the arid desert that was Italian cinema of the mid-1980s. The idea of focusing on a story with fantasy overtones, which might have seemed weird at first, was easily explainable with marketing issues—that is, aiming at a young audience.

The Italian Western was long gone, and adventure films often featured fantasy and horror elements after the success of Steven Spielberg's *Raiders of the Lost Ark* (1981), which had spawned a number of Italian rip-offs as well. And even though *Tex* had a steady fan base in Italy, Bonelli—who had become Italy's leading comic book publisher—had begun exploring new threads with new series such as Alfredo Castelli's *Martin Mystère* (started in 1982, about a professor who investigates unsolved mysteries, and whose stories dealt with UFOs, the paranormal, lost civilizations etc.). In 1986, the horror-themed *Dylan Dog* would commence publication, and soon become Italy's best-selling comic book ever.

The fact that *Tex*'s stories had sometimes included fantastic elements definitely helped. Moreover, another popular Bonelli comic, *Zagor*, was an odd mixture of Western, adventure, mystery and horror. However, despite what critics would say[2], it was Tessari himself who pointed at a debatable *fil rouge* between Tex and Indiana Jones, claiming in interviews of the period that Bonelli's comic book had predated Spielberg's film by a good 20 years or so and that his intention was to portray the hero as "some kind of Indiana Jones, but firmer, in the Wild West."[3]

That said, the references to Spielberg's film were actually few and far between, like the shots of the rapidly mummifying bodies, which somewhat recalled *Raiders of the Lost Ark*'s melting Nazis and the subterranean temple with a self-destruction mechanism. Yet such similarities were underlined and enhanced when it came to distribute the film abroad. A jaw-dropping French poster for the film has Gemma (looking more like Tom Berenger) wearing an Indiana Jones hat and coat (and, to top it all, holding a whip) inside what looks like a temple (of doom?). No mention of the film's Western nature can be found, save for the discreet presence of two Indian types in the background.

Tessari and his co-scriptwriters focused on three stories with decidedly fantastic undertones, namely *El Morisco* (#101), *Sierra Encantada* (Enchanted Sierra, #102) and *Il signore dell'abisso* (The Lord of the Deep, #103), written by Bonelli and drawn by comic book artist Guglielmo Lettieri. Filming took place in May and June 1985 in Italy (the interiors were shot at Cinecittà) and Spain, in the familiar exteriors of Colmenar and Hoyo de Manzanares, north of Madrid, and in the southern region of Almería, the setting of so many Euro Westerns, in the village of Fort Bravo, first seen in Giulio Petroni's *Death Rides a Horse*.

Yet, as soon as *Tex and the Lord of the Deep* begins, one senses that something has gone terribly wrong. Tessari had the story introduced by none other than Gian Luigi Bonelli, dressed up as an elderly Indian sitting by a fire inside a cave and narrating the whole tale to the camera, thus giving it a mythical resonance ("The story merges with the legend, in a time lost between magic and reality") and providing a nice homage to the character's own creator. It would have been a nice touch had the scene not featured distractingly ugly special effects of a flame that pops up right near the center of the frame. It is supposed to be a picture-in-picture, but this becomes clear only in the end when the Old Chief returns to wrap up the tale and we get to see Tex and friends in the flame's place.

The idea of blending genres looked tempting on paper. The story starts in a seemingly conventional way (with nods to Michael Curtiz's *The Comancheros*, 1961), yet Tessari and his scriptwriters throw in references to the Gothic and the sword-and-sandal. El Morisco (Peter Berling) is a re-imagining of the "mad doctor" figure, while the second half hints at the *peplum*, with its masked evil priestess (Russinova) and a mysterious villain inhabiting a multicolored cave which pays homage to the magical underworld as

Tex and the Lord of the Deep was given ample publicity in the media. Here is Gemma on the cover of the monthly magazine *Ciak* #3 (July 1985).

The Italian *locandina* for *Tex and the Lord of the Deep*.

seen in *Hercules in the Haunted World* (*Ercole al centro della terra*, 1961, Mario Bava) and *The Witch's Curse* (*Maciste all'inferno*, 1962, Riccardo Freda). Yet the mixture does not quite work. The blatantly naivete sounds forced and the overall feel is closer to the third-rate *Conan the Barbarian* rip-offs of the period, such as *Thor the Conqueror* (*Thor il conquistatore*, 1983, Tonino Ricci).

Even more debatable, however, was the choice on the part of the scriptwriters to retain *Tex*'s peculiar dialogue and style. Bonelli had his characters speak in a colorful language, full of over-the-top exclamations and typical catchphrases. Whenever they set foot in a Western town, be sure that our heroes yearn for a "three-finger high steak with a mountain of fried potatoes on top." All this is amusing and a welcome occurrence on paper, but on film it sounds forced and grating. It is as if Tessari was sticking to an impression of *Tex* as a comic book instead of devising his own cinematic interpretation of it. Which also meant that, with several exceptions—such as a steadicam sequence shot depicting Tex's arrival in town and meeting the local sheriff, perhaps a nod to a famous scene in Samuel Fuller's *Forty Guns* (1957)—many sequences were filmed as static *tableaux*, as if they were comic book panels brought to life, with a tendency toward emphasizing depth-of-field (with, say, Tex in the background shooting at a villain in close-up) and characters delivering their lines while standing perfectly still.

This might have worked if only the style, pacing and lighting had been up to the task, but most of the time *Tex and the Lord of the Deep* simply looks cheap and rushed, with indifferent cinematography and poor set-pieces. The Indian camp at the film's beginning is not that more convincing than the one seen in Ciro Ippolito's 1984 zero-budget Western spoof *Arrapaho*. The make-up effects (by the brothers Francesco and Gaetano Paolocci, who also helmed several Italian gory horror films of the period) are also disappointingly bad, and the mummified skulls look amateurish and unpersuasive.

The acting is either stilted or wooden. Gemma (who dubs himself despite not having a sufficiently powerful voice) repeats gestures and poses typical of the comic book character with awkward effect, and the other actors often sound ridiculously one-dimensional, while the emphasis on old-style, excessive stunts—with extras jumping into the air after explosions with an enthusiasm not seen since the days of Demofilo Fidani's Z-grade Westerns of the early 1970s—is another grating factor. Perhaps the real problem with *Tex and the Lord of the Deep* is that it just came out too late for its own good. The time for the magic and wonder had gone, and what was left was the flatness of a decade in which Italian genre cinema was almost totally devoured by television.

When asked about *Tex and the Lord of the Deep* by the Spanish film critic Carlos Aguilar, Gemma was candid about his feelings for the film:

> You know, I find it hard to talk about *Tex and the Lord of the Deep*, such are the bad memories it brings back to me. The idea was very good, to bring to the screen a classic of Italian popular culture […]. I was delighted to accept it, but I think that, first of all, they made a mistake by choosing to adapt that story, *Il signore dell'abisso*, because

there are much better ones in the series, and [several] less difficult to turn into a film. What is more, the producers failed to provide the budget, as they assured me there would be much more money than we actually had. For instance, in the Indian camp there had to be 20 tents, whereas we had just five, and when there should have been 40 horses, but you only saw eight. It was all like that. On top of it all, Tessari could not put the right care into filming, as he was propelled to work in a hurry.[4]

The critics ravaged the film and the box-office results were disappointing, despite a massive promotional campaign. And, of course, the planned series never took off.

Notes:
1. Curti, Roberto, *Il mio nome è Nessuno. Lo spaghetti western secondo Tonino Valerii* (Rome: unmondoaparte, 2008), p. 79.
2. See Aguilar, Carlos, "Tex e il signore degli abissi," in Festi and Scudiero, *Cinema & Fumetto*, p. 53.
3. Pulici, Davide, *Tex e il signore degli abissi*, in *Cinecomix*, Nocturno Dossier #2, July 2002, p. 56.
4. Aguilar, Carlos, *Giuliano Gemma. El factor Romano* (Almería: Diputación de Almería, 2003), p. 83.

1986

Three Supermen in S. Domingo
(*3 Supermen a Santo Domingo*)
Italy, color, 90 minutes

D: Italo Martinenghi. *S:* Italo Martinenghi; *SC:* Italo Martinenghi, Bitto Albertini, Antonio Cesare Corti; *DOP:* Piergiorgio Albertini; *M:* Stelvio Cipriani; *E:* Bitto Albertini, Italo Martinenghi.
Cast: Daniel Stephen [Daniel Ronald Stefanow] (Captain Brad Scott), Sal Borgese (Sal), Steven Martin [Stefano Martinenghi] (Steve), Gena Gas (Daia), Adalberto [Bitto] Albertini (American attaché).
Prod: Barbatoja Film.

Worldwide markets have been flooded with counterfeit dollars, which results in global inflation. The C.I.A. and the F.B.I. join forces to locate the gang of elusive counterfeiters and entrust captain Brad Scott with the mission of reuniting with his former partners, the masked "supermen" Sal and Steve, in order to solve the case. Through a Dominican girl named Daia, Brad and friends learn that the gang is based in Santo Domingo. Sal and Steve, though, are planning to steal the counterfeiting machine for their own profit. It turns out that the gang is maneuvered by the Russians and is located in a ship at the Santo Domingo dock. The three heroes succeed in their task, but the Russians capture Brad …

Italian DVD art for *3 Supermen in Santo Domingo* (1986), the last entry in the series

Produced by Italo Martinenghi's own company Barbatoja Film (based at the Isle of Elba, near the Tuscany coast), *Three Supermen in S. Domingo* marked the producer's last attempt at reviving the *Three Supermen* series, some 20 years after the first chapter. The film was clearly aimed at foreign (and specifically third-world) markets. Bitto Albertini, himself a veteran of the series, having directed no less than three entries (*3 Supermen a Tokyo*, *Three Supermen in the Jungle* and *Supermen Against the Orient*), worked alongside Martinenghi. Here Albertini figures not only as co-scriptwriter but also as co-editor, as well as actor in a secondary role. Furthermore, in a spirit of "all in the family" and further displaying the shoestring budget, Albertini's son Piergiorgio was the director of photography while his daughter Ornella took care of the make-up and art direction. Furthermore, Stefano Martinenghi also acted as cameraman for the scenes in which he was not performing.

The idea of reviving the series in an exotic setting (possibly attributable to Albertini) proved to be a bad one. The result is certainly not in the vein of Alexandre Dumas' *Twenty Years Later*. The storyline, replete with Cold War car-

Stefano Martinenghi (left), Sal Borgese and Daniel Stephen as the Three Supermen

icatures, is downright silly—yet, in a bit of unmotivated self-preservation, Martinenghi even throws in a disclaimer at the beginning that states that "any reference to maneuverings on the dollar is casual, knowing how the U.S. Treasury as well as the C.I.A [works]."

It gets worse from here.

The "humor" is kindergarten level (such as when Borgese and Martinenghi pop up in drag, yet are still wearing their supermen costumes underneath their female clothes, for instance), and the overall amateurishness is jaw dropping. Much of *Three Supermen in S. Domingo* takes place in hotel rooms like a cheap porn flick, while the story is sketched awkwardly in a series of badly concocted expository scenes (i.e. two characters talking in long shot with post-synch voice-over added), and the action stunts are poor beyond belief. The recycled footage from Albertini's *3 Supermen a Tokyo*, used here as flashbacks, looks like *Citizen Kane* in comparison.

In a cast of local non-professional extras (who often cannot keep a straight face during the action scenes—not that "one-take" Martinenghi would mind …), the only survivor from the past series is good ol' Sal Borgese as the mute of the trio. Borgese does his best to make the viewer oblivious of the overwhelming squalor with his usual pantomime routine and funny bits—in a scene he even makes a dog impression, sniffing like a truffle hound in search of mines in a minefield—but to no avail. Square-jawed Daniel Stephen, a survivor from Italian post-atomic and war film,

picks up the role of the F.B.I. agent who must recruit the two crooks. Once again, as in *Three Supermen at the Olympic Games*, Martinenghi cast his own son Stefano as one of the three leads, envisioning a career in the movie business for his offspring—an ill-fated attempt if ever there was one, as young Martinenghi proved to be absolutely disastrous in front of the camera, just as his father was behind it.

Three Supermen in S. Domingo was not even released theatrically in Italy, and would turn up only two decades later on DVD. It was not over, though, as Martinenghi tried yet again to recycle the *Three Supermen* franchise onto a different media—comic books, thus closing the circle. Starting in January 1989 the Italian company Star Comics published a series named *I fantastici 3 Supermen*, which later passed on to another publisher, Eclecta. The format was 9½" by 7" comprised of 48 pages in black-and-white, featuring poor scripts and terrible artwork. The scripts were by "George Stone" (that is, Giorgio Pedrazzi, a well-known *fumetti* author born in 1935 with a long career in popular and adults-only publications), based on stories by Martin Egg, that is Italo Martinenghi himself (although there are rumors that such stories were actually written by others).

The accent was on vulgar, crass humor with puerile hints at political satire. Issue #3 from 1991, *Missione un po' igienica* (A rather hygienic mission), deals with a laxative gas and ends with the world's main politicians suffering a collective attack of diarrhea. The magazine went on for four years, with at least 15 issues, before consigning itself to well deserved oblivion. Born as a fake adaptation of an imaginary comic book, the Fantastic Supermen ended up in a real one, for good.

In 1992 Martinenghi and son ended up in the news for a reason only partially related to the movies. Both were arrested after a police raid regarding bootleg copies of Walt Disney films, during which the authorities seized over 22,000 pirate videocassettes (of such films as *Bambi*, *Snow White and the Seven Dwarfs*, *Dumbo*, *Pinocchio*, *Fantasia*). It turned out that Martinenghi had requested official Siae seals[1] for old films to distribute in newsstands but instead used them to sell those old Disney classics instead, passing them off as official Disney releases (which according to Italian law must have the Siae seal on display)[2]. Martinenghi claimed that those films were public domain in Italy, according to a 1941 law. The 18-year-long trial ended with a sentence of discharge by the Supreme Court in February 2010[3]. Martinenghi had already passed away by then.

After giving up acting, Martinenghi, Jr. reinvented himself as an entrepreneur. He would later embark on a career in politics, first with Silvio Berlusconi's right-wing party Forza Italia—one would think that the myth of the Italian Superman was still fresh in his mind, given Berlusconi's own self-mythology as some sort of a secular messiah—and then running for mayor in 2009 with his own extreme right-wing movement Civiltà Italiana. Today he owns a bar at a beach in the isle of Elba, and bluntly refuses to speak of his past in the movies. Who could blame him?

Notes:
1. Siae—Società Italiana degli autori ed editori (Italian Society of authors and publishers)—is the intermediary between those and the consumers, managing the economic aspects and redistribution of the money obtained from the royalties to the authors and for them.
2. G. Am., "Falsi video Disney: giro da 7 miliardi," *Il Corriere della Sera*, 04/21/1992.
3. Guastella, Giuseppe, "Duplicava i film di Disney: assolto dopo 18 anni," *Il Corriere della Sera*, 02/20/2010.

1989

Valentina

Italy/France/Spain, color, TV series (13 episodes, 30 minutes each)

D: Giandomenico Curi and Gianfranco Giagni. *S:* Guido Crepax; *SC:* Gianfranco Manfredi and Gianfranco Giagni; *DOP:* Roberto Forges Davanzati; *M:* Fio Zanotti; *E:* Luigi Zitta.

Cast: Demetra Hampton (Valentina), Russel Case (Philip Rembrandt), Antonello Fassari (Checco), Mary Sellers

Film director Bitto Albertini takes a turn before the camera.

(Anita), Assumpta Serna (Baba Yaga), Regina Rodriguez (Tony), Kim Rossi-Stuart (Bruno), Mattia Sbragia, Giorgio Tirabassi, Guido Alberti, Eleonora Vallone, Sabrina Ferilli, Bruno Corazzari, John Karlsen, Ricky Gianco, Franco Diogene, Eva Robin's [Roberto Coatti].

Prod: Reteitalia.

In Milan fashion photographer Valentina Rossetti and her boyfriend, antique dealer Philip Rembrandt, face a series of adventures that often see the beautiful Valentina in peril, at the mercy of men and women who crave her beautiful body …

The 1980s was the decade that witnessed the definitive victory of television over the big screen in Italy. Box-office grosses had dropped, and—with the exception of comedies—genre cinema was gradually disappearing from screens. Silvio Berlusconi's Reteitalia invested in horror and *gialli* in order to lure a wider and younger audience, with dreary results, exemplified by Lamberto Bava's TV movies such as *Graveyard Disturbance* (*Una notte al cimitero*, 1987) or *Demons 3: The Ogre* (*La casa dell'orco*, 1987).

Over 20 years after its debut, Guido Crepax's *Valentina* still proved a marketable icon and gave way to a TV series. Accompanied by a considerable hype, the 13 episodes (25 to 30 minutes each) were broadcast between September 1989 and February 1990 on one of Berlusconi's channels, the youth-oriented Italia 1. Crepax was willing to give away the rights, as long as he would not be involved in the adaptations. The eclectic Gianfranco Manfredi—a singer-songwriter, writer, scriptwriter, actor and soon-to-be comic book writer—together with Gianfranco Giagni, a

Valentina and her camera, as visualized by Guido Crepax

former video maker who made his directorial debut with the promising horror film *The Spider's Labyrinth* (*Il nido del ragno*, 1988), concocted the scripts. Giagni also directed nine episodes, while the remaining four were helmed by Giandomenico Curi, a video maker and TV author and director, whose first film had been the juvenile comedy *Ciao ma'* (1988).

Valentina's troubles came right from the start, with the choice of the actress who would play the titular role. The casting of U.S. gymnast-turned-model Demetra Hampton, born in Philadelphia in 1968, came as a surprise to many fans of the comic. Even though the choice of an unknown, debuting actress—nevertheless, a well-known presence in Milan fashion shows—was a wise move on the part of the producers, Hampton was simply too far from Crepax's vision to be a convincing Valentina. Whereas the comic book character is thin and androgynous, Hampton was a healthy, buxom American girl with large shoulders and a square jaw, who would definitely look more at ease

Demetra Hampton as Valentina, with camera and very little else, in a publicity shot from the 1989 TV series

in some action/adventure flick. She was a beautiful girl, indeed, but she lacked the mystery, the allure and the subtle, lazy seductive power of Crepax's fashion photographer.

The rest of the cast was a journeyman one. As Valentina's boyfriend Philip Rembrandt, American actor Russel Case—seen in David Worth's *Warrior of the Lost World* (1983) and in Martin Scorsese's *The Last Temptation of Christ* (1988)—did not make much of an impression, while the series benefitted from a number of special guest stars and soon-to-be ones, such as Sabrina Ferilli, Kim Rossi-Stuart and transsexual Eva Robin's (seen in Dario Argento's *Tenebrae*, 1982).

The episodes followed Crepax's stories rather loosely. The first, Giagni's *Baba Yaga*, reprised the same comic that had been the source of Corrado Farina's 1973 film of the same name. The opening scene, as Valentina is almost run over by Baba Yaga's Rolls Royce, is very similar to Farina's film, but the differences soon become clear. Manfredi and Giagni abandoned the political and erotic overtones of their predecessor, even omitting one of the comic's most memorable moments—Valentina's boxing match scene in which she wears boxing gloves and shorts, and nothing else[1]—and focused on the lesbian attraction between the elderly witch and the young photographer. Valentina is lured into Baba Yaga's house (punctuated with such eerie detail as a floor completely littered with crystal glasses and a hole covered with an old carpet), made to wear a S/M outfit and imprisoned in a suspended box.

There is not much of a plot, however, given the episode's scant 30 minutes' duration. Another element that is lost is the doll that comes to life, memorably played in the 1973 film by Ely Galleani, and which here becomes a secondary detail. On the other hand, the scenes with Valentina's colleagues (played by Antonello Fassari and Mary Sellers) look like they were concocted mainly to pad out the running time, whereas Giagni had eyes mostly for Hampton's body (and specifically her gravity-defying ass). The resolution also looks rather abrupt and unsatisfying. Spanish actress Assumpta Serna (seen in Pedro Almodovar's grotesque psycho thriller *Matador*, 1986) plays Baba Yaga, and she is definitely too young-looking for the role, even though she wears the same old woman's clothes and veil as Carroll Baker in the earlier version.

From the very beginning it was clear that Giagni and Curi were going for a mixture of genres. The episodes are usually structured as mysteries of sorts, with distinct *giallo* and horrific elements and include nods to Argento's *oeuvre*. *Valentina assassina* features a razor-wielding killer, while a murder scene in *Rembrandt e le streghe* openly pays homage to *Suspiria*. However, the stories are rather bland, and the results are pretty disappointing, superficially enticing yet rather hollow at the core. Valentina is often seen talking to herself, in order to expose plot points (and make up for plot holes).

What is more, there was no trace of Crepax's style, which Farina had painstakingly tried to reproduce in the 1973 film. Most of the time Giagni and Curi opted for a look that was heavily reminiscent of MTV videos and hinted all too apparently at the directors' backgrounds as music video makers, with plenty of frantic camerawork, odd camera angles and the like—combined with Pio Zanotti's grating and very 1980-ish soundtrack, spiced with several hit songs (by Culture Club, Art of Noise, Simply Red) repeated over and over throughout the series.[2] The not-so-high budget also showed in the exterior scenes, while the editing was often slapdash.

The main problem, however, could be synthesized in one word: eroticism. Due to the limitations connected to *Valentina* being aimed at the small screen, nudity was tame (Hampton had only one full frontal nude scene in the whole series) and the makers preferred a glamorous approach—Valentina putting on her stockings and lingerie, *Playboy*-style, for instance—which was superficially enticing but ultimately cold and devoid of any real *frisson*. As a result, *Valentina* is closer to the many Italian erotic flicks of the period, all style over substance, than to Crepax's original and thought-provoking vision. Far from being the tormented, unsatisfied soul she was in the comics (and partly in Farina's film), Valentina became just the umpteenth T&A fodder for the mid-'80s generations, who were fed daily by Silvio Berlusconi's networks with scantily dressed babes (such as in the comedy show *Drive In*, 1983-1988, or in the satirical TV news *Striscia la notizia*, which started in 1988).

In a 2000 online interview, Guido Crepax commented diplomatically about the series that it was well scripted but had little resemblance to his original stories.

> I wanted to stay out of it, I didn't take part in the adaptations. I met Demetra Hampton: a beautiful girl but she was not fit to play Valentina, in my opinion. I would not say there is some other actress fit for the part, as there never was one. Sure, I had Louise Brooks in mind, but she was born in 1906 ...[3]

Despite being a moderate success, *Valentina* was not confirmed for a second season. What is more, it did not launch Hampton's career as expected—not the least because of her shortcomings as an actress. She took part in such trash as the painfully unfunny comedy *Saint Tropez, Saint Tropez* (1992, Castellano & Pipolo), the erotic drama *Kreola* (1993, Antonio Bonifacio) and the awful *Jurassic Park* spoof *Chicken Park* (1994, Jerry Calà), but soon her star waned. Hampton's name became news value again in 1998 when she escaped from justice with her lover, a local politician from Milan, who was to be imprisoned after being sentenced for corruption. In 2005 Hampton took part in a reality show, *La talpa* (The Mole), without making much of an impression.

As for Gianfranco Giagni, he shot his second feature—the political thriller *Nella terra di nessuno*—in 2001. As of today it remains his last fictional film, besides a number of interesting documentaries on Italian cinema. On the other hand, the experience led Manfredi to the comic book world, as he created the Western *Magico Vento* and scripted episodes for *Dylan Dog* and *Tex*.

Notes:
1. The scene was recycled in another episode, *Fotofinish*.
2. The list of episodes is as follows: *Baba Yaga, Il violoncello, Jack ama Lulù, Valentina non riposa, Per amore di Valentina, Farfalle, Fotofinish, L'altra, Rembrandt e le streghe, Valentina assassina, Caduta angeli, Ciao Valentina, Addio Valentina*.
3. Cassani, Alberto, "Intervista a Guido Crepax," *Ink* (www.inkonline.info), Spring 2000.

The German movie poster for Terence Hill's *Lucky Luke* (1991)

1991

Lucky Luke
(*Lucky Luke*)
Italy/U.S.A., color, 92 minutes

D: Terence Hill [Mario Girotti]. *S:* based on the comic book by Morris & Goscinny; *SC:* Lori Hill; *DOP:* Carlo Tafani and Gianfranco Transunto; *M:* Aaron Schroeder and David Grover; *E:* Eugenio Alabiso.

Cast: Terence Hill (Lucky Luke), Nancy Morgan (Lotta Legs), Roger Miller (Narrator), Fritz Sperberg (Averell Dalton), Dominic Barto (William Dalton), Bo Greigh (Jack Dalton), Ron Carey (Joe Dalton).

Prod: Paloma Films (Rome), Reteitalia (Milan).

In the Wild West, the white men and Indians are finally at peace. Life goes on quietly in Daisy Town, where Lucky Luke, the fastest gun in the West, is the new sheriff. However, Lucky must face the Daltons, four criminal brothers who are as ruthless as they are bungling, always failing in their elaborate deeds …

One of the most popular European comics ever, *Lucky Luke* debuted in 1946, the year of John Ford's *My Darling Clementine*. The overly slender cowboy, infallible with the gun (in one of the comic's trademark gags, he draws faster than his own shadow) and with a half-extinguished cigarette perpetually hanging from his lower lip, was the offspring of the Belgian comic artist Morris (born as Maurice de Bévère, 1923-2001) who in 1955 teamed up with the writer René Goscinny (1926-1977). If the idea of a Wild West reinvented by a couple of Europeans in a comic version was not enough, Morris and Goscinny injected the stories with surreal elements, by having Luke sided by a talking, chess-playing horse named Jolly Jumper and an incredibly stupid dog called Rantamplan, facing a quartet of clumsy antagonists, the Dalton family, who look like a Wild West version of Disney's Beagle Boys. After Goscinny's death in 1977, Morris collaborated with other writers—often prestigious ones, like the renowned novelists Daniel Pennac and Tonino Benacquista.

Lucky Luke was scarcely known in America but immensely popular in Europe and in French-speaking countries. It is understandable why Terence Hill decided to adapt it for the big screen. After all, Hill—real name Mario Girotti—was one of the icons of the Western/comedy blend that marked a vital turn of the screw for the genre in Italy, with his roles in the Trinity films (*My Name Is Trinity* and *Trinity Is STILL My Name!*, both directed by Enzo Barboni) as well as Tonino Valerii's *My Name Is Nobody* (*Il mio nome è Nessuno*, 1973).

With the decline of the Western and after separating from his long-time artistic half Bud Spencer, Hill moved toward other genres, always with an eye on the younger audiences. In 1980 he starred in Sergio Corbucci's superhero/cop comedy *Super Fuzz*, yet another attempt at winning the U.S. audiences, while his 1983 version of the classic *Don Camillo* (where he played a dynamic priest opposite a Communist mayor in a small Italian village) marked not only his debut behind the camera, but also, an ambitious bet as he tried to assess himself as an *auteur* for the masses. However, the results were disappointing. *They Call Me Renegade* (*Renegade—Un osso troppo duro*, 1987, Enzo Barboni), the road movie in which he played alongside his adoptive son Ross, further underlined Hill's aims toward the international market as well as his debt to Hollywood's imagery and epic.

Lucky Luke was the first non-animated adaptation of Morris and Goscinny's comic, following two feature-length cartoons dated 1971 (*Lucky Luke—Daisy Town*) and 1978 (*La Ballade des Daltons*), plus a 1984 animated series. Hill's film was actually based on the 1971 story, which had been turned into a comic book in 1982. The actor/director knew very well that with the death of genre cinema in Italy, it was preferable to devise the project for TV consumption. *Lucky Luke* was developed into a feature film which served as a pilot for a 13-episode series, each episode being a 90-minute film on its own, to be broadcast on Silvio Berlusconi's Fininvest network.

In order to ingratiate himself into the American market, Hill planned to shoot the film in the U.S.A. where he lived. It was to be a family effort. Hill would act as star, director and producer, his wife Lori would pen the script and he planned to cast Ross in one of the main roles. However, due to Ross Hill's tragic death in January 1990 at only sixteen, in a car accident, Hill entered a period of depression that affected the project deeply. The episodes were drastically reduced to only 8, while the pilot came out in theaters in summer 1991. The series featured two other directors, Richard Schlesinger and Ted Nicolaou, who helmed two and three episodes respectively, while Hill directed the remaining three. It premiered in Italy in March 1992 to lukewarm response.[1] On the other hand, *Lucky Luke* was a commercial success in France and Germany.

However, Hill's Lucky Luke has less in common with Morris & Goscinny's character than with the actor's previous incarnations as Trinity. Were it not for the presence of the comic's regular characters such as the Daltons and the talking horse, speaking with the voice of *King of the Road*'s Roger Miller[2], the two characters would be almost impossible to distinguish. Despite the impressive New Mexico setting, there is actually little left of Morris and Goscinny's character in the film, and much of the blame can be laid at the feet of the star himself. As one critic observed:

> Hill's Luke takes on a new connotation. He loses every hint at physical inade-

Terence Hill as Lucky Luke

One of Europe's most popular comics, *Lucky Luke* was created in 1946 by the Belgian comic artist Morris, who soon teamed up with René Goscinny.

quacy and the slightest touch of shadowiness, and Hill indulges in his own ever-magnetizing look, which is extraneous to the sad and solitary character that ended his stories under the stars, singing a song that went, "I'm a poor, lonesome cowboy in the West."[3]

The comic strip aspect is also rather dully exercised. Hill occasionally resorts to balloons and question marks that appear on characters' foreheads, but he fails to capture the strip's surreal humor. On the other hand, the Revisionist approach to the Western genre is given a sharp edge in the sequence in which one of the Daltons foretells the Apaches' bleak future as an ostracized people by the white man, and Hill intersperses the scene with inserts of the chaotic city life during the 20th century.

As for the rest of the cast, Nancy Morgan played Luke's love interest Lotta Legs, while Spaghetti Western fans will recognize one of the Daltons as Dominic Barto, who was in one of Hill's most enjoyable efforts, *Man of the East* (… *E poi lo chiamarono il magnifico*, 1972, Enzo Barboni).

Lucky Luke was adapted again for TV in 2004, with the French/German/Spanish series *Les Daltons* (2004, Philippe Haïm), starring Til Schweiger (*Inglourious Basterds*' Hugo Stiglitz) and for the big screen in 2009 (*Lucky Luke*, by James Huth), with Jean Dujardin (*The Artist*) in the titular role.

Notes:
1. The episodes were: *Who Is Mr. Josephs?* (*Chi è Mr. Josephs?*, d: Schlesinger), *Midsummer* (*Una notte di mezza estate a Daisy Town*, d: Hill), *Ghost Train* (*Il treno fantasma*, d: Nicolaou), *Ma Dalton* (*La mamma dei Dalton*, d: Schlesinger), *Cafe Olé* (*Caffè Olé*, d: Nicolaou), *Luke's Fiancée* (*Le fidanzate di Luke*, d: Nicolaou), *Grand Delusions* (*Magia indiana*, d: Hill), *Nobody's Fool* (*Pesce d'aprile*, d: Hill). *Lucky Luke* is available on home video in the U.S. on the Simitar label, and the eight episodes were released separately to DVD as well.
2. Miller also sings the opening theme *Lucky Luke Rides Again*, while Arlo Guthtrie sings *The Lonesomest Cowboy in the West*.
3. Bertolino, Marco and Ridola, Ettore, *Bud Spencer & Terence Hill* (Rome: Gremese, 2002), p. 74.

1992

DiaboliX (Colpo internazionale)
Italy, color, 110 minutes
D: Max Bellocchio [Alessandro Occhiobuono].
Cast: Babette Grey (Eva), Giancarlo Bini (Diabolix), Ugo Ross (Philip Perrel), Yves Baillat (Pierre Perrel), Marcello Fusi (Carlo Verdon), Angela Smith (Norma Martin), Don Fernando (Adriano), Sean Michaels (Tony), Béatrice Valle (Florence Vussi), Sally Palmer (Cop woman), Lynn Le May.
Prod: Showtime.

DiaboliX and Eva are enjoying a vacation in Rotterdam. Eva spends her time shopping while he is planning a new hit. However, whenever DiaboliX sneaks into the villas he plans to rob, he keeps bumping into people having sex …

In the early 1990s Italian porn was experiencing a renaissance of sorts due to the explosion of the home video market and the popularity of stars like Moana Pozzi (who would die of cancer in 1994, at only 33 years of age) and Selen (real name Luce Caponegro). Aristide Massaccesi resumed his hardcore career under the moniker Joe D'Amato, while directors like Mario Salieri and Silvio Bandinelli tried to shape a refined image of the adults-only Italian film, in stark contrast with the recent past.

In the States, porn filmmakers would often venture into hardcore parodies or remakes, with such outlandish results as Paul Norman's *Edward Penishands* (1991). Something similar happened with Franco Lo Cascio's trashy porn fairytales (*Le avventure erotiX di Cappuccetto Rosso* even included badly made animated inserts), but the most daring concept was carried out by Max Bellocchio, real name Alessandro Occhiobuono, one of the main figures of the 1990s Italian wave of porn. Taking inspiration from *Diabolik*, Bellocchio helmed a hardcore version of the Giussani sisters' comic, which gave away its inspiration from the very title—*DiaboliX*, with the final X replacing the "K" that had been a distinctive mark for the 1960s *fumetti neri*, so as to underline the film's explicitness.

Bellocchio's idea was a retaliation of sorts. As he would later claim, as a reader he was frustrated that Diabolik and Eva never got to have sex in the comic book. They were indeed shown a couple of times under the sheets, but—unlike Kriminal, for example—their sex life was basically implied, much to the chagrin of so many viewers who were dying to get a glimpse of Eva's curvaceous body. In Bellocchio's film, DiaboliX is the only character who does not take part in any explicit sex scene. As played by Giancarlo Bini, he is reduced to peeping on the couplings from behind doors or hidden inside cabinets.

The budget was about a hundred million *lire*, making it a sort of porn epic—even though Bellocchio had to replace Diabolik's trademark Jaguar E-Type with a more anonymous red Corvette. A CD was also released including four tracks (*Diabolix* in a "Club Mix" and "Techno Mix" and *Strange Feelings* in a "Vocal Version" and "Guitar Version"), written by Paul Manners and sung by Babette Grey, aimed at discos and clubs.

As an article of the period stated:

> The scenes are unambiguous. The actors are wearing the famous tight-fitting black suits; Eva Kant, played by Babette, wears a scarf tied at the nape; the thefts are always about diamonds. The producer even hired a Roman artisan to create latex masks imitating the exploits of the villain .... But between a theft and the other, there is plenty of room for the typical XXX footage.[1]

And yet Bellocchio had not considered the consequences that such a bold move—even the *DiaboliX* logo was identical to the original—would have had.

According to the director:

> The Giussani sisters, who created the comic book, wanted 30 *billion lire* in compensation. To think that my DiaboliX was the only one [in the cast] who did not f**k.[2]

The story goes that Luciana Giussani came across a description of *DiaboliX* in the erotic magazine *Blue* and was outraged to learn that her creation had become the subject of a porn flick. Giussani denounced the filmmakers and a judge seized the film (distributed in the home video circuit through the Riccione-based Cibii Italia) all over the country. As the magistrate declared to the press:

> I demanded the seizure of the videotape because I think that it was detrimental to the image of the character's creators as well as *Diabolik* itself, which is absolutely a [long] way from pornography.[3]

Bellocchio was not discouraged, though. "I just made a porn version of James Bond, shot in the States with a budget of 300,000 dollars," he claimed some time later.[4]

Notes:
1. a.t., "Vietato il porno Diabolik," *Il Corriere della Sera* 02/13/1993.
2. Giordano, Michele, *Moana e le altre. Vent'anni di cinema porno in Italia* (Rome: Gremese, 1997), p. 130.
3. a.t., "Vietato il porno Diabolik."
4. Giordano, *Moana e le altre*, p. 130.

Madness, a.k.a ***Eyes Without a Face***
(*Gli occhi dentro*, aka *Occhi senza volto*)
Italy, color, 83 minutes
D: Herik Montgomery [Bruno Mattei]. *S:* Angelo Longoni, Lorenzo De Luca; *SC:* Lorenzo De Luca; *DOP:* Luigi Ciccarese; *E:* Bruno Mattei.
Cast: Carol Farres [Monica Carpanese] (Giovanna Dei), Gabriele Gori (Nico Manelli), Emy Valentino (Emy), Antonio Zequila (Amedeo Callistrati), Anthony Berner [Achille Brugnini] (Marzio Mannino), Fausto Lombardi (Lorenzo Calligari).
Prod: Europe Communications (Rome).

Giovanna Dei is a young talented comics artist and the co-creator of the successful comic book "Doctor Dark," centered on a psychopathic killer with a split personality. A mysterious murderer is killing baby sitters in the same way as Doctor Dark does, by gouging their eyes out and employing an ancient Egyptian technique. In spite of the harsh criticism, Giovanna defends "Doctor Dark" at a press confer-

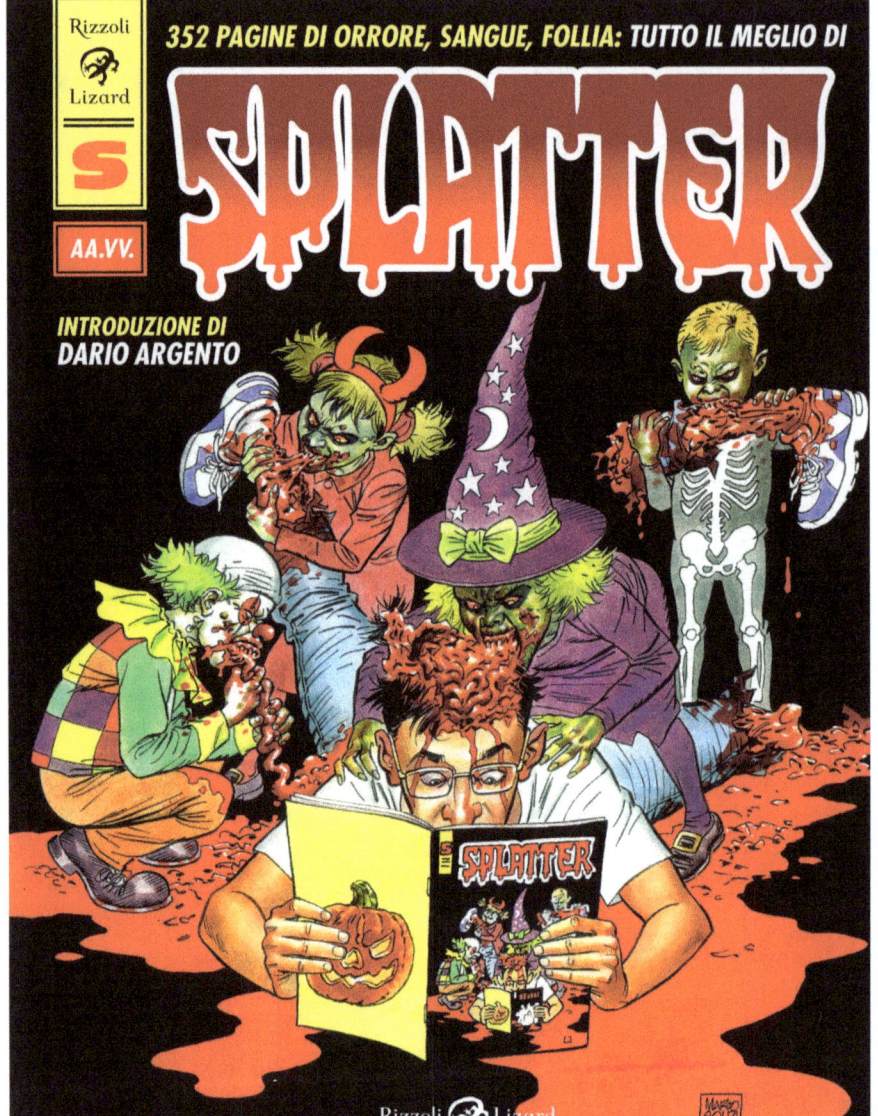

An over-the-top cover for the magazine *Splatter*, one of the hyper-violent horror comics that caused a heated controversy in the media, which in turn inspired the plot for Bruno Mattei's *Madness* (1992).

ence and decides to move out of town so as to keep on with her work in complete isolation. However, soon she finds herself persecuted by the madman, who leaves the victim's eyes in her study. The police sets a trap and captures a suspect, and Giovanna sails on a private cruise with her lover, Nico (who is "Doctor Dark's" writer) However, the suspected murderer turns out to be a mythomaniac journalist. The psycho is still at large, and the key to the solution lies in Giovanna's past ...

Much more than for its relevance (or rather, lack of) as a *giallo*, Bruno Mattei's *Gli occhi dentro* is interesting for its references to a heated controversy that broke out by the end of the 1980s, concerning hyper-violence in the media.

The key year was 1989, with the birth of an outrageously graphic comic anthology magazine significantly named *Splatter*. Published by ACME edizioni[1], it was the offspring of Paolo Di Orazio, a cartoonist and comics writer whose stories pushed the pedal of the grotesque and the shocking—a consequence of his background in hardcore porn *fumetti*. *Splatter* consisted of brief, over-the-top horror stories that were often "inspired" by either filmic or literary works. An infamous one was based on Stephen King's short story on self-cannibalism *Survivor Type*, albeit with a demented twist. The protagonist starts eating parts of his body not out of hunger, but because he is so narcissistic he finds his own meat more exquisite than anything else. Eventually, though, when he is physically unable to eat himself any longer, he can't help but throw himself into a garbage can. It was the kind of material that made parents raise an eyebrow. Even more controversial was Di Orazio's short stories anthology, *Primi delitti*, published as a supplement to *Splatter* and focused on murderous children.

The scandal arrived in Parliament, in 1990, with an MP accusing the book of incitement to crime. *Splatter* eventually closed down in 1991[2]. Meanwhile, a crusade to limit or ban violence and sex from the media resulted in the Mammì law (August 1990), which established a watershed. All the channels must broadcast "general audience" programs from 07:00 to 22:30. After 22:30, V.M.14 programs could be aired. V.M.18 programs were prohibited from television altogether. This resulted in a heavy back-draft in film production, as most films were primarily aimed at TV consumption.

If *Splatter* represented Italy's call to arms for the splatter-punk generation, around the same time Max Bunker took a stab at blood and gore with the self-labeled "hard-boiled comic" *Angel Dark*, focusing on grim, hyper-realistic stories about racism, cannibals, AIDS and drug addiction. Then there was *Dylan Dog*, whose philosophical and sociological digressions did not prevent the stories from featuring grim gory highlights. In short, violence was very much a primary feature in Italian comics of the period.

It is no wonder, then, that Lorenzo De Luca's script for *Gli occhi dentro* took inspiration from that controversy, basically using it to recycle the theme at the heart of Dario Argento's *Tenebrae* (*Tenebre*, 1982) with a comic book artist persecuted by a black-gloved killer who commits copycat murders inspired by her stories. If the press attacked Peter Neal for the violence and sexism of his books, in Mattei's film the protagonist Giovanna Dei faces a similar argument related to her character Doctor Dark (notice the double "D," as in Dylan Dog) in a heated press conference and similarly has to deal with a crazed journalist. De Luca goes so far as having Giovanna paraphrase almost to the letter Neal's question to Detective Germani ("If someone is killed with a Smith & Wesson revolver … Do you go and interview the president of Smith & Wesson?") as Giovanna tells the catatonic-looking Inspector: "When someone is killed with a power drill, are you investigating Black & Decker?" … a line which admittedly sounds quite a bit sillier.

Tenebrae resulted in a fascinating bout of self-examination on the part of Argento and presented a discourse on the relation between an author and his work, which could be read in many ways, even political ones, while *Gli occhi dentro* is just a Z-grade little *giallo* that relies on cheap psychoanalysis (with a nod to *Halloween*) to explain the reasons behind its mad killer's deeds. Besides *Tenebrae*, another reference is Julio Pérez Tabernero's gory Spanish *giallo Sexy Cat*, which features a very similar plot about a comic book character apparently coming to life and killing people. However, since Tabernero's film was never released in Italy, similarities may well have been coincidental. De Luca also reprises the third act from Phillip Noyce's *Dead Calm* (1989), but any attempt at creating suspense is let down by the transparent, telegraphed twist ending … which eventually (and no doubt involuntarily) seems to embrace the media's thesis that such works as *Splatter* and the like were indeed the result of sick minds.

As with the other films Mattei helmed in the early 1990s, *Gli occhi dentro* was a low-budget effort aimed primarily at foreign sales. As De Luca recalled, the scenario and the script were written in just one week:

> Bruno left me plenty of room to do what I wanted, as long as the movie did not cost too much and there were not too many characters. I had lots of fun, although being a low-budget film I was paid very little.[3]

The movie was shot with the same crew as Mattei's erotic thriller *Dangerous Attraction* (*Attrazione perversa*, 1992) and included some of the director's recurring actors, such as the enticing Monica Carpanese and the laughably wooden Zequila. Since this is a Bruno Mattei film, quality is an option *not* included in the package. The acting is terrible, the dialogue atrocious and the music score a hodgepodge of library cues. Luigi Ciccarese's blue-tinged photography does its utmost to create a suitably eerie mood, and it is the most tolerable thing about a film best forgotten.

The version released to home video in Italy (as *Eyes Without a Face*) was drastically re-edited from the one screened at film markets worldwide under the title *Madness*. First, and most importantly, it inexplicably includes two murder scenes lifted off Lamberto Bava's *A Blade in the Dark* (*La casa con la scala nel buio*, 1983), which replace the two murders shot by Mattei. In the original scenes a baby sitter looking for a child in a hangar during a go-kart race has her eyes gouged out and fragments of glass put into the empty sockets (shades of Michael Mann's *Manhunter*, 1986), while the second victim ends up with a syringe stuck in her jugular. *Eyes Without a Face* also lacks the moment in which Giovanna finds the victims' eyes in her apartment and the morgue scene in which an eyeless body is prepared for the autopsy, as well as an epilogue with a Coast Guard boat approaching the yacht where the final massacre has taken place.

Notes:
1. ACME also published the similarly themed *Mostri*, plus *Nosferatu*, a horror magazine that was intended as the answer to *Fangoria*, but only lasted 10 issues.
2. Over 20 years after its original run, *Splatter* was revived in 2013, with new material as well as reprints of the old stories. In 2015 a documentary entitled *Splatter: la rivista proibita*, about the mag's brief but controversial existence, has been put in production via crowd-funding by Stefano Cavalli.
3. Visani, Alex, "Intervista a Lorenzo De Luca," in www.alexvisani.it.

1994

Cemetery Man
(*Dellamorte Dellamore*)
Italy/France/Germany, color, 105 minutes
D: Michele Soavi. *S:* based on the novel by Tiziano Sclavi; *SC:* Gianni Romoli; *DOP:* Mauro Marchetti; *M:* Manuel De Sica; *E:* Franco Fraticelli.

Cast: Rupert Everett (Francesco Dellamorte), François Hadji-Lazaro (Gnaghi), Anna Falchi (The Woman), Mickey Knox (Commissioner Straniero), Barbara Cupisti (Magda), Stefano Masciarelli (The Mayor).

Prod: Audifilm, Urania Film, K.G. Productions, Canal+.

Francesco Dellamorte works as a gravedigger in the cemetery of the small town of Buffalora, isolated from the rest of the world and his only company is his retarded and mute aide Gnaghi. A strange "epidemic" has spread throughout the cemetery. Some of the dead—whom Francesco calls "returnees"—come back to life within seven days from death as bloodthirsty zombies. Francesco is forced to either shoot them in the head or destroy them and then bury the bodies again so that no one notices anything wrong. He spends his time reading the phone book, deleting from it the names of the citizens of Buffalora as soon as they die, collecting obituaries and attempting to assemble, without ever succeeding, a plastic model of a skull. His life radically changes after the encounter with an unhappy widow, with whom he

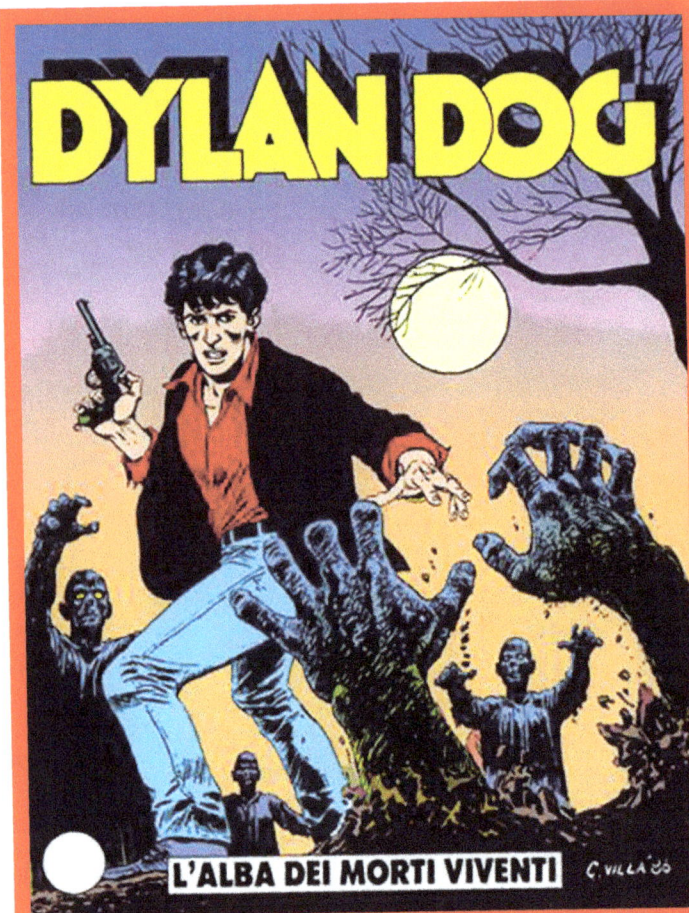

The cover for issue #1 of *Dylan Dog: Dawn of the Living Dead*, cover art by Claudio Villa

had become very popular after playing a tormented gay student in Mirek Kaniewska's *Another Country* (1984): Rupert Everett. With his angular cheekbones, raven dark hair and melancholic stare, Everett was the prototype of a romantic and accursed male beauty that perfectly fit Sclavi's character. Dylan Dog is a "detective of the paranormal"; based in his office in Craven Road, London, he investigates cases involving zombies, vampires, lycanthropes, ghosts and serial murderers. Dylan always wears a black sports jacket, red shirt, jeans and suede shoes. He is a teetotaler, a vegetarian and a non-smoker, drives an old Volkswagen Beetle whose number plate is 666, is an irresistible (if sometimes unwilling) womanizer and finally in his spare time plays the clarinet and tries to assemble a miniature galleon (which he never manages to finish). On top of that, Sclavi saddled his already offbeat hero with a comically annoying sidekick named Groucho who, believe it or not, is a dead ringer for Groucho Marx. Whenever he opens his mouth, it is either to chomp on his cigar or to hit the reader with one pun after another, even in the most inappropriate situations.

Dylan Dog was not a success. It was a thunderstorm, a mass phenomenon, an atomic bomb dropped into the

The suggestive cover for *Dylan Dog* #66, drawn by artist Angelo Stano

falls in love. However, the woman is bitten by her zombie husband and then killed by Francesco, who erroneously believes she is a "returnee." However, Francesco later falls for two more women who look exactly like her, with similarly tragic results. One day, the gravedigger meets the Grim Reaper, who suggests to him to "get on with the job" by killing living people. Francesco follows the advice and loses touch with reality even more. Eventually he decides to escape from Buffalora with Gnaghi. However, after they leave the village, Francesco comes to face a shocking truth …

In September 1986, newsstands welcomed the arrival of yet another series published by Sergio Bonelli, Italy's leading comic book publisher with such best sellers as *Tex*, *Zagor* and *Martin Mystère*. The new character had an odd-sounding name, *Dylan Dog*, and its adventures were deeply rooted in a genre that Bonelli had only marginally touched in his earlier comics: horror.

Dylan Dog was the brainchild of a very talented yet extremely elusive 33-year-old writer, Tiziano Sclavi. The name Dylan Dog (inspired by the poet Dylan Thomas) was the one Sclavi had given to all his "creatures" ever since his debut as a comics writer in the 1970s, and it was usually just a temporary one. This time the name stayed.

For the character's features, Sclavi and comic artist Angelo Stano took inspiration from a British actor who sleepy landscape of Italian popular comics. Sclavi's postmodernist approach allowed each story to be filled to the brim with reference and homages to (mostly) horror films and literature, and the mixture of splatter, humor, romanticism and philosophical antics proved to be irresistible to the audience. Within two years from its debut, the comic's popularity rocketed sky-high, with peaks of over 500,000 copies sold ... with the expected coda of psychoanalysts and sociologists commenting on the phenomenon and on the dangerous effects of such violent and bleak comics on the younger generations, as well as the proliferation of a new wave of horror comics (such as the self-explanatory *Splatter*, launched in June 1989, which became one of the media's favorite targets due to its overly graphic content). In the late 1980s, horror was definitely "in" again.

The success of *Dylan Dog* allowed Sclavi to release other pet projects. The novel *Nero* (1991, adapted into a film in 1992 by Giancarlo Soldi, featuring Hugo Pratt in a supporting role) and *Dellamorte Dellamore* followed in the wake. The latter, published in 1991 but actually written in 1983 and kept on the shelf for years, focused on a solitary gravedigger named Francesco Dellamorte (the surname reads as "Of death" in Italian, so that the novel's title becomes "Of Death and of Love") and was a one-of-a-kind zombie novel, mostly set in the cemetery of a small imaginary Northern Italian village, Buffalora, and more focused on philosophical speculation than zombie mayhem—even though there was just as much of the latter.

Before the novel was officially published, however, the character Francesco Dellamorte made a guest appearance in a special *Dylan Dog* issue, *Orrore nero* (July 1989), where he joins Dylan against a deadly menace. It was Sclavi's way of making the audience very much aware of Dellamorte's existence while at the same time underlining the analogies between his twin creations.

Indeed, Francesco Dellamorte had many things in common with Dylan Dog. Both have similar hobbies (Francesco is assembling a model of a human skull that he never manages to finish) and both have weird sidekicks that provide macabre comic relief. Dellamorte's is an obese, mute, developmentally challenged man who in the course of the novel utters only one word, "Gna." Francesco has appropriately nicknamed him Gnaghi. Ultimately both Dylan and Dellamorte share a similar relationship with death. Yet, whereas Dylan investigates nightmares, Dellamorte *lives* in them—what is more, he himself is a mystery of sorts and an unsettling one indeed. What is most frightening about the character, and the novel, is that at a certain point Dellamorte no longer sees any difference between life and death, as they ultimately become one and the same for him. It is a desperate world view that somehow synthesizes the author's pessimism; Sclavi suffered from bouts of depression over the years, and, as of today, he lives as a recluse with his family in a small Lombard town; he does not allow himself to be photographed or filmed.

Rupert Everett as Francesco Dellamorte, an undertaker who makes sure the dead stay dead ... with drastic methods, in Michele Soavi's *Cemetery Man* (1994)

In the early 1990s, with the advent of a film production leveled to the standards demanded by television—which meant that any attempt at excess would be banished—the horror genre was doomed to oblivion. The few examples that were produced in those years were anemic if not comatose—such as the overambitious ghost story *Il gioco delle ombre* (1991, Stefano Gabrini). The talented Mariano Baino had to expatriate in order to make his feature film debut, the confused yet visually striking Lovecraftian yarn *Dark Waters* (1993).

In such a desolated landscape, Michele Soavi's *Dellamorte Dellamore* (or, as it is known overseas, *Cemetery Man*) was a daring, Don Quixote-like project. Born in 1957, Soavi had made his first steps in the movie business in the late 1970s. After bit roles in such works as Lucio Fulci's *City of the Living Dead* and Ciro Ippolito's enjoyably trashy *Alien 2: On Earth* (*Alien 2—Sulla terra*, 1980) Aristide Massaccesi hired him as assistant director, bit part actor and screenwriter on no less than four films. Soavi then acted as Argento's aide on *Tenebrae* and *Phenomena* (1985), and was Lamberto Bava's assistant on *A Blade in the Dark*, where he also played a key role, and *Demons* (*Demoni*, 1985), where he turned up as the creepy masked guy who gives away movie tickets.

Soavi debuted behind the camera with a music video for Bill Wyman's *The Valley* (from the *Phenomena* soundtrack) and a documentary on Argento. Yet it was Massaccesi

A hot love-making scene occurring between Rupert Everett and Anna Falchi

again who offered him the chance to make his feature film debut. The clever, claustrophobic slasher film *Stagefright* (*Deliria*, 1987) gained him critical acclaim, and Soavi followed it with two horror films produced by Dario Argento, *The Church* (*La chiesa*, 1988) and *The Sect* (*La setta*, 1991). Both were uneven yet graced with sparks of brilliance, and they seemed to point at the filmmaker as being the next big thing in Italian horror cinema. Unfortunately, Soavi was born in the wrong place at the wrong time, as the Italian film industry was in a downward spiral.

For his fourth feature film as a director, Soavi and producer-cum-scriptwriter Gianni Romoli concocted an ambitious project. To adapt Sclavi's novel for the screen meant committing to a surreal, violent, gruesome kind of horror film, decidedly not the type of product that movie companies were dying for at the time. However, Soavi chose to underline the similarities between the two characters—not least because of understandable commercial reasons—and crafted Francesco Dellamorte as the on-screen incarnation of Dylan Dog. Therefore, there was only one actor he could and would cast for the role: Rupert Everett. The circle was over.

The director also made other radical moves, starting with the decision to adopt a comic book-like style, with camera angles, frame compositions and editing that paid direct homage to *Dylan Dog* as well as other comics. The gore would also be conspicuous, thanks to Sergio Stivaletti's special make-up effects.

Overall, *Cemetery Man* was a Gothic horror film, albeit a *sui generis* one—formally up-to-date and fit for the foreign markets, aimed at a young cinephile audience and containing thought-provoking political overtones. Soavi's surreal living dead epidemic can be easily read as an allegory of a rapidly zombified country. The film's theatrical distribution coincided with the rise to power of shady television mogul Silvio Berlusconi, who became Prime Minister just days after its release—incidentally and ironically, Berlusconi's own company had a part in producing *Cemetery Man*. Therefore, besides the expected gruesome antics à la George A. Romero—such as the many bullet-to-the-head scenes, a decapitation by shovel, and assorted zombie make-up effects—the core of the film was closer to the political flavor of early 1970s horror apologues, served within a virtuoso postmodernist package.

On the other hand, *Cemetery Man* played with one of Italian Gothic horror's recurrent obsessions, the idea of the female double as a manifestation of the uncanny, as depicted by such works as Mario Bava's *Black Sunday*, Antonio Margheriti's *The Long Hair of Death* (*I lunghi capelli della morte*, 1964), Mario Caiano's *Nightmare Castle* (*Amanti*

Anna Falchi returns from the dead

d'oltretomba, 1965) and Camillo Mastrocinque's *An Angel for Satan*. Soavi's film has Francesco Dellamorte face three different incarnations of the same ideal woman (all played by the gorgeous Anna Falchi) whom Francesco loves and eventually kills, again and again. It is a bizarre "eternal return" that hints at the incommunicability between the sexes as well as the vein of misogyny that characterizes the genre (and which is reprised here in a mocking way).

Soavi embraced Sclavi's flair for quotes and references … as well as the author's moralistic vision, even though the latter is concealed under a layer of black (and bleak) humor. He also inherited the novel's accursed romanticism and tendency for bombastic catchphrases, such as: "Each one of us does what he can so as not to think about life," "One is never different enough" or "Living dead or dying living, we are all equal."

However, Soavi ultimately failed to wholly capture *Dellamorte Dellamore*'s metaphysical anguish, which is often reduced to an abundance of self-satisfied symbols and calligraphic references to macabre icons. *Cemetery Man* is a visually striking yet somewhat cold sterile film, with its succession of references to other images which are stripped of their original context and value: Welles, Hitchcock, René Magritte's Surrealist painting *The Lovers* and Arnold Böcklin's eerie painting *Isle of the Dead* are reduced to mere pop icons and offered to the indifferent viewer in a jumble.

The film really comes alive only in its beautiful, moving ending, which has Dellamorte and Gnaghi on the edge of an abyss that marks the boundaries of their world. Here the allegory resounds loud and clear. Outside reality is ultimately an illusion, and what is left is our own internal crystal ball, where we build a universe of our own design, in the attempt to escape the awareness of our obvious mortality.

For all its qualities and shortcomings, *Cemetery Man* is an emblematic product of postmodern culture. Horror has become conventional, and as such it is allowed to poke fun at itself. We do not laugh at the gruesome excesses on screen but we laugh at their incapacity of shocking us. This somehow diminishes the impact of many impressive sequences, such as the couple of dead bikers rising from the grave, and hints at the film's main issue. Ultimately, *Cemetery Man* is infected by the very same epidemic it is depicting. Examples include Falchi's gratuitous nude scenes, which were one of the movie's selling points (Falchi was chosen over another candidate against Soavi's will, and she proved to be a less than mediocre actress), or the grating presence of TV comedian Stefano Masciarelli as the mayor. On the contrary, the French musician François Hadji Lazaro is a surprising find as the demented Gnaghi and manages to convey many of the film's most gruesome gags without betraying the spirit of Sclavi's book.

Rupert Everett is about to find out if love, with Anna Falchi, exists from beyond the grave.

As flawed as it may have been, *Cemetery Man* ultimately did not deserve to be the box-office disappointment it turned out, and over the years it has gained cult status—even in foreign countries. It is available on DVD in the U.S. on the Starz/Anchor Bay label, and a new release is long overdue. Michele Soavi's career did not benefit from it either. Due to family issues, the talented director stayed away from the cinema for a few years and later accepted assignments directing several mediocre TV films. His comeback to the big screen was the underrated political thriller *The Goodbye Kiss* (*Arrivederci amore, ciao*, 2006).

Cemetery Man and Francesco Dellamorte were later mentioned in two *Dylan Dog* issues. In *La donna che uccide il passato* (#94, July 1994) Dylan is in a cemetery, digging a grave, mumbling: "If my friend Dellamorte saw me … he'd think I'm trying to get his job!" In *Il compagno di scuola* (#205, September 2003) Dylan is tailing a man whom he eventually discovers to be a gravedigger. "So what?" he comments, "That's a job like any other … they even made a film on an Italian friend of mine!"

As for *Dylan Dog*, after an announced early 1990s TV series by Alberto Negrin (*Red Rings of Fear*) that never took off, it ultimately became a Hollywood movie in 2010. Starring—in an appalling casting choice—beefcake ex-Superman Brandon Routh, *Dylan Dog: Dead of Night* was nothing short of an abomination, betraying the original source to the point of insult. Not only did the film relocate Dylan Dog to New Orleans and (due to copyright issues) substitute Groucho with an undead assistant played by Sam Huntington, but it turned Sclavi's poetic, hopelessly bleak universe into some sort of a sub-par *Underworld* rip-off complete with an incredibly silly vampires-vs-werewolves plot and terrible attempts at tongue-in-cheek humor. The result was a deserved box-office flop, which has hopefully saved us from more of the same.

On the other hand, there are a number of fan-based films regarding *Dylan Dog*, solidifying the comic's still immense popularity among the younger generations. Denis Frison's *Dylan Dog—La morte puttana* (2012), starring the director himself, was overblown, with a running time of two hours and 10 minutes that had even the most fervent Dylan Dog devotees cringe in despair. In Summer 2014 Frison announced a sequel, again starring himself, with Dylan facing another horror icon, as the ominous title *Dylan Dog contro Freddy Krueger* suggested. The film is still in the making as of this writing. Two other projects ensued. The independent fan film *Dylan Dog—Vittima degli eventi* (Victim of the Events), directed by Claudio Di Biagio, has been financed through crowd-funding and distributed through the web. The cast features young actors such Valerio Di Benedetto (Dylan), Luca Vecchi (Groucho), alongside experienced actors as Alessandro Haber (Inspector Bloch) and Milena Vukotic. What is more, in the summer of 2014 indie "glam horror" filmmaker Domiziano Cristopharo (see *Bloody Sin*, 2013) shot *House of Shells*, an independently-made, non-profit short film focused on Sclavi's character and scripted by a trio of regular *Dylan Dog* writers: Andrea Cavaletto (who wrote a number of Cristopharo's films as well as the grim Chilean thriller *Hidden in the Woods*, 2012), Roberto Recchioni and Pasquale Ruju. Stefano Cassetti (the Devil in the NBC-produced remake of *Rosemary's Baby*) played the titular role, alongside Veronica Gentili. *House of Shells* was released directly on the web in January 2015.

1998

Laura non c'è

Italy, color, 90 minutes

D: Antonio Bonifacio. SC: Gianfranco Clerici and Daniele Stroppa; DOP: Silvano Tessicini; M: David Sabiu and Nek [Filippo Neviani]; E: Adriano Tagliavia.

Cast: Nicholas Rogers (Lorenzo), Gigliola Aragozzini (Laura), Francesco Apolloni (Luca), Laura Chiatti (Stefania), Federica Panicucci (Prof. Baldi), Nek [Filippo Nevani] (the real Lorenzo), Amadeus [Amedeo Sebastiani] (Doctor).

Prod: Edizioni Star Comics (Perugia), Gold Film (Rome).

A shootout takes place at a sort of nightclub, where several people die; the two hit men are looking for a man named Lorenzo. However, the shootout turns out to be part of a comic book that Lorenzo is drawing. Lorenzo's quiet life is plunged into turmoil by the arrival of Laura, a sweet girl with whom he falls in love immediately. Laura continually disappears and Lorenzo is never able to find her; what is more he is busy working on his comic book and has trouble with some loan sharks to whom he owes money. One day Laura shows up again. Lorenzo notices punctures in her arms and, assuming that she is a junkie, sends her away. Laura actually suffers from a severe form of diabetes, which worsens when she does not inject the insulin prescribed by her doctor. Soon Laura dies, and Lorenzo, overcome by grief and guilt, becomes obsessed with theories on reincarnation. He comes to believe that Laura has become reincarnated into his neighbor's cats. Eventually it turns out that the story of Lorenzo and Laura was part of the comic book "Laura Swan" that the real Lorenzo is drawing. Then a real Laura appears ...

Loosely inspired by the hit song of the same name by pop singer Nek (who co-wrote the score and turned up in a cameo at the film's end), *Laura non c'è* was produced by Star Comics, a small publishing house based in Perugia that acquired the rights to release Marvel comics in the late '80s, after the bankruptcy of Editoriale Corno, which had introduced Marvel superheroes to the Italian public in 1970. After the advent of Marvel Italia, which in 1994 took over the publication rights for all Marvel publications, Star acquired the rights from other U.S. comics companies, such as Image (*Spawn*, *Gen 13*) and Dark Horse, and launched several new magazines specializing in *manga*. It was a lucky bet, which coincided with the boom of Japanese comics in Italy and led to Star becoming the leading publishing company specialized in *manga* in Italy. The company's soaring position in the market allowed for an attempt at expanding into film production, which resulted in Bonifacio's film.

Formerly Aristide Massaccesi's assistant director, Bonifacio debuted with the erotic thriller *Appuntamento in nero* (1990) and went on to direct such diverse efforts as the teen comedy *Nostalgia di un piccolo grande amore* (1993), the erotic drama *Kreola* (1993, starring Demetra Hampton) and *The Strange Story of Olga O* (1995), a remake of sorts of *The Strange Vice of Mrs. Wardh*, starring Serena Grandi. The script, by Gianfranco Clerici (*Don't Torture a Duckling*; *Cannibal Holocaust*; *The New York Ripper* ...) and Daniele Stroppa (Lamberto Bava's *Delirium*; *Killing Birds*; *The House of Clocks* ...) develops a comics-related plot which goes to ridiculous lengths in its mixing of reality and fiction. It starts in a similar manner as the typical movie-within-a-movie situation (the *film noir*-like opening is revealed to be part of a comic in progress) and eventually concludes with exactly the same plot twist, as the whole story is revealed to be a comic book, *Laura Swan—investigatrice dell'occulto* (Laura Swan, Occult Investigator), which the *real* Lorenzo (played by Nek) was drawing ...

It is a Chinese box-like concept that would have made writer/director Charlie Kaufman proud, but here results in nothing more than a badly concocted syrupy melodrama aimed at teenagers, with laughable dialogue and low-level acting. Bonifacio's overuse of slow motion is utterly incomprehensible, and the many would-be stylish cross-dissolves and overlays are plain embarrassing. Similarly, the references to comics amount to a number of gratuitous unlikely low-angle shots, plus a number of blatant plugs to Star Comics' series *Lazarus Ledd* (a cardboard cutout of the eponymous hero is featured prominently in Lorenzo's room). The comic panels were drawn by Alessandro Bocci and are absolutely the best thing about the film.

The actors do not help. Nicholas Rogers, seen in Lamberto Bava's TV movie *The Cave of the Golden Rose 3* (*Fantaghirò 3*, 1993) is as wooden as a log. The cast also includes a number of cameos on the part of popular faces in showbiz, including the radio and TV show host Amadeus as Laura's doctor—all hopelessly amateurish. Overall, *Laura non c'è* very much recalls the kind of innocuous Neapolitan comedy-dramas made in the early 1980s, starring singer Nino D'Angelo and named after his songs, which were rather successful in the Southern Italian distribution circuit. Only, it is much worse.

Laura non c'è was a box-office flop. Its quick disappearance into oblivion proved once again, if any proof were needed, that the kind of popular cinema it represented had no place anymore in a market dominated by saturation selling and theater chain monopolies on the part of the big distribution companies. Star co-produced two more comics-unrelated titles: the comedy *Vacanze sulla neve* (1999, Mariano Laurenti) and the mystery *La donna del delitto* (2000, Corrado Colombo).

2002

Paz!

Italy, color, 102 minutes

D: Renato De Maria. *S:* Ivan Cotroneo and Renato De Maria, based on the works of Andrea Pazienza; *SC:* Ivan Cotroneo, Renato De Maria and Francesco Piccolo; *DOP:* Gian Filippo Corticelli; *M:* Riccardo Sinigallia and Francesco Zampaglione; *E:* Jacopo Quadri.

Cast: Claudio Santamaria (Pentothal), Flavio Pistilli (Massimo Zanardi), Matteo Taranto (Roberto Colasanti), Max Mazzotta (Enrico Fiabeschi), Rosalinda Celentano (Gianna), Fabrizia Sacchi (Lucilla), Iaia Forte (Headmaster), Roberto Citran, Vittoria Puccini, Antonio Rezza,

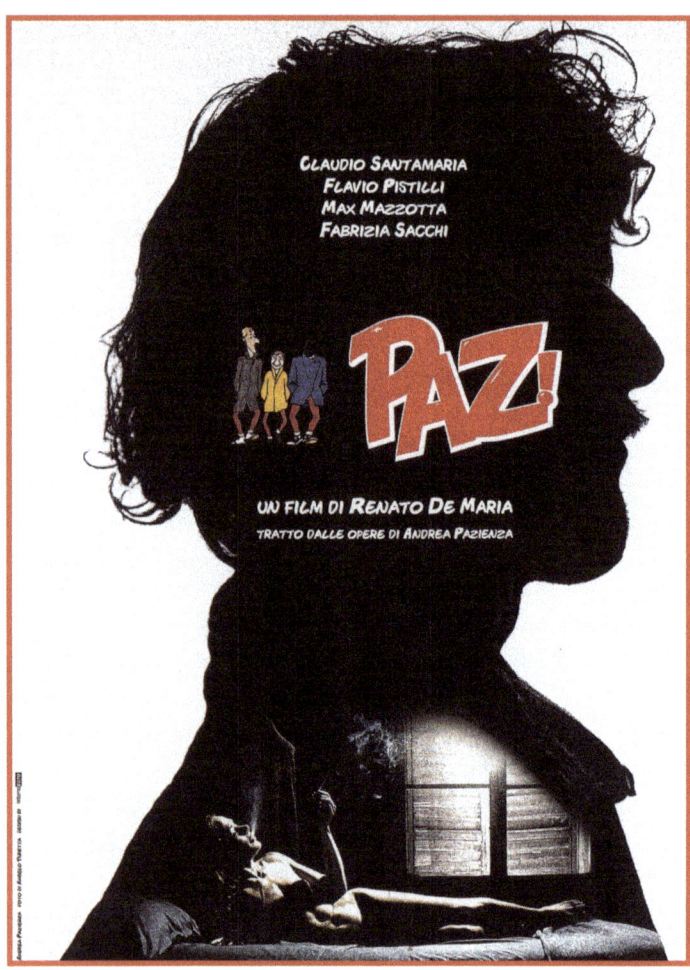

The Italian *locandina* for Renato De Maria's *Paz!* (2002), inspired by the works of Italy's most important comic artist of the 1980s, the late Andrea Pazienza

Ricky Memphis, Giorgio Tirabassi, Freak [Roberto] Antoni, Giovanni Lindo Ferretti.

Prod: Tangram Film Rai Cinema, Stream, ITC Movie.

In Bologna, 1977, high school student Zanardi and his schoolmates Colasanti and Petrilli spend their days doing drugs, bullying other students and looking for casual sex. An art student and comic artist nicknamed Pentothal feels lazy and depressed after being dumped by his girlfriend and does not take part in the students' protests against the government. Another student, Fiabeschi, is always looking for dope, fails an exam and keeps borrowing money from his girlfriend …

When he died of a heroin overdose in 1988, Andrea Pazienza was just 32. Yet he had been one of Italy's leading comic book artists for over a decade. Barely in his 20s, Pazienza became one of the keys personalities in the most important Italian comic magazines, such as *Alter Alter, Linus, Cannibale, Il Male* and *Frigidaire*. An incredibly prolific artist, he also designed film posters (for Fellini's *City of Women*, 1980) and record covers, leaving behind him a huge, multi-faceted body of work.

As comic book scholar Simone Castaldi put it, Pazienza was:

An artist gifted with a sharp sense of humor but also able to center his poetics on the little horrors of daily life [with a] knack for combining comedy with tragedy, Dadaist suggestions and journalistic approach […].[1]

Pazienza's works were deeply rooted in the social and political turmoil of late 1970s Italy, such as the riots of Bologna in 1977, which he portrayed in his first book-length work *Le straordinarie avventure di Pentothal* (1982). As Castaldi noted, *Pentothal* showed Pazienza's innovative approach to comics in many ways. First, because of the use of an autobiographical narrative, the titular character, Pentothal, is a student at Bologna's DAMS University (Drama, Art and Music Studies), the same school Pazienza attended, and he is a comic artist as well, which was a novelty in Italian comics. Second, the comic's contemporary historical background and its journalistic approach, which documented the rise and fall of the Bologna student movement (the violent clashes with the police, the student assemblies, the liberal use of drugs, the killing of a student activist by the police—whose death Pazienza included at the very last minute in the comic's closing panel) comes to the forefront. What is more, the artist adopted a stream-of-consciousness technique to make up for the lack of an actual plot with a non-linear narrative. Some wrote that Pazienza used the pencil the way Hendrix used the guitar. They were not wrong, after all.

Renato De Maria's film (his second after 1996's *Hotel Paura*) can be read as both an homage to Pazienza's work as well as a re-reading of his universe in cinematic terms. *Paz!* was a peculiar one-of-a-kind effort in the realm of Italian cinema of the early 2000s. A film that was not preoccupied with pleasing the audience or with blending comedy and drama in a grotesque manner. It was an attempt to make Pazienza's figure more popular among the younger generations as well as a way to look back and see what went wrong.

For the director who was Pazienza's friend and witnessed the same events as depicted in the artist's works, it was a heartfelt project, with a long and troubled genesis. Yet De Maria did not want to mount a traditional biopic and said:

> It seemed impossible to have an actor play Andrea. Whereas through his comics I had the chance to portray my own generation, thus giving the film a more universal point of view, that of youth in its most curious and experimental moments.[2]

Max Mazzotta as the perpetually stoned Fiabeschi in *Paz!*

For the film, De Maria gathered together many important personalities of the Italian underground culture, such as the late Roberto "Freak" Antoni (the leader of Bologna's pioneering tongue-in-cheek "demented" rock band Skiantos) and Giovanni Lindo Ferretti (the vocalist of Italy's most important punk band, CCCP Fedeli alla linea), as well as popular actors and musicians who played minor supporting roles. The result is surprisingly effective, since De Maria consciously avoids any nostalgic effect. For instance, the score puts together songs from the late 1970s and more recent ones, giving the story a timeless feel. As De Maria noted:

> I always thought of *Paz!* as a film indifferently projected to the future and the past ...

The setting is Bologna in 1977, during the days of the student revolts, which Pazienza recounted in *Le straordinarie avventure di Pentothal*. The main characters are taken from several of the artist's most important works and made to occupy the same narrative, even though they actually never interact during the 24-hour time span of the film. Pentothal comes from the 1982 book, while the parts with the wicked Zanardi and his two companions are taken almost verbatim from the grim 1983 stories *La proprietà transitiva dell'uguaglianza* (Zanardi and friends watch a soccer game on TV and then do drugs) and *Giallo scolastico* (the main plot about Zanardi and friends torturing the headmaster's cat and Zanardi losing his agenda in the process, which leads to an elaborate plan to get it back), whereas Fiabeschi was featured in the short story *Giorno* (Day), which appeared on *Frigidaire* in 1981 and which is also reprised to the letter, furnishing the film's tight time structure.

De Maria is surprisingly faithful to the original stories, and he manages to retain Pazienza's stark, vitriolic worldview. Therefore, *Paz!* is surprisingly frank and unpleasant, with an unexpected quota of full frontal male and female nudity and abundant references to drug use (although De Maria never actually shows the characters injecting heroin, but films the aftermath ... only their dilated pupils in extreme close-up); the use of hand-held camera shots and digital tape instead of film gives it an unpolished, rough look which fits well with Pazienza's panels.

What is more, De Maria is never, ever condescending toward the characters. For instance, the perpetually stoned Fiabeschi has a cinema exam, the results of which will determine his eligibility to avoid being drafted. The subject he is presenting is *Apocalypse Now* (in one of many deliberate anachronisms). All he knows about the film (which he invariably misspells as *Apocalypsy Now*) is that it was directed by Francis Ford Coppola and has music by The Doors, "and I don't even give a shit about it." When the all-too patient examiner finally rejects him, Fiabeschi bursts into a nonsense political tirade, accusing her of being a Fascist and attacking her with gratuitous insults, in a pathetic attempt at justifying his own failure.

As played by the beak-nosed, thin-mustached, lanky and curly-haired Max Mazzotta, who brings the role a much more clownish appearance compared with the comic, Fiabeschi becomes the film's central character and its more audience-friendly one.[3] Fiabeschi often nods to the camera, as if looking for the viewer's complicity in the least likely moments, such as while taking a leak at night or rolling a reefer. He keeps asking his girlfriend for money which he spends on drugs and is gleefully oblivious about the rest of the world—a world which is seemingly founded on anarchy, indifference, violence and prevarication. A world which Pentothal just cannot stand any longer—so much so that he is often seen sleeping, soon dreaming to be visited by the characters he creates in his strips (characters played by stage actor Antonio Rezza and rapper Frankie Hi-nrg MC); this is the ideal environment for someone like Zanardi.

Paz! is particularly successful in its portrayal of the evil Zanardi, with his "beaked nose and wolf eyes," as Pazienza defined it. A wicked and amoral student who performs cruel and Machiavellian practical jokes on the school professors (such as crucifying the headmaster's cat) with the help of two friends: the rich, handsome and sex-addicted Colasanti and the ugly and poor Petrilli. Zanardi was a key character to understand the generation that faced the 1980s—a young man with no ideals in a time of revolution (which he considered useless) and someone that most of all is terribly bored, to the point that he hurt people to just overcome his boredom. As Pazienza himself described him:

> Zanardi's principal characteristic is his inner void. The utter void that permeates his every action.

Notes:
1. Castaldi, *Drawn and Dangerous*, p. 78.
2. Sorrentini, Barbara, "Paz! Intervista al regista Renato De Maria," www.cinemaindipendente.it.
3. Mazzotta reprised the character of Fiabeschi for his directorial debut, the little-seen *Fiabeschi torna a casa* (2012). Here, the now 40-year-old Fiabeschi is totally disconnected to Pazienza's world, and he turns into a sort of Italian version of the Coen brothers' Jeffrey Lebowski.

2007

Le avventure di Diabetik

Italy, color, TV series (4 episodes, 18 minutes each)
D: Andrés Arce Maldonado and Federico Del Zoppo. *S and SC:* Adriano Ercolani and Stefano Poli; *DOP:* Federico Del Zoppo; *M:* Mal [Paul Bradley Couling] and Andrés Arce Maldonado; *E:* Iacopo Gianni and Silvia Giulietti.
Cast: Eva Henger (Eva Kunt), Enzo Salvi (Diabetik), Mariano D'Angelo, Diego Conte, Alessia Fabiani, Valerio Merola, Carolina Marconi.
Prod: Cine Storm Entertainment.

The voluptuous Eva Henger in *Le avventure di Diabetik*

Diabetik is a lazy, unlucky thief obsessed with food and women. He specializes in ambitious heists that always go wrong. His sidekick is the ravishing, intelligent and jealous Eva Kunt. Disappointed by Diabetik's continuous failings, she reproaches him all the time. Inspector Rinko is attempting to hunt down Diabetik and Eva …

The character Diabetik appeared for the first time in 1968, in the satirical magazine *Tilt*. The magazine was the offspring of Alfredo Castelli, who attempted to create an answer to U.S. magazines such as *Mad*, with an offbeat, surreal approach to humor. Curiously, Castelli had made his debut with a *Diabolik* spoof, *Scheletrino*, published as an appendix to a *Diabolik* issue, *La miniera di diamanti*, in January 1965. Together with former *Diabolik* writer Mario Gomboli, Castelli conceived a parody of Italy's most famous thief. Billed as "Il più diaboliko, il più demoniako, il più sataniko, il più kriminale mai apparso in un fumetto nero," ("The most diabolikal, demoniak, satanik, kriminal ever to appear in a *fumetto nero*"—note the tongue-in-cheek references to the season's most popular characters), Diabetik and his lover Eva Kunt (!) were introduced in a 24-page-long story titled *Dentiera di sangue* (Blood denture), drawn by Carlo Peroni.

Unfortunately it was to be the character's one and only appearance. *Tilt* lasted only one issue and soon became a much sought-after cult item, paving the way for similar experiments during the following decade. On the other hand Castelli would become one of Italy's leading comic book writers—in 1969 he created the revolutionary magazine *Horror*, while in 1982 he launched *Martin Mystère*. Among his body of work there is also a co-scriptwriting credit for Luigi Cozzi's feature film debut *Il tunnel sotto il mondo* (1969) … even though Castelli would rather pretend it never happened.

In 2007 Diabetik was revived for a TV series, *Le avventure di Diabetik*, starring comedian Enzo Salvi, who was and still is unfathomably popular among Italian audiences due to his TV appearances as a dumb working-class guy nicknamed "Er Cipolla," and for his supporting roles in many of the so-called *Cinepanettoni*—the vulgar, painfully unfunny comedies set in various exotic settings, so called because they are usually released on Christmas (hence the tell-tale reference to the traditional Italian Christmas *panettone* pie).

Why anyone would choose to do a *Diabolik* spoof as a TV series in 2007 is beyond this writer's guess. True, the Giussani character is still very popular today, but the authors were probably relying a bit too much on Salvi's debatable comic qualities. The four episodes—*Furto al museo* (Theft at the Museum), *La macchina invisibile* (The Invisible Car), *Tempesta di*

Diabetik, a *Diabolik* spoof created in 1968 by Alfredo Castelli, made its appearance in the satirical magazine *Tilt*.

sangue (Storm of Blood) and *Il calice della giovinezza* (The Cup of Eternal Youth) are so sloppily put together that they make Turkish superheroes films look like Spielberg in comparison. A case in point are Diabetik's recurrent visions—that is, four dancing ladies who pop up randomly for no apparent reason—caused by his frequent glycemic crises.

The direction strives for comic book-style camera angles and shots, with dreary results, while the writers keep returning to a lazily conceived recurring pattern. Diabetik—wearing his customary black outfit—is sitting on his sofa, bored (as the viewer soon will be), until his fiancée Eva (Eva Henger) turns on the TV. They watch the news and learn that something valuable is being exhibited or guarded in the town of Rezzanello (*Le avventure di Diabetik*'s answer to *Diabolik*'s Clerville): the World Cup, the Cup of Eternal Youth, a videogame and the Invisible Car. Obviously it is time for Diabetik and Eva to plan a new heist, which Inspector Rinko will stop just in time …

Despite the scant running time (18 minutes each), every episode seems to go on forever. It does not help that the plots feature useless characters such as a Sylvester Stallone-lookalike (who, in a bout of comic, er, genius on the part of the scriptwriters, keeps screaming "Adrianaaaaa!!" like Sly did in *Rocky*, 1976) and a dumb concierge (Carolina Marconi) who shares abysmal dialogue scenes with Eva. The Hungarian-born, ex-porn star-turned-TV-personality Eva Henger proved once again that she is one of the most beautiful women in Italian show business … and that she cannot act to save her life. Actually, her porn flicks featured better direction, acting and dialogue than *Le avventure di Diabetik*—and were definitely a lot more entertaining.

The icing on the cake is the title song, sung by former Primitives singer Mal, which mentions a "clinical mystery"—probably referring to why this abomination found its way to television and home video. Directors Andrés Arce Maldonado (who also co-wrote the score) and Federico Del Zoppo (who also acted as director of photography) did not learn their lesson, as they later helmed the bad-beyond-belief *Bastardi* (2008), which paired Franco Nero, Don Johnson, Giancarlo Giannini and, again, Eva Henger.

The Diabolikal Super-Kriminal
Italy, b&w/color, 73 minutes
D: SS-Sunda [Sandro Yassel Spazio].
Prod: Sinepathic Films.
A documentary on the 1960s photonovel Killing *and its makers.*

March 1966 saw the debut of one of the most controversial and notorious characters of the whole *fumetti neri* wave: *Killing*. Unlike other icons of the period such as *Diabolik*, *Kriminal* and *Mister X*, though, *Killing*—published by Edizioni Ponzoni and captioned "fotostorie del brivido" (Thrilling photo stories)—was not a comic book but a photonovel, featuring real actors.

Photonovels offered comic book-like versions of famous films and custom-made stories, often with the participation of popular actors, which were distributed to newsstands in Italy and France as well. In the early 1960s, though, beside the traditional syrupy Lancio photonovels, newsstands were filled with male-oriented, adults-only stuff such as the series *Malìa—I fotoromanzi del brivido*. Starting from February 1961, *Malìa* offered Gothic stories with such evocative titles as *L'urlo del vampiro* (The Vampire's Scream), *Il castello maledetto* (The Damned Castle), *Il risveglio di Dracula* (Dracula's Awakening), *Il regno del terrore* (The Reign of Terror) and *Il vampiro etrusco* (The Etruscan Vampire). As conceived by the magazine's editor-in-chief Umberto Paolessi with journalist and writer Giorgio Boschero, these *fotoromanzi* were photographed in the very same locations used for the Gothic horror films made during the decade. Photonovel versions of movies were also featured regularly in *Malìa*—such as *The Vampire and the Ballerina* (*L'amante del vampiro*, 1960, Renato Polselli), *The Playgirls and the Vampire* (*L'ultima preda del vampiro*, 1960, Piero Regnoli) and *Bloody Pit of Horror*.

The making of such sleazy photonovels was satirized in Gualtiero Jacopetti and Franco Prosperi's *Mondo cane 2* (1963) in a sequence:

> Depicting the making of a few sadistic-erotic *fumetti*, with several scantily dressed captive young women. This is supposed to be filmed from reality, but it's all fiction. The tortures are those of the Inquisition, anticipating certain torments shown in *Bloody Pit of Horror*. Among the damsels-in-distress we find the exotic Moa Tahi, also featured in Massimo Pupillo's cult movie.[1]

The following year, a similar idea was played for laughs. A sequence of *Totò contro i quattro* (1963, Steno) had Totò (playing a clumsy Commissioner) and Erminio Macario (as a private eye who eventually turns out to be an escaped lunatic) sneaking into a gloomy villa where a perverted nobleman is believed to be slaughtering young women. However, as the two bungling investigators will soon find out, the supposed Bluebeard is actually part of a Grand-Guignol-type photonovel that is being shot inside the villa. An enlightening dialogue exchange has the director yell:

"You are crazy! You ruined the best sequence in my photonovel!"

To which Totò replies:

"Photonovel … photonovel … so here you are making *fumetti*!"

"*Fumetti* or photonovel, what's the difference anyway?"

Killing was not the first photonovel of the period conceived as a counterpart to drawn comic books. In December 1965 the Florence-based publisher Sadea had launched the short-lived *Max*, a self-defined *fotoromanzo giallo*, which lasted only two issues. While in February 1966 it was the turn of publisher Furio Viano, with the similarly-themed *Genius* (82 issues till January 1970), which turned from *fotoromanzo* to out-and-out *fumetto*—and counted among its artists a young Milo Manara, who would later acquire fame as one of Italy's top comics artists. A masked man in a black suit and wearing a noose around his neck as if it were a tie, *Genius* was the umpteenth incarnation of the avenger who placed himself above the law and the stories involved mild erotic content. *Killing*, on the other hand, was something far more disturbing.

Apparently, *Killing* was basically more of the same … a sadistic genius of evil ("The King of Crime" as it was labeled in advertisements), a serial murderer whose deeds were graphically shown in detail, much to the audience's delight and to the chagrin of his sworn enemy Inspector Mercier. Like his contemporaries, Killing was also a master in disguise, and was able to assume other people's features by crafting masks through a flesh-like substance. Even its costume—a black leotard with white skeleton bones and a skull mask—evoked *déjà-vu*, patently recalling *Kriminal* as well as *Fantax*. However, *Killing* pushed the boundaries further than any of the other comics and photonovels of the period. It was erotic and violent to the point of unbridled sadism and made the most of its live-action concept. The result was something yet unseen, "a mythical character in a real-life squalid context," as comic writer Massimo Severano later put it. The skull mask itself looked only vaguely human, with oblong eyes and an unnerving evil grin that made Killing seem like an alien presence.

For *Killing*, Edizioni Ponzoni—a publishing house based in Milan that specialized in photonovels since 1950—put together a small task force that included writ-

S.S. Sunda's documentary on Italy's most controversial *fumetti neri*

ers Rocco Molinari, Attilio Mazzanti and Luigi Naviglio, special effects master Carlo Rambaldi and director Rosario Borrelli. Working with a more substantial budget than the standard *fotoromanzi*—each issue cost about three million *lire*, according to actor Vito Fornari—allowed them to achieve impressive results. For one thing, Rambaldi conceived Killing's costume and mask, as he was already an established name in Cinecittà, and despite the obvious nods to *Kriminal*, they were definitely upsetting and eye-catching. The mask, in particular, portrayed a deformed, grinning skull (which underwent four different incarnations throughout the series). The other striking element was a black belt with a "K" engraved in the buckle.

Borrelli (1927-2001), credited as Rosario Borelli, was a staple of photonovels, having appeared in the Ponzoni-published *Antar* (1964) as a Tarzan knock-off. He also had a career in the movies, mostly as a character actor in B-pictures (with such exceptions as Luchino Visconti's masterpiece *Rocco and His Brothers*), and even gained a marginal celebrity status as a singer, with the collaboration of the then still unknown Ennio Morricone. Borrelli's directorial efforts for *Killing* were among the reasons for the mag's success. The photo shoots were conceived and staged as film shootings, with multiple camera angles and a dynamic quality of the action that resulted in exciting frame compositions.

Borrelli also appeared in the series as an actor, together with an array of regulars that included Rico Boido (aka Rick Boyd), Erno Crisa, Renato Baldini, Gérard Landry, Alberto Farnese, George Hilton, Franco Jamonte, John Benedy (Giovanni Di Benedittis) and Paul Muller. Many of these were film actors, who agreed to work in photonovels (which were considered something of a subpar product, a poor surrogate of the real thing—that is, movies) in periods between shootings. The identity of the actor behind Killing's mask, however, was unknown—not only to the readers but to the crew as well, as Borrelli and Ponzoni demanded it be kept a secret with strict contract rules.

Explicit violence was an astonishingly eye-catching element. Borrelli and his acolytes pushed the pedal of Grand Guignol, having Killing employ such unusual weapons as butcher's hooks, harpoons, spears and pickaxes, whose aftermath was shown in all its gory glory. The graphic content—preferably directed against women—would prove an undeniable influence on Italy's very first splatter films such as Fernando di Leo's *Slaughter Hotel* (*La bestia uccide a sangue freddo*, 1971) and Mario Bava's *A Bay of Blood*, more so than the new wave of late 1960s U.S. horror movies.

Then, of course, there was sex. Ravishing beauties by the names of Luciana Paoli (as Killing's girlfriend Dana), Erna Schurer, Gabriella Giorgelli, Liliana Chiari, Annie Alberti (previously seen in the obscure Italian Gothic film *Tomb of Torture* and later the star of another adults-only photonovel, the French *Baby Colt*, directed by her husband Gérard Landry) and Magda Konopka enticed readers by appearing in provocative poses in their lingerie, or with their nudity scantily covered by judicious camera angles and carefully placed set props. Killing would not simply have sex with them. He used them, played with them, humiliated and tortured them. Then, he simply threw them away, like broken playthings.

As one critic stated:

> Whereas the most sophisticated characters—Kriminal, Diabolik, Satanik—underwent a deep psychological evolution and took upon themselves the evils of the century, of which they were both perpetrators and victims, the most embittered and fanatical remained, until they lasted, on Hitler-like positions. Crime, sadism, necrophilia, sexism, racism—all the ingredients of true crime and pulp fiction—converged in *Killing* [...]. Therefore, the season of *fumetti neri* and photonovels restored, in a country devoid of the Théatre du Grand Guignol, the right to popular, populist, sometimes even imaginative dirty tricks. If criminal comic books represented our own hard-boiled school and the Catholic version of the modern-day Gothic, adults-only photonovels killed the conviction that pictures and balloons could only be used to tell tear-jerking stories.[2]

Killing proved to be an astonishing success, and Ponzoni was quick in publishing it in France as well, where it reached a mind numbing printing of 700,000 copies. However, due to legal rights issues, the character's name was changed into *Satanik*. It also surfaced in Holland, Turkey, Colombia, Brazil and Argentina (as *Kiling*). Meanwhile similar photonovels turned up which capitalized on sex and violence. Most, like *P. 38*, *Racket* and *Ombra*, were lurid, crude hard-boiled tales, while others, like *Supersex*[3] and *Mantis*, had sci-fi undertones.

However, the magazine's emphasis on sex, sadism and violence did not pass unnoticed to the authorities. Soon *Killing* became one of the main targets for enraged newspaper articles about the debauched *fumetti neri*, which turned into a real witch hunt of sorts and caused the issues to be repeatedly seized by the authorities.

An article on the September 16, 1966 issue of *La Stampa*, one of Italy's most widespread newspapers, announced a trial against the "tales of sadism." The "Five Ks" (*Demoniak, Kriminal, Sadik, Satanik* and *Killing*) were accused of:

> Divulging works apt to perturb the common sense of decency and exalting crime. [Another *fumetto*, *Masokis*, whose female protagonist asked her friends and enemies to whip her bloodily, had recently been seized.] All these characters have in common not only the same alphabet letter but also the most complete exaltation of crime, violence, and the most un-nameable things about sex. Every value is completely overturned. The hero is an abject assassin who always manages to beat the law, and his female partner is the sample of everything a woman should not be. Never does their story become compelling; often it is just a jumble of absurdities that serve as a feeble screen to the images. [...] The frenzy comes at a climax in *Killing*, which has the aggravating factor of being a photonovel.[4]

Things did not fare better in France, where the magazine ceased publication, in June 1967, after just 19 issues. It was briefly replaced by a similarly conceived photonovel *Fatalik*, which even copied the cover design but nonetheless lasted only four issues.[5] In Italy, Ponzoni had to drastically tone down the violent content in order to save the day, but the move proved to be a commercial suicide, as the sales drastically diminished. Eventually *Killing* closed down in March 1969, after publishing issue #62. According to the authors, a planned film adaptation was dropped because of its overtly violent content. In Turkey, on the other hand, Kilink became the star of a number of films, starting with Yılmaz Atadeniz' *Kilink İstanbulda* (1967). (See **Appendix**)

Molinari attempted to launch other photonovels in the same vein. *Don Archer* was a James Bond lookalike starring Alberto Farnese and a group of scantily-dressed girls; however, it was a flop, partly because of its none-too-apt name ("Don," in Italian, stands for "priest").[6] On the other hand, *Wampir* (1971, not to be confused with a magazine of the same title which contained photonovel versions of horror films such as *Crypt of the Vampire* and *Frankenstein Meets the Wolf Man*) was a more explicitly horrific/erotic affair.

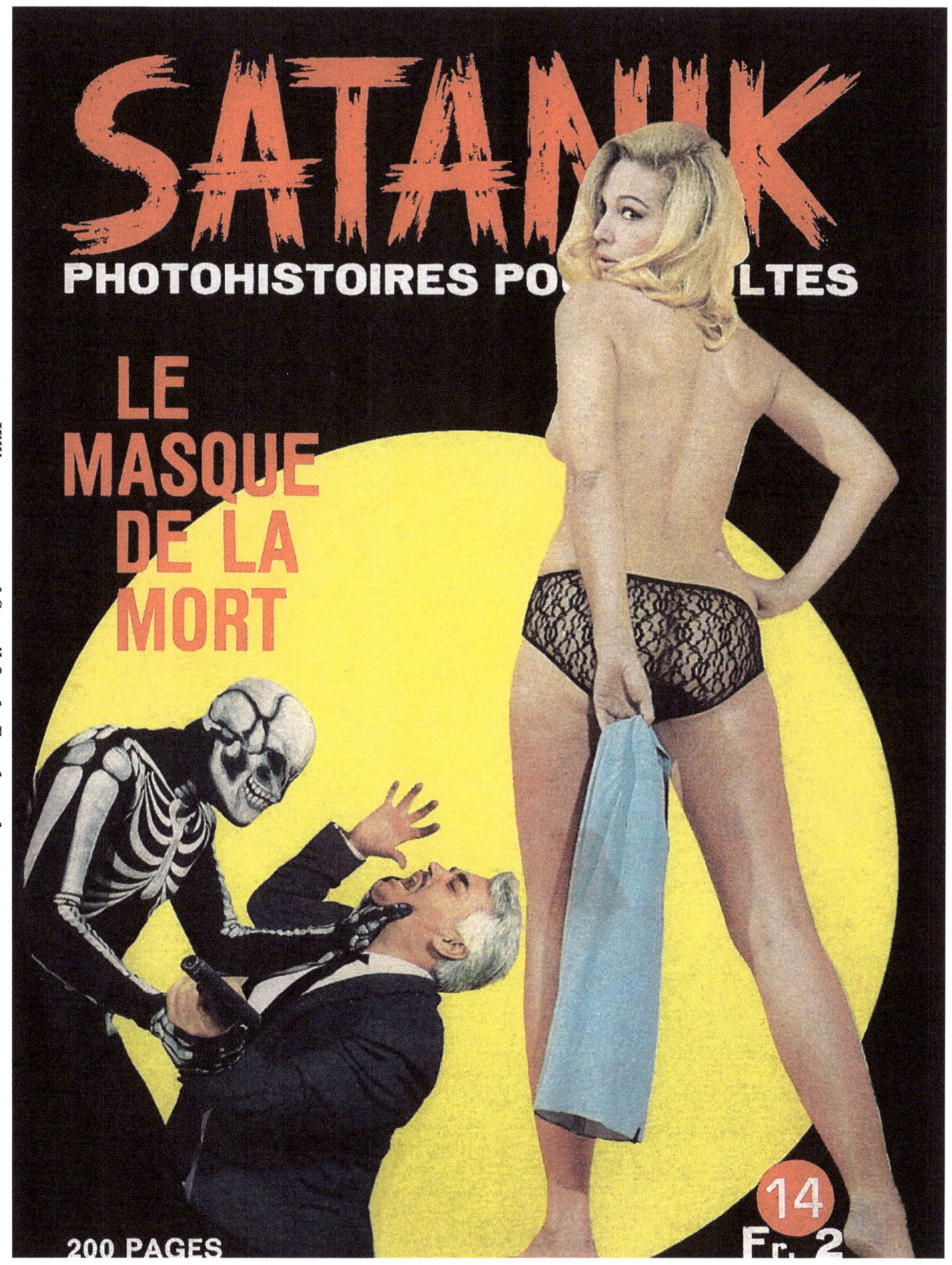

Killing was renamed Satanik for the French market.

Times were changing, the censorship was loosening and soon hardcore porn would find its way into Italian newsstands. Films were already being shot with more explicit inserts for the foreign market. Think of Filippo Ratti's Gothic horror film *The Night of the Damned*, which was obviously influenced by the atmosphere of photonovels of the period.

Just when nobody apparently remembered it any longer, *Killing* resurfaced across the ocean. It was released for the first time in English in the United States, this time dubbed as *Sadistik: The Diabolikal Super-Kriminal*, thanks to the efforts of publisher and comics creator Mort Todd, head of Comicfix, who acquired the rights in 2005. Todd also planned to develop an animated web series, *Sadistik Strip & Kill*, featuring Iggy Pop as the voice of Sadistik, but unfortunately, the project never took off.

Then, in 2007, Bologna-based comic artist and independent filmmaker SS-Sunda (real name Sandro Yassel Spazio, born in Araya, Venezuela in 1973) directed a documentary on the character, *The Diabolikal Super-Kriminal*, in which he interviewed members of the Ponzoni staff who worked on *Killing*, actors and actresses who took part in the photo shoots (Erna Schurer, Gabriella Giorgelli, Rico Boido, Paul Muller), Rosario Borrelli's son Giancarlo and fellow filmmakers such as Corrado Farina and Romano Scavolini.

Sunda's admiration for his subject matter is obvious. As he explained:

> Rosario Borrelli is no doubt the greatest photonovel director I've ever known. While it's true that, without such publications as *Diabolik* and *Kriminal*, *Killing* would never have existed, it is also true that without Borrelli we wouldn't have such photonovels as *Fatalik*, *Terrifik*, *Yorga*, *Namur*, etc. [...] Being myself a lover both of cinema and comics I've decided to use the best photonovel I've ever known in order to talk about a kind of cinema and a kind of comic that exists no more.[7]

As Sunda further elaborated:

> Another inspiring reason is about the '60s, the Beat Generation and the Flower Power movement. They fascinated me when I was a teenager and I still value them. I believe the (little) freedom we can enjoy now is due (a lot) to them. Cultural forefathers of mine have snubbed *Killing*. In fact, even if its form of expression was revolutionary, it still could only appeal to a public made of bourgeois, repressed by their own sick idea of women and eroticism. So, as much of a convicted hippy-freak that I am, I've decided to contribute to its reappraisal. 40 years later I consider it appropriate to fascinate a new kind of public, more sharpened. In short, I think *Killing* was too far ahead of its time; by this I don't mean the bourgeois thought has won, but only that the King of Crime is in the meantime psychotronic and hard-boiled, words not yet minted in 1966.[8]

Mixing stock footage, excerpts from newsreels, old 8mm films (from Corrado Farina's archives), interviews and newly-shot scenes (by Sunda himself) which recreate Killing's antics in a suitably old-fashioned, tongue-in-cheek manner, *The Diabolikal Super-Kriminal* is breezy and fast-moving all the way—so much so one wishes Sunda would have delved even deeper into the material and let us know more about that wonderfully weird world. The interviewees are often funny, candid, naive, enlightening and sometimes moving. Watching the now elderly John Benedy teach Sunda how to do a stunt in a photonovel, and thus savoring one more time the thrill of actually being in a movie, is a heart-warming moment, while Gabriella Giorgelli's recognition that those crappy photonovels were actually very well-made is surprisingly sincere, as is her passing comment about her "wasted talent," which sheds light on the sad decadence of so many have-beens of Italian genre cinema. The still-gorgeous Erna Schurer is perhaps the sweetest and most disenchanted of the lot, while Rico Boido still has an enthusiastic sparkle in his eyes when he recalls *Killing*'s adventurous antics. Accordingly, the director could not interview several of the original participants, such as George Hilton, who demanded money to speak about his early days working in the photonovels. Nevertheless, for the first time in over 40 years, Sunda managed to reveal the true identity of the man behind the mask ... Killing was played by Aldo Agliata, a little-known TV and photonovel actor who later became a sports journalist and talk-show host.

The ending itself, which comes with an in-joke teaser of a second film on the subject (*The Diabolikal Super-Kriminal Around the World*), feels almost like an abrupt wake-up call that makes one wish for more. That is exactly what readers at that time were experiencing, by ogling at those forbidden and evocative images of stylized violence and suggestive eroticism.

Notes:
1. Piselli, *Cinefumetto*, p. 15.
2. Lippi, Giuseppe, "Maschere e pugnali. Recital in tre parti," *Nocturno* #133, October 2013, p. 57.
3. Published by Rosario (Saro) Balsamo, who would later launch Italy's most famous pornographic magazine *Le Ore*, *Supersex* centered on the adventures of an intergalactic pilot whose starship crashes on our planet. In order to survive, Supersex has to move from one human body to the next (à la *The Hidden*). Also, in order to discharge his exceeding vital energy, he has to have sexual intercourse … *Supersex* lasted only six issues in 1967, but nine years later the photonovel would reappear in a hardcore version starring French porn star Gabriel Pontello.
4. e.don., "Il veleno dai fumetti," *La Stampa*, 09/16/1966.
5. Despite being published in France, *Fatalik* was another Italian product. It featured recurring photonovel faces such as the balding Romano Moraschini and a brief appearance by the Cuban-born Yuma Gonzalez.
6. In Argentina, *Don Archer* was mischievously re-titled *Satanik*. It was not the first time that such a thing happened. *Genius* came out in the South American country as *Goldrake*, that is the same name as the spy-erotic *fumetto* published by Renzo Barbieri.
7. Todd, Mort, "SS-Sunda Unmasked!," www-gosadistik.com, 06/11/2008. As for the other fotoromanzi Sunda mentions, *Terrifik*—which featured a masked rapist biker—came out in 1970 and lasted only one issue. It must not be confused with the 1992 comic mag of the same name published by Cenisio Editore. On the other hand, *Yorga* (a lizard man) and *Namur* (a masked, leather-clad female spy, portrayed by Gloria Gago) were made in Argentina and prove the strong influence that Italian photonovels had on the South American market.
8. Ibid.

2008

Capitan Basilico
Italy, color, 133 minutes

D: Massimo Morini. *S:* Massimo Morini; *SC:* Massimo Morini and Andrea Di Marco; *DOP:* Enzo Pirrone; *M:* Buio Pesto; *E:* Michele Badinelli.

Cast: Buio Pesto (Themselves), Massimo Bosso (Capitan Basilico), Andrea Di Marco (Informer), Walter "Ego" Filice, Giorgia Würth (Regina), Federica Ruggero (Lara Krapfen), Enrico Ruggeri, Giorgio Faletti, Ale & Franz [Alessandro Besentini, Francesco Villa], Elio e le Storie Tese, Piotta [Tommaso Zanella], Fausto Brizzi.

Prod: Associazione Buio Pesto (Genoa).

Capitan Basilico, the first Ligurian superhero, is dedicated to helping those in difficulty. However, he has to struggle with Regina, his beautiful but vengeful ex-girlfriend. In order to discredit him in front of his admirers, Regina performs a series of spectacular thefts, by making all of Liguria's most famous monuments disappear. Then she kidnaps Capitan Basilico, so as to permanently tarnish the reputation of the invincible hero. The police turn to Buio Pesto, a music combo from Genoa, since one of the band is a dead ringer for Capitan-Basilico. They have him dress like the superman so that the population will not be alarmed. With the help of a few kids, the musicians set out to locate the whereabouts of Capitan Basilico's prison, recover the monuments (which have been miniaturized by the thieves) and dismantle the unlikely array of supercriminals hired by Regina.

Buio Pesto is a no profit comedy/music dialectical combo based in Genoa, the capital of the Italian region Liguria. They formed in 1995, and their activity basically consists of concerts and special events, whose profits are donated to charity.

The eight musicians tried their hand at filmmaking for the first time in 2004, with the indie science-fiction spoof *Invaxön—Alieni in Liguria* (Invasion—Aliens in Liguria, 2004). Note that the word "Invasion" is spelled in Ligurian dialect, thus emphasizing the regional nature of the project. A modest, unassuming effort, it was a surprise box-office hit in the region (whereas it was not even distributed in the rest of Italy) and paved the way for a TV series.

The success convinced Buio Pesto to concoct another feature film. This time, the focus was on superheroes, following the flood of U.S. movies based on Marvel and D.C. Comics' characters. However, *Capitan Basilico*—directed by Buio Pesto's bandleader Massimo Morini—is quite another thing when compared with its illustrious American counterparts. A paunchy, mustached guy in a green suit, cloak and mask (not to mention his green baseball bat and vehicle), the titular Capitan Basilico (Captain Basil) is Ligurian to the bone—starting with his name, which makes reference to the main ingredient in Liguria's most popular culinary specialties, such as *pesto* sauce. Actually, our hero swallows *pesto* like Popeye does spinach. This provides him with … Godzilla-like breath, which comes in handy when it is time to tame a fire.

Despite the decidedly low budget, *Capitan Basilico* was a super-production of sorts. The filmmakers managed to gather 400 actors for the shoot, including a number of personalities—local politicians, football players, TV comedians, musicians … All agreed to take part in the film for free and are featured mostly in the first half-hour, which unrolls as a collection of vignettes about Captain Basil performing a variety of good deeds … like acting as a peacemaker between the members of a rock band who are arguing in the

An Italian ad for *Capitan Basilico* (2008), a superhero spoof concocted by the no profit combo Buio Pesto

studio about which chord to use in a song, or preventing a conjugal crisis caused by a suspicious SMS. The comedy, as can be deduced, is at the level of an amateur stage play, and so are the performances.

Even though one "actor" warns the audience at the beginning that: "If you are expecting to see Spiderman, Superman or Batman, you can leave now," several comic superheroes—or rather, a bunch of clumsy-looking impersonators pretending to be Wonder Woman, Captain America and Daredevil—actually turn up in brief cameos during a flashback sequence set at the Superhero Academy where our protagonist graduated and fell in love with Regina (the beautiful Giorgia Würth). On the other hand, the hero's female opponent—who acts out of jealousy—surrounds herself with a trio of demented thugs that include what looks like a developmentally challenged cousin of Agent Smith from *The Matrix* (1999) and a poor man's version of Angelina Jolie's titular character in *Lara Croft: Tomb Raider* (2001).

The many references are tongue-in-cheek and played down to the level of *Capitan Basilico*'s regional-based humor. Later on in the film, members of Buio Pesto show up dressed as Spiderman and Batman at Capitan Basilico's door, while another very Italian superhero is introduced with dubiously humorous results. His name is Capitan Ventosa (Captain Sucker), he comes from Milan and wears a … toilet sucker on top of his head. There is probably some unfathomable hint at between-the-lines feud between Milan and Genoa here—and more evidence of the film's parochialism.

Special effects, as expected, are entry level, with a fair use of computer-generated tricks including an animated title sequence that introduces the titular hero. Curiously, the idea of Regina miniaturizing the monuments she steals recalls the oft-seen devices seen in 1960s films such as *3 Supermen a Tokyo*.

As for Buio Pesto, they are introduced like characters from a children's cartoon, each with his or her own peculiarity (the pretty singer, the bickering guitar player, the over-the-top manager) which in one case gives way to a rather politically incorrect homophobic caricature, as the band's lead singer behaves like the prototypical pansy—referring to himself as a "she," making passes at every male in sight and spitting acidic comments about other women's clothes. Given that another character in the film is a black police inspector who is also the center of a number of

Capitan Basilico features references to the superhero universe as well as popular films such as *Star Wars* and *Scream*.

painfully unfunny gags about "niggers," one can easily deduce that the creators were definitely not going for subtlety and good taste.

As a result, *Capitan Basilico* is nothing more than a curio, and most of the gags will be lost on a non-Ligurian audience—hence the film's limited circulation. What is more, at 133 (!) minutes, the silly humor soon becomes repetitive, as the plot puts together a number of homages and parodies which are grating in their predictability. Examples? Capitan Basilico and his girlfriend are standing atop a boat's fore like Leonardo Di Caprio and Kate Winslet in *Titanic* (1997); the Captain's lookalike runs atop a flight of stairs like Sylvester Stallone did in *Rocky*, to the sound of Bill Conti's instantly recognizable theme. At a certain point a Darth Vader impersonator shows up with the requisite laser sword, followed by a bit featuring the Edvard Munch-masked villain from *Scream* (1996) making a prank phone call, in a gag blatantly lifted from … *Scary Movie* (2000). And so on, and on, and on we go. It takes great will power to get to the end, and the belief that a good deed will be rewarded in the next life—but hey, who said that an act of charity must become an endurance test?

The film spawned a sequel, *Capitan Basilico 2—I Fantastici 4+4* (2011).

2011

Capitan Basilico 2—I Fantastici 4+4

Italy, color, 131 minutes

D: Massimo Morini. *S and SC:* Massimo Morini, Andrea Di Marco, Mirko Gardella and Enrica Guidotti; *DOP:* Lorenzo Battilana; *M:* Buio Pesto; *E:* Michele BB Badinelli.

Cast: Buio Pesto (Themselves), Massimo Bosso (Capitan Basilico), Giorgia Würth (Regina), Luigi Marangon (BarMan), Matteo Lo Piccolo (Robin), Federica Ruggero (Lara Krapfen), Lazzaro Calcagno (Indiana Jones), Povia, Simone Cristicchi, Massimo Ranieri, Toto Cutugno, Mago Forest.

Prod: Associazione Buio Pesto.

Capitan Basilico must face a new criminal threat. The evil BarMan, one of his former classmates at the Superhero Academy, is in possession of a deadly weapon that can bend anyone to his will. BarMan kidnaps the Captain's girlfriend Regina and blackmails the green-dressed superhero. The band Buio Pesto is called into action to foil BarMan's plan. A series of adventures follows around Liguria.

The follow-up to 2008's *Capitan Basilico*, once again concocted by the band Buio Pesto as a means to collect money for charity, offers more of the same—that is, re-

Capitan Basilico 2 offers more of the same: a parade of unlikely superheroes and assorted film and comic spoofs.

gional humor, spoofs of superhero, assorted Hollywood flicks and a series of special participations from well-known actors, singers and showbiz personalities. For the occasion, Buio Pesto gathered 700 actors (mostly non-professionals) and 85,000 extras. This time, the most famous of the lot are the Neapolitan actor-cum-singer Massimo Ranieri (*Metello*, 1969; *Death Rage*, 1976), appearing as a fisherman, and pop singer Toto Cutugno, a well-known name among Italian immigrants abroad because of his songs based on traditional Italian values (such as the infamous *L'italiano*, 1983).

The title is a pun on the group "I 4+4 di Nora Orlandi," a well-known 1960s musical combo that featured the great Alessandro Alessandroni (the "whistle" in Ennio Morricone's scores for Sergio Leone's films, as well as a renowned film composer in his own right) and singer Nora Orlandi, whose angelic voice blessed many memorable Italian film scores such as *The Sweet Body of Deborah* (*Il dolce corpo di Deborah*, 1968, Romolo Guerrieri), *Double Face* (*A doppia faccia*, 1969, Riccardo Freda) and *The Strange Vice of Mrs. Wardh* (*Lo strano vizio della signora Wardh*, 1971, Sergio Martino). All things considered, it is the film's most salacious gag.

Once again the humor pokes fun at the superhero universe. BarMan (got the pun?) and his sidekick Robin (… Hood) gather a squad of villains that include Diabolik, Harry Potter, the Teletubbies (!) and Jack Sparrow's Pirates of the Caribbean. The level of the gags is more or less like the first episode, which means that, at a gargantuan length of 131 minutes, *Capitan Basilico 2—I Fantastici 4+4* is yet another endurance test for non-Ligurians and non-Buio Pesto fans. You have been warned.

Iros

Italy, color, Web Series (8 episodes, 25 minutes each)

D: Bob Ferrari. *S and SC:* Bob Ferrari, Davide Marcheselli and Carletto FX [Carlo Sagradini]; *DOP:* Marco Carroli; *M:* Gem Boy, Matteo Monti and Mecco; *E:* Rupert Blacksmith and Carletto FX.

Cast: Bob Ferrari (Jaxon Peel/Capitan Destino), Belinda Bertolo (Emma Pasternak), Carletto FX (Mente), Francesca Grandi (Dr. Tyrone), Giulio Colli (Richard Osumi).

Prod: Carmax/Kam/Hirin.

Home video: not available.

Jaxon Peel, an unassuming cleaner, is harassed by a life without urges, a tyrannical boss at work and a girlfriend who is too thoughtful. To escape from reality, Jaxon dreams of what his life would be like if he was a comic book hero. What he does not know, though, is that he really is a superhero, named Capitan Destino, who has been deprived of his memory by his deadly enemy, Black Tail. When his superpowers are restored, they are out of control, and real trouble begins for Jaxon ...

The mid-to-late 2000s saw the infusion of the web series as a way to make less expensive products that would be easier to distribute. Many young independent filmmakers opted for such a path, as a reaction to the stagnating situation in the Italian film industry. Such was the case with *Iros*, conceived, directed and starring Bob Ferrari. Self-described as "certainly the greatest living comedian among the totally unknown ones," Ferrari made his first steps in show business by authoring children's shows for television. He specialized in low-budget comedy shorts shot on digital cam, while making a living as a TV author and talk-show director.

Ferrari's dream project was a script that had been sitting on his shelf for no less than 10 years, about a guy who finds out by sheer chance that he has dormant superpowers, a fact which disrupts his life—a bit like M. Night Shyamalan's *Unbreakable* (2000), but played for laughs. However, the project was too costly, and Ferrari abandoned it. Ferrari explained:

> At the beginning it was called *Crypto Night*, and I had written it together with Davide Marcheselli. Then through my friend Belinda Bertolo I got in touch with Gem Boy's Carletto FX, who read the script and got crazy about it, so we decided to work again on it with his help."[1]

Carlo Sagradini, better known as Carletto FX, is the lead singer in the band Gem Boy, a combo devoted to spoofing (often in an overtly vulgar manner and with an emphasis on sex) famous pop and rock songs. As the dynamic duo joined forces to work on Ferrari's old script, in the meantime a new wave of film adaptation and TV series arose—including *Heroes* (2006), whose basic idea bore a passing resemblance to Ferrari's scenario. The NBC series not only pushed Ferrari to resume his old project, but also suggested its definitive title, which is a literal transcription of how Italians pronounce the term "Heroes" (note that in Italian the letter "i" is pronounced as the English "e").

Faced with the impossibility of finding a producer, Ferrari, Sagradini & Co. decided to finance the project and split the profits. Extras were called for an audition via a message on Facebook and on the authors' blogs, while shooting took place in the summer 2010 in Bologna, Imola and other sites in Emilia, with the participation of TV comedians as well as *Diabolik*'s regular drawing artist Giuseppe Palumbo. The finished film—blessed with the tagline "Compared with them, the Avengers are amateurs"—was screened at Bologna's Future Film Festival and distributed as an 8-part web series.

Ferrari himself played the lead, a sad and comic book-obsessed cleaning man named Jaxon Peel who, with the help of the comic book seller Mente (Sagradini), recovers his hidden superpowers, resumes his secret identity as Capitan Destino (Captain Destiny) and makes a mission out of finding all the "sleeper" superheroes who live a normal life without knowing about their own abilities. Such powers include hyper-sensible hearing, X-ray sight ("But … you told me you were a virgin!" Jaxon marvels when he gets to see beneath his girlfriend's clothes … and beyond) and other assorted capabilities.

Ferrari also pokes fun at Marvel and D.C.'s universe and at the often debatable film adaptations of the most popular superheroes. During an awkward dinner with his fiancée's parents at a restaurant, Jaxon dismisses Sam Raimi's *Spider-Man* (2002) as "bullshit" because it turns Peter Parker into a mutant who has the ability to generate organic webbing, unlike in the comic book, and proceeds to explain to his disgusted in-laws from which part of the body spiders actually generate their webs …

Despite its obvious budget shortcomings and amateurish acting, *Iros* is carefully shot and edited, with several amusing ideas and plenty of throwaway gags. It may well

The Italian poster for *Iros* (2011) features the tagline, "Expect the unexpected!"

be dumb (sometimes very much so), but overall it is fun—although it does lose some steam along the way. Ferrari, looking every bit the average overweight guy next door, comes up with several funny bits as the nerdy Jaxon, who keeps his comics everywhere (including the fridge, in a perhaps unintentional nod to *Thrilling*) and undergoes panic attacks whenever someone ignores his friendship requests on Facebook—which makes Capitan Destino much more grounded in reality than most of his peers.

Note:
1. Rinaldi, Andrea, "Gem Boy, *Iros* al cinema," *Il Corriere della Sera*, 01/13/2011.

The Last Man on Earth
(*L'ultimo terrestre*)
Italy 2011, color, 100 minutes

D: Gian Alfonso Pacinotti. *S:* loosely based on the graphic novel *Nessuno mi farà del male* by Giacomo Monti. *SC:* Gian Alfonso Pacinotti; *DOP:* Vladan Radovic; *M:* Valerio Vigliar; *E:* Clelio Benevento.

Cast: Gabriele Spinelli (Luca Bertacci), Anna Bellato (Anna Luini), Teco Celio (Giuseppe Geri), Stefano Scherini (The American), Roberto Herlitzka (Luca's father), Paolo Mazzarelli (Walter Rasini).

Prod: Fandango, Rai Cinema.

The landing of an extraterrestrial civilization on Earth, in Northeast Italy, has been announced on television, but the news failed to make much of an impression on the population. The solitary Luca Bertacci is equally unimpressed. He spends his time between an insignificant job at the local bingo hall and visits to his elderly father, and secretly spies on his beautiful neighborhood. The alien landing will change Luca's life for good. Luca's father finds one of the extraterrestrials near his farm. The man who has been living in solitude since being abandoned by his wife takes the alien home, hides it and takes care of it. Eventually, the alien—who is pacifistic and affectionate—takes the place of the elderly man's wife …

Born in Pisa in 1963, Gian Alfonso "Gianni" Pacinotti (nicknamed Gipi) is one of the most original voices in contemporary Italian comics, for his original drawing style (characterized by the use of oil and watercolor, in contrast with the overwhelming trend toward the digital) and for his tendency at blending adventure, realism and autobiography into his works. He was awarded prestigious European prizes, and his latest effort *unastoria* (2013) was the first graphic novel ever to be selected among the finalists of Italy's most important literary prize, Premio Strega.

For his debut behind the camera Pacinotti (who signed the film with his full name as opposed to Gipi, his trademark signature in comics) chose to adapt a colleague's work, Giacomo Monti's *Nessuno mi farà del male*, an anthology of graphic short stories centered on ordinary people—provincial teens, bartenders, waitresses, farmers, prosti-

The Italian poster for Gian Alfonso Pacinotti's *The Last Man on Earth* (2011)

tutes—observed during their everyday existence, so as to show vividly their misery and loneliness. Pacinotti's film retains the story's science fiction setting—albeit a *sui generis* one—but tells the story through the eyes of a solitary man, Luca, who is an alien of sorts because of his alexithymia, a personality disorder which consists of the inability to identify and describe emotions.

Despite the presence of UFOs (portrayed according to the standard appearances of aliens in the collective imagination from Roswell onwards), *The Last Man on Earth* is a symbolic parable that often borders on the grotesque and the absurd. The theme of the alien invasion is treated as a metaphor for a discourse on contemporary Italy, a weary and disillusioned country in a full-blown economic crisis, and one plagued by superficiality, materialism, machoism and xenophobic intolerance. People react to the arrival of extraterrestrials accordingly: "Now they're going to steal our jobs, as the Chinese did before them!" one complains. Aliens obviously stands for immigrants, and the feminine and maternal alien being who becomes Luca's father's housekeeper (and lover …) alludes to the Eastern European caregivers working in many North Italian families.

The film's main strength lies in its idiosyncratic style—with flash sequences which recall comic book panels and shots characterized by the use of light and color in accordance with the protagonist's emotional state—immensely aided by the top-notch cinematography (courtesy of Vladan Radovic) and by the eerie post-industrialist suburban locations. The casting is inspired: the weird-looking Gabriele Spinelli makes quite an impression as the misanthropic Luca, while veteran actor Roberto Herlitzka steals every scene he is in as Luca's father. On the other hand, Pacinotti's metaphors soon wear out their welcome, and after a very promising (and decidedly unpleasant) first half, the film trudges along uneasily from one vignette to the next, up to its cathartic but rather hasty ending.

Pacinotti's film was launched via a viral marketing campaign inspired by Orson Welles' radio broadcast of *War of the Worlds*. The UFO website *Esseri di Luce—Visitatori dalle Pleiadi* (Beings of Light—Visitors from the Pleiades) was launched, which contained footage of encounters with UFOs and videos of alien sightings in Italy were then posted on YouTube, followed by a clip of a Rai3 newscaster announcing on TV the arrival of extraterrestrials, which reached almost half a million clicks. The campaign gained the film's attention on the part of British newspaper the *Guardian*[1], but failed to do much for its commercial fortunes. *The Last Man on Earth* was screened at the 2011 Venice Festival, to favorable critical reactions, but it flopped at the box-office.

Note:

1. Hooper, John, *Italian alien film tries to ape Orson Welles radio play in web marketing*, The Guardian, 8/8/2011.

2013

Bloody Sin

Italy, color, 91 minutes

D: Domiziano Cristopharo. *S*: Domiziano Cristopharo and Nancy De Lucia; *SC:* L. Filippo Santaniello; *DOP:* Giuseppe Pignone; *M:* Kristian Sensini; *E*: Alessandro Giordani.

Cast: Lorenzo Balducci (Johnny Morghen), Nancy De Lucia (Helen), Roberta Gemma [Floriana Panella] (Barbara), Dallas Walker (Terence Fisher), Daniel Baldock (Mr. Lenzi), Clio Evans (Rita), Elda Alvigini (Fisher's mother), Ruggero Deodato (Inquisitor), Venantino Venantini (Priest), Maria Rosaria Omaggio (Miss Steele).

Prod: L. Filippo Santaniello, Domiziano Cristopharo, Filmon Aggujaro, Daniel Baldock.

In 1974 the American glamour magazine Bizarre *sends photographer Johnny Morghen, his assistant Helen, a model named Barbara and make-up artist Rita to Italy, in order to stage an erotic photo*

The British poster for *Bloody Sin* (2013)

shoot in an old castle in the village of Olevano. The place—which includes a torture chamber used by the Inquisition and recycled during the war by the Nazis, and has a grim history of torture and mayhem—is owned by ex-actor Terence Fisher, who lives there with his elderly mother. Fisher falls for Helen, who is a dead ringer for an old flame of his. Later on Johnny is found dead in mysterious circumstances. The survivors start suspecting one another, as there is a sadistic torturer who hides in the crypt, and Fisher conceals a horrible secret …

Labeled as "glam horror," indie filmmaker Domiziano Cristopharo's *Bloody Sin* (shot in 2010 but screened for the first time only in 2013, at Nice's Semaine du Cinéma Fantastique) harks back to Italy's adults-only comic books of the 1970s, namely *Oltretomba* (which also provides the film's subtitle). Debuting on June 1, 1971 *Oltretomba* marked the birth of a new publishing company, Ediperiodici, which was none other than a new incarnation of Erregi, the leading publisher in the market of adults-only comics, headed by Renzo Barbieri and Giorgio Cavedon. The following year marked the end of their commercial partnership, and Barbieri founded a new company, Edifumetto, which became Ediperiodici's biggest competitor throughout this decade and the next.

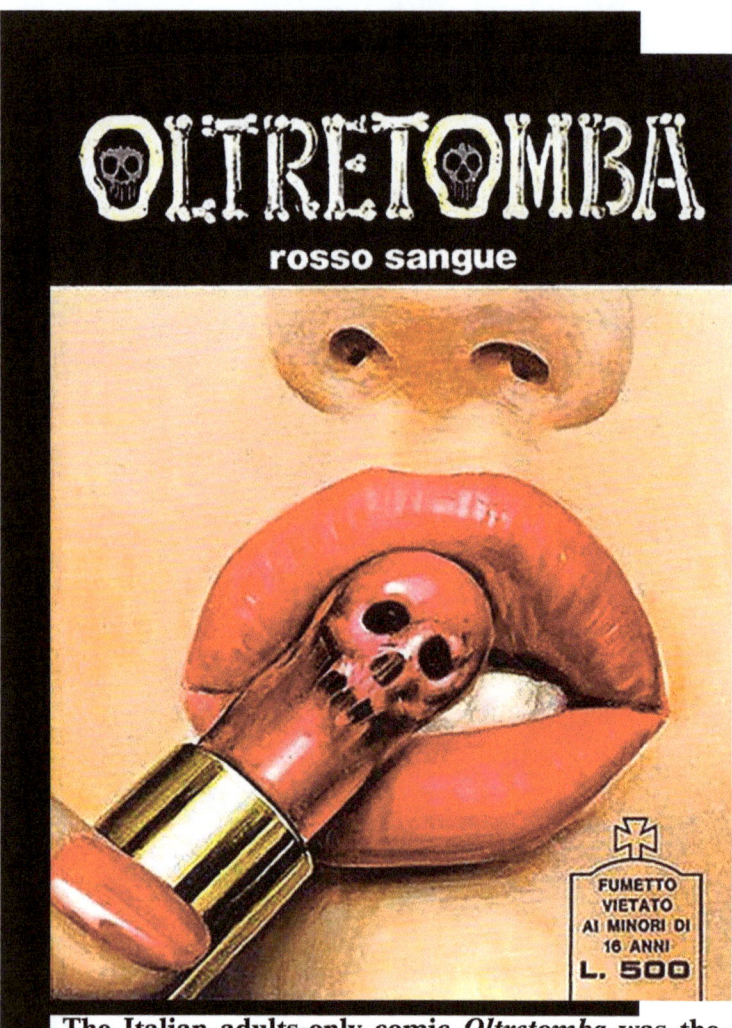

The Italian adults-only comic *Oltretomba* was the main inspiration for *Bloody Sin*.

Oltretomba was characterized by its anthology approach, with no recurring characters. The stories were focused on the macabre and the Grand Guignol and were often "inspired" by current horror films—although sometimes the contrary happened, as in the case of the aforementioned *Il grido del capricorno*. The erotic component got more and more important as the years went by, until *Oltretomba* actually became a quasi-hardcore *fumetto*. Its popularity was tremendous in Italy and in foreign countries as well. It was published also in Germany, France and Spain. In 1972 Ediperiodici launched a supplement, *Oltretomba Colore*, the first Italian adults-only comic in color, published until 1979 (80 issues overall) while 1973 saw the birth of *Oltretomba Gigante* (115 issues until January 1983). *Oltretomba* ceased publications in 1986, with issue #300.

With a clever move, the bulk of *Bloody Sin* takes place in 1974, the period where such comics were reaching their peak—just a step before turning into out-and-out hardcore porn, yet with an outstanding dose of graphic violence, sex and assorted perversions in their often over-the-top, no-holds-barred stories. A period, it must be added, which marked a significant evolution in Italian culture and society. In 1974 citizens were asked to vote in a referendum whether they wanted to repeal the 1970 government law that allowed divorce for the first time in Italy. The anti-divorce referendum, led by the Democrazia Cristiana party, was surprisingly voted down by 59% of the national electorate. The following year saw the Family Law Reformation Act, which introduced profound innovations concerning the relationship between spouses, between parents and children and between children born in and out of wedlock. The Feminist Movement was also gaining force in the early-to-mid 1970s.

Such a stark contrast between a society that was finally moving toward a more evolved vision of woman and marriage and the way popular culture exploited women's bodies was one of the factors that made the mid-1970s such a boiling period in Italy. "These are the seventies; women should not be objectified and looked upon as if they have no intelligence," as the adults-only comics publisher played by Maria Rosaria Omaggio points out, ending her monologue with the famous Feminist slogan: "Beware, behold, the witches are back!"

Like the director's earlier films—*House of Flesh Mannequins* (2009) and *The Museum of Wonders* (2010)—and similarly to his subsequent output, which includes the grim *Red Krokodil* (2012), *Bellerofonte* (2012) and *The Doll Syndrome* (2014)—*Bloody Sin* is distinguished by a frank, no-holds barred approach to the matter (which in Cristopharo's previous efforts had allowed for the inclusion of non-simulated sex scenes as well as extreme body art performances) which here benefits from a tongue-in-cheek approach, accomplished via the nod to the delirious stories concocted by *fumetti* writers and artists in the 1970s.

To achieve a comic-book feel, Cristopharo often intersperses live-action footage with comic book panels (courtesy of comic artist Maria Grazia Gianolla). The result, due also to the contemporary artwork (and the use of computer-generated colors), is not as atmospheric as it may have been. However, it provides for some nice narrative passages (not to mention a surprise ending) that make *Bloody Sin* look suitably sleek. Compared with the drab look of so many recent Italian independent horror films, Cristopharo shows a more careful approach to form, with an engrossing use of the split-screen, assorted editing tricks and colored filters (as much as the extreme low-budget and digital cinematography would allow …), as well as several striking visual bits, such as Walker's appearance in the climax, his face and body covered with blood and glitter. Add to this the clever use of singer Giovanna Nocetti's 1973 hit *Questo amore un po' strano* (This Somewhat Strange Love), a title that will prove to be definitely in tune with the film's theme.

Even though the director claimed: "The real shock is not caused by graphic violence, blood and horror, but

Maria Rosaria Omaggio as "Miss Steele" in a strikingly composed sequence from *Bloody Sin*

rather by the originality of the ideas we adopted in order to show all this," the story is actually an undeclared remake of sorts of Massimo Pupillo's *Bloody Pit of Horror*, with plenty of assorted homages to the glory days of Italian horror thrown in for good measure. For instance, for the scene where the protagonists reach the small Italian village where they will have to stage a photo shoot, Cristopharo recreates visuals that openly recall Bava's *Kill, Baby … Kill!* (*Operazione paura*, 1966); the arrival at the castle and the character of the old "countess" reprise *Lisa and the Devil* (*Lisa e il diavolo*, 1972); the necrophilia threesome between Fisher, Helen and the former's dead (and mummified) lover recalls both a notorious scene in Bava's film as well as Aristide Massaccesi's gory *Beyond the Darkness* (*Buio omega*, 1979), albeit with a twist; the notion that the castle is built on one of the Seven Gates of Hell winks at Fulci's *The Beyond* (*… E tu vivrai nel terrore! L'Aldilà*, 1981); a Nazi flashback hints at Liliana Cavani's *The Night Porter* (1974) and the Nazi-erotic thread that followed. And so on …

Such a jigsaw-like postmodernist approach to the narrative structure is not new to Cristopharo, whose previous films were also remakes of sorts of classic horror movies, with whole scenes and bits of dialogue restaged and reinvented in a similar manner. *House of Flesh Mannequins* was a reworking of *Peeping Tom* (1960), whereas *The Museum of Wonders* paid ample homage to *Freaks* (1932). Sometimes, the over-reliance on cinematic homages can become annoying. The trick of naming characters after horror icons (Steele, Fisher, Lenzi—not to mention "Johnny Morghen," a reference to the English alias of actor Giovanni Lombardo Radice, of *Cannibal Ferox* fame …) had a punch back when Joe Dante and John Sayles did it in *The Howling* (1981), but over 30 years later it is just old-hat.

Other cinematic homages are far less predictable and make for surprising results. The opening scene, with the main characters walking on an apparently endless countryside road, is an unexpected and amusing bow to Luis Buñuel's *The Discreet Charm of the Bourgeoisie* (1972) and hints at the filmmaker's sometimes Surrealist approach (with nods to video art as well) which gives way to some of *Bloody Sin*'s best moments. Take, for instance, the bizarre stop-motion sequence (by Paolo Gaudio), sort of Jan Švankmajer-meets-Robert Morgan, which ends up playing a vital role in the film's twist ending. For all its sense of *déjà-vu*, *Bloody Sin* moves at a brisk pace and accommodates several biting twists along the way—and, it must be added, dementedly grotesque ones, in the spirit of the old *Oltretomba* comics—besides the required amount of gore and sex. The over-the-top f/x are in league with early 1980s Italian splatter films, with hooks driven into the flesh, open skulls with exposed brains, a severed penis, a head transfixed by a long nail and other assorted graphic delights.

The cast is a mixed bunch. The drop-dead gorgeous porn actress Roberta Gemma—who willingly displays her voluptuous body for the camera and has a show-stopping bath scene—is a joy for the eyes, but her voice is obviously dubbed into English with rather uncomfortable results. The other young actors sometimes are too preoccupied with their English delivery than with anything else. On the other hand, Cristopharo puts together several cult figures of Italy's horror and exploitation cinema for amusing cameos: director Ruggero Deodato (as one of the inquisitors in the Middle Age prologue), character actor Venantino Venantini (as the other high priest) and actress Maria Rosaria Omaggio (Lenzi's *Nightmare City*, 1980) as the cigar-chomping Miss Steele.

2014

The Invisible Boy
(*Il ragazzo invisibile*)
Italy/France, color, 100 minutes
D: Gabriele Salvatores. S and SC: Alessandro Fabbri, Ludovica Rampoldi and Stefano Sardo; DOP: Italo Petriccione; M: Ezio Bosso, Federico De' Robertis; E: Massimo Fiocchi.
Cast: Ludovico Girardello (Michele), Valeria Golino (Giovanna), Fabrizio Bentivoglio (Basili), Christo Jivkov (Andrey), Noa Zatta (Stella), Vernon Dobtcheff (Claw), Kseniya Rappoport (Yelena), Riccardo Gasparini (Ivan).
Prod: Indigo Films (Rome), Rai Cinema (Rome), Faso Film (Rome), Babe Film (Paris).
In Trieste, Italy the 13-year-old Michele, the only son of Giovanna, a widowed police inspector, is the most unpopular kid at school, bullied by his classmates and ignored by Stella, the girl he has

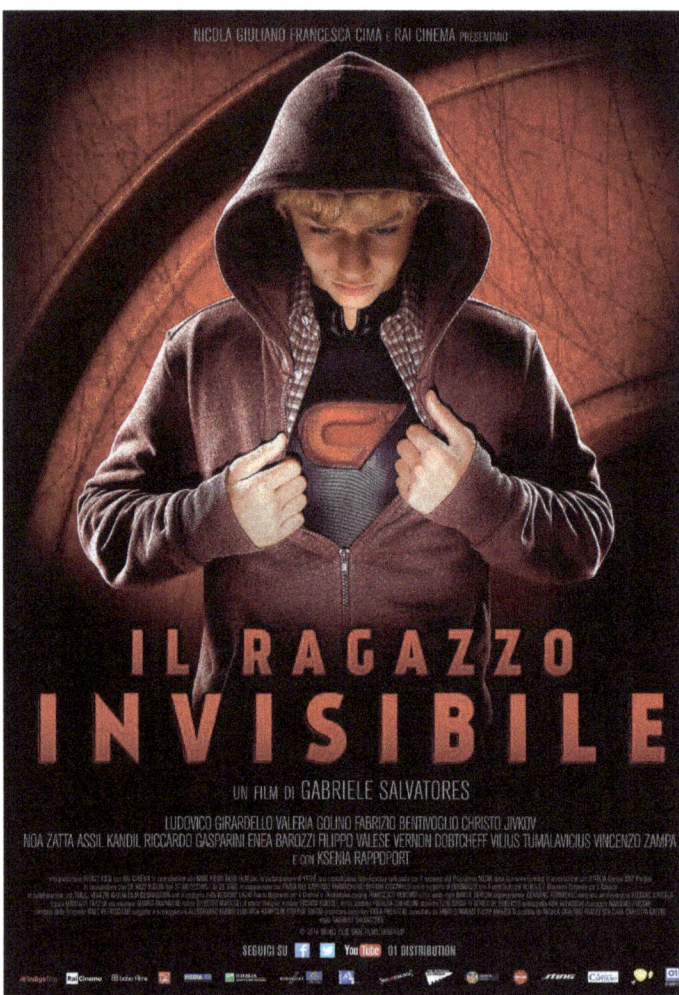

The Italian *locandina* for Gabriele Salvatores' coming-of-age superhero film, *The Invisible Boy*

a crush on. When the money he saved to buy a Spiderman costume for a Halloween party at Stella's house is stolen, Michele resorts to a cheap costume bought at a Chinese store. The party ends in disaster for him, but the next morning, when he wakes up, the boy discovers that he has become invisible. In his present state, Michele takes revenge on those who humiliated him, but once again he has to suffer another debasement when he unexpectedly becomes visible again (and totally naked) in the girls' dressing room. Later on, while invisible, Michele manages to become Stella's friend, but he also finds out that Giovanna adopted him. Meanwhile, someone is kidnapping Michele's classmates, and Stella is next. It turns out that the kidnappings are performed by a secret Russian army team, whose target is actually the invisible boy whose identity they have not determined yet. Michele meets his real father, Andrey, a blind Russian man who can read people's minds and who tells him the story of the "Specials," mutant individuals who developed superpowers after being exposed to nuclear radiation in Russia, trained as a secret weapon by the army. Michele, the son of two "Specials," was clandestinely taken away to Italy by his dad and abandoned in front of Giovanna's door. After evading capture, the boy teams up with classmate Ivan and finds out the kidnapped teens' prison, located in a ship harbored at the dock. There, he faces the villains' leader, an elderly man named Claw who has the power to control people's minds ...

For a filmmaker with a body of work as diverse as Gabriele Salvatores'—ranging from the Academy Award-winning war comedy-drama *Mediterraneo* (1991) to the dystopian sci-fi thriller *Nirvana* (1997), from the grotesquely nightmarish *Teeth* (*Denti*, 2000) to the grim *film noir Deadly Code*, aka *Siberian Education* (*Educazione siberiana*, 2013)—a teenage superhero adventure such as *The Invisible Boy* does not seem such a risky gamble after all. Still it is a risky one, especially considering the country in which it was made, the film industry where it has been developed and the audience to which it is aimed.

In press interviews, Salvatores has claimed that he made Italy's first superhero movie. As any reader of the present book has by now realized, that's not quite the case indeed. Nevertheless, even though Salvatores apparently forgot (or more likely, never even heard of them) such 1960s predecessors as *Flashman* or *Argoman the Fantastic Superman* (not to mention the *Three Supermen* series, for that matter) or the much more recent *Capitan Basilico* series, indeed *The Invisible Boy* is in many ways the first of its kind, a mainstream, big-budget attempt at a full-fledged fantasy adventure for the masses centered on a superhero—no, much more! An *Italian* superhero that lives in a real Italian town, today.

True, the *Capitan Basilico* diptych dealt with a similar theme, albeit in a context of parody, and so did the short film *Capitan Novara—Un giorno da supereroe*. But those were low or zero-budget flicks, indie or amateurish stuff with little or no room in the national market, and such movies came and went almost unnoticed (*Capitan Basilico* benefitting marginally from its regional setting, a bit like Mario Merola's crime melodramas did in the late 1970s). On the other hand, Salvatores' film displays a conspicuous budget, a cast featuring such popular names as Valeria Golino (of *Rain Man* fame), Fabrizio Bentivoglio (one of Italy's best actors and a Salvatores regular since 1989's amusing bittersweet road movie *Marrakech Express*) and Kseniya Rappoport (who appeared in Giuseppe Tornatore's sleazy thriller *The Unknown Woman*, 2006) and a special effects crew that can finally compete with Hollywood's very own. What is more, the project comes off as very ambitious in its multi-media format, featuring also a novel as well as a graphic novel of the same name which, in its creators' words, expand the film's landscapes.

Salvatores tries hard, he really does. As he stated:

> I liked the idea of confronting myself with the power of invisibility as a metaphor and depict the world of teenagers, with a true sounding and adventurous story [...]. There is also

Michele (Ludovico Girardello) plays the insecure teenager who discovers he has super powers.

Salvatores' teenage superhero sports an impressive costume.

the epic dimension of *Siberian Education*, which has always fascinated me, and to which I'm returning here, not only for the Eastern setting. In addition to these heroes of life, there are hints at authors that I love, such as Jack London and Joseph Conrad, as well as the theme of the role model and the secret friend, the mirror, the double, the person hidden inside you ... deep themes that I wanted to put in my film. There is also the theme of adolescent bullying, whence comes the challenge, the anger that one needs in order to react and shape another world for himself"[1]

The story of a teenage orphan, neglected by his widowed mom (Golino), bullied by his male classmates and rejected by the prettiest girl in the class, with whom he is hopelessly in love, is the obvious terrain for a meditation on coming of age in general and puberty in particular, with all its growing pains as well as the feelings of rebellion and rejection toward and from the parents. Salvatores stated his will to portray his self-labeled "Spaghetti-fantasy" without moving away from a realistic feel:

> We wanted to show that even in reality there is magic and vice versa.[2]

Too bad all this is rendered in the first half through a banal, often cringe-inducing series of vignettes replete with awkward dialogue and banally-sketched characters, such as Ivan, the bully who harasses the young hero at school and robs his pocket money (and who in turn is the son of a deadbeat jailbird and suffers from ADHD), or the haughty high-class kid stressed by an over-ambitious father. Michele himself is saddled with an absent father figure, who eventually shows up and becomes his mentor.

The didactic stress on the role of family in their kids' education as well as kids' often overlooked mental developmental disorders (such as Ivan's Attention Deficit Hyperactive Disorder) is the elephant in the room that often undermines Salvatores' attempts. What should come naturally feels often forced and hardly believable, as if the characters were (and actually, they are) just cyphers that represent a larger metaphoric scheme, whereas despite the filmmakers' efforts the "superheroes with super problems" angle is tired and worn. And when Salvatores attempts to address Michele's awaking sexuality, in the scene where the young invisible kid sneaks into the girls' dressing rooms, the result is an uncomfortable mixture between the open-

Invisibility has its advantages, as Michele soon finds out.

ing sequence of De Palma's *Carrie* (which however was an adult horror film) and some Japanese *Roman porno* such as *Invisible Man: Rape!* (1978, Isao Hayashi)—even though, it must be stressed, no female nudity is ever shown … even though Michele's bare ass pops up now and then in the film.

What is more, despite having directed a couple of impressive child centered dramas such as *I'm Not Scared* (*Io non ho paura*, 2003) and *As God Commands* (*Come Dio comanda*, 2008), Salvatores falters when it comes to directing his child actors. None of them is fully convincing and their delivery often comes off as either weak, forced or stilted, albeit both Ludovico Girardello and Noa Zatta have the right looks for the role. Their grown-up sidekicks fare better in comparison. As Michele's mother, the still-ravishing Valeria Golino displays once again her acting chops by playing a thankless role in a subdued way and emerging as protective and warm as requested without ever looking or sounding less than believable. Bentivoglio relishes his turn as a school psychiatrist who may or may not be one of the film's villains by hamming it all up with gusto and surviving potentially disastrous results by way of his self-ironic presence, myopic stare and somnolent delivery. As the main villain, Vernon Dobtcheff shows up perhaps too late in the story, but his Fagin-like looks hint at a Dickensian angle (more on this later) that is perhaps the picture's most interesting aspect.

Technically *The Invisible Boy* is top-notch and a product obviously conceived with an eye to the foreign markets. The impressive opening credit scene, with a crazed-looking sensitive "Special" frantically engraving signs with an owl on a white wall that eventually turns out to be part of a painting-like sketch of the town where Michele lives, immediately sets the tone of the story and contains a pointed reference to the act of creation and comics as well. Then, the young hero's first appearance as he rides his bike on the streets of Trieste to the sound of Gorillaz' *Clint Eastwood* provides not only an ironic yet catchy introduction but also a perfectly paced and edited showcase for the director's technical skills.

A longtime *fumetti* fan, Salvatores drew equally from popular comics as well as more ambitious ones.

> I was born in 1950, so as a kid the comics were always a part of my life. They are related to cinema, but the one I loved the most was "Corto Maltese" by Hugo Pratt, but I absolutely can't forget the French comic artists such as Moebius and Enki Bilal. Speaking of superheroes, I'd pick Flash Gordon. I was fascinated by the tribes, the falcon men, the lions …

Declarations such as these partly explain the somehow *retro* feel that *The Invisible Boy* conveys. As for movies, the director's eyes and reminiscences are firmly planted in the 1980s.

> I like very much the diversity in 1980s cinema, the coming of age in films like *The Goonies*. Steven Spielberg, he was the first to put together certain things, science fiction and the protagonists' everyday reality [...]. And I love *Let the Right One In* by Tomas Alfredson, Nolan, Tim Burton, Raimi ... [3]

Yet, at times Salvatores' clever style and self-conscious cinephile spirit turns out as oddly self-defeating. The many film buff references featured in the first part become distracting and unnecessary, often unmasking themselves as shortcuts to make lazily-written scenes seem more interesting than they are. Within a matter of minutes we are treated to not one but *two* nods to Kubrick's *The Shining* (Michele's classmate breaking into the toilet door, appearing in the crack and claiming he is the big bad wolf; a couple of girls dressed as the ghostly twins in the Overlook hotel during an ill-fated Halloween party scene), plus a recreation of the antique shop in Joe Dante's *Gremlins*, replete with an elderly Chinese who, like Robert De Niro's Louis Cypher in *Angel Heart*, peels a hard-boiled egg with his pinkie nail. Later on, as a bath-robed Michele finds out about his own invisibility by looking at the bathroom mirror while washing his teeth, Salvatore borrows an iconic image from Paul Verhoeven's *Hollow Man* (2000). On the other hand, Michele—wearing cap, scarf and shades to cover his invisible face—looks just like a miniature version of Chevy Chase in John Carpenter's *Memoirs of an Invisible Man* (1992) rather than the all-too-obvious (and perhaps too old) Claude Rains/James Whale reference. Similarly, the resort to syrupy foreign indie folk-rock songs on the soundtrack conveys a not very welcome feel of Sundance Film Festival fodder, so to speak. At one point the director even resorts to one of the oldest tricks in the book. As Michele is reading a superhero comic in his comics-filled (perhaps even too much so) bedroom and comes across the typical line where the hero deems his powers as a curse, a balloon pops up over his head. Intended as the umpteenth homage to the world of *fumetti*, the joke sounds ill conceived, especially within the story's realistic setting and feel.

The second half, mostly devoted to a simply-sketched action plot, has Salvatores embracing the spirit of a superhero film all the way, as Michele even dons a cool-looking costume whose molecules become invisible with him. Actually, the result is slightly more convincing and the script even has one or two tricks up its sleeve, with a couple of not-so-telegraphed twists along the way. Still, the best parts are the flashback scenes that portray the origins of Michele's superpowers as well as those of the other "Specials." Salvatores' film here draws from Marvel's *X-Men* but imbues the theme within a realistic setting, just like Bryan Singer did in his adaptation of Stan Lee's characters, as the superpowers are shown to be the consequence of a nuclear leak somewhere in Russia in the 1980s. The word Chernobyl is never spoken, but it is pretty clear throughout. Overall, though, the flashbacks almost come off as a rendition of the workhouse scenes in *Oliver Twist*. Besides being submitted to endless tests by masked guards, the young reclusive mutants are seen dining all together in an orphanage-like refectory like Dickens' children, and Salvatores even throws in a mutant version of the Artful Dodger in the shape of a kid with elongated arms à la Mr. Fantastic.

As the main location, the Northeast city of Trieste, near the border with Slovenia, provides a beautiful looking autumnal setting, with its elegant architectures and imposing docks; but one cannot help thinking what the result would have been had Salvatores filmed the story in the southern city of Naples, as he originally intended, thus providing a much warmer Italian feel, not to mention a more resounding contrast with the cold, de-saturated Eastern European flashbacks. One also wonders, since the film's main faults lie in the script, why Salvatore did not choose to adapt an existing comic book or at least collaborate with experienced comic book writers, as he did on the ensuing graphic novel, which was written by the renowned Sergio Bonelli collaborator Diego Cajelli and drawn by Giuseppe Camuncoli, Werther Dell'Edera and Alessandro Vitti, all of them boasting working experiences with Marvel and D.C. Comics.

Notes:
1. Andrea Giordano, "Gabriele Salvatores: "Il mio Ragazzo Invisibile supereroe contro i mostri di oggi, i bulli,"" *Il Corriere della Sera/Io Donna*, 12/03/2014.
2. Rosita Fattore, "Gabriele Salvatores scopre i superpoteri: "Anch'io vorrei essere un ragazzo invisibile,"" *La Repubblica*, 06/28/2014.
3. Giordano, "Gabriele Salvatores."

Appendix:
The Turkish "Melting Pot": When an Italian Antihero Meets An American Superhero in Turkey

by Kaya Özkaracalar

One of the photonovel series originating from Italy was *Killing*, featuring an antihero wearing a skull mask and a skeleton costume, whose popularity would reach international markets beyond its home country. *Killing* was obviously inspired (to put it politely!) from *Kriminal*, an Italian comic featuring a very similar antihero wearing a skull mask and a skeleton costume. *Kriminal* had been inspired from *Diabolik*, another and a better known Italian comic featuring an antihero wearing a black mask and a black costume. And the inspiration for *Diabolik* must have come from Fantômas, the seminal French pulp fiction antihero. Drawing from such a long line of successive inspirations, the Milanese publisher Ponzoni created *Killing* and its first issue hit the stands in March 1966. It would run for a total of 62 issues until 1969 and it was also published in several other countries. Its popularity was apparently most enduring in Latin America where additional Killing episodes would be produced when the original run of Italian stories ended. And yet, it was in Turkey where Killing would be adapted to the big screen—and not only once but in about a dozen movies most of which would be produced within a single year!

In Turkey, Killing was initially serialized in *Son*, a daily newspaper established in 1966. Feedback from the readers was apparently encouraging and *Son*'s publishers, the Simavi family, owners of the largest mass media group in Turkey at the time, would begin to publish *Killing* as a biweekly periodical under its own title in 1967. The wave of Turkish Killing movies would also spring up that year, but there is actually an overlooked indication that an earlier Turkish movie featuring Killing or perhaps a villain modeled from it might have been made in 1966. In 1993, veteran Turkish low-budget filmmaker Cevat Okçugil told the fanzine *Güzel* that he had made Turkey's first Killing movie as "İskelet Adam" (The Skeleton Man) in 1966. There is absolutely no record whatsoever regarding a movie titled as such, but in 1965-66, Okçugil made a series of obscure movies featuring a secret agent billed as "the Turkish James Bond" and one entry in this series, *Örümcek Adam* (Spider Man, 1966), features a villain clad in a costume with spider's web design; another one of the lesser-known entries, hypothetically speaking, may have featured a Skeleton Man as the villain and released under a title without explicit reference to its villain. The mystery regarding Okçugil's claim to have made the first Killing movie in Turkey is yet to be substantiated.

Sometime early in 1967, 35-year-old director Yılmaz Atadeniz saw the cinematic potential of Killing when it was still being serialized in the *Son* newspaper and he decided to make a film featuring this character. Quickly, the Killing project in his mind evolved into two movies to be shot back to back, one being the direct sequel of the other, somewhat in the fashion of the old American serials which he had enjoyed so much as a child. He would pit this novel character against a good, old-fashioned superhero. Having served as a director-for-hire for other producers up to that point in his career, Atadeniz resolved to produce this project himself and teamed with exhibitor İrfan Atasoy, who provided the finances. Immediately prior to the Killing project, Atasoy had acted in a supporting role in a movie he had produced and he assumed the role of the superhero in Atadeniz's initial Killing film(s). On May 29, on the anniversary of the Ottoman Turks' conquest of Constantinople (today's Istanbul), Atadeniz had his actor Yıldırım Gencer tour the old city region of Istanbul wearing Killing's suit, starting his trek from the ancient Byzantine walls from which the Turks had first entered the city. This publicity gimmick was a huge success and was widely covered in *Ses*, Turkey's best-selling entertainment magazine of the 1960s. However, not all the publicity around Atadeniz's Killing project was positive. An article published in the influential daily newspaper *Cumhuriyet* (that also covered the production of Turkish secret agent/spy and Western films) headlined as: "The worst of contemporary fashions in domestic cinema"; actually, despite the headline, the content of the article is more balanced as it links the attraction of contemporary popular figures as Killing to the attraction of ancient folk tales.

The debut of Simavis' biweekly *Killing* magazine on June 1 must have also raised the popularity of Killing and literally a Killing craze was going on in Turkey in the summer of 1967, with Killing costumed guests being the focus of attraction at masked balls held in Istanbul's high society as reported by the country's mainstream press. American science-fiction author Thomas M. Disch, who visited Istanbul in 1967, would write in his uncanny short story *The Asian Shore* that the skeleton-suited Killing was the principal figure of the new Turkish folklore. It seemed all was set for a successful release of Atadeniz's Killing films at the commencement of the 1967-1968 cinema season (until the 1990s, the summer months were considered the dead season for film-going in Turkey). Only one obstacle remained, the censorship, and Turkey's self-designated guardians of morality, law and order would indeed raise their eyebrows when faced with the Killing films.

Turkey's Central Film Control Commission, composed of representatives of the ministries of Interior Affairs, National Education and Tourism and Publicity, as well as members of the police force and the military met on Sept. 27[1] and viewed Atadeniz's two Killing films, *Kilink İstanbulda* (Kilink in Istanbul) and *Kilink Uçan Adama Karşı* (Kilink vs the Flying Man). In the end, the commission narrowly voted to allow distribution of the movie(s) on several conditions, with representatives of the military and National Education Ministry voting for an outright ban. First of all, the end of the first film was deemed "harmful to the country's security" and this mishap could be overcome only if the two movies were shown together; in other words, the inconclusive ending of the first part where the criminal Killing was still free couldn't be allowed to stand on its own and it had to be made sure that it was followed by the second part where Killing would eventually be overcome. Furthermore, the commission ordered several cuts in both films. One scene ordered for elimination involved Killing murdering a policeman. It was apparent that the censors were determined to prevent any suggestion of a criminal prevailing over the country's security forces. Other cuts were related to scenes of either violence and/or display of female flesh.

Meanwhile, a mainstream film company had also decided to cash in on the Killing craze and pulled together a comedy titled *Şaşkın Hafiye Kilink'e Karşı* (The Dumb Detective vs Kilink) starring Sadri Alışık, one of Turkey's biggest comedy stars of the era, as Killing's nemesis (in 1973, he would also star in a Turkish comedy feature film version of the popular TV series *Star Trek*, titled *Turist Ömer Uzay Yolunda*). The censors were even harsher on this outing and they voted unanimously on Oct. 12 to outright ban it on the grounds that it "encouraged crime," "caricaturized the police" and was "so horrifying as to give the youth nightmares." The filmmakers quickly re-fashioned their movie, cutting out scenes of murder by a ventilator and by strangulation, as well as adding new scenes of official police involvement in trailing and eventually capturing Killing and changing the occupation of the title hero from a private detective to an insurance agent (even though the title of the movie remained unchanged)! And yet, the censors were not still completely satisfied with the re-submitted movie and allowed it only by ordering a further cut of a scene where Killing stabs someone's hand.

Killing became an extremely popular figure in Turkey's culture. It first appeared in the daily newspaper *Son* and then as a biweekly periodical in 1967.

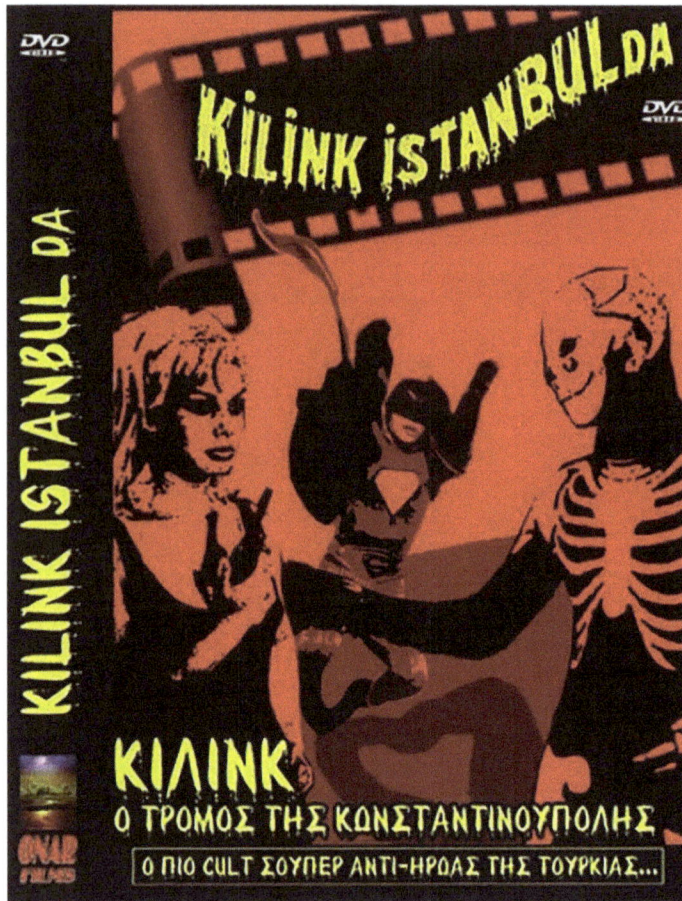

Kilink Istanbulda (1967, Yılmaz Atadeniz) was the first Turkish film based on the Killing character. It was released on DVD in Greece.

Director Yılmaz Atadeniz poses by the poster of his third Killing film, *Kilink Soy ve Öldür*.

Şaşkın Hafiye Kilink'e Karşı beat Atadeniz's Killing movies to the screens when it was released in five cinemas across Istanbul on Oct. 30, a wide release as any regular mainstream movie in terms of that year's release standards in Turkey. On that same day the Italian-made *Kriminal* (1966), an adaptation of the antihero comics which had served as the model for Killing in the first place, was also released in Istanbul re-titled as *Killing Istanbul'da*, on the basis that it was partially set in Istanbul and that the title character's mask and costume were indeed hardly distinguishable from Killing's! Furthermore, an obscure foreign movie re-titled as *Killing Atom Casusu* (Killing the Atom Spy) also appeared on the screen of a minor cinema in the city on the same day.

Atadeniz's Killing movies appear to have debuted in Ankara, Turkey's capital and second largest city, in November. *Kilink İstanbulda*'s Istanbul premier was held on Dec. 21 in the recently-established Işın cinema in the middle-income district Mecidiyeköy and it finally received a wide release on Dec. 25 by opening in four additional cinemas across the city, including the Lüks cinema in Beyoğlu, Istanbul's main entertainment center. Such a wide release for a B-movie was unprecedented in Turkey. It is difficult to establish with certainty from archival research of newspaper listings if *Kilink İstanbulda* was indeed paired with *Kilink Uçan Adama Karşı* as a double bill everywhere it opened as the censors had ordered. It popped up in several other Istanbul cinemas throughout the 1967-1968 season. In one cinema in a remote part of the city, it was re-titled as *Killing'in İntikamı* (The Revenge of Killing) for some unknown reason.

Both of Atadeniz's first two Killing movies were believed to be lost for more than 30 years. Encouraged by the revival of interest in his works following the publication of Pete Tombs' *Mondo Macabro* (1997), which covered Turkish bygone cine-fantastique along with similar fare from other parts of the globe, Atadeniz set out to locate prints of his films and found 16mm prints held in the collection of Cengiz Asena, a former film distributor in Ankara. While the *Kilink İstanbulda* print was in rough but presentable shape, the *Kilink Uçan Adama Karşı* print was incomplete. Thus, only *Kilink İstanbulda* was released on DVD format in Turkey in 2001. Later that year, the movie was also showcased at the Ankara Film Festival as part of a retrospective on

Turkish cine-fantastique, curated by the author of this article. Eventually, both *Kilink Istanbulda* and the available footage from *Kilink Uçan Adama Karşı* would be released on DVD in Greece. When *Kilink İstanbulda* was shown at the Istanbul Film Festival in 2014, the available material from *Kilink Uçan Adama Karşı* was also screened unannounced, leaving many spectators, who were uninformed about the movies' troubled history, puzzled.

Kilink İstanbulda, the spelling of the title character revised to avoid copyright infringement issues, is an odd movie because it brings together two very different popular fiction schools: the *noir* antihero school of largely European heritage and the mainstream superhero school of American heritage. The movie kicks off with Killing arriving in Istanbul, disguised as a mummified corpse lying in a casket and revived by a syringe administered by his lover, to get hold of a formula for a ray gun which would enable him to hold word domination. Orhan (played by İrfan Atasoy), the son of a scientist Killing murders, is visited by the apparition of an old wizard who tells him that he can transform into a super-strong Flying Man whenever he utters the magic word "Shazam." This transformation angle, complete with the keyword "Shazam," is directly lifted from the U.S. comics Captain Marvel and yet the Flying Man carries the letter "S" as logo on his suit, just like Superman does, and the Superman Sunday strips had indeed debuted in Turkey re-titled as *Uçan Adam* in 1956.

However, apart from the S logo on his suit, the Flying Man in this Killing movie doesn't really look like the Superman we know, as he wears a mask on his head! Nevertheless, this hybrid superhero falls on the trail of Killing to avenge his father. The single act of flying he performs consists of a few seconds of a horizontal medium-shot of his body poorly superimposed over a shot of a few clouds. More often, he goes around smacking and kicking the baddies in the traditional way.

The highlights of *Kilink İstanbulda* are the torture scenes in the cellar in Killing's hideout. There, Orhan's fiancée is initially tied onto a spinning rack that stretches her body. Subsequently, when her father and Orhan are also captured, she is flogged in their presence (pointedly, the censors had no objection to these scenes, presumably because the damsel-in-distress is fully clothed during the course of the torture sessions). In these cellar settings, *Kilink İstanbulda* does indeed approach the mood and the ambiance of the original Killing photonovels that abound in similar setups that, undoubtedly, were the real attraction of the series in addition to the grim figure of Killing himself. Whenever Orhan transforms into the Flying Man, *Kilink İstanbulda* transforms its mood and ambiance to that of vintage American serials. The almost equal weight Orhan/the Flying Man brings to the narrative with respect to that of Killing and, more significantly, the fact that the Flying Man is invincible, forces Killing's status to

A lobby card for *Kilink Istanbulda*

Dişi Kilink (Female Kilink), starring Gülgün Erdem, provided a spicy variation on the series by making Killing a woman.

be cut down from an antihero to that of a villain, and yet Killing is, unavoidably, such a grandiose dark character to fit into the pigeonhole of a mere villain and is undoubtedly the star attraction of the movie.

Kilink İstanbulda boasts a solid supporting cast. Muzaffer Tema (he was in Hollywood's *12 to the Moon* from 1960, credited as "Tema Bey") plays the professor, father of Orhan's fiancée and Hüseyin Peyda plays the police chief; both were seasoned veteran actors and, Suzan Avcı, who plays Killing's lover, was one of Turkish mainstream cinema's most sought after actresses for femme-fatale roles. However, one cast member who really shines in the movie, and especially outshines Avcı who doesn't have much to do, is Mine Soley. She plays the professor's assistant who falls for Killing's advances and is recruited to his side. Interestingly, her scantily clad pose in front of a mirror was ordered cut by the censors and yet such a scene is present in the currently available print of *Kilink İstanbulda* which, on the other hand, is indeed missing the murder of a policeman (hinted in a vague line by the police chief that one of his officers is missing and that Killing may be involved in his disappearance), similarly ordered cut by the censors.

Once her character is on Killing's team, Soley begins to play her role with astonishing relish, even her body language displaying, perhaps betraying, a delicious satisfaction in her new position.

Kilink İstanbulda ends with Killing and his entourage arriving at an island where he would experiment with the ray gun and lock up his captives at a dungeon-like cave archetypically decorated with chains hanging from the ceiling and torches protruding from the walls. *Kilink Uçan Adama Karşı* starts with a lengthy summary of the previous movie and then continues from where that one ended, rounding up that plot with a confrontation between the Flying Man and Killing, who manages to evade capture even though his plans for world domination have been demolished. Then, a new plot kicks off with Killing hatching a more modest plan in stealing the jewels of a visiting princess. That's where the currently available footage of *Kilink Uçan Adama Karşı* unfortunately ends. A few surviving stills depict a final confrontation between the Flying Man and Killing atop a tower. The censorship documents also reveal that there were brutal scenes in which Killing stuck a needle as well as a cigarette into the breasts of the princess and another girl, which were ordered cut together with a bath scene that still exists.

Atadeniz immediately followed these two Killing movies with a third one, *Kilink Soy ve Öldür* (Kilink Strip and Kill), which judging by the dates on censorship records, was pulled together in less than two months after the previous ones. *Kilink Soy ve Öldür* is markedly different from the earlier movies in more than one aspect. There is no superhero protagonist here and the main plot revolving around a microfilm of militarily strategic value has been adapted directly from an original *Killing* photonovel story, with elements from a few other original *Killing* stories integrated. However, violence is somewhat toned down. More significantly, the movie's finale is full of lines uttered by both Killing and his lover stating their love for the Turkish nation in general and especially acknowledging the talents of the Turkish police in particular! Atadeniz had apparently learned his lesson about the censors' soft spot and was either kissing-ass and/or subtly parodying their wishes ... The censors could spot only a few mild displays of female flesh to order cut—and yet, the military representative in the commission still voted for an outright ban as the dissenting opinion. Unlike Atadeniz' previous Killing movies, *Kilink Soy ve Öldür* was aired on a private TV channel in the 1990s and the available print is uncut.

It did not take long for other Turkish low-budget filmmakers to jump onto the Killing bandwagon. Çetin İnanç, Atadeniz's assistant in his first two Killing movies, shot *Kilink Caniler Kralı* (Kilink the King of the Murderers) for an obscure production company roughly at the same time Atadeniz was shooting *Kilink Soy ve Öldür*. Prolific producer-

The Italian comic *Zagor*, published in 1961, was very popular in Turkey, providing inspiration for no less than three films, all made in 1971.

director Aram Gülyüz, better known for his low-brow comedy films, introduced the novelty of a female Kilink in *Dişi Kilink* (Female Kilink), starring the 16-year-old Gülgün Erdem who, according to a published synopsis, plays a young woman bent on revenge after her face is disfigured by her husband who caught her cheating on him. *Dişi Kilink* escaped the wrath of the censors only narrowly in a 3-2 vote in which the movie was passed at the expense of suffering cuts involving a murder scene and another one where a severed head was seen inside a package. Neither *Kilink Caniler Kralı* nor *Dişi Kilink* have been available to the public in any format since their brief theatrical runs in Istanbul in the summer of 1968, even though a self-professed lost film hound claimed on Facebook in 2012 that he had found copies of both films. A more obscure title is *Kiling Sarışın Tehlike* (Kiling the Blonde Danger), which was banned outright unanimously by the censors in 1968 on the grounds that it was "full of obscene scenes from the beginning to the end." However, there are theatrical listings for this title in newspapers, so it may have been re-submitted at some point. Probably the most intriguing title among the Killing movies is producer-director Nuri Akıncı's *Kilink Frankeştayn ve Dr. No'ya Karşı* (Kilink vs Frankeştayn and Dr. No). After passing the censors at the expense of losing some murder footage, the film opened in Beyoğlu's central Lüks cinema, where *Kilink İstanbulda* had also played, on May 6, 1968 and is unfortunately now among the unavailable Killing movies. [Even though an online site since 2011 lists it, as well as *Kilink Caniler Kralı*, among its offerings, its owners do not really process orders and hence the listing appears to be a phony.]

Apart from Atadeniz's movies, the only two currently available Killing-related Turkish films are *Cango Korkusuz Adam* (Django the Fearless Man; produced in 1967, released in 1968) and *Sihirbazlar Kralı Mandrake Killing'in Peşinde* (Mandrake the King of the Magicians On the Trail of Killing; 1968), both pitting the photonovel antihero against heroes originating from different media. *Cango Korkusuz Adam* is one of the many Turkish Western films made from 1967 onward to ride on the popularity of Italian Spaghetti Westerns. Cango is the Turkish spelling of Django, the hero of several popular Spaghetti Westerns starting with the seminal *Django* (1966, Sergio Corbucci). Both the original *Django* and one of its in-name-only sequels had been released in Turkey in 1967. *Cango Korkusuz Adam* is an interesting and watchable Turkish Western that starts with a modestly spooky opening. Against a background of whirling wind sound effects mixed with wolves howling in the distance, a wealthy landowner announces to his guests at a late night gathering in his candle-lit mansion that he had discovered a new gold mine. After the guests leave, the mansion is raided by a gang of gunslingers led by a figure dressed in a skeleton costume and wearing a skull mask who kills the landowner. Cango (played by Tunç Oral), a relative of the murdered landowner, soon arrives in town to set the wrongs right. The gang's leader is never named as Killing, but he is referred to as "Ölüm Süvarisi" (the Death Rider). While long sections of the movie slide heavily into comedy via the antics of Cango's sidekick, there are several gruesome scenes as well, especially one where the Death Rider orders the hand of one of his henchmen to be cut off and then fed to his dog!

Cango Korkusuz Adam was produced by Nevzat Pesen's Pesen Film, scripted by Eşref Ekicigil and directed by Remzi Cöntürk [Jöntürk]. Pesen Film is not a Z-grade company and had made several mainstream movies as well, including some critically acclaimed ones. Eşref Ekicigil comes from a publishing background and the publishing company he co-founded with his brother had produced several comic titles beside a cinema journal. The Ekicigil brothers had entered the film business as producers and had almost certainly invested in *Cango Korkusuz Adam* as well. Jöntürk was a versatile director of an art direction background who worked in many different genres, one of his last movies being the Conan clone *Altar* (1985). A most surprising name in the credits of *Cango Korkusuz Adam* is Şerif Gören, who did the editing. Gören would soon start a bright career in directing, eventually helming *Yol* (1981),

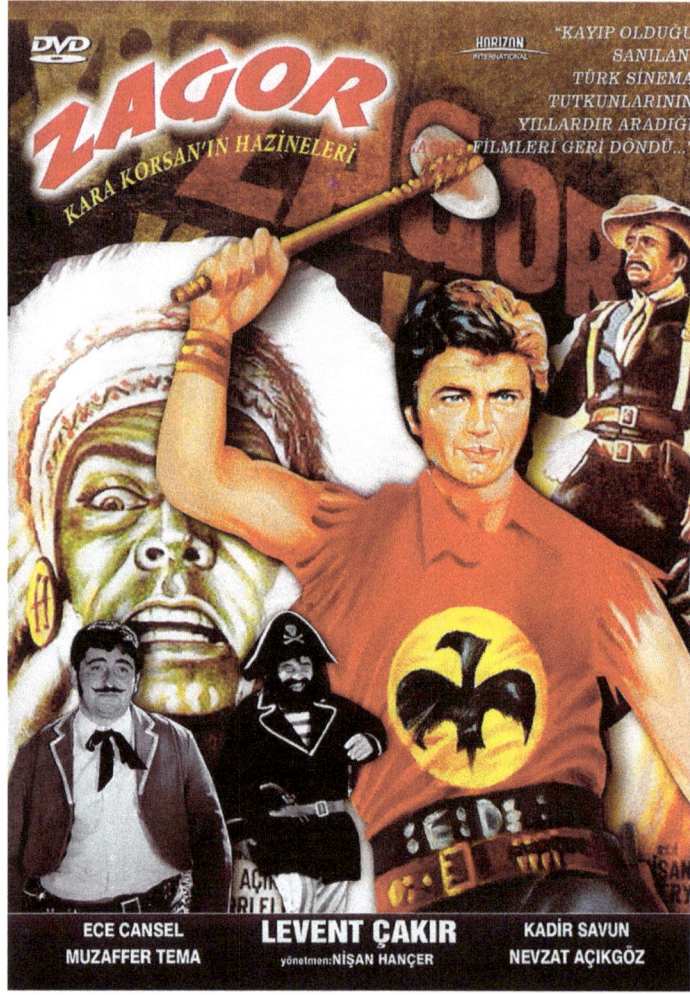

The DVD cover art for *Zagor: Kara Korsanın Hazineleri* (Zagor: The Treasures of the Black Pirate, 1971), starring Levent Çakır

Kaptan Swing was the Turkish version of another popular Italian comic, *Il Comandante Mark*.

which he directed from a script by then-imprisoned Yılmaz Güney, whose name the movie is more associated with, winning the Golden Palm award at the Cannes Film Festival. The Killing lookalike Death Rider is not featured in *Cango Korkusuz Adam*'s posters, so not many people caught up in the revival of interest in Killing movies in the late 1990s were aware of that fact then. When it was aired on a Turkish public TV channel in 2011, most Killing fans were caught by surprise.

Sihirbazlar Kralı Mandrake Killing'in Peşinde is apparently the last entry in the initial tidal wave of Killing movies produced in Turkey. While a Turkish film dictionary published by the Turkish filmmakers' union list it among movies made in 1967, the censors screened it well into 1968, on Aug. 28, so the movie must have been completed in 1968, but might have been announced in 1967 as a scheduled upcoming production. A short-lived *Sihirbazlar Kralı Mandrake* comics weekly published in Turkey early in 1968 might have been an impetus to have Killing face comic heroes of American origin and, if that was indeed the case, the 1967 date would be a mistake altogether. The movie was passed by the censors in a narrow 3-2 vote on the condition that two love-making scenes and one whipping scene would be cut, with representatives of the military and the education ministry voting for an outright ban. No listings for any theatrical release of *Sihirbazlar Kralı Mandrake Killing'in Peşinde* in Istanbul has so far turned out in research in newspaper archives, but it was at least released in the southeastern city of Adana in 1969. The movie itself was shot in the western coastal city of İzmir, rather than in İstanbul, a rarity for Turkish cinema.

Kemal Hakbilir produced this Killing movie with Mandrake the Magician; he was a little-known producer working for the obscure Mutlu Film, whose onscreen logo features an illustration of Lothar, Mandrake's sidekick. Oksal Pekmezoğlu, an illustrator by training who had picked up a career as a movie director after entering the Turkish film industry initially as a credits sequence artist, scripted and directed. Pekmezoğlu's prolific filmography encompasses titles from a wide variety of genres, but he is best known as one of the pioneers of the erotic comedies

The DVD sleeve for the Turkish Captain Swing movie, *Kaptan Swing: Korkusuz Kaptan* (Captain Swing: The Fearless Captain)

boom of the mid-1970s. Şerif Gören from *Cango Korkusuz Adam* is on the crew once again as the editor.

Killing in this outing runs a prostitution ring where customers are secretly filmed with hidden 8mm cameras, so that they can be blackmailed afterwards. Such lowly criminal activity on the part of Killing contrasts sharply with the larger-than-life persona of Killing of the photo-novels (and Atadeniz' Killing movies) where Killing was more of an amoral character than a mobster, wearing a gruesome costume and a mask. Actually the Killing of this Mandrake movie rarely wears his skull mask; he is either in normal clothes or in his skeleton costume without bothering to put on the skull mask. Such a visual presentation undercuts Killing as a faceless presence whose face, the conventional locus of identity, has given way to the archetypical image of the grinning skull. And yet, this Killing is not an ordinary mobster either, even without a costume. Scars on his back are revealed to be the result of flogging sessions in bed, a sample of which is very briefly onscreen, where he willingly submits to be flogged at the hands of one of his women. In one scene where Killing shows signs of undergoing an inner conflict on having someone tortured or killed, there is perhaps an attempt to portray him as an emotionally tortured soul as well, but if this was the intention of the filmmakers, it is not really driven home sufficiently because of either inept filmmaking or the incompleteness of the available print. Neither the causes nor origin of Killing's masochism nor any of its implications are developed to any degree.

Killing is not the only person at the receiving end of the whip in the movie, as a chained damsel-in-distress, probably a discontent prostitute, is violently flogged in a dingy-looking basement. In the absence of any costumed character, the damsel-in-distress scenes in the cellar have the look of early "roughie" films and have a certain nightmarish quality in their utter bleakness as distinct from the more marvelous nightmares. Later in the movie, Mandrake and Abdullah (the name of Lothar in the Turkish editions of Mandrake comics and consequently in this movie) are also chained in the same basement and flogged violently as well. In these scenes of Mandrake and Abdullah first raiding the cellar, fighting their way with Killing's henchmen only to be overpowered and flogged, quite a few of the on-screen male characters are shirtless with bared bodies from the waist up—hence these scenes are somewhat endowed with a faint gay radiance.

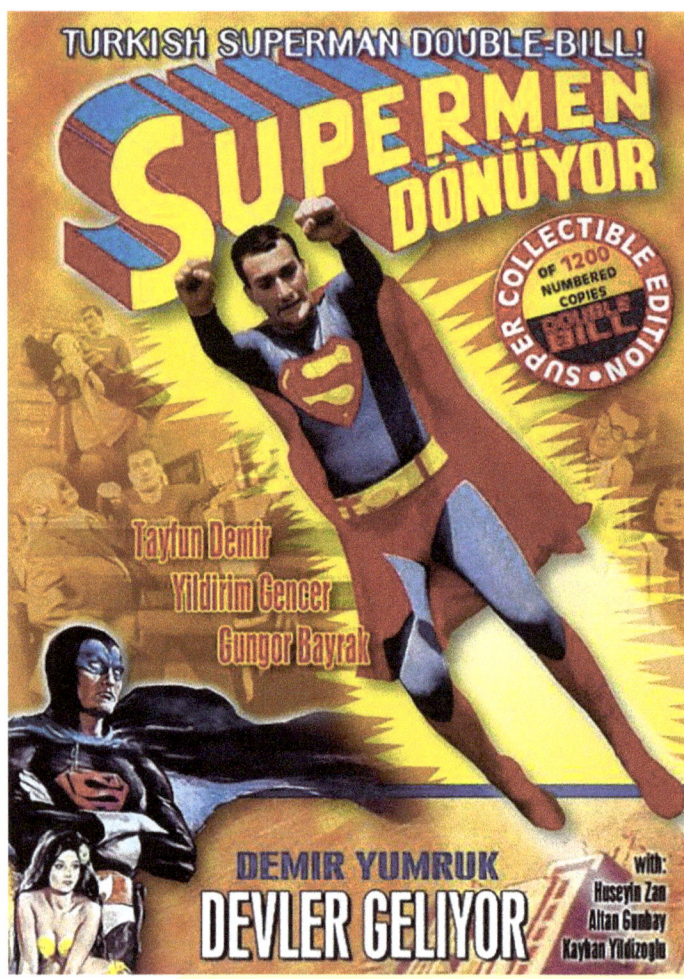

The DVD release of a Turkish Superman double bill: *Süpermen Dönüyor* (1979, Kunt Tulgar) and *Demir Yumruk: Dvler Geliyor* (1970, Tunç Basaran)

Mandrake (played by Güven Erte, a little-known actor whose only major role was in this movie) enters the plot after Killing steals the crown of a visiting Indian princess (played by Mine Mutlu, in one of her earliest roles, who would later become one of the starlets of Turkish erotic comedies). *Sihirbazlar Kralı Mandrake Killing'in Peşinde* is an odd movie not only because it brings together an Italian photonovel antihero and an American comics hero, but also because it is a hybrid of rather quite different cinematic narrative styles, veering even close to musical territory at one point when the initially platonic love-at-first-sight between Mandrake and the princess blossoms to intense intimacy. This blossoming is presented with dialogue-free cuddling and dancing at a seashore and a horse carriage ride around the city, all accompanied with an Indian song on the soundtrack! It should also be noted that the transition to the seashore scene is carried out in a quite deft move, as a shot of Mandrake and the princess sitting and chatting at a bar ends with a close-up of their cigarettes placed in a tray with their smoking tips facing each other at close proximity dissolves into a shot of Mandrake and the princess embracing each other.

Actor Saadettin Düzgün plays Mandrake's African sidekick Abdullah in blackface; that is, with his face and body literally painted in black. Blackface make-up for white actors portraying black characters had been predominantly used in American cinema (and theater) until the 1930s, due to insensitivity or racial discrimination when white actors sometimes played African-American roles. On the other hand, the reason for the low-budget *Sihirbazlar Kralı Mandrake Killing'in Peşinde*'s filmmakers to resort to blackface is probably the unavailability of any black actor at their disposal suitable to play the well-built Abdullah character, since Turkey doesn't have many black citizens. The portrayal of Abdullah is nevertheless quite stereotypical going beyond the blackface in keeping with his portrayal in vintage Mandrake comics (Lothar's rise to the status as Mandrake's dignified partner was a later evolution in the comic series).

Sihirbazlar Kralı Mandrake Killing'in Peşinde had never been aired on TV or released in VHS, but a 16mm print was rumored to be present in a private collection. Finally in 2009, veteran Z-grade filmmaker Kunt Tulgar, working as a middle-man for Onar Films, a Greece-based fan-driven venture which released a number of Turkish films on DVD, including Atadeniz's Killing movies, leased this print and had it transferred to a Betacam master which he delivered to Onar Films. However, fate decreed that the owner of Onar fell critically ill soon after receiving it and couldn't release any more DVDs. Nevertheless, a fan-subtitled copy appeared for those *who know where to look* circa 2011.

The movie's original running time is noted as 75 minutes in the censorship documents when it was viewed in 1968. The fan-subtitled copy's duration is only 56 minutes but a 61-minute master also exists, the difference between the two amount to one segment during which Killing's head henchman fatally stabs a woman in the back and wipes the blood from the blade of his knife, followed by the introduction of Mandrake and Lothar to the movie. Both copies include a scene where a woman is whipped, which fits the description of a scene ordered by the censors to be cut, and yet both versions are curiously missing the two sex scenes that were also ordered cut. Despite these deficiencies in its currently seen state, *Sihirbazlar Kralı Mandrake Killing'in Peşinde* still remains a captivating oddity and one can only wonder about its complete version.

It would take more than three years for a new Killing movie to be made in Turkey. In the meantime, Simavis' *Killing* biweekly had also ended its run in 1968 after a total of 19 issues, and another publisher, Ceylan Yayınları, would launch a new *Killing* biweekly in 1970. Finally, *Kiling Ölüm Saçıyor* (Kiling Spreads Death), starring Gülgün Erdem, appeared in the Rüya cinema located in Beyoğlu's main boulevard as part of a double bill with a Turkish comics adaptation, *Tarkan Viking Kanı* (1971; U.S. DVD title: *Tarkan vs the Vikings*) in 1972. *Kiling Ölüm Saçıyor* is notable as the only Killing movie helmed by a female director, Birsen Kaya. It was actually made in 1971, but initially banned by the censors for lack of police activity in its plot and subsequently passed only when resubmitted with new scenes featuring such activity! The final Turkish Killing movie to hit the screens[2] appeared as a martial arts effort, attempting to ride along the popularity of Chang Cheh's *One-Armed Swordsman* (1967) and its sequels. The movie was *Killing Kolsuz Kahramana Karşı* (Killing vs the Armless Hero, 1974). Sadly, both of these Killing movies from the 1970s are considered lost now.

Killing would not remain the sole Italian popular cultural item to be appropriated by Turkish low-budget filmmakers. From mid-1950s onwards, Italian comics have been enjoying a huge popularity in Turkey and had come to dominate the Turkish comics market much more so than their American counterparts (nevertheless, few, if any, of the Turkish readers were aware that these comics they cherished, all of which featured American heroes, were of Italian origin). The boom in comics publications in Turkey owes much to the success of *Tom Miks*, the Turkish edition of *Capitan Miki*, and *Teksas*, which featured Çelik Bilek, the Turkish edition of *Il Grande Blek*, both Western comics created by the Italian team collectively known as EsseGesse, published by Turkey's Ceylan Yayınları, the former from 1955 onwards and the latter from the next year onward, until 1987. For a generation whose childhood passed in the 1950s, the Turkish word for comics became synonymous with "Teksas-Tommiks," which came to be used as a catchword to refer to comics in general and not only to these two titles.

After the Killing movies, Yılmaz Atadeniz gave his assistant Çetin İnanç the chance to sit at the director's chair and commissioned him to make a film featuring Çelik Bilek. The resulting movie, however, apparently owes nothing to *Il Grande Blek*, which is set during the American War of Independence, other than the main protagonist's name being Çelik Bilek. Now considered lost, İnanç's *Çelik Bilek*, shot in 1967 and released in 1968, is referred to as a Western about a love affair between a gunfighter and the daughter of a landowner who doesn't approve of this relationship. Devising his plot around a popular theme in Turkish village drama films, placing it in a Western setting at a time when Spaghetti Westerns were popular, and naming it after a well-known comics hero, İnanç seems to have aimed to get the best of all worlds. His next go at another movie purportedly based on a comic *Kızıl Maske* (Red Mask, shot in 1968, released in 1969), again produced by Atadeniz, would also bear little resemblance to its source material, this time the American strip *The Phantom*. In 1971, İnanç also directed a movie titled *Kinova* and followed it the next year with two sequels, but, judging by their posters, these

Kinowa, yet another Italian comic which found a Turkish release as *Kinova*

now-lost movies had no connection with the Italian comics from which they took their title, as *Kinova* the comic (titled *Kinowa* in Italy) was in the Western genre while İnanç's films featured a masked hero in a modern-day setting. Despite these blemishes in his early career, İnanç has become a cult director today, largely on the basis of the re-discovery of his amazing *Dünyayı Kurtaran Adam* (The Man Who Saves the World, 1982), the so-called "Turkish Star Wars," in the 1990s by a new generation of astonished genre movie fans so eager to find a "Turkish Ed Wood."

Tommiks (the title spelled as a single-word from 1960s onwards), Ceylan Yayınları's other flagship comic series besides *Teksas*, would inevitably also attract the attention of Turkish low-budget filmmakers. *Maskeli Suvari Tommikse Karşı* (Lone Ranger vs Tommiks, 1969), produced, scripted and directed by Kayahan Arıkan, pits Capitan Miki (Tommiks) against the Lone Ranger (Maskeli Suvari), bringing together popular culture icons of Italy and the U.S. into a Turkish film. Altan Bozkurt plays the Lone Ranger and Capitan Miki plays Lami Ateş. Unfortunately it is a lost movie today like many others from those years, its theatrical poster indicates that Capitan Miki's two regular sidekicks from the original comics were also featured

3 Dev Adam (1973) featured Captain America and El Santo against an evil Spiderman.

in it, so the filmmakers must have paid at least some attention to their source model. In the same year, Arıkan also brought together two other popular culture icons in *Fantoma Supermen'e Karşı* (Fantoma vs Superman, 1969), pitting the French pulp fiction antihero Fantômas against Superman; Turkish filmmakers had earlier made a Fantômas movie featuring another American superhero, Batman, in *Fantoma İstanbul'da Buluşalım* (Fantomas Let's Meet in Istanbul, 1967, released in 1968). It seems the Turkish Z-grade films were a melting pot of popular culture. It should also be noted that Arıkan's jungle girl movie *Dişi Tarzan* (1972, released in 1973), starring Gülgün Erdem, was apparently inspired by the Italian *Samoa, regina della giungla* (1968, Guido Malatesta), which had been released in Turkey early in 1972 and/or *Gungala la pantera nuda* (1968, Ruggero Deodato), which had been re-released in the same year.

In 1970, Tay Yayınları, a newcomer to the Turkish comics market which immediately rose to prominence largely due to the glossy covers of its publications printed on highest quality paper and illustrated by top-notch Turkish artists, began publishing *Zagor* which became an instant hit. *Zagor* is another one of the Italian comics working within the Western genre and has become one of the most popular and enduring Italian comics of all times, still being published in Italy as well as in Turkey.

Turkish filmmakers made three Zagor movies in 1971. One of them, simply titled as *Zagor*, bears no relation to the comics besides the name of the title hero, played by the Iranian actor Cihangir Gaffari, and is a violent Western outing with a revenge plot. It was scripted and directed by Mehmet Arslan, who would soon rise to distinction in Turkish cinema with the Tarkan films based on a Turkish comics. Gaffari, who starred in many Turkish Westerns in the early 1970s, would later move to Western Europe and appear in Jess Franco's *Les Démons* (1972) under the pseudonym John Foster.

The other two Turkish Zagor movies are fortunately quite faithful to the comics: *Zagor—Kara Korsanın Hazineleri* (Zagor—The Treasures of the Black Pirate, 1971) and *Zagor—Kara Bela* (Zagor—The Black Trouble, 1971, released in 1973) star Levent Çakır as the title hero in his first starring roles. Çakır was an acrobat by training who had appeared in several Turkish action movies in supporting roles until these Zagor movies came about. His acrobatic talents were perfectly suitable for the multitude of fast-paced action scenes that are in tune with the fact that Zagor of the comics outwits his foes with his outstanding agility in fight and chase sequences. Nevzat Açıkgöz and Nuri Kırgeç, respectively, aptly play Zagor's two comical sidekicks from the comics, Çiko (Cico in Italian) and Kazmakürek Bill (Digging Bill). Kırgeç's Çiko especially shows an almost unbelievable likeness to Çiko in print. Beyond the contribution of appropriate castings, as well as decent costume and make-up, an equally significant factor in the success of these two movies as proper Zagor movies is the surprising fact that their scripts are indeed adaptations of specific Zagor comics stories.

Zagor—Kara Korsanın Hazineleri was adapted from the story *Le jene del mare* (#24, June 1967), where Zagor and Cico meet Digging Bill for the first time. The plot concerns the efforts of Zagor to bring Kazmakürek Bill, a treasure hunter, to court as a witness to clear the name of an innocent officer wrongly accused of murder. While *Zagor—Kara Korsanın Hazineleri* is of interest mainly to Zagor fans, *Zagor—Kara Bela* is arguably the better of the two Turkish Zagor movies starring Çakır. Adapted from the Zagor comics story *L'avvoltoio* (#22, April 1967), with elements from the "Satko" story interwoven into it, its plot revolves around a mysterious robber who terrorizes the natives with rape and murder. The chilling figure of the villain clad completely in black from head to toe is worthy of striking a chord with any fan of vintage *noir* pulp fiction and old serials based on or inspired from such sources. *Zagor—Kara Bela* is also noteworthy for its explicitly anti-racist stand regarding American natives. Nişan Hançeryan, who had earlier directed the obscure *Kara Atmaca* (Black Hawk, 1967), one of the first Turkish movies with a caped and masked hero, directed these two Zagor movies. After his performances in the Zagor movies, Çakır became the most sought-after actor for the masked hero genre, starring in *Süper Adam* (Super Man, 1971), *Kızıl Maske'nin İntikamı* (Revenge of the Red Mask [Turkish name for the Phantom], 1971) and *Yarasa Adam—Bedmen* (Bat Man, 1973, released in 1974), as well as several others.

Meanwhile, another Turkish publisher, Sümer Yayınevi, began to publish *Kaptan Swing*, the Turkish edition of *Il Comandante Mark*, another EsseGesse creation from Italy, in 1969. *Il Comandante Mark* is closely modeled on EsseGesse's earlier *Il Grande Blek*; it is also set during the American War of Independence, but the hero is of French origin here. Like the Zagor films starring Çakır, the Turkish Captain Swing movie, titled *Kaptan Swing—Korkusuz Kaptan* (Captain Swing—the Fearless Captain, 1971, released in 1972) is fairly faithful to its comic source. Swing's lover Betty (played by Gülgün Erdem) and his comical sidekicks, Mr. Blöf (Mr. Bluff; played by Ali Şen) and Native American Gamlı Baykuş (the Sorrowful Owl; played by Süleyman Turan) are in the movie, as well as the dog Puik. Actually, the movie opens with Swing rescuing Puik from "the Red Coats," British soldiers, who were about to use it as live target during shooting practice. After a lengthy series of comical scenes largely involving Gamlı Baykuş where Turan's somewhat campy performance may be tiresome to watch for those who do not like this strand of humor, the plot eventually hatches with Mr. Blöf being captured by the British and Swing rushing to rescue his compatriot.

Kaptan Swing—Korkusuz Kaptan is a relatively higher budget movie than all the rest of the Turkish movies based on or inspired from Italian comics, as evident in that it was shot in color while the others were in black-and-white. Furthermore, Swing is played by Salih Güney, a mainstream actor; he formerly played the Prince in the Turkish Snow White film *Pamuk Prenses ve 7 Cüceler* (1970, released in 1971), which would be released in Italy as *La Meravigliosa Favola di Biancaneve*. Critically acclaimed Turkish director

Captain America to the rescue in *3 Dev Adam*

Tunç Başaran is at the helm, but of special interest to exploitation cinema fans may be the fact that Vural Pakel penned the script and he would later collaborate with Italian exploitation producer-director Sergio Bergonzelli on two Turkish-Italian co-productions, *Şahit*, aka *La mondana nuda* (1978) and *Cümbüş Palas*, aka *Daniela Mini-Slip* (1979), as director of the Turkish footage in the former and as co-producer in the latter.

The last Turkish movie connected to Italian comics was *Şeytan Tırnağı* (Hangnail, 1972, released in 1973). The hero in this routine Western is named Tom Braks but actually has no relation with the title hero of *Tom Braks*, the Turkish edition of *Alan Mistero*, another EsseGesse creation.

Besides Killing and various Italian comics outlined above, several Italian movies with a comics-feel were also a source of inspiration, even to the point of being a model for Turkish low-budget filmmakers. Actually, the pseudo-superhero craze in Turkey in the late 1960s and early

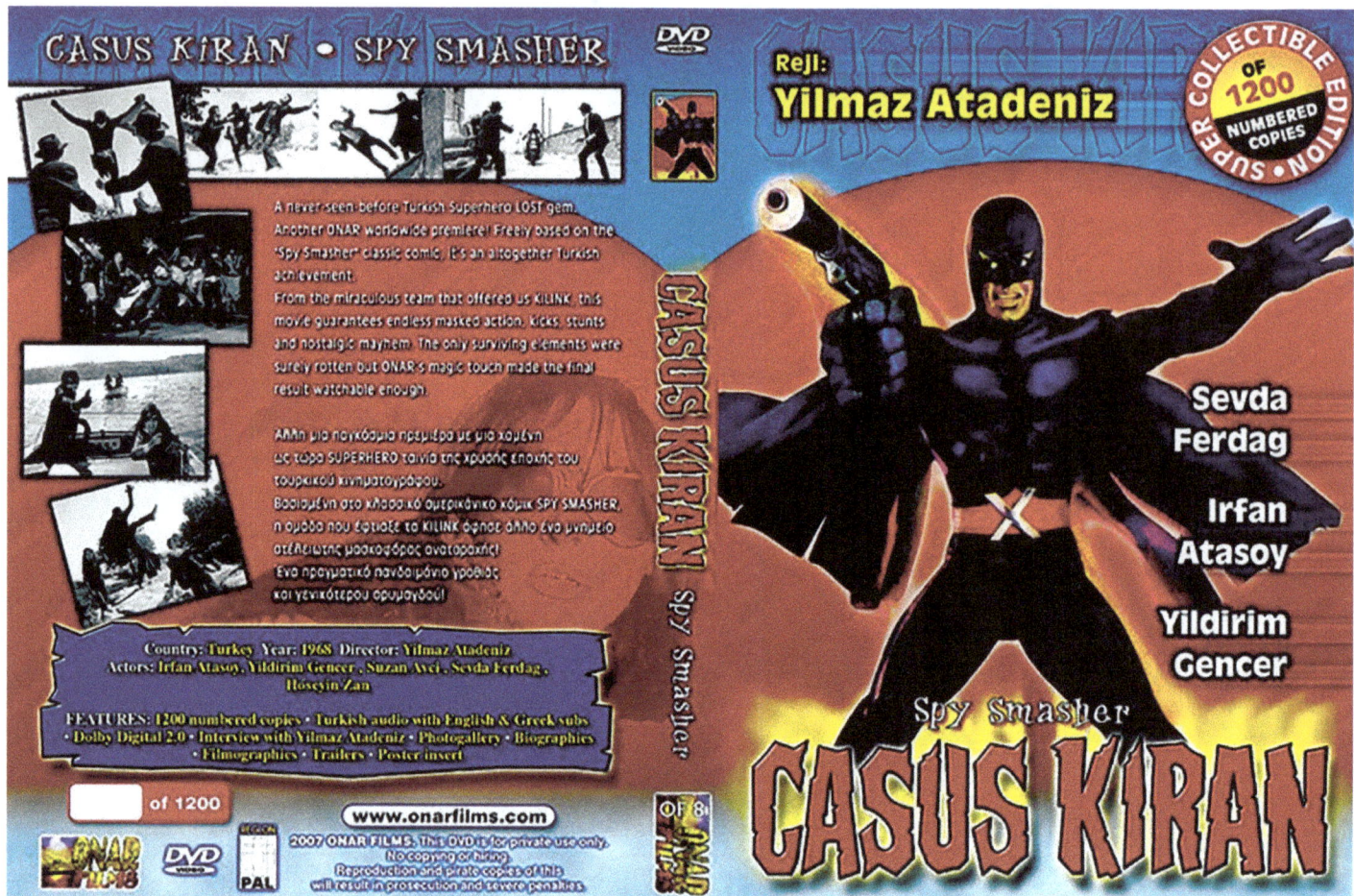

DVD cover art for Yılmaz Atadeniz' masked superhero film *Casus Kiran* (1968). Note the similarities with the poster art for *Avenger X*.

1970s owes a lot to the very similar and almost simultaneous craze in Italian cinema. Even when Turkish movies featured masked and costumed heroes of specifically American origin, chiefly Superman, they were molded very much in tune with the Italian films of the late 1960s, with masked and costumed heroes rather than adaptations of the American comics. Of course, this does not mean that the Italian films were the sole inspiration; for instance, the link between the release of the French Fantômas films in Turkey in 1966 and the production of *Fantoma İstanbul'da Buluşalım* in 1967 is self-evident and does not need elaboration, and certain directors' (chiefly Yılmaz Atadeniz's) nostalgia for old American serials which stem from fond childhood memories rekindled by their sporadic re-releases should also be taken into account. But Italian films seem to have been the determinant factor after 1968.

One crucial event appears to be the success enjoyed by *Superargo vs Diabolicus* (*Superargo contro Diabolikus*, 1966) in Turkey. It was released as *Hayaletin Tuzağı* (The Trap of The Ghost) on March 4, 1968 in the Yeni Ar cinema located in the Beyoğlu district and unexpectedly played for two consecutive weeks there. In those years, it was rather unusual for a foreign movie with no major stars from Hollywood to play for consecutive weeks in any Istanbul cinema, let alone a major one located in downtown Istanbul. *Hayaletin Tuzağı* was followed by *Şimşek Adam* (*Flashman*, 1967) two months later and *Argoman* (1967) and *Superman Geliyor* (*L'invincibile Superman*, 1968) in the 1968-69 season, all of which opened in Beyoğlu cinemas.

It was the popularity of these movies with Turkish audiences which provided the impetus for Turkish low-budget filmmakers to churn out a succession of masked and costumed hero flicks after the craze for Killing had been quickly depleted by the over-production of a large number of Killing movies within a very short span. The secret behind the dissimilarity of Turkish-made Superman or Phantom or other movies with their sources in American comics is their similarity to their Italian role models! In addition, Turkish low-budget filmmakers also made several masked and costumed hero flicks without giving lip service to American comics, apparently taking their cues in designing their heroes exclusively from similar Italian movies in general. Yet, the bizarre melting pot attitude often pops up; for instance Atadeniz' *Maskeli Şeytan* (The Masked Devil, 1970, released in 1971) features a comical side-kick who calls himself Red Kit, the Turkish name for the Belgian comics hero Lucky Luke. (It should be noted that Lucky Luke was popular enough in Turkey to give rise to two Red Kit movies as well.)

Another indication of the strong influence of Italian masked and costumed hero movies on Turkish low-budget filmmakers is that soon after *I fantastici 3 supermen* (1967) was released in Turkey in 1970 as *Üç Süpermen*, Turkish made movies featuring trios of masked and costumed heroes sprang up, beginning with Atadeniz's *Belanın Kralı* (King of Trouble, 1971), which admittedly was a non-conventional take on the trio concept as two members of the trio, headed by a male figure, were female. Judging by its poster, *Maskeli Üçler* (The Masked Three, 1971, released in 1972) may have also included a female member in its trio. The title of *3 Dev Adam* (3 Giant Men, 1973) also reflects a tendency to appear to appeal to the trio enthusiasm, even though in actuality the movie features a duo, an odd one at that—Captain America teaming up with Santo, the masked Mexican wrestler, fighting an evil Spider-Man as the villain!

The most direct appropriation of the Italians' 3 Supermen concept is *Çılgın Kız ve 3 Süper Adam* (The Crazy Girl and 3 Super Men, 1973). Made at a time when the craze for the masked and costumed hero flick was nearing its end, *Çılgın Kız ve 3 Süper Adam* is one of the crowning achievements of the Turkish Z-grade cinema in deliriousness. It stands apart from most of the rest of the Turkish low-budget masked and costumed hero movies for its abundance of pulp imagery, including some that appeal to certain guilty pleasures.

The opening of the movie showcases most of the goods the movie would deliver. During the opening credits, several people wearing green hoods and cloaks go down the stairs of an underground cavern (almost certainly an authentic Byzantine site) amid similarly-dressed partners-in-crime lined up along the way holding torches. A scantily-clad platinum blonde wearing cat's-eye spectacles, a cape and black boots is watching their arrival via a TV monitor together with a largely off-camera person who refers to her as Aphrodite. Then a meeting is held at the underground lair, presided over by a guy dressed in a red cloak and wearing a rubber devil's mask complete with horns, and the scantily clad lady acts as his second-in-command, referring to him as the Great Satan. The guys in green hoods and cloaks, who are referred to as X1 and the like by Aphrodite, report on their activities. When one member reports a failure of his mission, a tin-robot is summoned and the unfortunate guy is punished by being evaporated as the robot fires its ray gun.

The Great Satan explains that the ray gun is powered only to shoot three times, so they need to get possession of a certain ray material which powers the gun; once they have sufficient ray material, no one will be able to stand in their way of world domination. This premise is the one that drives the plot of the movie. The three supermen, led by Levent (yes, the main protagonist played by Levent Çakır is named Levent), and one of whom is mute (in line with one of the Italian three supermen being mute), go after this secret organization, engaging groups of green hooded and cloaked henchmen in several fast-paced chases and fights, including one lengthy sequence over rooftops. Somewhere along the way, Levent gets hooked up with a young woman named Emel (played by Emel Özden), "the crazy girl" in the title, who lives with her uncle and her private tutor. Emel is eventually (inevitably?) captured by the secret organization and brought to their lair and tied up naked on a rack while a masked ball complete with topless women is thrown elsewhere by the organization to celebrate the arrival of a large quantity of ray material from abroad. Will the supermen be able to rescue Emel and at the same time thwart the organization's deadly plans before it is too late? And discover the real identities of the Great Satan and Aphrodite?

As noted above, the magic of *Çılgın Kız ve 3 Süper Adam* lies not only in its showcasing of pulp imagery, but also in the fact they are also upgraded by somewhat unexpectedly more adult imagery. Initially, the pulp sensibility of the hooded, cloaked villains and the tin-robot with the ray gun, added to the slightly kinky outfit of Aphrodite—there is nothing surprising about the co-existence of pulp and kinky imagery as kink can also be seen as part of pulp. Then, topless nudity raises the stakes; however, the first instance of topless nudity, presented via an act with Levent acting as Peeping Tom, is not harmonious with the mood of the movie, as it is presented within a very mundane, banal framework. And yet, toward the finale, the nude bondage scene in the underground lair in the presence of Aphrodite, with Emel's nipples and crotch area carefully covered by ropes, explores the territory where pulp evolves into more unsavory imagery—and yet still stays clear of pornography or hardcore violence.

The poster of *Çılgın Kız ve 3 Süper Adam* carries the obscure "Emel Film" credit and the same credit also appears in the poster of *Yarasa Adam—Bedmen* from the same year, which also co-stars Emel Özden and indicates that this actress might have been involved in these two movies in a capacity beyond co-starring in them. *Çılgın Kız ve 3 Süper Adam* was produced by Müfit İlkiz, scripted by Volkan Kayhan and directed by Cavit Yürüklü. Exactly the same producer-writer-director trio had also made *Kızıl Maske'nin İntikamı* (The Revenge of The Red Mask [the Phantom], 1971) and *Süper Adam Kadınlar Arasında* (Super Man Among Women, 1972), which are most unfortunately lost movies today. *Çılgın Kız ve 3 Süper Adam* played for three weeks in three cinemas (one week in each) in the "old city" region of Istanbul in the 1973-74 season and was re-released

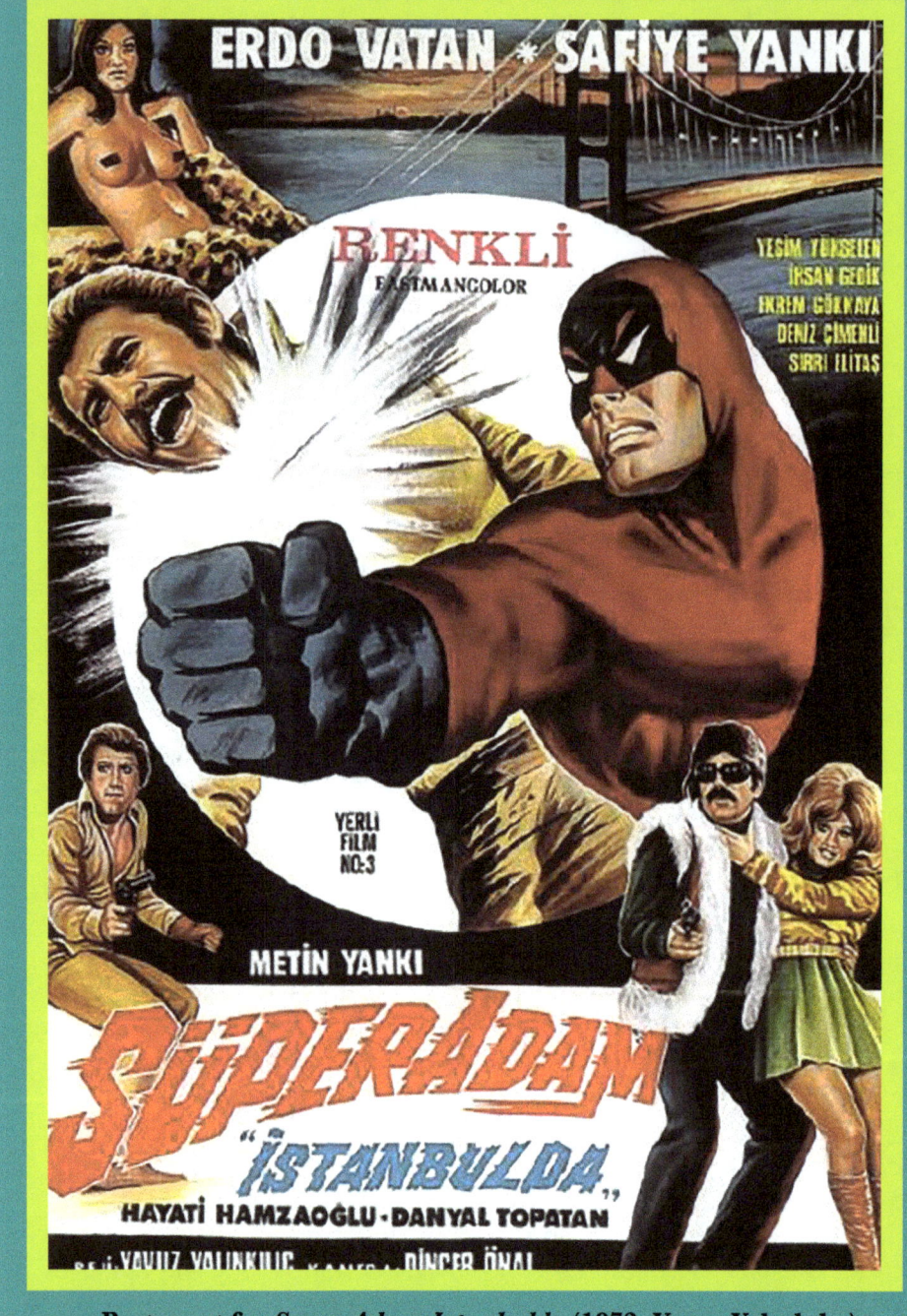

Poster art for *Super Adam Istanbulda* (1972, Yavuz Yalınkılıç)

there again in the summer of 1974. We owe the film's current availability to the fact that it was made available on home video in Turkey in 1983. Approximately 13 minutes of its footage would also be incorporated into *Üç Süpermen Olimpiyatlarda* (aka *Three Supermen at the Olympic Games*), and the brightness of the colors in the footage preserved in that patch-up movie is testament to how *Çılgın Kız ve 3 Süper Adam* originally looked marvelous in contrast to its own surviving worn-out dupe VHS tape with bleached colors.

Çılgın Kız ve 3 Süper Adam is one of the last entries in the Turkish low-budget cinema's output of costumed and masked hero films of the late 1970s and the early 1980s. While eroticism had been an ingredient in most of these movies with varying—and increasing—doses. The mid-1970s would see the proliferation of outright erotic comedies in Turkish cinema as costumed and masked hero films would largely disappear from Turkish screens. Once again, the huge popularity enjoyed by erotic comedy films arriving from Italy had provided the impetus for Turkish filmmakers to make their own products modeled on these commercially successful imports, but that's another story to tell at some other time.

Notes:

1. The censorship documents referred to in this article were kindly made available to the author by Dilek Kaya.

2. Decades after Killing had disappeared from Turkish screens, a little-known director named Esat Şekeroğlu, obviously inspired and encouraged by the revival of interest in vintage Killing movies, made *Bay Kilink* (2008, Mr. Kilink), which apparently remained commercially unreleased in any medium; it was eventually uploaded in entirety to YouTube and betrays an ignorance on what made Killing so special, as it is devoid of any sadistic element. In 2010, it was reported in the Turkish press that Şekeroğlu had began shooting a Killing movie titled *Kayıp Elmaslar* (Lost Diamonds). Since then, he frequently posts publicity material for several Killing titles on social media but yet no new Killing movie has been made available to this date.

Kaya Özkaracalar was born in 1968 in Istanbul. He was the editor of the quarterly *Geceyarısı Sineması* (1998-2004), Turkey's first journal on cinefantastique and exploitation cinema. He has been contributing articles and reviews to the monthly *Altyazı*, Turkey's leading cinema journal, since its inception in 2001. He is the author of two books, *Gotik* (2005) and *Geceyarısı Filmleri* (2007) and the chapters on Turkish horror films in *Fear Without Frontiers* (2003) and *European Nightmares* (2012). Holding a PhD degree for Graphic Design and Arts, Özkaracalar teaches courses on genre cinema at Istanbul's Bahçeşehir University.

Essential Bibliography

Books:

Aguilar, Carlos, *Mario Bava* (Madrid: Cátedra, 2013).

Aguilar, Carlos, *Giuliano Gemma. El factor Romano* (Almería: Diputación de Almería, 2003).

Aguilar, Carlos and Haas, Anita, *John Phillip Law. Diabolik Angel* (Pontevedra/Vizcaya: Scifiworld/Quatermass, 2008).

Albertini, Bitto, *Tra un ciak e l'altro. Storielle di Bitto Albertini* (Catania: Edizioni Boemi, 1998).

Anelli, Maria Teresa, Gabbrielli, Paola, Morgavi, Marta and Piperno, Roberto, *Fotoromanzo: fascino e pregiudizio* (Milan: Savelli Editori, 1979).

Barbiani, Laura and Abruzzese, Alberto, *Pornograffiti. Trame e figure del fumetto per adulti* (Rome: Napoleone, 1980).

Castaldi, Simone, *Drawn and Dangerous: Italian comics of the 1970s and 1980s* (Jackson MS: University Press of Mississippi, 2010).

Chiavini, Roberto, Lazzeretti Andrea, Somigli, Luca and Tetro, Michele, *Il cinema dei fumetti. Dalle origini a* Superman Returns (Rome: Gremese, 2007).

Codelli, Lorenzo, ed., *Nerosubrass* (Udine: Dino Audino Editore/Centro Espressioni Cinematografiche, 1996).

Curti, Roberto, *Il mio nome è Nessuno. Lo spaghetti western secondo Tonino Valerii* (Rome: unmondoaparte, 2008).

Curti, Roberto and Pulici, Davide, *Corrado Farina* (Milan: Nocturno Libri, 2000).

D'Amato, Rocco, *DizionHard. Il porno italiano in pellicola e videocassetta dalle origini al 1990* (Rome: RD'A Editions, 2003).

Della Casa, Stefano and Viganò, Dario E., eds., *Pop Film Art* (Rome: Mibac/Centro Sperimentale di Cinematografia/Cinecittà Luce/Edizioni Sabinae, 2012).

Fenton, Harvey, Grainger, Julian and Castoldi, Gian Luca, *Cannibal Holocaust and the Savage Cinema of Ruggero Deodato* (Surrey: FAB Press, 1999).

Festi, Roberto and Scudiero, Maurizio, eds., *Cinema & Fumetto. I personaggi dei comics sul grande schermo* (Trento: esaExpomostre, 2006).

Giordano, Michele, *Moana e le altre. Vent'anni di cinema porno in Italia* (Rome: Gremese, 1997).

Giusti, Marco, *007 all'italiana* (Milan: Edizioni ISBN, 2010).

Giusti, Marco, *Vado l'ammazzo e torno: Diario critico semiserio del cinema e dell'italia di oggi* (Milan: Edizioni ISBN, 2013).

Gomarasca, Manlio, *Umberto Lenzi* (Milan: Nocturno Libri, 2001).

Howarth, Troy, *The Haunted World of Mario Bava* (Baltimore MD: Midnight Marquee Press, 2014).

Lucas, Tim, *Mario Bava. All the Colors of the Dark* (Cincinnati OH: Video Watchdog, 2007).

Mencaroni, Luca, *Avventure Noir. Volume primo* (Bari: Mencaroni editore, 2013).

Mencaroni, Luca, *Avventure Noir. Volume secondo* (Bari: Mencaroni editore, 2013).

Mencaroni, Luca, *Immaginario Sexy. Guida ragionata ai tascabili erotici. Volume primo—Le edizioni Sessantasei/Erregi* (Bari: Mencaroni editore, 2014).

Moliterno, Gino, ed., *Encyclopedia of Contemporary Italian Culture*, 2003 (London: Routledge, 2003).

Origa, Graziano, ed., *Vietato ai minori. Il fumetto erotico italiano anni '70* (Milan: Rizzoli, 2007).

Pezzotta, Alberto, *Mario Bava* (Milan: Il Castoro, (1995) 2013).

Piselli, Stefano, ed., *Cinefumetto—Bizarre Sinema Archives* (Florence: Glittering Images, 2008).

Scaringi, Carlo; *Il mito Diabolik* (Rome: Gremese, 2003).

Scognamillo, Giovanni and Demirhan, Metir, *Fantastik Türk Sinemasi* (Istanbul: Kabalci, 1999).

Tombs, Pete, *Mondo Macabro. Weird & Wonderful Cinema Around the World* (New York: St. Martin's Griffin, 1998).

Zanatta, Sara, Zaghini, Samanta and Guzzetta, Eleonora, *Le donne nel fumetto: l'altra metà dei comics italiani. Temi, autrici, personaggi al femminile* (Latina: Tunué, 2009).

Essays, interviews and magazines' special issues:

Albiero, Paolo, "Un ragazzo di Calabria a Cinecittà," *Cine 70 e dintorni* #9, 2005. (Interview with Nick Nostro)

Aramu, Daniele, "Il ragazzo dei Parioli. Intervista a Ruggero Deodato," *Nocturno* #1, Summer 1996.

Blumenstock, Peter, "Margheriti – The Wild, Wild Interview," *Video Watchdog* #28, May/June 1995.

Cozzi, Luigi, "Intervista a Mario Bava," *Horror* #13, December 1970/January 1971.

Curti, Roberto and Di Rocco, Alessio, "'Maledizione!' The True Story Behind Seth Holt's Accursed Version of *Diabolik*," *Video Watchdog* #176, 2014.

Farina, Corrado, "Cinema italiano e fumetto: piccola cavalcata al confine tra gli anni 60 e 70," *FilmCronache* #2, 2006.

Farina, Corrado, "Selene bionda meteora," *Sgt. Kirk* #23, May 1969.

Garofalo, Marcello, "Le interviste celibi: Antonio Margheriti. La tecnica e gli effetti," *Segnocinema* #85, May/June 1997.

Giorgi, Andrea, "Eating Lenzi. Umberto Lenzi interviewed," *Necronomicon* #5, 1994.

Gomarasca, Manlio, "Culthard," *Nocturno Book* #1, 1997.

Gomarasca, Manlio, "Il cinema è quello che ci fa," in Gomarasca, Manlio, ed., "Fatti di cinema. Controcorrente 3," *Nocturno Dossier* #51, October 2006. (Interview with Alberto De Martino).

Gomarasca, Manlio and Pulici, Davide, eds., "Monsieur Cannibal. Il cinema di Ruggero Deodato," *Nocturno Dossier* #73, August 2008.

Gomarasca, Manlio, "Beyond the Screen. Il cinema di Ovidio G. Assonitis," in Gomarasca, Manlio and Pulici, Davide, eds., "Controcorrente 4," *Nocturno Dossier* #82, May 2009.

Grattarola, Franco, "Il dissacratore dei generi. Intervista con Guido Zurli," *Cine 70 e dintorni* #10, 2008.

Lippi, Giuseppe, "Maschere e pugnali. Recital in tre parti," *Nocturno* #133, October 2013.

Norcini, Matteo and Ippoliti, Stefano, "Piacere, Kramer… Frank Kramer," *Cine 70 e dintorni* #6, 2004. Pulici, Davide, "Killing for Culture. Il teschio turco," *Nocturno* #133, October 2013.

Online essays and interviews:

Azzano, Enrico and Meale, Raffaele, "Intervista a Bruno Bozzetto," www.quinlan.it, April 2014.

Cassani, Alberto, "Intervista a Guido Crepax," www.inkonline.info, Spring 2000.

Curti, Roberto, "The Wild, Wild World of Diabolik & Co.: Adults-only comic books on screen in the 1960s," www.offscreen.com, September 2002.

Ercolani, Eugenio, "Semplicemente cineasta! Intervista a Alberto De Martino," www.fascinationcinema.it.

Todd, Mort, "SS-Sunda Unmasked!," www-gosadistik.com, 06/11/2008.

Index

…e così divennero i 3 Supermen del West, see *The 3 Supermen in Y…e così divennero i 3 Supermen del West*, see *The 3 Supermen in the West*
…y así la armaron los 3 superhombres en el Oeste, see *The 3 Supermen in the West*
008: Operation Exterminate 51
10 162
110 pillole, Le (comic) 31, 54
12 to the Moon 230
1931: Once Upon a Time in New York 133
2001: A Space Odyssey 85, 161
3 Avengers 79
3 colpi di Winchester per Ringo 155
3 Dev Adam 71, 167, 236, 237, 239
3 Supermen a Santo Domingo, see *Three Supermen in S. Domingo*
3 Supermen a Tokio, see *3 Supermen a Tokyo*
3 Supermen a Tokyo 81, **128-129**, 135, 144, 187, 188, 214
3 Supermen Against the Godfather 81, 145, 157, **166-168**
3 supermen alle olimpiadi, see *Three Supermen at the Olympic Games*
3 supermen contro il padrino, see *3 Supermen Against the Godfather*
3 Supermen desafío al Kung Fu, Los, see *Supermen Against the Orient*
3 supermen en la selva, Los, see *Three Supermen in the Jungle*
3 Supermen in the West, The 81, 136, 143, **144-146**, 166, 181
5 Dolls for an August Moon 83
5 For Hell 81
8 ½ 10
Abatantuono, Diego 171, 174
Açıkgöz, Nevzat 236
Adam and Eve vs. Cannibals 180
Addio a Enrico Berlinguer, L' 160
Adios Sabata 82
Adventures of Phoebe Zeit-Geist, The (comic) 19
Âge d'or, L' 106
Agliata, Aldo 212
Agnello, Giancarlo 45
Agosti, Silvano 33
Aguilar, Carlos 186
Agus, Gianni 35, 177
Airport 147
Akıncı, Nuri 231
Al Bano, see Carrisi, Albano
Albanesi, Roberto 30
Al Capone (comic) 28
Alan Ford (comic) 33, 34, 41, 53, 73, 120, 121, 125
Alberti, Annie 210

Albertini, Adalberto "Bitto" 22, 24, 69, 70, 71, 128, 129, 135, 143, 148, 187, 188, 189
Alexander Nevsky 137
Alfredson, Tomas 225
Alice nel paese delle pornomeraviglie 172
Alien 2: On Earth 199
Alien from the Deep 180
Alika (comic) 26
Aliprandi, Marcello 33, 133
Alive or Preferably Dead 184
Alışık, Sadri 227
Allain, Marcel 95, 96, 97
Allen, Corey 150
Allen, Woody 69, 126, 128, 156
Alley Cats, The 117
Almodovar, Pedro 191
Almost Human 53
Alotta, Giuseppe 169
Altar 231
Altman, Robert 153
Alton, Walter George 162, 163
Amadio, Silvio 111
Amati, Edmondo 59, 78
Amazons Against Supermen, see *Super Stooges vs. the Wonder Women, The*
Amendola, Mario 131
Amore in prima classe, Un 175
Andenna, Ettore 108
Andreasi, Felice 153, 174
Andress, Ursula 27, 28, 130
Andrews, Dana 24
Angel Dark (comic) 196
Angel for Satan, An 115, 201
Angel Heart 225
Angelo, Luigi 161
Angiolini, Sandro 130
Annaud, Jean-Jacques 160
Antar (photonovel) 209
Antel, Franz 75
Anthony, Tony 133
Antonelli, Laura 153
Antoni, Roberto "Freak" 205
Antonioni, Michelangelo 63, 87
Ape Woman, The 87
Apocalittici e integrati (book) 136
Apocalypse Now 205
Apollinaire, Guillaume 84
Appuntamento in nero 203

Arbore, Renzo 159, 160
Arce Maldonado, Andrés 207
Arden, Mary 52
Ardisson, Giorgio 22
Arena, Maurizio 34, 156
Arendt, Hannah 152
Argento, Dario 20, 30, 37, 61, 76, 142, 173, 174, 176, 184, 191, 196, 197, 199, 200
Argento, Salvatore 30
Argoman superdiabolico, see *Argoman the Fantastic Superman*
Argoman the Fantastic Superman 22, 25, 33, **57-59**, 115, 168, 222, 238
Argos alla riscossa see *Santo contra las mujeres vampiro*
Argos contro le 7 maschere di cera see *Santo contra las mujeres vampiro*
Argos il fantastico Superman, see *Santo contra los asesinos de la Mafia*
Ariani, Giorgio 174
Arias, Victor Hugo 45
Arkın, Cüneyt 54, 146, 167, 168
Arrapaho 186
Arrriva Dorellik, see *How to Kill 400 Duponts*
Art School Confidential 38
Artist, The 194
Ary, Jacques 68
As God Commands 224
Asena, Cengiz 228
Asian Shore, The (short story) 227
Asino d'oro, L' 113
Assault with a Deadly Weapon 53
Asso di picche (comic) 15, 21, 22
Assonitis, Ovidio 147
Asterix & Obelix: Mission Cleopatra 41
Astrella (comic) 26
Atadeniz, Yılmaz 168, 210, 226, 227, 228, 230, 231, 233, 234, 235, 238, 239
Atasoy, İrfan 226, 229
Attacco! (Zen-Shin) 19
Attack of the Robots 124
Attraction 19, 65
Aulin, Ewa 64, 65
Autopsy 78
Autostrada del sole, L', see *Thrilling*
Avanti! 173
Avati, Pupi 122, 123
Avcı, Suzan 230
Avenger X 18, 20, **60-62**, 121, 238
Avram, Chris 94, 173
Avril, Jane [Maria Pia Luzi] 19
Avventure di Diabetik, Le **206-208**
Avventure di Jacques Douglas, Le (photonovel) 82
Avventure di Lucky Martin, Le (photonovel) 82
Avventure erotiX di Cappuccetto Rosso 172, 195
Avventuroso, L' (comic mag) 12

Awful Dr. Orlof, The 125
Ayach, Jean-Luc 109
Baba Yaga 27, **136-141**, 191
Baba Yaga, Devil Witch, see *Baba Yaga*
Babes in Toyland 43
Back to the Future Part III 145
Bad Blood 39
Baggio, Luca 41
Baila Guapa 54
Baker, Carroll 53, 138, 139, 191
Balcázar, Jaime Jesús 55
Baldini, Renato 62, 209
Balilla, Il (comic mag) 11
Ballade des Daltons, La 193
Ballard, James G. 176
Balsam, Martin 62
Balsamo, Rosario "Saro" 213
Balsamus l'uomo di Satana 122, 123
Balzarini, Gino 60
Bambi 189
Bambinaia, La, see *Caprice Italian Style*
Bandera Bandits 163
Banfi, Lino 154
Bang-Bang Kid, The 18
Bangkok, cita con la muerte 39
Baracco, Adriano 104
Baratto, Luisa (aka Liz Barrett) 66, 125
Barbarella (comic) 26, 27, 84, 85, 102, 103, 123
Barbarella (film) 9, 27, 29, **84-91**, 93, 102, 104, 107
Barbarella—Queen of the Galaxy, see *Barbarella* (film)
Barbey d'Aurevilly, Jules Amédée 17
Barbieri, Renzo 29, 31, 129, 130, 131, 171, 213, 219
Barboni, Enzo 164, 192, 193, 194
Barcarol, Bruno 64, 65
Bardot, Brigitte 85
Baron Blood 142, 180
Barrès, Maurice 17
Barrett, Liz, *see* Baratto, Luisa
Bartier, Pierre 111
Barto, Dominic 194
Başaran, Tunç 234, 237
Basta guardarla 19
Bastard, The 184
Bastardi 208
Bath-man dal pianeta Eros 25, 31, **168-170**
Batman (comic) 19, 22, 31, 33, 56, 58, 64, 67, 79, 148, 157, 169, 214, 236
Batman (TV series) 79, 102, 124
Batman XXX: A Porn Parody 40
Batman—The Movie 72
Battiato, Franco 139
Battle of the Amazons 147
Batzella, Luigi (aka Paolo Solvay) 30, 131
Bava, Lamberto 37, 108, 189, 197, 199, 203

Bava, Mario 9, 15, 18, 20, 38, 49, 61, 62, 68, 72, 79, 80, 83, 85, 87, 88, 90, 94, 99, 102-110, 120, 131, 142, 149, 172, 180, 200, 210, 221
Bay Kilink 240
Bay of Blood, A 131, 210
Bayrak, Güngör 168
Baytan, Natuk 146
Bazzoni, Luigi 77
Beast in Heat, The 131
Beast with a Gun 59
Beastie Boys, The (band) 108
Beatles, The (band) 26, 63
Bedi, Kabir 154
Belann Krali 239
Bellalta, José María 30
Belle de jour 104
Bellerofonte 220
Bellocchio, Marco 138
Bellocchio, Max, see Occhiobuono, Alessandro
Bellucci, Monica 109
Belmondo, Jean-Paul 28, 130
Benatti, Lorenzo 110
Benedy, John, *see* Di Benedittis, Giovanni
Benigni, Roberto 159, 171
Bentivoglio, Fabrizio 222, 224
Benussi, Femi 135
Berardi, Giancarlo 99, 110
Berenger, Tom 185
Berger, Helmut 59
Berger, William 184
Bergman, Ingmar 100
Bergonzelli, Sergio 54, 75, 237
Berling, Peter 185
Berlusconi, Silvio 36, 37, 109, 176, 189, 191, 193, 200
Berova, Olinka 28
Berruti, Giulio 139
Bertolo, Belinda 217
Beyond the Darkness 221
Beyond, The 221
Biancaneve (comic) 29, 151, 171
Biancaneve & Co…, see *Snow White and the 7 Wise Men*
Biancaneve e i sette nani 172
Bianchi Colombatto, Enrica (aka Erika Blanc) 83
Bianchi Montero, Roberto 94, 150, 171
Bianchi, Andrea 31
Bianchi, Mario 29, 118, 171
Bianchini, Paolo 8, 22, 24, 35, 65-67, 75-78, 124-125, 158-160
Big Ben Bolt (comic) 96
Big Deal on Madonna Street 171
Big Racket, The 159
Bilbao, Fernando 145
Bini, Alfredo 123
Bini, Giancarlo 195

Bird with the Crystal Plumage, The 30
Bird, Brad 127
Birkin, Jane 130
Bivio, Il 74
Black Box Affair 83
Black Deep Throat 118
Black Elk Speaks 139
Black Emanuelle 71
Black Emanuelle 2 71
Black Pirate, The 23
Black Sabbath 120
Black Sunday 15, 105, 180, 200
Blackmail (1974 film) 131
Blade in the Dark, A 197, 199
Blade Runner 175
Blanc, Erika, *see* Bianchi Colombatto, Enrica
Blasetti, Alessandro 40
Blood and Black Lace 49, 61, 180
Blood and Diamonds 62
Blood for a Silver Dollar 149
Blood For Dracula 138
Bloody Pit of Horror 66, 208
Bloody Sin 30, 202, **219-221**
Blow-up 63, 64, 87
Bludhorn, Charles 90, 103
Blue Is the Warmest Color 38
Blue Nude 39
Blues de la Calle Pop, The 39
Bob Crewe Generation, The (band) 88
Boccaccio '70 46
Bocci, Alessandro 203
Böcklin, Arnold 201
Boido, Federico "Rico" (aka Rick Boyd) 209, 212
Boldi, Massimo 153, 174
Bolero Film (photonovel) 12, 82, 83
Bologna, Ugo 156
Bolognini, Mauro 92
Bombolo, see Lechner, Franco
Bona, Giampiero 100
Bonelli, Gian Luigi 15, 182, 183, 184, 185, 186
Bonelli, Sergio 36, 198, 225
Bonifacio, Antonio 191, 203
Bonnie (comic) 28
Bonnie & Clyde 28
Bonvi, *see* Bonvicini, Franco
Bonvicini, Franco (aka Bonvi) 33, 34, 151, 152, 153, 154, 174
Borderie, Bernard 27, 62, 130
Borgese, Sal (Salvatore) 81, 128, 131, 135, 142, 143, 144, 145, 167, 168, 188
Borgia, Lucrezia 28
Born to Be a Warrior 118
Born to Fight 180
Borrelli, Rosario 209, 212

Bos, Roel (aka Glenn Saxson) 8, 50-52, 73-75
Boschero, Dominique 58, 59
Boschero, Giorgio 208
Bosic, Andrea 52, 73
Bouchet, Barbara 113
Boxer's Omen, The 143
Bozzetto, Bruno 33, 126-128, 159
Bozzoli, Flavio 110
Braña, Francisco "Frank" 144, 184
Brancaleone's Army 152
Brancucci, Ernesto 143, 145
Brass, Tinto 19, 62-65, 137, 140, 152
Braun, Axel, *see* Ferro, Alessandro
Braun, Lasse, *see* Ferro, Alberto
Brazzi, Oscar 151
Brazzi, Rossano 19
Brescia, Alfonso 75, 81, 143, 146-147, 149
Briganti, I (comic) 54
Brochero, Eduardo Manzanos 74, 121, 122
Brockmann, Jochen 79
Brody, Larry 109
Brooks, Louise 27, 63, 136, 191
Brown, Reb 179, 180
Browne, Roger 58, 59
Brugnolini, Sandro 112
Bruschini, Vito 118
Brynner, Yul 82
Bucceri, Franco 151
Bucci, Flavio 184
Buchs, Julio 124
Bufi Landi, Aldo 148
Buio Pesto (band) 40, 213-216
Bunker, Max *see* Secchi, Luciano
Buñuel, Luis 104, 106, 109, 221
Buono, Victor 118
Burton, Tim 225
Buscema, John 41
Buzzanca, Lando 28
Buzzati, Dino 12, 19
Cabiria 21
Caiano, Mario 131, 173, 200
Cajelli, Diego 225
Çakır, Levent 181, 236, 237, 239
Calamai, Clara 30
Caligula's Hot Nights 150
Caltiki, the Immortal Monster 68
Camuncoli, Giuseppe 225
Canalejas, José 145
Candela, Tony, *see* Canti, Rosato
Cango Korkusuz Adam 231, 232, 233
Cannata, Nino 44, 45
Cannavale, Enzo 174
Cannibal Ferox 53, 221
Cannibal Holocaust 134

Cannibale (comic mag) 35, 175, 176, 204
Cantafora, Antonio (aka Michael Coby) 142
Canti, Aldo (aka Nick Jordan) 22, 79, 80, 81, 117, 147, 148, 149, 167
Canti, Rosato (aka Tony Candela) 117
Cap (comic) 28
Capinera del mulino, La 44
Capitan Basilico 38, **213-215**, 222
Capitan Basilico 2—I Fantastici 4+4 38, **215-216**, 222
Capitan Miki (comic) 183, 235
Capitan Novara—Un giorno da supereroe 41, 222
Caplin, Elliot 96
Capone, Gino 133, 143
Caponegro, Luce (aka Selen) 31, 194
Capp, Al 34, 41, 136
Capponi, Pier Paolo (aka Norman Clark) 61
Capra, Frank 156
Capriccio all'italiana, see *Caprice Italian Style*
Caprice Italian Style 9, 33, **91-94**, 177
Caprioli, Vittorio 19
Capuano, Giosy 83
Capuano, Luigi 75
Capuano, Mario 83
Cara de oro, see *Goldface, the Fantastic Superman*
Carabbimatti, I 174
Carabbinieri, I 174
Carax, Leos 39
Card Dealer, The 142
Cardinale, Claudia 14
Carlini, Paolo 117, 158
Carnabuci, Piero 43
Carnimeo, Giuliano 174
Carogne si nasce 74
Carotenuto, Mario 175
Carpanese, Monica 197
Carpenter, John 225
Carpentieri, Luigi 152
Carpi, Arnaldo Piero "Pier" 33, 39, 99 100, 110, 121
Carrie 224
Carrisi, Albano (aka Al Bano) 172
Casa, Paolo 159
Case, Russel 191
Casini, Stefania 138
Cassetti, Stefano 202
Castagnini, Giuseppe 156
Castaldi, Simone 49, 54, 123, 204
Castel, Lou 19,
Castellari, Enzo G., see Girolami, Enzo
Castelli, Alfredo 99, 109, 110, 185, 206, 207
Castle of the Living Dead 62
Cat O' Nine Tails, The 61
Cat, The 59
Catacomba 30
Catherine of Russia 51

Cavaletto, Andrea 202
Cavallone, Alberto 19
Cavara, Paolo 76
Cave of the Golden Rose 3, The 203
Cavedon, Giorgio 28, 39, 129, 130, 131, 132, 219
Celentano, Adriano 28, 60, 176
Celi, Adolfo 102, 111, 133, 138, 158
Çelik Bilek 235
Cemetery Man 37, **197-202**
Cenerentola e il signor Bonaventura, see *Princess Cinderella*
Cerchio, Fernando 18, 72, 74
Cerimonia dei sensi, La 170
Cersosimo, Manlio (aka Mark Shanon) 169
Cervi, Gino 32, 40, 41
Cervi, Tonino 99, 100, 101, 102, 110
Chabat, Alain 41
Chaffey, Don 179
Chaplin, Charles 127, 145, 154
Chase, Chevy 225
Che fanno i nostri supermen tra le vergini della jungla?, see *Three Supermen in the Jungle*
Chi-hung, Kuei 143
Chiari, Liliana 210
Chiari, Walter 45, 46
Chiba, Sonny 108
Chicken Park 191
Christine, Katia 29
Church, The 200
Ciak si muore 20
Cianfriglia, Giovanni (aka Ken Wood) 55, 56, 57, 77, 124, 147, 162
Ciccarese, Luigi 197
Cimpellin, Leone 110
Cinesex (photonovel) 28, 130
Ciorciolini, Marcello (aka Frank Red) 83
Citizen Kane 188
City of the Living Dead 53
City of Women 204
Civirani, Osvaldo 28, 133, 155
Çılgın Kız ve 3 Süper Adam 181, 239, 240
Clark, Jim 149
Clark, Ken 59
Clark, Norman, see Capponi, Pier Paolo
Clark, Petula 46
Cleri, Dante 154
Clerici, Gianfranco 203
Cléry, Corinne 153, 180
Cloche, Maurice 18
Clockwork Orange, A (1971 film) 113, 170
Close Encounters of the Third Kind 160
Clowns, The 131
Coatti, Roberto (aka Eva Robin's) 191
Cobra, The 24
Coby, Michael, see Cantafora, Antonio

Codice d'amore orientale 123
Col cuore in gola, see *Deadly Sweet*
Collins, Alan, *see* Pigozzi, Luciano
Collins, Ray, see Zappietro, Eugenio
Colombini, Willy (aka Willy Newcomb) 128
Colombo, Corrado 203
Colombo, Furio 111
Colonna, Leone 159
Colonnese, Eugenio 57
Coluzzi, Francesca Romana 168
Comancheros, The 185
Comandante Mark, Il (comic) 232, 237
Come Play with Me 19, 153
Come rubammo la bomba atomica 151
Come rubare la corona d'Inghilterra, see *Argoman the Fantastic Superman*
Comencini, Luigi 46, 159
Commissario di ferro, Il 173
Compagnia della Forca, La (comic) 53
Conan the Barbarian 178, 186
Conjugal Bed, The 46
Connery, Sean 97, 116
Conquest 178
Conrad, Joseph 223
Constantine, Eddie 45, 124
Conte, Francesco Paolo 44
Conti, Bill 215
Continiello, Ubaldo 171
Cöntürk, Remzi 231
Cooper, Gary 15, 183
Coppola, Francis Ford 205
Coppola, Roman 108
Corbucci, Bruno 27, 34, 41, 130, 131, 132, 154, 171
Corbucci, Sergio 9, 35, 114, 145, 163, 164, 165, 166, 176, 177, 192, 231
Corman, Roger 34, 56, 90
Corona di ferro, La 40
Corriere dei Piccoli, Il (comic mag) 10, 11, 42
Corriere della Sera, Il 11
Corruption, The 175
Corteggi, Luigi 8, 16, 52, 119
Corti, Antonio Cesare 168
Cosmine (comic) 26
Costantino, Emma (aka Erna Schurer) 210, 212
Cosulich, Callisto 130
Cozzi, Luigi 104, 161, 206
Crash (novel) 176
Crash! Che botte strippo strappo stroppio, see *Supermen Against the Orient*
Crepax, Guido 19, 27, 36, 62, 63, 64, 65, 91, 136, 137, 138, 140, 141, 189, 190, 191
Crime Busters 164
Crisa, Erno 209
Crisanti, Gabriele 31, 65, 66, 76, 78

Crispino, Armando 76
Cristopharo, Domiziano 8, 30, 202, 219, 220, 221
Cronenberg, David 77
Crudo, Aldo 147
Crudup, Billy 109
Crypt of the Vampire 210
Cuatros Budas de Kriminal, Los, see *Marchio di Kriminal, Il*
Cümbüş Palas 237
Curtis, Betty [Roberta Corti] 98
Curtiz, Michael 185
Cushing, Peter 149
Cutugno, Toto 216
Cuvelier, Paul 84
D'Agostino, Antonio 25, 169, 170
D'Amato, Joe, *see* Massaccesi, Aristide
D'Angelo, Gianfranco 171
D'Angelo, Nino 203
D'Annunzio, Gabriele 17
Da Istanbul ordine di uccidere 133
Dacascos, Mark 109
Dalí, Salvador 19
Damiani, Damiano 12
Damiano, Luca, *see* Lo Cascio, Franco
Damned, The (1969 film) 130
Dane, Lawrence 162
Danger: Diabolik 9, 16, 18, 23, 38, 56, 87, 88, 93, **94-111**
Dangerous Attraction 197
Daniela Mini-Slip, see *Cümbüş Palas*
Dante, Joe 221, 225
Danton, Ray 23, 39
Dark Side of Love, The 175
Dassin, Jules 20
Date for a Murder 19
Dauphin, Claude 87
Davoli, Ninetto 92
Day the Sky Exploded, The 27
De Angelis, Vertunnio 23
De Bévère, Maurice (aka Morris) 192
De Concini, Ennio 152
De Coulteray, Georges 84
De Curtis, Antonio (aka Totò) 18, 92, 93, 94, 95, 145, 177, 208
De Fabritiis, Fabrizio 41
De Funès, Isabelle 137, 138, 139
De Funès, Louis 20, 99, 138
De Gaulle, Charles 83, 115
De Laurentiis, Dino 9, 18, 20, 24, 27, 29, 32, 56, 72, 85, 87, 88, 89, 90, 92, 93, 98, 99, 100, 101, 102, 103, 104, 108
De Luca, Lorenzo 196, 197
De Maria, Renato 38, 203, 204, 205
De Martino, Alberto 24, 35, 51, 160, 161, 162, 163, 173
De Massi, Barbara (aka Guia Lauri Filzi) 170
De Niro, Robert 59, 225

De Riso, Arpad 116
De Rita, Massimo 161
De Rossi, Patrizia (aka Patrizia Webley) 151
De Sade, Donatien-Alphonse-François 84, 130, 137
De Santis, Orchidea 117
De Sica, Vittorio 19, 46, 47, 68
De Sisti, Vittorio 29
Dead Calm 197
Dead stop—Le coeur aux lèvres, see *Deadly Sweet*
Deadly Chase 173
Deadly Code 222
Deadly Sweet 19, **62-65**, 137, 140
Death Laid an Egg 65
Death of a Soldier 180
Death on High Mountain 74
Death Rage 216
Death Rides a Horse 87, 185
Deathless Devil, The 182
Debord, Guy 111
Decameron n°4—Le belle novelle del Boccaccio 159
Decamerone nero, Il 123
Déclic, Le 31
Deep Red 30, 176
Del Buono, Ugo 44, 45
Del Zoppo, Federico 207
Delirium (1987 film) 203
Delitti, Amore e gelosia 39
Dell'Acqua, Alberto (aka Robert Widmark) 145
Dell'Acqua, Liliana 108
Dell'Edera, Werther 225
Dell'Orso, Edda 105
Dellamorte Dellamore (film), see *Cemetery Man*
Dellamorte Dellamore (novel) 199, 201
Delon, Alain 100
Demirhan, Metih 181
Demonia 150
Demons 37, 199
Demons 3: The Ogre 189
Demons, The (1972 film) 117
Deneuve, Catherine 28, 99, 103
Dennis Cobb—Agente SS 018 (comic) 22, 123
Deodato, Ruggero (aka Roger Rockfeller) 18, 27, 29, 33, 83, 113, 114, 115, 116, 132, 133, 134, 221
Desert Assault 68
Devia, Antonio 108
Devil in Love, The 28
Devil-Doll, The 128
Devil, Nicholas 26, 84
Devil's Man, The 24, **65-67**, 76, 77, 125
Devil's Wedding Night, The 29
Devilman Story, see *Devil's Man, The*
Di Benedetto, Valerio 202
Di Benedittis, Giovanni (aka John Benedy) 209, 212
Di Biagio, Claudio 202

Di Caprio, Leonardo 215
Di Leo, Fernando 61, 62, 117, 130, 159, 209
Di Orazio, Paolo 196
Diabolik (comic/character) 14, 15, 16, 17, 18, 19, 20, 23, 24, 31, 32, 33, 38, 44, 45, 47, 48, 49, 50, 52, 60, 61, 71, 72, 79, 84, 93, 94-111, 113, 116, 121, 122, 124, 132, 195, 206, 207, 210, 212, 216, 217, 226
Diabolik (film), see *Danger: Diabolik*
Diabolikal Super-Kriminal, The **208-213**
DiaboliX (Colpo internazionale) 31, **194-195**
Diamante Lobo 82
Diamond Peddlers, The 142
Diamond, Paul 109
Diamonds Are a Man's Best Friend 20
Dickens, Charles 225
Dimarno, Giacomo 123
Dionisio, Silvia 134
Dirty Dozen, The 81
Disch, Thomas M. 227
Discreet Charm of the Bourgeoisie, The 221
Dişi Kilink 230, 231
Dişi Tarzan 236
Divorce—Italian Style 14
Django 164, 231
Django Shoots First 51
Dolce Vita, La 15
Doll Syndrome, The 220
Dominò il vendicatore (comic) 28
Don Archer (photonovel) 210, 213
Don Camillo (1950s/1960s film series) 40
Don Camillo (1983 film) 193
Don't Torture a Duckling 203
Donan, J. Lee, see Loy, Mino
Donati, Ermanno 152, 153
Donati, Sergio 63
Donen, Stanley 176
Donna, il sesso e il superuomo, La, see *Fantabulous Inc.*
Donnarumma all'assalto 75
Donner, Richard 25
Door to Silence 150
Doors, The (band) 205
Dorelli, Johnny 32, 33, 71, 72, 159
Doria, Enzo 180
Double Face 216
Dr. Cyclops 128
Dr. Strangelove or: How I Learned to Stop Worrying and Love the Bomb 85, 87, 89, 111, 113
Dracula (novel) 138
Drei tolle Kerle, see *3 Supermen a Tokyo*
Dru, Joanne 166
Duel of Fire 51
Dufilho, Jacques 142, 143, 153
Dujardin, Jean 194
Dumas, Alexandre 34, 183, 187

Dumbo 189
Dünyayı Kurtaran Adam 235
Düzgün, Saadettin 234
Dylan Dog (comic) 36, 37, 38, 185, 192, 196, 198, 199, 200, 202
Dylan Dog contro Freddy Krueger 202
Dylan Dog—La morte puttana 202
Dylan Dog—Vittima degli eventi 202
Dylan Dog: Dead of Night 9, 202
È mezzanotte, butta giù il cadavere 118
Eastman, George, see Montefiori, Luigi
Eastwood, Clint 47, 68
Easy Life, The 19, 46
Eaten Alive 53, 173
Eco, Umberto 19, 136
Edward Penishands 195
Eisenstein, Sergei 137
Ekberg, Anita 15
Ekicigil, Eşref 231
El Gringo (comic) 183
Eleuteri Serpieri, Paolo 31
Ellin, Stanley 154
Emanuelle in America 59
Embalmer, The 20
Engagement Italiano 19
Enter the Seven Virgins 142
Epoxy (comic) 84
Ercoli, Luciano 61
Erdem, Gülgün 230, 236, 237
Erotic Adventures of Pinocchio, The 150
Erotic Rites of Frankenstein, The 39
Erte, Güven 234
Eureka (comic mag) 152
Eva la venere selvaggia 29
Everett, Rupert 199, 200, 202
Execution Squad 94
Exorciccio, The 159
Eyes Without a Face, see *Madness*
Facciolo, Enzo 99, 108
Faceless Monster, The, see *Nightmare Castle*
Faenza, Roberto 33
Fajardo, Eduardo 58
Falace, Paolo 108
Falchi, Anna 200, 201, 202
Falk, Lee 10, 22, 55, 79, 97, 111, 126, 148
Fall of the Roman Empire, The 71
Family Friend, The 149
Fanfani, Amintore 83
Fantabulous Inc. 33, **111-113**
Fantabulous, see *Fantabulous Inc.*
Fantasia 127, 189
Fantasia, Franco 62
Fantastic Argoman, The, see *Argoman the Fantastic Superman*
Fantastici 3 Supermen, I, see *Three Fantastic Supermen, The*

Fantax / Fantasm (comic) 16, 17, 48, 54, 208
Fantoma İstanbul'da Buluşalım 238
Fantoma Supermen'e Karşı 236
Fantomas (1964 film) 20, 66, 90, 100
Fantômas (character) 20, 24, 48, 66, 95, 96, 97, 99, 167, 226, 236, 238
Fargo (1996 film) 46
Farina, Corrado 26, 27, 33, 39, 100, 106, 136-141, 191, 212
Farmer, Philip José 172
Farnese, Alberto 209, 210
Fasan, Italo 95
Fassari, Antonello 191
Fatalik (photonovel) 210, 212, 213
Fearless Vampire Killers, The 120
Fellini—Satyricon 113, 130
Fellini, Federico 10, 11, 15, 19, 31, 39, 46, 59, 100, 113, 130, 131, 141, 159, 176, 204
Fellini: I'm a Born Liar 10
Fenech, Edwige 129, 153
Fenomenal e il tesoro di Tutankamen, see *Phenomenal and the Treasure of Tutankamen*
Ferilli, Sabrina 191
Ferrara, Romano 29, 114
Ferrari, Bob 217, 218
Ferreri, Marco 46, 87
Ferrero, Carlo 133
Ferretti, Giovanni Lindo 205
Ferro, Alberto (aka Lasse Braun) 40
Ferro, Alessandro (aka Axel Braun) 40
Ferroni, Giorgio 23, 149
Festa Campanile, Pasquale 176
Feuillade, Louis 13, 96,
Fiabeschi torna a casa 206
Fidani, Demofilo 186
Fidenco, Nico 143, 168
Field, Karin 117
Fifth Cord, The 77
Fighting Devil Dogs, The 66
Fitzcarraldo 162
Flash Gordon (1980 film) 91
Flash Gordon (comic) 10, 19, 99, 100, 224
Flashman 22, 33, **67-68**, 114, 173, 222, 238
Fleming, Ian 79
Flying Superboy, The 146
Fo, Dario 152
Fonda, Bridget 59
Fonda, Jane 26, 29, 85, 86, 87, 89, 90
Forbidden Photos of a Lady Above Suspicion, The 61
Ford, John 55, 166, 192
Forest, Jean-Claude 9, 26, 27, 84, 85, 89, 123
Formica, Daniele 108
Fornari, Vito 209
Fortune Cookie, The 112

Forty Guns 186
Foster, Harold 183
Foster, John see Gaffari, Cihangir
Four Times That Night 131
Fox, Charles 88
Franciosa, Massimo 19
Franco & Ciccio (Franco Franchi, Ciccio Ingrassia) 59, 83, 92
Franco, Jesús "Jess" 9, 39, 117, 124, 125, 131, 168, 236
Franju, Georges 83
Frankenstein Meets the Wolf Man 210
Freda, Riccardo 31, 32, 68, 120, 150, 152, 186, 216
Free Hand for a Tough Cop 53
Freud a fumetti 137
Freud, Sigmund 100, 138
Friend Is a Treasure, A 166
Frigidaire (comic mag) 34, 35, 123, 173, 175, 176, 204, 205
Frison, Denis 202
Frollo, Leone 28, 29, 151, 171
From Corleone to Brooklyn 53
Fuentes, Miguel Ángel 162, 163
Fulci, Lucio 150, 159, 173, 178, 199, 221
Full, Raymond, see Mussolini, Romano
Fuller, Samuel 186
Fumeria d'oppio 13
Fury in Marrakech 68
Fusco, Maria Pia 152
Futurama (animated TV series) 127
FX 18, Secret Agent 18
Gaffari, Cihangir (aka John Foster) 236
Gaiman, Neil 31
Gainsbourg, Serge 130, 169
Galeppini, Aurelio 15, 182, 183
Galimberti, Gilberto 57
Galleani, Ely 140, 191
Gangster venuto da Brooklyn, Un 155
Gans, Cristophe 109
Garassini, Sergio 44, 45
Garko, Gianni 81, 150
Gassman, Vittorio 19, 28, 46
Gastaldi, Ernesto 8, 68
Gates, Tudor 104
Gatling Gun 78
Gaudio, Paolo 221
Gemma, Giuliano 56, 163, 184, 185, 186
Gemma, Roberta, see Panella, Floriana
Gemser, Laura 71
Gencer, Yıldırım 226
Genius (photonovel) 208, 213
Gentili, Giorgio 18,
Gentili, Veronica 202
Gentilomo, Giacomo 22
George, Susan 163

Gerber, Gail 85, 86, 87, 88, 90
Gerini, Claudia 108
Germani, Gaia 61, 62
Germi, Pietro 14
Gesebel (comic) 26, 27, 85, 123
Ghione, Emilio 13
Ghost World 38
Giagni, Gianfranco 189, 190, 191, 192
Giallo a Venezia 31
Giannetti, Alfredo 19
Giannini, Giancarlo 108, 208
Gianolla, Maria Grazia 220
Giarda, Mino 55
Gicca Palli, Lorenzo "Enzo" 116, 155
Giliberti, Mario 95
Giochi proibiti de l'Aretino Pietro, I 151
Giorgelli, Gabriella 210, 212
Giorno dei ragazzi, Il (comic mag) 127
Gipi, *see* Pacinotti, Gian Alfonso
Giraldi, Franco 76
Girardello, Ludovico 223, 224
Giraud, Jean (aka Moebius) 224
Girl in Room 2A, The 20
Girl Who Knew Too Much, The 61
Giro girotondo... con il sesso è bello il mondo 151
Girolami, Enzo (aka Enzo G. Castellari) 159, 184
Girolami, Marino 34, 153, 154, 155
Girolami, Romolo (aka Romolo Guerrieri) 216
Girotti, Mario (aka Terence Hill) 35, 37, 38, 82, 128, 142, 145, 147, 156, 164, 165, 166, 192, 193, 194
Girotti, Massimo 19
Giuro che ti amo 151
Giussani, Angela 14, 38, 95, 96, 98, 99, 104, 108, 116, 195, 206
Giussani, Luciana 14, 31, 38, 95, 96, 98, 99, 104, 108, 116, 195, 206
Giusti, Marco 43
Gnoli, Domenico 19
Go with God, Gringo 50
Godard, Jean-Luc 111
Goethe, Johann Wolfgang 112
Goldface, il fantastico Superman, see *Goldface, the Fantastic Superman*
Goldface, the Fantastic Superman 22, 23, 24, **68-71**
Goldfinger 79, 97, 100, 130
Goldrake Playboy (comic) 28, 130
Golino, Valeria 222, 223, 224
Golon, Anne 27
Golon, Serge 27
Gomboli, Mario 109, 206
Gomorra (TV series) 38
Goodbye Kiss, The 202
Gören, Şerif 231, 233
Goscinny, René 38, 192, 193, 194
Gottfredson, Floyd 97
Gould, Chester 45
Governi, Giancarlo 174
Gozlino, Paolo (aka Paul Stevens) 68, 173
Grande Blek, Il (comic) 183, 235, 237
Grande quercia, La 180
Granger, Farley 94
Great Silence, The 164
Greci, Aldo 63
Green Hornet, The (TV series) 79, 143
Greganti, Roberta 108
Greggio, Ezio 72
Gremlins 225
Grey, Babette 195
Grieco, Sergio 22, 25, 58, 59
Grunt! 160
Guérin, Florence 31
Guerrieri, Romolo, *see* Girolami, Romolo
Guerrini, Mino 19, 153
Gülyüz, Aram 231
Güney, Salih 237
Güney, Yılmaz 232
Gungala la vergine della giungla 29
Gungala, the Black Panther Girl 29, 114, 236
Guzon, Andrea 168
H2S 33
Haber, Alessandro 202
Hadji Lazaro, François 201
Hakbilir, Kemal 232
Hamer, Robert 72, 95
Hampton, Demetra 37, 190, 191, 192, 203
Hançeryan, Nişan 237
Hannibal, Marc 147, 148
Hanno cambiato faccia, see *They Have Changed Faces*
Hard Time for Princes 19
Hardy, Oliver 154, 174
Harriman, George 136
Harris, Brad 22, 79, 80, 128, 135, 142
Harrison, Rex 115
Harrison, Richard 59, 111
Hauff, Werner 118
Hawks, Howard 166
Hayashi, Isao 224
Helen, Yes ... Helen of Troy 147
Hellström, Gunnar 30
Hellzapoppin' 74, 154
Hemmings, David 87, 89, 90
Henga, el cazador (comic) 178
Henger, Eva 206, 207, 208
Hepburn, Katharine 37
Hercules (1958 film) 55, 129
Hercules (1983 film) 161
Hercules Against the Moon Men 22
Hercules in the Haunted World 62, 186

Herlin, Jacques 83
Herlitzka, Roberto 219
Heroes (TV series) 38, 217
Hessa (comic) 28
Heston, Charlton 183
Heusch, Paolo 27
Heywood, Anne 138
Hidden in the Woods 202
High Infidelity 87
Hill, Ross 193
Hill, Terence, *see* Girotti, Mario
Hilton, George 23, 209, 212
Hipnos follia di massacro, see *Massacre Mania*
History of Violence, A 38
Hitchcock, Alfred 65, 90, 114, 201
Hitler, Adolf 28, 154, 210
Hoar Stevens, Thomas Terry (aka Terry-Thomas) 72
Hofbauer, Ernst 148
Hoffmann, E. T. A. 138
Hollow Man 225
Holt, Seth 100, 101, 102, 110
Horror (comic mag) 39, 110, 206
Hotel Paura 204
House of Clocks, The 203
House of Flesh Mannequins 221
House of Shells 202
How to Kill 400 Duponts 23, 32, 71, 72, 108, 159
Howling II: Stirba—Werewolf Bitch 180
Howling, The 221
Huerta, Rodolfo Guzmán (aka El Santo) 23, 55, 56, 57, 59, 68, 124, 167, 236, 239
Hunebelle, André 20, 66, 99
Hunters of the Golden Cobra 177
Huntington, Sam 202
Huth, James 194
I Am What I Am, see *Deadly Sweet*
I Married You For Fun 19
I'm Not Scared 224
Impariamo ad amarci: guida all'educazione sessuale 170
İnanç, Çetin 230, 235
Inanoglu, Türker 118, 157, 167
Incredible Paris Incident, The, see *Argoman the Fantastic Superman*
Incredible Shrinking Man, The 128
Incredibles, The 127
Infascelli, Roberto 28, 75
Inferno (1980 film) 173
Infierno virtual del Dr. Wong, El 39
Inglourious Basterds 194
Ingrid sulla strada 173
Innocenzi, Silvia 150
İnsanları Seveceksin 54
Invaxön—Alieni in Liguria 213
Inverse Canon, The 160
Invincibile Superman, L', see *Superargo and the Faceless Giants*
Invisible Boy, The 38, 39, **221-224**
Invisible Man, The (1933 film) 62
Invisible Man, The (novella) 68
Invisible Man: Rape! 224
Ippoliti, Silvano 64, 65
Ippolito, Ciro 186, 199
Ireland, John 132, 133, 134
Iros 38, **216-218**
Isabella (comic) 27, 130, 131, 132
Isabella—Mit blanker Brust und spitzem Degen, see *Ms. Stiletto*
Isabella, duchessa dei diavoli, see *Ms. Stiletto*
Israel, Víctor 144
Italian Spiderman 41
Jackie Brown 59
Jacovitti, Benito 97
Jacula (comic) 28, 29
Jamonte, Franco 209
Jancsó, Miklós 153
Jasset, Victorin 13
Jeva, Lino 110
Jewison, Norman 87
Jodelle (comic) 85, 111
Jodorowsky, Alejandro 31
Joe Crack (photonovel) 22
Johnson, Don 208
Jolanda (comic) 28
Jones, Dean 25
Jordan, Nick, *see* Canti, Aldo
Juliet of the Spirits 141
Jungla (comic) 29
Jurassic Park 191
Kakkientruppen 34, 153, **154-155**
Kane, Bob 64, 67
Kaplan, Jonathan 166
Kaptan Swing—Korkusuz Kaptan 233, 237
Kara Atmaca 237
Karoubi, Jimmy 100, 102
Kaufman, Charlie 203
Kaya, Birsen 235
Kaye, Danny 172
Kechiche, Abdellatif 38
Kelly, Grace 98
Kendall, Tony see Stella, Luciano
Khoshabe, Iloosh (aka Richard Lloyd) 155, 156
Kiefer, Warren 62
Kiling Ölüm Saçıyor 234, 235
Kiling Sarışın Tehlike 231
Kilink Caniler Kralı 230, 231
Kilink Frankeştayn ve Dr. No'ya Karşı 231
Kilink İstanbulda 210, 227, 228, 229, 230, 231
Kilink Soy ve Öldür 228, 230
Kilink Uçan Adama Karşı 227, 228, 229
Kill, Baby ... Kill! 221

Killer Reserved Nine Seats, The 133, 173
Killer Snakes 143
Killing (photonovel) 17, 20, 62, 157, 208-213, 226, 227, 229, 230, 235, 237, 238
Killing Atom Casusu 228
Killing Birds 203
Killing Kolsuz Kahramana Karşı 235
Killing'in İntikamı 228
Kind Hearts and Coronets 72, 95
King, Stephen 196
Kinowa (comic) 15, 183, 235
Kinski, Klaus 81, 116, 117, 118
Kirby, Jack 113
Kiss Kiss, Bang Bang 184
Kiss Me, Kill Me, see *Baba Yaga*
Kırgeç, Nuri 236
Kızıl Maske 167, 235
Kızıl Maske'nin İntikamı 237, 239
Klein, William 33
Klito-Bell, see *Bath-man dal pianeta Eros*
Knox, Mickey 134
Köksal, Yılmaz 181
Konopka, Magda 18, 121, 122, 123, 147, 210
Kowalski, Bernard 180
Krazy Kat (comic) 136
Kreola 191, 203
Kriminal (comic) 8, 15, 16, 17, 18, 22, 47, 48, 49, 50, 51, 52, 53, 54, 60, 93, 98, 99, 119, 120, 121, 123, 195, 209, 210, 226
Kriminal (film) 8, 18, **47-54**, 75
Kriminal Love—Amore carnale, see *Teufelscamp der verlorenen Frauen, Das*
Kriminal Porno, see *İnsanları Seveceksin*
Kriminaltango 48
Kristine la Superdonna (comic) 121
Kubrick, Stanley 85, 86, 111, 225
Kurosawa, Akira 100
Kyrou, Ado 84
L.S.D. 19
Lado, Aldo 184
Lady Football 168
Lady From Shanghai, The 179
Lambertini, Lamberto 108
Landi, Mario 31
Landis, John 135
Landry, Gérard 209, 210
Lange, Claudie 67, 68
Lara Croft: Tomb Raider 214
Last Cannibal World 134
Last Man on Earth, The (2011 film) **218-219**
Last Temptation of Christ, The 191
Lattuada, Alberto 24
Laura non c'è 202-203
Laurel, Stan 43, 154, 174

Laurenti, Mariano 203
Lauri Filzi, Guia, see De Massi, Barbara
Lavi, Daliah 80
Lavia, Gabriele 30
Law, John Phillip 9, 87, 88, 89, 90, 98, 99, 100, 102, 103, 104, 105, 106, 107, 108
Leblanc, Maurice 96
Lechner, Franco (aka Bombolo) 174
Lee, Bruce 141
Lee, Christopher 80
Lee, Margaret 23, 71, 72
Lee, Stan 22, 225
Left Hand of the Law, The 173
Legend of the 7 Golden Vampires, The 142
Lelli, Luciano 18
Lelouch, Claude 65
Lennon, John 16
Lenzi, Umberto 18, 23, 49, 50, 51, 52, 53, 61, 122, 173, 221
Leonardi, Sergio 19
Leone, Sergio 42, 44, 117, 183, 216
Leoni, Roberto 151
Lepori, Lorenzo 30
Leroy, Philippe 63
Let It All Hang Out, aka *The Man with the Golden Brush* 129
Let the Right One In 225
Leto, Marco 75
Lettieri, Guglielmo 185
Li'l Abner (comic strip) 34, 41, 136
Liberatore, Tanino 34, 35, 41, 175, 176, 177
Lichtenstein, Roy 64, 107, 111
Liebes Lager 155
Lieh, Lo 142
Linder, Christa 151
Liné, Helga 52, 62, 73
Linus (comic mag) 19, 27, 136, 204
Lionello, Oreste 69, 128, 171
Lippi, Giuseppe 107
Lisa and the Devil 221
Lisi, Virna 85, 100
Little Eye-Witness, The 118
Little Shop of Horrors, The (1960 film) 34
Live like a Cop, Die Like a Man 134
Lizzani, Carlo 46
Lloyd, Richard, see Khoshabe, Iloosh
Lo Cascio, Franco (aka Luca Damiano) 172, 195
Lo chiamavano Jeeg Robot 38
Lombardo Radice, Giovanni 221
London, Jack 223
Long Hair of Death, The 171, 200
Longo, Malisa 147
Loreley's Grasp, The 80
Loren, Sophia 85
Lorre, Peter 180

Lorys, Diana 66, 125
Losfeld, Éric 84, 91
Love, Lucretia 115, 133, 134
Loy, Mino (aka J. Lee Donan) 22, 68, 114, 173
Loy, Nanni 174
Luana, the Girl Tarzan 28, 29, 75
Lucarelli, Carlo 109
Lucifera (comic) 28, 131
Lucky Luke (1991 film) 37, 38, **192-194**
Lucky Luke (2009 film) 194
Lucky Luke (comic) 37, 38, 41, 192-194, 239
Lucky Luke—Daisy Town 193
Lucky the Inscrutable 9, 39
Lucrezia (comic) 28
Lungo giorno del massacro, Il 75
Luotto, Andy 159, 160
Lys, Ágata 144
M*A*S*H* 153
Macario, Erminio 208
Machen, Arthur 123
Macy, William H. 46
Mad Butcher, The 118
Mad Magazine (comic mag) 64
Madhouse (1974 film) 149
Madison, Guy 66, 67, 68, 124, 125
Madness, aka *Eyes Without a Face* 37, **195-197**
Maggi, Giuseppe 69
Magni, Enzo (aka Ingam) 29
Magnificent Seven, The 79
Magnifico texano, Il 75
Magnus, *see* Raviola, Roberto
Magritte, René 96, 201
Maiuri, Arduino "Dino" 104
Malabimba 31
Malatesta, Guido 29, 65, 236
Malavita attacca … la polizia risponde, La 173
Malcolm, Robert 142
Male, Il (magazine) 175, 204
Malerba, Luigi 24
Malìa (photonovel) 208
Malìa—Vergine e di nome Maria 75
Malicious 153
Malizia 2000 175
Man and a Woman, A 65
Man From Deep River, The 53
Man of Steel XXX: An Axel Braun Parody 40
Man of the East 194
Manara, Milo 10, 31, 173, 208
Mandrake (comic/character) 10, 47, 68, 111, 231, 232, 233, 234
Manfredi, Gianfranco 191, 192
Manfredi, Nino 46, 176
Manganelli, Giovanni 172
Mangano, Silvana 19, 47, 68, 93

Manhunter 197
Mankiewicz, Joseph Leo 83
Mann, Anthony 71
Mann, Michael 197
Marais, Jean 20, 66, 99
Marandi, Evi 23
Marceau, Marcel 87
March Or Die 166
Marchesi, Gino 97, 98
Marchesi, Marcello 57
Marchio di Kriminal, Il 18, 53, **72-75**, 121
Marcuse, Herbert 127, 138
Margheriti, Alberto 25, 36, 37, 66, 68, 114, 117, 123, 161, 171, 178, 179, 180, 200
Marischka, Franz 129
Marquand, Christian 86
Marrakech Express 222
Martin Mystère (comic) 110, 185, 198, 206
Martin, George, *see* Martínez Celeiro, Francisco
Martinelli, Elsa 102, 138,
Martinenghi, Italo 25, 135, 143, 144, 145, 157, 166, 167, 168, 181, 187, 188, 189
Martinenghi, Stefano 168, 181, 187, 188, 189
Martínez Celeiro, Francisco (aka George Martin) 116, 117, 128, 135, 142, 144, 145
Martinková, Susanna 150
Martino, Luciano 68
Martino, Sergio 68, 216
Marx, Groucho 198, 202
Marx, Karl 151, 153
Máscara de Kriminal, La, see *Kriminal*
Maschera nera (comic) 48, 183
Maskeli Şeytan 238
Maskeli Suvari Tommikse Karşı 235
Maskeli Üçler 239
Masokis (comic) 121, 210
Massaccesi, Aristide (aka Joe D'Amato) 59, 71, 169, 199, 203, 221
Massacre Mania 8, 24, 66, **75-78**
Massaro, Francesco 174
Master of Love 173
Mastrocinque, Camillo 115, 145, 201
Mastroianni, Marcello 10, 14, 15, 19
Mastrolorenzi, Sabrina 170
Matador 191
Matarazzo, Raffaello 13
Matrix, The 214
Mattei, Bruno 37, 180, 196, 197
Mattei, Giuseppe 80
Mauri, Roberto 29
Mazzanti, Attilio 209
Mazzotta, Max 205, 206
McCartney, Paul 16
McLeod, Norman Z. 172

McVicar, Daniel 108
Mediterraneo 38, 222
Meins, Gus 43
Mell, Marisa 23, 28, 98, 99, 100, 101, 103, 105, 122
Melloncelli, Cesare 60, 62
Melville, Herman 137
Memoirs of an Invisible Man 225
Ménard, Cathy 169
Mercier, Mario 84
Mercier, Michèle 27
Merli, Maurizio 77, 115, 165
Merola, Mario 81, 147, 222
Messalina (comic) 28
Messalina vs. the Son of Hercules 51
Messalina, Messalina! 154
Metello 216
Metz, Vittorio 58
Metzger, Radley 117
Mia Italida stin Ellada 51
Micalizzi, Franco 148
Mifune, Toshiro 163
Milian, Tomas 163, 174
Milius, John 178
Miller, Roger 193, 194
Mio sogno, Il (photonovel) 12
Miseria e nobiltà 93
Mission Stardust 39
Mission Top Secret 24, 68
Mister No (comic) 36
Mister Zehn Prozent – Miezen und Moneten, see *Psychopath* 116
Mister-X (comic) 16, 18, 60, 61, 62
Mister-X (film), see *Avenger X*
Mitchell, Gordon 115, 156
Miti, Michela 171
Moana l'isola del sogno 111
Modern Times 127
Modugno, Domenico 92
Modugno, Lucia 131
Moebius, *see* Giraud, Jean
Mogherini, Flavio 104
Molinari, Rocco 209, 210
Moliterno, Gino 13
Moll, Giorgia 83
Mondana nuda, La, see *Şahit*
Mondo Cane 2 208
Mondo di Yor, Il, see *Yor, the Hunter from the Future*
Monicelli, Mario 14, 46, 152, 184
Montefiori, Luigi (aka George Eastman) 138
Montesano, Enrico 176
Monti, Giacomo 218
Montorio, Giorgio 110
Moody, Lynne 147
Mora, Philippe 180
Moravia, Alberto 105

Morbidone, Il 19
Morbus Gravis (comic) 31
Morgan, Nancy 194
Morgan, Robert 221
Morini, Massimo 213
Moroni, Mario 20
Morricone, Ennio 105, 132, 209, 216
Morris, see De Bevere, Maurice
Mostro della domenica, Il, see *Caprice Italian Style*
Mostro, Il 72
Mouchot, Pierre 97
Mr. Billion 166
Mr. Freedom 33
Mr. Scarface 117
Mr. Superinvisible 25
Ms. Stiletto 29, **129-131**, 132, 171
Mucari, Carlo 184
Mücevher Hırsızları, see *Scoiattolo, Lo*
Mulargia, Edoardo 50
Muller, Paul 173, 209, 212
Murder Obsession 31
Murgia, Tiberio 14, 171
Murphy, Audie 83
Murphy, John Cullen 96
Museum of Wonders, The 220, 221
Mussolini, Benito 10, 45, 122
Mussolini, Romano (aka Raymond Full) 52, 122
Mutant Sexual Behaviour 170
Muti, Ornella 28, 31
Mutlu, Mine 234
My Name Is Nobody 192
My Name Is Trinity 34, 164, 165, 192
My Son, the Hero 184
Mysterious Doctor Satan 66, 182
Mystery Science Theater 3000 162, 163
N.P. il segreto 33
Naked and Cruel 71
Naked and Cruel 2 71
Naked Violence 61
Name of the Game is Kill!, The 30
Namur (photonovel) 212, 213
Nasca, Sergio 75
Nathan Never (comic) 36
Navarro, Marcel 97
Naviglio, Luigi 209
Necron (comic) 53, 54
Negrin, Alberto 202
Neihardt, John G. 139
Nek, see Neviani, Filippo
Nella misura in cui … 123
Nella terra di nessuno 192
Neri, Rosalba 39
Nero 199
Nero, Franco 19, 184, 208

Nest of Vipers 99
Neviani, Filippo (aka Nek) 203
New York Ripper, The 203
Nicolai, Bruno 115, 132
Nicolaou, Ted 193, 194
Nietzsche, Friedrich 17, 112
Night of the Damned, The 29, 212
Night Porter, The 221
Nightmare Castle 200
Nightmare City 53, 221
Nightmares Come At Night 125
Nirvana 222
Nixon, Richard 143
Nocetti, Giovanna 220
Noia, La (novel) 105
Nolan, Christopher 225
Norman, Paul 195
North by Northwest 70
Nosferatu (magazine) 197
Nosferatu the Vampyre 142
Nostro, Nick 22, 56, 57, 124
Noyce, Phillip 197
Nude for Satan 30
Nusciak, Loredana 57
O'Donoghue, Michael 19
O'Neal, Patrick 24
O'Shea, Milo 88, 89
O'Toole, Peter 34
Occhi dentro, Gli, see *Madness*
Occhiobuono, Alessandro (aka Max Bellocchio) 31, 195
Ogon batto 108
Okay sceriffo **43-44**
Okçugil, Cevat 226
Oliver Twist (novel) 225
Oltretomba (comic) 30, 219, 220, 221
Omaggio, Maria Rosaria 220, 221
Ombre 131
Once Upon a Time in the West 42, 133
One Million Years B.C. 179
One-Armed Swordsman 235
One-Dimensional Man (book) 127
Ongaro, Alberto 21, 22
Onibaba 117
Onofri, Fabrizio 100
Operation Counterspy 22
Operation Poker 59
Opiate '67 46
Oppini, Franco 174
Oral, Tunç 231
Ore, Le (adults-only mag) 213
Örümcek Adam 226
OS 117 (comic) 22
Özden, Emel 181, 239
Özkaracalar, Kaya 8, 9, 168, 240

Özlüer, Fuat 157
Özten, Filiz 181
Pabst, Georg Wilhelm 136
Pacinotti, Gian Alfonso (aka Gipi) 38, 218, 219
Pagano, Bartolomeo 21
Pakel, Vural 237
Palance, Jack 82, 183
Pallenberg, Anita 87, 88
Pallenberg, Rospo 109
Palmara, Mimmo 131
Paludetti, Franco 110
Pamuk Prenses ve 7 Cüceler 237
Panella, Floriana (aka Roberta Gemma) 221
Panic 173
Paolessi, Umberto 208
Paoli, Luciana 210
Paolocci, Francesco 186
Paolocci, Gaetano 186
Parada, Manuel 74, 122
Paranoia 53
Parenti, Neri 173
Parenti, Nicola Mauro 114, 115, 132, 133
Parolin, Aiace 141
Parolini, Gianfranco 22, 24, 79, 80, 81, 82, 128, 147
Pasolik—Il fumettok del brividok (comic) 33
Pasolini, Pier Paolo 92, 93, 123, 147
Pastrone, Giovanni 21
Patrick Still Lives 31
Paul, Gloria 81, 117, 128
Paulette (comic) 85
Paz! 38, **203-206**
Pazienza, Andrea 34, 35, 38, 175, 176, 177, 204, 205, 206
Pazzafini, Giovanni "Nello" 162
Peanuts (comic strip) 136
Pederiali, Giorgio (aka Rubino Ventura) 28, 151, 171
Pedersoli, Claudio (aka Bud Spencer) 82, 128, 142, 145, 147, 156, 164, 165, 166, 192
Pedrazzi, Giorgio 188
Pedrocchi, Luciano 12
Peellaert, Guy 111
Pekmezoğlu, Oksal 232
Penteado, Miguel 57
Perfect Crime, The 173
Peroni, Carlo 206
Perrault, Charles 93
Pesen, Nevzat 231
Petri, Elio 19, 184
Petroni, Giulio 87, 185
Pettigrew, Damian 10
Peyda, Hüseydin 230
Pezzotta, Alberto 104
Phantom, The (comic) 22, 24, 47, 56, 61, 79, 97, 99, 111, 124, 126, 161, 167, 235, 237, 238

Phenomena 37
Phenomenal and the Treasure of Tutankamen 20, 83, **113-115**, 116, 132
Piccioni, Fabio 30, 31, 40
Piccioni, Piero 81
Piccoli, Michel 102, 104
Piccolo Ranger, Il (comic) 43
Picture of Dorian Gray, The (novel) 119
Piedimonte, Gloria 54
Pignatelli, Micaela 71
Pigozzi, Luciano (aka Alan Collins) 66, 180
Pink Panther, The 116
Pinocchio (1940 film) 189
Pinocchio (book) 137
Piquer Simon, Juan 142
Pisano, Berto 124
Pistol for Ringo, A 184
Pisu, Mario 43
Pizzuti, Riccardo 147, 149
Planet of the Vampires 102, 105
Play It Again, Sam 156
Playgirls and the Vampire, The 150, 208
Pleasence, Donald 162
Pleasure, The 168
Plot of Fear 76
Poema a fumetti 19
Poggi, Nando 77
Poggi, Ottavio 56
Poli, Maurice 83
Polidoro, Gian Luigi 46, 47
Polizia selvaggia 118
Ponson du Terrail, Pierre Alexis 96
Pontello, Gabriel 169, 213
Ponzoni, Cochi 152, 153, 174
Poor But Beautiful 156
Porcaro, Giorgio 174
Potenza, Carlo 117
Povero Cristo 110
Power, Romina 172
Pozzetto, Renato 35, 152, 153, 174, 176
Pozzi, Moana 31, 123, 194
Prando, Francesco 108
Pratt, Hugo 9, 21, 22, 39, 199, 224
Pravda (comic) 85
Predoni del Sahara, I 65
Pregadio, Roberto 122
Preminger, Otto 87
Prete, Giancarlo 41
Price, Vincent 149
Princess Cinderella 12, 18, **42-43**
Principessa sul pisello, La 29, **149-151**, 171
Provocazione 123
PsicoVIP 127, 128
Psychopath 18, **115-118**

Pugni, dollari & spinaci 34, **155-156**
Pulp 173
Pumaman, The **160-163**, 173
Pupillo, Massimo 68, 208, 221
Purdom, Edmund 158
Purvis, Neal 90
Qua la mano 176
Quarry, Robert 149
Quattro del pater noster, I 132
Queens of Evil 99
Quelle strane occasioni 174
Quest for Fire 160
Questi, Giulio 65
Questo e quello 9, 35, 36, **175-177**
Questo sporco mondo meraviglioso 68
Quickly, spari e baci a colazione 19
Quiet American, The 83
Quiet Man, The 55
Quiet Place in the Country, A 19
Quiet Place to Kill, A 53
Radovic, Vladan 219
Rafelson, Bob 31
Raft, George 100
Ragazza di latta, La 33
Ragazzo invisibile, Il, see *Invisible Boy, The*
Raho, Umberto 62, 122
Raiders of the Lost Ark 177, 185
Raimi, Sam 217, 225
Rains, Claude 225
Rambaldi, Carlo 88, 209
Randall, Dick 118
Randall, Mónica 56, 57
Ranieri, Massimo 216
Rappoport, Kseniya 222
Rassimov, Ivan 53
Rassimov, Rada 76, 77
Rat Man 173
Ratti, Filippo (aka Peter Rush) 29, 212
Raviola, Roberto (aka Magnus) 15, 16, 18, 19, 22, 26, 27, 31, 33, 34, 47, 48, 49, 50, 52, 53, 54, 73, 98, 119, 120, 121, 123
Raymond, Alex 10
Re dei criminali, Il, see *Superargo and the Faceless Giants*
Recchioni, Roberto 202
Red Headed Corpse, The 123
Red Krokodil 220
Red Rings of Fear 202
Red River 166
Red Sun 163
Red, Frank, see Ciorciolini, Marcello
Redgrave, Vanessa 64
Reed, Carol 32
Reed, Dolly 29
Reeves, Steve 55

Refn, Nicolas Winding 90
Regnoli, Piero 24, 29, 150, 151, 171, 208
Reich, Wilhelm 111
Reitano, Mino 168
Renoir, Claude 90
Residencia para espias 125
Resnais, Alain 84, 150
Return of Ringo, The 184
Return of the Blind Dead 80
Revenge of Spartacus, The 59
Rezza, Antonio 205
Ribelli, Brigata Perlasca 44
Ricci, Tonino 186
Richards, Dick 166
Richards, Keith 88
Rififi in Amsterdam 59
Rigaud, George 78
Rigosi, Giampiero 109
Ring of Darkness 110
Risi, Dino 19, 28, 46, 59
Ritorno di Diavolik, Il, see *Ogon batto*
Rizzo, Alfredo 150
Rizzo, Giacomo 149
Robbe-Grillet, Alain 140
Robbery Roman Style 60
Roberts, Rocky 83
Robin's, Eva, see Coatti, Roberto
Robowar 180
Rocco and His Brothers 14, 209
Rockfeller, Roger, see Deodato, Ruggero
Rocky 207, 215
Rogers, Charles 43
Rogers, Nicholas 203
Roland, Gilbert 100
Rollin, Jean 26
Rolling Stones, The 88
Romanelli, Carla 115
Romanzo criminale (TV series) 38
Rome, Sydne 162
Romero, George A. 200
Romoli, Gianni 200
Rondi, Brunello 150, 173
Rooney, Mickey 28
Rose, William A. 20
Rosi, Francesco 160
Ross, Herbert 156
Rossellini, Isabella 159
Rossi-Stuart, Kim 191
Rossi, Fausto 148
Rossi, Franco 92
Rossi, Giorgio Carlo 147
Rostagno, Marco 26, 39
Routh, Brandon 202
Roy Colt and Winchester Jack 149

Ruju, Pasquale 202
Rumbera, La 123
Rush, Peter, see Ratti, Filippo
Russians Are Coming, the Russians Are Coming, The 87
Russinova, Isabel 184
Russo, Luigi 180
Sabatier, Jean-Marie 76
Sadik (comic) 16, 33, 44, 45, 46, 62, 210
Sadik (film), see *Thrilling*
Sadomania 168
Safari Express 184
Saga de Xam (comic) 26, 84, 85
Sagradini, Carlo 217
Şahit 237
Saint Tropez, Saint Tropez 191
Sala, Vittorio 20
Salce, Luciano 19, 172
Salò, or the 120 Days of Sodom 147
Salon Kitty 152, 153, 155
Salvatores, Gabriele 39, 222, 223, 224, 225
Salvatori, Renato 14
Salvi, Emimmo 34, 155, 156
Salvi, Enzo 206
Samantha (comic) 121
Sambrell, Aldo 124, 167, 168, 184
Samperi, Salvatore 19, 34, 151, 152, 153, 154, 174, 175
Samson and the Slave Queen 51
Sanchez, Pedro, see Spalla, Ignazio
Sancho, Fernando 76, 77, 144
Sandman, The (short story) 138
Sandokan the Great 51
Sandra of a Thousand Delights 50
Sandrelli, Stefania 14
Sansoni, Gino 95, 110, 121
Santercole, Gino 159
Santo contra las mujeres vampiro 57
Santo contra los asesinos de la Mafia 57
Santo en el museo de cera 57
Santo en el tesoro de Drácula 57
Santo, El, see Huerta, Rodolfo Guzmán
Santoni, Espartaco 70
Santoni, Tino 59
Saprofita, Il 75
Şaşkın Hafiye Kilink'e Karşı 227, 228
Satanik (comic) 15, 16, 18, 22, 50, 52, 93, 99, 119, 120, 121, 122, 123, 210
Satanik (film) 18, **118-123**, 147
Satanik il volto del male 123
Satan's Baby Doll 150
Sato, Hajime 108
Saxophone 153
Saxson, Glenn, see Bos, Roel
Sayles, John 221
Sbatti il mostro in prima pagina 138

Scali, Mireno 171
Scapagnini, Sergio 108
Scary Movie 215
Scattini, Luigi 39
Scavolini, Romano 19, 212
Schlesinger, Richard 193, 194
School of Erotic Enjoyment 75
Schultz, Charles 19, 136
Schurer, Erna, *see* Costantino, Emma
Sclavi, Tiziano 36, 37, 198, 199, 200, 201, 202
Scocchera, Fulvio 45
Scognamillo, Giovanni 167, 181
Scoiattolo, Lo 9, 118, **156-158**
Scola, Ettore 19, 28, 46
Sconosciuto, Lo (comic) 31, 53
Scopone Game, The 159
Scorsese, Martin 191
Scott Pilgrim vs. the World 38
Scotti, Tino 131
Scòzzari, Filippo 35, 123
Scream 215
Scream Blacula Scream 147
Scusi facciamo l'amore? 19
Secchi, Luciano (aka Max Bunker) 15, 16, 18, 22, 26, 33, 39, 47, 48, 49, 50, 52, 53, 54, 73, 98, 119, 120, 121, 122, 123, 152, 183, 196
Secondo tragico Fantozzi, Il 172
Secret Life of Walter Mitty, The 172
Secret of the Incas' Empire 82
Segar, Elzie C. 34, 156
Şekeroğlu, Esat 240
Selen, *see* Caponegro, Luce
Selene (comic) 26, 85
Sellers, Mary 191
Şen, Ali 237
Sequi, Mario 24
Serna, Assumpta 191
Settefolli 83
Seurat, Georges 90
Seven Bloodstained Orchids 61
Seven Golden Men 20, 83, 157
Seven Golden Men Strike Again 83
Seven Guns for the MacGregors 76, 78
Severini, Attilio 52, 70, 71, 157
Sexy Cat 197
Sexybell (photonovel) 19, 169
Şeytan Tırnağı 237
Shahn, Ben 137
Shakespeare, William 92
Shanon, Mark, *see* Cersosimo, Manlio
Shaw Brothers 25, 142, 143, 146, 147
She Wore a Yellow Ribbon 166
Sheik, The 153
Shindo, Kaneto 117
Shining, The (1980 film) 225
Shoot First … Ask Questions Later 163
Shyamalan, M. Night 217
Signor Robinson, mostruosa storia d'amore e d'avventure, Il 152
Sigpress contro Scotland Yard, see *Psychopath*
Sihirbazlar Kralı Mandrake Killing'in Peşinde 231, 232, 234
Silence of the Hams, The 72
Silva, Henry 24
Simenon, Georges 40
Singer, Bryan 225
Skay, Brigitte 131
Skidoo 87
Slaughter Hotel 209
Slave Girls of Sheba 117
Slave Queen of Babylon 111
Smith, Paul 142
Smoke Over London 63
Snake God, The 123
Snow White and the 7 Wise Men 28, **170-172**
Snow White and the Seven Dwarfs 189
So Sweet … So Perverse 53
So Sweet, So Dead 94
Soavi, Michele 37, 199, 200, 201, 202
Sogni mostruosamente proibiti 36, **172-174**, 176
Soldi, Giancarlo 199
Sollima, Sergio 23
Solvay, Paolo, *see* Batzella, Luigi
Sordi, Alberto 10, 11, 46, 63, 159
Sorel, Jean 100, 101, 102, 104
Southern, Terry 84, 85, 86, 87, 88, 89, 113
Souvestre, Pierre 95, 96, 97
Space Mutiny 180
Spalla, Ignazio (aka Pedro Sanchez) 144, 145
Sparagna, Vincenzo 35, 175
Specialty of the House, The (short story) 154
Spencer, Bud, *see* Pedersoli, Claudio
Spider-Man (2002 film) 217
Spielberg, Steven 185, 207, 225
Spies Like Us 135
Spina, Sergio 33, 111, 113
Spinelli, Gabriele 219
Spirits of the Dead 176
Splatter (comic mag) 196, 197, 199
Springer, Frank 19
Spy with Ten Faces, The 23
Squitieri, Pasquale 30
SS-Sunda, *see* Yassel Spazio, Sandro
Sssssss 180
Staccioli, Ivano 52, 67
Stagecoach 182
Stallone, Sylvester 207, 215
Stampa, La (newspaper) 95
Stander, Lionel 132, 134
Star Wars 34, 160, 161, 178, 180, 215

Stay Tuned for Terror 77
Steele, Barbara 15, 120, 180, 221
Stefanelli, Benito 162
Steiner, John 113, 134, 178, 180
Stella, Luciano (aka Tony Kendall) 22, 23, 79, 80
Steno, *see* Vanzina, Stefano
Stevens, Paul, *see* Gozlino, Paolo
Stoker, Bram 138
Stone Martin, David 137
Stone, Gidra 118
Stoppa, Paolo 42, 43
Storie Blu (comic) 30, 31
Strange Case of Dr. Jekyll and Mr. Hyde, The (novel) 119
Strange Story of Olga O, The 203
Strange Vice of Mrs. Wardh, The 203, 216
Stranger and the Gunfighter, The 144
Straordinarie avventure di Pentothal, Le (comic) 204, 205
Street Dance 162
Strike Commando 180
Stroppa, Daniele 203
Sturmtruppen (comic strip) 33, 34, 152, 153, 154, 174
Sturmtruppen (film) 34, **151-153**, 154, 174
Sturmtruppen 2—Tutti al fronte 34, 153, **174-175**
Süper Adam 237
Süper Adam Kadınlar Arasında 239
Super Agent Super Dragon 23
Super Fuzz 35, **163-166**, 192
Süper Selami 168
Super Seven Calling Cairo 59
Super Stooges vs. the Wonder Women, The 24, 81, 143, **146-149**, 167
SuperAndy, il fratello brutto di Superman 35, 125, **158-160**
Superargo and the Faceless Giants 22, 24, 57, 69, 76, 78, **123-125**
Superargo contro Diabolikus, see *Superargo vs. Diabolicus*
Superargo e i giganti senza volto
Superargo vs. Diabolicus 22, 23, **54-57**, 69, 124, 125, 238
Superargo, el gigante, see *Superargo and the Faceless Giants*
Superargo, el hombre enmascarado, see *Superargo vs. Diabolicus*
Superargo vs. Diabolicus
Superargo, see *Superargo and the Faceless Giants*
Supercolpo da 7 miliardi 69
Superdragon vs. Superman, aka *Bruce Lee Against Supermen* 143
Superman (1978 film) 25, 71, 158, 160, 161, 173
Superman (comic/character) 19, 21, 22, 157, 165, 168, 173, 181, 214, 229, 238
Superman el invencible, see *Superargo and the Faceless Giants*
Superman vs. Spider Man XXX: An Axel Braun Parody 40
Supermen Against the Orient 81, 136, **141-144**, 148, 187
Süpermen Fantoma'ya Karşı 167
Süpermenler, see *3 Supermen Against the Godfather*
Supersex (photonovel) 19, 169, 210, 213
Supersnooper, see *Super Fuzz*
Supersonic Man 142

Superuomini, superdonne, superbotte, see *Super Stooges vs. the Wonder Women*
SuperVIPs, The 33, **126-128**, 159
Suspiria 138, 173, 191
Švankmajer, Jan 221
Swan, Kitty 29
Sweet Body of Deborah, The 216
Swinburne, Algernon 17
Szu, Shih 142
Tabernero, Julio Pérez 197
Tahi, Moa 208
Tamburini, Stefano 34, 35, 41, 175, 176, 177
Tarantino, Quentin 59
Target 118, 157
Tarkan Viking Kanı 234
Tarzana the Wild Girl 29, 135
Tavella, Dino 20
Taylor, Robert 97
Tecnica di un amore 150, 173
Teeth 222
Teledrome, see *Massacre Mania*
Tema, Muzaffer 230
Ten Gladiators, The 79, 80
Tenebrae 196, 197, 199
Tenenti, Giancarlo 60, 62
Tenth Victim, The 19, 27
Teocoli, Teo 153
Terrifik (photonovel) 213
Terror in Rome 59
Terror of the Black Mask 23
Terry-Thomas, see Hoar Stevens, Thomas Terry
Tesoro di Dracula, Il see *Santo en el tesoro de Drácula*
Tessari, Duccio 36, 184, 185, 186, 187
Teufelscamp der verlorenen Frauen, Das 54
Teutscher, Pauline 169
Tex (comic) 15, 36, 43, 54, 182, 183, 184, 185, 186, 192, 198
Tex and the Lord from the Deep 36, **182-187**
Tex e il signore degli abissi, see *Tex and the Lord of the Deep*
They Call Me Renegade 193
Third Man, The 32
Thomas, Dylan 198
Thor the Conqueror 186
Three Fantastic Supermen in the Orient, The, see *Supermen Against the Orient*
Three Fantastic Supermen, The 22, 24, 33, 59, **78-81**, 144, 147, 222
Three Musketeers of the West, The 34, 41
Three Musketeers, The (novel) 34, 183
Three Superboys Strike Again, The 146
Three Superguys in the Snow 146
Three Superguys, The 146
Three Supermen at the Olympic Games 9, 81, 145, 168, **180-182**, 188, 240

Three Supermen in S. Domingo 81, 128, 135, 145, 168, 181, **187-189**
Three Supermen in the Jungle 81, **134-136**, 142, 144, 187
Three Supermen of the West, see *3 Supermen in the West, The*
Thrilling 32, 33, **44-47**, 218
Throne of Fire, The 178
Thunderball 56, 102, 111
Tichy, Gérard 57
Tiger Joe 177
Titanic 215
Today We Kill ... Tomorrow We Die! 99
Todd, Mort 8, 212
Tofano, Sergio 12, 42, 43
Tognazzi, Ricky 160
Tognazzi, Ugo 46, 87
Tolo, Marilù 100, 103
Tom Dollar **82-84**
Tomb of Torture 210
Tombs, Pete 8, 141, 181, 228
Tonelli, Bob 123
Topkapi 20, 114
Topolino (comic mag) 33, 43, 182
Toppi, Giove 10
Tornatore, Giuseppe 222
Torrisi, Pietro 57, 156
Totò contro i quattro 208
Totò, Peppino e le fanatiche 18
Totò, see De Curtis, Antonio
Tototruffa '62 145
Trafficone, Il 171
Tres supermen contra el padrino, Los, see *3 Supermen Against the Godfather*
Triangolo erotico 170
Trinity is STILL My Name! 45, 192
Trinity: Gambling for High Stakes 164
Trintignant, Jean-Louis 63, 64, 65
Trombetta, Piero 48
Truce, The 160
Tulgar, Kunt 181, 234
Tünaş, Erdoğan 157
Tunnel sotto il mondo, Il 206
Turan, Süleyman 237
Turist Ömer Uzay Yolunda 227
Twenty Years Later (novel) 187
Two Sane Nuts 146
Uberti, Emilio 45
Üç Süpermen Olimpiyatlarda, see *Three Supermen at the Olympic Games*
Uçak, Fikret T. 71, 167
Ukmar, Bruno 57
Ukmar, Franco 57
Ultimo terrestre, L', see *Last Man on Earth, The*
Umiliani, Piero 59, 74
Unbreakable 217

Uncanny, The (essay) 138
Uncle Was a Vampire 32, 59
Undertaker and His Pals, The 154
Underworld 202
Unger, Deborah Kara 109
Unknown Woman, The 222
Unnaturals, The—Contronatura 179
Uomo puma, L', see *Pumaman, The*
Uranella (comic) 26
Vacanze sulla neve 203
Vadim, Roger 9, 84, 85, 86, 87, 88, 89, 90, 103
Vai alla grande 175
Valentina (comic) 19, 27, 63, 91, 136, 137, 138, 139, 140, 141, 189, 190, 191
Valentina (TV series) 36, 37, **189-192**
Valentino, Rodolfo 153
Valerii, Tonino 184, 192
Valletti, Aldo 147
Vampire and the Ballerina, The 208
Vampirella (comic) 85
Vampiri, I 32, 120, 150, 152
Van Cleef, Lee 82, 87, 144
Van Hamme, Jean 84
Vanoni, Ornella 138
Vanzi, Luigi 133
Vanzina, Stefano (aka Steno) 59, 72
Vartan (comic) 28
Vartan, Sylvie 28
Vasile, Turi 138
Vecchi, Luca 202
Vedo nudo 28
Venantini, Venantino 100, 221
Ventura, Rubino, see Pederiali, Giorgio
Venus (comic) 26
Veo, Carlo 154
Verde, Dino 58, 59
Verdone, Carlo 171
Vergine, e di nome Maria, see *Malìa—Vergine e di nome Maria*
Verhoeven, Paul 225
Verne, Jules 137
Viaggia, ragazza, viaggia: hai la musica nelle vene 30
Viaggio a Tulum (graphic novel)
Viaggio di G. Mastorna, detto Fernet, Il
Vian, Boris 10, 31
Vicario, Marco 20, 83
Vieyra, Emilio 77
Vighi, Vittorio 152
Villa, Claudio 26
Villaggio, Paolo 10, 36, 152, 172, 173, 174, 176
Violent Naples 53, 115
Violent Rome 115
VIP, mio fratello superuomo, see *SuperVIPs, The*
VIP, My Brother Superman, see *SuperVIPs, The*
Visconti, Luchino 14, 46, 50, 130, 209

Vita sessuale di un vampiro see *Santo en el tesoro de Drácula*
Vitti, Alessandro 225
Vitti, Monica 9
Vittimista, Il, see *Thrilling*
Vivarelli, Piero 18, 52, 60, 61, 121, 122, 123
Voglio, Bianca Maria 108
Voice of the Moon, The 10
Voices from Beyond 150
Von Buttiglione Sturmtruppenführer 153
Von Cziffra, Géza 48
Von Däniken, Erich 161
Von Fürstenberg, Ira 24
Von Sacher Masoch, Leopold 84
Vukotic, Milena 202
Vulcan, Son of Giove 59, 155
Wacky Taxi 125
Wade, Robert 90
Walalla (comic) 28, 29
Wallach, Eli 163
Wampir (photonovel) 210
War Goddess 24, 147
War Gods of Babylon 111
Ward, Burt 67
Ward, Luca 108
Warhol, Andy 19, 104
Warrior of the Lost World 191
Wave of Lust 134
Wayne, Patrick 184
Web of the Spider 117
Wein, Len 41
Welcome America 118
Welles, Orson 32, 179, 201, 219
Wesselman, Tom 19
West and Soda 126
West, Adam 67
West, Judi 112
Westlake, Donald 109
Whale, James 62, 225
Whip and the Body, The 80, 180
White Collar Blues 172
White Fang 150
White Sheik, The 10, 11
Who Framed Roger Rabbit 32
Widmark, Robert, see Dell'Acqua, Alberto
Widower, The 59
Wild Dogs 83
Wild, Wild Planet 179
Williams, Fred 131
Williams, Guy 23
Wilson, John 181
Winslet, Kate 215
Witch's Curse, The 186
Witches, The 19, 47, 68, 92
Wolfman, Marv 41

Woman on Fire, A 130
Women in Cell Block 7 59
Wood, Edward D., Jr. 145, 181, 235
Wood, Ken, see Cianfriglia, Giovanni
Woods, Robert 8, 76, 77, 78
Worth, David 191
Wright, Edgar 38
Würth, Giorgia 214
Wyman, Bill 191
Yalınkılıç, Yavuz 181
Yankee 19, 63, 139
Yarasa Adam—Bedmen 237, 239
Yassel Spazio, Sandro (aka SS-Sunda) 209, 212, 213
Yayınları, Ceylan 235
Yayınları, Tay 236
Yeti 82, 166
Yilmaz, Atif 146
Yol 231
Yor, le chasseur du futur, see *Yor, the Hunter from the Future*
Yor, the Hunter from the Future 36, 161, **177-180**
Yorga (photonovel) 212, 213
Young, Terence 24, 147
Your Turn, Darling 62
Yueh, Hua 147
Yürüklü, Cavit 181, 239
Zac, Pino 92
Zagor (1971 film) 236
Zagor (comic) 9, 36, 185, 198, 231, 236
Zagor—Kara Bela 236
Zagor—Kara Korsanın Hazineleri 232, 236
Zakimort (comic) 16, 121
Zamagni, Riccardo 170
Zampa, Luigi 72
Zampaglione, Federico 108
Zane, Angio 44
Zaniboni, Sergio 108, 110
Zanotti, Pio 191
Zanotto, Juan 161, 178
Zappa, Frank 35, 175, 176, 177
Zappietro, Eugenio (aka Ray Collins) 36, 161, 178
Zapponi, Bernardino 176, 177
Zatta, Noa 224
Zavattini, Cesare 58
Zeglio, Primo 39, 111
Zemeckis, Robert 145
Zenabel 27, 115, **131-134**
Zequila, Antonio 197
Zingarelli, Italo 161
Zora la vampira (comic) 28, 29
Zora la vampira (film) 30
Zordon (comic) 131
Zorro the Fox 118
Zurli, Guido 18, 116, 117, 118, 157, 158, 167, 181
Zwigoff, Terry 38

Roberto Curti (1971) is an Italian film critic and historian. He has written a number of books on Italian and European genre cinema, including ITALIAN CRIME FILMOGRAPHY 1968-1980, ITALIAN GOTHIC HORROR FILMS, 1957-1969 and TONINO VALERII: THE FILMS. He has contributed essays to Midnight Marquee's THE HAUNTED WORLD OF MARIO BAVA, SO DEADLY, SO PERVERSE Vol.1 and SPLINTERED VISIONS.

If you enjoyed this book

Visit our website or
call, write or email
for a free catalog

Midnight Marquee Press, Inc.
9721 Britinay Lane
Baltimore, MD 21234
U.S.A.

www.midmar.com

410-665-1198

www.ingramcontent.com/pod-product-compliance
Lightning Source LLC
Chambersburg PA
CBHW051346110526
44591CB00025B/2928